INDIAN RELIGIONS

D1217141

INDIAN RELIGIONS

A HISTORICAL READER OF SPIRITUAL EXPRESSION AND EXPERIENCE

edited by

PETER HEEHS

NEW YORK UNIVERSITY PRESS
WASHINGTON SQUARE, NEW YORK

First published in the U.S.A. in 2002 by
NEW YORK UNIVERSITY PRESS
Washington Square
New York, N.Y. 10003

Copyright © 2002 by Peter Heehs
All rights reserved

Library of Congress Cataloging-in-Publication Data

Indian religions: a historical reader of spiritual expression and experience / edited by Peter Heehs
p. cm.
Includes bibliographical references and index.
ISBN 0-8147-3649-1 (alk. paper) — ISBN 0-8147-3650-5 (pbk. : alk. paper)
1. India-Religion. I. Heehs, Peter.

BL2003.3.I53 2002
294-dc21 2002022392

Printed in India

CONTENTS

EDITOR'S ACKNOWLEDGEMENTS

An anthology like this is only as good as the selections that make it up. I am grateful to the scholars who allowed me to use extracts from their translations, and to the organisations that made it possible for me to reproduce extracts from the works of their founders. Thanks also are due to the publishers who granted me permission to use works in which they hold copyright.

This book grew out of a suggestion by Rukun Advani of Permanent Black, whose encouragement did not falter during the many months it took to compile and write it. In gathering material I received much assistance from the librarians and staff of the French Institute of Pondicherry, the librarians and staff of the Sri Aurobindo Library, Pondicherry, and Patricia Meredith Greer. Ashok Acharya, David Slaney, Bob Zwicker, Bryce Grinlington and Madhumita Patnaik were kind enough to read all or part of the proofs. I am indebted to three of my colleagues at the Sri Aurobindo Ashram Archives for help with the typesetting: Matthijs Cornelissen, Chaitanya Swain and especially Ilavati Patel. The Sri Aurobindo Ashram bears no responsibility for the compilation, introduction or notes.

COPYRIGHT ACKNOWLEDGEMENTS

Some of the material reproduced within this book is, to the best of our knowledge, no longer under copyright. For material which remains under copyright, the editor and publishers gratefully acknowledge permission from copyright-holders to reproduce extracts, as listed below. Every effort was made to trace copyright-holders, as is evident from this list, but in some cases this was not possible at the time of going to press. Perceived omissions or errors, if brought to notice, will be rectified in subsequent printings.

To Agni, To Ushas, To Vishnu, To Soma. From *The Vedic Experience: Mantramañjari*, by Raimundo Panikkar copyright © 1977 by Raimundo Panikkar.

To Indra. From *The Secret of the Veda,* copyright © 1998 by Sri Aurobindo Ashram Trust. Reproduced with the permission of Sri Aurobindo Ashram Copyright Department.

The Unknown God, the Golden Embryo; Creation Hymn; The Long-Haired Ascetic. From *The Rig Veda: An Anthology* by Wendy Doniger O'Flaherty, copyright © 1981 Wendy Doniger O'Flaherty. Reproduced with the permission of Wendy Doniger.

The City of Brahman, From the Chandogya Upanishad, From the Shvetasvatara Upanishad. From *Hindu Scriptures*, edited by Dominic Goodall, copyright © 1996 J. M. Dent.

From the Kena Upanishad, The Isha Upanishad. From *Kena and Other Upanishads,* by Sri Aurobindo, copyright © 2001 Sri Aurobindo Ashram Trust; from *The Upanishads*, by Sri Aurobindo, copyright © 1972 Sri Aurobindo Ashram Trust. Reproduced with the permission of Sri Aurobindo Ashram Copyright Department.

From the Mundaka Upanishad, From the Kaivalya Upanishad. From *The Principal Upanishads*, translated by S. Radhakrishnan, first published in Great Britain 1953, reprinted 1978 by George Allen & Unwin Ltd.

From the Kundika Upanishad. *From The Samnyasa Upanisads.*

Hindu Scriptures on Asceticism and Renunciation by Patrick Olivelle, translated by Patrick Olivelle, copyright © 1992 Oxford University Press, Inc. Used by permission of Oxford University Press, Inc.

A Buddhist Account, Seeking and Enlightenment, The Summons to Teach, The Four Jhanas and Beyond, The Four Foundations of Mindfulness. From *The Middle Length Discourses of the Buddha: A New Translation of the Majjhima Nikaya,* translated by Bhikku Nanamoli and Bhikku Bodhi, copyright © 1995 Bhikku Bodhi. Used by permission of Wisdom Publications, Somerville, MA 02144, USA.

The Passing of the Buddha, Right Conduct for the Lay Person. From *The Long Discourses of the Buddha: A Translation of the Digha Nikaya*, by Maurice Walshe, copyright © 1987, 1995 Maurice Walshe. Used by permission of Wisdom Publications, Somerville, MA 02144, USA.

Turning the Wheel of Dhamma. From *The First Discourse of the Buddha*, by Dr Rewata Dhamma, copyright © 1997 Venerable Dr Rewata Dhamma. Used by permission of Wisdom Publications, Somerville, MA 02144, USA.

Nagasena on No-Self. From *Buddhist Scriptures* selected and translated by Edward Conze, copyright © 1959 Edward Conze.

One Monk, One Nun. From *Songs of the Sons and Daughters of Buddha*, translated by Andrew Schelling and Anne Waldman, copyright © 1996 Andrew Schelling and Anne Waldman. Reproduced with the permission of Andrew Schelling and Anne Waldman.

Fundamentals of Samkhya, Liberation in Samkhya. From *Classical Samkhya: An Interpretation of its History and Meaning*, by Gerald James Larson, copyright © 1969 author. Reproduced with the permission of Gerald James Larson.

Cessation of the Turnings of Thought, Freedom from Suffering by Active Performance of Yoga, The Eightfold Path of Yoga, Extraordinary Powers, Towards Pure Identity. From *Yoga: Discipline of Freedom: The* Yoga Sutra *Attributed to Patanjali*, by Barbara

Stoler Miller, copyright © 1995 Barbara Stoler Miller Testamentary Trust.

Beyond Life and Death, Freedom from Passion, The Path of Action, Inner Peace and Joy, Yoga Meditation, The Eternal Path, The Vision of the World-Spirit, Different Forms of Practice, The Cosmic Divine, The Supreme Secret. From *The Bhagavad Gita*, translated by Arthur Osborne and Prof. G. V. Kulkarni, copyright © Sri Ramanasramam.

The Heart Sutra, The Perfection of Patience, Emptiness, Suchness, Contemplation of Thought, The Perfection of Meditation, Perfection of Wisdom, The Provisional and the Final Nirvana, Devotion to Avalokiteshvara. From *Buddhist Texts through the Ages*, edited by Edward Conze *et al.* Published 1954 by Bruno Cassirer, Oxford, under the auspices of the Royal India, Pakistan and Ceylon Society.

Vimalakirti Replies to the Bodhisattva Manjusri. From Robert A. F. Thurman, translator, *The Holy Teaching of Vimalakirti: A Mahayana Scripture*. University Park, PA: Penn State University Press, pp. 46–7. Copyright © 1976 by The Pennsylvania State University. Reproduced by permission of the publisher.

A Bodhisattva's Self-realisation, Words and the Highest Reality. From *The Lankavatara Sutra: A Mahayana Text*, translated by Daisetz Teitaro Suzuki. Published 1932 by Routledge and Kegan Paul.

Supreme Enlightenment; As is Nirvana, So is Samsara, translated by David Snellgrove. From *Buddhist Texts through the Ages*, edited by Edward Conze *et al.* Published 1954 by Bruno Cassirer, Oxford, under the auspices of the Royal India, Pakistan and Ceylon Society. Reproduced with the permission of David Snellgrove.

Direct Personal Experience. From *The Concealed Essence of the Hevajra Tantra*, translated by G.W. Farrow and I. Menon, copyright 1992 © Motilal Banarsidass Publishers Pvt. Ltd. Reproduced by permission of Motilal Banarsidass.

The Bound Soul and its Liberation. From *Bhatta Ramakantha's*

Commentary on the Kiranatantra, edited and translated by Dominic Goodall, copyright © 1998 Institut Français de Pondichéry. Reproduced by permission of Institut Français de Pondichéry.

Supreme Delight. From *Vijnanabhairava or Divine Consciousness*, by Jaideva Singh, copyright © Motilal Banarsidass Publishers Private Limited. Reproduced by permission of Motilal Banarsidass.

Contemplation of the Supreme Lord, Fundamentals of Hathayoga, The Practice of Pranayama From *The Yoga Tradition*, by Georg Feuerstein. Copyright 1998 © Georg Feuerstein. Reproduced with the permission of Georg Feuerstein.

The Origin of Linga-Worship. From *Classical Hindu Mythology*, edited and translated by Cornelia Dimmitt and J.A.B. van Buitenen, copyright © 1978 Temple University.

For the Love of Krishna. From *Hindu Scriptures*, edited and translated by Dominic Goodall, copyright © 1996 J. M. Dent.

Nagarjuna. From *The Fundamental Wisdom of the Middle Way: Nagarjuna's Mulamadhyamakarika* by Jay L. Garfield, translated by Jay L. Garfield, copyright © 1995 Oxford University Press, Inc. Used by permission of Oxford University Press, Inc.

Shantideva. From *The Way of the Bodhisattva*, translated by the Padmakara Translation Group, copyright © 1997 The Padmakara Translation Group. Published by Shambhala Publications, Inc. Reproduced with the permission of the Padmakara Translation Group.

Vasubandhu. From *Seven Works of Vasubandhu: The Buddhist Psychological Doctor*, by Stefan Anacker, copyright © Motilal Banarsidass Publishers Private Limited. Reproduced by permission of Motilal Banarsidass.

Umasvati. From *That Which Is: Tattvartha Sutra*, translated by Nathmal Tatia, copyright © 1994 by Institute of Jainology. Reproduced with the permission of Institute of Jainology and International Sacred Literature Trust.

Amritachandra Suri. From *Anandachandrasuri's Laghutattvasphota*, edited by Padmanabh S. Jaini, copyright © 1978 Padmanabh S. Jaini. Reproduced with the permission of Padmanabh S. Jaini.

Shankara. From *A Thousand Teachings: The* Upadesasahasri *of Sankara*, translated and edited by Sengaku Mayeda, copyright © 1992 University of Tokyo Press.

Ramanuja. From *The* Gadya-traya *of Sri Ramanujacharya,* translated by M. R. Rajagopala Ayyangar. Published by M. R. Rajagopala Ayyangar.

Vasugupta. From *The Yoga Tradition*, by Georg Feuerstein, copyright © 1998 Georg Feuerstein. Reproduced with the permission of Georg Feuerstein.

Utpaladeva. Reprinted by permission from *Shaiva Devotional Songs of Kashmir: A Translation and Study of Utpaladeva's 'Shivastotravali'*, by Constantina Rhodes Bailly, the State University of New York Press © 1987, State University of New York, all rights reserved.

Abhinavagupta. Reprinted by permission from *The Triadic Heart of Siva: Kaula Tantricism of Abhinavagupta in the Non-Dual Shaivism of Kashmir*, by Paul Eduardo Muller-Ortega, the State University of New York Press © 1989, State University of New York. All rights reserved.

Nizam ad-din Awliya. From *Morals for the Heart*, translated by Bruce B. Lawrence, copyright © 1992 by Bruce B. Lawrence. Used by permission of Paulist Press. www.paulistpress.com

Sharafuddin Maneri. From *The Hundred Letters*, translated by Paul Jackson, S. J., copyright © 1980 by Paulist Press, Inc. Used by permission of Paulist Press. www.paulistpress.com

'Isa Jund Allah. From *Teachings of Sufism*, selected and translated by Carl W. Ernst, Ph.D., copyright © 1999 by Carl W. Ernst. Reprinted by arrangement with Shambhala Publications, Inc., Boston, www.shambhala.com

Dara Shikuh. From *Dara Shikuh: Life and Works*, translated by Bikrama Jit Hasrat, copyright © 1979 HASRAT, Bikrama Jit. Reproduced with the permission of Munshiram Manoharlal Publishers Pvt. Ltd.

Fatima Jahanara Begum Sahib. From *Readings from the Mystics of Islam*, by Margaret Smith. Published 1950 by Luzac & Company, London.

Shah Wali Allah. From *The Heritage of Sufism, vol. 3:Late Classical Persianate Sufism (1501–1750)*, edited by Leonard Lewisohn and David Morgan, copyright © 1999 Leonard Lewisohn and David Morgan. Reproduced by permission of Oneworld Publications.

Tirumular. From *Tirumantiram: A Tamil Scriptural Classic*, translated by Dr B. Natarajan, copyright © 1991 Sri Ramakrishna Math. Reproduced with the permission of Sri Ramakrishna Math, Chennai.

Sivavakkiyar, Pattinattar, Akkapey-cittar. From *The Poets of the Powers*, by Kamil V. Zvelebil, copyright © 1973 Kamil B. Zvelebil. Reproduced with the permission of Kamil V. Zvelebil.

Pampattic-cittar. From *dance, snake! dance!*, translated by David C. Buck, copyright © 1976 David Buck.

Songs of 'Jnandev'. From *Songs on Yoga: Texts and Teachings of the Maharashtrian Naths*, by Catharina Kiehnle, copyright © Catharina Kiehnle.

Lalla's Vakhs. From *To the Other Shore*, by Jaishree Kak Odin, copyright © 1999 Jaishree Kak Odin. Reproduced with the permission of Jaishree Kak Odin.

Songs of 'Chandidas'. From *Love Songs of Chandidas: The Rebel Poet-Priest of Bengal*, translated by Deben Bhattacharya, copyright © 1967, 1969 UNESCO.

Songs of the Bauls. From *The Mirror of the Sky: Songs of the Bauls of Bengal*, by Deben Bhattacharya, copyright © 1999 Deben Bhattacharya.

Appar, Sambandar. From *Poems to Siva: The Hymns of the Tamil Saints*, by Indira Viswanathan Peterson, published by Princeton University Press, copyright © 1989 by Princeton University Press. Reproduced by permission of Princeton University Press with the assistance of Indira Viswanathan Peterson.

Sundarar, Manikkavachakar (part), Tirumangai. From *Slaves of the Lord: The Path of the Tamil Saints,* by Vidya Dehejia, copyright © 1988 Vidya Dehejia. Reproduced with the permission of Vidya Dehejia.

Manikkavachakar (part). From *Hymns of the Dancing Shiva,* by Glen C. Yocum, copyright © 1982 Glen C. Yocum.

Manikkavachakar (part). From *Love of God according to Shaiva Siddhanta,* by M. Dhavamony, copyright © Oxford University Press.

Andal. Reprinted by permission from *Antal and Her Path of Love: Poems of a Woman Saint from South India*, by Vidya Dehejia, the State University of New York Press © 1990, State University of New York. All rights reserved.

Nammalwar. From *Hymns for the Drowning*, translated by A.K. Ramanujan, copyright © 1989 A. K. Ramanujan. Reproduced with the permission of Molly Daniels-Ramanujan.

Devara Dasimayya, Basavanna, Mahadeviyakka, Allama Prabhu. From *Speaking of Shiva*, translated by A. K. Ramanujan, copyright © 1973 A. K. Ramanujan. Reproduced with the permission of Molly Daniels-Ramanujan

Annamacharya, Purandardasa, Kanakadasa. From *Songs of Three Great South Indian Saints,* translated by William J. Jackson, copyright © 1998 Oxford University Press. Reproduced by permission of Oxford University Press, New Delhi, India.

Tyagaraja. From *Tyagaraja: Life and Lyrics*, by William J. Jackson, copyright © 1991 Oxford University Press. Reproduced by permission of Oxford University Press, New Delhi, India.

Jnandev. From *Shri Jnandev's Anubhavamrut: The Immortal*

Experience of Being, translated by Dilip Chitre, copyright © 1996 Dilip Chitre.

Chokhamela. From *Myths, Saints and Legends in Medieval India*, by Charlotte Vaudeville, copyright © 1996 Oxford University Press. Reproduced by permission of Oxford University Press, New Delhi, India.

Narsi Mehta. From *Gujarat and its Literature: From Early Times to 1852*, by Kanaiyalal M. Munshi, copyright © Bharatiya Vidya Bhavan.

Dayaram. From *The Poetics of Devotion: The Gujarati Lyrics of Dayaram*, by Rachel Dwyer, copyright © 2001 Rachel Dwyer. Reproduced with the permission of Rachel Dwyer.

Vidyapati. From *Love Songs of Vidyapati*, by Deben Bhattacharya, copyright © 1963 George Allen and Unwin, Ltd.

Chandidas. From *Love Songs of Chandidas: The Rebel Poet-Priest of Bengal*, translated by Deben Bhattacharya, copyright © 1967, 1969 UNESCO.

Govindadas. From *In Praise of* Krishna, translated by Edward Dimock and Denise Levertov (1997). Copyright © by Asia Society. Reprinted by permission.

Ramprasad. From *Ramprasad: The Melodious Mystic*, translated by Swami Budhananda, copyright © 1982 Secretary, Ramakrishna Mission, New Delhi. Reproduced with the permission of Ramakrishna Math, Chennai.

Surdas, Tulsidas. From *Songs of the Saints of India*, edited by John Stratton Hawley, translated by John Stratton Hawley and M. Juergensmeyer, copyright © 1988 Oxford University Press, Inc. Used by permission of Oxford University Press, Inc.

Mira Bai. From *The Devotional Poems of Mirabai*, translated by A. J. Alston, copyright 1980 © Motilal Banarsidass. Reproduced by permission of Motilal Banarsidass.

Kabir (part). Reprinted by permission from *Songs of Kabir from* *the Adi Granth*, translated by Nirmal Dass, the State University of New York Press © 1991, State University of New York. All rights reserved.

Kabir (part). From *The Bijak of Kabir*, translated by Linda Hess and Shukdev Singh, copyright © 1983 Linda Hess. Reproduced with the permission of Linda Hess.

Kabir (part). From *A Weaver Named Kabir*, by Charlotte Vaudeville, copyright © 1993 Oxford University Press. Reproduced by permission of Oxford University Press, New Delhi, India.

Raidas. From *The Life and Works of Raidas*, by Winand M. Callewaert and Peter G. Friedlander, © Authors. Reproduced with the permission of the authors.

Paltu Sahib. From *Saint Paltu: His Life and Teachings*, by Isaac A. Ezekiel, copyright © 1979 Radha Soami Satsang Beas. Reproduced with the permission of Radha Soami Satsang Beas.

Guru Nanak, Guru Ram Das, Guru Arjan, Guru Tegh Bahadur, Guru Gobind Singh. From *The Name of My Beloved: Verses of the Sikh Gurus*, translated by Nikky-Guninder Kaur Singh, copyright © 1995 by Nikky-Guninder Kaur Singh. Reproduced with the permission of Nikky-Guninder Kaur Singh.

Sultan Bahu. From *Death Before Dying: The Sufi Poems of Sultan Bahu*, translated by Jamal J. Elias, copyright © 1998 by The Regents of the University of California. Reprinted by permission of The Regents of the University of California.

Bulleh Shah. From *Bulleh Shah: The Love-intoxicated Iconoclast*, by J. R. Puri and T. R. Shangari, copyright © 1986 Radha Soami Satsang Beas. Reproduced with the permission of Radha Soami Satsang Beas.

Shah Abdul Latif. Khwaja Mir Dard (part). From *Pain and Grace: A Study of Two Mystical Writers of Eighteenth-Century Muslim India*, by Annemarie Schimmel, copyright © 1976 E.ÊJ. Brill. Reproduced with the permission of E. J. Brill.

Sachal Sarmast (part). From *Sindhi Literature*, by Annemarie

Schimmel, copyright © 1974 Otto Harrasowitz. Reproduced with the permission of Otto Harrasowitz.

Sachal Sarmast (part). From 'Sufism - II', by M. B. Butani, in *The Cultural Heritage of India*, copyright © 1956 The Ramakrishna Mission Institute of Culture, Calcutta.

Sachal Sarmast (part). From *Sachal Sarmast*, by Kalyan B. Advani, copyright © 1971 Sahitya Akademi.

Khwaja Mir Dard (part). From *Mystical Dimensions of Islam*, by Annemarie Schimmel. Copyright © 1975 by University of North Carolina Press. Used by permission of the publisher and the author.

Ghauth Ali Shah. From *Solomon's Ring: The Life and Teachings of a Sufi Master*, by Gul Hasan, translated by Hasan Askari, copyright © 1998 Hasan Askari. Reproduced by permission of AltaMira Press.

The Awakening, Ascension, From 'The Garland of Experience', The Universal True Creed. From Pathway to God Trod by Raamalinga Swaamikal, by G. Vanmikanathan, copyright © 1976 Ramalinga Mission.

From Sri Ramakrishna the Great Master, From The Gospel of Sri Ramakrishna. From *Sri Ramakrishna the Great Master*, by Swami Saradananda, translated by Swami Jagadananda, copyright © The President, Sri Ramakrishna Math; from *The Gospel of Sri Ramakrishna*, by Mahendranath Gupta, translated by Swami Nikhilananda, copyright © Sri Ramakrishna Math, Chennai. All reproduced with the permission of Sri Ramakrishna Math, Chennai.

From Uttarpara Speech, Extracts from Letters to Disciples, Sri Aurobindo's Teaching and Method of Practice, From the Life Divine, From Talks with Sri Aurobindo, Four Sonnets. From *Karmayogin*, by Sri Aurobindo, copyright © 1997 Sri Aurobindo Ashram Trust; Letters on Yoga, by Sri Aurobindo, copyright © 1970 Sri Aurobindo Ashram Trust; From On Himself, by Sri Aurobindo, copyright © 1972 Sri Aurobindo Ashram Trust; *The Life Divine*, by Sri Aurobindo, copyright © 1970 Sri Aurobindo Ashram Trust; from *Talks with Sri Aurobindo*, by Nirodbaran, copyright © 2001 Sri Aurobindo Ashram Trust; from *Sonnets*, by Sri Aurobindo, copyright © 1980 Sri Aurobindo Ashram Trust. All reproduced with the kind permission of Sri Aurobindo Ashram Copyright Department.

The Awakening, Who am I?, From Spiritual Instruction, From Maharshi's Gospel, From Talks with Sri Ramana Maharshi, Five Stanzas on the One Self. From *The Teachings of Bhagavan Ramana Maharshi in His Own Words,* edited by Arthur Osborne, copyright © Sri Ramanasramam; from *The Collected Works of Ramana Maharshi*, by Ramana Maharshi, sixth revised edition, copyright © 1996 Sri Ramanasramam; from *Maharshi's Gospel*, by Sri Ramana Maharshi, copyright © Sri Ramanasramam; from *Talks with Sri Ramana Maharshi*, copyright © Sri Ramanasramam. All reproduced with the permission of Sri Ramanasramam.

From the Sufi Message of Hazrat Inayat Khan. From *A Sufi Master Answers: On the Sufi Message of Hazrat Inayat Khan,* by Dr Elisabeth Keesing, copyright © Hazrat Inayat Khan Memorial Trust; from *The Heart of Sufism: Essential Writings of Hazrat Inayat Khan*, copyright © 1999 by The International Headquarters of the Sufi Movement. All reproduced with the permission of The International Headquarters of the Sufi Movement.

From In Quest of God, From In the Vision of God, From God-Experience. From *In Quest of God*, by Ramdas, copyright © Anandashram Trust; from *In the Vision of God*, copyright © Anandashram Trust; From *God-Experience*, volume 1, published by Anandasram, copyright reserved by the Publishers. Reproduced with the permission of Anandashram.

From Autobiography of a Yogi, Paramahansa Yogananda meets Anandamayi Ma. From *Autobiography of a Yogi*, by Paramahansa Yogananda, copyright © 1946 Paramahansa Yogananda, copyright © renewed 1974 Self-Realisation Fellowship.

Truth is a Pathless Land, The Core of Krishnamurti's Teaching. From *Total Freedom: The Essential Krishnamurti*, by J. Krishnamurti, published by HarperSanFrancisco, copyright © 1996 by Krishnamurti Foundation of American and Krishnamurti Foundation Trust, Ltd. Reproduced with the permission of Krishnamurti Foundation Trust, Brockwood Park, Bramdean, Hampshire SO24 0LQ, England.

The Awareness of What Is. From *The First and Last Freedom*, by J. Krishnamurti, copyright © 1954 Krishnamurti Foundation of America. Reproduced with the permission of Krishnamurti Foundation of America.

From Krishnamurti's Notebook, From Krishnamurti's Journal, From Krishnamurti To Himself. From *Krishnamurti's Notebook*, by J. Krishnamurti, copyright © Krishnamurti Foundation Trust, London; from *Krishnamurti's Journal*, by J. Krishnamurti, copyright © 1982 Krishnamurti Foundation Trust Ltd.; from *Krishnamurti To Himself: His Last Journal*, by J. Krishnamurti, copyright © 1987 by Krishnamurti Foundation Trust Limited. All reproduced with the permission of Krishnamurti Foundation Trust LImited, Brockwood Park, Bramdean, Hampshire SO24 0LQ, England.

Talks on Sadhana, Replies to Questions. From *Matri Vani, volume II*, by Anandamayi Ma, translated by Atmananda, compiled by Sister Uma, published by Shree Shree Anandamayee Charitable Society; from *As the Flower Sheds its Fragrance*, published Shree Shree Anandamayee Charitable Society; from *Words of Sri Anandamayi Ma*, by Anandamayi Ma, translated and compiled by Atmananda, published by Shree Shree Anandamayee Charitable Society.

From I Am That. From *I Am That*, by Sri Nisargadatta Maharaj, translated by Maurice Frydman, revised and edited by Sudhakar S. Dikshit, copyright © 1973 by Nisargadatta Maharaj, published by Chetana (P) Ltd., Bombay.

From Consciousness and the Absolute. *The Final Talks of Sri Nisargadatta Maharaj*, edited by Jean Dunn, copyright © 1994 by Imogene Dunn.

From Kundalini: The Evolutionary Energy in Man, From *Kundalini: The Evolutionary Energy in Man*, by Gopi Krishna, copyright ©

1967 by Gopi Krishna. Reproduced with the permission of Gene Kieffer.

From Later Writings. From *Kundalini Empowering Human Evolution: Selected Writings of Gopi Krishna*, copyright © by Gene Kieffer. Reproduced with the permission of Gene Kieffer.

Bhai Vir Singh: Four Poems. From *Bhai Vir Singh: Poet of the Sikhs*, translated by Gurbachan Singh Talib and Harbans Singh, with Yann Lovelock, copyright © Motilal Banarsidass. Reproduced by permission of Motilal Banarsidass.

Muhammad Iqbal: Five Poems. From *Tulip in the Desert: A Selection of the Poetry of Muhammad Iqbal*, translated by Mustansir Mir, translations © 2000 Mustansir Mir. Reproduced with the permission of Mustansir Mir.

Subramania Bharati: Three Poems. From *Poems of Subramania Bharati*, by Prema Nandakumar, translation copyright © 1977 UNESCO.

Introduction

The Jogi cries:
    "Gorakh, Gorakh!"
The Hindu utters
    the name of Ram,
The Mussalman repeats:
    "God is One!"
But the Lord of Kabir
    pervades all.[1]

Kabir, the fifteenth-century author of these lines, exemplifies the diversity of the religions of India and at the same time points to an all-pervading unity beyond religious formulations. Although influenced by each of the traditions he refers to—yoga, Hindu devotionalism and Islam—his teachings were not an amalgam of other people's ideas, but the result of his own practice and experience. Pervading all, "the Lord of Kabir" could be sought by means of one religion or another, but the best place to look, as he said elsewhere, was "in the heart of your heart".[2]

Kabir is just one of hundreds of men and women of South Asia who have given expression to personal experiences of an inner or higher or divine or absolute reality. Most of the religions of the region trace themselves back to such founder-figures. Selections from their written and spoken words are presented in the following pages.

Scope and Organisation

This reader is an attempt to present as much of the diversity of the Indian religious traditions as is possible in a single volume. Selections from around two hundred texts are included, written and oral, ancient and modern. The earliest ones were composed towards the end of the second millennium BCE, the latest at the end of the second millennium CE. The authors are from almost every corner of the subcontinent of South Asia. For convenience, the familiar term "India" is used for this region, but it should be understood that it is meant in its historical and not its political sense. In modern political terms, the authors lived in what are now the states of India, Pakistan and Bangladesh. Some of their texts drew nourishment from roots in central or western Asia; some spread their branches to Sri Lanka, Tibet, or even further afield; but all of them were fruits of the Indian soil.

The arrangement of the reader is historical, but strict chronology and rigid periodization are avoided. The material is arranged in five overlapping parts, called Foundations, Developments, Elaborations, Reformulations, and Continuity and Innovation. The markers of each part are date, language and tradition. The first part, Foundations, begins with the earliest surviving Indian religious text, the *Ṛg Veda*, and extends for some two millennia into the early centuries of the Common Era. Written in Sanskrit and two Prakrits, the texts included in this part document the beginnings of three religious traditions: Hinduism, Jainism and Buddhism, to use the modern names. The second part, Developments, covers some twelve hundred years, from just before the beginning of the Common Era until the end of the first millennium. During this period the foundational teachings of the vedic and upanishadic sages and of the earliest followers of the Buddha were developed in novel ways. Almost all the selections in this part were written in Sanskrit, ranging in style from the chaste classicism of the *Bhagavad Gītā* to the hybrid language of the Mahayana *sūtra*s and the rough vigour of the *tantra*s and *purāṇa*s. The third part, Elaborations, overlaps chronologically and developmentally with the second. For about a thousand years, from the second to the twelfth century, Sanskrit-knowing philosophers elaborated systems that defended and extended the insights of earlier Buddhist, Jaina and Hindu teachers. From the twelfth to the eighteenth centuries, Persian-knowing teachers did the same with a religious tradition whose foundations and early developments took place in Arabia and other lands to the west.

All the texts in the first three parts were composed in languages known by relatively small élite classes. In contrast, the texts included in the last two parts were sung or spoken or written in still-living languages of the subcontinent or (in a few recent cases) in English. The fourth part, Reformulations, begins with the poems and songs of Tamil *siddha*s and devotees, and includes works by mystics from Karnataka, Andhra, Maharashtra, Gujarat, Mithila,

Bengal, Kashmir, Punjab, Sind, and the Hindi- and Urdu-speaking North. Most of these texts give expression to the poet's *bhakti* or devotion to a particular form of the Divine, but some of them celebrate the Formless. Chronologically, they range from the sixth or seventh century up to the mid-nineteenth. The traditions chosen for inclusion comprise a dozen schools of Hinduism, several varieties of popular Sufism, and Sikhism. The fifth and last part, Continuity and Innovation, covers the mid nineteenth to late twentieth centuries. It includes works by sixteen mystics and poets from different parts of the subcontinent, who spoke Tamil, Bengali, Marathi, Punjabi, Urdu and other languages, and sometimes used English for their teachings.

In selecting material, preference has been given to what are often called (for want of better terms) the "mediaeval" and "modern" periods. Only about a third of the book (Parts 1 and 2) is devoted to the "classical" texts that for most people define what Hinduism, Jainism and Buddhism are. Frequently translated and widely published, these foundational texts do not need to be emphasised here.

The Sanskrit and Prakrit texts of the classical period share one characteristic: their actual authors were not historical individuals but generally nameless spokesmen of tradition. The second third of the book (Parts 3 and 4) is devoted to authors who lived between the end of the classical period and the beginning of modern times. With one or two exceptions, they are well attested historically, even if their dates are in dispute. Many of the authors in these parts are famous throughout India; others are little known outside their home provinces. The final third of the book (Part 5) comprises talks and writings of men and women who lived during the nineteenth and twentieth centuries. (No one living at the time this reader was compiled has been included.) Their works are given as much space as those of the more celebrated mystics of the past because their nearness to us in time gives their works an accessibility and relevance that older writings sometimes seem to lack.

The presentation of the texts is historical in the sense that it follows the roughly chronological lines indicated above. In addition, each text and each author is situated within the cultural, social or political history of a period and region. An attempt is made to bring out linkages between texts and authors of related traditions, as well as the often unacknowledged links between apparently unrelated traditions. Lines of historical development are sketched, but no attempt is made to plot the material into one historical narrative, with a single origin and direction. The emphasis rather is on the plurality of traditions. Texts from all the five "major" religions of the subcontinent are included. Of these, four are represented by a variety of subtraditions: orthodox and heterodox, classical and popular, public and transgressive. These subtraditions, rather than the religions themselves, are the units of the book's organisation. As a result, texts belonging to one religion are not necessarily grouped together. Buddhist texts, for example, are found in three separate places: Chapter 4 (Theravada Buddhism), Chapter 7 (Mahayana and Vajrayana Buddhism), and Chapter 10 (Spiritual Philosophies). The alternation of texts from different traditions should help the reader take note of parallel developments across religious boundaries.

The religions of India form such a vast area of study that it would be impossible to include selections dealing with every aspect of every tradition or even of selected traditions in a single volume. Every religion has a psychological, a practical, a mythic, an intellectual, an ethical, a legal and social, and an organisational side. Significant texts are associated with each of these aspects. Hinduism, for instance, has a large number of treatises dealing with ritual practice, huge compendia of myth and legend, whole libraries of philosophy, numerous ethical scriptures and many texts setting forth the intricacies of its laws and social organisation. Some of these texts are respected by many branches of Hinduism, others only by particular regional and sectarian groupings. Full coverage of all aspects of every important Hindu tradition would require more than one large volume, while Indian Buddhism and Islam, Jainism and Sikhism, would together require at least as much space.

In order to keep this reader to a manageable size, the editor has focused on one particular aspect of the religions of India: their psychological or experiential side. While by no means the whole of religion, the experiential side is regarded by many as being of central importance for at least four reasons. First, founders and adherents of many traditions, including all those covered by this book, see the ultimate goal of spiritual practice as a subjective or experiential state, to be obtained through individual effort or devotion. Secondly, many founders or innovators speak of subjective religious experiences as important means in their own spiritual practice and in the practices they recommend to their followers. Thirdly, many of these founders or innovators base their teachings on knowledge they say was obtained by means of subjective experience. Finally, the works in which these experience-based teaching are contained are among the high points of Indian religious literature, indeed of Indian literature in general. Each of these points will be discussed below. First, however, it is necessary to say something more about the preference given to the individual as opposed to the collective aspect of religion.

Collective and Individual Aspects of Religion: Social Science and Religion

Like all other expressions of human life, religion has a collective as well as an individual side. Even traditions that state their goals in individual terms, such as Buddhism, Jainism and some forms of Hinduism, grant an important role to the religious community and to collective forms of practice. So important indeed are the collective aspects of religion that most social scientists view religion primarily or entirely as a construction of social forces or entities. Cultural anthropologists see it as a chief determinant and expression of the structure and dynamics of a culture. Many sociologists, following Émile Durkheim, view it as a means by which society preserves its equilibrium. Some economists regard particular religions as consequences of particular socio-economic conditions; Marxists see it as a part of the ideology or false consciousness that keeps the exploited classes from realising their true condition. Historians, sifting through the documents of early civilisations, note that most of them were organised around their religions, and believe that the individual, as we now understand the term, is a relatively recent emergence. Recent cultural theorists go a step farther by asserting that the individual or "subject" is a modern cultural construct that in the postmodern age has effectively ceased to exist.

Despite their interest in the individual psyche, many psychologists also regard religion as a social construct — one that is at root illusory. Sigmund Freud gave definitive expression to this viewpoint when he wrote: "Religious conceptions originated in the same need as all other achievements of culture, from the necessity of defending oneself against the crushing superiority of nature" and "from the urge to correct the painfully felt imperfections of culture" (Freud 1961: 26–27; trans. Gay 1988: 530). To Freud and many other psychiatrists, religious experiences are manifestations or symptoms of underlying neuroses. More recently, some neurologists have tried to show that religious experience "can be explained in terms of neural networks, neurotransmitters and brain chemistry" (Vedantam 2001).

Practitioners of these disciplines view religion and its expressions in terms of theories that are believed to provide a complete explanation of human life and its products. They reduce religious phenomena to anthropological, sociological, economic, historical, psychological or neurological data, and in so doing deprive them of their religious character. While there is no universally accepted definition of "the religious", "the spiritual" or "the sacred", any acceptable definition would have to take seriously the claims of religious innovators, such as those whose works appear in this volume, that they are in contact with a reality that both includes and in some way exceeds the world around us. Theorists who explain religious phenomena in terms of social or psychological or neurological structures can sometimes tell us a great deal about how such phenomena emerge, but they often misrepresent the plain sense of the texts they criticise by imposing on them an alien interpretive framework.[3]

The selections in this reader are presented as religious documents and not as social-scientific data. Accordingly, in the notes that accompany the texts, little space is given to social-scientific theory. This does not mean that the presentation is free from theoretical assumptions. Every coherent presentation is based on assumptions, whether acknowledged or taken for granted. Here the working hypothesis is the one proposed, implicitly or explicitly, by the authors of the selected texts: that there is a religious or spiritual or sacred dimension of existence that both includes and in some sense exceeds the observable universe, and that it is possible for individuals to come into contact with it.

This hypothesis is consistent with the "radical empiricism" of William James, who attempted to study religious phenomena with the same rigour as he studied other aspects of human mind and life. According to James, "To be radical, an empiricism must neither admit into its constructions any element that is not directly experienced, nor exclude from them any element that is directly experienced" (1971: 25). In his *Varieties of Religious Experience*, James treated the writings of mystics as useful records of direct experiences. He summed up his attitude towards such material in a later essay: "One cannot criticise the vision of a mystic — one can but pass it by, or else accept it as having some evidential weight" (1912: 374). Not surprisingly, James's view of the relationship between individual religious experience and organised religion is different from that of most modern social theorists. He stated this view concisely in a letter of 1901: "The mother sea and fountain-head of all religions lie in the mystical experiences of the individual, taking the word mystical in a very wide sense. All theologies and ecclesiasticisms are secondary growths superimposed" (1920: 149). The selections in this book have sufficient "evidential weight" to establish a prima facie case for the existence of religious experience. They cannot prove, nor could any documentary evidence prove, the claim made by James in his letter,[4] but they do show that the experiences of religious founders and innovators have been a primary factor in the formulation of the goals, means and knowledge-claims of many spiritual traditions, and have been given expression in some of the most memorable literature of South Asia.

Goals: Liberation and Union

Many Indian traditions stress the importance of *mokṣa* or *mukti*: liberation of the individual from the cycles of rebirth. This goal is perhaps most explicit in Jainism and Buddhism. Jaina scriptures speak not only of *mokṣa* but also of *kevala* ("isolation" or "aloneness") (selections 24, 83). Buddhist texts speak especially of *nirvāṇa* or "extinction" (selections 28, 32, 63, 65, 80). The goal of liberation is found in some of the *upaniṣads* (selection 19), in Samkhya and Yoga (selections 40, 42), in the *Bhagavad Gītā* (selections 47, 49), in the *Śiva Sūtra* (selection 87), and in many modern texts (see for example selections 161, 168, 186). In other texts the goal put forward is not liberation from a painful or limited state, but calm or joyous union with the Absolute or Self or God (selections 11, 12, 15, 20, 21, 85, 103, 157, 163, 176). Some tantric texts promote the goal of liberation (selection 71); others combine or replace it with that of blissful union (selection 89, 97, 99, 104, 105) or masterful perfection (selections 68, 70, 100). In the devotional traditions, including those of the *sant*s and Sikhs, the goal is the ecstasy of closeness or union with the Divine (selections 55, 79, 88, 106–136, 137–141, 142–46, 154, 157, 173). Some sufis also speak of union with God or the Beloved (selections 90, 92, 94, 95, 150, 151, 152, 172).

These various conceptions of the goal of religious practice show some remarkable similarities across traditions, but it would be a mistake to think that the goals proposed were always precisely the same. It would not be wrong to conclude, however, that the goals are conceived as subjective or experiential states that are to be achieved by means of effort or grace.

Experiential Means

In most of the traditions included in this book, one who achieves the goal of liberation, unification or perfection does so by experiential means. The founders and renewers of the these traditions—those who are believed by the rank-and-file to have actually achieved the goal—state, or are made to state in traditional texts, that before reaching the ultimate goal they passed, spontaneously or by means of inner practice, through special subjective states, what nowadays we would call religious experiences.[5] When the time came for teaching, they exhorted others to seek these states, usually by following the same or a similar discipline.

Anubhava, the Sanskrit and modern north Indian word that corresponds most closely to our "experience", was not widely used for individual religious experience before the second half of the first millennium. Before then, terms denoting vision, direct witness, direct consciousness, direct knowledge or identity were used when speaking of the states that were prized and promoted by religious teachers.[6] The author of the *Śvetāśvatara Upaniṣad* says that when the embodied soul sees (*prapaśyet*) the real nature of the Self, the result is unity and freedom (selection 17). Similarly, the author of the *Maitrī Upaniṣad* says that when one sees (*paśyati*) the Brahman-source, one achieves unity in the Imperishable (selection 18). Early Theravada texts (for instance selection 28) stress that the Buddha mastered various teachings by "realising . . . with direct knowledge [*abhiññā*]", and then went on to attain the supreme deliverance of *nirvāṇa*. A later Mahayana *sūtra* has the Buddha declare that "the highest reality is to be attained by the inner realisation of noble wisdom" (selection 67). The *Sāṁkhya Kārikā* explains that the embodied being attains freedom in life through "the attainment of direct knowledge" (*samyagjñānādhigamād*) and then goes on to achieve full *kaivalya* (selection 40). The *Yoga Sūtra* describes *kaivalya* as "the power of consciousness in a state of true identity" (*svarūpapratiṣṭhā vā citiśaktiḥ*) (selection 45).

Individual experience plays an important role in all forms of tantric practice. The *Hevajra Tantra* says that the goal of Great Bliss is to be attained by "direct personal experience" (*svasaṁvedyād*) (selection 69); the *Dohākoṣa* says similarly that Great Bliss consists in "self-experience" (selection 70). The Hindu *Kulārṇava Tantra* explains that the awareness of the Absolute arises out of the pure experience of transcendental Being (selection 73). Texts of Nondual Kashmir Shaivism, which is rooted in the tantric tradition, stress the importance of experiential means for the attainment of freedom or union. The *Śiva Sūtra* says that by dwelling in the fourth or absolute state of consciousness, the practitioner is "released" and attains union with Shiva (selection 87). The Kashmiri philosopher Abhinavagupta explains that the yogin attains Self-knowledge by relaxing into the "direct experience of Bhairava [Shiva] in the form of consciousness" (*cidrūpa-sākṣad-bhairava*) (selection 89).

All but the last of these statements come from traditional or anonymous texts and might be regarded as prescriptive rather than descriptive—although it would not be unreasonable to think that many of the authors had experienced the states of which they spoke. The authors of most selected texts composed after the middle of the first millennium are known historical individuals, and when they speak of religious experiences, there is good reason to believe that they are describing states that they knew at first hand. The siddhas and yogis of the popular tantric traditions put many of their statements in experiential terms. "He is right there within you," Sivavakkiyar declares. "Stand still and feel him, feel!" (selection 98). The singers of the *bhakti* movement use intimate personal language to express the varied emotions of divine love and devotion. The cry of Manikkavachakar is representative: "You are my Lord who melting my bones entered my Self as a shrine" (selection 109). Ramanuja, the philosopher of *bhakti*, gives abstract expression to this "infinite and unsurpassed bliss of the experience of Bhagavan" (*bhagavad-anubhava*) (selection 86), but as a rule the poets of *bhakti* use the most concrete of language, speaking of seeing (selection 116), hearing (selections 120, 172), feeling (selection 114) and even tasting the forms of God. "He only can appreciate this who experiences it" (*sākṣa jyācī tyāsī manāmārjī*), says Bahina Bai of her "taste" of the divine consciousness (selection 126). Many *sants* and Sikhs use equally intense imagery to describe their devotion to the formless God (selections 137, 138, 140, 142), while others declare that no imagery is adequate: "This experience [*anabhai*] is such that it defies all description", sings Raidas of the unitive experience (selection 139). Some of the strongest human feelings are associated with erotic love, and a large number of bhaktas, sants, sufis and Sikhs use the language of human love to express their passion for the Divine (selections 107, 110, 112, 128, 129, 130, 132, 134, 135, 147, 148). The *sahajiyās* and *bāuls* combine this erotic devotionalism with the erotic methodology of the *tantras* (selections 104, 105).

The methodical disciplining of mind, emotions and body in order to attain experiential states has been a common theme in Indian religious traditions since the time of the *upaniṣads*. Meditative methods are alluded to in the *Chāndogya*, *Kaṭha* and other early *upaniṣads* (selections 11, 14), while later texts like the *Śvetāśvatara* and *Maitrī* present specific meditation techniques (selections 17, 18). Mahavira is said to have attained intuitive knowledge and *kevala* through the practice of psycho-physical austerities (selections 24, 25). Various meditative practices have formed part of Buddhist discipline from very early times (selections 35, 36, 38, 61). Methods for the attainment of *mokṣa* or *kaivalya* are given in the *Sāṁkhya Kārikā* and *Yoga Sūtra* (selections 40–43). The synthetic *Bhagavad Gītā* presents methods drawn from the upanishadic, Samkhya–Yoga and devotional traditions (selections 50, 53, 55). All forms of Tantrism, *haṭhayoga* included, are characterised by a reliance on psychological and psycho-physical techniques to achieve liberation and mastery (see for example selections 72–77, 101–103). Such techniques lie at the heart of philosophical systems like Kashmir Shaivism (selection 89), and are even found in the teachings of the Shattari and other sufi orders (selection 93). Masters of the *siddha*, *nāth* and *sant* traditions speak frequently of meditative and psycho-physical methods, as do virtually all the mystics of the modern period.

The works of these modern mystics were not transmitted orally, as were most earlier texts, but written down or recorded (in writing or on tape) and published during their lifetimes or afterwards. As a result, vast amounts of their direct teachings survive. These works, generally personal and often informal, contain many explicit references to their spiritual experiences. Scholars interested in modern theories of social constructivism might regard these as expressions of the nineteenth-century European "discourse of experience".[7] Others still under the sway of Freudianism or Marxism might consider them expressions of infant sexuality or post-feudal bourgeois mentality.[8] A more empirical approach would see them as recent examples of India's long tradition of basing spiritual teachings on individual spiritual experience.

Experience and Knowledge

The authority of the Veda is said to reside in the text itself, which is believed to be timeless and eternal. Most subsequent Indian teachings, even some that are ostensibly vedic, base themselves instead on experiential insights of the founders or renewers of the tradition. The *upaniṣads* never question the supernatural authority of the Veda, but many of them say also that spiritual knowledge is to be achieved experientially. The *Īśā Upaniṣad*, after acknowledging its debt to the givers of revealed knowledge, declares that Truth is to be attained by illuminated sight and through identity with the all-pervading Spirit (*yo'sāvasau puruṣaḥ so'hamasmi*) (selection 15). Theravada texts make it clear that that the Buddha's teachings were based on experiential insights. "The Dhamma I have attained", he is made to say in the *Majjhima Nikāya*, "is unattainable by mere reasoning, subtle, to be experienced by the wise" (selection 30). According to the *Yoga Sūtra*, the highest knowledge is not attainable by thought, but comes when "thought assumes the form of the spirit through consciousness that leaves no trace" (selection 45). In the post-classical yoga and devotional traditions, much stress is placed on the experiential sources of knowledge. After denying the efficacy of vedic study and practice, Sivavakkiyar declares, "Melt with the heart inside and proclaim the truth" (selection 98). A *nāth yogī* sings even more explicitly: "Know [that] positively with experience [*anubhava*]" (selection 102). The *sant* Dadu proclaims that he "found true knowledge" (*saṁcī mati āī*) when he "was one with Him" (*tab ham ek bhaye*) (selection 140). The Punjabi sufi Sultan Bahu (in a passage reminiscent of Sivavakkiyar's) says that "perfect knowledge is obtained . . . by those who close the revealed scriptures", for truth is to be found not by means of "rationality" but in "the glorious mystery of divine unity" (selection 147).

Most mystics of the modern period speak in unambiguous terms of the experiential basis of their teachings. Nisargadatta Maharaj states plainly that he is only able to teach "what I know from my own experience" (selection 186). Krishnamurti underlines the importance of the unaided individual: "Truth cannot be given to you by somebody. You have to discover it; and to discover, there must be a state of mind in which there is direct perception" (selection 178). Ramalinga declares that he attained the highest reach of knowledge "in the state of union with You [Shiva]" (selection 153).

Goals, Methods and Knowledge: Some Problems

The passages cited in the three preceding sections are enough to show that subjective religious experience has played a significant role in the formulation of the goals, methods and knowledge-systems of many religions traditions of South Asia. There are problems associated with each of these topics that the reader should be aware of while studying the texts. The brief selections in this book are not sufficient to settle all the questions that might be raised, but they can serve as useful and authentic materials when the questions are discussed.

Spiritual Goals: Immediate Awareness or Mediated Knowledge

Many founders and renewers of religious traditions state openly or imply that those who attain the goal of the tradition are in direct contact or union with a reality that comprehends all that is. It is generally, though not invariably, assumed that there is only one comprehensive reality.[9] It is apparent however that the nature of this reality is expressed differently by different traditions. There are, broadly speaking, three attitudes that may be taken in regard to this diversity of expression: (1) that there is only one reality and only one true formulation of its nature, all other formulations being false or at best incomplete; (2) that there is only one reality, and all formulations of its nature are various attempts to give form to a single truth, which is in essence beyond description; (3) that formulations of religious "truth" as well as the "reality" they speak of are plural and culturally specific. The first attitude is that of most traditional religions, in particular those based on a single infallible scripture. Tending towards bigotry or lukewarm toleration, it is of little interest in a book that seeks to highlight the diversity of Indian religions. The second attitude is the implicit stance of some liberal believers, and the explicit position of certain scholars of religion. It is sometimes referred to as "perennialism", since its proponents are said to endorse the views of Aldous Huxley in his *Perennial Philosophy* (1946).[10] This position is attractive to those who look on religious experience as a cross-cultural constant, and the reality experienced as a substrate underlying all religious traditions and showing their fundamental unity despite differences of expression. The third attitude, known as "contextualism" or "constructivism", is the position of some contemporary scholars of religion, and may be regarded as an extension to the field of religious studies of the social constructivism that is now the dominant framework in the humanities and social sciences.[11] It appeals to those who wish to emphasise the diversity of religious experience and expression, and fear that perennialist claims of universality amount in practice to the reduction of diversity to a single dominant model.

So much has been written on the question of universality vs. social construction in religion that it is not possible to do more here than sketch the principal lines of the debate and indicate what bearing the selections in this reader might have on it. The chief assumption of the perennialists is that there is a core religious experience (or range of experiences) that is essentially the same among mystics of all ages and cultures. This experience is direct, unmediated by language, and thus ineffable. Mystics who attempt to give expression to this experience, and to the knowledge that it grounds, are obliged to use their own language and (usually) to employ the terminology and figures of a particular religious system. As a result, their formulations differ, but the differences are matters of interpretation and not of essence. The core experience is always the same, as is the reality experienced. On the level of experience, all religions are fundamentally one.

Constructivists deny that there is a core religious experience that is identical across cultures. Their primary assumption, as stated emphatically by Stephen T. Katz, is: "*There are* NO *pure (i.e. unmediated) experiences*" (1978: 26; cf. Proudfoot 1985: 217). Linguistic and cultural mediation is a factor not only in the verbal expression of mystical experiences but also in the experiences themselves. The claims of mystics that their experiences are ineffable are incoherent and, given the amount they have written and spoken about them, absurd. The presumed distinction between the essence of the experience and its interpretation does not hold up. It follows that the experiences of different religious traditions are different from those of other traditions. There is no normative religious experience and no universal religion.

The difference between the perennialist and constructivist positions may be brought out by comparing statements explaining the relationship between the ultimate states as conceived in different religious traditions. William T. Stace, often cited as an typical perennialist, puts it this way: "Nirvana is the Buddhist interpretation of what Plotinus spoke of as union with the One, the Vedantist as realisation of identity with the Universal Self, the Christian as union with God" (1961: 199). Stephen Katz, the best-known constructivist, says rather: "'God' can be 'God', 'Brahman' can be 'Brahman' and *nirvāṇa* can be *nirvāṇa* without any reductionist attempt to equate the concept 'God' with that of 'Brahman', or 'Brahman' with *nirvāṇa*" (1978: 66). In their search for what Huxley calls "a Highest Common Factor in all . . . theologies" (1946: 1), perennialists treat the very different textual descriptions of Buddhist *nirvāṇa*, neo-platonic unity, upanishadic identity and Christian union as disparate interpretations of the same experience. But in seeking to get beyond "inessential" differences, they may be ignoring real and perhaps unresolvable divergences not only in forms of expression but also in the thing expressed. If we read early accounts of the Buddha's experience of *nirvāṇa* (see for example selection 28) and early statements of his spiritual teachings (see selections 29, 33, 37) we find that a great deal of stress is laid on what became known as the doctrine of *anattā* or "no-self". Can comparatists like Stace really be right in asserting that *nirvāṇa*, which assumes no-self, and the upanishadic experience of the self (see selections 11, 16, 19) are one experience differently interpreted? Even worse are attempts by proponents of a given position to reduce other positions to their own, as when a contemporary vedantist says that what the Buddha realised was "exactly the *ātman* of the Vedanta" (Dixit 1996: 103). Perennialists have been justly criticised for superficial reading of texts, reliance on inadequate translations and failure to master the systems of discourse of the traditions they profess to study. All this has allowed them to formulate generalisations that often do not stand up to informed criticism.

Much more than most perennialists, constructivist scholars

try to honour the particularity of the traditions they study, and to avoid making simplistic identifications on the basis of verbal resemblances. But they run into trouble when they say or imply that there is no relationship at all between such experiences as *nirvāṇa*, identity with *ātman–brahman*, union with God, etc. These experiences are described by most of those who have had them as all-inclusive. The systems of knowledge that are based on them are said to account for all that is. Brahman of the *upaniṣad*s, Buddha of the Mahayana, Krishna of the *Gītā*, Parama-Shiva of the shaiva *tantra*s, the Formless One of the *sant*s and Sikhs, Allah of the Muslims, the Christian God, etc., occupy the same ontological space. To say flatly that God is God and Brahman is Brahman is to assume a plurality of comprehensive realities. God and Brahman could be completely distinct entities only if both were human constructions — the usual reductionist position of Marxists, Freudians, and others.

The evident plurality of the forms of God, as conceived by different religions, does not rule out the possibility that there is a single comprehensive reality behind them all. There are a number of Indian precedents for this way of looking at things. Vaishnavas conceive of Vishnu as taking form in various incarnations — different faces of one divine principle. The twentieth-century mystic Sri Aurobindo writes that the Self, although without specific character, "bears and upholds the play of all character, supports a kind of infinite, one, yet multiple personality" (1999: 751). The similarities of the experiences of mystics of different cultures, despite differences of conception and expression, suggest that there may be a reality independent of culture that can be approached in different ways. Most constructivists do not deny that there are such things as mystical experiences, but by saying that such experiences are as much mediated by language and culture as other forms of experience, they make them something other than what mystics claim them to be.

An anthology consisting of translated extracts cannot hope to resolve all the issues raised by the perennialist–constructivist debate. All it can do is offer selections from texts in which founders, renovators and exponents of Indian religious traditions speak of their experiences and give expression to their understanding of life and the world. A number of statements in the selections seem to support the perennialists' views in regard to immediacy of experience, direct knowledge, and ineffability. This is not surprising:

the perennialist position was formulated by scholars who had immersed themselves in mystical literature and took the mystics at their word. Many passages in classic mystical literature do seem to allude to unmediated knowledge. To give one example, Meister Eckhart devotes the better part of a famous sermon to the question of mediation; in the course of this he says: "God the Father may speak His word there [in the ground of the soul], for *this* part is by nature receptive to nothing save only the divine essence, without mediation."[12] Since Eckhart is widely recognised as an authoritative Christian mystic, his statement lends support to the idea that mystical experience is linguistically and culturally unmediated. What do the mystics of India have to say about this question?

A number of citations reproduced above under the heading "Experience and Knowledge" indicate that the authors of important texts of the upanishadic, Theravada, Mahayana, Samkhya, Vajrayana and Kashmir Shaiva traditions accepted the existence of direct or unmediated knowledge and experience. The *Laṅkāvatāra Sūtra* explains that words cannot express the highest reality, which can only be attained by inner, non-linguistically mediated means (selection 67). The monistic philosopher Shankara argues: "If the light of *Ātman* which is Pure Consciousness were not eternal in one's own *Ātman*, it would be mediated by remembrance and the like and so it would be composite". Since *ātman* "exists for its own sake", it follows that the consciousness of *ātman* is uncomposite and unmediated (selection 85). The philosopher of *bhakti* Ramanuja speaks of knowledge by "direct vision" (selection 86), while the nineteenth-century *bhakta* and mystic Sri Ramakrishna makes reference to "immediate knowledge", "direct perception" and "direct self-existent truth consciousness" (selections 157, 158). The poet Tagore speaks similarly of receiving a "direct message of spiritual light" (selection 190). Mystics who emphasise intuitive knowledge rather than intuitive emotion, for example Sri Aurobindo, Ramana Maharshi, Krishnamurti, and Gopi Krishna, put even more stress on the attainment of direct truth-consciousness, direct perception, direct touch or contact, and so forth (selections 161, 166, 178, 188).

These examples indicate that a number of important Indian mystics acknowledged the existence of some form of direct or unmediated knowledge. No doubt their testimony cannot be taken uncritically. To begin with, most of them did not use the English words "direct" or "unmediated", but terms in Sanskrit and other languages that have been so translated.[13] Further, the fact that these authorities affirm the existence of unmediated experience does not in itself prove that such a thing exists. At best their statements can be taken as having "some evidential value", and used as a basis for further investigation.

Spiritual Methods: Liberation or Acculturation

Despite the striking similarities in the experience and expression of mystics of different traditions, it must be conceded that most members of a given tradition have experiences quite like those of their predecessors and less like or quite unlike those of mystics of other traditions. Constructivists explain this by saying that the mystics' background and training have a causal influence not only on their modes of expression but also on the experiences themselves. Gurus instruct their disciples as their gurus instructed them, transmitting what they themselves received. This instruction produces experiences of a similar kind. The practices recommended by various traditions, far from liberating practitioners into objectless awareness, simply acculturates them in a certain way, with the result that practitioners have experiences of the desired sort. As Katz confidently puts it: "It is in appearance only that such activities as yoga produce the desired state of 'pure' consciousness. Properly understood, yoga, for example, is *not* an *un*conditioning or *de*conditioning of consciousness, but rather it is a *re*conditioning of consciousness" (1978: 57).

The spiritual teacher (*ācārya, guru, murshid*) is held in extraordinary respect in most Indian spiritual traditions. Many disciples who have attained experiential knowledge attribute their success not their own efforts but to the guru's grace. The guru generally demands that disciples follow a certain discipline, judges their progress in accordance with traditional criteria, and certifies success or failure. This would seem to indicate that the disciples' experiences are not unmediated but determined by the guru's teaching. Accounts by modern yogis like Yogananda and Nisargadatta certainly emphasise the part of the guru in their attainment of experiential knowledge, but they also suggest that the role of the guru may be that of catalyst and not effective cause. Other mystics, for example Krishnamurti and Sri Aurobindo, took a direction radically different from the one proposed by early teachers and soon cut off all connection with them. Yet others — Ramana Maharashi, Anandamayi Ma, Swami Ramdas, Gopi Krishna — were able to attain realisation without a guru's assistance, while Ramakrishna had experiences first on his own, and later while following the instructions of gurus of various traditions.

The role of the guru in Indian religious traditions is clearly more complex than the constructivist position would permit. The guru does not seem to be an indispensable giver of tradition who enforces a specific pattern of experience and prevents all innovation. What about of the techniques that are transmitted by a guru's instruction or preserved in sacred texts? As noted above under the heading "Experiential Means", almost all the traditions dealt with in this reader have preserved and transmitted meditative, mantric, devotional, ritualistic or psycho-physical techniques that are meant to help practitioners get in direct touch with the Divine (variously conceived). A large number are these techniques are said to work by replacing the ordinary activities of mind, emotions and body with a state of quiet or dynamic openness to non-conceptual and non-verbal experience. They claim then to be means of restraining the ordinary forms of mediated conception and activity in order to provide access to unmediated experience. According to the *Kena Upaniṣad*, *brahman* is "hearing of our hearing, mind of our mind, speech of our speech" and so forth (selection 13). A later verse (2.3) states that *brahman* "is discerned by those who seek not to discern it". The *Śvetāśvatara Upaniṣad* recommends that the practitioner restrain the breath or life-force and "hold his mind in check"; to those who persist in such meditation, *brahman* will revealed (selection 17). The *Maitrī Upaniṣad* offers several methods of mind- and sense-restraint. A person who succeeds in a certain preliminary practice is urged to "continue void of conceptions" (*niḥsaṁkalpas tatas tiṣṭhet*) until the unconditioned Absolute (*turya*) is reached (selection 18). The suppression of mental activity and formations is also recommended by different schools of Buddhism and by Patanjali's Yoga. Theravada calming meditation is meant to take the practitioner beyond what is "conditioned and voluntarily produced" to what is permanent (selection 35); Theravada insight meditation requires the practitioner to observe the body, feelings, mind and mind-objects as they are, without active participation in their movements (selection 36). Similar practices are recommended in

Mahayana texts (see selections 60, 61). The *Yoga Sūtra*, which defines Yoga as "the cessation of the turnings of thought" (*citta-vṛtti-nirodha*), says that "a subliminal impression [*saṁskāra*] generated by wisdom stops the formation of other impressions", preparing the way for thought-free contemplation or *samādhi* (selection 41). The *Kulārṇava Tantra* declares that the yogin in *samādhi* is free from sensory impressions and mental conceptions (selection 73). The shaiva-tantric philosopher Abhinavagupta says that in the repose of meditation, the yogin enters "a state where there is no distinction", but only universal bliss (selection 89). Similarly the unlettered Kashmiri mystic Lalla sings: "Absorbed in bliss, I forgot the scriptures" and realised "consciousness-bliss" (*tsetan ānand*) (selection 103). Among modern teachers, Sri Aurobindo, Ramana Maharashi, Krishnamurti and Nisargadatta Maharaj declare that concept-free meditation opens the way to direct experience of that which is (selections 161, 166, 178, 186). If one assumes, like the neo-Kantian Katz, that unmediated experiences are impossible, one is obliged to say that practices like these constitute "reconditioning" rather than "deconditioning". The texts themselves suggest otherwise.

Robert K. C. Forman views the escape from ordinary sensory, verbal and conceptual activity into non-conceptual awareness as a sort of "forgetting", what Meister Eckhart calls *vergezzen* (1990: 30; 1998: 7). Forman's "forgetting model" is of some help in understanding certain forms of spiritual experience and practice. Along with the examples alluded to in the preceding paragraph, one might cite this passage from Sharafuddin Maneri: "On account of this forgetfulness, all awareness of self is lost. There is no calling upon the name or observance of customs; awareness of whether one exists or not; explanation, allusion, or divine throne!" (selection 92). There are however other forms of practice and experience that involve remembrance rather than forgetting. Examples are the repetition or contemplation of prayers or mantras or the Name (in Sufism this practice is called *dhikr*, literally "remembrance"), and the contemplation of visual or conceptual images. In several *upaniṣads*, the mystic syllable *om* (or *aum*) is put forward as the supreme object of contemplation; the *Muṇḍaka* says that contemplation of *aum* can propel the individual self into the *brahman* (selection 16). This use of *mantras* as a means for achieving spiritual ends is an important part of all forms of Tantrism (see for example selection 74). Another tantric technique is the mental visualisation of forms of divine power, such as Virochana Buddha or the Goddess as Shakti, or else the contemplation of the Absolute (selection 73). In the various paths of devotion, contemplation of forms of the godhead is the pre-eminent means of practice. Krishna declares in the *Bhagavad Gītā* that loving meditation on himself is better than the practice of yoga or dedicated work (selection 53). Vaishnava *bhaktas* from Andal to Dayaram give an intensely personal turn to this loving absorption in Krishna or other forms of Vishnu; shaiva bhaktas from Appar to Mahadeviyakka do the same with regard to Shiva. *Dhikr* is recommended by sufis from Hujwiri to Inayat Khan. The latter explains: "The whole idea of the Sufi is to cover his imperfect self even from his own eyes by the thought of God" (selection 172). Somewhat paradoxically, the *sants* and Sikhs counsel contemplation of the God without form, particularly as the Divine Name. These various traditions have their own patterns of practice and devotion, but there is considerable overlap among them. Narsi Mehta worships the visible Krishna but also cries "Let us see, but not with eyes, Him who is formless" (selection 127). Sai Baba of Shirdi counsels devotees to meditate on him as the Blissful Formless Being (*ānanda nirākāra*); if this proves impossible, they should picture his outward form "exactly as it is" (selection 159).

Reality, Truth and Verification

When mystics speak of their experiences, they imply or declare that the object of their experience is real, and that the knowledge that comes from the experience is true. Such claims raise difficult epistemological questions. Are mystics right in thinking that what they feel themselves to be in contact with is a (or *the*) reality? If it is real for them, is it necessarily real for others? Do their private experiences put them in a position to make claims about the nature of life and the world? If these truth-claims disagree with one another, are some or all of them refuted? Is there one Truth, or many truths, or is "truth" a human construction determined by social and political forces rather than anything inherent in the supposed source of truth?

The best way to begin an intellectual enquiry into these matters is to examine the textual evidence. In the *Chāndogya Upaniṣad*, Uddalaka Aruni tells his son and disciple Svetaketu that the "finest essence of things" is "the Real" (*satyam*, usually translated "the true"), and "the Self" (selection 11). The *Śvetāśvatara Upaniṣad* says that a person gains freedom when he or she "sees Brahman as It really is" (*brahmatattvam*) "by means of the self as it really is" (*ātmatattvena*) (selection 17). In a similar vein, the author of the *Bhagavad Gītā* says: "The unreal never is: the Real [*sataḥ*] never is not" (selection 46). The author of the *Kulārṇava Tantra* says that "the [ultimate] Reality shines forth of itself" (*svayaṁ tattvaṁ prakāśate*), not through "mental effort" but by its own self-nature (selection 73). Mystics of later traditions use a variety of words in a variety of languages to signify the "reality" they claim to be in contact with. Shah Abdul Latif cries in Sindhi: "Reality is one: do not be mistaken!" (selection 149). Ramana Maharshi writes in Tamil of the "Sole Reality" which "exists for ever", and which to him is the same as "the Self" (selection 171). Krishnamurti speaks in English of "that which is", "*what is*", or simply "that" (selection 178).

Most of the authors cited above belong to traditions classed as Hindu. As a rule, Hindu mystics speak of the Real as having some sort of positive existence. Buddhist mystics, on the other hand, generally speak of existence in negative terms, stressing the *un*reality or emptiness of things without proposing a "higher reality" beyond (selections 58, 61, 81) . The Prajnaparamita school introduces the term *tathatā* or "suchness" to signify that which is beyond verbal description (selection 59). To the Vijnanavada philosopher Vasubandhu, "suchness" is a quasi-positive term which he identifies with "perception-only" (selection 82). The *Laṅkāvatāra Sūtra* speaks of the "truth of the highest reality", which lies beyond positive as well as negative terms (selection 66).

Whether viewed negatively or positively, the real is not considered by many mystics to be something with specific qualities or properties. It is simply that which actually is. Their claim is that it is possible to have direct awareness of or to come into direct relationship with this reality. Since most believe that the reality can be known only by experiential means, they rarely argue the point. The real, they assert, has to be *realised*. This word crops up again and again in English translations of Indian spiritual texts, and also in texts written originally in English (23, 28, 66, 86, 103, 139, 148, 160, 170, 173, 176). To those who say that the mystic's reality is unsubstantial in comparison with the world as perceived by the senses, some mystics reply that the actual situation is the opposite.

Gopi Krishna speaks of being in contact with "a reality more solid than the material world" (selection 188). Nisargadatta Maharaj says similarly that the reality known by the *jñānī* is "more real" than the objects of the "ordinary consciousness" (selection 186). Nisargadatta also is emphatic that "the real is not imaginary, it is not a product of the mind" (selection 186). Vasubandhu distinguishes between "the constructed own-being", which is unreal, and the self-evidence of "suchness" (selection 82).

These various conceptions of "reality" are not necessarily incompatible with one another, though it must be admitted that it is not easy to reconcile the positive and negative approaches. When we come to claims about truth, however, we find that traditions and individuals offer a large number of apparently incompatible systems. Many *upaniṣads* speak of *satyam* or truth. In a notable passage, the *Muṇḍaka* declares: "Truth alone conquers, not untruth. By truth is laid out the path leading to the gods by which the sages who have their desires fulfilled travel to where is that supreme abode of truth" (selection 16). Mahavira is said to have realised the truth of things (selection 23); a Jaina text says of his teachings: "that is the truth, that is so, that is proclaimed this [creed]" (selection 26). The Buddha of the Theravada speaks of dependent origination as "the truth", and calls the primary doctrines of his *dhamma* "the four noble truths" (selections 30, 32). Mahayana texts like the *Saddharma-puṇḍarīka Sūtra* ("Sutra of the Lotus of the True Law") give quite different accounts of the Buddha's highest teaching. Even the *Guhyasamāja Tantra* says that its socially transgressive doctrines are an expression of "the great sacramental truth" (selection 68). Similarly, the Hindu *Mahānirvāṇa Tantra* says that its teachings are "the very truth" (selection 74).

When we come to texts written by historical individuals, we find a similar profusion of truth-claims. Shankara asserts that his view (*advaita vedānta*) is declared "from the standpoint of the highest truth" (selection 85). The Shattari sufi 'Isa Jund Allah distinguishes three levels of truth (selection 93); a later sufi, Shah Wali Allah, speaks of seven stages of perfection, at the top of which the Prophet stood at his side, while a voice cried: "Truth, truth, truth" (selection 96). Bulleh Shah speaks also of realising truth (selection 148), while Guru Nanak's greatest hymn is filled with references to the truth of the Name (selection 142). Ramana Maharshi, Nisargadatta Maharaj and other modern mystics all use words signifying "truth" to describe the world-views founded on their realisations. When Ramalinga Swami formulated a new religion he called it the Universal True Creed (selection 156).

All these mystics evidently felt that they were in experiential contact with a reality, and that as a result of this contact they had become aware of a truth which did not need intellectual justification. To many, such claims are unacceptable. Mystical experience, it is said, does not share with ordinary sensory experience the intersubjective verifiability that is necessary for general acceptance. But to argue this way is unduly to privilege one form of perception over another. Philosopher of religion William Alston shows that "unfavourable comparisons between mystical perception and sense perception" by naturalistic critics "either condemn the former for features it shares with the latter (the double standard) or unwarrantedly require the former to exhibit features of the latter (imperialism)" (1991: 253). If perceptual evidence provides grounds for belief, there is, prima facie, as much reason to accept mystical as sensory perceptual evidence. Most social scientists would argue however that it is possible to explain mystical experience in terms of psychological or sociological theory. When the supposed self-evidence of the experiences disappear, the truth-claims that are based on them are undermined. As for the religious "force" of the experience, this may, according to Wayne Proudfoot, be "accounted for by the fact that the criteria for identifying an experience as religious include reference to an explanatory claim. The experience is perceived by the subject as eluding explanation solely in terms of his own mental states but as having been produced in such a way that it supports his beliefs about the world, beliefs that are distinctive of the tradition within which it is being characterised as religious. The experience provides support for and conformation of those beliefs" (1985: 216). Proudfoot's argument depends on his assumption that there are no unmediated experiences. His conclusion that mystics' beliefs precede their experiences does not agree with statements made by mystics that their beliefs are the consequences of their experiences. It is true that many mystics have experiences within the framework of pre-existing belief systems, but this does not of itself prove that the experiences are the results of the beliefs. On the other hand, many mystics have experiences, and subsequently make truth-claims, that are the contrary of what they had hitherto accepted, for example, the Buddha, Appar, Vasubandhu,

Guru Nanak, Ramalinga Swami, Sri Aurobindo and Krishnamurti. Others who have no positive religious training or beliefs nevertheless have powerful mystical experiences, for example Ramana Maharshi and Gopi Krishna.

If it is true that mystical experience is the source of mystical knowledge, the most decisive way to verify mystical truth-claims is by means of mystical experience. No doubt the experiences of a Buddha or Nanak or Aurobindo are not in the reach of everyone, but these and other spiritual teachers insist that such states are the ultimate destiny of all aspiring humans. A preliminary decision to take seriously a mystic's account of his or her experience, the truth-claims based on the experience and the methods proposed for its attainment will depend on one's estimate of the authority of the mystic, the intellectual and emotional satisfactoriness of the truth-claims, and the utility of the methods in attaining the accepted goals.

There remains the problem of the variance of truth-claims of different mystics. It certainly is a fact that mystics describe "truth" in different ways. But it also is a fact that many mystics, particularly those living in multi-religious environments, are untroubled by the apparent differences, and provide ways to reconcile them. Many insist the differences between religions are nominal and not substantial. "Some call it Rama, some call it Khuda; some worship it as Vishnu, some as Allah", says Guru Arjan (*Ādi Granth*, p. 885, trans. Kaur Singh 37). Kabir similarly sings: "The Master of Hindus and Turks [Muslims] is one and the same" (selection 138). A number of Ramakrishna's parables touch on the same theme; in one he points out that what Hindus call *jal*, Muslims *pāṇi* and Christians *water* is always the same substance: so it is, he suggests, with the names and substance of God.

Another means of reconciliation is to distinguish between the paths, of which there are many, and the goal, which is one. Ramakrishna tells Keshab Sen: "God can be realised through all paths. It is like your coming to Dakshineswar by carriage, by boat, by steamer, or on foot. You have chosen the way according to your convenience and taste; but the destination is the same" (selection 158). In a similar vein, Ghauth Ali Shah says: "Let them all strive in their own ways towards that mystery — the traditionalists with their obedience to the law and ritual, and mystics with their meditations and aspirations, and the madmen with their eyes filled with wonder" (selection 152).

Other mystics stress the inadequacy of all formulations of truth and of all fixed paths to reach it. Truth is "limitless, unconditioned, unapproachable by any path whatsoever", says Krishnamurti; it is "pushed aside" rather than described "by symbols, words, images" (selections 177, 180). Many other mystics would agree: "Because the highest reality is an exalted state of bliss", says the author of the *Laṅkāvatāra Sūtra*, "it cannot be entered into by mere statements regarding it" (selection 67). Sri Aurobindo brushes aside the notion that "truth is a single idea that all must accept". Although "the fundamental truth of spiritual experience is one", he says, there are "numberless possibilities of variation of experience and expression" (selection 163).

These extracts from mystical literature do not solve all the problems raised by the diversity of religious truth-claims, but they suggest that solutions may yet be found. What is needed to proceed is "a pluralistic theory" of religion, such as the one proposed by philosopher of religion John Hick, which will help us "recognise and be fascinated by the manifold differences between the religious traditions, with their different conceptions, their different modes of religious experience, and their different forms of individual and social response to the divine", while at the same time remaining open to commonalities (2001: 566). The religions of India, in all their fascinating diversity, present the problems in their fullness, but they also hint that the similarities between traditions may be as important and as interesting as their differences.

The Literature of Indian Religion: Experience and Expression

Religious literature takes many forms: ritualism, mythology, sacred history, doctrine, ethical injunctions, social ordinances, and the expression of individual feelings and experiences. Because it emphasises individual expression, this reader gives little space to several sorts of religious literature. Few texts dealing exclusively with ritual, ethics or social organisation have been included. The vedic *saṁhitā*s are represented by a handful of hymns from the *Ṛg Veda* and an extract from the *Atharva Veda*. Epic literature finds place only in the extracts from the *Bhagavad Gītā*, mythology, only in some vedic and upanishadic passages and the two extracts from the *purāṇa*s. Other omissions might be noted; what is remarkable however is how much of the most important literature of Indian religions gives expression to spiritual experience or experience-based knowledge and emotion. It is open to question whether every example of such expression reproduced in this book is based on the author's first-hand experience. Much religious literature consists of traditional or even conventional wisdom passed down from teacher to student or disseminated in the form of books, songs or talks. It is all but impossible to say whether any particular expression of mystical knowledge or emotion is a transmission of this sort or is based on the author's experiential insight. Most of the selections seem to the editor to have the stamp of authentic experience. At the least they are authentic examples of experience-based spiritual literature.

Whatever their origin, most of the selections rank high as literature even when judged by "literary" criteria. If the aphorisms of the *Sāṁkhya Kārikā* and *Yoga Sūtra* and the writings of Vasubandhu and Shankara cannot be called masterpieces of *belles lettres*, they nevertheless are important examples of literary genres that have been much practised during the history of Indian literature. The same sort of apology does not need to be made for the works of the *bhakti* and yoga traditions that have been included. The sayings of Lalla and the virashaiva saints are among the masterpieces of Kashmiri and Kannada literature, while the songs of the nayanars and alvars, and the vaishnava devotees of Andhra, Maharashtra, Gujarat, Mithila, Bengal and the North are recognised as masterpieces of poetic expression in Tamil, Telugu, Marathi, Gujarati, Maithili, Bengali and Hindi. The works of Kabir are as much admired for their literary as their spiritual qualities, while the hymns of the Sikh gurus are foundation-stones of modern Punjabi literature. Bulleh Shah would also figure in any list of leading Punjabi poets, while Shah Abdul Latif remains the greatest name in Sindhi poetry, and Dard a major figure in Urdu literature. Rabindranath Tagore, Bhai Vir Singh, Muhammad Iqbal, and Subramania Bharati are generally acknowledged as the greatest twentieth-century writers of Bengali, Punjabi, Urdu and Tamil, while Sri Aurobindo and Krishnamurti are among India's most notable writers of English. By focussing on experience, this reader has been able to include many of the greatest literary expressions of the major Indian religions.

NOTES TO THE INTRODUCTION

1. Kabir, *Kabīr Granthāvali* 2, 128 and *Ādi Granth, rāg bhairo* 11; translation Vaudeville 1997: 240.

2. Kabir, *Kabīr Granthāvali* 2, 177 and *Ādi Granth, rāg bhibās* 2; translation Vaudeville 1997: 218.

3. An egregious example of such theory-laden interpretation is found in Kosambi 1975. The noted Marxist historian writes that the Buddha "expounded what seemed to him an underlying fundamental order in all nature (i.e. society). . . . This was a scientific advance, as it analysed, in a rather elementary way, the causes of social suffering and showed the way to its negation" (165). There is not the least evidence in the Pali Canon or contemporary texts that the Buddha meant anything like "social suffering" when he spoke of *dukkha*. A number of other examples of Marxist (or Marxist-Foucauldian) and Freudian "hermeneutics of suspicion" are found in recent studies of Ramakrishna Paramahansa. Partha Chatterjee (1994) and Sudhir Sarkar (1997) both regard the public figure of Ramakrishna as a creation of the Bengali middle class (more precisely, the Kolkata *bhadralok* or "respectable people"). "If Ramakrishna attracted bhadralok through his 'Otherness', this was to a considerable extent an Other constructed by the bhadralok themselves", writes Sarkar (285). Both critics focus on the key role played by the authors of the *Śrī Śrī Rāmakṛṣṇa Kathāmṛta* and *Śrī Śrī Rāmakṛṣṇa Līlāprasaṅga* in the construction of the popular image of Ramakrishna. Both also seek to situate Ramakrishna's practice and teachings within the economic and social world of colonial Bengal. Ramakrishna and others enter "the inner world of devotion, a personal relation of *bhakti* (devotion) with the Supreme Being" because the outer world of domestic responsibility is frustrating and unfulfilling. "The strategy of survival in a world that is dominated by the rich and the powerful is withdrawal", Chatterjee concludes (59). Writing as social historians of nineteenth-century Bengal, Sarkar and Chatterjee are not obliged to study the experiential sources of Ramakrishna's teachings, but by granting no autonomy to his inner life, they miss out on what may have been the most important factor in his appeal to his countrymen. The best Sarkar can do is to acknowledge in passing that "Ramakrishna's personal qualities" constitute a "by no means unimportant" issue (315). Scholar of religion Jeffrey Kripal gives much attention to Ramakrishna's experiences, but he looks at them from the standpoint of a rather dogmatic Freudianism. Reading closely the Bengali text of the *Kathāmṛta*, he isolates and interprets a number of passages that, "taken together", add up to what

he believes to be "a convincing argument for the 'secret' erotic nature of Ramakrishna's mystical experiences" (1995: 317). Kripal exposes this "secret" in a somewhat roundabout way; his disciples are less circumspect: the secret is that Ramakrishna was a homosexual. There is no direct evidence of this in the *Kathāmṛta* or anywhere else, and Kripal himself admits that his interpretations are often "speculative". The sensationalism of his approach vitiates the overall value of his book, which does make a number of interesting points, for instance that the official text of the *Kathāmṛta* tends to replace the "complexity and ambivalence" of the phenomenon of Ramakrishna with "monotone colors, simplicity and dogmatism" (171). Psychoanalytic theory is put to more productive use by the "post-Freudian" psychoanalyst Sudhir Kakar. Recognising that "theoretical uncertainties in contemporary psychoanalysis . . . threaten its basic paradigm", Kakar does not accept "the earlier equation of the mystical state with a devalued, if not pathological, regression comparable to a psychotic episode" (1991: 3–4). He does however draw on the insights of Freud and neo-Freudians like Bion and Lacan in his study of Ramakrishna's life, which includes an examination of his sexuality. But in the end Kakar avoids Freudian reductionism: "Mystic experience", he concludes, "is one and—in some cultures and at certain historical periods—the pre-eminent way of uncovering a vein of creativity that runs deep in all of us" (34).

4. The selections show that the practices and beliefs of many religious traditions, for example Jainism, Buddhism, Virashaivism and Bengal Vaishnavism, may be traced back to the experiences of their founders. They say nothing about the historical relationship between these foundational experiences and the "theologies and ecclesiasticisms" of the religions in question. There is no evidence that James's dictum applies to prehistoric religions in India and elsewhere, which seem to have been based on tribal cults rather than individual "mystical experiences". James's dictum does not adequately account for the importance of revealed scripture in such religions as vedic Hinduism, Islam, etc. There is no straightforward evidence that the *Ṛg Veda* (one or two hymns of the tenth book excepted) gave special importance to the attainment of subjective religious experiences; it stresses rather the correct performance of sacrificial rituals. (Spiritual or symbolic interpretations of the Veda expand on, but do not replace, this basic sense.) Ritualism remains an enormously important part of contemporary Hinduism, and also is found in such experience-based traditions as Jainism, Buddhism and Tantrism. The selections in this reader testify to the importance of experiential religion, but do not nullify the importance of other aspects: social, ethical, ecclesiastical, etc.

5. The English word "experience" began to be used for subjective spiritual states in the late seventeenth century (*OED*, s.v. "experience", significance 4b). The term "experience" (often accompanied by the adjectives "religious", "spiritual", or "mystical") was taken up by writers like William James in the nineteenth century, and since then has become the standard term, in scholarly as well as spiritual literature, for the special inner states attained by mystics and others by means of discipline or grace. Some recent Western writers have suggested that the term "religious experience", and perhaps also that to which it refers, is a modern Western invention, dating back no farther (in the opinion of Wayne Proudfoot [1985]) than the early nineteenth century. Robert H. Sharf, in several recent papers (for example Sharf 1995) extends this line of criticism to Far Eastern Buddhist religious experience, and in a more general article to Indian religious experience as well (Sharf 1998). In this article he asserts: "In the end there is simply no evidence of an indigenous Indian counterpart to the rhetoric of experience prior to the colonial period" (1998: 100). Sharf does not cite any Indian literature in support of this assertion, making do with a reference to a chapter of a book by Wilhelm Halbfass (1988: 378–402). Halbfass's chapter can only be said to support Sharf's argument if two-thirds of it is left unread. Halbfass begins his treatment of the Indian idea of experience by pointing out certain anachronisms and other flaws in the treatment of the concept by some late-nineteenth- and early-twentieth-century writers. He then goes on: "There can be no doubt that India has produced an extremely rich and complex legacy of ideas, doctrines, methods and practices related to religious, meditational and in general inner experience" (386), listing sources of such ideas, doctrines, methods and practices from all periods of Indian religious history, beginning with the Veda, continuing through the mediaeval philosophers and *bhakta*s, and finishing with modern times. Using the tools of textual and historical criticism, Halbfass corrects what he considers to be modern misreadings of this material, but he nowhere denies the existence of a "rhetoric of experience" in the pre-modern period. After noting that "there has been much vague rhetoric and more or less deliberate blurring of conceptual distinctions in the use of 'experience' ", he concludes that in such matters historical criticism may be "more shallow and parochial than its target" (402). Sharf, like Halbfass, has pointed out some significant instances of inexactness and vagueness in modern writing on religious experience, but his failure to cite any primary documents, and his misrepresentation of Halbfass's work, make it impossible to assign any value to his remarks on Indian religion.

6. While examining the citations that follow in the introduction, it is important to remember that almost all the texts from which they are extracted were written in languages that are quite different from English. In rendering these passages into English, the translators not only made use of nineteenth- and twentieth-century English vocabulary and syntax, but also drew on the categories of Western spiritual discourse. In a reader like this, there is no way (short of giving all the texts in the original languages) of avoiding problems of translation. As an acknowledgement of such difficulties, I have given the key words of many of the phrases cited in this introduction in the original languages. This should remind the reader that each of these phrases is part of a linguistic, textual and doctrinal or philosophical structure that differs in important respects from the structures of other languages and texts—even when the terms are, from the point of view of historical linguistics, the "same". The word *anubhava* occurs in late classical Sanskrit and (with slight phonetic variations) in modern north Indian languages. A translator of Ramanuja and a translator of Nisargadatta Maharaj might each use the word "experience" as the English equivalent of *anubhava*, but it should not be imagined that Ramanuja and Nisargadatta meant precisely the same thing when they said or wrote "*anubhava*". On the other hand, there is no compelling reason (unless one accepts as fact the claims of Foucauldian and other self-justifying theories of discourse) to believe that there were no commonalities between human consciousness and subjective experience in twelfth-century Srirangam and twentieth-century Mumbai.

7. See the works cited in note 5.

8. See the works cited in note 3.

9. In Jainism and Samkhya–Yoga, each soul or conscious being (called *jīva* in Jainism and *puruṣa* in Samkhya–Yoga) is eternally separate from every other soul. Liberation is a soul's realisation of its isolation (*kevala* or *kaivalya*) from nature (see Chapters 3 and 5). Thus it cannot be said that the comprehensive reality as visualised by these traditions is *one*. On the other hand, the plural souls of Jainism and Samkhya–Yoga cannot be said to be *different* from one another. Difference is found only in the realm of nature, the result, in Jainism, of the impurity of *karma*, in Samkhya–Yoga, of the imbalance of the three *guṇa*s.

10. The term "perennialist" is used mostly by opponents of the view, often with derogatory intent. Along with Huxley (1946), scholars frequently cited as holding the perennialist position are William T. Stace (1961), R. C. Zaehner (1994 [first published 1960]), Huston Smith, Mircea Eliade and others. Earlier scholars such as William James (1961

[first published 1902]) and Evelyn Underhill had many of the same assumptions as Stace and others later grouped together as perennialists. These scholars differ in many respects—Stace, for example, is basically monistic, while Zaehner is dualistic and theistic—but all of them agree in holding that (certain types) of religious experience occur without fundamental difference in mystics of various religious traditions. This position was predominant in discussions of religious experience during the 1960s and 1970s, but during the 1980s was replaced by the contextualist or constructivist view. During the 1990s, Robert K. C. Forman and others (Forman, ed., 1990 and 1998) tried to work out a viewpoint that conceded many of Katz's points but held on to the perennialist belief in the cross-cultural validity of certain forms of spiritual experience. Constructivist scholars see little difference between Forman's views and those of Stace-era perennialists.

11. The most important statements of the constructivist position in the field of religious studies are found in Katz, ed., 1978, and in subsequent volumes edited by Katz (e.g. Katz, ed., 1982). Katz prefers to call his position "contextualism"; "constructivism" is of broader application and relates Katz's view to that of the so-called postmodern discourse theorists, who stress the social construction of all forms of knowledge, and share many of Katz's assumptions. As is the case with "perennialist", "contextualist" and "constructivist" are umbrella terms covering a number of different stances. Most of those in this camp would agree, however, that no form of mystical experience is identical across cultures.

12. Meister Eckhart, Sermon 1 (Pf 1, QT 57), trans. Walshe 1957: 3. Eckhart of course did not say "without mediation". What he said, in Middle High German, was "àn allez mitel", which translates into modern German as "ohne alle Vermittlung" (J. Quint). An alternative English translations is "without means" (C. Evans). It seems fairly certain that Eckhart's meaning was that there is a form of communion between God and soul that is unmediated by thought, sense and language.

13. As an illustration of the problems involved in using translated terms when writing about mystical experience, one may examine the occurrences in this reader of the phrase "pure consciousness", often cited (notably in Forman, ed., 1990) as a key term in mystical studies. "Pure consciousness" is used by the translator of the *Kaivalya Upaniṣad* to render the Sanskrit terms *cinmātra* and *cit*; by the translator of the *Kuṇḍikā Upaniṣad* to render *(kevala) akhaṇḍabodha*; by the translator of the *Yoga Sūtra* to render *citi*; by the translator of the *Laghutattvasphoṭa*, again for *citi*; and by translators of the *Śiva Sūtra* and of Shankara's *Upadeśasāhasrī* to render

caitanya. (An equivalent phrase, "absolute consciousness", is used by the translator of Utpaladeva's *Śivastotrāvali* to render *viśvaikapūrṇā*.) Other Sanskrit terms sometimes translated by "pure consciousness" are *puruṣa* (in classical Samkhya), and *vijñaptimātratā* (in Vijnanavada Buddhism). In addition, translators of Ramakrishna, Ramana Maharshi and Nisargadatta Maharaj use "pure consciousness" as the equivalent of unspecified words or phrases in Bengali, Tamil and Marathi. All the Indian terms belong to different systems of spiritual knowledge, and it is unlikely that the mystics who employed them meant the very same thing by them: a Vijnanavada Buddhist would hardly say that *vijñaptimātratā* was the same as Patanjali's *citi*. It might nevertheless be argued that the terms are more or less synonymous, attempts in different discourse-systems to name a general power of unmediated and contentless consciousness. On the other hand, it might be charged that "pure consciousness" was used to translate the various Indian terms simply because the English phrase is often found in books about mysticism. It is probable that the translators were aware of the use of "pure consciousness" in English mystical discourse, but the very existence of that term, along with the various Indian terms, suggests that the idea of contentless consciousness is not confined to a single conceptual system, and that the faculty it presupposes may indeed be attainable by humans in different cultures.

WORKS CITED IN THE INTRODUCTION

William P. Alston, *Perceiving God: The Epistemology of Religious Experience*. Ithaca, NY: Cornell University Press, 1991.

Sri Aurobindo, *The Synthesis of Yoga*. Pondicherry: Sri Aurobindo Ashram, 1999.

Partha Chatterjee, *The Nation and its Fragments: Colonial and Postcolonial Histories*. Reprint edition. Delhi: Oxford University Press, 1994.

S. H. Dixit, "The Ātmavāda of Advaita Vedānta and the Anātmavāda of the Buddha". In Kalpakam Sankaranarayan et al., eds., *Buddhism in India and Abroad: An Integrating Influence in Vedic and Post-Vedic Perspective*. Mumbai: Somaiya Publications Pvt. Ltd., 1996, pp. 102–03.

Peter Gay, *Freud: A Life for Our Time*. New York: Norton, 1988.

Robert K. C. Forman, ed., *The Problem of Pure Consciousness*. New York: Oxford University Press, 1990.

Robert K. C. Forman, ed., *The Innate Capacity: Mysticism, Psychology and Philosophy*. New York: Oxford University Press, 1998.

Sigmund Freud, *The Future of an Illusion*, translated by James Strachey. New York: Norton, 1961.

John Hick, "Religious Pluralism". In M. Peterson et al., *Philosophy of Religion: Selected Readings*. Second edition. New York: Oxford University Press, 2001.

Sudhir Kakar, *The Analyst and the Mystic: Psychoanalytic Reflections on Religion and Mysticism*. New Delhi: Viking, 1991.

Jeffrey Kripal, *Kālī's Child: The Mystical and the Erotic in the Life and Teachings of Ramakrishna*. Chicago: The University of Chicago Press, 1995.

Wilhelm Halbfass, *India and Europe*. Albany, NY: State University of New York Press, 1988.

Aldous Huxley, *The Perennial Philosophy*. London: Chatto & Windus, 1946.

William James, "A Pluralistic Mystic". In *Essays and Studies*. New York: Longmans, Green and Co., 1912, pp. 371–411.

William James, "A World of Pure Experience". In *Essays in Radical Empiricism and A Pluralistic Universe*. Reprint edition. New York: Dutton, 1971, pp. 23–48.

William James, *The Letters of William James*, vol. II. Boston: Atlantic Monthly Press 1920.

William James, *The Varieties of Religious Experience: A Study in Human Nature*. Reprint edition. New York: Collier Books, 1961.

Stephen T. Katz, ed., *Mysticism and Philosophical Analysis*. New York: Oxford University Press, 1978.

Stephen. T. Katz, ed., *Mysticism and Religious Traditions*. New York: Oxford University Press, 1982.

Damodar Dharamanand Kosambi, *An Introduction to the Study of Indian History*. Reprint edition. Bombay: Popular Prakashan, 1975.

Wayne Proudfoot, *Religious Experience*. Berkeley: University of California Press, 1985.

Sumit Sarkar, *Writing Social History*. Delhi: Oxford University Press, 1997.

Robert H. Sharf, "Buddhist Modernism and the Rhetoric of Meditative Experience". *Numen* 42 (1995): 228–83.

Robert H. Sharf, "Experience". In *Critical Terms for Religious Studies*. Chicago: University of Chicago Press, 1998, pp. 94–116.

W. T. Stace, *Mysticism and Philosophy*. London: Macmillan, 1961.

Charlotte Vaudeville, *A Weaver Named Kabir*. Delhi: Oxford University Press, 1997.

Shankar Vedantam, "Tracing the Synapses of Spirituality". *Washington Post*, 17 June 2001, p. A01.

M. O'C. Walshe, ed. and trans., *Meister Eckhart: German Sermons and Treatises*, vol. 1. London: Watkins, 1979.

R. C. Zaehner, *Hindu and Muslim Mysticism*. Reprint edition. New Delhi: Research Press, 1999.

ON THE SELECTIONS, TRANSLATIONS AND EDITORIAL NOTES

The texts and authors chosen for inclusion in this reader are generally those regarded by the traditions in question to be the most important and most representative. For reasons explained in the Introduction, preference has been given to texts in which authors speak in the first person about their own experiences. Such texts usually require less knowledge of the technical vocabulary of the tradition than doctrinal statements or guides to practice, and thus are more accessible, and more interesting, to modern readers. Whether separate pieces or extracts from longer works, the selections had to be able to stand on their own with only a minimum of editorial explanation. The selections, finally, had to be from texts that have been adequately translated into modern English.

Even the best translation of a complex text written in a language very different from English can give only a rough approximation of its meaning. Faced with competing demands of readability and accuracy, translators adopt a variety of strategies to help them in their all-but-impossible task. Some, impressed by the linguistic and discursive particularity of their material, stay close to the letter of the text, often leaving technical terms untranslated, and supplying detailed notes and other explanatory aids. Others, banking on the similarities of human experience across temporal, spatial and linguistic boundaries, put their texts into straightforward modern English and hope for the best. The translations chosen for inclusion here are distinguished by accuracy as well as readability. Some, for example the renderings of three *upaniṣad*s by Purohit Swami and W. B. Yeats, often sacrifice verbal precision for ease of comprehension. Others, like the upanishadic translations of R. E. Hume and R. C. Zaehner, follow the texts closely but sometimes read awkwardly in English. The best translations combine a high degree of textual accuracy with straightforward idiomatic English.

Linguistic and other technical notes by the translators have been omitted. These generally require the rest of the explanatory material provided by the translators to make good sense. Readers are urged to turn to the complete translations for detailed information on texts, authors and terminology.

Most technical terms left untranslated by the translators, as well as those used by the editor in his notes, are defined in the Index and Glossary of Terms. Significant occurances of personal and geographical names and titles of works are listed in the Index of Proper Names.

In writing the notes that precede chapters, sections of chapters, and selections, the editor has made considerable use of the translators' introductions and notes, as well as the best recent monographs by specialists in the various fields. The editorial notes supply only basic factual information: dates, historical and theological/philosophical background, essential information on texts, terminology, etc. The works listed under Further Reading at the end of each chapter will provide interested readers with much more information on these and other topics.

ON TRANSLITERATION

The languages of India and Iran are written in a variety of scripts that differ considerably from the Roman script used for English and other European languages. All these languages contain sounds that are not found in English. To represent Indian and Persian writing in Roman script, scholars have devised systems of transliteration in which one Roman letter, with or without a diacritical mark, stands for one Indian or Persian letter. These systems enable those who know the languages concerned to spell Indian and Persian words precisely in Roman script, but they are less useful to those who do not know the phonetic systems involved. For the ordinary reader, an approximate transliteration, without diacritical marks, is generally preferable.

In reproducing extracts from translated texts, the editor has generally preserved the transliterations used by the translators. In a few cases, where translators used obsolete or incomplete transliteration-systems, the editor has modernised or completed them. In his notes, the editor has followed these rules: biographical, mythological and geographical names are transliterated using the "approximate" system, without diacritics or italics (Krishna, not *Kṛṣṇa*; Andal, not *Āṇṭāḷ*). Titles of books and technical terms are transliterated using the appropriate scholarly system, in italics. Terms used repeatedly (*bhakti*, *sant*) are sometimes printed in Roman rather than italic type.

Part One

Foundations

1

तत्सवितुर्वरेण्यं भर्गो देवस्य धीमहि। धियो यो नः प्रचोदयात्॥

Let us meditate on the glorious light of the divine Sun; may it illumine our minds.

Ṛg Veda 3.62.10

The Veda

THE SPIRITUAL beliefs and practices of the earliest humans in South Asia must be inferred from archaeological remains. Rock paintings in Mesolithic sites in different parts of the subcontinent suggest the performance of group rituals and dances, which were important aspects of prehistoric religion in most parts of the world. The burial practices of Neolithic pastoral civilisations in the Indus river valley and elsewhere point to a belief in an afterlife and the practice of what we would now call magic. The people of the mature Harappan civilisation, which flourished in Sind, Punjab, Gujarat and neighbouring regions during the third and second millennia BCE, evidently possessed a sophisticated religious system, but its exact nature is difficult to determine. Architectural features like the "great bath" at Mohenjo-daro and the "five altars" at Kalibangan are thought to have been used for ritual purposes. Some of the inscribed seals found in Harappan sites depict beings that clearly were regarded as sacred. Some modern writers have underlined apparent continuities between such figures and later Indian beliefs, but most archaeologists caution against anachronistic readings of this sort. "The famous seal from Mohenjo-daro showing a horned personage seated on a stool in what we would today call *baddhakoṇāsana* . . . cannot automatically be labelled 'the prototype of Siva as Pasupati'", notes Shereen Ratnagar (2001: 104), pointing out that the later Shiva Pashupati was associated with domestic animals and not the wild beasts depicted on the seal.

The earliest manifestation of Indian spirituality that has a clear connection with surviving beliefs and practices is the body of texts known as the Veda. Modern Hinduism defines itself as the religion of the Veda, and though most contemporary Hindu beliefs and practices emerged hundreds of years after the end of the vedic era, these texts are still regarded as the foundation and essence of the Hindu way of life. To the orthodox, the Veda is *apauruṣeya* — not a human composition but uncreated and self-existent. Viewed historically, vedic literature is a creation of the second and first millennia BCE. Attempts to date the texts more precisely suffer from a lack of hard evidence. There are no sure correlations between datable artefacts or events and the texts of the Veda itself. Certainly the vedic religion was well established by the time of the Buddha (sixth century BCE). Linguistic evidence suggests that the earliest vedic hymns are up to a thousand years older. Vedic Sanskrit is closely related to Avestan, the language of the scriptures of ancient Iran, and more remotely to Greek, Latin and other ancient European languages. Linguists have shown that these tongues all descend from a common source, which they call Indo-European. It is assumed that the speakers of Indo-European lived together in one region before dispersing in various directions. A great mass of archaeological and linguistic evidence suggests that their homeland lay somewhere between eastern Europe and central Asia, quite possibly the steppe to the north of the Caspian Sea. One branch of the Indo-European family moved south and east and later split into two sub-branches, one settling in Iran and the other in India. The people of the India group called themselves *āryāḥ* or Aryans; the Iranian group employed an almost identical term.

There has been an enormous amount of speculation concerning the anthropology and history of the Indo-Europeans and Aryans based on the Veda and other ancient texts. Much of this is suspect, since kinship of language does not necessarily imply kinship of blood. But it is clear that all branches of the Indo-European family shared a cultural inheritance that included not only language but also modes of life, social organisation, religious practices, etc. The Indo-Europeans were pastoral and mobile, yoked horses to chariots, counted their wealth in cattle, and sacrificed to gods of the heavens and the sun, etc. These and other characteristics set the Aryans apart from the people of the Harappan culture, which was urban, commercial, horseless, and apparently in a state of decline when the Aryans reached India.

The Aryans' first home in South Asia was Punjab and Haryana. Here, probably, they composed or compiled the hymnal portions of the Veda. During this period they were familiar with the Himalayas and the Yamuna, but had not yet proceeded as far east as the Ganges or as far south as the Vindhyas. Later they moved eastward into the Gangetic valley.

Vedic literature is divided into two main categories, the *saṁhitās* or "collections", most of which are in verse, and the commentaries or *brāhmaṇas*, most of which are in prose. The three main *saṁhitās* are the *Ṛg Veda*, the *Yajur Veda*, and the *Sāma Veda*; the *Atharva Veda*, a later text, is sometimes listed as the fourth. The *Ṛg Veda* consists of hymns, most of which are addressed to one or more gods. The *Yajur* and *Sāma Vedas* contain ritual formulas and chants, the *Atharva Veda*, mostly magical spells. The *brāhmaṇas* consist primarily of explanations of the elements of the sacrifice; appended to them are the more esoteric *āraṇyakas* ("forest books") and *upaniṣads*. Properly speaking, all of this is *Veda*; normally, however, when people speak of the Vedas, they are referring to the *saṁhitās* and in particular the *Ṛg Veda*, which is the most important of the *saṁhitās*. In the present chapter translations of all or parts of seven hymns of the *Ṛg Veda* are reproduced, along with one passage from the *Atharva Veda*. The *upaniṣads* are dealt with separately in the next chapter.

The word *veda* means "(sacred) knowledge". In the traditional account, the texts were "seen" by the *ṛṣis* or "seers", who were thus not authors but rather discoverers of pre-existent verities. Later traditions claiming descent from the Veda look on the entire vedic canon (inclusive of the *brāhmaṇas* and *upaniṣads*) as *śruti* or divine revelation, which is infallible and the source of all truth. In addition, the words and rhythms of the Veda were (and are) regarded as having special potency. Properly recited, vedic hymns bring about certain specified results: protection from harm, winning of cattle and other wealth, or positive psychological states. Over the centuries more importance has been attached to the memorisation and proper pronunciation of the hymns than to the full comprehension of their significance. The texts of the Vedas, independently preserved in regions as remote from each other as Tamil Nadu and Kashmir, hardly differ after millennia of oral transmission. On the other hand, the verbal significance of these texts has been in doubt for hundreds of years. Yaska, a vedic etymologist, wrote around 500 BCE: "The seers had direct intuitive insight. By oral instruction they handed down the hymns to later generations who were destitute of this insight. The later generations, declining in (power of) oral communication, repeated (compiled) this work, the Veda, and the auxiliary vedic treatises from memory, in order to illustrate (comprehend) their meaning" (Yaska, *Nirukta* 1.20, translated in Gonda 33).

Whatever else the *saṁhitās* and *brāhmaṇas* may have meant to the Aryans, they certainly were used to consecrate and direct the sacrificial rites that were the most important practices of their religion. Most of the hymns are addressed to a specific god or gods, each of whom has a special role to play. Agni, the god of fire, receives the sacrificial oblation and intercedes between the human and divine worlds; Indra, the god of the heavens, uses his might to defeat the enemies of the Aryans and to help those who approach him; Ushas, the goddess of dawn, brings illumination. There is no doubt that to most who participated in the sacrifice, these and other gods were supernatural powers that had to be appeased so that they would properly fulfil their roles. But to some worshippers they may also have symbolised spiritual or psychological faculties: Agni, the flame of aspiration, Indra, the divine mind, etc.

The *Ṛg Veda* consists of 1028 *sūkta*s or "hymns", which are grouped in ten *maṇḍala*s or "books". Books 2 to 7 are each devoted to hymns of certain family of *ṛṣi*s; these six books are thought to comprise the most ancient part of the *Ṛg Veda*. Books 1 and 8 are made up of hymns by *ṛṣi*s of different families. Book 9 consists entirely of hymns to Soma, while book 10 is made up of miscellaneous hymns, some containing sophisticated speculation on cosmological and metaphysical questions.

The text of the *Ṛg Veda* gives little information about how the vedic religion was lived by individual men and women. The *ṛṣi*s are known by clan and personal names, but little can be gathered about their personalities. The functions of different sorts of priests are set forth in detail, but we know nothing about their lives and thoughts. One of the few hymns that comes close to giving a credible picture of actual human beings is *Ṛg Veda* 10.136, which describes "long-haired" ascetics who seem similar to the actual renunciates mentioned in Buddhist and Jaina texts of the sixth century BCE. For the most part, however, modern notions of what the men and women of the vedic age were like have been determined by stereotypes found in literary works such as the *Rāmāyaṇa*, *Mahābhārata* and *purāṇa*s.

HYMNS OF THE VEDIC SACRIFICE

Sacrifice was central to the vedic religion, and most of the hymns of the *Ṛg Veda* have some direct or indirect connection with sacrificial ritual. Most are addressed to particular gods, who are summoned to the sacrifice and asked to participate. By the law of the sacrifice, when the gods receive the oblation, they become the allies and friends of humans. Reproduced here are translations of hymns to five vedic deities: Agni, Ushas, Soma, Vishnu and Indra.

[1]

To Agni

Fire or *agni* was given great importance in the vedic sacrificial religion. As the power who brings the gods to the sacrifice, he is the intermediary between them and human beings. This hymn, the very first in the *Ṛg Veda saṁhitā*, is a straightforward invocation, summoning Agni to his duties as "minister of the sacrifice". Translated by Raimundo Panikkar.

I magnify the Lord, the divine,
the Priest, minister of the sacrifice,
the offerer, supreme giver of treasure.

Worthy is the Lord to be praised
by living as by ancient seers.
He makes present for us the Gods.

The Lord brings us riches, food
in daily abundance, renown,
and hero sons to gladden our hearts.

Only that worship and sacrifice
that you, Lord, guard on every side
will reach the heavenly world of the Gods.

May the Lord, wise and true offerer,
approach, most marvelous in splendor,
encircled with his crown of Gods!

Whatever gift you may choose
to give, O Lord, to your worshiper,
that gift, refulgent One, is true.

To you, dispeller of the night,
we come with daily prayer
offering to you our reverence.

For you are Lord of sacrifice,
enlightener, shepherd of the world,
who wax mighty in your own abode.

So, like a father to his sons,
be to us easy of entreaty.
Stay with us, O Lord, for our joy.

[2]
To Ushas

The importance of the sun in vedic religion and mythology is demonstrated by the large number of hymns addressed to solar deities—Mitra, Varuna, Savitri, Ushas, and others. Some of the most beautiful hymns of the Veda are to Ushas or Dawn, the bringer of light. In this hymn from the seventh book of the *Ṛg Veda*, Ushas is pictured as a "Lady of Light". Translated by Raimundo Panikkar.

Dawn comes shining
like a Lady of Light,
stirring to life all creatures.
Now it is time
to kindle the Fire.
The light of Dawn scatters the shadows.

Her face turned toward
this far-flung world,
she rises, enwrapped in bright garments.
Shining with gold,
with rays of light bedecked,
she sends forth the world on its course.

Our Lady of Light
brings the Eye of the Gods,
as she rides her white, beautiful steed.
Dawn shines apparent,
bestowing on all men
her store of marvelous treasure.

Come with your bounty;
drive away foes.
Grant us secure and lush pastures.
Disperse those who hate us.
O bountiful One,
give to your singer reward.

Beam forth your light
to guide and sustain us,

prolonging, O Goddess, our days.
    Give to us food,
    grant to us joy,
chariots and cattle and horses.

    Lady nobly born,
    Daughter of Heaven,
worshiped by all the illustrious,
    grant us your blessings,
    riches and wealth.
Now and forever protect us!

[3]

To Vishnu

Comparatively unimportant in the Veda, where he has vaguely solar characteristics, Vishnu later developed into one of the great gods of classical Hinduism. In this hymn, from the first book of the *Ṛg Veda*, Vishnu is celebrated for his most famous deed: measuring out the earth, mid-worlds and heaven in three giant strides. Translated by Raimundo Panikkar.

I will proclaim the mighty deeds of Viṣṇu
who measured out the earthly regions and propped
the heavens above, accomplishing in his course
    three mighty strides.

For this his prowess Viṣṇu is acclaimed.
He inhabits the mountains, like a savage beast
wandering at will; in his three mighty paces
    are set all worlds.

Now may my prayer ascend to the far-striding
Viṣṇu, the Bull, who dwells upon the mountains,
to him who unaided measured with threefold step
    these far-flung spheres.

The marks of his three strides are filled with honey
imperishable; each is cause of joy.

Alone he supports the three spheres — Earth and Sky
and all things living.

May I attain to Viṣṇu's glorious mansion
where the faithful rejoice, where, close beside the Strider,
within his highest footstep springs the well
of purest honey!

O for your realms where dwell the tireless oxen
abundantly furnished with horns, whence shine
from the highest step of the widely striding Hero,
his multiple splendors!

[4]

To Soma

An entire book of the *Ṛg Veda* is made up of hymns to Soma, the ambrosial drink of the gods. There has been much speculation as to the exact nature of the *soma* beverage. Many scholars believe it was a psychoactive drug, similar to those used in religious rituals in other parts of the world. Some writers however prefer to view *soma* as a symbol of the divine delight of existence, pointing out the evident connection between the vedic *soma* and the *ānanda* or bliss that is spoken of in the *upaniṣad*s and elsewhere. This selection, comprising six verses from *Ṛg Veda* 9.133, was translated by Raimundo Panikkar.

Where the priest, reciting the metrical word
and handling the pressing stone, exults in Soma,
through Soma creating, O Purifier, bliss,
flow, Soma-juice, for Indra's sake!

Where light unfailing ever shines,
where dwells the Sun, in that deathless world
place me, O Purifier, beyond harm's reach.
Flow, Soma-juice, for Indra's sake!

Where the Son of Vivasvat holds sway,
the shrine of heaven where the waters flow
ever young and fresh, there make me immortal.
Flow, Soma-juice, for Indra's sake!

Where Men move at will, in the threefold sphere,
in the third heaven of heavens, where are realms full of light,
in that radiant world make me immortal.
 Flow, Soma-juice, for Indra's sake!

In the place of vows and eager longings,
the realm of the golden Sun, of libations
and fullness of joy, there make me immortal.
 Flow, Soma-juice, for Indra's sake!

Where happiness and joy abound,
pleasures and delights, where all desires
find their fulfillment, make me immortal.
 Flow, Soma-juice, for Indra's sake!

[5]

To Indra

More vedic hymns are addressed to Indra than to any other god. He is the lord of the heavens, leader of the gods of the storm, and victor over the enemies of the Aryan people. Those who perform the vedic sacrifice offer the *soma* to him in the hope that he will act generously in return. But just as *soma* can be viewed both as a psychoactive drug and as the delight of the divine, so Indra can be conceived both as the anthropomorphic King of Heaven and as the Lord of Divine Mind. In his *Secret of the Veda*, the twentieth-century mystic Sri Aurobindo proposed a two-levelled interpretation of the Veda, in which the hymns have at once an outward ritualistic and an inner spiritual meaning. Aurobindo argued that ancient religious cults, such as the Eleusinian mysteries of Greece, used this sort of system of dual significances to preserve the inner secrets of the Mysteries. He also pointed out that the use of dual senses (*śleṣa* or equivoque) is a characteristic of Sanskrit literature of all periods. His reading, while controversial and not generally accepted, seeks to explain the spiritual authority that has been accorded to the Veda by Indian mystics from at least the time of the *upaniṣad*s. In the following selection, Aurobindo translates a single hymn to Indra twice: first according to the ritualistic interpretation formalised by the mediaeval commentator Sayana, and then according to his own psychological or spiritual interpretation.

The doer of [works that have] a good shape, Indra, we call daily for protection as [one calls] for the cow-milker a good milch-cow.

Come to our [three] libations, drink of the Soma, O Soma-drinker; the intoxication of thee, the wealthy one, is indeed cow-giving.

Then [standing] among the intelligent people who are nearest to thee, may we know thee. Do not [go] beyond us [and] manifest [thyself to others, but] come to us.

Come to him and question about me, the intelligent one, [whether I have praised him rightly or not], — to the intelligent and unhurt Indra who gives to thy friends [the priests] the best wealth.

Let of us [i.e. our priests] speak [i.e. praise Indra], — and also, O you who censure, go out [from here] and from elsewhere too, — [our priests] doing service all about Indra.

O destroyer [of foes], may even our enemies speak of us as having good wealth, — men [i.e. our friends will say it of course]; may we be in the peace [bestowed] by Indra.

Bring this Soma, that wealth of the sacrifice, the cause of exhilaration to men, [the Soma] that pervades [the three oblations] for Indra who pervades [the Soma-offering], that attains the rites and is friendly to [Indra] who gives joy [to the sacrificer].

Drinking of this, O thou of many actions, thou becamest a slayer of Vritras [i.e. enemies led by Vritra] and didst protect entirely the fighter in the fights.

O Indra of many actions, for enjoyment of riches we make thee abundant in food who art strong in the battles.

Sing to that Indra who is a protector of wealth, great, a good fulfiller [of works] and a friend of the sacrificer.

–

The fashioner of perfect forms, like a good yielder for the milker of the Herds, we call for increase from day to day.

Come to our Soma-offerings. O Soma-drinker, drink of the Soma-wine; the intoxication of thy rapture gives indeed the Light.

Then may we know somewhat of thy uttermost right thinkings. Show not beyond us, come.

Come over, question Indra of the clear-seeing mind, the vigorous, the unoverthrown, who to thy comrades has brought the highest good.

And may the Restrainers say to us, "Nay, forth and strive on even in other fields, reposing on Indra your activity."

And may the fighters, doers of the work, declare us entirely blessed, O achiever; may we abide in Indra's peace.

Intense for the intense bring thou this glory of the sacrifice that intoxicates the Man, carrying forward on the way Indra who gives joy to his friend.

When thou hadst drunk of this, O thou of the hundred activities, thou becamest a slayer of the Coverers and protectedst the rich mind in its riches.

Thee thus rich in thy riches we enrich again, O Indra, O thou of the hundred activities, for the safe enjoyment of our havings.

He who in his vastness is a continent of bliss, — the friend of the Soma-giver and he carries him safely through, — to that Indra raise the chant.

LATER HYMNS

The tenth book of the *Ṛg Veda* is generally thought to have been composed centuries after the others. It contains a number of hymns that anticipate the *upaniṣad*s in speculating on the origins of the universe. Translations of two of the most striking of these, the Hymn to Hiranyagarbha (the "Golden Embryo"), and the enigmatic Hymn of Creation, are reproduced below. They are followed by another hymn from the tenth book, which speaks of the practices of ascetics who seemed to care little about the orthodox sacrifice.

[6]
The Unknown God, the Golden Embryo

Much of the mythology of ancient cultures is concerned with the beginnings of things. How did the universe arise out of nothingness or whatever it was that preceded the beginning of Time? This hymn and the next are attempts to provide answers to this question. *Hiraṇya* means "golden", *garbha* can mean "womb" or "embryo" or "child": hence Hiranyagarbha is the Shining Source of everything. Because its characteristics are unknown and probably unknowable, the seer of this hymn ended every verse but the last with the phrase "who is the god whom we should worship with the oblations". Later the force of this question was blunted by treating the word "who" (*ka*) as a proper noun: "Ka is the god we should worship". Translated by Wendy Doniger.

In the beginning the Golden Embryo arose. Once he was born, he was the one lord of creation. He held in place the earth and this sky. Who is the god whom we should worship with the oblation?

He who gives life, who gives strength, whose command all the gods, his own, obey; his shadow is immortality—and death. Who is the god whom we should worship with the oblation?

He who by his greatness became the one king of the world that breathes and blinks, who rules over his two-footed and four-footed creatures—who is the god whom we should worship with the oblation?

He who through his power owns these snowy mountains, and the ocean together with the river Rasā, they say; who has the quarters of the sky as his two arms—who is the god whom we should worship with the oblation?

He by whom the awesome sky and the earth were made firm, by whom the dome of the sky was propped up, and the sun, who measured out the middle realm of space—who is the god whom we should worship with the oblation?

He to whom the two opposed masses looked with trembling in their hearts, supported by his help, on whom the rising sun shines down—who is the god whom we should worship with the oblation?

When the high waters came, pregnant with the embryo that is everything, bringing forth fire, he arose from that as the one life's breath of the gods. Who is the god whom we should worship with the oblation?

He who in his greatness looked over the waters, which were pregnant with Dakṣa, bringing forth the sacrifice, he who was the one god among all the gods—who is the god whom we should worship with the oblation?

Let him not harm us, he who fathered the earth and created the sky, whose laws are true, who created the high, shining waters. Who is the god whom we should worship with the oblation?

O Prajāpati, lord of progeny, no one but you embraces all these creatures. Grant us the desires for which we offer you oblation. Let us be lords of riches.

[7]

Creation Hymn

Among the most famous of the hymns of the *Ṛg Veda*, the Creation Hymn also is one of the least typical. The language of the Veda is almost always concrete, with the certitude that comes from concreteness. In the tenth book of the *Ṛg Veda*, however, there are a number of hymns that exhibit sophisticated abstract thinking. The most famous and most intriguing example is the so-called Creation Hymn (*Ṛg Veda* 10.129). Both in approach and tone it anticipates the speculations of the early *upaniṣads*. Here even the gods are posterior to the act of creation, about which nothing can be known. Translated by Wendy Doniger.

There was neither non-existence nor existence then; there was neither the realm of space nor the sky which is beyond. What stirred? Where? In whose protection? Was there water, bottomlessly deep?

There was neither death nor immortality then. There was no distinguishing sign of night nor of day. That one breathed, windless, by its own impulse. Other than that there was nothing beyond.

Darkness was hidden by darkness in the beginning; with no distinguishing sign, all this was water. The life force that was covered with emptiness, that one arose through the power of heat.

Desire came upon that one in the beginning; that was the first seed of mind. Poets seeking in their heart with wisdom found the bond of existence in non-existence.

Their cord was extended across. Was there below? Was there above? There were seed-placers; there were powers. There was impulse beneath; there was giving-forth above.

Who really knows? Who will here proclaim it? Whence was it produced? Whence is this creation? The gods came afterwards, with the creation of this universe. Who then knows whence it has arisen?

Whence this creation has arisen—perhaps it formed itself, or perhaps it did not—the one who looks down on it, in the highest heaven, only he knows—or perhaps he does not know.

[8]

The Long-haired Ascetic

The ascetics described in this hymn seem to be precursors of the renunciates mentioned in some of the *upaniṣads* and in the *sūtras* of Jainism and Theravada Buddhism. Their outward appearance is considered worthy of remark: they are clothed in the wind (compare the "sky-clad" or naked ascetics of Jainism) or wear robes dyed red or perhaps ochre. More remarkable however are their spiritual practices. They do not put their reliance in the gods or the sacrifice, but advance on the strength of their austerities, aided perhaps by a psychoactive drug. Their mastery of the "wind", which seems to increase their powers of vision, may be an early form of the practices formalised in the later *prāṇāyāma* of *haṭhayoga* (see Chapter 8). Translated by Wendy Doniger.

Long-hair holds fire, holds the drug, holds sky and earth. Long-hair reveals everything, so that everyone can see the sun. Long-hair declares the light.

These ascetics, swathed in wind, put dirty red rags on. When gods enter them, they ride with the rush of the wind.

"Crazy with asceticism, we have mounted the wind. Our bodies are all you mere mortals can see."

He sails through the air, looking down on all shapes below. The ascetic is friend to this god and that god, devoted to what is well done.

The stallion of the wind, friend of gales, lashed on by gods — the ascetic lives in the two seas, on the east and on the west.

He moves with the motion of heavenly girls and youths, of wild beasts. Long-hair, reading their minds, is their sweet, their most exciting friend.

The wind has churned it up; Kunamnamā prepared it for him. Long-hair drinks from the cup, sharing the drug with Rudra.

FROM THE *ATHARVA VEDA*

Most of the hymns of the *Ṛg Veda* are intended to promote the general welfare of worshippers. Most of those in the *Atharva Veda* are directed towards the satisfaction of specific desires or the removal of specific ills. Its primary contents are spells and incantations meant to help the user obtain a son or ward off danger or cure disease. This is an aspect of South Asian religion that presumably preceded the *Ṛg Veda* and reappeared later in the *tantras*. The *Atharva Veda* also contains a few remarkable hymns filled with the sort of cosmological speculation found also in the tenth book of the *Ṛg Veda* and the earlier *upaniṣads*. The selection below is from such a hymn.

[9]

The City of Brahman

This extract is from a hymn of the *Atharva Veda* dealing with the Primal Man, whose members were fashioned by a power referred to as "Brahman". In the *Ṛg Veda* this key term denotes the divine (creative) word, in the *upaniṣads*, the Absolute Spirit. Here it appears to be a great creative power that gives form to the manifested world. Translated by R. C. Zaehner.

By whom was this earth established?
By whom were the heavens fixed on high?
By whom was this atmosphere, this wide expanse,
Established above, athwart?

By Brahman was this earth established;
Brahman the heavens fixed on high;
Brahman this atmosphere, this wide expanse,
Established above, athwart.

Atharvan sewed up his head and heart:
A wind, rising above the brain, expelled [it] from the head.

Atharvan's head assuredly
Is a casket of the gods, close sealed:
This head the bread of life (*prāṇa*) protects;
So too do food and mind.

Brought forth above, brought forth athwart,
All cardinal points did Man pervade—
[Yes, Man] who Brahman's city (*pur*) knows,
By which he is called "Man" (*puruṣa*).

Whoso that city of Brahman truly (*vai*) knows
As swathed in immortality,
To him do Brahman and the Brāhmans give
Sight, life (*prāṇa*), and progeny.

Neither sight nor life desert the man
Before old age sets in,

Who the city of Brahman knows
By which he is called "Man".

The city of the gods which none lays low in battle
Has circles eight and portals nine:
In it is a golden treasure-chest —
Celestial, suffused with light.

In this golden treasure-chest, three-spoked and thrice supported —
In this there is a being strange (*yakṣa*) possessed of self (*ātmanvat*):
That is what knowers of Brahman know.

Into this radiant [city], — yellow, gold,
Compassed with glory round about,
The city unsubdued
Brahmā has entered in!

FURTHER READING

Source Materials

Sri Aurobindo, *The Secret of the Veda*. Pondicherry, India: Sri Aurobindo Ashram, 1998.

Wendy Doniger [O'Flaherty], *The Rig Veda: An Anthology*. New Delhi: Penguin Books India, 1994.

Dominic Goodall, ed., *Hindu Scriptures*. London: Phoenix, 1996.

Raimundo Panikkar, *The Vedic Experience: Mantramañjarī*. Reprint edition. Pondicherry: All India Books, 1977.

Other Works

Jan Gonda, *Vedic Literature (Saṃhitās and Brāhmaṇas)*. Wiesbaden: Otto Harrassowitz, 1975.

Rajesh Kochhar, *The Vedic People*. Hyderabad: Orient Longman, 2000.

Shereen Ratnagar, *Understanding Harappa: Civilisation in the Greater Indus Valley*. New Delhi: Tulika, 2001.

Sources of Texts and Translations

1	*Ṛg Veda* 1.1	Panikkar 329
2	*Ṛg Veda* 7.77	Panikkar 169
3	*Ṛg Veda* 1.154	Panikkar 152–53
4	*Ṛg Veda* 9.113.6–11	Panikkar 634–35
5	*Ṛg Veda* 1.4	Aurobindo 257–60
6	*Ṛg Veda* 10.121	Doniger 27–28
7	*Ṛg Veda* 10.129	Doniger 25–26
8	*Ṛg Veda* 10.136	Doniger 137–38
9	*Atharva Veda* 10.2.24–33	Goodall 23–24

2

यदात्मतत्त्वेन तु ब्रह्मतत्त्वं दीपोपमेनेह युक्तः प्रपश्येत्।
अजं ध्रुवं सर्वतत्त्वैर्विशुद्धं ज्ञात्वा देवं मुच्यते सर्वपापैः॥

When by means of the true nature of the self, as with a lamp,
a man practising yoga sees here the true nature of *brahman*,
he is freed from all fetters, for he has known God, unborn,
steadfast, unsullied by all objects.

Śvetāśvatara Upaniṣad 2.15

The Upanishads

BY THE END of the vedic period, that is, around 700–600 BCE, the centre of Aryan culture had shifted eastwards from Punjab to the Ganges–Yamuna basin. The kingdoms of this region, notably the powerful Kuru–Panchala alliance, patronised and protected the vedic priesthood. The status of priests and kings was given religious sanction in the system of the four *varṇa*s or social orders: *brāhmaṇa*s or priests, *kṣatriya*s or warriors, *vaiśya*s or tradesmen, and *śūdra*s or labourers. Members of the first three orders were allowed to hear the Veda; *śūdras* and non-Aryans were not. Mentioned first in a symbolic hymn in the tenth book of the *Ṛg Veda*, the *varṇa*-system soon became hereditary and inflexible, and eventually degenerated into the present system of caste.

The *brāhmaṇa* portion of the Veda, consisting primarily of prose commentaries on the hymns, codified the ritual religion. A related sort of text, the *āraṇyaka*s or "forest books", were concerned especially with the hymns' esoteric or allegorical meaning. Some of them also contained mystical and philosophical speculations; such portions were often named *upaniṣad*s. Eventually a large number of *upaniṣad*s were composed. Some of them are integral parts of the Veda, others apparently had an independent origin, though they were later assigned to one *veda* or another. All of them are concerned not with the vedic ritual in itself, but with the secret knowledge that is said to underlie it.

The word *upaniṣad* is made up of the word-elements *upa*, *ni*, and *sad*, which are generally explained as meaning "sitting down near". The picture this evokes is a group of students at the feet of their instructor in a secret teaching "session". In the *upaniṣads* themselves, the term denotes "secret knowledge" or "secret teaching". This esoteric instruction was reserved for qualified students, who had proved to their teachers that they were ready to receive it. Since the *upaniṣads* are found at the end of the vedic corpus, they are known collectively as *vedānta*, "the end of the Veda". This term is also explained as meaning "the culmination of the Veda", since the *upaniṣads* are said to contain the Veda's culminating wisdom. Like the *saṁhitās* and *brāhmaṇas*, the *upaniṣads* are *śruti* or revealed scripture. To those who accept the truth of the Veda, they require no proof; rather they are cited to prove or disprove other assertions. The orthodox justify the unchallengeable authority assigned to the *upaniṣads* and other forms of *śruti* by saying that they were *seen* by the ancient sages. Some modern admirers of the *upaniṣads* say rather that they embody the results of their authors' spiritual experiences.

The *upaniṣads* deal with a large number of topics in a rather unsystematic manner. For centuries, students have concentrated on a selection of these topics and tried to systematise them. These attempts do not do justice to the entire upanishadic corpus, but they do highlight, in a useful way, the characteristic ideas of these texts. For the last two thousand years there has been general agreement that the central concept of the *upaniṣads* is *brahman*, the absolute ground of all that is. Badarayana, the author of the *Vedānta Sūtra* (c. 500–200 BCE), declared that all the verses of the *upaniṣads* are worthy of credence, but gave most of his attention to selected passages dealing with *brahman*. All schools of Vedanta philosophy, from Shankara's to Sri Aurobindo's, regard the *upaniṣads* as privileged sources of spiritual truth, whose central term is *brahman*. Modern scholars like Paul Deussen, Robert E. Hume, and S. Radhakrishnan agree that the idea of *brahman* is the core of what they call the "philosophy of the *upaniṣads*".

Brahman denotes the spaceless and timeless Spirit; but the term itself has a history in time. In the earlier portions of the Veda, it meant "prayer" or "sacred word" and the power that this word contained. Later it came to signify the origin of the universe, and still later the mysterious fundamental principle that underlies the world and everything in it. According to the *Chāndogya Upaniṣad* (6.2.1), *brahman* is "One without a second". This Unity is not knowable by ordinary means. In the paradoxical expression of the *Kena Upaniṣad*, it is "other than the known" and at the same time "above the unknown" (see selection 13). Only those who have received the secret knowledge passed down from olden times, can know the *brahman* by becoming one with it. For the Self or *ātman* is identical with *brahman*.

Ātman is the second most important term of the *upaniṣads*. Derived from a root that also is the source of the the verb "to breathe", *ātman* is the self or soul of the human individual. It is also, as Uddalaka Aruni tells his son Svetaketu in the *Chāndogya*, the "finest essence" of every object. "The whole universe has this [essence] as its Self," Uddalaka continues. "That is the Real: That is the Self: That *you* are, Svetaketu!" (selection 11). The terms *ātman* and *brahman* are often treated as synonyms, though they generally occur in specific contexts—*brahman* in passages dealing with cosmology, *ātman* in presentations of what we would now call psychology. Nevertheless, it is clear from various texts that the two are identical: "this *ātman* is *brahman*" (selection 19).

Because it is the Absolute, *ātman–brahman* does not have attributes. As a result it is often described by negatives: "This is the teaching: 'Not this, not this', for there is nothing higher than this [negative teaching]" (*Bṛhadāraṇyaka Upaniṣad* 2.3.6). Elsewhere, however, there are passages describing the nature of *brahman* in positive terms. It is ancient, self-existent and limitless. It is absolute truth and consciousness. Perhaps most remarkably, it is identified as pure joy or delight (*ānanda*). A celebrated passage of the *Taittirīya Upaniṣad* (reproduced as selection 12) describes the joy of the Spirit as 100^{11} times greater than the greatest joy an ordinary human can attain. One who knows this self-existent joy "fears nothing".

Since *ātman–brahman* is all that is, it follows that the diversity of the universe is only an appearance. How this world of manifestation came into being is a mystery that a number of *upaniṣads* attempt to explicate. Several passages propose a theory of a dual *brahman*: one formless and the other formed. "That which is the formed", explains the *Maitrī Upaniṣad* (6.3), "is unreal", while "that which is the formless is real". Other texts suggest that the manifested world is the creation of a power of illusion, known as *māyā*. This notion was fleshed out by the eighth-century philosopher Shankara, and eventually became the keynote of the predominant interpretation of Vedanta. Other passages of the *upaniṣads*, for instance the opening of the *Īśā* (selection 15), grant derivative reality to the manifested world as a creation of *brahman* as the Lord.

Although centrally interested in the reality behind cosmic and individual phenomena, the *upaniṣads* also have much to say about the nature and destiny of the human being. Two important concepts that emerged in later vedic literature are the basis of the *upaniṣads*' theories of eschatology and ethics. These concepts are *karma* and rebirth. The word *karma*, from the verbal root *kṛ*, "to do", means "action". In the ritual portions of the Veda it refers to the right performance of the sacrifice. In some of the *upaniṣads* the sense is extended to cover every action of life. What one does, determines one's future condition in this life or in another. A portion of the individual survives the death of the body, and, after a time, is reborn in another body, whose quality is a reflection of the quality of his former deeds: "Those whose conduct here has been good will quickly attain a good womb; . . . but those whose conduct has been evil here will attain an evil womb" (*Chāndogya Upaniṣad* 5.10.7). This process is then repeated, each birth paving the way for the next in a cycle called *saṁsāra*. The only means of escape from this endless round is the attainment of the knowledge of *brahman*. When this happens, the last seeds of *karma* are consumed, and the individual achieves *mokṣa* or liberation. These ideas have played an enormously important role in all subsequent religious thought in India, not only in the traditions that descend from the Veda, but also in heterodox systems like Jainism and Buddhism.

Since *ātman–brahman* is at once the object of spiritual knowledge, the source of spiritual delight, and the key to the release from *karma*, it clearly is of the utmost importance for humans to put themselves into contact with it. The *upaniṣads* give a number of methods for doing this. To begin with, the aspirant must hear the secret teachings of the *upaniṣads* from the lips of a qualified teacher. Then he must meditate on them in order to grasp their inner meaning, for the secrets of the *upaniṣads* lie beyond the range of senses, thoughts and words (see selection 13). The Formless One, says the *Śvetāśvatara Upaniṣad*, is not to be seen with the eye; but "those who know him through heart and mind as abiding in the heart become immortal" (4.20). The same *upaniṣad* provides a number of disciplines for helping the "mind and heart" achieve this intuitive knowledge. These are similar to the methods promoted by the schools of Samkhya and Yoga (see Chapter 5). Several of the later, theistic *upaniṣads* introduce another idea: that the knowledge of *brahman* can best be obtained by the grace of God.

About the intuitive knowledge itself, the *upaniṣads* say little, but what they do say is often phrased in experiential terms. The unitary knowledge is like the wholeness one gains in dreamless sleep; or like the state experienced by a man who makes love with his wife; or like the peace of eternity.

There are all told more than a hundred *upaniṣads*. Of these, twelve or thirteen are considered "major" or "classical". The earliest ones, written mostly in prose, and clearly parts of the *brāhmaṇas* and *āraṇyakas*, were composed towards the end of the vedic period, that is, around 700–500 BCE. The great metrical *upaniṣads* appeared in the four or five centuries that followed, while the last major *upaniṣads* were composed in prose just before or after the start of the Common Era. Other texts calling themselves *upaniṣads* continued to appear for almost a millennium.

EARLY PROSE UPANISHADS

Scholars agree that the *Bṛhadāraṇyaka* and *Chāndogya Upaniṣads* are the earliest surviving upanishadic texts. They seem to have been composed during the eighth or seventh centuries BCE. By far the longest of the *upaniṣads*, they are in fact compilations of teachings from various sources and not unitary compositions. The *Taittirīya Upaniṣad* is more compact and from a slightly later period.

[10]

From the *Bṛhadāraṇyaka Upaniṣad*

The "Great *Āraṇyaka Upaniṣad*" occurs as the last section of *Śatapatha Brāhmaṇa* of the *Śukla Yajurveda*. At once an *āraṇyaka* and an *upaniṣad*, it illustrates well the position of the older *upaniṣads* within the vedic corpus. This selection, like much of the *brāhmaṇa* literature, uses myth to explain an imponderable question, in this case the creation of the world. Translated from the Sanskrit by Purohit Swami and W. B. Yeats.

In the beginning all things were Self, in the shape of personality. He looked round, saw nothing but Himself. The first thing he said was, "It is I." Hence "I" became His name. Therefore even now if you ask a man who he is, he first says, "It is I", and gives what other name he has. He is the eldest of all. Because he destroyed all evil, he is called the first Person. He who knows this, destroys all evil, takes the first rank.

He became afraid; loneliness creates fear. He thought: "As there is nothing but myself, why should I be afraid?" Then his fear passed away; there was nothing to fear, fear comes when there is a second.

As a lonely man is unhappy, so he was unhappy. He wanted a companion. He was as big as man and wife together; He divided himself into two, husband and wife were born.

Yādnyawalkya said: "Man is only half himself; his wife is the other half."

They joined and mankind was born.

She thought: "He shall not have me again; he has created me from himself; I will hide myself."

She then became a cow, he became a bull; they joined and cattle were born. She became a mare, he a stallion; she became a she-ass, he an ass; they joined and the hoofed animals were born. She became a she-goat, he a goat; she became a ewe, he a ram; they joined and goats and sheep were born. Thus He created everything down to ants, male and female.

Then he put his hand into his mouth and there created fire as if he were churning butter. He knew that He was this creation; that He created it from Himself; that He was the cause. Who knows, finds creation joyful.

When they say: "Sacrifice to this or that god," they talk of separate gods; but all gods are created by Him, and He is all gods.

Whatever is liquid He created from His seed. Everything in this world is eater or eaten. The seed is food and fire is eater.

He created the gods; created mortal men, created the immortals. Hence this creation is a miracle. He who knows, finds this miracle joyful.

This world was everywhere the same till name and shape began; then one could say: "He has such a name and such a shape." Even today everything is made different by name and shape.

Self entered into everything, even the tips of finger-nails. He is hidden like the razor in its case. Though He lives in this world and maintains it, the ignorant cannot see Him.

When he is breathing, they name Him breath; when speaking, they name Him speech; when seeing, they name Him eye; when hearing, they name Him ear; when thinking, they name Him mind. He is not wholly there. All these names are the names of His actions.

He who worships Him as the one or the other is ignorant, is imperfect; though he attain completely one or the other perfection. Let him worship Him as Self, where all these become the whole.

This Self brings everything; for thereby everything is known. He is the footprint that brings a man to his goal. He who knows this attains name and fame.

This Self is nearer than all else; dearer than son, dearer than wealth, dearer than anything. If a man call anything dearer than Self, say that he will lose what is dear; of a certainty he will lose it; for Self is God. Therefore one should worship Self as Love. Who worships Self as Love, his love never shall perish.

It is said everything can be got through the knowledge of Spirit. What is that knowledge?

In the beginning there was Spirit. It knew itself as Spirit; from that knowledge everything sprang up. Whosoever among gods, sages and men, got that knowledge, became Spirit itself. Sage Wāmadewa knew it and sang "I was Manu; I was the sun."

Even today he who knows that he is Spirit, becomes Spirit, becomes everything; neither gods nor men can prevent him, for he has become themselves.

[11]

From the *Chāndogya Upaniṣad*

This "*upaniṣad* of the *chandogyas*" (singers of the vedic chant) belongs to the *Sāma Veda*. The following extract from its sixth book contains one of the best-known explications of the nature of the *ātman* or Self. Translated by R. C. Zaehner.

[Once upon a time] there lived [a man called] Śvetaketu Āruṇeya. To him his father said: "Śvetaketu, you should [now] live the life of a chaste student of sacred knowledge. No one in our family, my dear boy, is uneducated, a [mere] hanger on, as you might say, of the Brāhman class."

So at the age of twelve he went to [a master], and when, at the age of twenty-four, he had studied all the Vedas, he returned, conceited, priding himself on his learning, and obdurate.

Then his father said to him: "Śvetaketu, my boy, since you are now conceited and obdurate, and pride yourself on your learning, did you also ask about that teaching by which what had [hitherto] not been heard, is heard; what had [hitherto] not been thought of, is thought of; and what had [hitherto] not been known, is known?"

"Now, sir, what manner of teaching is that?"

"My dear boy, just as all that is made up of clay can be known by one lump of clay—its modifications are verbalizations, [mere] names—the reality is just 'clay-ness'.

"And, dear boy, just as all that is made of copper can be known by one copper ornament—its modifications are verbalizations, [mere] names—the reality is just copper.

"And, dear boy, just as all that is made of iron can be known by one pair of nail-scissors—its modifications are verbalizations, [mere] names—the reality is just iron—so, dear boy, is that teaching."

"Now, I am sure those venerable gentlemen did not know this; for if they had known it, why should they not have told me? Do you, sir, then tell me."

"My dear boy, I will", said he. . . .

Uddālaka Āruṇi said to his son, Śvetaketu: "My child, learn from me the true nature of sleep.

"When a man is properly (*nāma*) asleep (*svapiti*), then, dear boy, is he suffused in Being—he will have returned to his own (*svam apīta*). That is why it is said of him '*svapiti*, he is asleep'; for he will have returned to his own (*svam apīto bhavati*).

"Just as a bird, tied to a string, will fly around in all directions and finding no resting-place anywhere else, will resort to the very [string] that keeps it captive, so too, my dear, the mind will fly around in all directions and, finding no resting-place anywhere else, will come to rest in the breath of life; for, my child, the mind is the captive of the breath of life.

"[Now,] dear boy, learn from me about hunger and thirst. When a man is really hungry, it is the water that carries off what he has eaten. For just as we speak of a carrier off of cattle or a carrier off of horses or a carrier off of men, so do we speak of water as a carrier off of food.

"In this context, my dear boy, you must know that this [body] is a sprout which has sprung up; and there is no [sprout] without a root.

"What could its root be but food? So too, my child, [if you think of] food as a sprout, then you must look for water as its root; and, dear boy, [if you think of] water as the sprout, then you must look for light-and-heat as its root; and, dear boy, [if you think of] light-and-heat as the sprout, you must look for Being as its root.

"My dearest child, all these creatures [here] have Being as their root, Being as their resting-place (*āyatana*), Being as their foundation.

"Now, when a man is really thirsty, it is the light-and-heat that carries off what he has drunk. For just as we speak of a carrier off of cattle or a carrier off of horses or a carrier off of men, so too do we speak of light-and-heat as a carrier off of water.

"In this context, my dear boy, you must know that this [body] is a sprout which has sprung up; and there is no [sprout] without a root.

"What could its root be but water? And, my child, [if you think of] water as the sprout, you must look for light-and-heat as its root; and, dear boy, [if you think of] light-and-heat as the sprout, you must look for Being as its root.

"My dearest child, all these creatures [here] have Being as their root, Being as their resting-place, Being as their foundation.

"My dear boy, I have already told you how each of these substances (*devatā*) [itself] becomes threefold when it enters into the sphere of man.

"My dear boy, when a man dies, his voice is absorbed (*sampad-*) into the mind, his mind into breath, breath into light-and-heat and light-and-heat into the highest substance.

"This finest essence, — the whole universe has it as its Self: That is the Real: That is the Self: That *you* are, Śvetaketu!"

"Good sir, will you kindly instruct me further?"

"I will, my dear child', said he.

"As bees, dear boy, make honey by collecting the juices of many trees and reduce the juice to a unity, yet [those juices] cannot perceive any distinction there [so that any of them might know:] 'I am the juice of this tree', or 'I am the juice of that tree', [so too], my dearest boy, all these creatures [here], once they have merged (*sampad-*) into Being do not know that they have merged into Being.

"Whatever they are in this world, whether tiger or lion, wolf or boar, worm or moth, gnat or fly, that they become again (*ā-bhū*).

"This finest essence — the whole universe has it as its Self: That is the Real: That is the Self: That *you* are, Śvetaketu!"

"Good sir, will you kindly instruct me further?"

"I will, my dear child", said he.

"[Look at] these rivers, my dear: from east to west, from west to east they flow — from ocean to ocean they go. They become the ocean itself so that, once there, they no longer know: 'This one am I, that one am I.'

"Even so, my dear, all these [living] creatures, arising out of Being, do not know that they have arisen out of Being.

"Whatever they are in this world, whether tiger or lion, wolf or boar, worm or moth, gnat or fly, that they become again.

"This finest essence — the whole universe has it as its Self: That is the Real: That is the Self: That *you* are, Śvetaketu!"

"Good sir, will you kindly instruct me further?"

"I will, my dear child," said he.

"[Look at] this great tree, my dear. If you were to strike at its root, it would bleed but live on; if you were to strike it in the middle, it would bleed but live on; if you were to strike it at the top, it would bleed but live on. Strengthened by the living Self, it still stands, drinking in the moisture and exulting.

"If life leaves one of its branches, it dries up; if it leaves a second, that too dries up; if it leaves a third, that too dries up. If it leaves the whole [tree], the whole [tree] dries up. This, my dear boy, is how you ought to understand it," said he.

"When the life has gone out of it, this [body] dies; [but] the life does not die.

"This finest essence — the whole universe has it as its Self: That is the Real: That is the Self: That *you* are, Śvetaketu!"

"Good sir, will you kindly instruct me further?"

"I will, my dear child," said he.

"Bring me a fig from over there."

"Here you are, sir."

"Cut it open."

"[There it is,] cut open, sir."

"What do you see there?"

"These rather small seeds, sir."

"Would you, please, cut one of them up?"

"[Here is one,] cut up, sir."

"What do you see there?"

"Nothing at all, sir."

Then he said to him: "My dear boy, it is true that you cannot perceive this finest essence, but it is equally true that this huge fig tree grows up from this same finest essence.

"My dear child, have faith.

"This finest essence — the whole universe has it as its Self: That is the Real: That is the Self: That *you* are, Śvetaketu!"

"Good sir, will you kindly instruct me further?"

"I will, my dear child", said he.

"Put this piece of salt in the water and come to me tomorrow morning."

[Śvetaketu] did as he was told. [Then his father] said to him:

"[Do you remember] that piece of salt you put in the water yesterday evening? Would you be good enough to bring it here?"

He groped for it but could not find it. It had completely dissolved.

"Would you please sip it at this end? What is it like?" he said.

"Salt."

"Sip it in the middle. What is it like?"

"Salt."

"Sip it at the far end. What is it like?"

"Salt."

"Throw it away, and then come to me."

He did as he was told; but [that did not stop the salt from] remaining ever the same.

[His father] said to him: "My dear child, it is true that you cannot perceive Being here, but it is equally true that it *is* here.

"This finest essence — the whole universe has it as its Self: That is the Real: That is the Self: That *you* are, Śvetaketu!"

"Good sir, will you kindly instruct me further?"

"I will, my dear child", said he. . . .

[12]

From the *Taittirīya Upaniṣad*

This extract comprises the second of the three books of this *upaniṣad*, which belongs to the *Kṛṣṇa Yajur Veda*. It contains classic presentations of two important upanishadic ideas: the hierarchy of *puruṣa*s or conscious beings (here translated "Selves"), and the nature of the divine *ānanda* or delight of existence (here translated "Joy"). Translated by Purohit Swami and W. B. Yeats.

May He protect us both. May He take pleasure in us both. May we show courage together. May Spiritual knowledge shine before us. May we never hate one another.

May peace and peace and peace be everywhere.

He who knows Spirit knows the foundation. Here is my authority: "He who knows Spirit as that boundless wise reality, hidden in the heart's cavern, gets all that he wants."

Out of Spirit came air, out of air, wind; out of wind, fire; out of fire, water; out of water, earth; out of earth, vegetation; out of vegetation, food; out of food, man;

Man's elemental Self comes from food: this his head; this his right arm; this his left arm; this his heart; these legs his foundation. Here is my authority:

"From food are born all creatures; they live upon food, they are dissolved in food. Food is the chief of all things, the universal medicine.

"They who think of food as Spirit, shall never lack. From food all beings are born, all beings increase their bulk; all beings feed upon it, it feeds upon all beings."

The elemental Self is from food, but within it lives its complement and completion, the living Self. The living Self grows up side by side with the elemental Self. Prāṇa is its head, Wyāna its right arm, Apāna its left arm, air its heart, earth its foundation. Here is my authority:

"Gods, men, beasts, live by breath. Breath is life and is called the giver of Life."

The living Self is the soul of the elemental Self, but within it lives its complement and completion, the thinking Self. The thinking Self grows up side by side with the living Self. Meditation is its head, ritual its right arm, prayer its left arm, admonition of the Wedas its heart, Sage Atharwāngiras its foundation. Here is my authority:

"He who knows the spiritual joy mind cannot grasp nor tongue speak, fears nothing."

The thinking Self is the soul of the living Self, but within it lives its complement and completion, the knowing Self. The knowing Self grows up side by side with the thinking Self. Faith is its head, right its right arm, truth its left arm, concentration its heart, discrimination its foundation. Here is my authority:

"Knowledge runs to sacrifice and incites action. Gods worship knowledge as the highest expression of Spirit. The steadfast worshipper of Spirit, as knowledge, goes beyond all evil, gets everything he wants."

The knowing Self is the soul of the thinking Self, but within it lives its complement and completion, the joyous Self. The joyous Self grows up side by side with the knowing Self. Satisfied desire is its head, pleasure its right arm, contentment its left arm, joy its heart, Spirit its foundation. Here is my authority:

"He who denies Spirit, denies himself; he who affirms it, affirms himself."

This joyous Self is the soul of the knowing Self.

Does an ignorant man attain Spirit after death or only a wise man?

God thought: "I would be many; I will procreate." And in the heat of his meditation created everything; creating everything He entered into everything; entering into everything He took shape yet remained shapeless; took limits yet remained limitless; made his home, yet remained homeless; created knowledge and ignorance; reality, unreality; became everything; therefore everything is reality. Here is my authority:

"In the beginning there was no creation; then creation came. He created Himself, out of Himself. Hence He is called Self-Creator."

Everything is Self-created. He is that essence. Drinking that essence, man rejoices. If man did not lose himself in that joy, he could not breathe; he could not live. Self is the sole giver of joy.

When man finds invisible, nameless, homeless, shapeless, invulnerable rock, he is no longer terrified. To doubt Spirit is to live in terror. For that man, thinking himself wise, who doubts Spirit, Spirit becomes terror itself. Here is my authority:

"Through terror of God, sun shines, rain pours, fire burns, wind blows, death speeds."

What is joy?

Think of a young man, well read, ambitious, firm, strong, noble; give him all the wealth of the world, call him one unit of human joy.

Multiply that joy a hundred times, and call it one unit of the joy of those brought to the celestial choir by their good deeds. A man full of revelation, but without desire, has equal joy.

Multiply that joy a hundred times, and call it one unit of the joy of choir-born spirits. A man full of revelation, but without desire, has equal joy.

Multiply that joy a hundred times, and call it one unit of the joy of the fathers, living in their eternal paradise. A man full of revelation, but without desire, has equal joy.

Multiply that joy a hundred times, and call it one unit of the joy of heaven-born gods. A man full of revelation, but without desire, has equal joy.

Multiply that joy a hundred times, and call it one unit of the joy of gods brought to godhead by their good deeds. A man full of revelation, but without desire, has equal joy.

Multiply that joy a hundred times, and call it one unit of the joy of ruling gods. A man full of revelation, but without desire, has equal joy.

Multiply that joy a hundred times, and call it one unit of the joy of Indra, god of Power. A man full of revelation, but without desire, has equal joy.

Multiply that joy a hundred times, and call it one unit of the joy of Brihaspati, who has taught the gods. A man full of revelation, but without desire, has equal joy.

Multiply that joy a hundred times, and call it one unit of the joy of Prajāpati, maker of gods. A man full of revelation, but without desire, has equal joy.

Multiply that joy a hundred times, and call it one unit of the joy of Spirit. A man full of revelation, but without desire, has equal joy.

He who lives in man, He who lives in the sun, are one.

He who knows this, cries goodbye to the world; goes beyond elemental Self, living Self, thinking Self, knowing Self, joyous Self. Here is my authority:

"He who knows the spiritual joy mind cannot grasp nor tongue speak, fears nothing."

Should he do wrong, or leave good undone, he knows no remorse. What he does, what he does not, is sanctified; what he does not, what he does, is sanctified.

METRICAL UPANISHADS

Short, clear and for the most part unencumbered by the now-mysterious terminology of the vedic sacrifice, the metrical *upaniṣad*s are those most frequently read by modern students of this literature. Somewhat younger than the great prose *upaniṣad*s, they are among the earliest Indian texts to give expression to theism and devotionalism. Composed mostly in the straightforward *śloka* form, they contain poetry of great evocative power.

[13]

From the *Kena Upaniṣad*

This *upaniṣad* is generally considered to be the bridge between the early prose and later poetic *upaniṣad*s. It is divided into four parts, two in verse and two in prose. The first part, reproduced here, analyses the various instruments of knowledge, showing how each assumes an unchanging essence that "sees sight", "hears hearing", and so forth. Translated by Sri Aurobindo.

By whom missioned falls the mind shot to its mark? By whom yoked moves the first life-breath forward on its paths? By whom impelled is this word that men speak? What god set eye and ear to their workings?

That which is hearing of our hearing, mind of our mind, speech of our speech, that too is life of our life-breath and sight of our sight. The wise are released beyond and they pass from this world and become immortal.

There sight travels not, nor speech, nor the mind. We know It not nor can distinguish how one should teach of It: for It is other than the known; It is there above the unknown. It is so we have heard from men of old who declared That to our understanding.

That which is unexpressed by the word, that by which the word is expressed, know That to be the Brahman and not this which men follow after here.

That which thinks not by the mind, that by which the mind is thought, know That to be the Brahman and not this which men follow after here.

That which sees not with the eye, that by which one sees the eye's seeings, know That to be the Brahman and not this which men follow after here.

That which hears not with the ear, that by which the ear's hearing is heard, know That to be the Brahman and not this which men follow after here.

That which breathes not with the breath, that by which the life-breath is led forward in its paths, know That to be the Brahman and not this which men follow after here.

[14]

From the *Kaṭha Upaniṣad*

This *upaniṣad* is presented in the form of a dialogue between Nachiketas, a young seeker of spiritual knowledge, and Yama, the god of Death. Having been given three boons by Death, Nachiketas requests welfare for his father, the knowledge of the vedic sacrifice, and finally, the knowledge of what happens after death. Yama tries to dissuade him from seeking this secret knowledge, offering him instead sons, grandsons, desirable women, cattle, elephants, horses, land and gold — indeed anything Nachiketas can think of. The young man insists that he does not want things that give temporary fulfilment, but rather the secret of immortality. The extract that follows comprises the first part of Death's reply to Nachiketas. Translated by Purohit Swami and W. B. Yeats.

Death said: "God made sense turn outward, man therefore looks outward, not into himself. Now and again a daring soul, desiring immortality, has looked back and found himself.

"The ignorant man runs after pleasure, sinks into the entanglements of death; but the wise man, seeking the undying, does not run among things that die.

"He through whom we see, taste, smell, feel, hear, enjoy, knows everything. He is that Self.

"The wise man by meditating upon the self-dependent, all-pervading Self, understands waking and sleeping and goes beyond sorrow.

"Knowing that the individual self, eater of the fruit of action, is the universal Self, maker of past and future, he knows he has nothing to fear.

"He knows that He himself born in the beginning out of meditation, before water was created, enters every heart and lives there among the elements.

"That boundless Power, source of every power, manifesting itself as life, entering every heart, living there among the elements, that is Self.

"The Fire, hidden in the fire-stick like a child in the womb, worshipped with offerings, that Fire is Self.

"He who makes the sun rise and set, to Whom all powers do homage, He that has no master, that is Self.

"That which is here, is hereafter; hereafter is here. He who thinks otherwise wanders from death to death.

"Tell the mind that there is but One; he who divides the One, wanders from death to death.

"When that Person in the heart, no bigger than a thumb, is known as maker of past and future, what more is there to fear? That is Self.

"That Person, no bigger than a thumb, burning like flame without smoke, maker of past and future, the same today and tomorrow, that is Self.

"As rain upon a mountain ridge runs down the slope, the man that has seen the shapes of Self runs after them everywhere.

"The Self of the wise man remains pure; pure water, Nachiketas, poured into pure water."

[15]

Īśā Upaniṣad

The only *upaniṣad* that occurs as part of a vedic *saṁhitā* (that of the *Śukla Yajur Veda*), the *Īśā Upaniṣad* is always printed first in Indian collections. It is centrally concerned with the relations between the creative Lord and the manifested universe. Consisting of only eighteen stanzas, it is printed here in its entirety. Translated by Sri Aurobindo.

All this is for habitation by the Lord, whatsoever is individual universe of movement in the universal motion. By that renounced thou shouldst enjoy; lust not after any man's possession.

Doing verily works in this world one should wish to live a hundred years. Thus it is in thee and not otherwise than this; action cleaves not to a man.

Sunless are those worlds and enveloped in blind gloom whereto all they in their passing hence resort who are slayers of their souls.

One unmoving that is swifter than Mind, That the Gods reach not, for It progresses ever in front. That, standing, passes beyond others as they run. In That the Master of Life establishes the Waters.

That moves and That moves not; That is far and the same is near; That is within all this and That also is outside all this.

But he who sees everywhere the Self in all existences and all existences in the Self, shrinks not thereafter from aught.

He in whom it is the Self-Being that has become all existences that are Becomings, for he has the perfect knowledge, how shall he be deluded, whence shall he have grief who sees everywhere oneness?

It is He that has gone abroad — That which is bright, bodiless, without scar of imperfection, without sinews, pure, unpierced by evil. The Seer, the Thinker, the One who becomes everywhere, the Self-existent has ordered objects perfectly according to their nature from years sempiternal.

Into a blind darkness they enter who follow after the Ignorance, they as if into a greater darkness who devote themselves to the Knowledge alone.

Other, verily, it is said, is that which comes by the Knowledge, other that which comes by the Ignorance; this is the lore we have received from the wise who revealed That to our understanding.

He who knows That as both in one, the Knowledge and the Ignorance, by the Ignorance crosses beyond death and by the Knowledge enjoys Immortality.

Into a blind darkness they enter who follow after the Non-Birth, they as if into a greater darkness who devote themselves to the Birth alone.

Other, verily, it is said, is that which comes by the Birth, other that which comes by the Non-Birth; this is the lore we have received from the wise who revealed That to our understanding.

He who knows That as both in one, the Birth and the dissolution of Birth, by the dissolution crosses beyond death and by the Birth enjoys Immortality.

The face of Truth is covered with a brilliant golden lid; that do thou remove, O Fosterer, for the law of the Truth, for sight.

O Fosterer, O sole Seer, O Ordainer, O illumining Sun, O power of the Father of creatures, marshal thy rays, draw together thy light; the Lustre which is thy most blessed form of all, that in Thee I behold. The Purusha there and there, He am I.

The Breath of things is an immortal Life, but of this body ashes are the end. OM! O Will, remember, that which was done remember! O Will, remember, that which was done, remember.

O god Agni, knowing all things that are manifested, lead us by the good path to the felicity; remove from us the devious attraction of sin. To thee completest speech of submission we would dispose.

[16]

From the *Muṇḍaka Upaniṣad*

A relatively late *upaniṣad*, the *Muṇḍaka* appears to have been an independent composition rather than a part of the older vedic corpus. It contains a number of remarkable passages dealing in a straightforward way with the great upanishadic concepts. The first of the passages reproduced below deals with the *brahman*, the second with the knowledge of the Self or *ātman*. Translated by S. Radhakrishnan.

Manifest, well-fixed, moving, verily, in the secret place [of the heart] such is the great support. In it is centred all this which moves, breathes and winks. Know that as being, as non-being, as the supreme object to be desired, as the highest beyond the reach of man's understanding.

What is luminous, what is subtler than the subtle, in which are centred all the worlds and those that dwell in them, that is the imperishable *Brahman*. That is life, that is speech and mind. That is true, that is immortal, O beloved, that is to be known, know [that].

Taking as the bow the great weapon of the Upaniṣads, one should place in it the arrow sharpened by meditation. Drawing it with a mind engaged in the contemplation of that [*Brahman*], O beloved, know that Imperishable *Brahman* as the target.

The syllable *aum* is the bow: one's self, indeed, is the arrow. *Brahman* is spoken of as the target of that. It is to be hit without making a mistake. Thus one becomes united with it as the arrow [becomes one with the target].

He in whom the sky, the earth and the interspace are woven as also the mind along with all the vital breaths, know him alone as the one self. Dismiss other utterances. This is the bridge to immortality.

Where the arteries of the body are brought together like the spokes in the centre of a wheel, within it [this self, moves about] becoming manifold. Meditate on *aum* as the self. May you be successful in crossing over to the farther shore of darkness.

He who is all-knowing, all-wise, whose is this greatness on the earth, in the divine city of Brahmā, in the ether [of the heart] is that self-established.

He consists of mind and is the leader of life and body and is seated in food [i.e. the body] controlling the heart. The wise perceive clearly by the knowledge [of *Brahman*] the blissful immortal which shines forth.

The knot of the heart is cut, all doubts are dispelled and his deeds terminate, when He is seen — the higher and the lower.

In the highest golden sheath is *Brahman* without stain, without parts; Pure is it, the light of lights. That is what the knowers of self know.

The sun shines not there, nor the moon and stars, these lightnings shine not, where then could this fire be? Every thing shines only after that shining light. His shining illumines all this world.

Brahman, verily, is this immortal. In front is *Brahman*, behind is *Brahman*, to the right and to the left. It spreads forth below and above. *Brahman*, indeed, is this universe. It is the greatest.

*

Two birds, companions [who are] always united, cling to the self-same tree. Of these two, the one eats the sweet fruit and the other looks on without eating.

On the self-same tree, a person immersed [in the sorrows of the world] is deluded and grieves on account of his helplessness. When he sees the other, the Lord who is worshipped and his greatness, he becomes freed from sorrow.

When a seer sees the creator of golden hue, the Lord, the Person, the source of Brahmā, then being a knower, shaking off good and evil and free from stain, he attains supreme equality with the lord.

Truly it is life that shines forth in all beings. Knowing him, the wise man does not talk of anything else. Sporting in the self, delighting in the self, performing works, such a one is the greatest of the knowers of *Brahman*.

This self within the body, of the nature of light and pure, is attainable by truth, by austerity, by right knowledge, by the constant [practice] of chastity. Him, the ascetics with their imperfections done away, behold.

Truth alone conquers, not untruth. By truth is laid out the path leading to the gods by which the sages who have their desires fulfilled travel to where is that supreme abode of truth.

Vast, divine, of unthinkable form, subtler than the subtle. It shines forth, farther than the far, yet here near at hand, set down in the secret place [of the heart] [as such] even here it is seen by the intelligent.

He is not grasped by the eye nor even by speech nor by other sense-organs, nor by austerity nor by work, but when one's [intellectual] nature is purified by the light of knowledge then alone he, by meditation, sees Him who is without parts.

The subtle self is to be known by thought in which the senses in five different forms have centred. The whole of men's thought is pervaded by the senses. When it [thought] is purified, the self shines forth.

Whatever world a man of purified nature thinks of in his mind and whatever desires he desires, all these worlds and all these desires he attains. Therefore, let him who desires prosperity worship the knower of the self.

[17]

From the *Śvetāśvatara Upaniṣad*

Clearly influenced by the dualism later given classic expression by the *saṁkhya* and *yoga* schools of philosophy (see Chapter 5), the *Śvetāśvatara Upaniṣad* brings to the foreground the idea of the Absolute as a personal deity. In the first passage below, the *upaniṣad* speaks of the relationship between *brahman* and the Lord, who is sometimes referred to as Śiva. In the second passage, the *upaniṣad* gives detailed instructions in meditation, by which the aspirant can achieve union with the highest. Translated by R. C. Zaehner.

The One, [himself] uncoloured,
Widely disposes colours manifold
By the practice (*yoga*) of his power
(Now hidden is his purpose!):
Into Him all things dissolve at the end [of time],
[As] in the beginning [all things from Him emerged]:
He is God! May He conjoin us with a lucid mind (*buddhi*)!

That assuredly is fire, That the sun,
That the wind, and That the moon;
That is the Pure, That Brahman,
That is the waters, That the Lord of Creatures!

Thou art woman, Thou art man,
Thou art the lad and the maiden too,
Thou art the old man tottering on his staff:
Once born thou comest to be, thy face turned every way!

A dark-blue moth art Thou, green [parrot] with red eyes,
Pregnant with lightning — seasons, seas:
Thyself beginningless, all things dost Thou pervade;
From Thee all worlds were born.

With the one unborn female, red, white and black,
Who gives birth to many a creature like unto herself,
Lies the one male unborn, taking his delight.
Another Male unborn forsakes her, for she has had her pleasure.

Two birds, close-linked companions,
Cling to the selfsame tree;
Of these the one eats of the sweet fruit,
The other, nothing eating, looks on intent.

On the selfsame tree a person is plunged in [grief],
Mourning his lack of mastery, perplexed;
When he sees the other, the Lord, rejoicing
In his majesty, his sorrow melts away.

That syllable of the Vedic hymn (*ṛc*) whereon
In highest heaven all the gods are seated—
What shall the Vedic hymns avail the man
Who knows not Him [who indwells that syllable]?
The men who know it, lo, they are here assembled!

Hymns, sacrifices, rites and ordinances,
What was and what is yet to be,
[All] that the Vedas proclaim—
All this does He who is possessed of creative power (*māyā*) emit
From that [same syllable]; and by the same creative power (*māyā*)
The other is therein constrained.

Creative power (*māyā*) is Nature (*prakṛti*), this must be known,
And He who possesses it (*māyin*) is the Mighty Lord:
By things that are but parts of Him
This whole world is pervaded.

It is He alone who approaches every womb,
In Him [alone] does this universe grow together and dissolve;
He is the Lord who grants [us] favours,
God, the adorable:
Discerning Him a man wins peace for ever.

He, of gods the source and origin,
All-sovereign Rudra, mighty Seer,
Of old beheld the Golden Embryo when he was born:
May He conjoin us with a lucid mind!

King of the gods is He,
All worlds in Him are fixed!
His is the kingdom over fourfooted and twofooted beasts:
To what God shall we offer our oblations?

More subtile than the subtile, in the midst of chaos
All things He emanates — how manifold his forms! —
All things encompasses [though He is but] One:
Whoso should know Him, *Śiva*, the Benign, wins peace forever.

For sure protector of the world in time is He,
Sovereign of all, hidden in all creatures;
In Him are seers of Brahman and the gods united:
By knowing Him death's fetters are cut loose.

By knowing *Śiva*, the Benign, in all creatures hidden,
Surpassing subtile, even as cream surpasses butter,
By knowing God, the One Encompasser of all,
A man is from all fetters freed.

He is God, All-maker, of exalted Self (*mahātman*),
Forever dwelling in the hearts of men,
By heart and thought and mind to be conceived of:
Whoso knows this becomes immortal.

When there is no darkness, no day nor night,
No Being, no Not-Being — Śiva alone (*kevala*) [is this];
This the imperishable, this the choice [light] of Savitṛ:
From this primeval wisdom (*prajñā*) issued forth!

Above, athwart, or in the middle —
Nowhere hath anyone caught hold of him:
Of Him there is no likeness,
Great Glory is his name.

His form cannot be glimpsed,
None may see Him with the eye:
Whoso should know Him with heart and mind
As dwelling in the heart, becomes immortal! . . .

*

Holding the body straight with head, neck and chest in line,
With senses and the mind withdrawn into the heart,
Let a wise man on Brahman's raft cross over
All the rivers [of this life] so fraught with peril.

Restraining here his breath, his movements well controlled,
Let a wise man breathe in through the nostrils, his breath reduced;
Free from distraction, let him hold his mind in check
Like a chariot harnessed to vicious steeds.

Let him meditate in a clean and level [spot]
From pebbles, fire and gravel free,
Pleasing to the mind by reason of [soft] sounds,
Water and dwelling-places, not offensive to the eye—
A secret spot protected from the wind.

Fog, smoke, sun, fire and wind,
Fire-flies, lightning, crystal, and the moon—
In Yoga these are the visions (*rūpa*) that anticipate
The [fuller] revelations [seen] in Brahman.

When the fivefold attributes (*guṇa*) of Yoga come to be and grow,
[The attributes] of earth, water, fire, wind and space—
Then is there no sickness, age or death
For him who has won himself a body of Yogic fire.

Lightness, good health, freedom from harassment,
A clean complexion and a pleasant voice,

A fragrant odour and but slight excretions
Announce the first steps on Yoga['s path].

Even as a mirror with dirt begrimed
Shines brightly once it is well cleaned,
So too the embodied soul, once it has seen
Self as it really is (*tattva*),
Becomes one, its goal achieved, from sorrow free.

When by means of self as it really is as with a lamp
An integrated (*yukta*) man sees Brahman as It really is (*tattva*),

[Then will he know] the unborn, undying God, the Pure,
Beyond all essences as they really are,
[And] knowing Him, from all fetters he'll be freed.

This is the God who pervades all regions:
He is the first-born, He is in the womb.
He is born indeed and will be born again:
Over against [his] creatures does He stand,
His face turned every way.

This is the God in fire and in the waters;
The whole world has He entered;
In healing plants is He, He it is in the trees:
To this God all hail, all hail!

LATE PROSE UPANISHADS

The language of the later prose *upaniṣad*s is markedly different from that of the earliest texts. Derivative and sometimes repetitive, they typify a stage when the upanishadic revelation was becoming conventionalised. Nevertheless, they contain many passages of great significance and force.

[18]

From the *Maitrī Upaniṣad*

Not always counted among the major *upaniṣad*s, the *Maitrī* or *Maitrāyaṇīya Upaniṣad* is a late work that often quotes the classical *upaniṣad*s. This passage provides a number of methods for achieving union with the One. The elements of the "sixfold Yoga" mentioned here are almost identical with the last six elements of the eightfold yoga of Patanjali (see selection 43). Translated by Robert E. Hume.

Verily, in the beginning this world was Brahma, the limitless One — limitless to the east, limitless to the south, limitless to the west, limitless to the north, and above and below, limitless in every direction. Truly, for him east and the other directions exist not, nor across, nor below, nor above.

Incomprehensible is that supreme Soul (Ātman), unlimited, unborn, not to be reasoned about, unthinkable — He whose soul is space (*ākāśātman*)! In the dissolution of the world He alone remains awake. From that space He, assuredly, awakes this world, which is a mass of thought. It is thought by Him, and in Him it disappears.

His is that shining form which gives heat in yonder sun and which is the brilliant light in a smokeless fire, as also the fire in the stomach which cooks food. For thus has it been said: "He who is in the fire, and he who is here in the heart, and he who is yonder in the sun — he is one."

To the unity of the One goes he who knows this.

The precept for effecting this [unity] is this: restraint of the breath (*prāṇāyāma*), withdrawal of the senses (*pratyāhāra*), meditation (*dhyāna*), concentration (*dhāraṇā*), contemplation (*tarka*), absorption (*samādhi*). Such is said to be the sixfold Yoga. By this means

> When a seer sees the brilliant
> Maker, Lord, Person, the Brahma-source,
> Then, being a knower, shaking off good and evil,
> He reduces everything to unity in the supreme Imperishable.

For thus has it been said: —

> As to a mountain that's enflamed
> Deer and birds do not resort —
> So, with the Brahma-knowers, faults
> Do never any shelter find.

Now, it has elsewhere been said: "Verily, when a knower has restrained his mind from the external, and the breathing spirit (*prāṇa*) has put to rest objects of sense, thereupon let him continue void of conceptions. Since the living individual (*jīva*) who is named 'breathing spirit' has arisen here from what is not breathing spirit, therefore, verily, let the breathing spirit restrain his breathing spirit in what is called the fourth condition (*turya*)." For thus has it been said: —

> That which is non-thought, [yet] which stands in the midst of thought,
> The unthinkable, supreme mystery! —
> Thereon let one concentrate his thought
> And the subtile body (*liṅga*), too, without support.

Now, it has elsewhere been said: "One may have a higher concentration than this. By pressing the tip of his tongue against the palate, by restraining voice, mind, and breath, one sees Brahma through contemplation." When through self, by the suppressing of the mind, one sees the brilliant Self which is more subtile than the subtile, then having seen the Self through one's self, one becomes self-less (*nir-ātman*). Because of being selfless, he is to be regarded as incalculable (*a-saṁkhya*), without origin — the mark of liberation (*mokṣa*). This is the supreme secret doctrine (*rahasya*). For thus has it been said: —

For by tranquillity (*prasāda*) of thought
Deeds (*karman*), good and evil, one destroys!
With soul (*ātman*) serene, stayed on the Soul (Ātman),
Delight eternal one enjoys!

[19]

Māṇḍūkya Upaniṣad

This short prose *upaniṣad*, given here in its entirety, deals with the inner significance of the mystic syllable OM. According to Sanskrit phonetics, OM breaks down into the letters *a*, *u*, and *m*. In the *upaniṣad* these symbolise the three conscious states of waking, dreaming and dreamless sleep. The Absolute lies beyond all three. It is incommunicable, but can be known by experience. Translated by Robert E. Hume.

Om! — This syllable is this whole world.

Its further explanation is: —

The past, the present, the future — everything is just the word *Om*.

And whatever else that transcends threefold time — that, too, is just the word *Om*.

For truly, everything here is Brahma; this self (*ātman*) is Brahma. This same self has four fourths.

The waking state (*jāgarita-sthāna*), outwardly cognitive, having seven limbs, having nineteen mouths, enjoying the gross (*sthūla-bhuj*), the Common-to-all-men (*vaiśvānara*), is the first fourth.

The dreaming state (*svapna-sthāna*), inwardly cognitive, having seven limbs, having nineteen mouths, enjoying the exquisite (*pravivikta-bhuj*), the Brilliant (*taijasa*), is the second fourth.

If one asleep desires no desire whatsoever, sees no dream whatsoever, that is deep sleep (*suṣupta*).

The deep-sleep state (*suṣupta-sthāna*), unified (*ekī-bhūta*), just (*eva*) a cognition-mass (*prajñāna-ghana*), consisting of bliss (*ānanda-maya*), enjoying bliss (*ānanda-bhuj*), whose mouth is thought (*cetas-*), the Cognitional (*prājña*), is the third fourth.

This is the lord of all (*sarveśvara*). This is the all-knowing (*sarva-jña*). This is the inner controller (*antar-yāmin*). This is the source (*yoni*) of all, for this is the origin and the end (*prabhavāpyayau*) of beings.

Not inwardly cognitive (*antaḥ-prajña*), not outwardly cognitive (*bahiḥ-prajña*), not both-wise cognitive (*ubhayataḥ-prajña*), not a cognition-mass (*prajñāna-ghana*), not cognitive (*prajña*), not non-cognitive (*a-prajña*), unseen (*a-dṛṣṭa*), with which there can be no dealing (*a-vyavahārya*), ungraspable (*a-grāhya*), having no distinctive mark (*a-lakṣaṇa*), non-thinkable (*a-cintya*), that cannot be designated (*a-vyapadeśya*), the essence of the assurance of which is the state of being one with the Self (*ekātmya-pratyaya-sāra*), the cessation of development (*prapañcopaśama*), tranquil (*śānta*), benign (*śiva*), without a second (*a-dvaita*) —[such] they think is the fourth. He is the Self (*Ātman*). He should be discerned.

This is the Self with regard to the word *Om*, with regard to its elements. The elements (*mātra*) are the fourths; the fourths, the elements: the letter *a*, the letter *u*, the letter *m*.

The waking state, the Common-to-all-men, is the letter *a*, the first element, from *āpti* ("obtaining") or from *ādimatvā* ("being first").

He obtains, verily, indeed, all desires, he becomes first—he who knows this.

The sleeping state, the Brilliant, is the letter *u*, the second element, from *utkarṣa* ("exaltation") or from *ubhayatvā* ("intermediateness").

He exalts, verily, indeed, the continuity of knowledge; and he becomes equal (*samāna*); no one ignorant of Brahma is born in the family of him who knows this.

The deep-sleep state, the Cognitional, is the letter *m*, the third element, from *miti* ("erecting") or from *apīti* ("immerging").

He, verily, indeed, erects (*minoti*) this whole world, and he becomes its immerging—he who knows this.

The fourth is without an element, with which there can be no dealing, the cessation of development, benign, without a second.

Thus *Om* is the Self (Ātman) indeed.

He who knows this, with his self enters the Self—yea, he who knows this!

MINOR UPANISHADS

Products of the Common Era, the hundred or more minor *upaniṣads* have no direct relation to the Vedic corpus. Accordingly they were not cited or commented on by the great exponents of vedantic philosophy. Their language is more formalised and less subtle than that of the classical *upaniṣads*; as a result, they present fewer difficulties of comprehension to the modern reader.

[20]

From the *Kaivalya Upaniṣad*

Classified as a *śaiva upaniṣad* because it visualises *brahman* in the form of the god *Śiva*, the *Kaivalya* undertakes to show the way to absolute aloneness or *kaivalya*, a term used also by followers of the Samkhya and Jaina philosophies. Translated by S. Radhakrishnan.

The world which shines in the states of waking, dream and dreamless sleep, knowing that it is *Brahman* who I am, one is freed from all fetters.

In the three states of consciousness whatever appears as the object of enjoyment, or the enjoyer or the enjoyment, I am different from them, the witness [thereof], pure consciousness, the eternal *Śiva*.

From me all proceed, in me all exist, and to me all return. That *Brahman* without a second am I.

I am subtler than the subtle, greater than the great. I am this manifold universe. I am the ancient, the person. I am the lord of golden hue. I am *Śiva*.

I am without hands and feet, of inconceivable powers. I see without eyes. I hear without ears. I know [all]. I am of one form. None knows me. I am always pure consciousness.

I am the One to be known through the many Vedas. I am the maker of the Vedānta and the knower of the Vedas. Merit or demerit I have none [do not affect me]. There is no destruction for me, no birth or body, senses or intellect.

I have not earth, water, fire, air, ether. Knowing the nature of the Supreme Self, dwelling in the cave of the heart, stainless without a second; the witness of all, free from [the duality of] existent and non-existent, he obtains the pure nature of the Supreme Self.

[21]

From the *Kuṇḍikā Upaniṣad*

Modern scholars speak of the *Kuṇḍikā* and related texts as *saṁnyāsa upaniṣads*, because they counsel the absolute renunciation of the world (*saṁnyāsa*). In this *upaniṣad*, as in the *Kaivalya*, the first person singular is freely used. Translated by Patrick Olivelle.

Stirred by the wind of illusion,
the waves of the whole universe
Repeatedly rise and fall
within me, the ocean of total bliss.

As the sky is not tied to a cloud,
so to the body I am not tied.
Awake, dreaming, or deep in sleep,
how could I its qualities have?

Like the sky am I,
far beyond the reach of time.
Like the sun am I,
other than the illumined.
Like a hill am I,
forever unchangeable.
Like the sea am I,
without a farther shore.

I am Nārāyaṇa! Naraka I killed!
I am Puruṣa! Citadels I laid waste!
I am the Lord!

I am pure consciousness, the witness of all!
I am free from the thought of "I" and "mine"!
    I have no lord!

The witness is different; he is untouched
    by the qualities of things witnessed.
Like a lamp, the unchanging and impartial man
    is not touched by the duties of home.

Let this insentient body
    wallow in water or on land.
By its qualities I am not touched,
    as space by the qualities of a pot.

I do not act, I do not change.
    I have no parts. I have no form.
I am eternal, I have no thought.
    I am unique, I have no support.

All are myself and I am all!
    I am unique and I transcend all!
I am my own eternal bliss,
    pure undivided consciousness!

Seeing me alone everywhere,
    knowing myself to be unique,
Enjoying the bliss of myself,
    I become free from every thought.

Walking, standing, or sitting down,
    sleeping, or doing anything else,
Let a wise sage live as he likes,
    ever delighting in himself.

That is the secret teaching.

FURTHER READING

Source Materials

Sri Aurobindo, trans., *The Upanishads*. Pondicherry: Sri Aurobindo Ashram, 1972.

Dominic Goodall, ed., *Hindu Scriptures*. London: Phoenix, 1996.

Robert Ernest Hume, trans., *The Thirteen Principal Upanishads*. Reprint edition. Delhi: Oxford University Press, 1998.

Patrick Olivelle, trans., *Saṃnyāsa Upaniṣads: Hindu Scriptures on Asceticism and Renunciation*. New York: Oxford University Press, 1992.

Purohit Swami and W. B. Yeats, trans., *The Ten Principal Upanishads*. Reprint edition. London: Faber and Faber, 1997.

S. Radhakrishnan, trans., *The Principal Upanishads*. Reprint edition. New Delhi: HarperCollins India, 1999.

Other Works

Paul Deussen, *The Philosophy of the Upanishads*. Reprint Edition. New Delhi: Oriental Books Reprint Corporation, 1979.

Patrick Olivelle, trans., *Upaniṣads*. Oxford: Oxford University Press, 1996.

Sources of Texts and Translations

10 *Bṛhadāraṇyaka Upaniṣad* 1.4.1–10	Purohit and Yeats 119–22
11 *Chāndogya Upaniṣad* 6.1; 6.8–13	Goodall 132, 136–39
12 *Taittirīya Upaniṣad*, part 2	Purohit and Yeats 69–74
13 *Kena Upaniṣad*, part 1	Aurobindo 145–46
14 *Kaṭha Upaniṣad* 2.1	Purohit and Yeats 55–56
15 *Īśā Upaniṣad*	Aurobindo 63–68
16 *Muṇḍaka Upaniṣad* 2.2.1–12; 3.1.1–10	Radhakrishnan 682–85, 686–89
17 *Śvetāśvatara Upaniṣad* 4.1–20; 2.8–17	Goodall 194–97, 190–191
18 *Maitrī Upaniṣad* 6.17–20	Hume 435–36
19 *Māṇḍūkya Upaniṣad*	Hume 391–93
20 *Kaivalya Upaniṣad* 17–23	Radhakrishnan 930–31
21 *Kuṇḍikā Upaniṣad*	Olivelle 127–28

3

सयंकडं नन्नकडं च दुक्खं आहंसु विज्जाचरणं पमोक्खं।

Misery is produced by one's own actions, not by those of anyone or anything else; but right knowledge and right conduct lead to liberation.

Sūtrakṛtāṅga 1.12.11

Jainism

DURING the sixth and fifth centuries BCE, the central and eastern Gangetic plains saw an extraordinary upsurge of intellectual and spiritual innovation. This period was in fact a time of revolutionary change in intellectual and spiritual practice and thought across Asia. In China, it was the age of Lao Tzu and Confucius; in Persia, of Zoroaster; in Israel, of the later prophets; in Asia Minor, of the pre-Socratic philosophers. In India, the chief manifestations of this so-called "Axial Age" were, on the one hand, the *upaniṣad*s, and on the other, a number of heterodox or non-vedic teachings, the most enduring of which were Jainism and Buddhism.

The social conditions of the lower Ganges valley favoured the development of new ways of thought. Vedic orthodoxy was not yet entrenched in the region, and *kṣatriya*s vied with *brāhmaṇa*s for social predominance. Trade was on the rise and prosperous town-based tradesmen were free to patronise teachers who held unorthodox views. In the sixth and fifth centuries BCE, a number of such teachers were active in the kingdoms of Kosala, Kashi, Vrijji and Magadha (roughly, eastern Uttar Pradesh and Bihar). Most of them practised asceticism, accepted a theory of the cycle of rebirth, and looked forward to escape from its bondage. (In this they were like the sages of the *upaniṣad*s; unlike them, however, they rejected the authority of the Veda.) Several of them developed theories about the ultimate stuff of the universe. (In this they were like the Ionian philosophers; unlike them, however, they rated introspective knowledge higher than intellectual reason.) Among themselves, they differed chiefly in the importance they assigned to individual action. One doubted its very reality, another was antinomian, yet another rigidly fatalistic. Finally there were two who taught that a life of right action, informed by right beliefs and right knowledge, could lead to liberation from the cycle of rebirth. These two were Vardhamana, the founder of Jainism, and Siddhattha Gotama, the founder of Buddhism.

Vardhamana, later called Mahavira, is said to have been born in 599 BCE near what is now the city of Patna. (This would make him an elder contemporary of the Buddha, as Buddhist sources show him to be. Some scholars, however, believe Mahavira to have been the younger, and adjust the year of his birth accordingly.) Vardhamana's father was a clan chieftain; his mother, the sister of a local ruler. Both parents were members of an ascetic order that had been founded by a teacher named Parshvanatha two centuries earlier. Vardhamana grew up in comfort, married, and had a daughter. Then, at the age of thirty, he renounced the world and took to a life of severe asceticism. For a year he wore clothes; when they wore out, he went naked and possessionless. Exposed to the elements, to attacks by insects, to the injury and abuse of men, he bore all with patience and equanimity, eating nothing but what was offered him by others, and often observing long fasts. He continued this life for more than twelve years. Finally, in the thirteenth year, while fasting and meditating, he achieved the state of omniscience or *kevala* (literally "aloneness"). As a result of this victory over the lower principles of existence, he was called "Victor" (*Jina*) or "Fordmaker" (*Tīrthaṅkara*) or "Great Hero" (*Mahāvīra*). Those who follow the path of this Jina are known as Jainas.

According to Jaina tradition, Mahavira was the twenty-fourth and last Jina of the present world-cycle. The twenty-third was Parshvanatha, whose historicity is generally acknowledged. The others are said to have lived thousands or millions of years ago, and thus escape the scrutiny of the historian. Mahavira is regarded not so much as the founder of the Jainism as its renewer, a human being who by his own efforts rediscovered the Truth that periodically is made available to humanity. For thirty years after his attainment of *kevala*, Mahavira taught his path to men and women without regard to caste. In his seventy-second year, he left his body by means of voluntary self-starvation, obtaining *mokṣa* or complete liberation. As a *siddha* or Perfect One he dwells on the very top of the universe in a state of unadulterated bliss.

It is said that during his lifetime, Mahavira made converts of 14,000 monks and 36,000 nuns, along with thousands of laymen and laywomen. For several hundred years, the Jaina community transmitted the teachings of their founder orally. During this time, several councils were held to fix the canon. Towards the end of the third century BCE, the religion was patronised, and perhaps embraced, by Chandragupta, the Mauryan ruler who made Magadha the centre of the first pan-Indian empire. But around this same time, Jainism suffered a schism. According to one account, during a famine in Bihar, a group of monks migrated to Karnataka. When they returned years later, they found that the monks who had stayed behind no longer followed the founder's rules. In particular, the northern group had taken to wearing clothing, while Mahavira had been utterly possessionless. Moreover, they had adopted certain beliefs that the southern group found unacceptable. Noteworthy among these was the idea that women (who had to be clothed) could attain the highest realisation. These and other minor differences led to an irreconcilable split between the Digambara or "sky-clad" monks, who go naked, and the Swetambara or "white-clad" monks, who wear white clothing. The schools developed separate canons, but these exhibit no fundamental differences in basic points of doctrine.

Jaina monks of both schools must take a series of extremely strict vows, the most important of which is to "desist from the knowing or intentional destruction of all great lives" — that is, roughly, animals and humans — to "neither kill nor cause others to kill", refraining "from all such activities, whether of body, speech or mind" (Jaini 1994: xxix). To assist themselves in this effort, many Swetambara monks and nuns wear masks and carry whisk-brooms, to prevent them from breathing in or treading on small life-forms. Beyond such visible expressions of sanctity, Jaina monastics undergo various austerities and practise special forms of meditation. About these, little information is given in the texts, the methods being transmitted orally. The texts do distinguish four forms of meditation (*dhyāna*), two negative and two positive. The negative ones, which are to be avoided, are concentration on what is unpleasant, and dwelling upon the causing of injury. The positive ones, which are to be cultivated, are concentration on points of doctrine, and pure concentration, leading to *kevala-jñāna* or omniscience.

By means of such practices, monastics climb the fourteen rungs of the ladder of existence. Laypersons too can make progress in a number of ways: by keeping lay vows, by undertaking fasts, by practising daily meditation, and by devotional practices, which are regarded as forms of meditation. The five lay vows (less severe forms of the monastic vows) are avoidance of violence, lying, stealing, illicit sex, and attachment to possessions. Lay meditation is known as *sāmāyika* or "maintaining equanimity for a fixed period of time", traditionally forty-eight minutes.

The philosophy of Jainism encourages its adherents to be spiritually self-reliant. It has no priesthood in the sense of a class of specialists whose intercession is required by others. Neither does it recognise gods to whom petitions may be addressed (though it must be added that modern Jaina temples contain images of numerous gods, many of them borrowed from Hinduism). The twenty-four Tirthankaras are not regarded as agents who intercede on behalf of their followers. Having attained *kevala*, they are free from attachment to the earth and its creatures; but they do serve as exemplars of right conduct and right spiritual effort.

Most Jaina temples contain images of Tirthankaras that are meant to serve as examples of the liberated state. In practice these images, as well as those of Hindu deities, are worshipped in the hope of divine response. Some of these images, notably the carvings that fill the delicate temples of Gujarat and Rajasthan and the colossal statue at Sravana Belagola in Karnataka, are among the high points of Indian sculpture. Other important contributions of Jainism to Indian culture are various philosophical and literary texts written in Sanskrit and regional languages (see Chapter 10). The influence of Jaina ethics has been even more significant. The doctrine of *ahiṁsā*, as understood by Jainas, has helped vegetarianism spread into most parts of the subcontinent. Numerically small — less than one half of one percent of the Indian population — the Jaina community is prominent in business, education and government. The religion's pessimistic worldview has attracted few converts, but the example of its founder has been and remains influential.

The extant Swetambara canon consists of 43 texts (13 others are said to have been lost). Chief among the surviving texts are the eleven *aṅga*s or "limbs". The most ancient of these are the *Ācārāṅga Sūtra* and *Sūtrakṛtāṅga* (see selections 23, 26 and 27). The other extant division of texts is known as the *Aṅgabāhya* or subsidiary canon. This has five main divisions. One, the *Chedasūtra*, includes the *Kalpa Sūtra*, which comprises biographies of the Jinas, lists of saints, etc. (see selections 22 and 24). All the texts are written in a Prakrit or vernacular language known as *Ardha-māgadhī*. This probably was very similar to the language Mahavira spoke as he wandered around eastern India. Jainas do not believe that the existing texts are their founder's exact words; but they do consider them an adequate record of the utterances of one who spoke from a state of omniscience.

THE LIFE AND SELF-DISCIPLINE OF MAHAVIRA

The story of Mahavira's life is recounted in different parts of the Jaina canon. Along with traditional biographical materials, most of the sources include legendary and doctrinal accretions.

[22]

The Going Forth of Mahavira

The main Swetambara account of the life of Mahavira is found in the *Kalpa Sūtra*. Not as old as other parts of the canon, the *Kalpa Sūtra* contains a great deal of legendary material, but it may be assumed to provide an adequate account of the outlines of the founder's life. This selection tells part of the story of Mahavira's renunciation. Translated from the Ardha-magadhi by Hermann Jacobi.

The Venerable Ascetic Mahāvīra belonged to the Kāśyapa gotra. His three names have thus been recorded: by his parents he was called Vardhamāna; because he is devoid of love and hate, he is called Śramaṇa [i.e. Ascetic]; because he stands fast in midst of dangers and fears, patiently bears hardships and calamities, adheres to the chosen rules of penance, is wise, indifferent to pleasure and pain, rich in control, and gifted with fortitude, the name Venerable Ascetic Mahāvīra has been given him by the gods. . . .

The Venerable Ascetic Mahāvira — clever, with the aspirations of a clever man, of great beauty, controlling [his senses], lucky, and modest; a Jñātṛ Kshatriya, the son of a Jñātṛ Kshatriya; the moon of the clan of the Jñātṛs; a Videha, the son of Videhadattā, a native of Videha, a prince of Videha — had lived thirty years in Videha when his parents went to the world of the gods [i.e. died], and he with the permission of his elder brother and the authorities of the kingdom fulfilled his promise. . . .

Then the Venerable Ascetic Mahāvīra . . . went right through Kuṇḍapura to a park called the Shaṇḍavana of the Jñātṛs and proceeded to the excellent tree Aśoka.

There under the excellent tree Aśoka he caused his palankin to stop, descended from his palankin, took off his ornaments, garlands, and finery with his own hands, and with his own hands plucked out his hair in five handfuls. When the moon was in conjunction with the asterism Uttaraphalgunī, he, after fasting two and a half days without drinking water, put on a divine robe, and quite alone, nobody else being present, he tore out his hair and leaving the house entered the state of houselessness.

The Venerable Ascetic Mahāvīra for a year and a month wore clothes; after that time he walked about naked, and accepted the alms in the hollow of his hand. For more than twelve years the Venerable Ascetic Mahāvīra neglected his body and abandoned the care of it; he with equanimity bore, underwent, and suffered all pleasant or unpleasant occurrences arising from divine powers, men, or animals.

[23]
The Austerities of Mahavira

This selection from the *Ācārāṅga Sūtra*, one of the oldest parts of the Swetambara canon, tells of the austerities Vardhamana underwent during the twelve years that followed his renunciation. Much stress is laid in the text on the outward manifestations of equality: indifference to discomfort, persecution, and social contacts. The future Jina went without food and water for extended periods; when he did eat, the food was often stale and tasteless. Occasionally a hint is given of the psychological rewards he gained from these austerities: intuitive knowledge, calm, and finally liberation. Translated by Hermann Jacobi.

As I have heard it, I shall tell how the Venerable Ascetic, exerting himself and meditating, after having entered the order in that winter, wandered about,

"I shall not cover myself with that robe," only in that winter [he used it]. He had crossed [the saṁsāra] for the rest of his life. This [refusing of dress] is in accordance with his doctrine.

More than four months many sorts of living beings gathered on his body, crawled about it, and caused pain there.

For a year and a month he did not leave off his robe. Since that time the Venerable One, giving up his robe, was a naked, world-relinquishing, houseless [sage].

Then he meditated [walking] with his eye fixed on a square space before him of the length of a man. Many people assembled, shocked at the sight; they struck him and cried.

Knowing [and renouncing] the female sex in mixed gathering places, he meditated, finding his way himself: I do not lead a worldly life.

Giving up the company of all householders whomsoever, he meditated. Asked, he gave no answer; he went, and did not transgress the right path.

For some it is not easy [to do what he did], not to answer those who salute; he was beaten with sticks, and struck by sinful people.

Disregarding slights difficult to bear, the Sage wandered about, [not attracted] by story-tellers, pantomimes, songs, fights at quarter-staff, and boxing-matches.

At that time the son of Jñātṛ saw without sorrow [or pleasure]

people in mutual conversation. Jñātṛputra obtained oblivion of these exquisite sorrows.

For more than a couple of years he led a religious life without using cold water; he realised singleness, guarded his body, had got intuition, and was calm. . . .

Practising the sinless abstinence from killing, he did no acts, neither himself nor with the assistance of others; he to whom women were known as the causes of all sinful acts, he saw [the true state of the world].

He did not use what had expressly been prepared for him; he well saw [that bondage comes] through action. Whatever is sinful, the Venerable One left that undone: he consumed clean food.

He did not use another's robe, nor does he eat out of another's vessel. Disregarding contempt, he went with indifference to places where food was prepared.

Knowing measure in eating and drinking, he was not desirous of delicious food, nor had he a longing for it. A sage should not rub his eyes nor scratch his body. . . .

He sometimes lodged in workshops, assembling-places, wells, or shops; sometimes in manufactories or under a shed of straw.

He sometimes lodged in travellers' halls, garden-houses, or towns; sometimes on a burying-ground, in relinquished houses, or at the foot of a tree.

In these places was the wise Śramaṇa for thirteen long years; he meditated day and night, exerting himself, undisturbed, strenuously.

The Venerable One, exerting himself, did not seek sleep for the sake of pleasure; he waked up himself, and slept only a little, free from desires.

Waking up again, the Venerable One lay down, exerting himself; going outside for once in a night, he walked about for an hour.

In his resting-places he sustained fearful and manifold calamities; crawling or flying animals attack him.

Bad people, the guard of the village, or lance-bearers attack him; or there were domestic temptations, single women or men;

Fearful and manifold [calamities] of this and the next world; pleasant and unpleasant smells, and manifold sounds:

Always well controlled, he bore the different sorts of feelings; overcoming carelessness and pleasure, the Brāhmaṇa wandered about, speaking but little.

In the resting-places there once, in a night, the single wanderers asked him [who he was, and why he was there]; as he did not answer, they treated him badly; but he persevered in his meditations, free from resentment. . . .

The Venerable One was able to abstain from indulgence of the flesh, though never attacked by diseases. Whether wounded or not wounded, he desired not medical treatment.

Purgatives and emetics, anointing of the body and bathing, shampooing and cleansing of the teeth do not behove him, after he learned [that the body is something unclean].

Being averse from the impressions of the senses, the Brāhmaṇa wandered about, speaking but little. Sometimes in the cold season the Venerable One was meditating in the shade.

In summer he exposes himself to the heat, he sits squatting in the sun; he lives on rough [food]: rice, pounded jujube, and beans.

Using these three, the Venerable One sustained himself eight months. Sometimes the Venerable One did not drink for half a month or even for a month.

Or he did not drink for more than two months, or even six months, day and night, without desire [for drink]. Sometimes he ate stale food.

Sometimes he ate only the sixth meal, or the eighth, the tenth, the twelfth; without desires, persevering in meditation.

Having wisdom, Mahāvīra committed no sin himself, nor did he induce others to do so, nor did he consent to the sins of others.

Having entered a village or a town, he begged for food which had been prepared for somebody else. Having got clean food, he used it, restraining the impulses.

When there were hungry crows, or thirsty beings stood in his way, where he begged, or when he saw them flying repeatedly down,

When a Brāhmaṇa or Śramaṇa, a beggar or guest, a caṇḍāla, a cat, or a dog stood in his way,

Without ceasing in his reflections, and avoiding to overlook them, the Venerable One slowly wandered about, and, killing no creatures, he begged for his food.

Moist or dry or cold food, old beans, old pap, or bad grain, whether he did or did not get such food, he was rich [in control].

And Mahāvīra meditated [persevering] in some posture, without the smallest motion; he meditated in mental concentration on [the things] above, below, beside, free from desires.

He meditated free from sin and desire, not attached to sounds or colours; though still an erring mortal (*chadmastha*), he wandered about, and never acted carelessly.

Himself understanding the truth and restraining the impulses for the purification of the soul, finally liberated, and free from delusion, the Venerable One was well guarded during his whole life.

[24]

Kevala and Moksha

This passage from the *Kalpa Sūtra* (which in the text comes just after what is reproduced as selection 22) recounts the two climactic moments of Mahavira's life: his attainment of *kevala* in his forty-second year, and his passage into *mokṣa* or liberation thirty years later. The literal meaning of *kevala* is "aloneness" or "isolation". When the soul has been freed from the last trace of karmic matter, it stands alone, fully conscious and thus omniscient. After attaining this state, Mahavira taught his doctrine and practice to men and women in eastern India. Finally, in his seventy-second year, he died in a town in central Bihar called Papa or Pava. According to Jaina tradition, after his soul left its body, it rose upward to the very top of the universe (*loka ākāśa*). Here it will dwell forever, motionless and freed from bondage. Translated by Hermann Jacobi.

The Venerable One lived, except in the rainy season, all the eight months of summer and winter, in villages only a single night, in towns only five nights; he was indifferent alike to the smell of ordure and of sandal, to straw and jewels, dirt and gold, pleasure and pain, attached neither to this world nor to that beyond, desiring neither life nor death, arrived at the other shore of the saṁsāra, and he exerted himself for the suppression of the defilement of Karman.

With supreme knowledge, with supreme intuition, with supreme conduct, in blameless lodgings, in blameless wandering, with supreme valour, with supreme uprightness, with supreme mildness, with supreme dexterity, with supreme patience, with supreme freedom from passions, with supreme control, with supreme contentment, with supreme understanding, on the supreme path to final liberation, which is the fruit of veracity, control, penance, and good conduct, the Venerable One meditated on himself for twelve years.

During the thirteenth year, in the second month of summer, in the fourth fortnight, the light [fortnight] of Vaiśākha, on its tenth day, when the shadow had turned towards the east and the first wake was over, on the day called Suvrata, in the Muhūrta called Vijaya, outside of the town Jṛmbhikagrāma on the bank of the river Rijupālika, not far from an old temple, in the field of the householder Sāmāga, under a Sal tree, when the moon was in conjunction with the asterism Uttaraphalgunī, [the Venerable One] in a squatting position with joined heels, exposing himself to the heat of the sun, after fasting two and a half days without drinking water, being engaged in deep meditation, reached the highest knowledge and intuition, called Kevala, which is infinite, supreme, unobstructed, unimpeded, complete, and full.

When the Venerable Ascetic Mahāvīra had become a Jina and Arhat, he was a Kevalin, omniscient and comprehending all objects; he knew and saw all conditions of the world, of gods, men, and demons: whence they come, whither they go, whether they are born as men or animals (cyavana) or become gods or hell-beings (upapāda), the ideas, the thoughts of their minds, the food, doings, desires, the open and secret deeds of all the living beings in the whole world; he the Arhat, for whom there is no secret, knew and saw all conditions of all living beings in the world, what they thought, spoke, or did at any moment.

In that period, in that age the Venerable Ascetic Mahāvīra stayed the first rainy season in Asthikagrāma, three rainy seasons in Campā and Pṛshṭicampā, twelve in Vaiśālī and Vāṇijagrāma, fourteen in Rājagṛha and the suburb of Nālandā, six in Mithilā, two in Bhadrikā, one in Ālabhikā, one in Paṇitabhūmi, one in Śrāvastī, one in the town of Pāpā in king Hastipāla's office of the writers: that was his very last rainy season.

In the fourth month of that rainy season, in the seventh fortnight, in the dark [fortnight] of Kārttika, on its fifteenth day, in the last night, in the town of Pāpā, in king Hastipāla's office of the writers, the Venerable Ascetic Mahāvīra died, went off, quitted the world, cut asunder the ties of birth, old age, and death; became a Siddha, a Buddha, a Mukta, a maker of the end [to all misery], finally liberated, freed from all pains.

THE TEACHINGS OF MAHAVIRA

It is central to the Jaina view of things that the universe is uncreated. There is, accordingly, no creator God. Innumerable souls or *jīva*s, each eternally separate, exist. Not only human, animal and vegetable organisms, but also things like earth, fire and water have souls. In their nature, these souls are perfectly conscious; but this consciousness is covered over, in different degrees in different individuals, by matter, in particular the fine matter of *karma*. Since any violence towards life, especially in its higher forms, produces a great influx of *karma*, non-violence or *ahiṁsā* is of the utmost importance to Jainas. Full liberation can only be achieved by monks (and, according to the Swetambaras, nuns) who follow an arduous self-discipline.

[25]
A Buddhist Account

In Theravada *sutta*s, Mahavira is referred to as Nigantha Nataputta. He was one of the six heterodox teachers active around the time that the Buddha attained *nirvāṇa*, whose doctrines the Buddha criticised. In the *Cūḷadukkhakkhandha Sutta* of the *Majjhima Nikāya*, the Buddha tells of a meeting with a group of Niganthas (that is, Jainas) who "were practising continuous standing, rejecting seats, and were experiencing painful, racking, piercing feelings due to exertion". He asked them why they were doing this. The passage that follows is their reply. Jaina authors sometimes cite this as an adequate expression of the thought of Mahavira — though in citing it they drop the dismissive "claims to have" of the first sentence. Translated from the Pali by Bhikkhu Ñāṇamoli and Bhikkhu Bodhi.

"Friend, the Nigaṇṭha Nātaputta is omniscient and all-seeing and claims to have complete knowledge and vision thus: 'Whether I am walking or standing or asleep or awake, knowledge and vision are continuously and uninterruptedly present to me.' He says thus: 'Nigaṇṭhas, you have done evil actions in the past; exhaust them with the performance of piercing austerities. And when you are here and now restrained in body, speech, and mind, that is doing no evil actions for the future. So by annihilating with asceticism past actions and by doing no fresh actions, there will be no consequence in the future. With no consequence in the future, there is the destruction of action. With the destruction of action, there is the destruction of suffering. With the destruction of suffering, there is the destruction of feeling. With the destruction of feeling, all suffering will be exhausted.' This is [the doctrine] we approve of and accept, and we are satisfied with it."

[26]

Ahimsa

Jaina doctrine deals with a vast range of subjects: morality, monastic practice, lay practice, soteriology, philosophy, cosmology, etc. The main moral teachings of Mahavira are summed up in the five great vows: non-violence, non-stealing, non-lying, sexual purity, and non-possession. Of these, non-violence or *ahiṁsā* is given special prominence. This passage from the *Ācārāṅga Sūtra* calls *ahiṁsā* "the eternal law", a phrase that occurs also in Buddhist and Hindu texts. The spirit of non-violence has done much across the centuries to foster a respect for nature that has helped preserve India's ecological balance. In the political field, *ahiṁsā* has proved to be an effective tool in the hands of leaders like Mahatma Gandhi, Martin Luther King, Jr. and Nelson Mandela. Translated by Hermann Jacobi.

The Arhats and Bhagavats of the past, present, and future, all say thus, speak thus, declare thus, explain thus: all breathing, existing, living, sentient creatures should not be slain, nor treated with violence, nor abused, nor tormented, nor driven away.

This is the pure, unchangeable, eternal law, which the clever ones, who understand the world, have declared: among the zealous and the not zealous, among the faithful and the not faithful, among the not cruel and the cruel, among those who have worldly weakness and those who have not, among those who like social bonds and those who do not: "that is the truth, that is so, that is proclaimed in this [creed]."

Having adopted [the law], one should not hide it, nor forsake it. Correctly understanding the law, one should arrive at indifference for the impressions of the senses, and "not act on the motives of the world." . . .

What has been said here, has been seen [by the omniscient ones], heard [by the believers], acknowledged [by the faithful], and thoroughly understood by them. Those who acquiesce and indulge [in worldly pleasures], are born again and again. "Day and night exerting thyself, steadfast," always having ready wisdom, perceive that the careless [stand] outside [of salvation]; if careful, thou wilt always conquer. Thus I say.

[27]

Steps towards Liberation

This passage from the *Sūtrakṛtāṅga*, one of the oldest parts of the Swetambara canon, lists steps that Jainas should take in order to prepare themselves for the "distant end" of liberation. As in many Jaina texts, the accent is on outward forms of practice — non-violence, self-control, detachment — though there are also occasional references to the importance of meditation. Translated by Hermann Jacobi.

When a wise man, in whatever way, comes to know that the apportioned space of his life draws towards its end, he should in the meantime quickly learn the method [of dying a religious death].

As a tortoise draws its limbs into its own body, so a wise man should cover, as it were, his sins with his own meditation.

He should draw in, as it were, his hands and feet, his mind and five organs of sense, the effect of his bad Karman, and every bad use of language.

The virtuous exert themselves with regard to the distant end [viz. Liberation]. One should live indifferent to one's own happiness, calm, and without any attachment.

Do not kill living beings, do not take what is not freely given, do not talk false, treacherous speech! This is the Law of him who is rich in control.

Do not desire by words or thoughts what is a transgression [of the Law]; guarding yourself in all ways, and subduing [the senses], practise control.

A man who guards his self and subdues his senses, abhors all sins, past, present, and future ones.

Benighted men of wrong faith, [though] they be renowned as heroes, exert themselves in a bad way, which will have, in all respects, evil consequences for them.

Wise men of right faith, who are renowned heroes, exert themselves in a good way which will have no [evil] consequences whatever for them.

Penance is of no good if performed by noble men who have turned monks [for the sake of fame]; but that penance of which nobody else knows anything [is meritorious]. Do not spread your own fame!

A pious man should eat little, drink little, talk little; he should always exert himself, being calm, indifferent, a subduer [of his senses], and free from greed.

Meditating and performing religious practices, abandoning his body, regarding forbearance as the paramount duty, a monk should wander about till he obtains liberation.

FURTHER READING

Source Materials

Hermann Jacobi, trans., *Jaina Scriptures*. Volumes 22 and 45 of *The Sacred Books of the East*. Reprint edition. Delhi: Motilal Banarsidass, 1968.

Bhikkhu Ñāṇamoli and Bhikkhu Bodhi, trans., *The Middle Length Discourses of the Buddha*. Somerville, MA: Wisdom Publications, 1995.

Other Works

Helmuth von Glasenapp, *Jainism: An Indian Religion of Salvation*, translated from the German by Shridhar B. Shrotri. Reprint edition. Delhi: Motilal Banarsidass, 1999.

Padmanabh S. Jaini, *The Jaina Path of Purification*. Reprint edition. Delhi: Motilal Banarsidass, 1998.

Padmanabh S. Jaini, "The Jaina Faith and its History". In Umasvati, *That Which Is*, translated by Nathmal Tatia. San Francisco: HarperCollins, 1994, pp. xxv – xxxxiii.

Sources of Texts and Translations

22 *Kalpa-sūtra* 5.108, 110, 115 – 117	Jacobi, vol. 22: 255 – 260
23 *Ācārāṅga-sūtra* 1.8.1.1 – 10; 1.8.2.2 – 11; 1.8.4.1 – 16	Jacobi, vol. 22: 79 – 83, 85 – 87
24 *Kalpa-sūtra* 5.119 – 123	Jacobi, vol. 22: 262 – 265
25 *Majjhima Nikāya* 1.92 – 93	Ñāṇamoli and Bodhi 187 – 88
26 *Ācārāṅga-sūtra* 1.4.1	Jacobi, vol. 22: 36 – 37
27 *Sūtrakṛtāṅga* 1.8.15 – 26	Jacobi, vol. 45: 299 – 301

4

किं पन वासेट्ठ अत्थि कोचि तेविज्जानं ब्राह्मणानं एकब्राह्मणो
पि येन ब्रह्मा सक्खिदिट्ठो ति ?
नो हिदं भो गोतम।

But, Vāseṭṭha, is there then a single one of these Brahmins
learned in the three Vedas who has seen Brahmā face to face?
No, Reverend Gotama.

Dīgha Nikāya: *Tevijja Sutta* 12

Theravada Buddhism

BUDDHISM emerged from the same social, intellectual and spiritual milieu as Jainism. It is remarkable that the founders of these two religions, both of which are still practised after two thousand five hundred years, were alive at the same time in the same general region of north India. Both renounced comfortable lives in order to find release from the impermanence and suffering of existence. Both practised extreme forms of discipline; but the Buddha discovered that extreme asceticism was a hindrance on the path to liberation. His "middle way" between self-indulgence and self-defeating austerity eventually became the predominant religious system of Asia, though it had all but died out in its Indian homeland before its late-twentieth-century revival.

Siddhattha Gotama,[1] the future Buddha or "enlightened one", was the son of the ruler of a small "republic" in the lowlands of what is now

[1] The scriptures of the two main branches of Indian Buddhism were written in two different languages, Pali and Sanskrit. As a result there are Pali and Sanskrit variants for most names and terms found in accounts of the Buddha's life and teachings. "Siddhattha Gotama" is Pali, for example, while "Siddhartha Gautama" is Sanskrit. Since the selections in the present chapter are drawn from the Pali Canon, I follow the translators in using the Pali forms in these notes. When necessary, I give also the Sanskrit forms, which are generally better known in the English-speaking world.

southern Nepal and northern Bihar. The year of his birth is uncertain. Most historians favour a date around 566 BCE, but some would move it up, or back, by sixty years or more. As noted in the previous chapter, the kingdoms of Kosala, Kashi and Magadha, where the Buddha passed his active life, were at the end of the sixth and the beginning of the fifth century BCE in a state of intellectual and spiritual ferment. Buddhist scriptures mention six heterodox teachings that were current in the region at the time, one of which was Jainism. These teachings shared with the *upaniṣads* (some of which date from the same period) an interest in the make-up of the universe, the nature of causality, and the way to obtain liberation from the rounds of rebirth. Many teachers, both vedic and non-vedic, advocated psycho-physical techniques such as meditation and breath-control as means to achieve this end.

The essentials of Siddhattha's life, so far as they can be disengaged from the legends that have encrusted them, are as follows. The son of a tribal chieftain, he was brought up in comfort, and shielded from the harsh realities of life; but while still a young man he became acutely aware of the transience and sorrow of existence. Leaving his father's house and his young wife and child, he went forth to seek enlightenment. As a wandering mendicant, he met teachers and mastered their disciplines, but remained unsatisfied. Going off on his own, he passed years in the practice of fasting and other austerities. Realising in the end that he was making himself too weak for spiritual effort, he resumed a more normal way of life. Applying himself to meditation with renewed vigour, he succeeded in seeing into the true nature of things, achieving the freedom of *nibbāna* (Skt. *nirvāṇa*). According to tradition, this enlightenment came in a place now known as Bodh Gaya (near Gaya, in Bihar) when he was in his thirty-fifth year. From this point onward, he was no longer addressed as Siddhattha Gotama but by titles such as the Buddha ("the awakened one") or the Tathagata ("the one who has thus gone").

For the remainder of his life, the Buddha taught his Way or *dhamma* (Skt. *dharma*) to all who desired to learn it. Disciples gathered around him, becoming the nucleus of his *sangha* or spiritual community. For those who wished to devote themselves entirely to the *dhamma*, he established a rule of life or *vinaya*; but he also gave his teachings to lay men and women of all castes. Unlike many spiritual teachers, he did not name a successor; before his passing he told his followers that the *dhamma* and the *vinaya* would now be their guides. He is said to have died at the age of eighty, or around 486 BCE. By tradition, his last words were a summary of his teaching: "All conditioned things are of a nature to decay—strive on untiringly."

The Buddha gave his teachings in the form of conversations and discourses. He spoke not in Sanskrit, the language of the vedic priesthood, but a related vernacular. His words were transmitted orally for some three hundred years before finally being written down in Sri Lanka. The literary language used, based on a north-west Indian vernacular, became known as *pāḷi-bhāsā* ("canon-language"). Pali was probably close to the dialect the Buddha spoke, and it is reasonable to assume that the early works of the Pali Canon preserve the spirit, if not the exact letter, of his words.

The Pali Canon comprises an enormous mass of literature that was compiled over several centuries. Early on it was divided into three main parts, known as *piṭaka*s or baskets. The *Tipiṭaka* (Skt. *Tripiṭaka*) or Three Baskets consists of the *Sutta Piṭaka* or Discourses, the *Vinaya Piṭaka* or Monastic Rule, and the *Abhidhamma Piṭaka* or Scholastic Treatises. Each of the Baskets is subdivided in various ways. Most of the discourses of the *Sutta Piṭaka*, for example, are grouped by length in the *Dīgha Nikāya* or Long Collection, the *Majjhima Nikāya* or Middle-Length Collection and the *Khuddaka Nikāya* or Short Collection. The last includes the famous *Dhammapada*, an anthology of ethical teachings, and the *Theragāthā* and *Therīgāthā* or "Hymns of the Elder Monks and Elder Nuns" (see selection 38). A later, non-canonical but very influential work is the *Milinda-pañha* or "Questions of King Milinda" (see selection 37).

The Buddha's *dhamma* is regarded as the fruit of his own experience, "a description of a path seen by himself", as the philosopher Dharmakirti wrote. But in formulating his teaching, he drew upon, and reacted against, many contemporary practices and conceptions. The idea that action (*kamma*, Skt. *karma*), bears fruit in this life or another, resulting in a cycle of rebirths (*saṁsāra*) from which the wise desire release, was common to many vedic and non-vedic teachings. The Buddha took it for granted but rejected the upanishadic teaching that there is a Permanent behind the flux of *saṁsāra*. The intuition on which his teachings rest is that all things and beings are impermanent (*anicca*, Skt. *anitya*). Since all is subject to change, there can be no fundamental substance, as several vedic and non-vedic schools proposed, and no changeless self, as some *upaniṣad*s declared. What is *anicca* is *anattā*, "not-self". Whatever appears to be lasting is a ceaseless succession of instants; whatever appears to be substantial is an ever-changing compound. Further, since all things are subject to change, they are all at root unsatisfactory. What is *anicca* and *anattā* must bring *dukkha* (Skt. *duḥkha*): suffering, misery, pain. The root cause of this unsatisfactoriness is desire or craving, and craving comes into existence because of ignorance (*avijjā, Skt. avidyā*). Upon ignorance depends karma, upon karma depends consciousness—and so on down to death, sorrow and despair (see selection 29). Since suffering is born of craving, the way to eliminate suffering is to eliminate craving. And the way to this is to follow the Buddha's eightfold path: (1) right understanding, (2) right resolve, (3) right speech, (4) right action, (5) right livelihood, (6) right effort, (7) right mindfulness, and (8) right meditation. The Buddha summed up these teachings in the Four Noble Truths: (1) existence is suffering, (2) suffering is caused by craving, (3) there is a means by which craving can be eliminated, and (4) this means is the Noble Eightfold Path.

When one has succeeded in eradicating craving in all its forms, one achieves the state that the Buddha achieved at Bodh Gaya: *nibbāna*. Although by far the best-known term in the Buddhist vocabulary, *nibbāna* is perhaps the least well understood. This is because, as the Buddha himself explained (selection 30), *nibbāna* cannot be attained "by mere reasoning" but only by intuitive experience. The Buddha described *nibbāna* mostly in negative terms: as freedom from craving, anger and hatred; but he sometimes spoke of it as a state of bliss and deathlessness. Even this positive formulation proved too abstract for most of his followers, and by the second century CE we find *nibbāna* described as "a glorious city, stainless and undefiled, pure and white, unageing and deathless" (*Milinda-pañha* 5.6). It is possible for humans to achieve a form of *nibbāna* while still living. Those who do so are known as *arahants* (Skt. *arhats*). Unqualified *nibbāna*, the final release from the rounds of rebirth, is obtained only when a fully enlightened being passes away. This is called *parinibbāna* (see selection 31).

Buddhism eventually developed a philosophical system of great complexity; but the Buddha himself discouraged metaphysical speculations, because they "do not conduce to profit, are not concerned with the holy life, do not tend to . . . the perfect wisdom, to *nibbāna*" (*Saṁyutta Nikāya* 437). His concern was therapeutic: to provide a way for sentient beings to escape from suffering. The way he taught was the Noble Eightfold Path, the elements of which are sometimes placed in three categories: two dealing with wisdom (*paññā*, Skt. *prajñā*), three dealing with virtue (*sīla*), and three dealing with concentration (*samādhi*). Wisdom, in this sense, means understanding and accepting the Buddha's *dhamma*; virtue is the carrying out of his ethical teachings; concentration is the practice of the psycho-physical disciplines without which the goal cannot be reached.

A sizeable proportion of the Pali Canon is devoted to ethical teachings. The *vinaya* or rule of the order is made up of sundry regulations governing every aspect of life. More general ethical guidelines are found in other Pali scriptures. An example is the *Sigālaka Sutta* (selection 34), which deals with the proper conduct of the lay practitioner. Once the aspirant has been made ready by the practice of virtue, she or he can profitably begin concentration. Two main types are described in the Pali scriptures: *samatha* or "calming" meditation, and *vippasanā* or "insight" meditation (see selections 35 and 36).

For some two hundred years after the passing of the Buddha, his *dhamma* was just one among the heterodox systems of north India. Then, in the third century BCE, it was granted special patronage by the Mauryan emperor Ashoka. From that moment, the Buddha's *dhamma* began its spread across Asia. Besides codifying and transmitting their master's teachings, his early followers produced some original works, notably the scholastic writings of the *Abhidhamma Piṭaka*. In time, differences in interpretation and practice emerged. This led to the formation of various schools, traditionally numbered as eighteen. The school claiming to represent the unadulterated teachings of the Buddha, called the *Theravāda* or School of the Elders, is the only one of these that has survived. Theravada Buddhism, and the canon on which it is based, spread eventually to Sri Lanka, Burma, Thailand, Cambodia and Laos. The other main branch of Buddhism, the *Mahāyāna*, is based on a separate set of scriptures, most of which were written originally in Sanskrit (see Part 7). In the course of time, Mahayana Buddhism spread from India to Central Asia, China, Korea, Japan, Vietnam and Tibet.

Buddhism was a major cultural force in India for sixteen hundred years, from the fourth century BCE to around 1200 CE. The chief reasons for its decline were the emergence of new forms of Hinduism, and the hostile impact of Islam. But it might also be said that its own characteristics helped bring about its undoing. By putting a premium on the monastic life, it lost out to the more affirmative teachings of popular Hinduism. And the concentration of its membership, and wealth, in monasteries, made it an easy target for militant Islam. Theravada writers try to explain away their Dhamma's pessimism, but it is hard to deny that the Buddha of the Pali Canon sees little value in "what is subject to birth", that is, human life and its activities. Nevertheless, for almost a millennium and a half, much of the most important literature, philosophy, architecture, sculpture and painting in South Asia was produced by Buddhists, while the religious and societal structures that the Buddha set in place changed the social and cultural landscape of the subcontinent, and beyond, in countless ways.

THE LIFE OF THE BUDDHA

Nowhere in the Pali Canon is the life of the Buddha recounted in a continuous narrative. Several *sutta*s deal with specific incidents in his life, others allude to specific persons and places. There is undoubtedly a factual substratum to this material, but much of it is obviously legendary. In later accounts, notably Ashwaghosha's *Buddhacarita* (first or second century CE), the legend of the Buddha's earthly existence was given definitive form. These accounts have little historical but much evocative value. The bare fact that Siddhattha Gotama became obsessed with the transient nature of existence is made memorable when presented in the story of the Four Signs, in which the pampered young prince sees in succession an old man, a sick man, a corpse and a religious mendicant, after which he decides to renounce the world. The extracts in this section, all from early strata of the Pali Canon, deal in semi-legendary fashion with several important incidents in the Buddha's life.

[28]

Seeking and Enlightenment

This passage from the *Majjhima Nikāya* of the *Sutta Piṭaka* begins with the Buddha's departure from his parents' house, and ends with his attainment of *nibbāna*. Readers familiar with the legendary narrative will notice the absence of such incidents as the Great Departure from the palace and the temptation by Mara, the Evil One. The teachers Alara Kalama and Uddaka Ramaputta may have been Siddhattha's actual teachers; if not, they represent the masters of philosophy and practice under whom he certainly studied. Translated from the Pali by Bhikkhu Ñāṇamoli and Bhikkhu Bodhi.

"Bhikkhus, before my enlightenment, while I was still only an unenlightened Bodhisatta, I too, being myself subject to birth, sought what was also subject to birth; being myself subject to ageing, sickness, death, sorrow, and defilement, I sought what was also subject to ageing, sickness, death, sorrow, and defilement. Then I considered thus: 'Why, being myself subject to birth, do I seek what is also subject to birth? Why, being myself subject to ageing, sickness, death, sorrow, and defilement, do I seek what is also subject to ageing, sickness, death, sorrow, and defilement? . . .

"Later, while still young, a black-haired young man endowed with the blessing of youth, in the prime of life, though my mother and father wished otherwise and wept with tearful faces, I shaved off my hair and beard, put on the yellow robe, and went forth from the home life into homelessness.

"Having gone forth, bhikkhus, in search of what is wholesome, seeking the supreme state of sublime peace, I went to Āḷāra Kālāma and said to him: 'Friend Kālāma, I want to lead the holy life in this Dhamma and Discipline.' Āḷāra Kālāma replied: 'The venerable one may stay here. This Dhamma is such that a wise man can soon enter upon and abide in it, realising for himself through direct knowledge his own teacher's doctrine.' I soon quickly learned that Dhamma. As far as mere lip-reciting and rehearsal of his teaching went, I could speak with knowledge and assurance, and I claimed, 'I know and see'—and there were others who did likewise.

"I considered: 'It is not through mere faith alone that Āḷāra Kālāma declares: "By realising for myself with direct knowledge, I enter upon and abide in this Dhamma." Certainly Āḷāra Kālāma abides knowing and seeing this Dhamma.' Then I went to Āḷāra Kālāma and asked him: 'Friend Kālāma, in what way do you declare that by realising for yourself with direct knowledge you enter upon and abide in this Dhamma?' In reply he declared the base of nothingness.

"I considered: 'Not only Āḷāra Kālāma has faith, energy, mindfulness, concentration, and wisdom. I too have faith, energy, mindfulness, concentration, and wisdom. Suppose I endeavour to realise the Dhamma that Āḷāra Kālāma declares he enters upon and abides in by realising for himself with direct knowledge?'

"I soon quickly entered upon and abided in that Dhamma by realising for myself with direct knowledge. Then I went to Āḷāra Kālāma and asked him: 'Friend Kālāma, is it in this way that you declare that you enter upon and abide in this Dhamma by realising for yourself with direct knowledge?' — 'That is the way, friend.' — 'It is in this way, friend, that I also enter upon and abide in this Dhamma by realising for myself with direct knowledge.' — 'It is a gain for us, friend, it is a great gain for us that we have such a venerable one for our companion in the holy life. So the Dhamma that I declare I enter upon and abide in by realising for myself with direct knowledge is the Dhamma that you enter upon and abide in by realising for yourself with direct knowledge. And the Dhamma that you enter upon and abide in by realising for yourself with direct knowledge is the Dhamma that I declare I enter upon and abide in by realising for myself with direct knowledge. So you know the Dhamma that I know and I know the Dhamma that you know. As I am, so are you; as you are, so am I. Come, friend, let us now lead this community together.'

"Thus Āḷāra Kālāma, my teacher, placed me, his pupil, on an equal footing with himself and awarded me the highest honour. But it occurred to me: 'This Dhamma does not lead to disenchantment, to dispassion, to cessation, to peace, to direct knowledge, to enlightenment, to Nibbāna, but only to reappearance in the base of nothingness.' Not being satisfied with that Dhamma, I left it and went away.

"Still in search, bhikkhus, of what is wholesome, seeking the supreme state of sublime peace, I went to Uddaka Rāmaputta and said to him: 'Friend, I want to lead the holy life in this Dhamma and Discipline.' Uddaka Rāmaputta replied: 'The venerable one may stay here. This Dhamma is such that a wise man can soon enter upon and abide in it, himself realising through direct knowledge his own teacher's doctrine.' . . .

"I soon quickly entered upon and abided in that Dhamma by realising for myself with direct knowledge. Then I went to Uddaka Rāmaputta and asked him: 'Friend, was it in this way that Rāma declared that he entered upon and abided in this Dhamma by realising for himself with direct knowledge?' — 'That is the way, friend.' . . . 'So you know the Dhamma that Rāma knew and Rāma knew the Dhamma that you know. As Rāma was, so are you; as you are, so was Rāma. Come, friend, now lead this community.'

"Thus Uddaka Rāmaputta, my companion in the holy life, placed me in the position of a teacher and accorded me the highest honour. But it occurred to me: 'This Dhamma does not lead to disenchantment, to dispassion, to cessation, to peace, to direct knowledge, to enlightenment, to Nibbāna, but only to reappearance in the base of neither-perception-nor-non-perception.' Not being satisfied with that Dhamma, I left it and went away.

"Still in search, bhikkhus, of what is wholesome, seeking the supreme state of sublime peace, I wandered by stages through the Magadhan country until eventually I arrived at Senānigama near Uruvelā. There I saw an agreeable piece of ground, a delightful grove with a clear-flowing river with pleasant, smooth banks and nearby a village for alms resort. I considered: 'This is an agreeable piece of ground, this is a delightful grove with a clear-flowing river with pleasant, smooth banks and nearby a village for alms resort. This will serve for the striving of a clansman intent on striving.' And I sat down there thinking: 'This will serve for striving.'

"Then, bhikkhus, being myself subject to birth, having understood the danger in what is subject to birth, seeking the unborn supreme security from bondage, Nibbāna, I attained the unborn supreme security from bondage, Nibbāna; being myself subject to ageing, having understood the danger in what is subject to ageing, seeking the unageing supreme security from bondage, Nibbāna, I attained the unageing supreme security from bondage, Nibbāna; being myself subject to sickness, having understood the danger in what is subject to sickness, seeking the unailing supreme security from bondage, Nibbāna, I attained the unailing supreme security from bondage, Nibbāna; being myself subject to death, having understood the danger in what is subject to death, seeking the deathless supreme security from bondage, Nibbāna, I attained the deathless supreme security from bondage, Nibbāna; being myself subject to sorrow, having understood the danger in what is subject to sorrow, seeking the sorrowless supreme security from bondage, Nibbāna, I attained the sorrowless supreme security from bondage, Nibbāna; being myself subject to defilement, having understood the danger in what is subject to defilement, seeking the undefiled supreme security from bondage, Nibbāna, I attained the undefiled supreme security from bondage, Nibbāna. The knowledge and vision arose in me: 'My deliverance is unshakeable; this is my last birth; now there is no renewal of being.'"

[29]

The Discovery of Dependent Origination

Dependent origination or causal genesis (*paticca-samuppāda*) is the key to the Buddha's explanation of the world. As he says in the *Majjhima Nikāya* (28.28): "One who sees dependent origination sees the Dhamma, and who sees the Dhamma sees dependent origination." All the elements of existence arise in a linked chain of conditions, each dependent on the one preceding it. The root of all is ignorance (*avijjā*), the end result, suffering and despair. In the formal presentation of this theory, there are precisely twelve links in the chain: ignorance, *kamma*, consciousness, name and form, the organs of sense, contact, sensation, desire, attachment, existence, birth, death. According to tradition, the Buddha discovered this principle just after his attainment of *nibbāna*. The following account of this discovery, from the *Mahāvagga* section of the *Vinaya Piṭaka*, was translated by Henry Clarke Warren.

At that time The Buddha, The Blessed One, was dwelling at Uruvelā at the foot of the Bo-tree on the banks of the river Nerañjarā, having just attained the Buddhaship. Then The Blessed One sat cross-legged for seven days together at the foot of the Bo-tree experiencing the bliss of emancipation.

Then The Blessed One, during the first watch of the night, thought over Dependent Origination both forward and back: —

On ignorance depends karma;
On karma depends consciousness;
On consciousness depend name and form;
On name and form depend the six organs of sense;
On the six organs of sense depends contact;

On contact depends sensation;
On sensation depends desire;
On desire depends attachment;
On attachment depends existence;
On existence depends birth;
On birth depend old age and death, sorrow, lamentation, misery, grief, and despair.

Thus does this entire aggregation of misery arise. But on the complete fading out and cessation of ignorance ceases karma; on the cessation of karma ceases consciousness; on the cessation of consciousness cease name and form; on the cessation of name and form cease the six organs of sense; on the cessation of the six organs of sense ceases contact; on the cessation of contact ceases sensation; on the cessation of sensation ceases desire; on the cessation of desire ceases attachment; on the cessation of attachment ceases existence; on the cessation of existence ceases birth; on the cessation of birth cease old age and death, sorrow, lamentation, misery, grief, and despair. Thus does this entire aggregation of misery cease.

Then The Blessed One, concerning this, on that occasion, breathed forth this solemn utterance,—

"When to the strenuous, meditative Brāhman
There come to light the elements of being,
Then vanish all his doubts and eager questions,
What time he knows *The Elements have Causes*."

Then The Blessed One, during the middle watch of the night, thought over Dependent Origination both forward and back:— On ignorance depends karma. . . . Thus does this entire aggregation of misery arise. But on the complete fading out and cessation of ignorance ceases karma. . . . Thus does this entire aggregation of misery cease.

Then The Blessed One, concerning this, on that occasion, breathed forth this solemn utterance,—

"When to the strenuous, meditative Brāhman
There come to light the elements of being,
Then vanish all his doubts and eager questions,
What time he knows *How Causes have an Ending*."

Then The Blessed One, during the last watch of the night, thought over Dependent Origination both forward and back: — On ignorance depends karma. . . . Thus does this entire aggregation of misery arise. But on the complete fading out and cessation of ignorance ceases karma. . . . Thus does this entire aggregation of misery cease.

Then The Blessed One, concerning this, on that occasion, breathed forth this solemn utterance, —

"When to the strenuous, meditative Brāhman
There come to light the elements of being,
Then scattereth he the hordes of Māra's army;
Like to the sun that lightens all the heavens."

[30]

The Summons to Teach

Although supernatural, the gods of Buddhism are insubstantial, like all else in *saṁsāra*. In this selection (which occurs in the *Majjhima Nikāya* just after the passage reproduced as selection 28), the god Brahma Sahampati persuades the Buddha to give the *dhamma* to suffering beings. This may be read as the Buddha's spirit of compassion compelling him to devote himself to others. After learning (by supernatural means) that Alara Kalama and Uddaka Ramaputta have died, he decides to give the *dhamma* first to five ascetics with whom he had practised earlier. Going from Uruvela to Varanasi (Benares), he gives them the teaching in the "Turning the Wheel of Dhamma" discourse (see selection 32). Translated by Bhikkhu Ñāṇamoli and Bhikkhu Bodhi.

"I considered: 'This Dhamma that I have attained is profound, hard to see and hard to understand, peaceful and sublime, unattainable by mere reasoning, subtle, to be experienced by the wise. But this generation delights in adhesion, takes delight in adhesion, rejoices in adhesion. It is hard for such a generation to see this truth, namely, specific conditionality, dependent origination. And it is hard to see this truth, namely, the stilling of all formations, the relinquishing of all attachments, the destruction of craving, dispassion, cessation, Nibbāna. If I were to teach the Dhamma, others would not understand me, and that would be wearying and troublesome for me.' . . .

Considering thus, my mind inclined to inaction rather than to teaching the Dhamma.

"Then, bhikkhus, the Brahmā Sahampati knew with his mind the thought in my mind and he considered: 'The world will be lost, the world will perish, since the mind of the Tathāgata, accomplished and fully enlightened, inclines to inaction rather than to teaching the Dhamma.' Then, just as quickly as a strong man might extend his flexed arm or flex his extended arm, the Brahmā Sahampati vanished in the Brahma-world and appeared before me. He arranged his upper robe on one shoulder, and extending his hands in reverential salutation towards me, said: 'Venerable sir, let the Blessed One teach the Dhamma, let the Sublime One teach the Dhamma. There are beings with little dust in their eyes who are wasting through not hearing the Dhamma. There will be those who will understand the Dhamma.' . . .

"Then I listened to the Brahmā's pleading, and out of compassion for beings I surveyed the world with the eye of a Buddha. Surveying the world with the eye of a Buddha, I saw beings with little dust in their eyes and with much dust in their eyes, with keen faculties and with dull faculties, with good qualities and with bad qualities, easy to teach and hard to teach, and some who dwelt seeing fear and blame in the other world. . . . Then I replied to the Brahmā Sahampati in stanzas:

'Open for them are the doors to the Deathless,
Let those with ears now show their faith.
Thinking it would be troublesome, O Brahmā,
I did not speak the Dhamma subtle and sublime.' . . .

"I considered thus: 'To whom should I first teach the Dhamma? Who will understand this Dhamma quickly?' It then occurred to me: 'The bhikkhus of the group of five who attended upon me while I was engaged in my striving were very helpful. Suppose I taught the Dhamma first to them.'" . . .

[31]

The Passing of the Buddha

This passage is from the *Mahāparinibbāna Sutta* of the *Dīgha Nikāya*, which is believed to descend from a chronicle composed by the Buddha's earliest disciples. It relates the Buddha's last moments on earth and his entry into final *nibbāna*. The *jhāna*s and higher levels he passes through on his way are at the same time subjective states (see selection 35) and levels of the Theravada cosmos. Translated by Maurice Walshe.

And the Lord said to Ānanda: "Ānanda, it may be that you will think: 'The Teacher's instruction has ceased, now we have no teacher!' It should not be seen like this, Ānanda, for what I have taught and explained to you as Dhamma and discipline will, at my passing, be your teacher. . . . "

Then the Lord addressed the monks, saying: "It may be, monks, that some monk has doubts or uncertainty about the Buddha, the Dhamma, the Sangha, or about the path or the practice. Ask, monks! Do not afterwards feel remorse, thinking: 'The Teacher was there before us, and we failed to ask the Lord face to face!'" At these words the monks were silent. The Lord repeated his words a second and a third time, and still the monks were silent. Then the Lord said: "Perhaps, monks, you do not ask out of respect for the Teacher. Then, monks, let one friend tell it to another." But still they were silent.

And the Venerable Ānanda said: "It is wonderful, Lord, it is marvellous! I clearly perceive that in this assembly there is not one monk who has doubts or uncertainty. . . . " "You, Ānanda, speak from faith. But the Tathāgata knows that in this assembly there is not one monk who has doubts or uncertainty about the Buddha, the Dhamma or the Sangha or about the path or the practice. Ānanda, the least one of these five hundred monks is a Stream-Winner, incapable of falling into states of woe, certain of Nibbāna."

Then the Lord said to the monks: "Now, monks, I declare to you: all conditioned things are of a nature to decay—strive on untiringly." These were the Tathāgata's last words.

Then the Lord entered the first jhāna. And leaving that he entered the second, the third, the fourth jhāna. Then leaving the fourth jhāna he entered the Sphere of Infinite Space, then the Sphere of Infinite Consciousness, then the Sphere of No-Thingness, then the Sphere of Neither-Perception-Nor-Non-Perception, and leaving that he attained the Cessation of Feeling and Perception.

Then the Venerable Ānanda said to the Venerable Anuruddha: "Venerable Anuruddha, the Lord has passed away." "No, friend Ānanda, the Lord has not passed away, he has attained the Cessation of Feeling and Perception."

Then the Lord, leaving the attainment of the Cessation of Feeling and Perception, entered the Sphere of Neither-Perception-Nor-Non-Perception, from that he entered the Sphere of No-Thingness, the Sphere of Infinite Consciousness, the Sphere of Infinite Space. From the Sphere of Infinite Space he entered the fourth jhāna, from there the third, the second and the first jhāna. Leaving the first jhāna, he entered the second, the third, the fourth jhāna. And, leaving the fourth jhāna, the Lord finally passed away.

THE TEACHINGS OF THE BUDDHA

A large number of sermons are attributed to the Buddha by the Theravada tradition and still more by the Mahayana tradition. The body of doctrine they present is vast and complex. The two selections reproduced here are among the most famous and the most fundamental in the entire Pali Canon.

[32]

Turning the Wheel of Dhamma

The Buddha's teachings are summed up in a *sutta* called *Dhammacakkappavattana* or "Turning the Wheel of Dhamma", which forms part of the *Saṁyutta Nikāya*. By tradition it was the first sermon he delivered after his enlightenment. This discourse contains a classic presentation of the Middle Path and the Four Noble Truths. It begins, like most *sutta*s, with the phrase "Thus have I heard", indicating that the reciter had received it in direct transmission from the Buddha and his followers. Reproduced here in its entirety, it exhibits one of the most striking characteristics of Pali writing: the repetition of words, phrases and even long passages. Doubtless intended as aids to memorisation, these repetitions must have added to the solemnity of group recitations, but can be tedious to modern readers. Often elided by translators (and compilers), they have been preserved in the present translation, which is by Dr. Rewata Dhamma.

Thus have I heard: At one time the Blessed One was staying at Deer Park, in Isipatana (the Sage's Resort) near Varanasi.

Then the Buddha addressed the five ascetics: "O bhikkhus, one who has gone forth from worldly life should not indulge in these two extremes. What are the two? There is indulgence in desirable sense objects, which is low, vulgar, worldly, ignoble, unworthy, and unprofitable and there is devotion to self-mortification, which is painful, unworthy, and unprofitable.

"O bhikkhus, avoiding both these extremes, the Tathāgata has realized the Middle Path. It produces vision, it produces knowledge, it leads to calm, to higher knowledge, to enlightenment, to nibbāna.

"And what is that Middle Path, O bhikkhus, that the Tathāgata has realized? It is simply the Noble Eightfold Path, namely: Right understanding, right thought, right speech, right action, right livelihood, right effort, right awareness, and right concentration. This is the Noble Eightfold Path realized by the Tathāgata. It produces vision, it produces knowledge, it leads to calm, to higher knowledge, to enlightenment, to nibbāna.

"This, O bhikkhus, is the Noble Truth of suffering (*dukkha*): Birth is suffering, aging is suffering, sickness is suffering, death is suffering, sorrow, and lamentation, pain, grief, and despair are suffering, association with the unloved or unpleasant condition is suffering, separation from the beloved or pleasant condition is suffering, not to get what one wants is suffering. In brief, the five aggregates of attachment are suffering.

"This, O bhikkhus, is the Noble Truth of the origin of suffering: It is craving which produces rebirth, bound up with pleasure and greed. It finds delight in this and that, in other words, craving for sense pleasures, craving for existence or becoming and craving for nonexistence or self-annihilation.

"This, O bhikkhus, is the Noble Truth of the cessation of suffering: It is the complete cessation of suffering; giving up, renouncing, relinquishing, detaching from craving.

"This, O bhikkhus, is the Noble Truth of the path leading to the cessation of suffering. It is simply the Noble Eightfold Path, namely: Right understanding, right thought, right speech, right action, right livelihood, right effort, right awareness, and right concentration.

"This is the Noble Truth of suffering. Thus, O bhikkhus, concerning things not heard before, there arose in me the vision, the knowledge, the wisdom, the insight, and the light.

"This is the Noble Truth of suffering, which should be fully understood. Thus, O bhikkhus, concerning things not heard before, there arose in me the vision, the knowledge, the wisdom, the insight, and the light.

"This is the Noble Truth of suffering, which has been understood. Thus, O bhikkhus, concerning things not heard before, there arose in me the vision, the knowledge, the wisdom, the insight, and the light.

"This is the Noble Truth of the Origin of Suffering. Thus, O bhikkhus, concerning things not heard before, there arose in me the vision, the knowledge, the wisdom, the insight, and the light.

"This is the Noble Truth of the origin of suffering, which should be abandoned. Thus, O bhikkhus, concerning things not heard by me before, there arose in me the vision, the knowledge, the wisdom, the insight, and the light.

"This is the Noble Truth of the origin of suffering, which has been abandoned. Thus, O bhikkhus, concerning things not heard before, there arose in me the vision, the knowledge, the wisdom, the insight, and the light.

"This is the Noble Truth of the cessation of suffering. Thus, O bhikkhus, concerning things not heard before, there arose in me the vision, the knowledge, the wisdom, the insight, and the light.

"This is the Noble Truth of the cessation of suffering, which should be realized. Thus, O bhikkhus, concerning things not heard before, there arose in me the vision, the knowledge, the wisdom, the insight, and the light.

"This is the Noble Truth of the cessation of suffering, which has been realized. Thus, O bhikkhus, concerning things not heard before, there arose in me the vision, the knowledge, the wisdom, the insight, and the light.

"This is the Noble Truth of the path leading to the cessation of suffering. Thus, O bhikkhus, concerning things not heard before, there arose in me the vision, the knowledge, the wisdom, the insight, and the light.

"This is the Noble Truth of the path leading to the cessation of suffering, which should be developed. Thus, O bhikkhus, concerning things not heard before, there arose in me the vision, the knowledge, the wisdom, the insight, and the light.

"This is the Noble Truth of the path leading to the cessation of suffering, which has been developed. Thus, O bhikkhus, concerning things not heard before, there arose in me the vision, the knowledge, the wisdom, the insight, and the light.

"As long, O bhikkhus, as my vision of true knowledge was not fully clear in these three aspects and in these twelve ways regarding the Four Noble Truths, I did not claim to have realized the perfect enlightenment that is supreme in the world with its devas, māras and brahmās, in this world with its recluses and brāhmaṇas, with its princes and men.

"But when, O bhikkhus, my vision of true knowledge was fully clear in these three aspects and in these twelve ways regarding the Four Noble Truths, then I claimed to have realized the perfect enlightenment that is supreme in the world with its devas, māras and brahmās, in this world with its recluses and brāhmaṇas, with its princes and men.

"Indeed, a vision of true knowledge arose in me thus: My mind's deliverance is unassailable. This is the last birth. Now there is no more becoming."

Thus the Buddha spoke. The group of five bhikkhus was glad and acclaimed his words. While this doctrine was being expounded, there arose in the Venerable Kondañña the pure, immaculate vision of the truth and he realized, "Whatsoever is subject to causation is also subject to cessation."

When the Buddha expounded the discourse, thus putting into motion the turning of the wheel of Dhamma, the devas of the earth exclaimed: "This excellent wheel of Dhamma, which could not be expounded by any ascetic, brāhmaṇa, deva, māra or brahmā in this world, has been put into motion by the Blessed One at Deer Park, in Isipatana, near Varanasi."

Hearing this, the devas Catumahārājika, Tavatiṃsā, Yāmā, Tussitā, Nimmānarati, Paranimmitavasavati, and the brahmās of Brahmāpārisajjā, Brahmāpurohitā, Mahābrahmā, Parittābhā, Appamāṇabhā, Ābhassarā, Parittasubhā, Appamāṇasubhā, Subhakiṇṇā, Vehapphalā, Avihā, Atappā, Sudassā, Sudassī, and Akaniṭṭhā also raised the same joyous cry.

Thus, at that very moment, at that very instant, this joyous cry extended as far as the brahmā realm. These ten thousand world systems quaked, tottered, and trembled violently. A radiant light, surpassing the radiance of the devas appeared in the world.

Then the Buddha said, "Friends, Kondañña has indeed understood. Friends, Kondañña has indeed understood." Therefore, the Venerable Kondañña was named Aññāsi Kondañña — "Kondañña who understands."

[33]

The Fire-Sermon

According to tradition, the *Adittapariyaya Sutta* or "Fire Sermon" was delivered near Uruvela a short while after the "Turning the Wheel of Dhamma" sermon. In it, the Buddha explains that all beings are on fire with passion, hatred and infatuation (*lobha*, *dosa* and *moha*, otherwise translated "greed", "hate", and "delusion"). When one has divested oneself of these "three roots of evil", one becomes free from the "taints" and escapes from the cycle of rebirth. The text, from the *Mahāvagga* section of the *Vinaya Piṭaka*, was translated by Henry Clarke Warren.

Then The Blessed One, having dwelt in Uruvelā as long as he wished, proceeded on his wanderings in the direction of Gayā Head, accompanied by a great congregation of priests, a thousand in number, who had all of them aforetime been monks with matted hair. And there in Gayā, on Gayā Head, The Blessed One dwelt, together with the thousand priests.

And there The Blessed One addressed the priests: —

"All things, O priests, are on fire. And what, O priests, are all these things which are on fire?

"The eye, O priests, is on fire; forms are on fire; eye-consciousness is on fire; impressions received by the eye are on fire; and whatever sensation, pleasant, unpleasant, or indifferent, originates in dependence on impressions received by the eye, that also is on fire.

"And with what are these on fire?

"With the fire of passion, say I, with the fire of hatred, with the fire of infatuation; with birth, old age, death, sorrow, lamentation, misery, grief, and despair are they on fire.

"The ear is on fire; sounds are on fire; . . . the nose is on fire; odors are on fire; . . . the tongue is on fire; tastes are on fire; . . . the body is on fire; things tangible are on fire; . . . the mind is on fire; ideas are on fire; . . . mind-consciousness is on fire; impressions received by the mind are on fire; and whatever sensation, pleasant, unpleasant, or indifferent, originates in dependence on impressions received by the mind, that also is on fire.

"And with what are these on fire?

"With the fire of passion, say I, with the fire of hatred, with the fire of infatuation; with birth, old age, death, sorrow, lamentation, misery, grief, and despair are they on fire.

"Perceiving this, O priests, the learned and noble disciple conceives an aversion for the eye, conceives an aversion for forms, conceives an aversion for eye-consciousness, conceives an aversion for the impressions received by the eye; and whatever sensation, pleasant, unpleasant, or indifferent, originates in dependence on impressions received by the eye, for that also he conceives an aversion. Conceives an aversion for the ear, conceives an aversion for sounds, . . . conceives an aversion for the nose, conceives an aversion for odors, . . . conceives an aversion for the tongue, conceives an aversion for tastes, . . . conceives an aversion for the body, conceives an aversion for things tangible, . . . conceives an aversion for the mind, conceives an aversion for ideas, conceives an aversion for mind-consciousness, conceives an aversion for the impressions received by the mind; and whatever sensation, pleasant, unpleasant, or indifferent, originates in dependence on impressions received by the mind, for this also he conceives an aversion. And in conceiving this aversion, he becomes divested of passion, and by the absence of passion he becomes free, and when he is free he becomes aware that he is free; and he knows that rebirth is exhausted, that he has lived the holy life, that he has done what it behooved him to do, and that he is no more for this world."

Now while this exposition was being delivered, the minds of the thousand priests became free from attachment and delivered from the depravities.

THE PRACTICE OF VIRTUE AND MEDITATION

In several places in the *suttas*, the Buddha lays down a method of *anupubbasikkhā* or gradual training. This begins with the hearing and acceptance of the *dhamma* and ends with the attainment of liberation. Having entered the order, the novice must follow the prescribed rules of discipline in order to purify his or her conduct and livelihood. This practice of virtue or *sīla* becomes the basis for a fruitful practice of meditation or *samādhi*, by which the novice obtains contentment, restraint of the senses, and mindfulness. Extracts from different *suttas* dealing with morality and meditation are reproduced below.

[34]

Right Conduct for the Lay Person

Of the three divisions of Buddhist practice — morality, meditation and wisdom — the most fundamental is morality or virtue. The primary rules of conduct are the five *sīla*s: avoidance of killing, theft, sexual misconduct, harmful speech and intoxication. Those who have entered the order must follow a code consisting of 277 regulations. The life of the layperson is also governed by rules, but they are less stringent and permit the performance of family duties. This selection, an extract from the *Sigālaka Sutta* of the *Dīgha Nikāya*, gives the chief prohibitions that a householder must observe in the form of numbered groups. Subsequent paragraphs (not reproduced) show that the lay practitioner was encouraged to form sincere, warm and lasting relationships with parents, teachers, wife, children and friends. Translated by Maurice Walshe.

"Young householder, it is by abandoning the four defilements of action, by not doing evil from the four causes, by not following the six ways of wasting one's substance — through avoiding these fourteen evil ways — that the Ariyan disciple covers the six directions, and by such practice becomes a conqueror of both worlds, so that all will go well with him in this world and the next, and at the breaking-up of the body after death he will go to a good destiny, a heavenly world.

"What are the four defilements of action that are abandoned? Taking life is one, taking what is not given is one, sexual misconduct is one, lying speech is one. These are the four defilements of action that he abandons." . . .

"What are the four causes of evil from which he refrains? Evil action springs from attachment, it springs from ill-will, it springs from folly, it springs from fear. If the Ariyan disciple does not act out of attachment, ill-will, folly or fear, he will not do evil from any one of the four causes." . . .

"And which are the six ways of wasting one's substance that he does not follow? Addiction to strong drink and sloth-producing drugs is one way of wasting one's substance, haunting the streets at unfitting times is one, attending fairs is one, being addicted to gambling is one, keeping bad company is one, habitual idleness is one. . . . "

[35]

The Four *Jhānas* and Beyond

Pali texts speak of two sorts of meditation: *samatha* or "calming" meditation, and *vipassanā* or "insight" meditation. Descriptions of calming meditation feature the four inner states known as *jhānas* (Skt. *dhyānas*). In stock descriptions of the *jhānas*, such as this one from the *Aṭṭhakanāgara Sutta* of the *Majjhima Nikāya*, each *jhāna* is shown to exhibit increasing freedom from affect, until full equanimity is reached. Translated by Bhikkhu Ñāṇamoli and Bhikkhu Bodhi.

"Venerable Ānanda, has any one thing been proclaimed by the Blessed One who knows and sees, accomplished and fully enlightened, wherein if a bhikkhu abides diligent, ardent, and resolute, his unliberated mind comes to be liberated, his undestroyed taints come to be destroyed, and he attains the supreme security from bondage that he had not attained before?"

"Yes, householder, one such thing has been proclaimed by the Blessed One."

"What is that one thing, venerable Ānanda?"

"Here, householder, quite secluded from sensual pleasures, secluded from unwholesome states, a bhikkhu enters upon and abides in the first jhāna, which is accompanied by applied and sustained thought, with rapture and pleasure born of seclusion. He considers this and understands it thus: 'This first jhāna is conditioned and volitionally produced. But whatever is conditioned and volitionally produced is impermanent, subject to cessation.' Standing upon that, he attains the destruction of the taints. But if he does not attain the destruction of the taints, then because of that desire for the Dhamma, that delight in the Dhamma, with the destruction of the five lower fetters he becomes one due to reappear spontaneously [in the Pure Abodes] and there attain final Nibbāna without ever returning from that world. . . .

"Again, with the stilling of applied and sustained thought, a bhikkhu enters and abides in the second jhāna. . . . He considers this and understands it thus: 'This second jhāna is conditioned and volitionally produced. . . .'

"Again, with the fading away as well of rapture, a bhikkhu . . . enters upon and abides in the third jhāna. . . . He considers this and understands it thus: 'This third jhāna is conditioned and volitionally produced. . . .'

"Again, with the abandoning of pleasure and pain . . . a bhikkhu enters upon and abides in the fourth jhāna. . . . He considers this and understands it thus: 'This fourth jhāna is conditioned and volitionally produced. But whatever is conditioned and volitionally produced is impermanent, subject to cessation.' Standing upon that, he attains the destruction of the taints. But if he does not attain the destruction of the taints, then because of that desire for the Dhamma, that delight in the Dhamma, with the destruction of the five lower fetters he becomes one due to reappear spontaneously [in the Pure Abodes] and there attain final Nibbāna without ever returning from that world.

"This too is the one thing proclaimed by the Blessed One who knows and sees, accomplished and fully enlightened, wherein if a bhikkhu abides diligent, ardent, and resolute, his unliberated mind comes to be liberated, his undestroyed taints come to be destroyed, and he attains the supreme security from bondage that he had not attained before. . . . "

[36]

The Four Foundations of Mindfulness

Samatha meditation is a powerful tool, but on its own it might lead to attachment to inner states that, like everything else in *saṁsāra*, are subject to cessation. *Vipassanā* meditation works not by passing into unusual states of consciousness, but by observing one's daily physical and mental states — bodily sensations, feelings, mind, mental objects — with minute and detached attention. A classic presentation of *vipassanā* meditation is found in the *Satipaṭṭhāna Sutta* of the *Majjhima Nikāya*. The following extract from that text includes a summary of the "four foundations of mindfulness", and part of a more detailed account of the first one, "contemplating the body as a body". The full descriptions of the rest of the first foundation, and all of the second, third and fourth foundations, are omitted for want of space. Translated by Bhikkhu Ñāṇamoli and Bhikkhu Bodhi.

"Bhikkus, this is the direct path for the purification of beings, for the surmounting of sorrow and lamentation, for the disappearance of pain and grief, for the attainment of the true way, for the realisation of Nibbāna — namely, the four foundations of mindfulness.

"What are the four? Here, bhikkhus, a bhikkhu abides contemplating the body as a body, ardent, fully aware, and mindful, having put away covetousness and grief for the world. He abides contemplating feelings as feelings, ardent, fully aware, and mindful, having put away covetousness and grief for the world. He abides contemplating mind as mind, ardent, fully aware, and mindful, having put away covetousness and grief for the world. He abides contemplating mind-objects as mind-objects, ardent, fully aware, and mindful, having put away covetousness and grief for the world.

"And how, bhikkhus, does a bhikkhu abide contemplating the body as a body? Here a bhikkhu, gone to the forest or to the root of a tree or to an empty hut, sits down; having folded his legs crosswise, set his body erect, and established mindfulness in front of him, ever mindful he breathes in, mindful he breathes out. Breathing in long, he understands: 'I breathe in long'; or breathing out long, he understands: 'I breathe out long.' Breathing in short, he understands: 'I breathe in short'; or breathing out short, he understands: 'I breathe out short.' He trains thus: 'I shall breathe in experiencing the whole body [of breath]'; he trains thus: 'I shall breathe out experiencing the whole body [of breath].' He trains thus: 'I shall breathe in tranquillizing the bodily formation'; he trains thus: 'I shall breathe out tranquillizing the bodily formation.' Just as a skilled turner or his apprentice, when making a long turn, understands: 'I make a long turn'; or, when making a short turn, understands: 'I make a short turn'; so too, breathing in long, a bhikkhu understands: 'I breathe in long' . . . he trains thus: 'I shall breathe out tranquillizing the bodily formation.' . . .

"Bhikkhus, if anyone should develop these four foundations of mindfulness in such a way for seven years, one of two fruits could be expected for him: either final knowledge here and now, or if there is a trace of clinging left, non-return. . . . "

VOICES FROM THE SANGHA

The most important teachings in the Pali Canon are presented in the form of utterances attributed to the Buddha or his chief disciples. There are also a number of authoritative teachings that are put in the mouths of less exalted personages. Two examples of such texts are reproduced here.

[37]

Nagasena on No-Self

The *Milinda-pañha* or "Questions of King Milinda" is written in the form of a dialogue between the monk Nagasena and the Bactrian-Greek King Menander (Pali: Milinda). Menander (second century BCE) was the ruler of a kingdom in what is now northern Pakistan and southern Afghanistan. (The area had been one of the conquests of Alexander the Great; later it passed into the hands of the so-called Indo-Greek kings, of whom Menander is the best known.) Menander is supposed to have been converted to Buddhism by the monk Nagasena, and the *Milinda-pañha* purports to be a record of the monk's teachings to the king. It was composed during the early centuries of the Common Era, and is one of the masterpieces of Pali prose. This extract deals with one of the most problematic concepts of Theravada Buddhism: *anattā* or the non-existence of the self. The difficulty, as Milinda points out, is that without a self there would seem to be no basis for moral action or responsibility. It will be noted that Nagasena avoids answering the king's question directly; instead he deconstructs (rather literally) the notion of self by comparing it to a chariot, which in fact is just a name for its parts, just as "Nagasena" is a name for the collection of the monk's attributes. Translated by Edward Conze.

The Venerable Nagasena stayed at the Sankheyya hermitage together with 80,000 monks. King Milinda, accompanied by a retinue of 500 Greeks, went up to where he was, gave him a friendly and courteous greeting, and sat on one side. Nagasena returned his greetings, and his courtesy pleased the king's heart. . . .

And King Milinda asked him: "How is your Reverence known, and what is your name, Sir?" "As Nagasena I am known, O great king, and as Nagasena do my fellow religious habitually address me. But although parents give such names as Nagasena, or Surasena, or Virasena, or Sihasena, nevertheless this word 'Nagasena' is just a denomination, a designation, a conceptual term, a current appellation, a mere name. For no real person can here be apprehended." But King Milinda explained: "Now listen, you 500 Greeks and 80,000 monks, this Nagasena tells me that he is not a real person! How can I be expected to agree with that!" And to Nagasena he said: "If, most reverend Nagasena, no person can be apprehended in reality, who then, I ask you, gives you what you require by way of robes, food, lodging, and medicines? Who is it that consumes them? Who is it that guards morality, practises meditation, and realizes the [four] Paths and their Fruits, and thereafter Nirvana? Who is it that kills living beings, takes what is not given, commits sexual misconduct, tells lies, drinks intoxicants? Who is it that commits the five Deadly Sins? For, if there were no person, there could be no merit and no demerit; no doer of meritorious or demeritorious deeds, and no agent behind them; no fruit of good and evil deeds, and no reward or punishment for them. If someone should kill you, O Venerable Nagasena, he would not commit any murder. And you yourself, Venerable Nagasena, would not be a real teacher, or instructor, or ordained monk! You just told me that your fellow religious habitually address you as 'Nagasena'. What then is this 'Nagasena'? Are perhaps the hairs of the head 'Nagasena'?" — "No, great king!" "Or perhaps the hairs of the body?" — "No, great king!" "Or perhaps the nails, teeth, skin, muscles, sinews, bones, marrow, kidneys, heart, liver, serous membranes, spleen, lungs, intestines, mesentery, stomach, excrement, the bile, phlegm, pus, blood, grease, fat, tears, sweat, spittle, snot, fluid of the joints, urine, or the brain in the skull — are they this 'Nagasena'?" — "No, great king!" — "Or is form this 'Nagasena', or feeling, or perceptions, or impulses, or consciousness?" — "No, great king!" — "Then is it the combination of form, feelings, perceptions, impulses, and consciousness?" — "No, great king!" — "Then is it outside the combination of form, feelings, perceptions, impulses, and consciousness?" — "No, great king!" — "Then, ask as I may, I can discover no Nagasena at all. Just a mere sound is this 'Nagasena', but who is the real Nagasena? Your Reverence has told a lie, has spoken a falsehood! There really is no Nagasena!"

Thereupon the Venerable Nagasena said to King Milinda: "As a king you have been brought up in great refinement and you avoid roughness of any kind. If you would walk at mid-day on this hot, burning, and sandy ground, then your feet would have to tread on the rough and gritty gravel and pebbles, and they would hurt you, your body would get tired, your mind impaired, and your awareness of your body would be associated with pain. How then did you come — on foot, or on a mount?"

"I did not come, Sir, on foot, but on a chariot." — "If you have come on a chariot, then please explain to me what a chariot is. Is the pole the chariot?" — "No, reverend Sir!" — "Is then the axle the chariot?" — "No, reverend Sir!" — "Is it then the wheels, or the framework, or the flag-staff, or the yoke, or the reins, or the goad-stick?" — "No, reverend Sir!" — "Then is it the combination of pole, axle, wheels, framework, flag-staff, yoke, reins, and goad which is the 'chariot'?" — "No, reverend Sir!" — "Then is this 'chariot' outside the combination of pole, axle, wheels, framework, flag-staff, yoke, reins, and goad?" — "No, reverend Sir!" — "Then, ask as I may, I can discover no chariot at all. Just a mere sound is this 'chariot'. But what is the real chariot? Your Majesty has told a lie, has spoken a falsehood! There really is no chariot! Your Majesty is the greatest king in the whole of India. Of whom then are you afraid, that you do not speak the truth?" And he exclaimed: "Now listen, you 500 Greeks and 80,000 monks, this king Milinda tells me that he has come on a chariot. But when asked to explain to me what a chariot is, he cannot establish its existence. How can one possibly approve of that?"

The five hundred Greeks thereupon applauded the Venerable Nagasena and said to king Milinda: "Now let your Majesty get out of that if you can!"

But king Milinda said to Nagasena: "I have not, Nagasena, spoken a falsehood. For it is in dependence on the pole, the axle, the wheels, the framework, the flag-staff, etc., that there takes place this denomination 'chariot', this designation, this conceptual term, a current appellation and a mere name". — "Your Majesty has spoken well about the chariot. It is just so with me. In dependence on the thirty-two parts of the body and the five Skandhas there takes place this denomination 'Nagasena', this designation, this conceptual term, a current appellation and a mere name. In ultimate reality, however, this person cannot be apprehended. And this has been said by our Sister Vajira when she was face to face with the Lord:

'Where all constituent parts are present,
The word "a chariot" is applied.
So likewise where the skandhas are,
The term a "being" commonly is used.'"

"It is wonderful, Nagasena, it is astonishing, Nagasena! Most brilliantly have these questions been answered! Were the Buddha himself here, he would approve what you have said. Well spoken, Nagasena, well spoken!"

[38]

One Monk, One Nun

The *Khuddaka Nikāya* of the *Sutta Piṭaka* consists of fifteen short didactic texts, among which are the *Theragāthā* and *Therīgāthā*. Written as early as the third century BCE, these "Songs of the Elder Monks" and "Songs of the Elder Nuns" tell the stories of some three hundred members of the early *sangha*. Whether or not they are factual, they have the immediacy and poignancy of personal accounts. Translated by Andrew Schelling and Anne Waldman.

Dead to the world and its troubles
he recites mantras
mind unruffled
shaking distractions away
like the wind god
scatters a few
forest leaves

*

It's been twenty-five years since I became a nun
But I'm still restless
No peace of mind — not even one moment
(*she snaps her fingers*)
Every thought's of sex
I hold out my arms
Cry out like a madwoman
Then I go into my cell
But I heard Dhamma-Dinna preach
and she taught me impermanence
I sat down to meditate:
I know I've lived before
My celestial eye has been purified
I see I see other lives past and present
I read other minds present and past
The ear element is purified
I hear I hear I can really hear

FURTHER READING

Source Materials

Edward Conze, trans., *Buddhist Scriptures*. Harmondsworth, England: Penguin Books, 1976.

Rewata Dhamma, trans., *The First Discourse of the Buddha*. Somerville, MA: Wisdom Publications, 1997.

Bhikkhu Ñāṇamoli and Bhikkhu Bodi, trans., *The Middle Length Discourses of the Buddha*. Somerville, MA: Wisdom Publications, 1995.

Andrew Schelling and Anne Waldman, trans., *Songs of the Sons and Daughters of Buddha*. Boston: Shambhala Publications, 1996.

Maurice Walshe, trans., *The Long Discourses of the Buddha*, Somerville, MA: Wisdom Publications, 1995.

Henry Clarke Warren, trans., *Buddhism in Translation*. Cambridge, MA: Harvard University Press, 1947.

Other Works

David Kalupahana, *A History of Buddhist Philosophy*. Reprint edition. Delhi: Motilal Banarsidass, 1994.

Damien Keown, *Buddhism: A Very Short Introduction*. Oxford: Oxford University Press, 1996.

Sources of Texts and Translations

28	*Majjhima Nikāya* 1.163–67	Ñāṇamoli and Bodhi 256–60
29	*Mahāvagga* 1.1	Warren 83–85
30	*Majjhima Nikāya* 1.167–70	Ñāṇamoli and Bodhi 260–63
31	*Dīgha Nikāya* 2.154–56	Walshe 269–71
32	*Saṁyutta Nikāya (Dhamma-cakkapavattana Sutta)*	Dhamma 17–20
33	*Mahāvagga* 1.21	Warren 351–53
34	*Dīgha Nikāya* 3.181–82	Walshe 461–62
35	*Majjhima Nikāya* 1.349–51	Ñāṇamoli and Bodhi 454–56
36	*Majjhima Nikāya* 1.55–62	Ñāṇamoli and Bodhi 145–55
37	*Milinda-pañha* 2.1.1	Conze 146–49
38	*Thera-gāthā* 1.2; *Therīgāthā* 5.38	Schelling and Waldman 9, 89

5

यत्सांख्यैः प्राप्यते स्थानं तद्योगैरपि गम्यते।
एकम् सांख्यं च योगं च यः पश्यति स पश्यति॥

The status attained by those who follow the Samkhya is reached also by those who practise Yoga. One sees truly who sees Yoga and Samkhya as one.

Bhagavad Gītā 5.5

Samkhya and Yoga

SYSTEMATIC philosophy in South Asia had its beginnings in the centuries just before and after the start of the Common Era. Earlier literature, for example the *upaniṣad*s, the Jaina *sūtra*s and the Theravada *sutta*s, contained philosophical passages of considerable depth, but the presentation was unmethodical and intermixed with what we would now call mythology. Philosophy properly speaking, the reasoned examination of the principles of things, began with the formulation of the six schools of orthodox (vedic) thought, and the systematic presentation of Buddhist, Jaina and other non-vedic doctrines.

The six orthodox schools are all concerned with salvation or liberation, but they conceive of it in very different terms. *Pūrva Mīmāṁsā* and *Uttara Mīmāṁsā* (the latter also called *Vedānta*) see the Veda as the eternal repository of Truth, and view the right performance of vedic rituals, or the right comprehension of the ideas of the *upaniṣad*s, as the proper means of salvation. *Nyāya* and *Vaiśeṣika* stress the liberative power of the right understanding of logic and ontology. *Sāṁkhya* and *Yoga* seek freedom by bringing about the separation of the conscious soul from matter. Of all the schools, Samkhya and Yoga are most concerned with the attainment of salvation by means of human effort. Vedanta, particularly as interpreted by Shankara and later philosophers, places a great deal of stress on liberation, but sees it as proceeding ultimately from the sacred word of the Veda. Samkhya and Yoga acknowledge the importance of revealed scripture, but they rely on intellectual discrimination and also (in the case of Yoga) on psycho-physical practices to achieve the highest aim.

The primary texts of all the orthodox schools are collections of highly condensed statements known as *sūtras* (literally, "threads"). These terse, occasionally enigmatic aphorisms sum up the tenets of the system in a memorable way, but offer little by way of explanation. The work of bringing out the meaning of the *sūtras* was left to teachers and commentators. Later developments in the schools are represented less by original texts than by commentaries and commentaries on commentaries.

The primary texts of Samkhya and Yoga are the *Sāṁkhya Kārikā* of Ishwarakrishna and the *Yoga Sūtra* of Patanjali. Both are thought to have been composed around the third century CE, though the schools themselves are much older. The seeds of the ideas that were elaborated in Sankhya and Yoga are found in the later *upaniṣads* and in Jaina and Buddhist texts. The similarities between Jainism and Samkhya are especially striking. Both are radically dualistic and atheistic systems that see salvation as the separation of soul from matter, leading to isolation (*kevala* or *kaivalya*) and final liberation (*mokṣa*). There are also parallels between the heterodox schools and Yoga. Some passages in the *Yoga Sūtra* echo passages in Jaina and Buddhist texts, and those texts make reference to the sort of psycho-physical techniques that are systematised in the *Yoga Sūtra*. Such techniques have undoubtedly been practised in South Asia from very early times.

Philosophically, Samkhya and Yoga are almost identical. Both view the world in terms of a fundamental duality: soul and matter. In Samkhya, these two principles are called *puruṣa* ("male", "person") and *prakṛti* ("primordial matter", sometimes translated as "nature"). The number of souls is infinite, and each soul is eternally distinct. When a soul comes into contact with matter, its consciousness is obscured. The result is bondage and suffering. The way for the soul to escape from suffering is to realise its difference from nature. In Samkhya, this is done by means of discrimination; Yoga offers in addition various psycho-physical techniques as aids in the task of liberation and as means to attain extraordinary powers. Yoga also (unlike the atheistic Samkhya) gives a limited role to *Īśvara* or God in the attainment of liberation.

THE SYSTEM OF SAMKHYA

Samkhya is probably the older of the two systems, and provides the philosophical basis for both. It takes its name from a word that means "summing up" or "counting". From this appears its later senses: the enumeration of the principles of existence and their analysis as a means of achieving freedom. Samkhya recognises twenty-five principles or *tattvas*, of which only two are permanent: (1) *puruṣa* and (2) *prakṛti*. When soul comes into contact with matter, a process of manifestation begins. First comes (3) intellect or *buddhi*, followed by (4) ego-sense or *ahaṁkāra*, which is the source of all the rest: (5) mind (sometimes called the sixth sense); (6–10) the five subtle substances (light, sound, etc.); (11–15) the five instruments of sense (sight, hearing, etc.); (16–20) the five instruments of action (speaking, grasping, etc.); and finally (21–25) the five elements (ether, air, etc.) that compose the material world. All of these, intellect and mind included, lack consciousness, because they emerge from *prakṛti*, which is inherently unconscious. It is *puruṣa* that lends consciousness to *prakṛti* and its products, but by so doing it becomes bound and suffers.

The process of manifestation is not creation, but the emergence of effects pre-existent in the cause. This process comes about as a result of the disequilibrium of the three *guṇas* or modes of nature. The first *guṇa*, *sattva*, is present in all that is clear and illuminated; the second, *rajas*, in things that are dynamic; the last, *tamas*, in all that is dark and inert. When the three are in a state of balance, there is no manifested world; when that balance is disturbed, the process of manifestation begins. It goes on until a soul, by means of its intellect, becomes aware of its eternal distinctness from matter. In this way it achieves isolation (*kaivalya*) and liberation (*mokṣa*). Once again, it is absorbed in pure, objectless consciousness, untouched by suffering.

In Samkhya, as in Jainism, the goal is a negative state: not a realisation of what is, but an understanding of what is not. The soul becomes aware of what always has been the case: its fundamental separation from matter. This awareness marks the end of manifested existence. Only soul and indeterminate matter remain. Despite this negative aim and its dry, analytical approach, Samkhya was one of South Asia's most prominent systems of thought for more than a thousand years. Its terminology—the three *guṇas*, *buddhi*, *ahaṁkāra*, *manas*—was taken up by the *Bhagavad Gītā*, the *tantras*, and the *purāṇas*, and through them has entered common parlance. The school itself ceased to be a living force after the sixteenth century, but it lives on as the philosophical framework of the still vigorous system of Yoga.

[39]

Fundamentals of Samkhya

These passages from the beginning of the *Sāṁkhya Kārikā* give the bases of Samkhya's view of the world. The first two verses explain that the fundamental suffering of existence (called, as in Buddhism and Jainism, *duḥkha*) cannot be removed by perceptible means, such as drugs, nor by imperceptible means, such as scripture. The only effective means is to become aware of the difference between nature and conscious soul. The third verse presents the twenty-five elements of existence: conscious soul; primordial nature; "the seven" (intellect, ego-sense, mind, and the four subtle elements); and "the sixteen" (the other elements in four groups of four). The next pair of verses introduces the concept of the constituents or modes of nature. The last pair explains the relationship between *puruṣa* and *prakṛti* which leads to cosmic manifestation. The conscious but immobile *puruṣa* and the unconscious but active *prakṛti* are compared to a blind man and a lame man who are bound to each other. Translated from the Sanskrit by Gerald James Larson.

Because of the torment of the threefold suffering, [there arises] the desire to know the means of removing it. If [it is said that] this [desire — i.e., inquiry] is useless because perceptible [means of removal are available], [we say] no, since [perceptible means] are not final or abiding.

The revealed [or scriptural, means of removing the torment] are like the perceptible [— i.e., ultimately ineffective], for they are connected with impurity, destruction and excess; a different and superior method is the [discriminative] knowledge of the manifest (*vyakta*), the unmanifest (*avyakta*) and the knowing one [or knower — i.e., *puruṣa*].

Primordial nature (*mūlaprakṛti*) is uncreated. The seven — the great one (*mahat*), etc. — are both created and creative. The sixteen are created. *Puruṣa* is neither created nor creative. . . .

[Both] the manifest and unmanifest are [characterized by the] three *guṇa*s ("qualities" or "strands"); undiscriminating; objective; general; non-conscious; productive; the *puruṣa* is the opposite of them, although similar [to the *avyakta*].

The *guṇa*s, whose natures are pleasure, pain and indifference, [serve to] manifest, activate and limit. They successively dominate, support, activate, and interact with one another. . . .

Because of the proximity [or association] of the two — i.e., *prakṛti* and *puruṣa* — the unconscious one appears as if characterized by consciousness. Similarly, the indifferent one appears as if characterized by activity, because of the activities of the three *guṇa*s.

The proximity [or association] of the two, which is like that of a blind man and a lame man, is for the purpose of seeing the *pradhāna* and for the purpose of the isolation of the *puruṣa* from this [association] creation proceeds. . . .

[40]

Liberation in Samkhya

These fourteen consecutive verses, which come towards the end of the *Sāṁkhya Kārikā*, present Samkhya's view of the process of liberation. The association of *prakṛti* with *puruṣa* brings about manifestation and its resultant suffering. But from another point of view, the whole purpose of the manifestation is for *prakṛti* to bring about the release of *puruṣa*. Once a *puruṣa* has understood its separateness from *prakṛti*, the process of manifestation ceases, just as a dance-performance ceases after the dancer has been seen by the audience. In fact, however, there is no "liberation", because *puruṣa* was never bound in the first place. The activities of the embodied soul continue after its liberation because of the force of past "impressions" (*saṁskāras*, a term used also in Buddhism, Yoga and other systems). When the liberated soul casts off its body, it achieves perfect isolation from matter and escapes from the cycle of rebirth. Translated by Gerald James Larson.

The *puruṣa*, which is consciousness, attains there the suffering made by decay and death; until deliverance of the subtle body; therefore, suffering is of the nature of things.

This creation, brought about by *prakṛti*—from the great one (*mahat*) down to the specific gross elements—[functions] for the sake of the release of each *puruṣa*; [this is done] for the sake of another, as if it were for her own [benefit].

As the unknowing [or unconscious] milk functions for the sake of the nourishment of the calf; so the *prakṛti* functions for the sake of the release of the *puruṣa*.

As [in] the world [a man] engages in actions for the sake of the cessation of a desire; so also does the *prakṛti* function for the sake of the release of the *puruṣa*.

As a dancer ceases from the dance after having been seen by the audience; so also *prakṛti* ceases after having manifested herself to the *puruṣa*.

[She] (*prakṛti*), possessed of the *guṇas* and helpful in various ways, behaves selflessly for the sake of him [*puruṣa*], who is without the *guṇas* and who plays no helpful part.

It is my thought that there is nothing more delicate than *prakṛti*, who [says to herself] "I have been seen," and never again comes into the sight of *puruṣa*.

Nothing, therefore, is bound; nothing released, likewise not any thing transmigrates. [Only] *prakṛti* in its various forms transmigrates, is bound and is released.

Prakṛti binds herself by herself by means of seven forms (*rūpa* or *bhāva*); she releases herself by means of one form (*rūpa* or *bhāva*) for the sake of each *puruṣa*.

Thus, from the study [or analysis] of the principles (*tattva*s), the "knowledge" [or salvation-knowledge] arises, "I am not, nothing belongs to me, I do not exist," [and this "knowledge"] is complete because free from error, pure and solitary (*kevala*).

Then, the *puruṣa*, comfortably situated like a spectator, sees *prakṛti* whose activity has ceased due to the completion of her purpose, and who has turned back from the seven forms (*rūpa* or *bhāva*).

[Says the] indifferent one [or spectator], "I have seen [her]"; the other ceases [saying], "I have been seen." Though the two are still in proximity, no [further] creation [takes place].

Having arrived at the point at which virtue, etc., has no [further] cause, because of the attainment of direct knowledge (*samyagjñānādhigamād*), the endowed body [i.e., the body in association with *puruṣa*] yet continues because of the force of past impressions (*saṁskāras*), like a potter's wheel.

With the cessation of *prakṛti* due to its purpose having been accomplished, [the *puruṣa*] on attaining separation from the body, attains isolation (*kaivalya*) which is both certain and final.

THE YOGA OF PATANJALI

The Sanskrit word *yoga* is related to the English word "yoke", and like it implies "joining together" or "union". Any means by which the individual is united to the truth of existence can be called a *yoga*. The classical system of Yoga, as set forth in the *Yoga Sūtra*, is similar to the system of Samkhya, but it includes a number of psycho-physical techniques meant to hasten the process of liberation. Some of these go back at least as far as the first millennium BCE. Methods similar to those detailed in the *Yoga Sūtra* are mentioned in certain Theravada *sutta*s and late *upaniṣad*s, and are hinted at in earlier vedic texts.

The *Yoga Sūtra* itself was composed during the second or third century CE. It is attributed to Patanjali, about whom nothing is known. The same name was borne by one or more earlier writers, which has led to confusions of attribution. The Patanjali of the *Sūtra* (who may or may not have been a single person) uses Samkhya as a framework for a systematisation of meditative and occult practices. He assumes that his listeners are familiar with concepts like *puruṣa*, *prakṛti*, the twenty-five *tattvas*, the *guṇas*, etc., and so mentions them only in passing. His chief concern is to present ways for the individual soul to effect its separation from the workings of nature, in particular the *cittavṛttis* or "turnings of thought". This leads to isolation (*kaivalya*) and liberation (*mokṣa*). The main ways for bringing this about are "ascetic practice, study of sacred lore, and dedication to the Lord of Yoga" (*YS* 2.1). Since Yoga is an orthodox system, "sacred lore" presumably would refer to the Veda, but no vedic scripture is cited in the text, and study in general is given little importance. The Lord of Yoga or Ishwara — the only important concept Patanjali did not borrow from the Sankhya — is a "special sort of *puruṣa*" unaffected by the forces of corruption. Devotion to him can help the practitioner, but Patanjali does not dwell long on this. Most of his text is concerned with various forms of "ascetic practice" or *tapas*. In a famous passage, he presents a series of such practices that form an eightfold scale, beginning with moral principles and observances, and ending with spiritual absorption.

Two of the eight "limbs" of Yoga seek mastery of the body by means of postures or *āsanas* and breath-control or *prāṇāyāma*. These practices, passed over quickly by Patanjali, became the focus of the system of *haṭhayoga*, which was given definitive form around the eleventh century (see Chapter 8). Patanjali's attitude towards the body is inconsistent. On the one hand he considers it a sink of impurity, on the other hand an instrument of liberation. He also mentions the possibility of its transformation into a thing of beauty, grace, strength and indestructibility (*YS* 3.46). This physical transformation became a major point of interest in Nath Yoga and other postclassical systems of yogic discipline (see Chapter 12).

A revival of Patanjali's yoga began at the end of the nineteenth century, when the *Yoga Sūtra* was translated and commented on by Swami Vivekananda, a disciple of Paramahansa Ramakrishna (see Chapter 17). Vivekananda called his book *Raja-Yoga*, one of many names by which the yoga of Patanjali is known. His reading of the text was strongly influenced by the Vedanta philosophy, of which he was a great modern proponent. In this vedantic form, Patanjali's teachings became a major ingredient of the eclectic version of yoga that spread from India to other parts of the world during the twentieth century. In this contemporary blend, the classical yoga of Patanjali, which is life-denying both in practice and in aim, has been given an affirmative turn more in line with the interests of modern practitioners. But it has retained its basic focus: the practice of mental and physical discipline in order to achieve psychological freedom.

[41]

Cessation of the Turnings of Thought

The opening aphorisms of the *Yoga Sūtra* are concerned with the halting of the ordinary activity of thought. In Yoga, as in Sankhya, mind and even the higher intellect are regarded as components of material nature that have no consciousness of their own. Consciousness belongs only to *puruṣa* (here translated as "spirit"), which in the manifested world is bound to *prakṛti* or unconscious matter. When the "turnings of thought" are completely halted, and even the seeds of future activity destroyed, spirit becomes again what it always has been, an inactive witness of nature. This is what Patanjali calls "yoga". Translated from the Sanskrit by Barbara Stoler Miller.

This is the teaching of Yoga.

Yoga is the cessation of the turnings of thought.

When thought ceases, the spirit stands in its true identity as observer to the world.

Otherwise, the observer identifies with the turnings of thought. . . .

Cessation of the turnings of thought comes through practice and dispassion.

Practice is the effort to maintain the cessation of thought.

This practice is firmly grounded when it is performed for a long time without interruption and with zeal.

Dispassion is the sign of mastery over the craving for sensuous objects.

Higher dispassion is a total absence of craving for anything material, which comes by discriminating between spirit and material nature. . . .

The profound clarity of intuitive cognition brings inner tranquility.

Here wisdom is the vehicle of truth.

It has a different scope than scriptural or inferential knowledge because its object is singular.

A subliminal impression generated by wisdom stops the formation of other impressions.

When the turnings of thought cease completely, even wisdom ceases, and contemplation bears no seeds.

[42]

Freedom from Suffering by Active Performance of Yoga

In Samkhya and Yoga, as in Buddhism and Jainism, the most salient characteristic of existence is *duḥkha* or suffering. According to Buddhism, the origin of suffering is desire; according to Yoga, it is the connection between the observer (*puruṣa*) with the observed (*prakṛti*). In both systems the origin of *duḥkha* is ignorance. There are also similarities in the means of deliverance recommended by the two systems. In Buddhism, the aspirant is asked to follow the eightfold path, which culminates in right meditation or *samādhi*. In Yoga, the aspirant is instructed to follow a somewhat different eightfold path, which also culminates in *samādhi*. But the aim of yoga meditation is conceived in terms that a Buddhist would not accept: as the separation of an eternal conscious self from unconscious matter. The purpose of Patanjali's Yoga is to bring about this separation by means of understanding, devotion and practice. Translated by Barbara Stoler Miller.

The active performance of yoga involves ascetic practice, study of sacred lore, and dedication to the Lord of Yoga.

Its purpose is to cultivate pure contemplation and attenuate the forces of corruption.

The forces of corruption are ignorance, egoism, passion, hatred, and the will to live. . . .

All life is suffering for a man of discrimination, because of the sufferings inherent in change and its corrupting subliminal impressions, and because of the way qualities of material nature turn against themselves.

Suffering that has not yet come can be escaped.

The cause of suffering, which can be escaped, is the connection between the observer and the phenomenal world.

The phenomenal world consists of material elements and sense organs characterized by their clarity, activity, or stillness; this world can serve the goals of sensual experience or spiritual liberation. . . .

In its essence the phenomenal world exists only in relation to an observer.

Even if the phenomenal world ceases to be relevant for an observer who has realized freedom, it continues to exist because it is common to other observers.

The connection between the observer and the phenomenal world causes a misperceived identity between active power and its master.

The cause of this connection is ignorance.

When there is no ignorance, there is no such connection — the freedom of the observer lies in its absence.

The way to eliminate ignorance is through steady, focused discrimination between the observer and the world.

[43]

The Eightfold Path of Yoga

The yoga of Patanjali is often called the *Aṣṭāṅga* or "Eight-limbed" yoga on account of the following passage, which describes eight successive stages of yogic practice. These eight limbs are (1) moral principles (*yama*), (2) observances (*niyama*), (3) posture (*āsana*), (4) breath-control (*prāṇāyāma*), (5) withdrawal of the senses (*pratyāhāra*), (6) concentration (*dhāraṇā*), (7) meditation (*dhyāna*), and pure contemplation (*samādhi*). Many of these activities have parallels in Jaina and Buddhist practice. For example the fivefold "great vow of yoga" is identical with the "great vow" of Jainism. The first five limbs are regarded as preparatory stages, the last three as yoga properly speaking. Translated by Barbara Stoler Miller.

When impurity is destroyed by practicing the limbs of yoga, the light of knowledge shines in focused discrimination.

The eight limbs of yoga are moral principles, observances, posture, breath control, withdrawal of the senses, concentration, meditation, and pure contemplation.

The moral principles are nonviolence, truthfulness, abjuration of stealing, celibacy, and absence of greed.

These universal moral principles, unrestricted by conditions of birth, place, time, or circumstance, are the great vow of yoga.

The observances are bodily purification, contentment, ascetic practice, study of sacred lore, and dedication to the Lord of Yoga. . . .

The posture of yoga is steady and easy. . . .

When the posture of yoga is steady, then breath is controlled by regulation of the course of exhalation and inhalation. . . .

When each sense organ severs contact with its objects, withdrawal of the senses corresponds to the intrinsic form of thought. . . .

Concentration is binding thought in one place.

Meditation is focusing on a single conceptual flow.

Pure contemplation is meditation that illumines the object alone, as if the subject were devoid of intrinsic form.

Concentration, meditation, and pure contemplation focused on a single object constitute perfect discipline.

[44]

Extraordinary Powers

Most of the third book of the *Yoga Sūtra* is concerned with the development of extraordinary powers of the mind and body. Such powers are often regarded as distractions on the spiritual path. One is free from danger if one cultivates detachment not only from the ordinary workings of nature but from these extraordinary workings as well. Translated by Barbara Stoler Miller.

The turning of thought without reference to the external world is called "the great disembodied thought"; from this the veil that obscures the light is destroyed.

From perfect discipline of the gross, intrinsic, subtle, relational, and purposive aspects of the elements of matter, one attains mastery over them.

Then extraordinary powers appear, such as the power to be as small as an atom, as well as bodily perfection and immunity from the constraints of matter. . . .

From dispassion even towards these powers, freedom of the spirit occurs with the destruction of the seeds of sin.

[45]

Towards Pure Identity

In this closing passage of the *Yoga Sūtra*, Patanjali describes the highest reach of yogic knowledge, which is obtained by means of separation of the conscious soul from the workings of nature. Thought (*citta*) is part of nature, and so is inherently unconscious. It is impossible to perceive thought by means of thought, for then another thought would be needed to perceive the perceiving thought, and so on infinitely. Thought becomes aware of its own intelligence by assuming the form of spirit by means of *citi* or pure consciousness. *Citi* is not personal consciousness but something that moves towards complete isolation (*kaivalya*) of spirit and a knowledge that is practically infinite. This movement is the reversal of the development of the manifested world out of the conjunction of spirit and matter, leading in perfect self-awareness by the liberated spirit. Translated by Barbara Stoler Miller.

The spirit, never subject to change, is master of the turnings of thought, which it always knows.

Since thought is an object of perception, it cannot illuminate itself.

Nor can both thought and its object be comprehended simultaneously.

If a thought is the object of another thought, there is an infinite regression from intelligence to intelligence, and a confusion of memory.

Awareness of its own intelligence occurs when thought assumes the form of the spirit through consciousness that leaves no trace. . . .

One who sees the distinction between the lucid quality of nature and the observer ceases to cultivate a personal reality.

Then, deep in discrimination, thought gravitates toward freedom. . . .

Then the infinity of knowledge, released from impurities that obscure everything, leaves little to be known.

This infinite knowledge means an end to the sequence of transformations in material things, their purpose now fulfilled.

Sequence corresponds to a series of moments perceivable at the end of a process of transformation.

Freedom is a reversal of the evolutionary course of material things, which are empty of meaning for the spirit; it is also the power of consciousness in a state of true identity.

FURTHER READING

Source Materials

Gerald James Larson, *Classical Sāṃkhya: An Interpretation of its History and Meaning*. Delhi: Motilal Banarsidass, 1969.

Barbara Stoler Miller, trans., *Yoga: Discipline of Freedom: The Yoga Sutra Attributed to Patanjali*. New York: Bantam Books, 1998.

Other Works

Mircea Eliade, *Yoga: Immortality and Freedom*. Princeton, NJ: Princeton University Press, 1973.

Georg Feuerstein, *The Yoga Tradition: Its History, Literature, Philosophy and Practice*. Prescott, AZ: Hohm Press, 1998.

Swami Vivekananda, *Rāja-Yoga*. In *The Complete Works of Swami Vivekananda*, vol. I, pp. 119–313. Calcutta: Advaita Ashrama, 1989.

Sources of Texts and Translations

39	*Sāṁkhya-kārikā* 1–3, 11–12, 20–21	Larson 257–58, 262, 265–66
40	*Sāṁkhya-kārikā* 55–68	Larson 277–80
41	*Yoga-sūtra* 1. 1–4, 12–16, 47–51	Miller 29, 32, 42
42	*Yoga-sūtra* 2. 1–3, 15–18, 21–26	Miller 44, 47, 49, 50
43	*Yoga-sūtra* 2. 28–32, 46, 49, 54; 3.1–4	Miller 51–53, 56–57, 59–60
44	*Yoga-sūtra* 3. 43–45, 50	Miller 69–70, 72
45	*Yoga-sūtra* 4. 18–22, 25–26, 31–34	Miller 79–80, 82–83

Part Two

Developments

6

श्रुतिविप्रतिपन्ना ते यदा स्थास्यति निश्चला।
समाधावचला बुद्धिस्तदा योगमवाप्स्यसि॥

When your intellect, bewildered now by scripture, stands firm and unmoved in concentration, then you will attain the status of yoga.

Bhagavad Gītā 2.53

The Bhagavad Gita

BY THE SECOND century BCE, a number of distinct but related spiritual traditions coexisted in the subcontinent. Those we have considered so far — vedic formalism, vedantic asceticism, the world-denying heterodoxies of the Jainas and Buddhists, the liberative philosophies and practices of Samkhya and Yoga — were transmitted by means of specialised texts to relatively limited audiences. But there also were teachings that were spread by less exclusive means, offering direct and simple worship of popular deities. Prominent among these were the cults of Narayana, Vasudeva and Krishna. These names eventually were applied to a single deity, who became one of the most popular gods of Hinduism. Krishna's rise from a pastoral *devatā* to the supreme god of Vaishnavism was due largely to the stories of his life and deeds told in the great Indian epic, the *Mahābhārata*. The most famous and most significant episode of this epic is the *Bhagavad Gītā*.

The *Mahābhārata* is based on a dim recollection of events that took place in north India around 1000 BCE. A semi-legendary account of those events became the core of an epic of the clan of the Bharatas, which took definite shape around 400 BCE. Since the text of this poem was not sacrosanct, later poets were free to add lines, passages and even whole episodes, until the heroic epic of the Bharatas grew into the *Mahābhārata* or Great Bharata, which at 70,000 (or more) stanzas is the longest poem in the world.

The central narrative of the epic recounts the war of succession between two branches of the royal family of Hastinapura (near modern Delhi). On the one side are the Kauravas, sons of Dhritarashtra, on the other the Pandavas, their cousins. Cheated of their kingdom, the Pandavas must regain it by force of arms. Militarily outnumbered, they are strengthened by the virtue of their cause, and by the advice of their friend Krishna, who (unbeknownst to them) is the God of Gods. On the day of the battle which will decide the future of the world, Arjuna, one of the Pandava brothers, asks Krishna, who is acting as his charioteer, to take him between the two armies. There he is overcome by dejection. How, he asks Krishna, can he slay in battle his gurus, kinsmen, and friends? Laying down his divine bow and arrows, he refuses to fight.

The first part of Krishna's answer to Arjuna occupies twenty-eight stanzas at the beginning of Book Two (selection 46). Death is inevitable, says Krishna, but the immortal spirit is indestructible. Arjuna is a warrior, a *kṣatriya*, and his duty is to fight. To a *kṣatriya*, righteous battle is a door open to heaven. If Arjuna were to abandon his duty, other warriors would say that he had run away out of fear, and his name would be dishonoured forever. Let him fulfil his duty as a *kṣatriya* by taking part in the battle. Slain, he will win glory in heaven, victorious, he will win glory on the earth.

This answer is all that is required by the situation in the epic; but Krishna uses it as a springboard to deeper considerations. Up to the end of the sixth book, he is concerned mainly with the relative merits of the paths to liberation put forward by Samkhya and Yoga. In the *Gītā*, these two terms have special meanings. By "Samkhya" is meant all forms of liberative philosophy, not just classical Samkhya but also the soteriological doctrines of the *upaniṣads*, etc. Krishna refers to these as *jñānayoga* (the yoga of knowledge). "Yoga" includes, among other things, the path to union by means of action, called in particular *karmayoga* (the yoga of action). One of Krishna's first aims is to establish a synthesis of these two paths. In Books Five and Six, he presents methods of self-discipline that would not be out of place in the *upaniṣads*, but at the same time he declares that those who follow the path of knowledge need not withdraw from the world. What is needed, he explains, is the renunciation not of action but of the desire for the fruits of the action. To those who follow the way of vedic sacrifice, "action" means the correct performance of ritual or social duties. This ordinarily is done selfishly, for personal gain. Giving an allegorical explanation to "sacrifice", Krishna insists that action should indeed be done, but without regard for the fruits. The true sacrifice is the offering of everything one does to the Supreme.

While discussing the question of sacrifice, Krishna begins to reveal what will emerge as his "most secret" teaching: that he himself is identical with the Supreme, and that the best way to approach the highest is to approach Krishna with love and devotion. "In whatever ways humans approach me, in those very ways I receive them with love", he says (4.11). And in the same book he alludes to his real identity by saying: "Whenever there is a decay of righteousness (*dharma*) and an increase of unrighteousness, I cast myself forth into birth. For the protection of the good and the destruction of the evil, for the sake of establishing righteousness, I am born from age to age" (4.7–8).

In these stanzas are contained the two distinctive teachings of the *Gītā*: salvation by means of devotion or *bhakti*, and the incarnation of God in the form of *avatāra*s. The way of devotion was not originated by the *Gītā*. *Bhakti* and cognate terms are mentioned in the *Śvetāśvatara Upaniṣad* and in certain Buddhist texts, and devotion doubtless was of importance in the cults of Vasudeva and Narayana. But it is in the *Gītā* that it is decisively put forward as a preferred method of salvation. It is a path that is open to all human beings, not just those of the higher castes. "Whosoever takes refuge in me", Krishna tells Arjuna, "whether they be born in sin or are women or traders or even labourers, they also reach the highest goal" (9.32).

The idea that the Divine can take human form may have been hinted at in earlier scriptures, but it was first given prominence by the *Gītā*. The idea that Vishnu takes birth in a series of avatars, of whom Krishna is one, was a later development; but already in the *Gītā*, Krishna stands forth as an embodiment of the Divine. Puzzled by Krishna's statements on the subject, Arjuna asks for clarification. By way of answer, Krishna reveals to him his Universal Form, first as Time the Destroyer, and then, at Arjuna's request, in his more approachable human-divine form. This theophany, perhaps the most detailed description of the appearance of God in world literature, occupies the best part of Book Eleven. What follows is anticlimactic. Krishna reverts to comparatively dry explanations of the nature of the cosmos in terms of Samkhya philosophy, though in chapter fifteen, he goes beyond the categories of Samkhya by declaring that there exists a Supreme Purusha beyond both the changeful *puruṣa*, which is caught in the web of nature, and the changeless *puruṣa*, which is separate and free. This Supreme Soul is none other than Krishna. Those who worship him are freed from delusion.

In the final chapter of the *Gītā*, Krishna recapitulates his teachings. The paths of works and knowledge and devotion each can lead to the Supreme, but the simplest and greatest of them is the path of devotion. In his closing speech, Krishna gives to Arjuna, who is dear to him, his "supreme word". All a devotee has to do is to think constantly of Krishna and offer his actions as a sacrifice to him. Krishna will do the rest. "Abandoning all *dharma*s, take refuge in me alone. I will free you from sin and error. Do not grieve" (18.66).

For perhaps two millennia, the *Gītā* has been a central text of Hinduism, commented on by many of the greatest names of Indian philosophy, and read daily by countless devotees. Commentators intent on establishing their interpretations have missed the text's synthetic character. Shankara, the great proponent of monistic Vedanta, emphasised passages that speak of the way of knowledge, and played down those that promote the ways of action and devotion. His rival Ramanuja stressed the devotional side of the text, while modern commentators like Bankim Chandra Chatterjee, Bal Gangadhar Tilak, and M. K. Gandhi turned the *Gītā* into a gospel of duty. All these interpretations are correct as far as they go, but they do not give the whole of the *Gītā*'s message. Among recent writers, Sri Aurobindo probably went furthest in bringing out the *Gītā*'s many-sidedness, but even he did not exhaust its riches. Although it contains a number of passages that now strike a discordant note, such as those that seem to defend the system of caste, the *Gītā* remains a useful guide to life, a storehouse of profound philosophy, and a devotional poem of great power and beauty.

PASSAGES FROM THE BHAGAVAD GITA

The text of the *Gītā* consists of seven hundred stanzas, occupying eighteen chapters of the sixth book of the *Mahābhārata*. Critical scholars believe that the *Gītā* belongs to a strata of the epic composed between the second century BCE and the second century CE. Wide-ranging in its concerns and interests, it is at once a guide to life according to the Aryan *dharma*, a book of philosophy incorporating the insights of Samkhya and Vedanta, and a an inspiring work of devotion. Some scholars believe that these various elements are by different hands, that the *Gītā* as we know it is a composite text that took shape over many years. This theory is historically plausible, but it gives insufficient credit to the greatest achievement of the text as we now have it: its successful synthesis of a number of important strands of early Indian spirituality. Whether by one or several hands, the *Gītā* is best read as a unified whole.

The following selections, drawn from nine of the *Gītā*'s eighteen books, were translated from the Sanskrit by Arthur Osborne and G. V. Kulkarni.

[46]

Beyond Life and Death

After Arjuna tells Krishna that he refuses to fight and possibly kill his gurus and kinsmen, Krishna's first response is to remind him that death itself is unreal. The *ātman* or inner spirit never dies. This "dweller in the body" abandons one body and enters another just as people take off one set of clothing in order to put on another. The outer form changes, the spirit is forever unchanged.

Although you speak of wisdom you grieve for those who need no grief. The wise grieve neither for the dead nor the living.

Never was a time when I did not exist, nor you, nor these lords of men, nor shall we ever hereafter cease to be.

As the Embodied passes through childhood, youth and old age in this body, so does it take on a new body; the wise man is not confused by this.

The sense-contacts it is, Son of Kunti, that cause heat and cold, pleasure and pain. They come and go and are impermanent. Bear with them, O Bharata.

The wise man whom these perturb not, O Chief of Men, who remains the same in pleasure and pain, he it is who fits himself for eternal life.

The unreal has no being, the Real no non-being. These two facts the Truth-seers perceive.

Know That which pervades all this to be indestructible. That immutable none can destroy.

It is these bodies of the eternal, indestructible, incomprehensible Embodied that are said to come to an end.

He who considers That to slay and he who considers It to be slain are alike in error. It slays not, nor is It slain.

That is not born, nor does It ever die; nor, having been, does It ever cease to be. That unborn, eternal, abiding, primeval Being is not slain when the body is slain.

Knowing It to be indestructible, eternal, beginningless, immutable, whom can a man slay or cause to be slain, O Son of Pritha?

Just as a person casts off worn-out garments and puts on others that are new, so does the Embodied cast off worn-out bodies and take on new.

Weapons cleave Him not, fire burns Him not, waters drench Him not, wind dries Him not.

Invulnerable He is, not to be burnt, not to be drenched or dried. He is eternal, all pervading, changeless, motionless, enduring.

He is said to be unmanifest, beyond thought, immutable. Knowing Him to be so you should not grieve.

Even if you consider That evermore coming to birth and evermore dying, still should you not grieve, O Mighty-Armed;

For to him who is born death is indeed certain, and to him who dies birth is certain. Therefore should you not grieve for the inevitable.

[47]

Freedom from Passion

Arjuna, puzzled by Krishna's abstract words, asks him for a straightforward description of the man of stable mind: how does he speak, how does he sit, how does he act? Krishna replies that such a man is to be known by inner and not by outward signs. His mind is equanimous, untroubled by joy or sorrow, freed from bondage, withdrawn from outer things, concentrated in the self.

When a man casts out all desires of the mind, O Son of Pritha, and is content in himself he is said to be steadfast in wisdom.

He who is undismayed in grief and controlled amid pleasures, from whom lust, fear and anger have passed away, he it is who is called a Sage of steadfast wisdom.

He who is free from attachment, who accepts good and evil alike without exultation or loathing, his mind it is that is established in wisdom.

He who withdraws his senses from sense-objects as a tortoise draws in its limbs, he it is who is established in wisdom.

Sense objects withdraw from him who abstains from them, but their attraction remains. On seeing the Supreme even this goes.

Even though a man strives and is wise, O Son of Kunti, the impetuous senses forcibly distract his mind.

Restraining them all, let him remain steadfast, concentrated on Me, for he whose senses are under control is established in wisdom.

When the mind dwells on sense-objects attachment to them arises. From attachment springs desire, from desire anger.

From anger springs delusion, from delusion forgetfulness, from forgetfulness weakness of mind; and from weakness of mind a man perishes.

But he who moves among sense-objects with his mind and senses controlled, free from desire and aversion, attains serenity.

In serenity comes the cessation of all grief, for the mind of such a one is soon stabilised.

The uncontrolled have no wisdom and the uncontrolled have no concentration. Without concentration there is no peace; and what happiness can there be without peace?

When the mind follows the wandering senses it carries away the understanding, as winds do a ship upon the waters.

Therefore, O Mighty-Armed, he whose senses are withdrawn from sense objects is established in wisdom.

When it is night for all beings the self-controlled is awake; when all beings are awake it is night for the Sage who sees.

He attains peace whom all desires enter as waters do the ocean, leaving it undisturbed though ever being filled, not he who desires desire.

He attains peace who abandons all desires, acting without attachment, free from "I" and "mine."

This is the Divine State (*brāhmī sthitiḥ*), O Son of Pritha, which having attained a man is free from delusion. Abiding in it even at the end [of life] he attains Brahma-Nirvana.

[48]

The Path of Action

In the *Gītā* the word "Samkhya" is used for any way of liberation that relies on intellectual discrimination. If not otherwise qualified, the word "Yoga" means action done as a means of attaining union. Krishna refers to such dedicated action as *karmayoga*, and he devotes much of the third and fourth books to a discussion of its nature. It is not necessary to withdraw from all action, as the *sannyāsin* or ascetic does, in order to be free from the results of action. Since life in the world is impossible without action, the best course is to act without desire.

In this world a twofold path was taught by me of old, O Blameless One; the path of knowledge for introverts and the path of action for extroverts.

Not by refraining from activity does a man attain freedom from action, nor by mere renunciation does he gain perfection.

Indeed, no one can remain even for a moment really inactive, for one is driven helplessly to action by the qualities of Nature.

The deluded person who controls his physical organs but lets his mind brood on the objects of sense is known as a hypocrite.

He it is who excels, Arjuna, who controls his senses with his mind and employs his physical organs in karma yoga without attachment.

Perform your allotted duty, for action is better than inaction. Even the preservation of life in the body is impossible without action.

People in this world are fettered by action unless it is performed as a sacrifice. Therefore, O Son of Kunti, let your action be sacrifice free from attachment. . . .

For him, however, who rejoices only in the Self, is gratified with the Self and content with the Self no action is incumbent.

He has nothing to gain by actions done or to lose by those undone. He is not dependent on any one for the achievement of any object.

Therefore without attachment perform always the actions that are incumbent, for by disinterested activity man attains the Supreme.

It was by action that Janaka and others attained perfection. Perform actions, therefore, you also, as an example to mankind.

[49]

Inner Peace and Joy

One who escapes from attachment by means of the *yoga* of action finds inner peace and joy. The dweller in the body sits in the nine-gated city (the body with its nine apertures) undisturbed by the movements of the organs of sense and action. On occasion, the sage shuts all doors to the outside world and, by means of techniques like breath-control, strives to attain oneness with the Supreme.

Renouncing attachment, yogis engage in activity with the body, the mind (*manas*) the intellect (*buddhi*), or simply the sense organs, for the sake of purification.

He who is integrated in Union (*yuktaḥ*) attains abiding Peace relinquishing attachment to the fruits of action, while the nonintegrated (*ayuktaḥ*) is bound by attachment to the fruits through desire.

The self-controlled one who has mentally renounced all activity dwells peacefully in the city of the nine gates [the body], neither acting nor causing to act.

The Supreme Self (*prabhuḥ*) creates neither agency nor action for people, nor unites action with its fruit; it is one's own nature (*svabhāva*) which does so.

The Universal Self (*vibhuḥ*) takes over neither the evil nor the good of any man. Wisdom (*jñāna*) is veiled by unwisdom (*ajñāna*); thereby are men deluded.

But in those whose unwisdom is destroyed by wisdom, that wisdom, like the sun, reveals the Supreme (*param*).

Mind fixed on That, self merged in That, directed and devoted to That, their sins dissolved by wisdom, they go whence there is no return.

The wise (*paṇḍitāḥ*) see with an equal eye a learned and modest Brahmin, a cow, an elephant, a dog and an outcast.

Even in this life those whose mind is equipoised have overcome phenomenal existence (*sarga*). Flawless and uniform is Brahman; hence in Brahman are they established.

The knower of Brahman, established in Brahman, steadfast and clear of mind, neither exults over a pleasant event nor grieves over an unpleasant.

Unattached to outer contacts, he finds happiness in Self; united with Brahman, he enjoys eternal bliss.

The pleasures of the senses are sources of misery, O Son of Kunti, being ephemeral. A wise man (*budhaḥ*) does not delight in them.

He who, even before being set free from the body, can resist the force of desire and anger is in a state of integration (*yuktaḥ*); such a one is happy.

That yogi whose happiness is inward, whose joy and whose light are inward, attains Brahma-Nirvana and becomes Brahman.

Those Sages (*ṛṣis*) attain Brahma-Nirvana whose imperfections are destroyed, their doubts torn aside, their minds controlled, and who seek the well-being of all creatures.

Brahma-Nirvana lies around those who have freed themselves from anger and desire, who have subdued their minds and have known the Self.

The Sage (*muni*) who, intent on Liberation (*mokṣā*), has overcome desire, fear and anger, who turns away from outer things and sits with gaze fixed between the eyebrows and with out-going and in-coming breath made equal in the nostrils, is for ever free.

Knowing Me as the enjoyer of sacrifices and austerities, the Great Lord of all the worlds, the Friend of all beings, he attains Peace.

[50]

Yoga Meditation

In this passage, Krishna instructs Arjuna in a special technique of yoga meditation. The aspirant is to concentrate on Krishna within. This will lead to absorption in what he calls *brahma-nirvāṇa* ("extinction in the *brahman*"), a term that in effect unites the goals of Buddhism and Vedanta.

Sitting alone, in solitude, the yogi should meditate with body and mind controlled, free from desire and possessiveness.

He should assume a firm posture (*āsana*) in a clean place, neither too high nor too low, on kusha grass covered with a deerskin and a cloth.

Seated there, with concentrated mind, thoughts and senses under control, he should practise yoga to purify himself.

With body, head and neck erect, motionless, gazing at the tip of his nose and not looking about,

Serene and fearless let him sit, firm in his vow of celibacy, with mind controlled and turned to Me, integrated and intent on Me alone.

Thus, ever at one, the yogi of controlled mind attains to the supreme peace of Nirvana, which is in Me.

[51]

The Eternal Path

Krishna gives a more advanced technique of meditation in this passage from the eighth book of the *Gītā*. A *yogī* who passes away while absorbed in perfect concentration reaches a state superior even to the world of the creator-god Brahma. From this state there is no return to the world of birth and death. Krishna, who (as Arjuna will soon learn) is none other than the Supreme, uses the personal pronoun "me" to refer to this status.

I will briefly describe to you that state which knowers of the Vedas call eternal (*akṣara*), which passion-free Sages enter, and in quest of which men observe celibacy (*brahmacarya*).

He who, at the time of leaving the body, closes all the gateways of the senses, fixing his mind in his heart and his life-breath in his head and, remembering Me, utters the Divine Monosyllable OM, he attains the Supreme State.

To him who dwells constantly on Me alone in fixed attention I am readily accessible, O Son of Pritha.

Having attained to Me, the Great Ones (*mahātmas*) do not return to birth, which is the domain of suffering and impermanence, for they have entered the Supreme State.

From Brahmaloka downwards, all worlds involve rebirth, Arjuna; but on attaining to Me, O Son of Kunti, there is no return to birth.

[52]

The Vision of the World-Spirit

The eleventh book of the *Gītā*, here reproduced in its entirety, consists of Krishna's revelation of his universal form to Arjuna. Here, as elsewhere in the *Gītā*, Krishna is referred to as "Sri Bhagavan". Some of the stanzas are spoken by Sanjaya, the charioteer of Dhritarashtra, who recites the entire text of the *Gītā* to him.

Krishna's *visva-rūpa* encompasses the whole universe, which he both creates and destroys. This vision of Krishna as Time the Destroyer Godhead is too much for Arjuna to bear, and he asks to see again the familiar human form of his friend. Krishna complies with this request, and reminds Arjuna at the end that the surest way to attain the vision of the Supreme is by means of love and devotion.

Arjuna said:

By the profound explanation of the Self that you have made out of grace towards me, my delusion has been quite dispelled.

I have heard from you at length of the origin and dissolution of beings, O Lotus-Eyed, as also of Your imperishable Majesty.

As You have declared of Yourself, so it is, Divine Lord. But I long to see Your Heavenly Form, O Supreme Being.

If You deem it possible for me to see it, O Lord, then, Lord of Yoga, show me Your Imperishable Self.

Sri Bhagavan said:

Behold My divine forms, O Son of Pritha, hundreds and thousands of them, of many sorts, many colours, many shapes.

Behold Adityas, Vasus, Rudras, Asvins and Maruts. Behold also, O Bharata, many wonders not seen before.

Behold here today, O Gudakesa, the entire universe, moving

and unmoving and whatever more you would see, all centred in My body.

But you cannot see Me with these eyes of yours. I will give you divine sight: behold My Divine Power.

Thus speaking, O king, Hari, the great Lord of Yoga, showed the son of Pritha the Supreme Divine Form.

With innumerable mouths and eyes, innumerable wondrous sights, innumerable divine ornaments, innumerable divine weapons brandished.

Wearing heavenly garlands and attire, anointed with celestial unguents, wondrous, resplendent, boundless, facing all ways.

If the splendour of a thousand suns were to blaze forth simultaneously in the sky it would be like the splendour of that Great One.

Then in the body of the God of gods the Pandava beheld the entire [universe] in one form divided into many.

The Wealth-Winner (Arjuna), astounded and hair standing on end, bowed his head before the Lord and with joined hands spoke.

Arjuna said:

O God, I see all the gods in Your body as well as the multitudes of beings of all kinds and the God Brahma on his lotus seat and all the Sages and celestial serpents.

I see You of boundless form on every side, with numberless arms, bellies, mouths and eyes, O Lord of the Universe, O Cosmic Form; no end, no middle, no beginning do I see to you.

I see You with diadem, mace and disc, a radiance blazing everywhere, hard to look upon, dazzling like blazing fire and sun, immeasurable.

You are the Eternal Supreme to be realized, the ultimate Treasure of the Universe, the Imperishable, Lord of eternal Dharma. You are, I believe, the Primordial Purusha.

I see You with no beginning, no middle, no end, infinite in power, with countless arms, with the sun and moon for eyes, flaming fire for mouth, scorching this universe with Your radiance.

The space between heaven and earth and all the [four] quarters are pervaded by You alone. At sight of Your wondrous, terrifying form the three worlds tremble.

Behold galaxies of gods entering into You! Some in fear extol You with palms folded, companies of Maharshis and Siddhas crying

"All Hail!" extol You with their hymns.

The Rudras, Adityas, Sadhyas, Viswedevas, the two Asvins, the Maruts, the Ancestors, the hosts of Gandharvas, Yakshas, Asuras and Siddhas, all gaze astounded at You.

O mighty-armed, seeing Your huge form with myriad faces, eyes, feet, with myriad bellies bearing fearful tusks, the worlds are horrified. So too am I.

Seeing You reaching the sky, blazing with many colours, mouth wide open, with large fiery eyes, I am terrified at heart and find no courage or peace, O Vishnu!

Seeing Your jaws terrible with tusks flaming like the fires of Cosmic Death, I find no directions of space and know no peace. Be gracious, O Lord of gods, refuge of the worlds!

And all these sons of Dhritarashtra and hosts of the kings of earth, with Bhishma, Drona, Sutaputra and the warrior chiefs of our side also rush headlong into Your fierce tusked jaws, terrible to behold. Some are to be seen caught in the gaps between the teeth, their heads crushed to powder.

As the torrents of many rivers hasten to the ocean, so do these heroes of the world of men into Your flaming jaws.

As moths plunge swiftly to their doom in a blazing fire, so do these men speed to their doom in Your jaws.

Devouring all the worlds on every side with Your flaming jaws, You lick them up. Your radiance lights the whole world while scorching it, O Vishnu.

Tell me who You are with so terrible a form. I bow down to You, Great God. Be gracious to me. I seek to know You, the Primal Being; I do not know Your nature.

Sri Bhagavan said:

I am Time the mighty Destroyer of worlds engaged now in world destruction. Even without you none of these warriors in hostile armies shall survive.

Arise therefore and win fame. Conquer your enemies and enjoy a prosperous kingdom. By Me alone these have been already slain. Be merely the instrument, Left-Handed One [capable of shooting arrows with the left hand].

Slay Drona, Bhishma, Jayadratha, Karna and other great warriors slain already by Me. Have no fear. Fight and you shall conquer the enemy in battle.

Sanjaya said:

Hearing these words of Kesava, the Crowned One joined his hands and, trembling, prostrated before him again and then said in a choked voice, overcome by fear:

It is but right, O Hrishikesha, that the world is delighted and rejoices in Your praise, the demons flee to all sides in fear and the hosts of the siddhas bow down to You.

Why should they not bow down to You, Great One, Originator even of Brahma? O Unbounded God of gods, Refuge of the worlds, You are the Eternal Being, the Non-Being, and the Supreme beyond both.

You are the Primal God, the Primordial Purusha, the Supreme Refuge of this universe. You are the Knower and what is to be known, the Supreme abode; all this universe is pervaded by You with Your endless forms.

You are Vayu (Wind), Yama (Death), Agni (Fire), Varuna (oceans), the Moon, Prajapati (the First Ancestor) and the Great Grand Sire. Salutations to You! A thousand times and ever again salutations to You.

Salutations to You before, behind and on every side, All-in-all, of endless power, Immeasurable; You pervade all and thus are all.

For whatever I have rashly or lightly said, calling You "Krishna, Yadava, friend," treating You as a friend, ignorant of this greatness of Yours, for any disrespect I have shown in play or repose, when sitting or at meals, O Achyuta, alone or in company, I now implore You, the Immeasurable, for pardon.

You are the Father of this world, of the moving and unmoving, its great and revered Guru. There is none equal to You in the three worlds, who then can surpass You, Lord of Boundless Might?

Therefore, bowing down to You and prostrating my body at Your feet, I crave forgiveness, Adorable Lord. Bear with me, as a father with his son, as a friend with his friend, as a lover with his beloved.

I rejoice that I have seen what none have seen before, and yet my mind is shaken with fear. Show me only Your usual form. Be gracious, Lord God, Refuge of the worlds.

Let me see You in the same form as before, four-armed wearing a crown, and with mace and disc in hand, O Thousand-Armed Cosmic Form.

Sri Bhagavan said:

Out of grace for you, I have shown you by My yogic power this supreme form of Mine, splendid, universal, infinite, primeval, never before seen by any other.

I am not to be seen in such form by any other than you, great hero of the Kurus, whether through the Vedas or through sacrifice or study [of scriptures], or gift or ritual or severe austerity.

Be not afraid or bewildered at having seen this terrible form of Mine. With fear dispelled and heart made glad behold My usual form again.

Sanjaya said:

Having spoken thus to Arjuna, Vasudeva showed again in usual form. In that gentle form the Great One calmed his fear.

Arjuna said:

Now that I again see this gentle human form of Yours, O Janardana, I am composed again and restored to my own nature.

Sri Bhagavan said:

Very hard it is to see the form of Mine which you have seen. Even the gods ever long to see this form.

I am not to be seen in such form as you have seen Me by study of the Vedas or by austerity or gifts or sacrifice.

Only by unswerving devotion can I be known and truly seen in this form, Arjuna, and even be entered into, O Tormentor of the Foe.

He who performs actions for Me, takes Me for his Goal, is devoted to Me and is free from attachment and aversion towards all beings, he comes to Me, O Pandava.

[53]

Different Forms of Practice

The twelfth book of the *Gītā* deals with the yoga of devotion, *bhakti-yoga*. In this passage, it offers a variety of practices for those who follow this path. The easiest and most direct way is to surrender oneself to Krishna. If this proves impossible, one can try various yogic techniques, or simply do all one does as an offering to the Supreme.

Those who fixing their minds on Me meditate on Me with steadfastness and who have supreme faith, I deem to be the highest among yogins.

Those who steadfastly meditate on the Imperishable, the Indescribable, the Unmanifest, Immutable, Omnipresent, the Unthinkable, stable and Immovable, Eternal, — having their senses under control, even-minded under all circumstances, engaged in the welfare of all beings — they reach only Me.

More difficult is the task of those whose minds are set on the Unmanifest; the Goal, the Unmanifest, is hard to attain for the embodied beings.

But those who surrendering all actions to Me, meditate upon Me and worship Me with single-minded devotion, whose hearts are fixed on Me, I speedily rescue from the ocean of death-bounded samsara.

Fix your thought on Me alone, center your mind and reason on Me. Then, without doubt, you will abide in Me.

If you cannot fix your mind steadily on Me, Oh Dhananjaya, then seek to reach Me by the yoga of constant practice (*abhyāsayoga*).

If you are unable to practise that yoga either, then practise performing actions for My sake. This will help you to attain perfection.

If you are unable to do even this, then taking refuge in Me, self-controlled, abandon the fruit of all actions [performed entirely without selfish motives as service to God].

Better indeed is knowledge than practice; meditation better than knowledge; the abandonment of the fruit of action better than meditation. Peace results from this abandonment.

[54]

The Cosmic Divine

In the *Kaṭha Upaniṣad*, the universe is described as a giant asvattha or fig tree, with its roots above (in the transcendent) and its branches below (in the world of life and death). Borrowing this image, the *Gītā* transforms it into a symbol of the manifested world, which must be cut down with the axe of non-attachment. By this means, the soul attains liberation. Krishna further explains that each soul is a small part of himself. After occupying a body for a time, the soul leaves it for another. Only those who strive for union with the Supreme are aware of the soul's comings and goings.

The asvattha [tree] with roots above and branches below is said to be imperishable. The Vedas are its leaves. He who knows this knows the Vedas.

Its branches spread above and below, growing well on *guṇas* (the three qualities of Prakriti). The objects of the senses are its foliage and its roots stretch below in the world of men leading to actions which are binding.

Its [real] form cannot be ascertained here, nor its end, nor beginning, nor support. After cutting this deep-rooted asvattha tree with the strong [unfailing] sword of non-attachment, that state should be sought on attaining which one does not return [to this world], saying "I surrender myself completely to that Supreme Being (Purusha) from which this ancient activity [of creation] began to flow."

The undeluded, those who are free from pride and ignorance, who have overcome the evil of attachment, who are ever devoted to the Self, who have turned away from desires and are entirely beyond the dualities of pleasure and pain, attain that imperishable state.

Neither sun, nor moon, nor fire illumine this state, on attaining which one does not return. And this is My supreme abode.

A fragment of Myself, eternal [like Myself] becomes the jiva (the individual self) in the world and attracts to itself the six sense-organs, including the mind, based on Prakriti.

When the Lord (Ishwara) takes a body and also when He leaves it [*lit.* ascends] He takes these [the six organs] and departs, like the wind that takes [and wafts] scents from their receptacles [flowers, etc.].

Presiding over the ear, the eye, the skin, the tongue, the nose and the mind He enjoys the sense-objects [so long as he is in a body].

The extremely deluded persons do not perceive Him [as the indwelling Self] when in association with the gunas He ascends [from a body] or dwells [in one] or experiences [sense-objects]; only those who have the eye of wisdom see.

With great effort Yogis see Him dwelling within themselves, but unenlightened persons, even if they strive, cannot see Him.

The lustre in the sun which illumines the whole world and that which is in the moon and the fire, know that to be My lustre.

[55]
The Supreme Secret

In the closing passage of the *Gītā*, Krishna sums up the various means by which union with the Supreme can be attained. The aspirant can proceed by way of meditative knowledge or love of God or selfless work. But the best way of all is to surrender everything to Krishna. This, Krishna tells Arjuna, is the supreme secret. Whatever happens on the battlefield, Arjuna is sure to attain the highest, because Krishna looks after those who are dear to him.

Know from Me in brief, O son of Kunti, how a man, who has attained perfection, realizes Brahman, — which is the highest consummation of the yoga of wisdom.

One endowed with extremely pure reason, controlled in mind by steadfastness and abandoning objects of senses such as sound etc., dispelling attachment and aversion, resorting to a solitary place, eating little, speech, body and mind subdued, always engages in the yoga of meditation and is dispassionate leaving aside egoism, violence, arrogance, lust, anger and greed, free from the feeling of "mine" and full of peace, he is fit for becoming One with Brahman.

Becoming One with Brahman, the serene self neither grieves nor desires. Treating all alike, he attains the highest devotion to Me.

Through devotion he knows Me and My nature in truth and [thus] knowing Me in truth [or in essence] he forthwith enters into Me.

And he, performing all actions with Me as his refuge and support, through My grace attains the eternal and imperishable abode.

Mentally surrendering all actions to Me, regarding Me as the Supreme, always concentrating your mind on Me, fix your heart ever on Me.

With mind reposed in Me, you will cross over all the difficulties through My grace; but if you do not hear Me through egotism, you will perish.

If out of egotism you decide not to fight, this resolve of yours is in vain [or futile]. Nature (Prakriti) will compel you to fight.

That which you do not wish to perform from delusion, O son of Kunti, bound as you are by your duty inherent in your nature, you shall do even against your will.

The Lord resides in the hearts of all, O Arjuna, revolving all creatures by Prakriti as if mounted on a machine.

Surrender unto Him with all your heart, O Bharata. Through His grace you will attain supreme peace and the perennial abode.

This wisdom, the secret of secrets, I have divulged to you. Reflect over this thoroughly and act as you please.

Listen again to My Supreme Word, the most secret of all. I shall tell you what is beneficial to you as you are My beloved and firm friend.

Fix your thought on Me; be devoted to Me; worship Me and bow down to Me. Indeed [thus] you will reach Me. This I truly promise to you, [as] you are dear to Me.

Leaving aside all dharmas, surrender to Me, as your sole Refuge. I shall relieve you of all [your] sins; do not grieve.

FURTHER READING

Source Materials

Arthur Osborne and G. V. Kulkarni, trans. *The Bhagavad Gita*. Tiruvannamalai: Sri Ramanasramam, 1973.

Other Works

Sri Aurobindo, *Essays on the Gita*. Pondicherry: Sri Aurobindo Ashram, 1997.

W. M. Callewaert and Shilanand Hemraj, *Bhagavadgītānuvāda: A Study in Transcultural Translation*. Ranchi: Satya Bharati Publication, 1983.

Sources of Texts and Translations

46 *Bhagavad Gītā* 2.11–27	Osborne and Kulkarni 10–13
47 *Bhagavad Gītā* 2.55–72	Osborne and Kulkarni 19–21
48 *Bhagavad Gītā* 3.3–9, 17–20	Osborne and Kulkarni 22–23, 25
49 *Bhagavad Gītā* 5.11–29	Osborne and Kulkarni 38–42
50 *Bhagavad Gītā* 6.10–15	Osborne and Kulkarni 44–45
51 *Bhagavad Gītā* 8.11–16	Osborne and Kulkarni 59–60
52 *Bhagavad Gītā* 11	Osborne and Kulkarni 80–88
53 *Bhagavad Gītā* 12.2–12	Osborne and Kulkarni 89–90
54 *Bhagavad Gītā* 15.1–12	Osborne and Kulkarni 102–04
55 *Bhagavad Gītā* 18.50–66	Osborne and Kulkarni 123–25

7

तद् यथापि नाम शारिपुत्र सूर्यमण्डलमुदयत् सर्वजम्बुद्वीपमवभासेन स्फुटीकरोति। एवमेव शारिपुत्र बोधिसत्त्वो महासत्त्वः षट्सु पारमितासु चरित्वा सत्त्वान् परिपाच्य बुद्धक्षेत्रं परिशोध्य . . . अपरिमाणान् सत्त्वान् परिनिर्वापयति।

The sun, when it has risen, radiates its light over the whole of the continent of Jambudvipa. Just so the Bodhisattva, after he has accomplished the practices which lead to the full enlightenment of Buddhahood, leads countless beings to Nirvana.

Pañcaviṁśatisāhasrikā Prajñāpāramitā

Mahayana & Vajrayana Buddhism

UNDER the patronage of Ashoka, Buddhism spread throughout north and south India and into Sri Lanka. This expansion continued even after the fall of the Mauryan Dynasty in the middle of the second century BCE. By that time the *dharma* had become particularly well entrenched in the North-West. This region was a hub of international trade, and the new religion followed the caravans into Central Asia and points east and west. At the same time, ideas from Persia, Greece and the Middle East followed the trade routes back to India, and had some influence on the doctrines that were developing in the land of the historical Buddha.

The growth of trade meant also that there was a large class of people ready to support a religious and social system that rejected the brahminical claim to divinely sanctioned status. Thanks to mercantile and state patronage, *vihāra*s of brick and stone replaced the temporary structures meant to shelter wandering monks during the monsoon. Some of these *vihāra*s included *stupa*s or shrines that housed relics of the Buddha. Around such centres, communities of monks grew up that became focal points for the intellectual and spiritual developments that marked the next stage of Buddhist history.

During the first five centuries after the Buddha's *parinirvāṇa*, a series of councils were held to settle controversial issues. The details of these councils are now uncertain, but it is apparent that new approaches were developing, some of which were unacceptable to the School of the Elders (*Sthaviravāda*, Pali: *Theravāda*). The end result was a schism between the older schools, represented primarily by the Theravada, and the newer ones, which called themselves the *Mahāyāna* or Great Vehicle.

The original differences between the schools seem to have been over relatively minor matters of monastic discipline; but before long new texts offering a new set of ideas were competing with the Pali Canon. Written in Sanskrit, these "Words of the Buddha" (*Buddhavacana*s) were supposed to have been spoken by the Buddha to close disciples but not made public during his lifetime. Those who accepted the new teachings regarded the older ones not as false but incomplete, a lesser vehicle or *Hīnayāna*.

The doctrines of the Theravada and the Mahayana differ chiefly in their views of the nature of the Buddha and of the goal of Buddhist practice. In the texts of the Theravada, the Buddha is a human who achieved *nirvāṇa* by his own effort; he thus became a perfected being or *arhat*. On his death, he obtained the full liberation of *parinirvāṇa*. Freed from rebirth, he had no further contact with the world. Those who accepted the Buddha's *dharma* could also become *arhat*s by following the eightfold path. When they died, they too were lost to the world. To followers of the Mahayana, it was inconceivable that the Buddha could cease to be. His body was the manifestation of an immortal principle. This idea of a transcendent Buddha developed into that of the "five celestial Buddhas", and eventually into innumerable Buddhas; at the same time, the *bodhisatta*s or Buddhas-to-be of Theravada lore evolved into heavenly *bodhisattva*s, "those whose essence is enlightenment".

The bodhisattva ideal became the distinctive term of the Mahayana. On the threshold of *nirvāṇa*, the bodhisattva turns back, postponing his own salvation until all sentient beings have been saved. Great bodhisattvas like Manjusri ("Gentle Glory") and Avalokitesvara ("He who looks down") are not just models of conduct and attainment, but responsive godheads who can be approached by means of devotion. In their wisdom and mercy, they use appropriate methods or "skilful means" (*upāyakauśalya*) to help suffering humanity.

To some extent, these Mahayana doctrines may have arisen or developed under the influence of ideas originating in Persia or further west, just as the religions of those regions were influenced by Mahayana concepts. There may, in addition, have been mutual exchanges between the indigenous devotional cults of the shaivas and bhagavatas (see Parts 8 and 9) and the devotional strand of the Mahayana. But for the most part, the growth of Mahayana was a natural development of Buddhism. The ideal of the *arhat* began to seem too austere, the goal of personal salvation too selfish, to have been the full message of the Buddha, who after all had been driven by *karuṇā* or compassion to give his teachings to humanity.

The Buddha of the Mahayana exists in three dimensions: earthly, heavenly, and transcendental. In each sphere, he has a corresponding body: the *nirmāṇakāya* or physical body, the *sambhogakāya* or heavenly body of bliss, and the *dharmakāya* or cosmic body. In the last, he is always present in his true nature; in the first, he manifests among creatures to teach them the *dharma*; in the second, he enjoys heavenly bliss and gives to the Bodhisattvas "the doctrine which is associated with the six Perfections and which ends in the Knowledge of the Omniscient One after the attainment of the supreme and perfect *bodhi*" (*Saddharma-puṇḍarīka Sūtra*, section 17).

Everyone who enters the Mahayana becomes a bodhisattva in principle; but there are ten *bhūmi*s or stages of bodhisattvahood that must be passed through before the highest is reached. These stages are described differently in different scriptures, but they always involve a graded cultivation of the necessary qualities and attitudes. Mahayana authors, with their fondness for numbered lists, specify thirty-seven "*dharma*s" (practices and principles) needed for the attainment of enlightenment. First on most of the lists are the four *smṛti-upasthāna*s: attending carefully to one's body, feelings, thoughts, and mental phenomena. (These are the same as the four *satipaṭṭhāna*s of the Theravada; see selection 36.) The *smṛti-upasthāna*s are followed by the four right efforts, the four steps to psychic power, the five special qualities, the five special powers, the seven factors or conditions of enlightenment, and finally the elements of the eightfold path.

The fully developed Bodhisattva is possessed of six or ten perfections (*pāramitā*s). The six primary ones — the main factors in the bodhisattva's discipline — are the perfections of generosity, virtue, patience, courage, meditation, and wisdom. These are described in great detail, and at considerable length, in various Mahayana writings. One entire class of texts, representing the first stage of Mahayana literature, deals especially with the Perfection of Wisdom, *prajñāpāramitā*.

The most important *sūtra*s of the *Prajñāpāramitā* school were written between 100 BCE and 150 CE. Their principal contribution to Buddhist doctrine and practice is the concept of *śūnyatā* or emptiness. Given classic formulation in the *Heart Sutra* and other *Prajñāpāramitā* texts (see selections 56 and 58), *sūnyatā* became the central idea of the *Mādhyamika* school of philosophy, as developed by Nagarjuna and his followers. The other main school of Mahayana philosophy, the *Yogācāra* or *Vijñānavāda*, deals centrally with the idea of "mind-itself", which had been hinted at earlier in the *Laṅkāvatāra Sūtra* (selections 66, 67). A third important trend, synthesising much of what came before, looks back to the *Saddharma-puṇḍarīka Sūtra* or *Lotus Sutra* (selections 63, 64). This scripture is especially popular in China and Japan, as is the *Vimalakīrti Sūtra* (selection 65), which shows that a gifted lay practitioner is not inferior to the greatest Bodhisattvas.

The history of Mahayana Buddhism in South Asia lasted close to a millennium. During much of this period, it and the Theravada coexisted peacefully, monks of both schools sometimes living together in the same monasteries. Before it died out in its homeland in the twelfth century, Buddhism had become a pan-Asian phenomenon. The Mahayana entered Central Asia before the start of the Common Era, and from there spread to China, Korea and Japan. In the seventh century, a special type of the Mahayana known as the Vajrayana (see below) was transmitted from Bengal to Tibet. Buddhists in many of these places venerate adepts of Indian origin as the bringers of the *dharma* to their countries; and they all honour India as the home of the historical Buddha.

PRAJNAPARAMITA TEXTS

Prajñāpāramitā, the Perfection of Wisdom, is one of the six chief "perfections" of the bodhisattva. The term gave its name to a class of Buddhist Sanskrit literature that began to appear around the first century BCE, and to the school of the Mahayana based on it. Of unknown authorship, the *Prajñāpāramitā* texts are sometimes attributed to the philosopher Nagarjuna (see Chapter 10). They include the early *Aṣṭasāhasrikā-prajñāpāramitā Sūtra* or *Perfection of Wisdom Sutra in 8,000 Lines*, and later works like the *Śatasāhasrikā-prajñāpāramitā Sūtra* or Perfection of Wisdom Sutra in 100,000 Lines. The number and size of these texts necessitated the creation of epitomes and digests. The most famous of these is the *Prajñāpāramitā-hṛdaya-sūtra* or *Sutra on the Heart of the Perfection of Wisdom*, generally known in English as the *Heart Sutra*.

[56]

The Heart Sutra

Set in the form of a speech by the Bodhisattva Avalokitesvara to Sariputra, a disciple of the Buddha, the *Heart Sutra* gives in brief the fundamentals of Mahayana doctrine from the point of view of the *Prajñāpāramitā* school. All is emptiness: the five "heaps" or *skanda*s that make up the individual are empty, the innumerable "*dharma*s" or constituents of phenomenal existence are likewise empty — yet this emptiness is not different from form. The closing *mantra* (rendered "spell" by the translator) is believed to have great salvific powers. The Sanskrit text is here translated in its entirety by Edward Conze.

Homage to the Perfection of Wisdom, the lovely, the holy!

Avalokita, the holy Lord and Bodhisattva, was moving in the deep course of the wisdom which has gone beyond. He looked down from on high; he beheld but five heaps; and he saw that in their own being they were empty. Here, O Sariputra, form is emptiness and the very emptiness is form; emptiness does not differ from form, nor does form differ from emptiness; whatever is form, that is emptiness, whatever is emptiness, that is form. The same is true of feelings, perceptions, impulses and consciousness. Here, O Sariputra, all dharmas are marked with emptiness, they are neither produced nor stopped, neither defiled nor immaculate, neither deficient nor complete. Therefore, O Sariputra, where there is emptiness there is neither form, nor feeling, nor perception, nor impulse, nor consciousness; no eye, or ear, or nose, or tongue, or body, or mind; no form, nor sound, nor smell, nor taste, nor touchable, nor object of mind; no sight-organ element, and so forth, until we come to: no mind-consciousness element; there is no ignorance, nor extinction of ignorance, and so forth, until we come to, there is no decay and death, no extinction of decay and death; there is no suffering, nor origination, nor stopping, nor path; there is no cognition, no attainment and no non-attainment.

Therefore, O Sariputra, owing to a Bodhisattva's indifference to any kind of personal attainment, and through his having relied on the perfection of wisdom, he dwells without thought-coverings. In the absence of thought-coverings he has not been made to tremble, he has overcome what can upset, in the end sustained by Nirvana. All those who appear as Buddhas in the three periods of time,—fully awake to the utmost, right and perfect enlightenment because they have relied on the perfection of wisdom. Therefore one should know the Prajnaparamita as the great spell, the spell of great knowledge, the utmost spell, the unequalled spell, allayer of all suffering, in truth,—for what could go wrong? By the Prajnaparamita has this spell been delivered. It runs like this: Gone, gone, gone beyond, gone altogether beyond, O what an awakening, all hail!

[57]

The Perfection of Patience

A second important digest of *Prajñāpāramitā* thought is the *Vajracchedikā-prajñāpāramitā-sūtra* or "Diamond-cutter Sutra", generally known in English as the *Diamond Sutra*. It was composed before 400 CE, when a Chinese translation appeared. The text remains popular in East Asia, being particularly well respected by the Zen school of Japan. The subject of the passage reproduced below is the perfection of patience or forbearance (*kṣānti pāramitā*), the third of the six perfections of the Bodhisattva. Alluding to incidents in his former lives, the Buddha explains that to have perfect patience is the same as having no self. Freed from personal reactions, the Bodhisattva can lift up his thought to supreme enlightenment. Translated by Edward Conze.

THE LORD: A Tathagata's perfection of patience is really no perfection. Because, Subhuti, when the king of Kalinga cut my flesh from every limb, at that time I had no notion of a self, or of a being, or of a soul, or of a person, nor had I any notion or non-notion. And why? If, Subhuti, at that time I had had a notion of self, I would also have had a notion of ill-will at that time. If I had had a notion of a being, of a soul, of a person, then I also would have had a notion of ill-will at that time. And why? By my superknowledge I know the past, five hundred births, and how I have been the Rishi, "Preacher of Patience". Then also I have had no notion of a self, or of a being, or a soul, or a person. Therefore then, Subhuti, a Bodhisattva, a great being should, after he has got rid of all notions, raise his thought to the supreme enlightenment. Unsupported by form a thought should be produced, unsupported by sounds, smells, tastes, touchables or mind-objects a thought should be produced, unsupported by dharma a thought should be produced, unsupported by no-dharma a thought should be produced, unsupported by anything a thought should be produced. And why? What is supported has no support.

[58]

Emptiness

Śunyatā or emptiness is the key concept of the *Prajñāpāramitā* school and of the Madhyamika philosophy that is based on it. An extension of the Theravada notion of "no-self", *śūnyatā* implies that things and beings lack independent reality. The comprehension of this concept frees one from attachment to the things of the world. So viewed, the Mahayana doctrine of *śūnyatā* has an ethical force similar to that of the power of *samatā* or equality of the *Bhagavad Gītā*, e.g. 12.18–19: "The one who is equal to friend and foe, honour and insult, heat and cold, pleasure and pain, free from attachment, accepting equally praise and blame, silent, content with whatever comes, homeless, firm in mind, full of devotion, that one is dear to Me [Krishna]." The *Gītā* and the *Prajñāpāramitā* school were roughly contemporaneous. The following passage from *Prajñāpāramitā* literature is taken from the *Śikṣāsamuccaya*, an eighth-century anthology compiled by the philosopher Shantideva (see Chapter 10). Translated by Edward Conze.

One who is convinced of the emptiness of everything is not captivated by worldly dharmas, because he does not lean on them. When he gains something he does not rejoice, when he does not gain it he is not depressed. Fame does not make him proud, lack of fame does not depress him. Scorn does not cow him, praise does not win him over. Pleasure does not attract, pain does not repel him. One who in such a way is not captivated by the worldly dharmas is said to be one who knows emptiness. So one who is convinced of the emptiness of everything has no likes or dislikes. For he knows that that which he might like is just empty, and he sees it as just empty. But one does not know emptiness if he likes or dislikes any dharma. Neither does one know it if he quarrels or disputes with anyone. For one would know that that also is just empty, and would see it as just empty.

[59]

Suchness

Another important term in *Prajñāpāramitā* and other Mahayana literature is *tathatā* or "suchness". Suchness is simply the way things are. In this passage from the *Aṣṭasāhasrikā-prajñāpāramitā Sūtra*, the Buddha equates *tathatā* with supreme enlightenment, which is beyond the reach of words. The Bodhisattva approaches, but does not enter, supreme enlightenment by "dwelling in" mental activities connected with Suchness. Translated by Edward Conze.

SUBHUTI: It is wonderful to see the extent to which the Tathagata has demonstrated the true nature of all these dharmas, and yet one cannot properly talk about the true nature of all these dharmas (in the sense of predicating distinctive attributes to separate real entities). As I understand the meaning of the Tathagata's teaching, even all dharmas cannot be talked about in any proper sense?

THE LORD: So it is, for one cannot properly express the emptiness of all dharmas in words.

SUBHUTI: Can something have growth, or diminution, if it is beyond all distinctive words?

THE LORD: No, Subhuti.

SUBHUTI: But if there is no growth or diminution of an entity which is beyond all distinctive words, then there can be no growth or diminution of the six perfections. And how then could a Bodhisattva win full enlightenment through the force of these six perfections, if they do not grow, and how could he come close to full enlightenment, since, without fulfilling the perfections, he cannot come close to full enlightenment?

THE LORD: So it is, Subhuti. There is certainly no growth or diminution of a perfection-entity. A Bodhisattva who practises perfect wisdom, who develops perfect wisdom, and who is skilled in means, does obviously not think that "this perfection of giving grows, or diminishes". But he knows that "this perfection of giving is a mere word". When he gives a gift he dedicates to the supreme enlightenment of all beings the mental activities, the productions of thought, the roots of good which are involved in that act of giving. But he dedicates them in such a way that he respects the actual reality of full enlightenment. And he proceeds in the same way when he takes upon himself the moral obligations, when he perfects himself in patience, when he exerts vigour, enters into the trances, practises perfect wisdom, develops perfect wisdom.

SUBHUTI: What then is this supreme enlightenment?

THE LORD: It is Suchness. But Suchness neither grows nor diminishes. A Bodhisattva, who repeatedly and often dwells in mental activities connected with that Suchness, comes near to the supreme enlightenment, and he does not lose those mental activities again. It is certain that there can be no growth or diminution of an entity which is beyond all words, and that therefore neither the perfections, nor all dharmas, can grow or diminish. It is thus that, when he dwells in mental activities of this kind, a Bodhisattva becomes one who is near to perfect enlightenment.

[60]

Contemplation of Thought

Like many other mystical teachings, the texts of *Prajñāpāramitā* school are much concerned with the relation between thought and that which is beyond thought's range. This passage from the

Śikṣāsamuccaya gives a method of introspection similar to the "mindfulness" or *vipassanā* meditation of the Theravada (see selection 36). The practitioner is encouraged to plumb the nature of thought; this leads to the discovery that thought is not really different from its object. Translated by Edward Conze.

He searches all around for his thought. But what thought? It is either passionate, or hateful, or confused. What about the past, future or present? What is past that is extinct, what is future that has not yet arrived, and the present has no stability. For thought, Kasyapa, cannot be apprehended, inside, or outside, or in between both. For thought is immaterial, invisible, non-resisting, inconceivable, unsupported and homeless. Thought has never been seen by any of the Buddhas, nor do they see it, nor will they see it. And what the Buddhas never see, how can that be an observable process, except in the sense that dharmas proceed by way of mistaken perception? . . .

Thought, though one searches for it all round, cannot be found. What cannot be found, that cannot be apprehended. What cannot be apprehended, that is not past, future or present. What is not past, future or present, that is beyond the three dimensions of time. What is beyond the three dimensions of time, that neither is nor is not.

Searching for thought all round, he does not see it within or without. He does not see it in the skandhas, or in the elements, or in the sense-fields. Unable to see thought, he seeks to find the trend of thought, and asks himself: Whence is the genesis of thought? And it occurs to him that "where there is an object, there thought arises". Is then the thought one thing, and the object another? No, what is the object, just that is the thought. If the object were one thing, and the thought another, then there would be a double state of thought. So the object itself is just thought. Can then thought review thought? No, thought cannot review thought. As the blade of a sword cannot cut itself, as a finger-tip cannot touch itself, so a thought cannot see itself. Moreover, vexed and pressed hard on all sides, thought proceeds, without any staying power, like a monkey or like the wind. It ranges far, bodiless, easily changing, agitated by the objects of sense, with the six sense-fields for its sphere, connected with one thing after another. The stability of thought, its one-pointedness, its immobility, its undistraughtness, its one-pointed calm, its non-distraction, that is, on the other hand, called mindfulness as to thought.

[61]
The Perfection of Meditation

The fifth perfection of the Bodhisattva is *dhyāna-pāramitā*, the Perfection of meditation. In this passage from the *Śikṣāsamuccaya*, the Buddha explains to Subhuti how an aspirant Bodhisattva develops perfect meditation by means of mindfulness, and through perfect meditation gains perfect equanimity. Translated by Edward Conze.

THE LORD: When he practises the perfection of meditation for the sake of other beings his mind becomes undistracted. For he reflects that "even worldly meditation is hard to accomplish with distracted thoughts, how much more so is full enlightenment. Therefore I must remain undistracted until I have won full enlightenment." . . . Moreover, Subhuti, a Bodhisattva, beginning with the first thought of enlightenment, practises the perfection of meditation. His mental activities are associated with the knowledge of all modes when he enters into meditation. When he has seen forms with his eye, he does not seize upon them as signs of realities which concern him, nor is he interested in the accessory details. He sets himself to restrain that which, if he does not restrain his organ of sight, might give occasion for covetousness, sadness or other evil and unwholesome dharmas to reach his heart. He watches over the organ of sight. And the same with the other five sense-organs,—ear, nose, tongue, body, mind.

Whether he walks or stands, sits or lies down, talks or remains silent, his concentration does not leave him. He does not fidget with his hands or feet, or twitch his face; he is not incoherent in his speech, confused in his senses, exalted or uplifted, fickle or idle, agitated in body or mind. Calm is his body, calm is his voice, calm is his mind. His demeanour shows contentment, both in private and public. . . . He is frugal, easy to feed, easy to serve, of good life and habits; though in a crowd he dwells apart; even and unchanged, in gain and loss; not elated, not cast down. Thus in happiness and suffering, in praise and blame, in fame and disrepute, in life or death, he is the same unchanged, neither elated nor cast down. And so with foe or friend, with what is pleasant or unpleasant, with holy or unholy men, with noises or music, with forms that are dear or undear, he remains the same unchanged, neither elated nor cast down, neither gratified nor thwarted. And why? Because he sees all dharmas as empty of marks of their own, without true reality, incomplete and uncreated.

[62]

Perfection of Wisdom

At an early stage of the Perfection of Wisdom literature, the sixth Perfection, *Prajñāpāramitā*, was personified as a goddess. (Later on she became a favourite subject in Buddhist painting and sculpture.) In this passage from the *Aṣṭasāhasrikā-prajñāpāramitā Sūtra*, the Buddha tells Subhuti that the Perfection of Wisdom, is ineffable, yet still attempts to describe her in terms of the fundamental emptiness of the *skandha*s, elements and sense-fields. Translated by Edward Conze.

SUBHUTI: Is it at all possible, O Lord, to hear the perfection of wisdom, to distinguish and consider her, to make statements and to reflect about her? Can one explain, or learn, that because of certain attributes, tokens or signs this is the perfection of wisdom, or that here this is the perfection of wisdom, or that there that is the perfection of wisdom?

THE LORD: No indeed, Subhuti. This perfection of wisdom cannot be expounded, or learnt, or distinguished, or considered, or stated, or reflected upon by means of the skandhas, or by means of the elements, or by means of the sense-fields. This is a consequence of the fact that all Dharmas are isolated, absolutely isolated. Nor can the perfection of wisdom be understood otherwise than by the skandhas, elements or sense-fields. For just the very skandhas, elements and sense-fields are empty, isolated and calmly quiet. It is thus that the perfection of wisdom and the skandhas, elements and sense-fields are not two, nor divided. As a result of their emptiness, isolatedness and quietude they cannot be apprehended. The lack of a basis of apprehension in all Dharmas, that is called "perfect wisdom". Where there is no perception, appellation, conception or conventional expression, there one speaks of "perfect wisdom".

THE LOTUS SUTRA

The *Saddharma-puṇḍarīka Sūtra* or "Sutra of the Lotus of the True Law", generally known in English as the *Lotus Sutra*, took shape over two or three centuries. The early chapters seem to have been composed in the first century BCE, the later ones around the second century of the Common Era. The *sūtra* was translated into Chinese about 250 CE, and remains enormously popular in China and in Japan, where it is the principal text of the Tendai and Nichiren sects. In it the Buddha is presented as an immortal, transcendent being who reveals the highest *dharma* to *arhat*s, *bodhisattva*s, and *buddha*s. His earlier teachings, he explains, were just temporary expedients he had created by his power of "skilful means" (*upāyakauśalya*), just as a father might build one or more toy vehicles to lure his sons out of a burning building.

[63]

The Provisional and the Final Nirvana

In this extract, the Buddha discourses on the difference between the provisional forms of *nirvāṇa*, which are available to those who follow lesser paths, and the final *nirvāṇa*, which is gained by those who see all *dharma*s as one. Translated by Edward Conze.

In the world, deluded by ignorance, the supreme all-knowing one,
The Tathagata, the great physician, appears, full of compassion.

As a teacher, skilled in means, he demonstrates the good Dharma:
To those most advanced he shows the supreme Buddha-enlightenment.

To those of medium wisdom the Leader reveals a medium enlightenment.
Another enlightenment again he recommends to those who are afraid of birth-and-death.

To the Disciple, who has escaped from the triple world, and who is given to discrimination
It occurs: "Thus have I attained Nirvana, the blest and immaculate."

But I now reveal to him that this is not what is called Nirvana,
But that it is through the understanding of all dharmas that deathless Nirvana can be attained.

To him the great Seers, committed to compassion, will say:
"Deluded you are, and you should not think that you have won gnosis.

"When you are inside your room, enclosed by walls,
You do not know what takes place outside, so tiny is your mental power. . . .

"If you wish to win omniscience, then you should aspire to superknowledge,
And then reflect, in the forest, on the emission of the superknowledges,
The pure dharma, by which you will gain the superknowledges."

When he has grasped the meaning [of this advice], and gone to the remote forest, he will reflect, well concentrated,
Before long he attains the five superknowledges, endowed with virtues.

Just so with all the Disciples who have formed the notion that they have attained Nirvana.
To them the Jina teaches This is a temporary repose, not the final Nirvana.

As a device of the Buddhas it was introduced. But outside this principle of all-knowledge,
They teach, there is no [final] Nirvana. Exert yourselves on behalf of that! . . .

And who knows that the triple world, without exception, has such an own-being,
And is neither bound nor freed, he does not discern Nirvana [as separate from the triple world].

He knows that all dharmas are the same, empty, essentially without multiplicity.
He does not look towards them, and he does not discern any separate dharma.

Then, greatly wise, he sees the Dharma-body, completely.
There is no triad of vehicles, but here there is only one vehicle.

All dharmas are the same, all the same, always quite the same.
When one has cognized this, one understands Nirvana, the deathless and blest.

[64]
Devotion to Avalokitesvara

A remarkable feature of *The Lotus Sutra* is the importance it gives to devotion. In the Theravada, as in the Sankhya and Yoga systems, devotion hardly finds a place. There are strands of devotional religion in the vedic *saṁhitā*s and *brāhmaṇa*s, the later *upaniṣad*s, and even in the *Theragāthā*; but in these texts other tools of salvation — ritualistic in the case of the *Ṛg Veda*, discriminative in the case of the *upaniṣad*s and *Theragāthā* — are emphasised. In the last chapters of the *Lotus Sutra* devotion to Avalokitesvara and reliance on his grace are given special emphasis. This may be compared to the exaltation of *bhakti* in the final chapter of the *Bhagavad Gītā*, a contemporary text to which the *Lotus Sutra* is often compared. In this passage from the twenty-fourth chapter of the *sūtra*, Avalokitesvara is extolled as beautiful, powerful and beneficent. Recollection of him and his qualities will lead the worshipper to the goal. Translated by Edward Conze.

O you, whose eyes are clear, whose eyes are friendly,
Whose eyes betray distinguished wisdom-knowledge;
Whose eyes are pitiful, whose eyes are pure,
O you, so lovable, with beautiful face, with beautiful eyes!

Your lustre is spotless and immaculate,
Your knowledge without darkness, your splendour like the sun,
Radiant like the blaze of a fire not disturbed by the wind,
Warming the world you shine splendidly.

Eminent in your pity, friendly in your words,
One great mass of fine virtues and friendly thoughts,
You appease the fire of the defilements which burn beings,
And you rain down the rain of the deathless Dharma.

In quarrels, disputes and in strife,
In the battles of men, and in any great danger,
To recollect the name of Avalokitesvara
Will appease the troops of evil foes.

His voice is like that of a cloud or drum;
Like a rain-cloud he thunders, sweet in voice like Brahma.

His voice is the most perfect that can be.
So one should recall Avalokitesvara.

Think of him, think of him, without hesitation,
Of Avalokitesvara, that pure being.
In death, disaster and calamity
He is the saviour, refuge and recourse.

As he who has reached perfection in all virtues,
Who looks on all beings with pity and friendliness,
Who is virtue itself, a great ocean of virtues,
As such Avalokitesvara is worthy of adoration.

He who is now so compassionate to the world,
He will a Buddha be in future ages.
Humbly I bow to Avalokitesvara
Who destroys all sorrow, fear and suffering.

THE VIMALAKIRTI SUTRA

From the earliest days of Buddhism, a role was given to the lay follower; but in the texts of the Theravada and some forms of the Mahayana, it is understood that the highest goal can only be reached by those who have given up the world. In the *Heart Sutra*, however, the celestial Buddha declares that the goal of enlightened Buddhahood is available to all beings, laypersons no less than monks and nuns. A text composed around the same time as the end of the *Lotus Sutra* assigns an even higher status to the lay practitioner. The *Vimalakīrti-nirdeśa-sūtra* or "Sutra of the Instruction of Vimalakirti", generally known in English as the *Vimalakirti Sutra*, was written in Sanskrit around the beginning of the second century. The original text has been lost, but the *sūtra* is preserved in Chinese, Japanese and Tibetan translations.

[65]

Vimalakirti Replies to the Bodhisattva Manjusri

The Vimalakirti of the *sūtra* is a pious layman living in the city of Vaishali. Learning that this exemplary Buddhist was feeling unwell, the Buddha asked a number of disciples and bodhisattvas to inquire after his health. All replied that they were unworthy of calling on one who had bested them in religious debate in the past. Finally the Bodhisattva Manjusri agrees to speak with Vimalakirti. A conversation ensues in which many points of Mahayana doctrine, such as the concept of Emptiness, are explicated. In the following extract from the fifth chapter of the *sūtra*, Vimalakirti explains to Manjusri the true nature of liberation (*nirvāṇa*), "liberative technique" (*upāya*), and wisdom (*prajñā*). Translated from the Tibetan version by Robert A. F. Thurman.

"What is bondage? And what is liberation? To indulge in liberation from the world without employing liberative technique is bondage for the bodhisattva. To engage in life in the world with full employment of liberative technique is liberation for the bodhisattva. To experience the taste of contemplation, meditation, and concentration without skill in liberative technique is bondage. To experience the taste of contemplation and meditation with skill in liberative technique is liberation. Wisdom not integrated with liberative technique is bondage, but wisdom integrated with liberative technique is liberation. Liberative technique not integrated with wisdom is bondage, but liberative technique integrated with wisdom is liberation.

"How is wisdom not integrated with liberative technique a bondage? Wisdom not integrated with liberative technique consists of concentration on voidness, signlessness, and wishlessness, and yet, being motivated by sentimental compassion, failure to concentrate on cultivation of the auspicious signs and marks, on the adornment of the buddha-field, and on the work of development of living beings — and it is bondage.

"How is wisdom integrated with liberative technique a liberation? Wisdom integrated with liberative technique consists of being motivated by the great compassion and thus of concentration on cultivation of the auspicious signs and marks, on the adornment of the buddha-field, and on the work of development of living beings, all the while concentrating on deep investigation of voidness, signlessness, and wishlessness — and it is liberation.

"What is the bondage of liberative technique not integrated with wisdom? The bondage of liberative technique not integrated with wisdom consists of the bodhisattva's planting of the roots of virtue without dedicating them for the sake of enlightenment, while living in the grip of dogmatic convictions, passions, attachments, resentments, and their subconscious instincts.

"What is the liberation of liberative technique integrated with wisdom? The liberation of liberative technique integrated with wisdom consists of the bodhisattva's dedication of his roots of virtue for the sake of enlightenment, without taking any pride therein, while forgoing all convictions, passions, attachments, resentments, and their subconscious instincts."

THE LANKAVATARA SUTRA

The *Saddharma-laṅkāvatāra-sūtra*, or "Sutra of the Appearance of the True Law in Lanka", generally known in English as the *Lankavatara Sutra*, was probably written in the fourth century CE. It deals with a variety of Mahayana themes, but is noted especially for its treatment of cognition. The idea of "mind-only", which became central to the Vijnanavada school of philosophy, was presented, somewhat unsystematically, in this *sūtra*. Roughly speaking, the theory of "mind-only" is a form of subjective idealism. No external objects exist, only absolute Mind.

[66]

The Bodhisattva's Self-realisation

In this passage from section 35 of the *sūtra*, the Buddha explains to the bodhisattva Mahamati that realisation of "Mind itself" frees one from "false imaginings" (which are illustrated in the sequel by a series of metaphors: a dream, a painting, water-bubbles, etc.) This realization opens the way to liberation. Translated from the Sanskrit by D. T. Suzuki.

At that time Mahāmati the Bodhisattva-Mahāsattva again said this to the Blessed One: Pray tell me, Blessed One, about the attainment of self-realisation by noble wisdom, which does not belong to the path and the usage of the philosophers; which is devoid of [all such predicates as] being and non-being, oneness and otherness, bothness and not-bothness, existence and non-existence, eternity and non-eternity; which has nothing to do with the false imagination, nor with individuality and generality; which manifests itself as the truth of highest reality; which, going up continuously by degrees the stages of purification, enters upon the stage of Tathagatahood; which, because of the original vows unattended by any striving, will perform its works in infinite worlds like a gem reflecting a variety of colours; and which is manifested [when one perceives how] signs of individuation rise in all things as one realises the course and realm of what is seen of Mind itself, and thereby I and other Bodhisattva-Mahāsattvas are enabled to survey things from the point of view which is not hampered by marks of individuality and generality nor by anything of the false imagination, and may quickly attain supreme enlightenment and enable all beings to achieve the perfection of all their virtues.

Replied the Blessed One: Well done, well done, Mahāmati! and again, well done, indeed, Mahāmati! Because of your compassion for the world, for the benefit of many people, for the happiness of many people, for the welfare, benefit, happiness of many people, both of celestial beings and humankind, Mahāmati, you present yourself before me and make this request. . . .

Mahāmati, since the ignorant and the simple-minded, not knowing that the world is what is seen of Mind itself, cling to the multitudinousness of external objects, cling to the notions of being and non-being, oneness and otherness, bothness and not-bothness, existence and non-existence, eternity and non-eternity, as being characterised by self-nature which rises from discrimination based on habit-energy, they are addicted to false imaginings.

[67]

Words and the Highest Reality

One of the most important problems of the mystic philosopher is the relationship between words and the supreme reality. Under the influence of twentieth-century philosophy, many contemporary theorists assert that all experience, the mystic's included, is linguistically mediated. A number of mystics, however, make the explicit claim that their experiences are ineffable, that is, beyond the range of language. In this selection, the Buddha explains to Mahamati that words cannot express the highest reality, which can only be obtained by inner realisation. Translated by D. T. Suzuki.

Then Mahāmati said: Again, Blessed One, are words themselves the highest reality? or is what is expressed in words the highest reality?

The Blessed One replied: Mahāmati, words are not the highest reality, nor is what is expressed in words the highest reality. Why? Because the highest reality is an exalted state of bliss, and as it cannot be entered into by mere statements regarding it, words are not the highest reality. Mahāmati, the highest reality is to be attained by the inner realisation of noble wisdom; it is not a state of word-discrimination; therefore, discrimination does not express the highest reality. And then, Mahāmati, words are subject to birth and destruction; they are unsteady, mutually conditioning, and are produced by the law of causation. And again, Mahāmati, what is mutually conditioning and produced by the law of causation cannot express the highest reality, because the indications [pointing to the distinction between] self and not-self are non-existent. Mahāmati, words are these indications and do not express [the highest reality].

Further, Mahāmati, word-discrimination cannot express the highest reality, for external objects with their multitudinous individual marks are non-existent, and only appear before us as something revealed out of Mind itself. Therefore, Mahāmati, you must try to keep yourself away from the various forms of word-discrimination.

VAJRAYANA BUDDHISM

Around the fourth century, a new class of Mahayana texts began to appear. Known as *tantra*s, these treatises were concerned with the power of verbal formulas (*mantra*s), sacred diagrams (*yantra*s, *maṇḍala*s), and esoteric worship. The deities to be invoked were forms of the five heavenly Buddhas long familiar to the Mahayana, as well as female energies, called *Tārā*s or Saviouresses, who had become associated with them; but in the *tantra*s these deities were visualised in terrible forms, similar to those of *Śiva* and *Śakti*, the terrible divinities of the tantric cults that began to emerge in Hinduism around this time (see Chapter 8). In both Buddhist and Hindu *tantra*s, the uniting of the male and female principles is seen as the source of cosmic creation. And since all divine principles have their counterparts on the human level, this process can be duplicated by properly initiated worshippers.

The doctrines and practices described in the Buddhist *tantra*s are known as the *vajrayāna* ("path of the thunderbolt"), or *mantrayāna* ("path of the mantra"), or simply as tantric Buddhism. This became the dominant form of the religion in eastern India in the eighth century, and remained active in the region until Indian Buddhism was extinguished four centuries later. By then, the Vajrayana had spread to Tibet, where it merged with other forms of the Mahayana and with traditional Tibetan shamanism to form a distinctive school of Buddhism that persists to this day.

Both Buddhist and Hindu Tantrism drew on a fund of knowledge and practice that had been conserved and transmitted for centuries by aboriginal cults, wandering sages, and mystic schools. The use of spells and the propitiation of wrathful deities is at least as old as the *Atharva Veda*, and texts as diverse as the *upaniṣad*s, the *Yoga Sūtra* and the *purāṇa*s, as well as certain Theravada and Mahayana *sūtra*s, speak of occult powers — *iddhi*s, *ṛddhi*s, *siddhi*s — that sometimes emerge in those who practice spiritual disciplines. These can be deliberately developed in those who desire them, but many masters, like the Buddha of the Pali Canon, advised against their cultivation, since they were no help on the path to *nirvāṇa*, and could become dangerous distractions.

Those who formulated the Buddhist *tantra*s saw the question from another point of view. All available energies should be put to work in the difficult task of liberation. It is a central doctrine of the Mahayana that enlightenment (*nirvāṇa*) is not different from the world (*saṁsāra*). It follows that the things and forces of the world can be used to achieve liberation. By means of esoteric practices, the human body, which is a microcosm of the universe, can be filled with energy and bliss. Even things usually regarded as the antithesis of spirituality, such as sensory and sensual pleasures, can be used to obtain freedom, as a thorn can be used to remove another thorn. It is only a step from this to the idea that it is *only* through enjoyment of what is forbidden by conventional society, as well as conventional Buddhism, that liberation can be achieved. All forms of discipline, asceticism and self-control are useless. It is "by the enjoyment of all desires, to which one devotes oneself as one pleases . . . that one may speedily gain Buddhahood" (selection 68). This is a far cry from the Buddha's discovery that desire was the cause of the suffering of existence.

The dangers of Tantric Buddhism do not end in the possibility of moral collapse. By opening the door to powerful forces, the tantric can endanger himself and others. Used improperly, a tantric spell might rebound against the user. Performed improperly, a tantric ritual might invoke the wrong sorts of energies, or leave the practitioner depleted or mired in ordinary attachments. To prevent such outcomes, the *tantra*s insist that only those who have been initiated by a qualified guru, and who practise under his or her direction, can safely take up this practice. For this reason these texts were not widely disseminated, but reserved for the use of initiates. Without a guru's instruction, the systems of symbols that make up the texts are meaningless. Accordingly, as a scholar of the Vajrayana notes, "There are serious problems in studying the Tantric literature. Because of the syncretic and deliberately mystifying nature of such texts as the *Guhyasamājatantra*, their sentences, although relatively simple in language complexity, continually need the guru's oral expansion and authoritative commentary" (Wayman 1999: 54). Such expansion and commentary is impossible in an introductory reader like this. The texts that follow are given as examples of a special type of Indian spirituality that to be fully understood would have to be studied in greater depth.

[68]

Supreme Enlightenment

The earliest surviving Buddhist *tantra*, and one of the most important, is the *Guhyasamāja Tantra* or "Treatise of the Secret Conclaves". Composed in Sanskrit in the fourth or fifth century, it is sometimes ascribed to the sage Asanga, who (in history as opposed to myth) was one of the founders of the Yogachara school of philosophy. This extract, comprising the whole of chapter seven of the *tantra*, lays down general principles of tantric practice: the power of *mantras*, the harnessing of desire, the worship of the five meditational Buddhas. Translated from the Sanskrit by David Snellgrove.

Then the Lord who is ruler of the Body, Speech and Mind of all the Tathagatas, expounded this chapter on supreme enlightenment, the mantra-practice of the great sacramental truth.

"By the enjoyment of all desires, to which one devotes oneself just as one pleases, it is by such practice as this that one may speedily gain Buddhahood.

"With the enjoyment of all desires, to which one devotes oneself just as one pleases, in union with one's chosen divinity, one worships oneself, the Supreme One.

"One does not succeed by devoting oneself to harsh discipline and austerities, but by devoting oneself to the enjoyment of all desires one rapidly gains success.

"Don't move your lips for the eating of food you've begged, nor should you be attached to these offerings. It is by moving one's lips in the recitation of mantras that the body becomes whole and confirmed in the enjoyment of all desires.

"One gains enlightenment, when one has first attained to a condition of well-being of Body, Speech and Mind. Otherwise untimely death will certainly bear its fruit in hell.

"Buddhas and Bodhisattvas, followers of the Mantra-practice supreme, have attained to the supreme place of the Dharma by devoting themselves to all desires.

"Those who aspire to the five kinds of knowledge should always devote themselves to the five kinds of desirable things. They should gratify the Bodhisattvas, and gladden them with the sun of enlightenment.

"Knowing Form to be threefold, one should worship it, identifying oneself with the worship, for this is that knowing Lord, the Great Buddha Vairocana.

"Knowing Sound to be threefold, one should entrust it to the divinities, for this is that Lord, the Great Buddha Ratnasambhava.

"Knowing Smell to be threefold, one should entrust it to the Buddhas, Bodhisattvas and the rest, for this is that Lord, the Great Buddha Amitabha.

"Knowing Taste to be threefold, one should entrust it to the divinities, for this is that Lord, the Great Buddha Amoghasiddhi.

"Knowing Touch to be threefold, one should entrust it to one's own Buddha-family, for this is that adamantine Lord, endowed with the form of Akshobhya.

"Form and Sound and the other three, one should always endow with Thought, for of all those Five Buddhas Thought is the secret essence."

[69]

Direct Personal Experience

Among the terrible forms of the Supreme in Tantric Buddhism is Hevajra, an emanation of the celestial Buddha Akshobhya. The *Hevajra Tantra*, composed in the eighth or ninth century, presents a system of tantric practice that includes the recitation of mantras, the creation of consecrated spaces, and mystic sexual rites. The following passage from the eighth chapter of this work gives a typically tantric explanation of the nature of individual consciousness and the means by which it can achieve union with the Supreme. As often in Buddhist Tantrism, the final goal of union is referred to as *mahāmudrā* (the "Great Seal"), which is associated with the female sexual energy and with *Prajñā*, the goddess of Wisdom. Translated from the Sanskrit by G. W. Farrow and I. Menon.

"This whole universe arises from me. The three realms arise from me. I pervade all there is and this visible world consists of nothing else." The yogī who reflects in this manner and attentively practises will without doubt attain the accomplishment, even if he is a person of low merit. He should think in this manner, whether eating, drinking, bathing, awake or asleep. Then the eager seeker of the Mahāmudrā will attain the eternal.

The yogī conceives of the whole of existence in such a way that it is not emanated by the mind. Such an emanation through the understanding of the nature of all things, is no emanation at all.

Whatever exists, moving or stationary, grass, shrubs, creepers etc. are all conceived of as the supreme principle which is one's own very nature.

Among them there is one, higher than which there is no other, the Great Bliss which is known through direct personal experience. The Accomplishment comes about from direct personal experience and emanation is itself one of direct personal experience.

Karma consists of this direct personal experience and Karma arises from perception. One is oneself the Destroyer, the Creator, the King and the Lord.

In that delightful experiential state all passion, anger, envy, delusion and pride cannot even be compared to one-sixteenth part.

The Knowledge that arises from the Source of Nature is space-like and also consists of Means. It is there in the Source of Nature that the three worlds arise having the nature of Wisdom and Means.

Bhagavān is of the nature of Semen; that Bliss is the Beloved. Semen is free from [the notions of] one and many. Originating from the "moment" the bliss is the one supreme erotic delight.

This Knowledge is one of direct personal experience and is beyond the scope of verbal communication. This direct personal experience is the process of empowerment for it is at one with the knowledge of the Omniscient One.

THE WAY OF THE MAHASIDDHAS

Late Buddhist tantric texts mention eighty-four *mahāsiddha*s or "Great Perfected Ones". The term *siddha*, used in Jainism and Hinduism as well as in Buddhism, means a person who has mastered various extraordinary powers, and through them gained access to high spiritual states, and even, it is believed, to physical immortality. The way of the *mahāsiddha*s dispenses with dialectics and intricate practices, promoting instead the natural or easy (*sahaja*) way. The final stage of the path is the attainment of the innate (*sahaja*) nature of existence, which is characterised by *mahāsukha* or "great bliss". Between the eighth and eleventh centuries, a body of literature in the Apabhramsa language was composed in eastern India that was attributed to the Buddhist *mahāsiddha*s. One of the greatest of these

Perfected Ones was Saraha, who, unlike most of the *siddha*s mentioned in conventional lists, was apparently a historical figure.

[70]

As is Nirvana, so is Samsara

Saraha was a contemporary of King Dharmapala, who ruled Bengal from around 770 to 810. His songs are found in the anthology known as *Caryāpada* and in a three-part cycle of his own composition known as the *Dohākoṣa* or "Song Treasury". The songs deal in an accessible way with the great themes of tantric Buddhism: the non-difference of *nirvāṇa* and *saṁsāra*, the mutuality of emptiness and compassion, and the attainment of *mahāsukha* or Great Bliss. These stanzas from the *Dohākoṣa* were translated by David Snellgrove from an early Tibetan translation, which is in a better state of preservation than the Apabhramsa original.

Even as water entering water
Has an identical savour,
So faults and virtues are accounted the same
As there's no opposition between them.

Do not cling to the notion of voidness,
But consider all things alike.
Indeed even the husk of a sesame-seed
Causes pain like that of an arrow.

One thing is so, another is not so.
The action is like that of a wish-granting gem.
Strange how these pandits go to grief through their own errors,
For in self-experience consists this great bliss.

In it all forms are endowed with the sameness of space,
And the mind is held steady with the nature of this same sameness.
When the mind ceases thus to be mind,
The true nature of the Innate shines forth.

In this house and that the matter is discussed,
But the basis of the great bliss is unknown.

The world is enslaved by thought, Saraha says,
And no one has known this non-thought. . . .

As is Nirvana, so is Samsara.
Do not think there is any distinction.
Yet it possesses no single nature,
For I know it as quite pure.

Do not sit at home, do not go to the forest,
But recognize mind wherever you are.
When one abides in complete and perfect enlightenment,
Where is Samsara and where is Nirvana? . . .

He who clings to the Void
And neglects Compassion,
Does not reach the highest stage.
But he who practises only Compassion
Does not gain release from toils of existence.
He, however, who is strong in practice of both,
Remains neither in Samsara nor in Nirvana.

FURTHER READING

Source Materials

Edward Conze, David Snellgrove, et. al., trans., *Buddhist Texts Through the Ages*. Oxford: Bruno Cassirer, 1954.

G. W. Farrow and I. Menon, trans., *The Concealed Essence of the Hevajra Tantra*. Delhi: Motilal Banarsidass, 1992.

Daisetz Teitaro Suzuki, trans., *The Laṅkāvatāra Sūtra: A Mahāyāna Text*. Reprint edition. Delhi: Motilal Banarsidass, 1999.

Robert A. F. Thurman, trans., *The Holy Teaching of Vimalakīrti: A Mahāyāna Scripture*. University Park, PA: Penn State University Press, 1976.

Other Works

Har Dayal, *The Bodhisattva Doctrine in Buddhist Sanskrit Literature*. Reprint edition. Delhi: Motilal Banarsidass, 1999.

Alex Wayman, *Yoga of the Guhyasamājatantra: The Arcane Lore of Forty Verses: A Buddhist Tantra Commentary*. Delhi: Motilal Banarsidass, 1999.

Sources of Texts and Translations

56 *Prajñāpāramitāhṛdaya*	Conze et al. 152–53
57 *Vajracchedikā-sūtra* 14e	Conze et al. 137–38
58 *Śikṣāsamuccaya* 264	Conze et al. 163–64
59 *Aṣṭasāhasrikā* 18.348–51	Conze et al. 179–80
60 *Śikṣāsamuccaya* 233–34	Conze et al. 162–63
61 *Śikṣāsamuccaya* 202–03	Conze et al. 138–39
62 *Aṣṭasāhasrikā* 7.177	Conze et al. 149–50
63 *Saddharmapuṇḍarīka* 5.59–83 passim	Conze et al. 124–27
64 *Saddharmapuṇḍarīka* 24.20–27	Conze et al. 195–96
65 *Vimalakīrti-nirdeśa-sūtra*, ch. 5	Thurman 46–47
66 *Laṅkāvatāra-sūtra* 35	Suzuki 78–79
67 *Laṅkāvatāra-sūtra* 33	Suzuki 77
68 *Guhyasamāja-tantra* 7	Conze et al. 221–23
69 *Hevajra-tantra* 1.8.39–49	Farrow and Menon 101–106
70 *Dohākoṣa* 74–78, 102–03, last	Conze et al. 234, 238, 239

8

श्रुतिस्मृतिपुराणादौ मयैवोक्तं पुरा शिवे।
आगमोक्तविधानेन कलौ देवान् यजेत् सुधीः॥

O Blissful One, I [Shiva] have already foretold in the *vedas*, *smṛtis* and *purāṇas* that in this *kali* age the wise shall worship the gods according to the method enjoined in the *tantras*.

Mahānirvāṇa Tantra 2.8

The Tantras

SANSKRIT texts similar to the Buddhist *tantras*, but promoting the worship of the great gods of Hinduism, began to appear towards the end of the first millennium. The earliest surviving Hindu *tantras* appear to be later than the *Guhyasamāja Tantra* and other early Vajrayana texts, but it does not necessarily follow that Hindu Tantrism derives from the Buddhist variety. Rather, both appear to incorporate elements of earlier systems of practice that may be non-Aryan or even pre-Aryan. Whatever its origins, Tantrism was well established by the eighth century CE, and for the next five centuries was a dominant tendency in Hinduism and Buddhism, and even had some influence on Jainism. Hindu Tantrism was especially strong in the border regions of the North-East, especially Assam and Bengal, and the North-West, notably Kashmir. In these areas it interacted with Buddhist Tantrism, while both forms drew on, and influenced, the religions of Central Asia and Tibet.

Given the number and diversity of Hindu tantric texts, one is obliged to speak not of a single tantric system but of many different ones. To begin with, there are three main classes of tantric literature according to the divinity featured: Shiva, Vishnu or Shakti (the Goddess in the form of power). Most modern writing about Hindu Tantrism has dealt with the shakta schools, and has focused on narrow range of practices, in particular those related to ritual sexuality. In the West, tantric yoga means little more than "the yoga of sex", while in India another stereotype prevails equating

Tantrism with black magic. It is true that some *tantra*s prescribe ritualised sexual practices, but these are directed towards the attainment of beatitude and freedom and not just heightened sexual pleasure. It is also true that tantric spells and diagrams are sometimes used to obtain earthly rewards or inflict harm on others, but such misapplications do not define what Tantrism is any more than stories of alchemists or mad scientists define modern science.

The word *tantra* comes from a root meaning "to spread" or "to expand" and may be understood to mean "that by which knowledge is spread". Many different sorts of works are called *tantra*s; those that form the basis of Hindu Tantrism are ritualistic treatises said to have been revealed by Shiva, Vishnu or the Goddess. Since it rejects the supremacy of the Veda, Tantrism is technically heterodox, though as time went on tantric texts tended to assert that they supplemented but did not supplant the vedic revelation.

The chief purpose of all *tantra*s is to present the rituals of esoteric cults, which are said to be more effective than the rituals of the Veda, particularly in this present, debased age. Generally speaking, the Hindu *tantra*s are anti-ascetic and anti-metaphysical. In contrast to the world-negating attitude of the Vedanta, Jainism, Buddhism and Samkhya – Yoga, Tantrism does not just accept life but embraces it in all its diversity. More: it asserts that the very things that bind ordinary people are means of release to tantric initiates. Sexual energy, for example, should not be shunned but channelled. The body is not an obstacle but a vessel for receiving the bliss and power of the Divine.

The philosophy of the *tantra*s is borrowed from Samkhya – Yoga; but in Tantra the inactive Purusha of Samkhya – Yoga is replaced by the Lord and his Female Power, who in shaiva and shakta Tantrism are called Shiva and Shakti. The world and all it contains is the result of their union. By means of the techniques revealed in the *tantra*s, the human aspirant or *sādhaka* can achieve perfection or *siddhi*.

The bulk of most *tantra*s is made up of rituals and *mantra*s intended to produce specific effects. The language is highly technical and often makes use of opaque symbols that are meant to conceal the inner meaning from the profane. It therefore is essential for the aspirant to be initiated by a competent guru. Mere book learning counts for little, as a tantric text declares: "The fool who, overpowered by greed, acts after having looked up [the matter] in a written book, without having obtained it from the guru's mouth, he also will certainly be destroyed" (Brooks xii).

The golden age of Hindu Tantrism was from around 900 to 1300 CE. This was also, and not by mere coincidence, the golden age of temple-building in India. The Vedic religion had no need of temples. The rituals of mediaeval Hinduism, most of which are based on tantric lore, required permanent sacred structures with halls for congregational ceremonies. The rulers of the kingdoms that succeeded the Gupta dynasty, and contemporary kingdoms in the South, gained glory and merit by constructing temples in accordance with the principles laid down in tantric literature. The images that adorn these structures and are the foci of their worship were also produced in accordance with tantric teachings. The tantric inspiration of the temples of Khajuraho (tenth century) and Konarak (thirteenth century) is obvious; but tantric principles also underlie the less voluptuous iconography of most later Hindu sculpture and architecture, as well as much current Hindu ritual.

Tantric cults became less prevalent after the fourteenth century, due in part to the rise of devotional (*bhakti*) cults; but by then many tantric ideas had been absorbed by mainstream Hinduism. More overt Tantrism survived in the popular yoga movements that began to spread after the eleventh century (see Chapter 12). The songs of Lalla, Kabir, the Tamil *siddha*s and the *bāul*s are all full of tantric motifs.

The selections that follow are intended to provide a general idea of the mediaeval shaiva and shakta tantric traditions. Philosophical passages that give the general principles of the tradition have been given preference over technical ones.

SHAIVA TANTRAS

According to most authorities there are eighteen *śaiva tantra*s, also known as *śaiva āgamas* ("traditional scriptures of the shaiva cults"). Written in Sanskrit in northern India during the second half of the first millennium, they are looked upon as the foundational texts of the school of spiritual philosophy known as Shaiva Siddhanta. Nowadays this term is used mostly of a dualistic school, most of whose texts were written in Tamil in south India. This Tamil Shaiva Siddhanta is often distinguished from the non-dual Shaivism of Kashmir (see Chapter 10); however, the roots of both schools lie in the earlier Sanskrit shaiva *tantra*s, among which the *Kiraṇa Tantra* (fifth to ninth centuries) has an important place.

[71]

The Bound Soul and its Liberation

The philosophy of Shaiva Siddhanta is based on that of the Samkhya. The universe consists of conscious soul and unconscious matter. The supreme soul or *Parama-śiva* is forever free; human and other lower souls are bound. The following passage from the first book of the *Kiraṇa Tantra* explains the nature of this bondage and the way of liberation. It is in the form of a dialogue between Garuda, the winged vehicle of Vishnu, and Shiva. Translated from the Sanskrit by Dominic Goodall.

GARUDA: [I]n order to remove my doubts, tell me what sort of entity is this bound soul (*paśuḥ*)? How is he bound? and how released?

THE LORD: The bound soul is eternal, has no form, is without knowledge, is devoid of activity and of qualities, is impotent and [all-]pervasive. It is situated [variously] in the belly and at the [upper] edge of *māyā* and in deliberation among [effects, which can be grouped under the heading] experience [of accumulated *karman*] and [the faculties of sense and action, which can be grouped under the heading] the means [to experience].

Kalā from Śiva joins this impure [soul]. The bound soul's consciousness is empowered by this [*kalā*], the sphere [of the operation of his senses] is made known by *vidyā* and it is also stained by passion. And matter (*pradhānaṁ ca*), which consists of the *guṇa*s [viz. *sattva*, *rajas* and *tamas*] [is joined with the soul]. And the soul is bound through its connection with the organs [of sense and action] beginning with *buddhi* and with the army [of gross and subtle elements].

Then by the embrace of binding fate it is also bound to that [*karman*] which it has itself accumulated. Because of the effect [of *māyā*] which is the division of time he is deluded in experience by [the *tattva* of] time.

Thus bound with the *tattva*-elements the [soul that is] naturally enveloped [becomes] partially equipped of knowledge, linked to a [gross] body, embraced by experience [generated out] of *māyā* and [thus] absorbed by that [*māyā*].

Then [the soul] experiences his entire experience, composed of happiness and other such [experiences] according to his *karman*.

When [good and bad] actions have become equal because of an intense descent of power [which in turn comes about] through the power of the maturation of *mala*, the soul is initiated by his guru and becomes omniscient like Śiva and devoid of parviscience, filled with the unfolding of the [innate] nature of Śiva and [if he receives the less intense kind of initiation by which he does not immediately relinquish his physical body] then he does not [after death] continue to be involved in *saṁsāra*.

Thus the soul bound by the sequence [of bonds starting with *kalā*] is liberated according to the sequence [of events starting with the maturation of *mala*]. The soul is taught to have three conditions; [that of] the *kevala*, the *sakala* and the pure soul. . . .

[72]

Supreme Delight

The *Kiraṇa Tantra* is one of several shaiva *tantra*s that are spoken of with esteem by the great philosopher and tantric adept Abhinavagupta (see Chapter 10). Another is the *Vijñāna-bhairava*, a short text written in the seventh or eighth century. The name means "the supreme consciousness of Shiva", from *vijñāna*, the highest consciousness, and *Bhairava*, a name of Shiva as the supreme Reality. The *Vijñāna-bhairava* claims to be a summary of the now-lost *Rudrayāmala Tantra*. Written in the form of a dialogue between Shakti and Shiva, it gives in brief 112 techniques of tantric yoga. Eleven of these are explained in the following selection. All show how ordinary physical delight can be raised by tantric concentration to its divine equivalent. Translated from the Sanskrit by Jaideva Singh.

When by stopping the opening of all the senses the current of all sensory activity is stopped, the *prāṇaśakti* moves slowly upward [in the middle *nāḍī* or *suṣumnā* from *mūlādhāra* towards *brahmarandhra*], then in the upward movement of *prāṇaśakti*, there is felt a tingling sensation [at the various stations in the middle *nāḍī*] like the one created by the movement of an ant [over the body]. At the moment of that sensation, there ensues supreme delight.

One should throw [i.e. concentrate] the delightful *citta* in the middle of *vahni* and *viṣa* both ways whether by itself or permeated by *vāyu* (*prāṇic* breath), one would then be joined to the bliss of sexual union.

At the time of sexual intercourse with a woman, an absorption into her is brought about by excitement, and the final delight that ensues at orgasm betokens the delight of Brahman. This delight is [in reality] that of one's own Self.

O goddess, even in the absence of a woman, there is a flood of delight, simply by the intensity of the memory of sexual pleasure in the form of kissing, embracing, pressing, etc.

On the occasion of a great delight being obtained, or on the occasion of delight arising from seeing a friend or relative after a long time, one should meditate on the delight itself and become absorbed in it, then his mind will become identified with it.

When one experiences the expansion of joy of savour arising from the pleasure of eating and drinking, one should meditate on the perfect condition of this joy, then there will be supreme delight.

When the *yogī* mentally becomes one with the incomparable joy of song and other objects, then of such a *yogī*, there is, because of the expansion of his mind, identity with that [i.e. with the incomparable joy] because he becomes one with it.

Wherever the mind of the individual finds satisfaction [without agitation], let it be concentrated on that. In every such case the true nature of the highest bliss will manifest itself.

When sleep has not yet fully appeared, i.e. when one is about to fall asleep, and all the external objects [though present] have faded out of sight then the state [between sleep and waking] is one on which one should concentrate. In that state the Supreme Goddess will reveal Herself.

One should fix one's gaze on a portion of the space that appears variegated with the rays of the sun, lamp, etc. At that very place, the nature of one's essential Self will manifest itself.

SHAKTA TANTRAS

The great gods of purano-tantric Hinduism, Brahma, Vishnu, and Shiva, each have consorts who are considered their active powers. Shiva's is known by various names — Parvati, Uma, Devi, Durga — but these are all different aspects of the one Shakti or Power who is the source of cosmic creation. Cults devoted to Shakti became prominent in north India around 1000 CE. Their *tantra*s, like those of the shaiva cults, place Shiva and Shakti at the head of the cosmic order, but with reversed priority. Shiva is regarded as the cause of bondage, Shakti of liberation.

There are many schools of shakta Tantrism. Among the most prominent are the *kaula* schools, which take their name from *kula*, a word that can mean "grouping", "family", "clan", "spiritual lineage" or "undifferentiated energy". The scriptures of *kaula* Tantrism contain technical descriptions of the rituals preferred by the teachers of this tradition. These include the famous or infamous five M's — ritualised drinking of wine (*madya*), eating of meat, fish and parched grain (*māṁsa*, *matsya* and *mudrā*), and extramarital sexual intercourse (*maithuna*). These acts, all of which break more or less stringent Hindu taboos, are meant to liberate the *sādhaka* or practitioner from the constraints of ordinary morality, clearing the way for the workings of a higher energy. But the texts make it clear that they should only be performed by initiates under the guidance of a guru; otherwise they are simple self-indulgence.

In all forms of Tantrism, great importance is given to body and its perfection. The human organism, which is a microcosm of the universe, is visualised as consisting of five *koṣa*s or "sheaths", only the most outward of which is composed of physical substance. Within the other sheaths are various systems of subtle energies: the five or ten subtle breaths, the thirty-five million *nāḍī*s or channels of subtle force, and the six or seven *cakra*s or plexuses. The Shakti is viewed as lying dormant within the lowest of these *cakra*s, coiled up in the form of a snake. As a result of certain techniques, this *kuṇḍalinī-śakti* can be made to rise. She awakens the energies of all the *cakra*s, rising eventually to the thousand-petalled lotus above the head, bringing boundless knowledge and freedom.

[73]

Contemplation of the Supreme Lord

One of the most important texts of the *kaula* school of shakta Tantrism is the *Kulārṇava Tantra*, which was composed between the tenth and fourteenth centuries. In this selection from the ninth book of that text, Shiva explains to Shakti some of the principles of *kaula yoga*. Translated by Georg Feuerstein.

One should contemplate the supreme Lord [who is] impartite Being-Consciousness-Bliss lacking hands, feet, belly, face, and so forth and consisting entirely of [unmanifest] light.

He does not rise; he does not sink; he does not undergo growth; he does not undergo diminution. Himself being resplendent, he illumines others, without performing [any actions whatsoever].

When the infinite, luminous, pure, transcendental (*agocara*) Being is experienced purely by the mind, then the [arising] wisdom is designated as the Absolute (*brahman*).

The *yogin* who knows the singular splendor (*dhāman*) of the supreme entity (*jīva*), [which is] immovable like stone [or like] the discontinued motion of the wind [i.e., windstillness], is called a knower of Yoga.

That meditation that is devoid of its essence but illuminating and steady like the unruffled ocean is styled "ecstasy" (*samādhi*).

The [ultimate] Reality shines forth of itself, not by any mental effort (*cintana*) whatsoever. When Reality shines forth of itself, one should immediately assume its form.

He who abides sleeplike in the dream and waking state, without inhaling or exhaling, is certainly liberated.

He who is like a corpse, having the "wind" [i.e., the breath and subtle life energy] and the mind merged in his Self, with the host of senses motionless, he is clearly called "liberated while alive."

[The *yogin* in the ecstatic state] does not hear, smell, touch, see, or experience pleasure and pain, and his mind does not conceptualize.

He experiences nothing and, like a log, does not comprehend [anything]. Thus, with the [individual] self merged into Shiva, [the *yogin*] is here called "ecstasy abiding" (*samādhi-stha*).

As water poured into water, milk into milk, and ghee into ghee becomes indistinguishable, so [also is the merging of] the individual self with the supreme Self.

Just as through the capacity for meditation a worm comes to be a bee, so a man, through the capacity for ecstasy, will assume the nature of the Absolute (*brahman*).

The knower of Reality (*tattva*) obtains a crore of virtues, which are the fruit of vows, rites, austerities, pilgrimages, gifts, worship of the deities, and so forth.

The natural state (*sahaja-avasthā*) is highest; meditation and concentration are middling; recitation and praising are low; sacrificial worship is lowest.

Thinking (*cintā*) about Reality is highest; thinking about recitation is middling; thinking about the textbooks (*śāstra*) is low; thinking about the world is lowest.

A crore of ritual worships (*pūjā*) is equal to one hymn of praise (*stotra*); a crore of hymns of praise is equal to one recitation (*japa*); a crore of recitations is equal to one meditation; a crore of meditations is equal to one [moment of complete] dissolution (*laya*) [into the transcendental Self].

Mantra is not superior to meditation; a deity is not superior to the Self; worship is not superior to application [of the limbs of Yoga]; reward is not superior to contentment.

Inaction is supreme worship; silence is supreme recitation; nonthinking is supreme meditation; desirelessness (*anicchā*) is the supreme fruit.

The *yogin* should daily practice the worship at twilight without ablutions and *mantras*, [and he should practice] asceticism (*tapas*) without sacrifices (*homa*) and rituals of worship (*pūjā*), and worship without garlands.

[He who is] indifferent, unattached, free from desire (*vāsana*) and superimposition (*upādhi*), absorbed in the essence of his innate [power] is a *yogin*, a knower of the supreme Reality.

The body is the abode (*ālaya*) of God (*deva*), O Goddess! The psyche is God Sadā-Shiva. One should abandon the offering-remains of ignorance; one should worship with the thought "I am He."

The psyche is Shiva; Shiva is the psyche. The psyche is Shiva alone. The [unliberated] psyche is known as the fettered beast (*paśu*). Sadā-Shiva is one who is released from [all] bonds (*pāśa*).

Rice is imprisoned in the husk; when the husk is gone, the grain [becomes visible]. [Similarly,] the psyche is known as imprisoned by karma; Sadā-Shiva is [that Reality which is eternally] free from [the "husk" of] karma.

God abides in fire in the heart of devout worshipers (*vipra*) who have themselves awakened to the likeness (*pratimā*) [within], who know the Self everywhere.

He who is the same in praise and abuse, cold and heat, joy and sorrow, and [who is always the same] toward friend and foe is chief among *yogins*, beyond excitement and nonexcitement.

The *yogin* who is desireless and always content, seeing the same [in all], with his senses controlled and sojourning as it were in the body knows the supreme Reality.

He who is free from thought, free from doubt, unsullied by desire and superimposition (*upādhi*), and immersed in his innate essence is a *yogin* who knows the supreme Reality.

As the lame, blind, deaf, timid, mad, dull-witted, etc., live, O Mistress of Kula, so [lives] the *yogin* who knows the [ultimate] Reality.

He who is keen on the supreme bliss produced by the five seals (*mudrā*) is chief amongst *yogins*; he perceives the Self within himself.

[74]

The Worship of Brahman

The *Mahānirvāṇa Tantra* is a rather late *tantra* of the *kaula* school. Its date is uncertain. Some scholars place it in the twelfth century, others believe it was composed as late as 1750. During the early nineteenth century, when Tantrism was in general disrepute, the *Mahānirvāṇa Tantra* was put forward by members of the educated class of Bengal as a comparatively inoffensive text, and since then has achieved wide circulation in a translation by Sir John Woodroffe. In this passage from that translation, Shiva relates to Shakti part of the philosophical basis of Tantrism. The terminology shows a clear Vedantic influence.

Listen, then, O Beloved of My life! to the most secret and supreme Truth, the mystery whereof, O propitious One, has nowhere yet been revealed.

Because of My affection for Thee I shall speak to Thee of that Supreme Brahman, Who is Being-Consciousness in the form of the universe and Who is dearer to Me than life itself. O Maheśvarī! the unchanging eternal, conscious world-pervading Brahman may be known in Its real Self or by Its external signs. That Which is without difference, pure being and beyond both mind and speech, Which truly is in the three worlds of appearance, is the Brahman according to Its real nature. That Brahman is known in ecstasy by those who look upon all things alike, who are above all contraries, devoid of all wandering thought, free of all ignorance regarding body and self. That same Brahman is known from His external signs, from Whom the whole universe has sprung, in Whom when so sprung It exists, and into Whom all things return. That which is known by yoga-experience may also be perceived from these external signs. For those who would know Him through these external signs, for them Sādhana is enjoined.

Attend to me, Thou, O dearest One! while I speak to Thee of such Sādhana. And firstly, O Ādyā! I tell Thee of the Mantroddhāra of the Supreme Brahman. Utter first the Praṇava, then the words "Being" and "Consciousness," and after the word "One" say "Brahman". *Oṁ Saccidekam Brahma.*

This is the Mantra. These words, when combined according to the rules of Sandhi, form a Mantra of seven letters. If the Praṇava be omitted, it becomes a Mantra of six letters only. This is the most excellent of all the Mantras, and the one which immediately bestows Dharma, Artha, Kāma, and Mokṣa. In the use of this Mantra there is no need to consider whether it be efficacious or not, or friendly or inimical, for no such considerations affect it. Nor at initiation into this Mantra is it necessary to make calculations as to the phases of the Moon, the propitious junction of the stars, or as to the Signs of the Zodiac. Nor are there any rules as to whether the Mantra is suitable or not. Nor is there need of the ten Saṁskāras. This Mantra is in every way efficacious in initiation. There is no necessity for considering anything else. Should one have obtained, through merit acquired in previous births, an excellent Guru, from whose lips this Mantra is received, then life indeed becomes fruitful, and the worshipper, receiving in his hands Dharma, Artha, Kāma, and Mokṣa, rejoices both in this world and the next.

He whose ears this great jewel of Mantra reaches is indeed blest, for he has attained the desired end, being virtuous and pious, and is as one who has bathed in all the sacred places, been initiated in all Yajñas, versed in all Scriptures, and honoured in all the worlds. Happy is the father and happy the mother of such an one — yea, and yet more than this. his family is hallowed, and the gladdened spirits of the Pitṛs rejoice with the Devas, and in the excess of their joy sing: "In our family is born the most excellent of our race, one initiate in the Brahma-mantra. What need have we now of Piṇḍa offered at Gayā, or of Śrāddha, Tarpaṇa, pilgrimage at holy places; of what use are alms, Japa, Homa, or multiplicity of Sādhana, since now we have obtained imperishable satisfaction by the Sādhana of this good son?"

Listen, O Devī! Adored of the world, whilst I tell You the very truth, that for the worshippers of the Supreme Brahman there is no need for other religious observances. At the very moment of initiation into this Mantra the disciple is Brahman, and for such an one, O Devī what is there to attain in the three worlds?

[75]

Kaula Worship

In these brief passages from the *Mahānirvāṇa Tantra*, Śiva explains to the Goddess the necessity and nature of *kaula* worship. As the Christian New Testament (*Titus* 1.15) says, "Unto the pure all things are pure." Translated by John Woodroffe.

In this Kali Age, O Devī! success is achieved by Kaulika worship alone, and therefore should it be performed with every care. By it, O Devī! is acquired knowledge of Brahman, and the mortal who has gained it, is of a surety whilst living freed from future births and exonerated from the performance of all religious rites. According to human knowledge the same thing appears to be pure and same impure, but when Brahma-jñāna has been acquired there is nothing either pure or impure. For to him who knows that the Brahman is in all things and eternal, what is there that can be impure? Thou art in the form of all, and above all Thou art the Mother of all. If Thou art pleased, O Queen of the Devas! then all are pleased.

*

Without Kulācāra, O Devī! the Śakti-Mantra is powerless to give success, and therefore the Sādhaka should practise Śakti-Sādhanā with Kulācāra rites. O Ādyā! the five essential Elements in the worship of Śakti have been prescribed to be Wine, Meat, Fish, parched Grain, and the Union of man with woman. The worship of Śakti without these five elements is but the practice of evil magic. That Siddhi which is the object of Sādhana is never attained thereby, and obstacles are encountered at every step. As seed sown on barren rocks does not germinate, so worship without these five elements is fruitless.

HATHAYOGA

The psycho-physical aspects of Tantrism were developed by the teachers of the *haṭhayoga* school. Gorakshanatha (or, in Hindi, Gorakhnath), the semi-legendary founder of Hathayoga, is supposed to have lived in eastern India in the tenth, eleventh or twelfth century. His name is found on lists of the *siddha*s of Vajrayana Buddhism, and his yoga certainly draws from the traditions that gave rise to Hindu as well as Buddhist Tantrism.

In Hathayoga the body is viewed as the tool *par excellence* of the *sādhaka*. Its techniques include purifications, postures or *āsana*s, breath control or *prāṇāyāma*, sense-withdrawal, meditation and *samādhi*. Five of these are identical with five of the "limbs" of Patanjali's yoga (see Chapter 5). The purifications are methods for cleansing the internal and external organs; they include *trāṭak* or gazing at a fixed point, which is said to cure diseases of the eye. The *āsana*s, by far the most widely practised hathayogic techniques, include dozens of postures of varying difficulty that have beneficial effects on different parts of the body. Related to them are more advanced physical manoeuvres known as "seals" and "locks". The heart of hathayogic practice is *prāṇāyāma* or "extension of the breath". The breath is drawn in, held and expelled in various rhythms and patterns of repetition. This purifies and stimulates the entire system. As in Patanjali's yoga, the "higher" limbs of sense-withdrawal, meditation and *samādhi* are stages of progress that culminate in the attainment in union with the Absolute.

[76]

Fundamentals of Hathayoga

One of the oldest and most important texts of Hathayoga is the *Gorakṣa Śataka*, which is attributed to Gorakshanatha himself. It consists of a hundred stanzas explaining the terminology and techniques of the system. These seven verses from the beginning of the text were translated by Georg Feuerstein.

The most excellent ones resort to Yoga, which is the fruit of the wish-fulfilling tree of revelation (*śruti*), whose branches are frequented by the twice-born, and which pacifies the tribulations of existence.

They name posture, breath restraint (*prāṇa-samrodha*), sense-withdrawal, concentration, meditation, and ecstasy as the six limbs of Yoga. . . .

The "prop" (*ādhāra*) is the first center; *svādhiṣṭāna* is the second. Between them is the perineum named *kāma-rūpa*.

The four-petaled lotus called "prop" is at the place of the anus (*guda-sthāna*). In the middle of it is said to be the "womb" (*yoni*) praised by adepts under the name of desire (*kāma*).

In the middle of the "womb" stands the great phallus/symbol [of Shiva] facing backward. He who knows the disk, which is like a [brightly shining] jewel, in [its] head is a knower of Yoga.

Situated below the penis is the triangular city of fire, flashing forth like lightning bolts and resembling molten gold.

When in the great Yoga, in ecstasy, [the *yogin*] sees the supreme, infinite, omnipresent Light, he does not experience [any further] coming and going [i.e., births and deaths in the finite world].

[77]

The Practice of Pranayama

This passage, which includes the concluding stanzas of the *Gorakṣa Śataka*, presents a particular technique of *prāṇāyāma*. Translated by Georg Feuerstein.

Placing the right [lower] leg on top of the left [thigh] and the left [lower leg] on top of the right [thigh], firmly grasping the big toes with the hands crossed behind the back, while placing the chin on the chest, he should look at the tip of the nose. This is said to be the [*baddha* or "bound"] lotus posture, which removes various kinds of diseases. . . .

The *yogin* [seated in] the bound lotus posture should fill in the life force through the lunar [nostril] and then, after holding it according to his capacity, expel it again through the solar [nostril].

Meditating on the moon disk, the nectar that resembles [white] curd or is like cow's milk or silver, [the *yogin* practicing] breath control should be happy.

Drawing in the breath (*śvāsa*) through the right [nostril], he should fill the abdomen gradually. Having retained it according to the rules, he should expel it again through the lunar [nostril].

Meditating on the solar circle, which is a mass of brightly burning flames located at the navel, the *yogin* practicing breath control should be happy.

When the breath is filtered through the *iḍā* [i.e. the left nostril], he should expel it again through the other [nostril]. Sucking the air in through the *piṅgalā* [i.e. the right nostril] he should, after holding it, release it again through the left [nostril]. By meditating on the two disks — of the sun and the moon — according to the rules, the host of channels become pure after three months.

By purifying the channels, [the *yogin*] achieves health, the manifestation of the [subtle inner] sound (*nāda*), [the ability to] hold the "wind" according to capacity, and the flaring up of the [inner] fire.

FURTHER READING

Source Materials

Georg Feuerstein, *The Yoga Tradition: Its History, Literature, Philosophy and Practice*. Prescott, AZ: Hohm Press, 1998.

Dominic Goodall, ed. and trans., *Bhaṭṭa Rāmakaṇṭha's Commentary on the Kiraṇatantra*. Pondicherry: Institut Français de Pondichéry, 1998.

Jaideva Singh, *Vijñānabhairava or Divine Consciousness*. Delhi: Motilal Banarsidass, 1998.

John Woodroffe, *The Great Liberation (Mahanirvana Tantra)*. Reprint edition. Madras: Ganesh and Company, 1993.

Other Works

George Weston Briggs, *Gorakhnāth and the Kānphaṭa Yogīs*. Reprint edition. Delhi: Motilal Banarsidass, 1998.

Douglas Renfrew Brooks, *The Secret of the Three Cities: An Introduction to Hindu Śākta Tantrism*. Chicago: University of Chicago Press, 1990.

Sources of Texts and Translations

71	*Kiraṇa-tantra* 1.14–23	Goodall 190–221 passim
72	*Vijñāna-bhairava* 67–76	Singh 64–71
73	*Kulārṇava-tantra* 9.5–16, 33–49	Feuerstein 490–91, 494–95
74	*Mahānirvāṇa-tantra* 3.5–24	Woodroffe 30–37
75	*Mahānirvāṇa-tantra* 4.20–24, 5.21–24	Woodroffe 86–87, 67–68
76	*Gorakṣa-śataka* 6–7, 17–21	Feuerstein 533, 534–35
77	*Gorakṣa-śataka* 12, 96–101	Feuerstein 533, 545

9

ध्यायन्कृते यजन्यज्ञैस्त्रेतायां द्वापरेऽर्चयन्।
यदाप्नोति तदाप्नोति कलौ संकीर्त्त्य केशवम्॥

The reward that one obtains in the *kṛta* age by meditation, in the *treta* by sacrifice, in the *dvāpara* by adoration, one receives in the *kali* age merely by reciting the names of Krishna.

Viṣṇu Purāṇa 6.12.17

The Puranas

MYTH has been a part of Indian religion since the time of the Veda, if not earlier. The vedic *saṁhitā*s and *brāhmaṇa*s, the *upaniṣad*s, Jaina and Buddhist texts, the epics and the *tantra*s all contain mythical accounts of the doings of gods, sages and heroes, and mythical explanations of the nature and workings of the cosmos. The principal sources of Indian mythology, however, are the collections known as *purāṇa*s or "ancient stories". Compiled for the most part between 300 and 1000 CE, they contain material that goes back as far as the *Ṛg Veda*. The *purāṇa*s were important elements in the Hindu revival of the first millennium, when a resurgent vedic religion, often in a popular form, began to turn back the tide of Buddhism and Jainism.

There are, according to tradition, eighteen major and eighteen minor *purāṇa*s. Composed in simple, rather undistinguished Sanskrit verse, they appealed to people previously thought unfit for vedic teachings, in particular women and the lower castes. Like the epics and law-books, they were regarded as "recollection" (*smṛti*) and not "revelation" (*śruti*). As a result the texts were freely altered and enlarged over a period of centuries. In time, however, some members of the devotional cults, and later even theologians and commentators, began to speak of them as being equal in sanctity to revealed scripture.

According to the classical definition, *purāṇa*s deal with five things:

the creation of the universe, its destruction and recreation, genealogies of gods and heroes, the *manvantaras* or cosmic ages, and the deeds of gods, sages and kings. In fact, along with these typically mythic topics, the *purāṇas* contain discussions of society, law, holy places, sacrifices, sects and everything else that a Hindu needs to know in order to act correctly in the world. They are scriptures not of personal spiritual experience but of *dharma*. As a result, despite their enormous importance in contemporary Hinduism, they fall for the most part outside the limits of this anthology. The *purāṇas* are, however, important expressions of devotional religion or *bhakti*, and offer glimpses of the ascetic life through the window of myth. Our contemporary notions of the powers and practices of Hindu holy men and holy women are formed largely on the puranic model.

In the *purāṇas*, the major vedic gods — Agni, Indra, Mitra-Varuna and so forth — were supplanted by a new pantheon consisting of Brahma, Vishnu and Shiva, along with their consorts and offspring. Vishnu and Shiva, the most important of these deities, had risen from a secondary status in the Vedas to the position of the supreme gods of the bhagavata and shaiva cults. The esoteric side of these cults was given expression in the secret teachings of the *tantras* (see Chapter 8). The exoteric side consisted of the devotionalism and rituals taught in the *puraṇas* and in the songs of the *bhaktas* (see Chapter 13).

SHIVA IN THE PURANAS

Shiva is a god of contrasts. The name means "the Auspicious One", but auspiciousness is just one side of his complex personality. He also is Rudra, "the Howler", the embodiment of all that is fearsome and unpredictable. Shiva is the ascetic, lost in meditation on mount Kailasa; but he is also the storehouse of generative power, whose symbol is the *liṅga* or phallus.

[78]

The Origin of Linga-Worship

The worship of the *liṅga* is the central ritual act of all forms of Shaivism. The radical meaning of *liṅga* is "mark" or "sign", hence "penis", which is the mark of manhood. The central icon in any Shiva temple is an upright shaft that is evidently a stylised image of a phallus, though it is not necessarily perceived as such by modern worshippers. In many early cultures, the power of generation was worshipped as a phallus; *liṅga*-worship has presumably the same origin. This selection from the *Śiva Purāṇa* gives a less anthropological explanation of the origin of this cult. It is of interest also for the picture it gives of the life of ascetic sages, who developed formidable powers by means of yogic practices. These powers however are as nothing compared to the limitless energy of Shiva. Note that *Śaṅkara* and *Hara* are two of Shiva's many names. Translated by Cornelia Dimmitt and J. A. B. van Buitenen.

There is a beautiful Pine Forest where certain virtuous sages, always loyal to Śiva, used to occupy themselves continually with meditation on him. Those lords of seers performed worship to Śiva three times a day and praised him continuously with all kinds of divine hymns.

Once upon a time all those chief brahmins, devotees of Śiva, intent upon meditation on Śiva, went into the forest to gather fuel. Meanwhile Śankara adopted a misshapen body in order to test them and appeared there colored blue and red. Utterly resplendent in appearance, he was naked and decked out in ornamental ashes. Holding his penis in his hand he made lewd gestures. Thus Hara himself went to the forest in an affectionate mood, thinking to do a favor to his devotees who lived there, and with whom he was well pleased.

When they saw him, some of the wives of the sages were terrified. But others, amazed and excited, sought to approach him. While some of the women embraced him and others grasped his hand, they lost themselves in rivalry with one another. At this moment the eminent seers returned. When they beheld this revolting person, they were upset and overcome with anger. Much aggrieved, all the sages, fooled by Śiva's trick, cried out, "Who is this? Who is this?"

When that pure, naked man said nothing at all, the noble seers spoke to that terrible apparition, "Your behavior is disgusting! You are ruining the way of the Veda! Therefore that penis of yours shall fall to the ground!"

When they said this, the *liṅga* of the pure Śiva's supernatural body fell off at once. Blazing like fire, that penis, or *liṅga*, burned up everything in its way. Wherever it went it burned things down. Śiva's fiery *liṅga* went to the netherworld and to heaven. It traveled throughout the world but nowhere did it come to rest. The worlds grew troubled and the sages unhappy. No one could find shelter, neither gods nor seers.

All the gods and seers, not recognizing Śiva, were miserable. They assembled and quickly went together to Brahmā for refuge.

When they arrived the brahmins honored and hymned Brahmā the creator and told him all that happened. When he heard what they said, he recognized that they had been deluded by Śiva's illusion. Worshipping Śankara, he said to the excellent seers:

"O brahmins, you are wise but you have done a contemptible thing, you who are so critical when the ignorant act this way! Who can hope for his own well-being after obstructing the god Śiva? One who does not welcome a guest in the middle of the day has his good *karman* taken away, and after leaving to that man his own evil *karman*, the guest departs. How much worse, then, is it to deny hospitality to Śiva!

"As long as Śiva's *liṅga* roams the three worlds there will be no prosperity. This is the truth I speak. You should do whatever is necessary to pacify Śiva's penis. O sages, consider carefully what is to be done."

Thus addressed, the seers bowed to Brahmā and said, "What shall we do, lord? Show us our duty!" After these lords of seers had spoken, Brahmā, grandfather of all the worlds, himself addressed the seers: "Go and worship the mountain-born goddess. You must placate Śiva! When she assumes the form of a vulva the penis will become calm. Listen to the rule I tell you now. If you treat her with affection, she will be agreeable.

"Put a jar filled with water from a sacred ford, *dūrvā* grass and barley in the center of a splendid eight-petalled diagram. Cast a spell on the jar with vedic *mantras*, doing worship according to the rules of *śruti*, and while recollecting Śiva. Anoint the *liṅga* with that water, O supreme seers. When it is consecrated with Śatarudrīya *mantras*, it will come at last to rest. After putting in place the mountain-girl in the form of a *yoni*, place the blessed shaft on top of it and once more cast a spell on it. Propitiate the supreme lord with perfumes, sandal wood, flowers and incense and with the *pūjā* of food and other goods. Placate him with prostrations, hymns, holy songs and instruments. Then perform the *svastyayana* ceremony for godspeed and cry out:

"'Victory! Be gracious, lord of gods who brings happiness to the world! You are the creator, protector, and destroyer who is beyond OṂ. You are the beginning of the world, the womb of the world, the interior of the world. Be at peace, great lord! Protect all the worlds!'

"When you follow this procedure, well-being will return to the world, without a doubt. The three worlds will not decay and felicity will prevail. . . . After gratifying the daughter of the mountain and also the one whose banner bears the bull by the preceding rule, the supreme *liṅga* will be brought to rest."

After this the gods and sages propitiated the mountain-born girl and Śiva according to the injunction dictated by the *mantras* for the sake of Dharma. . . .

When the penis was pacified, prosperity returned to the world, O brahmins, and that *liṅga* became famous in the three worlds as Hatakṣema, or Śivā-Śiva. Because the *liṅga* is worshiped, happiness abounds in the triple world in every way.

VISHNU IN THE PURANAS

To those who adore him, Vishnu is no less powerful than Shiva; but he is always mild and approachable, especially in the form of his *avatāra*s or incarnations. By the time of the *purāṇa*s, the list of Vishnu's *avatār*s had been standardised. The most popular of all of them was Krishna, whose life is recounted in many Puranic texts, notably the *Viṣṇu Purāṇa*, *Bhāgavata Purāṇa* and the *Harivaṁsa*.

The *Bhāgavata Purāṇa* is the most popular and most influential of all the *Purāṇa*s. Composed in south India between the eighth and eleventh centuries, it is the supreme expression in Sanskrit of the *bhakti* movement that began in the Tamil country a century or two earlier. Later commentators, such as the Vedantin Vallabhacharya, accorded it equal status to that of the *upaniṣad*s and other revealed scriptures. The account of Krishna and the *gopī*s in the *Bhāgavata* became the basis of much later *bhakti* poetry, as well as the source of many of the motifs of Rajasthani and Pahari miniature painting.

[79]

For the Love of Krishna

The tenth book of the *Bhāgavata Purāṇa* gives the standard account of the childhood and youth of Krishna. Growing up a simple cowherd in Gokula, he amused himself with the other *gopāla*s. When he reached young manhood, he won the hearts of the *gopī*s by his beauty and by the sound of his flute. This selection, from the thirty-second and thirty-third chapters of the tenth book, tells of the unspeakable joys of union that the *gopī*s experienced, after having suffered the unbearable pain of Krishna's absence. Translated from the Sanskrit by Dominic Goodall.

Thus the Gopīs loudly lamented, singing and babbling in various ways, yearning for a sight of Kṛṣṇa.

And Śauri (Kṛṣṇa) appeared to them, a love god for the god of love himself, incarnate before their very eyes, garlanded, clothed in yellow, and with a smile on His lotus-face.

When they saw their love had come, the women's eyes grew large with delight, and all stood up in the same instant like the limbs of the body when the breath of life enters them.

One [Gopī] joyfully took Śauri's lotus-hand in her clasped hands. Another lifted on her shoulder His arm smeared with sandal.

Another slender [Gopī] took the chewed remains of His betel nut in her clasped hands. One, feverish [with love], pressed His lotus foot (*aṅghri*) to her breasts.

One, distracted with the violence of her love, knitted her brow, bit her lips, and stared at Him as though she would kill Him by onslaughts of sidelong glares.

Another could not be satisfied, though she drank in the nectar of the lotus of His [very] face and savoured it with unblinking eyes, like the sages (*santaḥ*) [who contemplate merely] His feet.

One took Him into her heart through the orifices of her eyes, shut them, and remained (*āste*) embracing Him there, all the hairs of her body on end, immersed in bliss like a yogin.

All were enraptured at the sight of Him, a feast for the eyes, and shook off the pain [they had suffered] from separation from Him, like people who reach the All-knowing one (*prājñam*).

Their grief cast off, they surrounded Acyuta, and the Lord shone brightly like the [Supreme] Soul (*puruṣa*) surrounded by His powers.

The immanent Lord came with them to the banks of the Yamunā (*kālindī*), where there were bees and a breeze fragrant with blossoming white jasmine (*kunda*) and coral-tree flowers — [banks that were] kindly, because the darkness of the dusk was dispelled by the clusters of rays of the autumn moon, [and] whose gentle sands had been smoothed out by the hands of waves of the dark river.

The pain in the [Gopīs'] hearts was shaken off in the bliss of beholding Him, and they attained the summation of all their desires, just as the Vedas. With their upper garments that were flecked with sandal-paste from their breasts they prepared a place for the soul's friend (*ātmabandhave*) to sit.

There the Lord God, who has a seat made for Him in the hearts of masters of yoga, sat down, and in this assembly of Gopīs He shone in His form that is the one focus of [true] beauty in all the three worlds.

They honoured Him who inflamed them with love by caressing His hands and feet on their laps; they laughed, shot playful glances at Him, and their brows flickered and they praised Him, and said, a little reproachfully:

The Gopīs spoke:

"Some people love in return [only] those who love them, and some, the opposite. Others love neither [those who love them nor those who do not]. Tell us truly, sir, [why is this?]"

The Lord spoke:

"My friends, those who love in reciprocation are striving only for their own ends. There is no [loving] friendship (*sauhṛdam*), no moral behaviour (*dharma*) in that, merely serving one's own ends and nothing else.

"People who, like parents, love those who do not [necessarily or at first] love them are full of compassion. In this there is moral behaviour (*dharma*) beyond reproach and loving friendship, my lovely-waisted ones.

"[Now] some people, who do not love even those who love them and still less those who do not, are people [sufficient in themselves] who delight in themselves, [or] they are people who have obtained all that they require, [or] they are ungrateful, [or] they wrong their elders.

"But I do not [always visibly] love [in return] creatures even when they love me, in order that they may continue to follow me (*anuvṛttivṛttaye*), just as a poor man who gains wealth and loses it is then aware of nothing else, sunk in anxious thought about that [lost wealth].

"In the same way I loved you, my women, and concealed [the fact, so that it was] beyond your knowing — [you,] who for my sake gave up this world, your traditions (*veda*) and your relatives in order to follow me. My loves, you should not be angry with me, your lover.

"I cannot, even in the life-span of Brahmā, make return to you, whose devotion (*saṃyuj*) to me is irreproachable, for you have sundered the unwearing fetters [that bound you] to your homes. May that be your reward."

*

The Gopīs heard these delightful words of the Lord and forgot the pain of their separation [from Him], their desires increasing at [the touch of] His body.

There Govinda began the game of the Rāsa dance with those jewels of women, who linked their arms together, devoted and joyful.

Kṛṣṇa set in motion the festival of the Rāsa that was made beautiful by the circles of Gopīs. The Lord of yoga entered between each pair among them and put an arm about each one's neck, [so that] each woman thought Him next to herself. The sky was crowded with the hundreds of celestial chariots of the gods and their wives, who were filled with curiosity.

Then the kettle drums sounded, showers of blossoms fell and the greatest of the celestial musicians (*gandharvapatayaḥ*) and their women sang of His spotless glory.

A confused noise of the bangles, anklets and girdles of the women and their lovers arose in the circle of the Rāsa game.

The Lord, the son of Devakī, shone with intense brightness among them, like a great emerald amidst golden jewels.

With the movements of their feet, the shaking of their arms, their smiles and flickering brows, their flexing waists, fluttering stoles, and earrings that swung at their cheeks, the women of Kṛṣṇa shone out as they sang, like streaks of lightning in a mass of cloud, their faces glowing and the knots of their girdles worked loose.

They sang out loud with impassioned voices as they danced, thrilled at Kṛṣṇa's caresses, in love with love, so that this [whole world] was filled with their song.

One [Gopī] with Mukunda sang out (*unninye*) an unmixed range of notes, and He was pleased and honoured her, [saying,] "Well done! well done!" [Then] she sang out the same [in] the [rhythmic cycle called] *dhruva* and [then] too he honoured her.

Another, exhausted by the Rāsa, put her arm around the shoulder of the Kṛṣṇa (*gadābhṛtaḥ*) who stood to her side, as her [loose] bracelets and jasmine flowers slipped down.

She smelt Kṛṣṇa's arm, placed across one of her shoulders, fragrant as a lotus and smeared with sandal paste, and, as the hairs of her body stood on end, ah! she kissed it.

[One Kṛṣṇa] gave His chewed betel nut to another, as she pressed her cheek to His — [her cheek] which was adorned with the [reflected] glimmer of her earrings as they were tossed about in the dance.

One weary [Gopī] pressed to her breasts the soothing lotus-hand of the Kṛṣṇa (*Acyuta*) who stood at her side, [all the while] singing and dancing with jingling anklet and girdle[-bells].

The Gopīs [each] attained Acyuta, Lakṣmī's only beloved, as their lover, and they played, singing His praises with His arms around their necks.

The Gopīs, their garlands slipping from their hair, their faces glowing with perspiration, their cheeks [adorned] with the tips of curls of their hair and with lotus-blooms hung at their ears, danced with the Lord in the Rāsa gathering — [a gathering] in which bees were the singers accompanied by the sounds of their bangles and anklets as instruments.

Thus the Lord of Lakṣmī (*rameśaḥ*) played with the beauties of Vraja like a child confused with His own reflections [in a mirror], with laughter, unrestrained love-games, fond looks, caresses and embraces.

Their senses were in turmoil at the intense pleasure [they felt] from the touch of His body [and] the women of Vraja, whose garlands and ornaments had [already] slipped off, became incapable of setting straight their hair, their veils or their breast-cloths, O great Kuru.

FURTHER READING

Source Materials

Cornelia Dimmitt and J. A. B. van Buitenen, trans., *Classical Hindu Mythology: A Reader in the Sanskrit Purāṇas*. Philadelphia: Temple University Press, 1978.

Dominic Goodall, ed. and trans., *Hindu Scriptures*. London: Phoenix, 1996.

Other Work

Wendy Doniger [O'Flaherty], trans., *Hindu Myths: A Sourcebook Translated from the Sanskrit*. Harmondsworth: Penguin Books, 1975.

Sources of Texts and Translations

78	*Śiva Purāṇa, Koṭirudra Saṁhitā* 12.6–54	Dimmitt and van Buitenen 203–05
79	*Bhāgavata Purāṇa* 10. 32.1–22, 33.1–18	Goodall 386–91

Part Three

Elaborations

10

सर्वस्यात्मत्वाच्च ब्रह्मास्तित्वप्रसिद्धिः। सर्वो ह्यात्मास्तित्वं प्रत्येति न नाहमस्मीति। यदि हि नात्मास्तित्वप्रसिद्धिः स्यात् सर्वो लोको नाहमस्मीति प्रतीयात्। आत्मा च ब्रह्म।

The existence of the Brahman is well known, because it is the Self of all; for we all feel that our Self exists; no one says, "I am not". If the existence of the Self were not well known, everyone would feel: "I do not exist". And that Self is the Brahman.

Shankara, Commentary on *Brahma Sūtra 1.1.1*

Spiritual Philosophies

MOST FORMS of Indian spirituality have insisted that enlightenment is beyond the reach of intellect, but many of them have developed intellectual systems that formalise the teachings of their founders. These philosophies are intended to help the mind by correcting false views and showing the way to the truth revealed by the fundamental teachings. As part of this task, they have examined all the questions that humans have grappled with since they began to reflect about themselves and their place in the universe: the characteristics and constituents of existence; the nature and limits of knowledge and language; and the right way to achieve the good life.

The foundations of Indian philosophy were laid in the first millennium BCE in the teachings of the upanishadic sages and of heterodox masters like Mahavira and the Buddha. Its superstructure was erected between 200 and 1200 CE by theorists working within the vedic, Jaina, Buddhist and tantric traditions. So rich a diversity of views was put forward that it is difficult to speak of "Indian philosophy" as a whole; still, most of these systems had several features in common. First, they were less concerned with creating something entirely new than with providing the correct interpretation of foundational texts. As a result, the main form of philosophical discourse was the commentary. A few exceptional thinkers, such as Nagarjuna and Abhinavagupta, created independent works, but even these were said to be mental elaborations of more-than-mental teachings. In spite of this subservience to sacred authority, Indian philosophers did not lack originality. Once they had shown that their thinking was rooted in a timeless past, they were free to extend it in new directions.

The foundational texts—the *upaniṣads*, the Jaina and Buddhist *sūtra*s, the *śaiva āgama*s—are all concerned with salvation. It follows that salvation, in one form or another, is the declared aim of most schools of Indian philosophy. By means of right knowledge, the individual (real or apparent) casts off limitation and achieves *mokṣa*. It should not be concluded from this, however, that all Indian philosophers were theologians. A few, like the thinkers of the materialistic *cārvāka* school, were aggressively non-religious. Others, like the specialists in logic and epistemology, were often more interested in the technical problems of their disciplines than in the spiritual aims it professed to serve. And even those philosophers who followed a spiritual path did not let their beliefs become an excuse for sloppy thinking.

The systems of philosophy included in this chapter are those in which the spiritual orientation is most apparent. They are arranged, as is the custom, by religion. This highlights common origins and acknowledged influences, but it obscures the fact that for hundreds of years Indian philosophers of all traditions debated with, and borrowed from, one another. Indian philosophy remained fruitful for as long as it did because of this cross-fertilisation.

MAHAYANA BUDDHIST PHILOSOPHIES

The Buddha discouraged philosophical speculation as a distraction on the path to *nirvāṇa*, but he touched on many of the questions that have always fascinated philosophers: the nature of the human being, causality and necessity, correct action and thought. The importance of these matters, and the difficulty of the path to *nirvāṇa*, led some of those who followed his *dharma* to construct cosmological and metaphysical systems of enormous range and complexity.

Buddhist philosophy properly speaking may be said to begin with the Abhidharma schools of the Theravada. Later came the more systematic Sarvastivada or realist school and the Sautrantika school, which attempted to recover the original sense of the *sūtra*s. These schools remained active well into the first millennium; but from the time of the appearance of the *Prajñāpāramitā Sūtra*s, the most influential Buddhist systems were created by Mahayana thinkers. Two traditions stand out: the Madhyamika or Shunyavada system, which was founded by Nagarjuna in the second or third century, and the Vijnanavada or Yogachara system, which was formalised by Asanga and Vasubandhu a century or two later.

Madhyamika Buddhism tried to find a middle path between the belief that nothing at all exists, and the belief that beings and things are real. The Buddha had shown, in his doctrine of dependent origination (see selection 29), that nothing has independent existence. Madhyamika thinkers, following the lead of the *Prajñāpāramitā* literature (which they regarded as the higher teaching of the Buddha), asserted that apparent entities are devoid of "self-nature". On the level of conventional appearances, all is empty (*śūnya*). Any statement on this level is relative and can, by means of dialectical argument, be reduced to absurdity. The way is then opened to the awareness of emptiness, which is an important precondition for entry into *nirvāṇa*. From the ordinary point of view, *nirvāṇa*, the ultimate truth of being, is regarded as the opposite of *saṁsāra*, the conventional truth of appearances. At root, however, *nirvāṇa* and *saṁsāra* are one.

Around the fifth century, two schools of interpretation of Madhyamika Buddhism became distinguished. One of them, the Prasangika school, emphasised Nagarjuna's method of *reducio ad absurdum* (*prasaṅga*). The doctrines of this school were developed by Chandrakirti in the seventh century, and given their supreme literary expression by Shantideva in the beginning of the eighth.

Madhyamika thinkers took negative dialectics as far as they could go; but they left unanswered a number of questions about cognition and consciousness. If mind was simply empty, and truth forever ineffable, who was it that needed to seek *nirvāṇa*, and by what methods could it be sought? Between the second and fourth centuries, texts like the *Sandhinirmocana* and *Laṅkāvatāra Sūtra*s (see Chapter 7) looked into such matters and introduced a new set of concepts for dealing with them. The only reality is consciousness (*vijñāna*). External objects appear only in the act of apprehension and thus cannot be said to be real. These and related ideas were formalised in the fourth or fifth centuries in a system that became known as the "Doctrine of Consciousness" (*Vijñānavāda*) or (because of the importance it gave to yogic introspection) as "The Practice of Yoga" (*Yogācāra*). Vijnanavada and Madhyamika Buddhism coexisted in India for more than five centuries, and remain influential in Tibet and the Far East as the philosophical bases of most schools of Mahayana Buddhism.

[80]

Nagarjuna

Nagarjuna's dates are conventionally given as 150 to 250 CE, but he might have been born a century earlier or later. According to the hagiographies that are the only sources of information on his life, he was born a south Indian brahmin. Of the many works attributed to him, only two survive in the original Sanskrit. The best known of these is the *Mūlamadhyama-kārikā* or "Fundamental Treatise on the Middle Way". The twenty-fifth and culminating chapter of this work examines the concept of *nirvāṇa.* It begins with an objection raised by a hypothetical opponent: If, as the Madhyamikas claimed, there is nothing that rises up or passes away, how can we speak of *nirvāṇa*? Nagarjuna uses his dialectical tools to show that *nirvāṇa* cannot be said to exist, or to not exist, or both, or neither. Translated from the Tibetan version by Jay L. Garfield.

If all this is empty,
Then there is no arising or passing away.
By the relinquishing or ceasing of what
Does one wish nirvāṇa to arise?

If all this is nonempty,
Then there is no arising or passing away.
By the relinquishing or ceasing of what
Does one wish nirvāṇa to arise?

Unrelinquished, unattained,
Unannihilated, not permanent,
Unarisen, unceased:
This is how nirvāṇa is described. . . .

That which comes and goes
Is dependent and changing.
That, when it is not dependent and changing,
Is taught to be nirvāṇa.

The teacher has spoken of relinquishing
Becoming and dissolution.
Therefore, it makes sense that
Nirvāṇa is neither existent nor nonexistent.

If nirvāṇa were both
Existent and nonexistent,
Passing beyond would, impossibly,
Be both existent and nonexistent.

If nirvāṇa were both
Existent and nonexistent,
Nirvāṇa would not be nondependent.
Since it would depend on both of these.

How could nirvāṇa
Be both existent and nonexistent?
Nirvāṇa is uncompounded.
Both existents and nonexistents are compounded.

How could nirvāṇa
Be both existent and nonexistent?
These two cannot be in the same place.
Like light and darkness.

Nirvāṇa is said to be
Neither existent nor nonexistent.
If the existent and the nonexistent were established,
This would be established.

If nirvāṇa is
Neither existent nor nonexistent,
Then by whom is it espounded
"Neither existent nor non-existent"?

Having passed into nirvāṇa, the Victorious Conqueror
Is neither said to be existent
Nor said to be nonexistent.
Neither both nor neither are said.

So, when the victorious one abides, he
Is neither said to be existent
Nor said to be nonexistent.
Neither both nor neither are said.

There is not the slightest difference
Between cyclic existence and nirvāṇa.
There is not the slightest difference
Between nirvāṇa and cyclic existence.

Whatever is the limit of nirvāṇa,
That is the limit of cyclic existence.
There is not even the slightest difference between them,
Or even the subtlest thing. . . .

Since all existents are empty,
What is finite or infinite?
What is finite and infinite?
What is neither finite nor infinite?

What is identical and what is different?
What is permanent and what is impermanent?
What is both permanent and impermanent?
What is neither?

The pacification of all objectification
And the pacification of illusion:
No Dharma was taught by the Buddha
At any time, in any place, to any person.

[81]
Shantideva

The author of the *Bodhicaryāvatāra* (*Entering the Path of Enlightenment*) lived during the first half of the eighth century. He is said to have been born in Saurashtra, to have practised some form of Mahayana or tantric *sādhana*, and to have become a monk at the university of Nalanda. While there he compiled a digest of Mahayana teachings (the *Śikṣāsamuccaya*, see Chapter 7) and wrote the *Bodhicaryāvatāra*. The ninth chapter of this work, from which this selection is drawn, deals with *prajñā* or Wisdom. After exposing the weaknesses of different vedic and Buddhist schools, Shantideva shows that no indubitable statement can be made about mind or any other entity. One is left with the liberating awareness of Emptiness. The *Bodhicaryāvatāra* was translated in Tibetan soon after its composition, and is esteemed by all schools of Tibetan Buddhism. The present translation was made from the Tibetan version by the Padmakara Translation Group.

The source of sorrow is the pride of saying "I,"
Fostered and increased by false belief in self.

To this you may say that there's no redress,
But meditation on no-self will be the supreme way. . . .

The subject of sensation has no real existence,
Thus sensation, likewise, has no being.
What damage, then, can be inflicted
On this aggregate deprived of self?

The mind within the senses does not dwell;
It has no place in outer things, like form,
And in between, the mind does not abide:
Not out, not in, not elsewhere can the mind be found.

Something not within the body, and yet nowhere else,
That does not merge with it nor stand apart—
Something such as this does not exist, not even slightly.
Beings have nirvāṇa by their nature.

If consciousness precedes the cognized object,
With regard to what does it arise?
If consciousness arises with its object,
Again, regarding what does it arise?

If consciousness comes later than its object,
Once again, from what does it arise?
Thus the origin of all phenomena
Lies beyond the reach of understanding.

"If this is so," you say, "the relative will cease,
And then the two truths—what becomes of them?
If relative depends on beings' minds,
This means nirvāṇa is attained by none."

This relative is just the thoughts of beings;
That is not the relative of beings in nirvāṇa.
If thoughts come after this, then that is still the relative;
If not, the relative has truly ceased. . . .

When nonbeing prevails, if there's no being,
When could being ever supervene?

For insofar as entity does not occur,
Nonentity itself will not depart.

And if nonentity is not dispersed,
No chance is there for entity to manifest.
Being cannot change and turn to nonbeing,
Otherwise it has a double nature.

Thus there is no being,
Likewise no cessation.
Therefore beings, each and every one,
Are unborn and are never ceasing.

Wandering beings, thus, resemble dreams
And also the banana tree, if you examine well.
No difference is there, in their own true nature,
Between the states of suffering and beyond all sorrow.

Thus, with things devoid of true existence,
What is there to gain, and what to lose?
Who is there to pay me court and honors,
And who is there to scorn and to revile me?

Pain and pleasure, whence do these arise?
And what is there to give me joy and sorrow?
In this quest and search for perfect truth,
Who is craving, what is there to crave?

[82]
Vasubandhu

The founders of the Vijnanavada school, Asanga and Vasubandhu, are supposed to have been half-brothers. They were born in Peshawar, apparently in the fourth or fifth century. Vasubandhu, who wrote an important digest of Sarvastivada thought, was (according to the story) converted to the Mahayana by Asanga. After his conversion he wrote a number of key Vijnanavada works, one of which is the *Triṁśikā-kārikā* or "Treatise in Thirty Verses". This contains a classic presentation of the Vijnanavada concept of consciousness. Translated by Stefan Anacker.

Whatever range of events is discriminated by whatever
discrimination
is just the constructed own-being, and it isn't really to be found.—

The interdependent own-being, on the other hand, is the
discrimination which arises from conditions,
and the fulfilled is its [the interdependent's] state of being
separated always from the former [the constructed].

So it is to be spoken of as neither exactly different nor
non-different from the interdependent,
just like impermanence, etc., for when one isn't seen, the other is.

The absence of own-being in all events has been taught with a
view towards
the three different kinds of absence of own-being in the three
different kinds of own being.

The first is without own-being through its character itself, but the
second
because of its non-independence, and the third *is* absence of
own-being.

It is the ultimate truth of all events, and so it is "Suchness", too,
since it is just so all the time, and it's just perception-only.

As long as consciousness is not situated within perception-only,
the residues of a "dual" apprehension will not come to an end.

And so even with the consciousness: "All this is perception-only",
because this also involves an apprehension,
for whatever makes something stop in front of it isn't situated in
"this-only".

When consciousness does not apprehend any
object-of-consciousness, it's situated in "consciousness-only",
for with the non-being of an object apprehended, there is no
apprehension of it.

It is without citta, without apprehension, and it is supermundane
knowledge;
it is revolution at the basis, the ending of two kinds of
susceptibility to harm.

It is the inconceivable, beneficial, constant Ground, not liable to
affliction,
bliss, and the liberation-body called the Dharma-body of the Sage.

JAINA PHILOSOPHY

The teachings of Mahavira, considered by Jainas to be expressions of his omniscient consciousness, are preserved to some extent in the surviving canons of the Swetambara and Digambara schools. Around these canonical texts grew up an extensive secondary literature of commentaries and expositions; but the systematic presentation of Jaina thought had to wait till the beginning of the first millennium, when it was summed up by Umasvati in the *Tattvārthādhigama Sūtra* or "Manual for Understanding All that Is". This work, and Jaina philosophy in general, is structured around seven *tattva*s or principles, which can be linked together in seven propositions to provide a summary of the Jaina view of existence. The soul (*jīva*) is of the nature of consciousness. Lifeless substance (*ajīva*) is inert and unconscious. Souls come into contact with substance by means of influx (*āsrava*) of karma, which in Jainism is a fine form of matter. As a result there is bonding (*bandha*) of inert substance to the soul. It is possible to put a stop (*saṁvara*) to the influx of karma. Residual karma too can fall away (*nirjarā*). As a result, the soul achieves liberation (*mokṣa*) from karmic bondage, and lives forever in bliss.

Because of the importance of knowledge in the Jaina scheme of things, Jaina philosophers did much work in epistemology and logic. They arrived at a stance called *anekāntavāda* or non-absolutism, according to which all knowledge (with the exception of a Jina's omniscience) is partial and context-dependent. According to Jaina logicians, there are not two but seven possibilities of predication: a statement may be true, not-true, both true and not-true, indescribable, true but indescribable, not-true but indescribable, and true-and-not-true but indescribable. Similarly, there are seven possible ways of approaching a subject of study according to the viewpoint of the enquirer. This relativistic approach to conventional knowledge made it possible for Jaina thinkers to regard the views of their opponents not as outright falsehoods but partial truths; but the only view that could be considered wholly true is the view that is in accord with the Jinas' omniscience.

[83]

Umasvati

The author of the *Tattvārthādhigama Sūtra* (generally abbreviated to *Tattvārtha Sūtra*), is believed by Jainas to have lived in the second or third century, though some modern scholars place him in the fourth or fifth. His work is the only philosophical text that both Swetambaras and Digambaras regard as authoritative. Written in Sanskrit in the *sūtra* style, it sums up in 350 aphorisms the main points of Jaina doctrine. The last of its chapters, dealing with *mokṣa* or liberation, is given here in full. Translated by Nathmal Tatia.

Omniscience arises when deluding karma is eliminated and, as a result, knowledge-covering, intuition-covering and obstructive karma are eliminated.

There is no fresh bondage because the causes of bondage have been eliminated and all destructive karmas have worn off.

The elimination of all types of karma is liberation.

When the five states in all their varieties and also the state of being worthy of liberation cease, with the exception of the perfect enlightened world-view, perfect knowledge, perfect intuition and the state of being liberated, then there is liberation.

When all karmic bondage is eliminated, the soul soars upwards to the border of cosmic space.

The soul soars up by virtue of the antecedent impetus, separation from karmic particles, severance of the karmic bondage and its innate mode of upward flight.

Because of these factors, it is like the potter's wheel set in motion, like the gourd with dissolved earthen layers, like the castor seeds released from the pod and like the flame of fire.

The liberated soul cannot go outside cosmic space because there is no medium of motion beyond.

The state of the liberated soul is considered through twelve gateways of investigation: place, time, realm of birth, gender or dress, ford, conduct, mode of enlightenment through self or others, knowledge, height, interval, number and relative numerical strength of the liberated souls in the preceding eleven gateways.

[84]

Amritachandra Suri

The *stotra* or hymn of praise became a popular form of Sanskrit composition towards the end of the first millennium. Hindus addressed them to the gods and sages, Buddhists to the Bodhisattvas, and Jainas to the Tirthankaras. One of the finest examples of Jaina *stotra* literature is the *Laghutattvasphoṭa* or "Brief Exposition of Reality" by the Digambara philosopher Amritachandra Suri, who lived between the tenth and twelfth centuries. Like other examples of this literary form, Amritachandra's *stotra* is at once an expression of devotional feeling and a summary of doctrine for the lay believer. Here he speaks of the pure consciousness of the Jina and its relationship to external objects. Translated by Padmanabh Jaini.

O Lord! You illuminate the whole universe with your supramundane brilliance. [And this brilliance is even further] ornamented by the light of knowing your self. You refrain eternally from vitiating attachments to the objects known; you are seen to be one who is distinct [from these, though cognizing them].

Although your pure consciousness has turned away from [the desire to know] all external objects, it [nevertheless] acquires the wondrous glory [of simultaneously cognizing them]. This [cognizing] in no way defiles your pure consciousness, for that consciousness is ever the same.

These objects possess their own forms, external [to the cognizing knowledge]. But [when reflected] in your [pure consciousness], they assume the form of that very knowledge [i.e. they become modification of consciousness]. [And yet] you [remain] one undivided mass of consciousness; hence there is neither delusion, aversion, nor attachment [in you].

O Lord! The massive impact of external objects simply brightens the light of your knowledge; [for] you are endowed with the rich blooming of the bud of pure consciousness, which opens under the force [of external factors, as does the bud of a flower in response to wind, sunlight, etc.].

O Lord Jina! That crystal clearness which characterizes the external objects [i.e. the knowables] is identical with the internal clarity of the knower [i.e. objects are seen exactly as they are]. But this clear light of yours is not seen by those who are attached to external objects [i.e. those whose minds are not pure].

O Jina! I describe your splendour to the best of my ability, [a splendour] seen in the holy assembly as you [sit and] enjoy the various forms of bliss attained through your skilfulness in means [i.e. those deeds which engender the Tīrthaṅkara's majesty].

VEDANTIC PHILOSOPHIES

Systems based on the orthodox vedic schools of philosophy were comparative latecomers on the Indian philosophical scene, but they have outlived most of their competitors. To many people today Indian philosophy is identical with Vedanta. Not only is it the basis of most contemporary spiritual teachings in the Hindu tradition, but also it is an important element of the general Indian worldview. Some of the reasons for this success are non-philosophical: the departure of Buddhism from its homeland, the premature end of Shaivism in Kashmir, the marginalisation of Jainism, and the promotion of Vedanta by key figures in the nineteenth- and twentieth-century movement of Indian cultural nationalism. But the staying-power of Vedanta is due also to its successful handling of the main problems of life and thought, and its ability to combine mystical insight with intellectual soundness.

The philosophies of Vedanta are based on the teachings of the *upaniṣad*s, particularly as formalised in the *Brahma Sūtra* or *Vedānta Sūtra* of Badarayana (fifth to third century BCE). This phase of Vedanta is closely related to the philosophy of Mimamsa, first formalised by Jaimini, who was roughly contemporaneous with Badarayana. Both systems are based on the Veda, but Mimamsa gives its attention to the earlier portions (the *brāhmaṇa*s and hymns), while Vedanta is concerned with the "end (*anta*) of the Vedas", that is, the *upaniṣad*s. Regarding the Vedas to be authorless and eternal, Mimamsa counsels the performance of sacrifice in order to achieve heavenly rewards. Vedanta accepts the final authority of the Veda, but promotes the attainment of liberation in the form of union or relationship with *brahman* or with God.

All schools of Vedanta claim to give the correct interpretation of the *Brahma Sūtra*, the *upaniṣad*s, and the *Bhagavad Gītā*. The schools' distinctive viewpoints are set forth in commentaries on these works. The first school to emerge was Advaita or non-dualism, which was formalised by Gaudapada in the seventh century, and systematised and defended by Shankara in the eighth. Much influenced by Madhyamika and Vijnanavada Buddhism, Gaudapada argued that the things of the world are unreal, like objects seen in dream. They are superimposed on Brahman by *māyā*, the power of illusion. Shankara developed Gaudapada's ideas into a formidable system, having as its centrepiece a theory of error that explains the origin of the world's appearances. Brahman alone exists; it is changeless and eternal. The phenomenal world is superimposed on Brahman by means of *avidyā* or ignorance, just as an illusory snake is projected onto a stick by a frightened traveller. The way to escape from ignorance is to hear and reflect on the truth of passages from the *upaniṣad*s that assert the identity of Brahman and the individual. Meditation and spiritual experience are aids in this search for liberation.

Advaita Vedanta has been influential for thirteen hundred years. The idea that the world is an illusion is today familiar to millions who have never read a word of Shankara's philosophy. Advaita helped bring about a revival of vedic religion towards the end of the first millennium, and was a significant factor in the decline of Buddhist philosophy in India. Ironically, Shankara's opponents refer to him as a crypto-Buddhist, since his denial of reality to the phenomenal world seems to them Mahayana in vedic clothing. Shankara also denied ultimate reality to God, the creator and maintainer of the universe; but God, in the forms of Vishnu, Shiva and the Goddess, was affirmed by the tantric and devotional cults that were becoming important at the time that Shankara wrote. It was therefore inevitable that his interpretation of Vedanta would not be the final one.

There are a half-dozen important schools of Vedanta besides Advaita. All grant some form of reality to the world and affirm the existence of a divine Being with whom humans can enter into relation. The most influential of these schools is the "qualified non-dualism" (*Viśiṣṭādvaita*) of Ramanuja. Strongly influenced by the poetry of the Alvars (see Chapter 13) and the Tantrism of the Pancharatra sect, Ramanuja forged a synthesis of vaishnava religion and upanishadic monism. Brahman is related to the finite world as the soul is related to the body. Although utterly dependent on the Lord, the world is not unreal. By means of devotion and surrender to the Lord, the individual becomes absorbed in a blissful contemplation of God's perfection. Ramanuja's synthesis brought devotional religion (*bhakti*) into the vedic fold and later fostered its spread in northern India.

[85]

Shankara

Born in a village in Kerala towards the beginning of the eighth century, Shankara packed an enormous amount of intellectual and practical activity in his short lifetime. Besides writing many important works, he voyaged around India, debating with all comers and (according to tradition) founding monasteries in the North, South, East and West. His commentaries on the *Brahma Sūtra*, several *upaniṣad*s and the *Bhagavad Gītā* remain touchstones in any consideration of Vedanta. A large number of other works are ascribed to him; of these, only the

Upadeśasāhasrī ("A Thousand Teachings") is certainly his composition. The *Upadeśasāhasrī* is divided into two parts, one in verse and the other in prose. In the first passage below, the tenth chapter of the metrical part, the speaker gives expression to the knowledge of one who has realised oneness with Brahman. The next passage, from the fourth book of the prose part, shows how a guru brings a student to this realisation by means of dialectical reasoning. Both passages were translated from the Sanskrit by Sengaku Mayeda.

The highest [*Brahman*]—which is of the nature of Seeing, like the sky, ever-shining, unborn, one alone, imperishable, stainless, all-pervading, and non-dual—That am I and I am forever released. Om.

I am Seeing, pure and by nature changeless. There is by nature no object for me. Being the Infinite, completely filled in front, across, up, down, and in every direction, I am unborn, abiding in Myself.

I am unborn, deathless, free from old age, immortal, self-effulgent, all-pervading, non-dual; I am neither cause nor effect, altogether stainless, always satisfied and therefore [constantly] released. Om.

Whether in the state of deep sleep or of waking or of dreaming, no delusive perception appears to pertain to Me in this world. As those [three states] have no existence, self-dependent or other-dependent, I am always the Fourth, the Seeing and the non-dual.

The continuous series of pains due to the body, the intellect and the senses is neither I nor of Me, for I am changeless. And this is because the continual series [of pain] is unreal; it is indeed unreal like an object seen by a dreaming man.

It is true that I have neither change nor any cause of change, since I am non-dual. I have neither good nor bad deeds, neither final release nor bondage, neither caste nor stages of life, since I am bodiless.

Since I am beginningless and attributeless, I have neither action nor result [of action]. Therefore I am the highest [*Ātman*], non-dual. Just as the ether, though all-pervading, is not stained, so am I not either, though abiding in the body, since I am subtle.

And I am always the same to [all] beings, the Lord, for I am superior to, and higher than, the perishable and the imperishable. Though I have the highest *Ātman* as my true nature and am non-dual, I am nevertheless covered with wrong knowledge which is nescience.

Being perfectly stainless, *Ātman* is distinguished from, and broken by, nescience, residual impression, and actions. Being filled with powers such as Seeing, I am non-dual, standing [perfect] in my own nature and motionless like the sky.

He who sees *Ātman* with the firm belief "I am the highest *Brahman*" "is born no more" [Kaṭha Upaniṣad 1.38], says the *Śruti*. When there is no seed, no fruit is produced. Therefore there is no birth, for there is no delusion. . . .

This view which has been declared by me from the standpoint of the highest truth is the supreme [view] as ascertained in the Vedānta. If a man has firm belief in it, he is released and not stained by actions, as others are.

*

A certain student, who was tired of transmigratory existence characterized by birth and death and was seeking after final release, approached in the prescribed manner a knower of *Brahman* who was established in *Brahman* and sitting at his ease, and asked him, "Your Holiness, how can I be released from transmigratory existence? I am aware of the body, the senses and [their] objects; I experience pain in the waking state, and I experience it in the dreaming state after getting relief again and again by entering into the state of deep sleep again and again. Is it indeed my own nature or [is it] due to some cause, my own nature being different? If [this is] my own nature, there is no hope for me to attain final release, since one cannot avoid one's own nature. If [it is] due to some cause, final release is possible after the cause has been removed."

The teacher replied to him, "Listen, my child, this is not your own nature but is due to a cause."

When he was told this the pupil said, "What is the cause? And what will remove it? And what is my own nature? When the cause is removed, the effect due to the cause no [longer] exists; I will attain to my own nature like a sick person [who recovers his health] when the cause of his disease has been removed."

The teacher replied, "The cause is nescience; it is removed by knowledge. When nescience has been removed, you will be released from transmigratory existence which is characterized by birth and death, since its cause will be gone and you will no [longer] experience pain in the dreaming and waking states."

The pupil said, "What is that nescience? And what is its object?

And what is knowledge, remover of nescience, by which I can realize my own nature?"

The teacher replied, "Though you are the highest *Ātman* and not a transmigrator, you hold the inverted view, 'I am a transmigrator.' Though you are neither an agent nor an experiencer, and exist [eternally], [you hold the inverted view, 'I am] an agent, an experiencer, and do not exist [eternally]'—this is nescience." . . .

To this the pupil replied, "Your Holiness, the delusion has gone thanks to your gracious assistance; but I am in doubt as to how I am transcendentally changeless."

"How?"

"Sound and other [external objects] are not self-established, since they are not conscious. But they [are established] through the rise of notions which take the forms of sound and other [external objects]. It is impossible for notions to be self-established, since they have mutually exclusive attributes and the forms [of external objects] such as blue and yellow. It is, therefore, understood that [notions] are caused by the forms of the external objects; so, [notions] are established as possessing the forms of external objects, *i.e.*, the forms of sound, etc. Likewise, notions, which are the modifications of a thing (= the intellect), the substratum of the 'I'-notion, are also composite, so it is reasonable that they are non-conscious; therefore, as it is impossible that they exist for their own sake, they, like sound and other [external objects], are established as objects to be perceived by a perceiver different in nature [from them]. If I am not composite, I have pure consciousness as my nature; so I exist for my own sake. Nevertheless, I am a perceiver of notions which have the forms [of the external objects] such as blue and yellow [and] so I am indeed subject to change. [For the above reason, I am] in doubt as to how [I am] transcendentally changeless."

The teacher said to him, "Your doubt is not reasonable. [Your] perception of those notions is necessary and entire; for this very reason [you] are not subject to transformation. It is, therefore, established that [you] are transcendentally changeless. But you have said that precisely the reason for the above positive conclusion—namely, that [you] perceive the entire movement of the mind—is the reason for [your] doubt [concerning your transcendental changelessness]. This is why [your doubt is not reasonable].

"If indeed you were subject to transformation, you would not perceive the entire movement of the mind which is your object, just as the mind [does not perceive] its [entire] object and just as the senses [do not perceive] their [entire] objects, and similarly you as *Ātman* would not perceive even a part of your object. Therefore, you are transcendentally changeless." . . .

"If so, Your Holiness, I am of the nature of transcendentally changeless and eternal perception whereas the notions of the intellect, which have the forms of [external objects] such as sound, arise and end with the result that my own nature which is perception falsely appears [as perceiver]. Then what is my fault?"

[The teacher replied,] "You are right. [You] have no fault. The fault is only nescience as I have said before."

[The pupil said,] "If, Your Holiness, as in the state of deep sleep I undergo no change, how [do I experience] the dreaming and waking states?"

The teacher said to him, "But do you experience [these states] continuously?"

[The pupil answered,] "Certainly I do experience [them], but intermittently and not continuously."

The teacher said [to him,] "Both of them are adventitious [and] not your nature. If [they] were your nature [they] would be self-established and continuous like your nature, which is Pure Consciousness. Moreover, the dreaming and waking states are not your nature, for [they] depart [from you] like clothes and so on. . . .

. . . If apprehension, *i.e.*, the light of *Ātman* which is Pure Consciousness, were not eternal in one's own *Ātman*, it would be impossible for *Ātman* to exist for Its own sake; as It would be composite like the aggregate of the body and senses, It would exist for another's sake and be possessed of faults as we have already said."

"How?"

"If the light of *Ātman* which is Pure Consciousness were not eternal in one's own *Ātman*, it would be mediated by remembrance and the like and so it would be composite. And as this light of Pure Consciousness would therefore not exist in *Ātman* before Its origination and after Its destruction, It would exist for another's sake, since It would be composite like the eye and so on. And if the light of Pure Consciousness exists in *Ātman* as something which has arisen, then *Ātman* does not exist for Its own sake, since it is established according to the existence and absence of that light of Pure Consciousness that *Ātman* exists for Its own sake and non-*Ātman* exists for another's sake. It is therefore established that *Ātman* is the eternal light of Pure Consciousness without depending upon anything else." . . .

Here [the pupil] objected, saying, "It is contradictory to say that Apprehension is the result of the means of knowledge and that It is by nature the transcendentally changeless and eternal light of Ātman."

To this [the teacher] said, "It is not contradictory."

"How then [is it not contradictory]"?

"Although [Apprehension] is transcendentally changeless and eternal, [It] appears at the end of the notion [forming process] due to sense-perception and other [means of knowledge] since [the notion-forming process] aims at It. If the notion due to sense-perception and other [means of knowledge] is non-eternal, [Apprehension, though eternal,] appears as if it were non-eternal. Therefore, [Apprehension] is figuratively called the result of the means of knowledge."

[The pupil said,] "If so, Your Holiness, Apprehension is transcendentally changeless, eternal, indeed of the nature of the light of *Ātman*, and self-established, since It does not depend upon any means of knowledge with regard to Itself; everything other than This is non-conscious and exists for another's sake, since it acts together [with others]."

And because of this nature of being apprehended as notion causing pleasure, pain, and delusion, [non-*Ātman*] exists for another's sake; on account of this very nature non-*Ātman* exists and not on account of any other nature. It is therefore merely non-existent from the standpoint of the highest truth. Just as it is experienced in this world that a snake [superimposed] upon a rope does not exist, nor water in a mirage, and the like, unless they are apprehended [as a notion], so it is reasonable that duality in the waking and dreaming states also does not exist unless it is apprehended [as a notion]. In this manner, Your Holiness, Apprehension, *i.e.*, the light of *Ātman*, is uninterrupted; so It is transcendentally changeless, eternal and non-dual, since It is never absent from any of the various notions. But various notions are absent from Apprehension. Just as in the dreaming state the notions in different forms such as blue and yellow, which are absent from that Apprehension, are said to be non-existent from the standpoint of the highest truth, so in the waking state also, the various notions such as blue and yellow, which are absent from this very Apprehension, must by nature be untrue. And there is no apprehender different from this Apprehension to apprehend It; therefore It can Itself neither be accepted or rejected by Its own nature, since there is nothing else."

[The teacher said,] "Exactly so it is. It is nescience that is the cause of transmigratory existence which is characterized by the waking and dreaming states. The remover of this nescience is knowledge. And so you have reached fearlessness. From now on you will not perceive any pain in the waking and dreaming states. You are released from the sufferings of transmigratory existence."

[The pupil said,] "Om."

[86]

Ramanuja

Said to have lived from 1017 to 1137, Ramanuja was born in Sriperumbudur (near Chennai) and died in the temple-city of Srirangam. His main works are a commentary on selected verses from the *upaniṣad*s, a commentary on the *Brahma Sūtra*, and a commentary on the *Gītā* that highlights the devotional content of that work. His followers also count among his writings three prose works, the *Gadya-traya*. Some scholars disbelieve this ascription; but even if not by him, the texts making up the *Gadya-traya* are fine expressions of the devotional core of his thinking. This extract from the *Śaraṇagati-gadya* ("Prose Poem on Surrender") is in the form of a dialogue between Ramanuja and the Lord. Translated by M. R. Rajagopala Ayyangar.

Thou art the Father of the world, of those that move and those that do not move; Thou art the object of homage and reverence to all of them; Thou art the Preceptor and the one to whom supreme reverence is due. There is no one equal to Thee; how [then] could there be any one greater than Thee in all the three worlds, O Thou of unequalled might? . . .

Pardon all the varied and innumerable offences committed [by me] from beginningless time with the mind, the speech and the body — countless sins of omission and commission — sins against Thee, sins against Thy devotees and [other] unpardonable sins — sins some of which have begun to yield their fruit, and some which have not — sins that were committed in the past, that are committed at present and sins that will be committed in future — pardon all of them without exception. . . .

Enable me to acquire the parabhakti referred to in three places in the Gita: — "I am capable of being attained, O Partha, by sole and exclusive devotion [bhakti] to me", "I can be attained by sole and exclusive devotion [bhakti]", "Having realised the pure self within him and with his mind unclouded by karma or suffering [of any kind] he neither grieves [at any sad event] nor desires anything [of worldly gain]. Having become indifferent to all things [desired by others] he soon attains devotion [bhakti] to me".

Make me attain the sole character of one who has parabhakti, parajnana, and paramabhakti.

Having attained the infinite and unsurpassed bliss of the experience of Bhagavan, full, continuous, eternal, clear and having no other end in view — the experience which has resulted from parabhakti, parajnana and paramabhakti, may I become the eternal servant of Bhagavan finding my sole joy in fulfilling all His purposes in all states and situations without any exception, owing to the infinite and unequalled delight arising from such an experience!

Though you are lacking in all the requisites which are enjoined as the means for attaining such service of mine, though you are overcome by endless sins which stand in the way of [obtaining] that service, though you are guilty of innumerable offences against me, though you are guilty of innumerable offences against my devotees, though you are guilty of innumerable offences of an unpardonable nature, though your inner nature is deluded by perverse conceit continuing from beginningless time, which is the effect and the cause of these offences, though you are bound by perverse mental impressions which have been from beginningless time and which are the effect and the cause of the offences and the conceit, though you are bound by the form of prakriti which is conducive to them, though you are beset by obstacles standing in the way of exclusive and everlasting parabhakti, parajnana and paramabhakti towards my two lotus-like feet — obstacles which are of the nature of the contraction of true knowledge arising from the experience of pleasures and pains due to the body, to animals and the gods, from the experience of their causes and likewise from the experience of other sense-objects fit to be discarded — since you have uttered the *dvaya*, whatever may be the manner [of the utterance], you will, solely as the result of my compassion, get rid, without any exception, of all obstacles as well as their causes that stand in the way of exclusive and everlasting parabhakti, parajnana, and paramabhakti towards my two lotus-like feet and you will win, by my grace, exclusive and everlasting parabhakti, parajnana and paramabhakti towards my two lotus-like feet and by my grace alone, you will have a vision, just as they are, of my essential nature [svarupa], of my form, of my attributes, of the nitya-vibhūthi [Vaikuntha] and Līlā-vibhūti [this world] and all the accompaniments thereof in all their fullness; you will then realise by direct vision that your essential nature consists in being controlled by me and in being solely and exclusively devoted to my service. With the sole and exclusive enjoyment of me, with the sole and exclusive joy of serving me and with the full, continuous, eternal, distinct, infinite and unequalled joy of experiencing me without any other end in view, you shall become my eternal servant finding your sole delight in rendering all forms of service without any exception and appropriate to all states and situations — delight which arises from the infinite and unsurpassed joy of such an experience of me.

Such, indeed, you have become.

Devoid of the slightest trace of sufferings or obstacles due to the body, the animals or the gods, remain happy here at Srirangam itself until the body is cast off, ever uttering the *dvaya* in this way with careful attention to its meaning.

At the time of the body falling off [from you] and solely as a result of my compassion, having a distinct vision of me alone and with perfect knowledge, without deviating from previous discipline and previous longing, casting off lightly this prakriti both in its gross and in its subtle form as if it were a worn out garment, you will, at that very moment, become my eternal servant finding sole and exclusive joy in rendering all forms of service without exception suited to all states and situations — joy arising from boundless and unsurpassed love resulting from the full, continuous, everlasting, distinct, boundless and unsurpassed delight of experiencing me which is the effect of exclusive and everlasting parabhakti, parajnana, and paramabhakti seeking no other end and which will be attained by my grace.

Have no doubts about this.

"I have never told a falsehood before nor shall I tell [one] in the future." "Rama never deviates from what he has said once." "To one who seeks succour from me as a suppliant, though only once, and says 'I am Thine', I vouchsafe freedom from the fear of all beings." "Having given up all rites [of expiation], seek me alone as the means of your salvation. I will release you from all sins. Do not grieve." These words were [all] uttered by myself.

Hence be free from all doubts in regard to your having the true knowledge, the true vision and the true attainment of myself, and remain happy.

NON-DUAL KASHMIR SHAIVISM

The basis of all forms of shaiva philosophy and religion are the *tantras* or *āgamas* that extol the glory of Shiva and of Shakti, his creative energy. (Selections from two shaiva *tantras* are reproduced and discussed in Chapter 8.) Written in Sanskrit in north India between the fourth and eighth centuries, these texts are considered by worshippers of Shiva to be revealed scriptures. Though diverse in form and emphasis, they have a number of common features. Their cosmological structure is similar to that of Samkhya – Yoga, but it includes eleven "higher" *tattvas*, making a total of thirty-six cosmic principles. The ultimate reality is Parama-Shiva, who comprehends both Shiva and Shakti. The individual *jīva* or soul is bound by a triple impurity to limitation and suffering. Liberation is achieved when, by the power of Shakti, *jīva* is united with Shiva.

At present there are three main schools of shaiva philosophy and religion in India: Tamil Shaiva Siddhanta, Kashmir Shaivism and Virashaivism. Each of these may be referred to as a school of Shaiva Siddhanta, but that term is now applied mostly to the dualistic school that developed in Tamil Nadu from around the sixth century, whose primary texts are written in the Tamil language. (One of these texts is the *Tirumantiram*; see selection 97.) The second school took shape in Kashmir in the eighth century. Unlike Tamil Shaiva Siddhanta, this Kashmiri school, whose principal texts are written in Sanskrit, is non-dualistic. Extracts from a few texts of Non-Dual Kashmir Shaivism are discussed below. Virashaivism, the youngest of the three shaiva schools, took a distinct form in Karnataka in the twelfth century; its primary texts are the Kannada *vacanas* of Basavanna and others, which are discussed in Chapter 13.

Non-dual Kashmir Shaivism traces itself to the *Śiva Sūtra* of Vasugupta, which is dated to the mid eighth century. This text, together with the shaiva *āgamas*, mark the first phase of the development of the school. The second stage is represented by the *Spanda* literature, which elaborates on the *Śiva Sutra*, while the final phase, spanning the ninth to eleventh centuries, comprises the various systematic schools or "tendencies" of Kashmir Shaivism. The most important of these is the Pratyabhijna system, which was founded by Somananda (c. 875 – 925), formalised by

Utpaladeva (c. 900–950), and fully developed by Abhinavagupta (c. 900–950).

At the time that Non-Dual Kashmir Shaivism arose, Mahayana Buddhism had been a force in the region for a millennium, latterly in its Vijnanavada form. A more recent influence was the non-dual Vedanta of Shankara, who is said to have visited Kashmir in the eighth century. Non-dual Shaivism agrees with Vijnanavada Buddhism in holding that external things exist because they are perceived to exist by consciousness. It agrees with non-dual Vedanta in holding that the ultimate reality is One. It differs from both in asserting that the One Reality is Shiva, who creates, by means of his Shakti, a real world not different from himself. Unlike Buddhism and Advaita, Non-dual Shaivism conceives of liberation in positive as well as negative terms. The liberated soul enjoys perfect inner freedom but also participates joyfully in a world that is recognised as being the manifestation of Shiva. This recognition or *pratyabhijñā*, which gives the school its name, is the key to its soteriology. The soul is bound because it has forgotten its true nature. When it recognises that *saṁsāra* is not an independent reality but simply Shiva's play, it is released into freedom and bliss. The soul (*jīva*) realises its oneness with the Ultimate (*Śiva*). This recognition comes through a descent of the divine Shakti (*śaktipāta*), either by a guru's initiation or by the Shakti's grace.

[87]

Vasugupta

Kashmiri shaivas believe that the text of the *Śiva Sūtra* was revealed to Vasugupta by Shiva, who thus is the true author of the text. It can nevertheless be dated to the mid eighth century—after the period of the shaiva *āgama*s and before the later philosophical systems. In less than eighty aphorisms, it lays down the basic tenets of Kashmir Shaivism. Commentators and exegetes later expounded Vasugupta's aphorisms at considerable length. The extracts from the *Śiva Sūtra* reproduced below give the basis of the Kashmir shaiva view of liberation. Translated from the Sanskrit by Georg Feuerstein.

The Self (*ātman*) is [pure] Consciousness (*caitanya*).

[Finite] knowledge is bondage.

The source [of the manifest world together with its] collocation [of manifest effects] is embodied in [limited] activity (*kalā*).

The matrix [of sound] is the foundation of [conditional] knowledge.

The [spontaneous] flashing-forth (*udyama*) [of the transcendental Consciousness] is Bhairava.

Upon [ecstatic] union with the "wheel" (*cakra*) of powers, [there comes about] the abolition of the universe [as a distinct object of consciousness].

[Even] during the differentiation [of consciousness into the three modes of] waking, dream sleep, and deep sleep, [there is continuous] emergence of enjoyment of the Fourth [i.e., absolute Reality].

*

[The adept] considers pleasure and pain as external.

Free from these, he is indeed alone (*kevalin*).

However, the dynamic [or karmic] self [i.e., the unenlightened personality] is afflicted by delusion.

Upon the eclipse of differentiation [based on the unenlightened mind, the adept acquires] the capacity for [bringing forth] other creations.

The power of creation [is well established] on account of one's own experience [in dreams and meditation, etc.].

[There should be] animation of the three states [of unenlightened consciousness] by the principal [State, which is Reality itself]. . . .

For him who is in the condition of being rooted in that [Fourth, or ultimate Reality, there results] termination of individuality (*jīva*) owing to the ending of that [desire for contact with objects].

Then, he who has the elements for his covering is released, mighty, supreme, and the same as the Lord [i.e., Śiva].

[88]

Utpaladeva

Although the Pratyabhijna school of Kashmir Shaivism is said to have been founded by Somananda, it was his disciple, Utpaladeva, who gave it its distinctive form, developing the doctrine of "recognition" in works like the *Īśvara-pratyabhijñā-kārikā*. Along with his philosophical writings, Utpaladeva composed a number of *stotra*s or hymns of praise. The *stotra* was an appropriate form for him to use, since he saw devotion to Shiva as the supreme way to achieve liberation. The selection below gives a glimpse of his experience of union. Translated from the Sanskrit by Constantina Rhodes Bailly.

Lord! When the objective world has dissolved
Through a state of deep meditation
You stand alone —
And who does not see you then?
But even in the state of differentiation
Between the knower and the known,
You are easily seen by the devotees. . . .

Meditation on you
Washes away both delights and sorrows
As a river stream
Washes away high lands and low lands alike.

For those who feel no separation from you
And for whom you are dearer than their own souls —
What cannot be said
Of the abundance of their happiness!

I roar! Oh, and I dance!
My heart's desires are fulfilled
Now that you, Lord,
Infinitely splendid,
Have come to me.

In that state, O Lord,
Where nothing else is to be known or done,
Neither *yoga*
Nor intellectual understanding
Is to be sought after,
For the only thing that remains and flourishes
Is absolute consciousness.

[89]

Abhinavagupta

The greatest philosopher of the Pratyabhijna school, and one of the greatest in Indian philosophy, Abhinavagupta lived from around 975 to 1025. Encyclopaedic in his mastery of existing systems of philosophy, he studied Vijnanavada Buddhism and Jainism as well as all forms of northern Shaivism. Among his teachers was Lakshmangupta, a disciple of Utpaladeva's. In addition, Abhinavagupta was an adept in *kaula* Tantrism; his philosophy unites the insights of Pratyabhijna with the practical methods of the *tantras*. His works include commentaries on Utpaladeva's *Īśvara-pratyabhijñā-kārikā*, and treatises on philosophy and aesthetics. All are difficult works, which resist presentation in the form of extracts. The first two selections below are from the *Mālinī-vijaya-vārtika*, the third from the *Parātriṁśikā-vivaraṇa*, and the last from the *Tantrāloka*. Together they give some idea of Abhinavagupta's philosophical breadth and tantric realisation. All translated from the Sanskrit by Paul Eduardo Muller-Ortega.

The light is one, and it cannot ever be divided, and for this reason there is no possible division capable of sundering the non-duality, the Lord, beautiful with light and bliss. But [someone might object] space, time, forms, knowledge, qualities, attributes, distance, and so on are usually considered to be diversifying elements. Not so [we reply], because that which so appears is nothing but the light. If the light were not such, then non-duality would be useless. Difference then is only a word devoid of reality. But even if we admit a portion of reality to differences, then according to what we have said, it will have its basis only in non-duality. This is a pot, this is a cloth, the two are different one from the other. The two are different from other cognizing subjects, the two are different even from me. All these notions are nothing but the one light, which by its own intrinsic nature displays itself in this way.

*

When the yogin begins to expand the face or sphere of consciousness, all the channels of the senses flow into the inner circle (*cakra*). Then the channels of the senses forcibly expand with an expansion whose nature is the absence of the variety or differences of the objects of sense. The multiplicity of objects, such as blue, yellow, the relationship of subject and object, and so forth, begin at once to disappear because they are in a state of expectancy facing towards consciousness. At that very moment, by means of the *mudrā* which bestows direct experience and which he obtained from the tradition that stems from the very mouth of the *yoginī*, he seals the All. The *yogin* directly relaxes into the direct experience of Bhairava in the form of consciousness, the ruler of All. That yogin, filled with wonder attains knowledge of his own Self. The water-tank is empty even if it is joined with a quantity of water swelling up with various objects. The water which is found in the tank cannot pour forth from there elsewhere. It is incompetent to fill the tank even with continued exertion. But when, because of the liquid that results from the shower of rain which falls into the essence of the door of the inner portion, the tank is filled quite full, then the streams of water flow fully in all directions. Thus, because of the violent force of its own light, consciousness begins to manifest itself. If even for an instant the sense objects would all together turn to repose in consciousness, which illuminates all things as being nondifferent from itself, then *māyā* disappears and the plane of Bhairava shines forth brilliantly.

*

The tantric practitioner who has penetrated into the Heart whose essence is pure existence and potency, who because of the particular efficacy of the practice of the ritual of adoration is capable of remembering perfectly the *mantra*, thus attains to a very high degree the potency of the *mantra* which is the reality known as the Heart. By the peculiar efficacy of the ritual of adoration he crosses over completely, either by himself or as a result of the clear and pristine lotus-word of the teacher, and obtains the power of the *mantra*, whose essential characteristic is the Heart, and in this way he attains liberation in this very life.

*

This supreme wheel goes out from the Heart through the spaces of the eyes, and so forth, and ranges over the various objects of the senses. Because of the wheel's rays of light, a form whose nature is of the light of the moon, sun, and fire is established in those objects by regular degrees in conjunction with manifestation, maintenance, and dissolution. In this way, as this wheel falls on the various objects of the senses (such as sound) by way of the sense-capacity openings, one should recognize that sensory object as identical with the wheel. Thus, wherever the universal wheel falls, by this methodical practice it falls in its entirety like the universal monarch. In this way, the whole multitude of paths is effortlessly dissolved in the great wheel of Bhairava which is contained in consciousness. Then — even when all this has come to an end and all that is left are latent impressions—one should meditate on the great wheel which revolves and is the overflowing of the true Self. Because of the dissolution of all that could be burned, and because of the destruction of even the remaining latent impressions, the practitioner should meditate on that wheel as becoming calm, then as pacified, then as tranquil quietude itself. By this method of meditation, the entire universe is dissolved in the wheel, in that consciousness. Consciousness then shines alone, free of objects. Then, because of the essential nature of consciousness, manifestation occurs once again. That consciousness is the great Goddess. Continually causing the universe to become absorbed in his own consciousness, and continually emitting it again, the practitioner would become the perpetual Bhairava. The *yogin* should meditate on the wheel with three rays or spokes, then on one with four, with five, with fifty, sixty-four, one hundred, or one thousand. He should meditate with an undistracted mind on the wheel with innumerable thousands of rays. There is no limitation at all to the universal power of the great Lord, the great God, the Lord of consciousness, whose consciousness is always trembling and shining brilliantly. For his powers are the entire world and the great Lord is the possessor of those powers. This is what Śrī Kaṇtha has stated in the *Māṅgala Śāstra*. This is the first method, the method of meditation taught to me by Śambhunātha when I had pleased him, and it was taught to him by Sumati. These hints will be useful in practicing the other meditations as well, which without succession may be placed among the highest methods that lead to the Supreme. Now, as has been seen, the activities of the vital breath are the rising breath and so on. We will now describe how the Supreme may be unfolded when one employs the vital breath. At first abiding in the Heart, due to a repose in the mere emptiness, in the portion of the knower alone, in the innate bliss, he experiences a state known as "devoid of bliss." Then, when the vital breath rises, he experiences in the "knowable object" the bliss that arises from another. In this condition of the bliss that arises from another, he abides at ease in the *apāna*, which is filled with the infinite portions of the knowable, and he is embellished with the moon of the *apāna*. Having attained the level of the *samāna*, he abides wholly absorbed in the unification of the infinite rays of the knowable objects. He becomes one who is composed of the bliss of *brahman*. He is totally dedicated to devouring the limiting forces of the streams of the knowable objects and the means of knowing; he reposes in the fire of the *udāna* and comes to know the great bliss. Then, having entered this repose, and when the great flames begin to abate, the great pervasion which is beyond all qualifications ensues, and this is called the *vyāna*, the unlimited. Then, indeed, the bliss of consciousness occurs which is not strengthened by what is inert. For here indeed there is no possibility whatsoever of a difference which would be formed of the insentient. That is a state where there is no distinction, where everything appears shining on all sides, where consciousness is unstruck, and fed by the supreme nectar. There one does not meet with any "realizations" in the proper sense of the word at all. This condition taught to me by Śambhunātha is known as the universal bliss. The repose in this state may be obtained by employing the pronunciation of the Heart. The complete repose in this state corresponds to the attainment of the condition of the Supreme. These are the six states which arise from the ascension of the vital breath into our different internal abodes, even if in essence our essential nature, flowing out of the Heart, is always one.

FURTHER READING

Source Works

Stefan Anacker, trans., *Seven Works of Vasubandhu: The Buddhist Psychological Doctor*. Second edition. Delhi: Motilal Banarsidass, 1998.

M. R. Rajagopala Ayyangar, ed. and trans., *The Gadya-Traya of Sri Ramanujacharya*. Madras: M. R. Rajagopala Ayyangar, n.d.

Constantina Rhodes Bailly, ed. and trans., *Shaiva Devotional Songs of Kashmir: A Translation and Study of Utpaladeva's* Shivastotravali. Albany, NY: State University of New York Press: 1987.

Jay L. Garfield, *The Fundamental Wisdom of the Middle Way: Nāgārjuna's* Mūlamadhyamakārikā. New York: Oxford University Press, 1995.

Georg Feuerstein, *The Yoga Tradition*. Prescott, AZ: Hohm Press, 1998.

Padmanabh S. Jaini, ed. and trans., *Amṛtachandrasūri's Laghutattvasphoṭa*. Ahmedabad: L. D. Institute of Indology, 1978.

Sengaku Mayeda, trans., *A Thousand Teachings: The* Upadeśasāhasrī *of Śaṅkara*. Albany, NY: State University of New York Press, 1992.

Paul Eduardo Muller-Ortega, *The Triadic Heart of Śiva: Kaula Tantricism of Abhinavagupta in the Non-Dual Shaivism of Kashmir*. Albany, NY: State University of New York Press, 1989.

Padmakara Translation Group, trans., *The Way of the Bodhisattva: A Translation of the* Bodhicharyāvatāra. Boston: Shambhala, 1999.

Nathmal Tatia, trans., *Tattvārtha Sūtra: That Which Is*. San Francisco: HarperCollins, 1994.

Other Works

Stephen H. Phillips, *Classical Indian Metaphysics*. Chicago: Open Court, 1995.

Jaideva Singh, trans., *Pratyabhijñāhṛdayam: The Secret of Self-Recognition*. Delhi: Motilal Banarsidass: 1998.

Cyril Velkiath, *The Mysticism of Rāmānuja*. New Delhi: Munshiram Manoharlal, 1993.

Sources of Texts and Translations

80	*Mūlamadhyamakārikā* 25. 1–3, 9–20, 22–24	Garfield 73–76
81	*Bodhicaryāvatāra* 9.77,101–07, 147–52	Padmakara 148, 151–52, 158
82	*Triṁśikā-kārikā* 20–30	Anacker 188–89
83	*Tattvārtha-sūtra* 10	Tatia 253–57
84	*Laghutattvasphoṭa* 4.20–25	Jaini 36–38
85	*Upadeśasāhasrī* 1.10.1–10. 14; 2.2.45–50, 74–75, 84–89, 100–01, 109–111	Mayeda 123–24, 234–35, 239–40, 241–42, 244–45, 247–48
86	*Śaraṇagatigadya* 8, 10, 14–16, 17–23	Ayyangar 10–14
87	*Śiva-sūtra* 1.1–7; 3.33–38, 41–42	Feuerstein 358–59, 365–66
88	*Śivastotrāvali* 1.8; 3.9–12	Bailly 30, 40
89	*Mālinī-vijaya-vārtika* 1.620–30; *Mālinī-vijaya-vārtika* 2.95–103; *Parātriṁśikā-vivaraṇa*; *Tantrāloka*	Muller-Ortega 97, 192–93, 161, 197–98

11

آن راه بسوی کعبه برود این بسوی دوست

That way to the Ka'ba leads, this one to the Friend!

Fawā'id al-Fu'ād, Majlis 28

Indo-Persian Sufism

SUFISM is the English word for a widespread system of spiritual belief and practice that took form within the religious and cultural framework of Islam. Sufism is often described as the mystical side of Islam, and this is adequate as a brief description so long as it is remembered that some Muslims have considered and still consider Sufism to be un-Islamic, while some who consider themselves sufis deny that they are Muslims. It cannot however be denied that Sufism has been an important strain of Islamic thought and practice for more than a millennium, and that most of the well-known sufis of Arabia, Persia, India and elsewhere have been devout Muslims.

The Arabic for Sufism is *taṣawwuf*, a word that comes, like *ṣūfī*, from *ṣūf* or "wool" — evidently an allusion to the rough woollen garments worn by early Muslim ascetics. Sufism arose during the first Muslim century as a reaction against the worldliness of the successors of the Prophet, who suddenly found themselves in possession of an empire. Sufism's early ascetic practices were mellowed by the introduction of a gospel of love, and justified by a comprehensive philosophy. It is probable that sufi asceticism and devotion were influenced by eastern Christianity, and that its philosophy drew on Neo-Platonism. It is even possible that some of its monistic or pantheistic tendencies developed under the indirect influence of Buddhism or Vedanta. But Sufism's core has always been Muslim. The Prophet Muhammad experienced divine illumination and received the word of God in the form of the *Qur'ān*, and Muhammad and his Book have always been the principal points of reference for sufis in all parts of the world.

Sufism is a path (*ṭarīqa*) that leads from absorption in the lower self to closeness or union with God. It begins when the aspirant is accepted by a guide (*shaykh* or *pīr*) and is initiated into a particular mode of practice. *Dhikr* or the remembrance of God, often in the form of repetition of His names, is a fundamental practice in all forms of Sufism. Another that is widespread, though always controversial, is *samā'* or listening to spiritually inspiring music. Such preliminary methods prepare the seeker for the higher stages of the path, which are described in great detail by sufi writers. Ascending stage by stage, the human soul draws near to God or even feels that she has dissolved in a blissful state of union. A major step along the way is the state known as *fanā'* or annihilation. The tenth century Iraqi sufi al-Junayd distinguished three stages of *fanā'*: annihilation of characteristics, annihilation of pleasures, and annihilation of consciousness.

The religion of Muhammad first entered South Asia when Arabs penetrated Sind in the eighth century. Three hundred years later, Central Asian Turks used Afghanistan as a staging point for raids into the Indian interior. But it was not until the beginning of the thirteenth century that a permanent Muslim government was established in Delhi. For the next six hundred years, one Muslim dynasty or another was the dominant political force in northern India. During this period, Islamic culture extended itself gradually from the ruling élite to segments of the general populace. Sufis played an important role in this dissemination.

During the early stages of its development, Sufism was transmitted mainly by individual masters to small groups of disciples. By the time it entered India, the first of the fraternal orders or *silsilah* had been founded, and from this time forward, the transmission of doctrine and practice was along the lines of the various orders. Those active in India included the Qadiriyah, the Naqshbandiyah, the Shattariyah and above all the Chishtiyah. Their continuity, established rituals, and missionary spirit helped spread Sufism, and with it Islam, throughout the subcontinent. People were attracted by the sufis' preaching of universal brotherhood, and won over by the holiness of individual masters, whose tombs became places of pilgrimage and worship.

There are two main strands of Sufism in South Asia. One was the high-culture tradition of the urban élite, who spoke and wrote in Persian; the other, the popular traditions of those who spoke and sang in the regional languages: Sindhi, Punjabi, old Hindi, Urdu, Bengali. The first or Indo-Persian strand is the subject of this chapter, the second strand is dealt with in Chapter 16.

Indo-Persian Sufism may be viewed as having three phases: one that developed while Punjab was under Afghan rule, another that flourished during the Delhi Sultanate, and a third that prevailed during the Mughal Dynasty.

EARLY SOUTH ASIAN SUFISM

Economic and political relations between Punjab and Afghanistan have always been close. In the beginning of the eleventh century, the two formed parts of a single entity: the empire of Mahmud of Ghazni. Mahmud made his capital a centre of power and culture, but he did so at the expense of India, where he is remembered as a plunderer and destroyer. Quite different is the reputation of one of his younger contemporaries, the sufi Abu al-Hasan, known as al-Hujwiri, who is remembered as Data Ganj Bakhsh, "the giver who bestows treasure". A century after Hujwiri's death, Khwaja Muinuddin Chishti, who brought the Chishtiyah to India, stopped to pray at Hujwiri's tomb before proceeding further south, because he felt that Data Ganj Bakhsh had spiritual authority over the subcontinent.

[90]
Al-Hujwiri

Hujwiri was born in a village near Ghazni around 1009. Some thirty years later he was sent by his *shaykh* to Lahore, and he spent the better part of his life in this city, dying there in 1073. Widely travelled in the Islamic world, and widely read in Arabic and Persian, he was well acquainted with the varieties of Sufism current in his day. Towards the end of his life, he presented this knowledge in his masterwork, the *Kashf al-Mahjub* or "Uncovering of Veils". The first comprehensive manual of Sufism in Persian, the *Kashf al-Mahjub* is still regarded as a classic statement of the "sober" school of al-Junayd of Baghdad. Unlike his "intoxicated" disciple al-Hallaj, who was executed for heresy for proclaiming "I am the Creative Truth", Junayd counselled restraint in the seeking and expression of mystical states. To him, and to Hujwiri, intoxication was a preliminary stage, sobriety a precondition for the annihilation of self in God. In the last eleven chapters of his book, each of which is called the "uncovering" of a veil, Hujwiri deals with various points of sufi doctrine and practice, such as the love of the soul for God, the function of reason, and the attainment of ecstasy through music and other means. The four passages making up this selection were translated from the Persian by Reynold A. Nicholson.

My Shaykh, who followed the doctrine of Junayd, used to say that intoxication is the playground of children, but sobriety is the death-field of men. I say, in agreement with my Shaykh, that the perfection of the state of the intoxicated man is sobriety. The lowest stage in sobriety consists in regarding the powerlessness of humanity: therefore, a sobriety that appears to be evil is better than an intoxication that is really evil. It is related that Abú 'Uthmán Maghribí, in the earlier part of his life, passed twenty years in retirement, living in deserts where he never heard the sound of a human voice, until his frame was wasted and his eyes became as small as the eye of a sack-needle. After twenty years he was commanded to associate with mankind. He resolved to begin with the people of God who dwelt beside His Temple, since by doing so he would gain a greater blessing. The Shaykhs of Mecca were aware of his coming and went forth to meet him. Finding him so changed that he hardly seemed to be a human creature, they said to him: "O Abú 'Uthmán, tell us why you went and what you saw and what you gained and wherefore you have come back." He replied: "I went because of intoxication, and I saw the evil of intoxication, and I gained despair, and I have come back on account of weakness." All the Shaykhs said: "O Abú 'Uthmán, it is not lawful for anyone after you to explain the meaning of sobriety and intoxication, for you have done justice to the whole matter and have shown forth the evil of intoxication."

Intoxication, then, is to fancy one's self annihilated while the attributes really subsist; and this is a veil. Sobriety, on the other hand, is the vision of subsistence while the attributes are annihilated; and this is actual revelation. It is absurd for anyone to suppose that intoxication is nearer to annihilation than sobriety is, for intoxication is a quality that exceeds sobriety, and so long as a man's attributes tend to increase he is without knowledge; but when he begins to diminish them, seekers [of God] have some hope of him. . . .

There are two kinds of intoxication: (1) with the wine of affection (*mawaddat*) and (2) with the cup of love (*maḥabbat*). The former is "caused" (*ma'lúl*), since it arises from regarding the benefit (*ni'mat*); but the latter has no cause, since it arises from regarding the benefactor (*mun'im*). He who regards the benefit sees through himself and therefore sees himself, but he who regards the benefactor sees through Him and therefore does not see himself, so that, although he is intoxicated, his intoxication is sobriety.

Sobriety also is of two kinds: sobriety in heedlessness (*ghaflat*) and sobriety in love (*maḥabbat*). The former is the greatest of veils, but the latter is the clearest of revelations. The sobriety that is connected with heedlessness is really intoxication, while that which is linked with love, although it be intoxication, is really sobriety. When the principle (*aṣl*) is firmly established, sobriety and intoxication resemble one another, but when the principle is wanting, both are baseless. In short, where true mystics tread, sobriety and intoxication are the effect of difference (*ikhtiláf*), and when the Sultan of Truth displays his beauty, both sobriety and intoxication appear to be intruders (*ṭufaylí*), because the boundaries of both are joined, and the end of the one is the beginning of the other, and beginning and end are terms that imply separation, which has only a relative existence. In union all separations are negated, as the poet says—

> When the morning-star of wine rises,
> The drunken and the sober are as one.

*

Man's love towards God is a quality which manifests itself in the heart of the pious believer, in the form of veneration and magnification, so that he seeks to satisfy his Beloved and becomes impatient and restless in his desire for vision of Him, and cannot rest with anyone except Him, and grows familiar with the remembrance (*dhikr*) of Him, and abjures the remembrance of everything besides. Repose becomes unlawful to him and rest flees from him. He is cut off from all habits and associations, and renounces sensual passion and turns towards the court of love and submits to the law of love and knows God by His attributes of perfection. It is impossible that Man's love of God should be similar in kind to the love of His creatures towards one another, for the former is desire to comprehend and attain the beloved object, while the latter is a property of bodies. The lovers of God are those who devote themselves to death in nearness to Him, not those who seek His nature (*kayfiyyat*), because the seeker stands by himself, but he who devotes himself to death (*mustahlik*) stands by his Beloved; and the truest lovers are they who would fain die thus, and are overpowered, because a phenomenal being has no means of approaching the Eternal save through the omnipotence of the Eternal. He who knows what is real love feels no more difficulties, and all his doubts depart. Love, then, is of two kinds—(1) the love of like towards like, which is a desire instigated by the lower soul and which seeks the essence (*dhát*) of the beloved object by means of sexual intercourse; (2) the love of one who is unlike the object of his love and who seeks to become intimately attached to an attribute of that object, e.g. hearing without speech or seeing without eye. And believers who love God are of two kinds — (1) those who regard the favour and beneficence of God towards them, and are led by that regard to love the Benefactor; (2) those who are so enraptured by love that they reckon all favours as a veil (between themselves and God) and by regarding the Benefactor are led to [consciousness of] His favours. The latter way is the more exalted of the two.

*

When reason is gone as far as possible, and the souls of His lovers must needs search for Him, they rest helplessly without their faculties, and while they so rest they grow restless and stretch their hands in supplication and seek a relief for their souls; and when they have exhausted every manner of search in their power, the power of God becomes theirs, i.e. they find the way from Him to Him, and are eased of the anguish of absence and set foot in the garden of intimacy and win to rest. And reason, when it sees that the souls have attained their desire, tries to exert its control, but fails; and when it fails it becomes distraught; and when it becomes distraught it abdicates. Then God clothes it in the garment of service (*khidmat*) and says to it: "While thou wert independent thou wert veiled by thy faculties and their exercise, and when these were annihilated thou didst fail, and having failed thou didst attain." Thus it is the allotted portion of the soul to be near unto God, and that of the reason is to do His service. God causes Man to know Him through Himself with a knowledge that is not linked to any faculty, a knowledge in which the existence of Man is merely metaphorical. Hence to the gnostic egoism is utter perfidy; his remembrance of God is without forgetfulness, and his gnosis is not empty words but actual feeling.

*

It is a well-known story that Junayd and Muḥammad b. Masrúq and Abu 'l-'Abbás b. 'Aṭá were together, and the singer (*qawwál*) was chanting a verse. Junayd remained calm while his two friends fell into a forced ecstasy (*tawájud*), and on their asking him why he did not participate in the audition (*samá'*) he recited the word of God: "*Thou shalt think them* [the mountains] *motionless, but they shall pass like the clouds*" (*Qur'ān* xxvii, 90). *Tawájud* is "taking pains to produce *wajd*", by representing to one's mind, for example, the bounties and evidences of God, and thinking of union (*ittiṣál*) and wishing for the practices of holy men. Some do this *tawájud* in a formal manner, and imitate them by outward motions and methodical dancing and grace of gesture: such *tawájud* is absolutely unlawful. Others do it in a spiritual manner, with the desire of attaining to their condition and degree. The Apostle said, "He who makes himself like unto a people is one of them," and he said, "When ye recite the Koran, weep, or if ye weep not, then endeavour to weep." This tradition proclaims that *tawájud* is permissible. Hence that spiritual director said: "I will go a thousand leagues in falsehood, that one step of the journey may be true."

SUFISM DURING THE DELHI SULTANATE

During the period of the Delhi Sultanate (1206–1526), Muslim rule was established over most of northern India, and often extended into the West and South as well. In these generally stable conditions, Indian Sufism took root and flourished. The arrival in Ajmer of Khwaja Muinuddin Chishti towards the beginning of the thirteenth century facilitated this advance. The Chishti order he brought from Afghanistan soon became the most important in South Asia. Its emphasis on the attainment of unity with God and its rejection of property and the use of force fostered the peaceful spread of Sufism throughout Rajasthan, Punjab and Uttar Pradesh.

[91]

Nizam ad-din Awliya

The most famous of the Indian Chishti *shaykhs* was Nizam ad-din Awliya. Born in Budaun (Uttar Pradesh) around 1243, he became a disciple of Shaykh Farid ad-din of Ajodhan (west Punjab) while still a young man. Appointed as Farid ad-din's successor, he settled in Delhi, where he died in 1325. In the capital, Awliya lived a simple, saintly life, studying, practising his discipline, and transmitting the Chishti teachings through daily conversations. Some of these were recorded by one of his disciples, the poet Amir Hasan Suzji. The resulting book, the *Fawā'id al-Fu'ād* or "Morals of the Heart", is the finest Indian example of the *malfuzāt* or collection of edifying discourses. In the following selections from the *Fawā'id al-Fu'ād*, Awliya deals with spiritual and practical problems with insight, urbanity and wit. He refers often to the experiences of other sufis, but rarely to his own, except when speaking of himself as a disciple of Shaykh Farid ad-din. Translated from the Persian by Bruce B. Lawrence.

I obtained the good fortune of kissing his feet. He discussed a group of indifferent believers, to wit, those who make the canonical pilgrimage but on their return immerse themselves in worldly concerns. I submitted: "I would be surprised if any group attached to the master would journey in that direction [i.e., to Mecca]." At the time that I was speaking, my friend Malih was with me. Continuing to address the master, I said: "Broken-hearted though I be, I once heard from my friend Malih a phrase that has made a lasting impression on me. The phrase that Malih told me was this: 'Someone goes on the pilgrimage who has not found a spiritual guide.'" When the master — may God remember him with favor — heard this phrase, his eyes filled with tears. On his blessed tongue came this line of poetry:

That way to the Ka'ba leads, this one to the Friend!

Then he remarked that after the death of Shaykh al-Islam Farid ad-din — may God sanctify his lofty secret — he had had a strong urge to make the canonical pilgrimage. "I said to myself: 'First I will go to Ajodhan to visit the tomb of the Shaykh.' In short, when I had paid my respects to Shaykh al-Islam, I achieved my purpose. Nothing more remained [to be done]. Another time, the same desire [to make the pilgrimage] arose. Again, I visited the tomb of Shaykh al-Islam and fulfilled my goal."

*

"Patience is this," he said, "that when something odious happens to you, you bear with it and do not complain. As for contentment, that is when something odious happens to you and you do not regard it as odious, but instead act as if that misfortune had never befallen you!"

"The theologians," he went on, "deny this meaning of contentment. They maintain that it is inconceivable that something odious might afflict a person without that person perceiving it as odious. The rejoinder to their denial is this," he explained. "Many times it happens that a traveler will have a thorn lodge in his foot. His foot may even begin to bleed, but he is hurrying along so fast, and is so preoccupied with reaching his destination, that he does not take notice of what has happened to his foot. Only later does he become aware of pain. Also, there are many instances of a soldier having been wounded, but because he is so engaged in combat, at first he remains unaware of his wound. Only on returning home does he realize what has happened to him. Now, if you reflect on the lesson of these incidents in which pain goes unnoticed, you will understand how much more that same reflex characterizes one who is preoccupied with meditating on God.

After that he spoke about Qazi Hamid ad-din Nagauri—may God be merciful to him. "He was sitting in a certain place when a man came to punish him for wrongs he had allegedly committed. That man rained blows on Qazi Hamid ad-din, hitting him a thousand times. Yet the Qazi let out no cry nor did any sign of pain appear on his face. Afterward, when they brought him to the political tribunal, he was asked, 'How is it that you experienced no pain from this beating?' 'At the moment that I was being pummeled,' replied Qazi Hamid ad-din, 'my beloved was keeping watch over me. Under his gaze no pain could reach me.'" Then on the tongue of the master—may God remember him with favor—came this blessed utterance: "If such protection is provided under the gaze of a human beloved, how much more protected is one under the gaze of the divine Beloved?"

Conversation next turned to trust. The master observed that there are three stages of trust. (1) The first is the relation of a client to his advocate. That advocate is both knowledgeable of the law and well disposed toward him. The client has faith in the outcome, saying to himself, "I have a lawyer who both knows his business and is my friend." In short, the client has trust, even though from time to time he may ask that advocate a question or suggest to him that he argue the case in a particular manner or offer a specific motion. Such is the first stage of trust for a Sufi adept: He also has trust, but at the same time he asks favors of God. (2) The second stage of trust is the relationship of a nursing child to its mother. It also has trust but it does not question. Never does it say to its mother: "Give me milk at such-and-such a time." When hungry, it simply cries. It does not implore. It does not say: "Give me milk." Its heart has total confidence in the compassion of its mother. (The same is true for the Sufi adept at the second stage of trust.) (3) As for the third stage, it is this: that the adept conducts himself like the corpse in the hands of a washerman. That corpse asks no questions.

It does not move on its own. It responds to every wish and to every initiative of the washerman. This is the third stage of trust. It is the highest, and its attainment represents a lofty spiritual station for the Sufi adept.

*

He was then prompted to tell a story . . . the gist of which, thank God, I have remembered. This is the story. "There once was an Israelite ascetic. For years he had scrupulously obeyed God. Then one day a message came to the prophet of that time: 'Go tell that ascetic: "What do you gain from those discomforts caused by your strict observance? I have not created you but for chastisement!"' As soon as the prophet had given this message to the ascetic, the ascetic got up and began to twirl around. 'Why,' asked the prophet, 'did this disclosure make you so happy that you've started dancing?' 'At least He has remembered me,' replied the ascetic. 'He has taken me into account; I have experienced His reckoning!

Though He speaks of killing me,
That He speaks is thrilling to me.'"

*

Discussion turned to the difference between sainthood (*walayat*) and saintdom (*wilayat*). The master explained: "The saint possesses both *walayat* and *wilayat* at the same time. *Walayat* is that which masters impart to disciples about God, just as they teach them about the etiquette of the Way. Everything such as this which takes place between the Shaykh and other peoples is called *walayat*. But that which takes place between the Shaykh and God is called *wilayat*. That is a special kind of love and when the Shaykh leaves the world, he takes his *wilayat* with him. His *walayat*, on the other hand, he can confer on someone else, whomever he wishes, and if he does not confer it, then it is suitable for God Almighty to confer that *walayat* on someone. But the *wilayat* is the Shaykh's constant companion; he bears it with him [wherever he goes].

[92]

Sharafuddin Maneri

Just as Awliya's *Fawā'id al-Fu'ād* is the finest example of an Indian sufi's discourses, so the letters of his younger contemporary Sharafuddin Maneri are the best Indian example of a sufi's epistolary instructions. Born in a town near Patna in 1263, Maneri went to Sonargaon, east Bengal, for his early education, and then to Delhi in search of a master. He saw the famous *shaykh*s of the capital, Awliya included, but remained dissatisfied until he met and was accepted by the Firdausi master Najibuddin. Returning to Bihar, Sharafuddin began to live as an ascetic in the forest and in the Rajgir Hills. Eventually his disciples persuaded him to settle in the town of Bihar Sharif, where he died at an advanced age in 1381. Among his followers was the provincial governor Qazi Shamsuddin, to whom he addressed the letters collected in the *Maktūbāt-i ṣadī* or *Hundred Letters*. These are more in the nature of essays than personal communications, but they are certainly informed with Maneri's personal experience and wisdom. Translated from the Persian by Paul Jackson.

In the name of God, the Merciful, the Compassionate!

May the bounty of God be upon you, my brother Shamsuddin, both in this world and the next! It should be known, at the very beginning, that belief in the unity of God can be divided into four stages. In the first of these a person proclaims "There is no god but God!" (*Qur'ān* 47:19) but his heart is devoid of faith. Such belief is hypocrisy and will prove profitless in the next life. In the second stage a person both proclaims "There is no god but God!" and believes in his heart that this is so. This type of belief can be either conventional — as is true for ordinary people — or supported by rational proofs — as is the case of the learned. This is the way belief normally manifests itself. In truth it can be said: Come, open your eyes and see that each particle of dust, if you look carefully, contains a world-revealing cup. Sufis say that such faith prevents people from falling into crass polytheism and saves them from languishing eternally in hell. It also ensures entrance into paradise. Although this type of belief is more beneficial and enduring than the first, there is still an element of instability about it. The highest form of belief is for you, my friend, not this, which is fit for old women!

The third stage is said to be reached when a person's soul is illuminated in such a way that he is able to perceive every action flowing from a single source and deriving from a single agent. This firm belief is different from the faith of common people and the faith of the learned, both of which are constricted. This elevates the heart. It is the contemplation of a light that effaces creatures! There is a similar difference between the person who believes that a certain gentleman is in an inn because somebody told him (just as the person of conventional faith inherits what he believes from his father or mother or someone else) and the person who, upon seeing the gentleman's horse and servants at the door of the inn, infers that the owner himself must be inside. This is the view and belief of the learned, but it contains a great amount of imitation. From the vantage point of someone who has actually seen the man, however, both beliefs are on the same footing; that is, they are equally defective. A believer who has attained the third stage is like the man who actually sees the gentleman in the inn. He is a Sufi who, in this stage, sees creatures and experiences the Creator, in the sense that he perceives that they all come from Him. This very discrimination, however, indicates that the state of complete unification has not yet been attained.

Sufi masters are of the opinion that, in the fourth stage, such a surfeit of the dazzling divine light becomes manifest to the pilgrim that every single existing particle that lies within his vision becomes concealed in the very luster of that light just as particles in the air are lost to sight on account of the brightness of the light emanating from the sun. This occurs not because the particles have ceased to exist but rather because the intensity of the sunlight makes it impossible that anything other than this concealment should result. In the same way, it is not true that a person becomes God—for God is infinitely greater than any man—nor has the person really ceased to exist, for ceasing to exist is one thing, and becoming lost to view quite another!

> Before your Unique Being, there is neither old nor new:
> Everything is nothing, nothing at all! Yet He is what He is.
> How then can we remain separate from You?

When "I" and the "You" have passed away, God alone will remain!

When you look into a mirror you do not see the mirror for the simple reason that your attention has become riveted on your own handsome reflection. You would not, however, go on to say that the mirror has ceased to exist, or that it has become beautiful, or that beauty has become a mirror. In a similar fashion, one can contemplate God's almighty power in the whole gamut of creation, without any distinction. Sufis describe this state as that of being entirely lost to oneself in contemplation of the Unique Being!

A person who attains such a blessed state says:
"His very brilliance blinds me to whatever descends!"

Many have lost their balance here; for without the ever-present help of God's grace and favor, as well as the assistance of a spiritual guide, no one can traverse this wilderness. The guide should be a person who has passed through the ups and downs of the Way and tasted the unique sweetness of his all-demanding Majesty, as well as the pleasure of his intoxicating Beauty, and himself have attained enlightenment. This is the meaning of the following story. One day, Mansur al-Hallaj saw a famous Sufi, Ibrahim, wandering about in a wilderness. He inquired what he was about. "I am treading the path that leads to perfect trust in God," he replied. Mansur exclaimed, "If your whole life were to be passed in doing justice to this stage of trusting in God, then how would you ever reach that of being lost in divine contemplation?" It has been noted that fostering any sort of desire is really a waste of time, since it will be but a hindrance to contemplation.

Some people are admitted into the royal Presence for an hour a week; others, for an hour or two a day; while yet others are absorbed in divine contemplation for the great part of their time. Beyond these four stages is one known as "losing consciousness of being lost in divine contemplation." This is due to the total absorption of the understanding of the pilgrim, which leads him to forget himself altogether, in the heightened awareness of the King who is unsurpassable in beauty and power! In an instant, the pilgrim is himself borne off to the concealment of nothingness! Everything slips away from him for, if he were to know anything else, then, in the opinion of Sufis, it would be a sign of the distinction between seeing God apart from creation and seeing creation rooted in God! Hence we can understand how a person can lose sight of both himself and the entire creation in the dazzling light of God! The last vestige of self-awareness is itself lost in the rapture of this union.

When you lose yourself in God, you proclaim the divine Unity.
Lose the sense of "being lost" — that is complete detachment!

Hence it is that he forgets himself and the entire creation on account of this dazzling divine light. On account of this forgetfulness, all awareness of self is lost. There is no calling upon the name or observance of customs; awareness of whether one exists or not; explanation, allusion, or divine throne! In this world, all things pass away (*Qur'ān* 55:26). There is no splendor except at this stage. Here, "everything perishes except His essence" (*Qur'ān* 28:88). Here alone is God actually seen face to face. Apart from here, one finds no trace of the Truth! "I am the Holy One!" The absolutely unhampered realization of the Unique Being occurs only in this stage.

Do not delude yourself, instead remember,
Not everyone who gets lost in God becomes God!

Consider an example from the world around us: the nut consists of (1) the outer shell, (2) the inner skin, (3) the kernel, and (4) the essence of the kernel itself, its oil. All four constitute the nut, but each is different in its importance and possible uses, as anyone can easily see. In a similar fashion all the aforementioned refer to belief in divine Unity, although in degrees, fruits, benefits, and gains there are thousands of distinctions. This letter should be given careful, detailed consideration, for it will be found to be the foundation of all stages, states, activities, and ecstatic phenomena. It will also help the reader to understand the sayings and allusions of religious leaders, when he peruses their writings, for that is what God is like. They will not fall into error. Also, it can throw light upon the foundation and lawfulness of verses dealing with divine Unity and its various degrees, a matter in which one and all can be deceived and in which contradictions may arise.

Brother, you are now but an ant, yet you can become a Solomon. Do not be preoccupied with your sinfulness. Though you might now be fainthearted, you can develop great courage. Do not lay stress on your present impure and mean condition, but rather on what it is possible for you to achieve. For many long years there have been followers of the Way. Consider Adam; he came from mud and water. Though an orphan raised by Abu Talib, Muhammad became the messenger of God. From Azar the idol-maker came Abraham, the Friend of God. Consider also how polytheists have become monotheists; unbelievers, believers; sinners, followers of the Way, and mischief-makers, peacemakers!

Neither is God's might dependent on man's obedience, nor is His Grace determined by man's sin. . . .

*

Brother Shamsuddin, may God Almighty grant you the blessing of union with Him! Realize that union with the Lord is not of the same kind as when your body is joined to another, nor your accidents with others, or your substance with your body, or knowledge with the thing known, or willing with the thing willed. "God Almighty is more exalted than that!" (*Qur'ān* 17:4, 43). This word *union* occurs in the Law and public discourse, and is also well known among the Sufis. It means "being joined to the Lord." What does it mean to be joined to the Lord? It means that, for the sake of God, one is cut off from what is in any way base. Being closely united would mean becoming lost in the very depths of God! To this corresponds a great freedom from preoccupation with things other than God. On the other hand, to the extent that a person becomes free from preoccupation with God, to the same extent he becomes separated from Him.

One can learn from this saying of Harisa: "Surely I see the throne of my Master." It so happened that, to the extent that Harisa was not united to this world, he was closely united to the Hidden One. Muhammad the Chosen One was detached from both worlds in order to be intimately united with God. If his secret leaked out, he would say, "I take refuge in You from You!" When he said these words, it was clear that nothing remained in his secret thoughts that was other than God.

Separation from this world restores union with God. Again there is the saying of Abdullah ibn Umar. As he was performing the circumambulation of the Kaaba, he said: "I was lost in the vision of the Lord in that place." This means that his personality was lost in the Law, while his secret thoughts were immersed in the Truth. Absorption in the Law is superseded by absorption in the Truth. A person is no longer aware of either house or greeting. So engrossed does he become in God that he hears no greeting, and his veneration of the Lord of the house reaches such a stage that there remains no memory of even the house! This is the sense of "I see God Himself in that house!" But when the person who had greeted him and not been vouchsafed a reply came, he was full of complaints and reproaches against him. When Umar came to the place, he said nothing. This became an argument in favor of the claim made by Abdullah, since the masters of jurisprudence argue that when it is necessary to speak, no reply becomes the reply. In short, every spiritually endowed person arrives at the point of return to the Lord. "Surely the ultimate point of return is to your Lord" (*Qur'ān* 53:42). In the beginning, the first covenant was "Am I not your Lord?" (*Qur'ān* 7:171). Just as spiritual nature was prepared for a lump of clay, so on the pinnacle of human nature was showered the leaven of everything leavened! "God created the universe in darkness, but then sprinkled his light upon it." One gulp from the cup of "Am I not" gives so much pleasure to his palate that throughout his entire lifetime it can never be erased from his soul. Indeed, his life consists of that delight and the desire of that Light is like the center and treasure of his own being. He is not inclined toward this world and is unable, even for a moment, to abandon that wine!

> Your lovers have been intoxicated from eternity.
> They have come, their heads swaying with "Am I not?"
> Imbibing this wine and savoring its fragrance,
> They become spiritual sots due to "Am I not?"

Those people are like moths sacrificing their lives out of love — for the yoke of yearning for God himself has fallen upon their necks in the covenant of "Am I not?" Here, many feathers and wings strain after Him. The veils of the beauty of the glorious Candle are shed, so that "whoever comes even a hand's breadth toward Me, toward him do I advance a yard" takes him by the hand! From the many stirrings of a heart, yearning for God Himself is like a rope between the two worlds, for it draws a person to the very edge of union and says, "How far could one reach with these weak wings and feathers? You have drawn aside the veils of My beauty, but you cannot fly in the atmosphere of My divine substance with these paltry wings and feathers!" Those required there are earned on the battlefield by "those people who struggle on Our behalf" (*Qur'ān* 29:69). As the *Qur'ān* goes on to promise, "Certainly I shall show them the way!" Wings and feathers of another hue shall I bestow upon you by scattering my own illuminations — "God guides by His own light whomsoever He wishes" (*Qur'ān* 24:35).

If the most exalted of angels, jinn, and men were gathered together, they could not confer on a single slave the enjoyment of the illumination of the Lord God, nor even enough desire for Him to enable a slave to venture a few footsteps upon the Divine Expanse. Undoubtedly this is a better desire than any concerned with creatures, and a form of slavery that is really a liberation from slavery and from oneself. Such people have the habit of directing all their desires toward the Divine World. One breath of theirs is equivalent to all the affairs of both worlds. The following verse hints at the intensity of their renunciation:

> In one breath the Sufis celebrate two feasts,
> While spiders tear flies to pieces!

At every moment a Sufi dies, only to obtain a new form of existence, coming further under the control of the desire of self-effacement and absorption in God. From that effacement one goes for a different type of stroll in the Divine World, under the influence of a strong yearning. "God effaces or establishes whatever He pleases" (*Qur'ān* 13:39). At every step absorption and affirmation are obtained, so that the Sufi celebrates two feasts there: one that of absorption, and the other a feast of affirmation. At this stage, it is fitting that he should be called "the Spirit of God" or "the Word of God"; such a title will become like a robe that fits him perfectly.

O brother, this work is scarcely compatible with having the sash of lordship tied to one's turban! For when that beloved one, Adam, came to heaven, he looked around and said: "These itching feet of mine cannot remain in the bonds of a stirrup. And this head of mine, filled with the effects of love, cannot bear the weight of the crown. I have been given an erect stature, that I may stand upright and alone, just like the letter *alif*." Causes and effects are fit only for the fire. He said "Here am I!" to love, and bade adieu to the eight heavens. While he was passing through heaven, along with his crown and robe of honor, Adam was in the rank of those near to God. When he entered upon the Way of seeking, he was not aware of things that still lay concealed. Hence it has been said:

> Do you know the precondition for entering a tavern?
> First lay aside your crown, your belt, and your turban!

Every particle of the being of Adam raised this primeval slogan of love:

> I will sorely try your heart with the anguish of love;
> Even today I shall demand your very life's blood!

SUFISM DURING THE MUGHAL DYNASTY

During the reign of the great Mughal emperors (1526–1707), Muslim rule in India reached its high-water mark. Sufis of the various orders were active throughout the empire, and, unlike their pre-Mughal predecessors, they were in contact with Hindus and members of other religions. This led to various forms of syncretism as well as orthodox reactions. The emperor Akbar (reigned 1556–1605) founded a short-lived cult called the *Dīn-i Ilāhī* or Divine Faith, which grafted cuttings from Zoroastrianism, Jainism and other religions on a Sufi–Muslim stock. Some members of the urban élite saw resemblances between Advaita Vedanta and the ontological monism of the Iberian sufi Ibn al-Arabi. Dara Shikuh, son of the emperor Shah Jahan, translated the *Bhagavad Gītā* and some *upaniṣads* into Persian. Sufis of several orders, notably the Shattariyah, practised forms of spiritual discipline that were akin to, or borrowed from, Indian yoga. Sufis far from the urban centres, who spoke and wrote in regional languages, were influenced by and influenced Hindu *bhaktas*, *sants* and Sikhs. Against such eclecticism, the Punjabi *shaykh* Ahmad Sirhindi raised the standard of orthodoxy. The existential unity (*waḥdat al-wujūd*) of Ibn al-Arabi was pantheistic, he said. Correctly viewed, divine unity was a matter of experience (*waḥadat al-shuhud*). For thus vindicating Islamic monotheism, Sirhindi was given the title "The Renovator of the Second Millennium", but eclecticism and synthesis continued. Coming of age during the break-up of the Mughal empire which followed the death of Aurangzeb, Shah Wali Allah sought ways to reconcile differences between sufis and between them and other Muslims. According to him, unity of existence and unity of experience were both true and not contradictory. Changing conditions required that religious law be interpreted by scholars who were able to balance the conflicting demands of orthodoxy and modernity. This approach opened the door to reform in Islamic South Asia.

[93]

'Isa Jund Allah

The sufis of the Shattari order stress the attainment of divine knowledge and union through meditation and personal experience. Some South Asian Shattaris adopted yoga-like practices including breath-control and physical postures. The Shattari master 'Isa Jund Allah (d. 1622), who lived in Burhanpur (Madhya Pradesh), left two manuals in Persian on specialised meditation techniques. These are based, philosophically, on the works of Ibn al-Arabi. On the practical side, they have similarities to techniques found in the writings of Jewish Kabbalists and Indian tantrics. Translated from the Persian by Carl W. Ernst.

The three levels of truth. . . . One encounters his own master, either in person or at a distance. When this becomes established in the heart, he then concentrates on having the same kind of encounter with the revered Prophet (may God bless him and grant him peace). When this too becomes natural, he attains "the encounter with his Lord, so let him act rightly" (*Qur'ān* 18:110). "Acting rightly" here means meditation, which is just like "presence" in the saying "There is no real ritual prayer without presence of the heart." This is on the first level, that of the religious law. In the religious law, only presence is established in the heart, and witnessing and quietude follow. When one attains witnessing, vision takes place; this is described by the saying, "The Prophet is totally absorbed in ritual prayer." This process takes place on all three levels: in the religious law (*shari'at*), on the spiritual path (*tariqat*), and in the spiritual reality (*haqiqat*).

Political and spiritual authority of the Prophet. On the topic of witnessing, the revered Prophet said, "One who has seen me has seen God." The explanation is as follows. In the Holy Scripture, it is said, "Obey God, obey the Messenger, and those who hold authority" (*Qur'ān* 4:59). In the religious law, "those who hold authority" means the ruler, who is called the interpreter of the religious law. On the spiritual path, he is called a master. It is a religious duty to carry out both these forms of authority. This authority is of two types, external and internal. External authority is the religious law, which everyone carries out. Internal authority is the spiritual path, which the masters enact, and this authority does not reach perfection except through meditation, which is being in the divine presence.

Spirit, heart, and body, and the three levels of truth. All the wayfarers and upholders of God's unity say that there are three meanings in the Qur'anic verse just quoted: (1) "Obey God" is the station of the spirit. (2) "Obey the Messenger" is the station of the heart. The bodily form of the divine essence is fixed in the heart, but it is veiled from the five senses. It sees without the eye, hears without the ear, and speaks without the tongue. The inner divine archetype is hidden from the outer senses. The heart is its roof material, comparable to a canopy over a throne, for "the heart of the believer is the canopy of God Most High." (3) "Those who hold authority" is the station of the body, and the body is the station of the religious law. The action of this station is performed with bodily limbs. But the station of the spiritual path is the heart, and the action of its station is performed by meditation. On the level of reality, all is spirit, and this is not even attained by annihilation in annihilation. Here, understanding is impotent and imagination fails. This station is not easily attained except through perfect love, for it is the station of the spirit. One obtains this authority by the vision of realities. Here there is universal understanding, so that one truly knows.

Divine attributes and the emanation of the human form. The spirit is in the form of the body. These are the three levels of the descent of the divine essence [spirit, heart, and body]. (1) The spirit exists in the station and level of absolute singleness. (2) The heart is in the secret reality of unity and in the station of unity, but absolute singleness is higher than unity. (3) Part of the spark of the light of the divine essence, the seven chief names of God that they call the "seven mothers," manifested itself in the bodily form of Muhammad and Adam. The light of Muhammad simultaneously illuminated all things through these seven chief names of God: Knowing, Hearing, Seeing, Speaking, Willing, Living, and Powerful. It was to that bodily form that Muhammad alluded by saying, "I was a prophet when Adam was between water and clay." The "seven mothers" descended into existence through the Five Presences [i.e., God's essence, the spiritual world, the imaginal world, the bodily world, and the Perfect Human]. Necessarily, when these descend from the divine presence, they are five. The descents of Muhammad, the Perfect Human, are in the hidden realm of the divine essence, but his appearance is by means of the spirit, the imaginal, and the bodily. As one master has said, "The fifth presence [i.e., the Perfect Human] comprehends these other presences." If one has this vision by lofty insight and manifestation, where can intellectual understanding fit, except in the perfect, comprehensive, and practicing knower of God? Sayyid Ni'mat Allah has said:

Since I saw Your beauty in manifestation,
I saw and witnessed the Beloved's face.
Then I looked upon the seeing eye,
And I saw a bodily form as essential meaning.

[94]

Dara Shikuh

Eldest son of the Emperor Shah Jahan, Muhammad Dara Shikuh was born near Ajmer in 1615. Given to the study of religious works from his youth, he was initiated into the Qadiri order at the age of 25. After writing several works on sufi doctrine, he began to examine other traditions. His study of Hindu scriptures, and meetings with Hindu holy men, led to translations of the *Bhagavad Gītā* (1650) and fifty *upaniṣads* (1657). He also wrote a treatise on comparative religion called *Majma'-ul-Baḥain* or "Mingling of the Two Oceans" (1656). Around this time, the illness of Shah Jahan led to a struggle for succession among his four sons. The eventual victor, Aurangzeb, was as intolerant as Dara Shikuh was liberal. After the ascension of Aurangzeb, a *fatwā* was passed accusing Dara Shikuh of heresy. He was executed in 1659. Dara Shikuh's Persian poems, of which these quatrains and *ghazal* are examples, are not master-works of religious thought or literature, but they do give expression to an eclectic spirituality that was perhaps three hundred years ahead of its time. Translated from the Persian by Bikrama Jit Hasrat.

O, thou, who seekest God everywhere,
Thou verily art the God and not separate from Him.
Already in the midst of a boundless ocean,
Thy quest resembles the search of a drop for the ocean!

*

Like an ocean is the essence of the Supreme Self,
Like forms in water are all souls and objects.
The ocean, heaving and stirring within,
Transforms itself into drops, waves, and bubbles.

*

In separation from thee, I have suffered pangs of anxiety,
In union with thee, I have lost my own consciousness:
Then happiness dawned upon my soul and became my lot,
Now shall I pass my days in peace, both in body and mind!

*

Whosoever recognised this, carried the day,
He who lost himself, found Him.

He who sat at the foot of the wine jar,
Won over the Sāqī, the wine and the cup.

And he who sought him not within his own self,
Passed away, carrying his quest along with him.

And he who knew not this secret,
When turned to dust, carried his desire unfulfilled.

Qādirī found his Beloved within his own self:
Himself of good disposition, he won [the favour of] the Good.

[95]

Fatima Jahanara Begum Sahib

Dara Shikuh was close to his sister Jahanara, and he persuaded her to become a disciple of one of his Qadiri masters, though she already was a member of the Chishti order. After her father Shah Jahan's deposition and Dara's execution, Jahanara remained at Shah Jahan's side during his imprisonment. Her final years, until her death in 1681, were passed in quiet devotion. In her *Risālat al-Ṣāḥibiyya* or "Treatise of the Sahib", Jahanara wrote in passing of her own experiences. This passage from the *Ṣāḥibiyya*, though somewhat conventional in its language, gives a good idea of the discipline and devotion of a sufi initiate. Translated from the Persian by Margaret Smith.

I offer a thousand praises and thanks to God the Incomparable, for it was He Who, when my life was being spent to no purpose, led me to give myself to the great search for Him, and Who, after that, let me attain to the high degree of Union with Himself. He it was Who enabled me to quench my thirst in the ocean of Truth and the fountain of Gnosis and thereby granted me the unending happiness and state of blessedness, which are to be found by one who drinks from these. I pray that God Most High will let me walk in the Path which leads, like *Ṣirāt*, to Paradise, with firm step and unfaltering courage, and to taste the delight of continual recollection of Himself.

Praise be to God for His grace in what He has given to me. I have been granted full and perfect apprehension of the Divine Essence, as I had always most earnestly desired. That one who has not attained to knowledge of the Absolute Being is not worthy to be called a man — he belongs to the type of those of whom it is said: "They are like the beasts of the field and are even more ignorant." But he to whom this supreme happiness has been granted has become a perfect man and the most exalted of created beings, for his own existence has become merged in that of the Absolute Being. He has become a drop in the ocean, a mote in the rays of the sun, a part of the whole. In this state, he is raised above death and the fear of punishment, above any regard for Paradise or dread of Hell. Whether woman or man, such a one is the most perfect of human beings. This is the grace of God which He gives to whom He wills.

[96]

Shah Wali Allah

Born in Delhi in 1703, four years before the death of Aurangzeb, Shah Wali Allah reached adulthood at a time of political and social instability. Before the end of his life, the Mughals had lost control of the Deccan and much of northern India, and Delhi had been sacked by Nadir Shah. Wali Allah's chief concern was to put a stop to the political and spiritual decline he saw around him. His many works include a Persian translation of the *Qur'ān*, legal commentaries, theological argumentation, and mystical treatises. In his "Divine Inspirations" (*al-Tafhīmāt al-ilāhiyya*), he described his *ṭarīqa* or path, a word that can refer both to individual progress and to an organised way or order. Using a device common in sufi literature, he distinguished seven stages of ascent. The first three are "true faith", "opening of the breast", and "drawing near [to God] through supererogatory actions". Three of the remaining four stages are described in the following extracts. Translated from the Persian by Marcia K. Hermansen.

According to us, wisdom is "existential drawing-near" (*qurb al-wujūd*). Its essence consists of the person's remaining as he was pre-eternally insofar as his fixed essence (*'ayn thābita*) is worshipping and prostrating before God, drawn near to Him, transcending evil and corruptions. This represents the condition of the preceding types of knowledge, the place to find complete sinlessness, and the location of the previous positions.

Once I had attained this station, the science of the divine names was disclosed to me, as well as the science of bringing into existence and drawing nearer to God, the divine legislation, the last days, the wonders of the human being. . . . The saints have continued to stand firm in their faith, and they have deeply sought out the annihilation of the rational soul. Annihilation (*fanā'*) is a garment and an inner aspect, and their state is never completely free from focusing on it. Faith is an outer dress and an overt thing towards which their references were directed and their expressions were targeted, until the Sufis came along. . . .

Then *Shaykh Aḥmad Sirhindī* [d. 1035/1625] came along and foretold the reappearance of Jesus, peace be upon him, and the light of prophecy shone upon him in its generality. Then the lights of the unseen flowed over me and I attained the station of wisdom (*ḥikma*) and on that day I was made the deputy of Joseph, because he is the one who possessed wisdom (*ḥikma*) among the Prophets.

*

The fifth stage is the "drawing-near" through the obligatory acts of worship. The Prophet said, in a *ḥadīth qudsī*, "I have not brought near to my servant anything dearer to me than performing what I had made obligatory on him."

My Lord made me understand, may His majesty be exalted, that whatever [divine] name should come to dominate a person, the signs of this would be that he would be able to effect his desire in the world and that he would be forced to some strong vision. When I had completed this cycle I made a covenant on the following matters:

1. That my heart and physical form would be totally devoted constantly to worship;
2. that if anyone needs me or is attracted to me for support, either in matters of faith only, or in other ways of drawing nearer to God [Sufism], I will prevent him from worshipping or asking for help from any other than God and from having doubts, fleeting thoughts, and other related matters;
3. that there can be no connection of love between me and another person unless this is permeated by the coloring of God;
4. to follow the path of the prophets and their practice;
5. not to be one of the "*ulamā*" thriving in worldly life, inclined to the world and its offspring in knowledge and dealings.

*

The seventh is the stage of perfection. The Prophet said, "Many men have been perfected and among women only Khadīja bint

Khawlaid, Miryam daughter of 'Imrān, Āsiya the wife of Pharaoh and Fāṭima daughter of Muḥammad." Its essence is uniting the worshipper with his perfections that reach out towards God, imploring Him with the tongue of their capacities so that He bestows a new level of perfection obtained from mixing of these six [previous] elements in the emanation of a sanctified form upon them. The beloved of God [set out] in this cycle, then he kept on developing until he became the seal of the prophets.

When this stage began for me, I saw [a vision] while I was sitting after the afternoon prayer, as if my clothing had been removed until I was completely naked. Then there appeared a theophany of the Prophet and he stood at my left side. I put on the clothing of validation, and the lowest level of the spirit (*nasama*) uttered a cry saying, "Truth, truth, truth." Then it became calm and this was an emanation of validation, comprehensively. Then an emanation of eternal blessing descended from above and on my right and on my left, transcending all verbal expressions and beyond all description, so praise be to God, Lord of the worlds. This is the end of what I wanted to explain with respect to the *ṭarīqa* that was bestowed on me, as a totality, on the basis of allusion and symbol.

FURTHER READING

Source Materials

Carl W. Ernst, *Teachings of Sufism*. Boston: Shambhala, 1999.

Bikrama Jit Hasrat, ed. and trans., *Dārā Shikūh: Life and Works*. Reprint edition. Delhi: Munshiram Manoharlal, 1982.

Marcia K. Hermansen, "Contemplating Sacred History in Late Mughal Sufism: The Case of Shāh Wāli Allāh of Delhi". In Leonard Lewisohn and David Morgan, eds., *The Heritage of Sufism, volume 3: Late Classical Persianate Sufism (1501–1750)*. Oxford: Oneworld, 1999.

Paul Jackson, trans., *The Hundred Letters*. New York: Paulist Press, 1980.

Bruce B. Lawrence, trans., *Morals for the Heart*. New York: Paulist Press, 1992.

Reynold A. Nicholson, trans., *Revelation of the Mystery*. Reprint edition. Accord, NY: Pir Press, 1999.

Margaret Smith, *Readings from the Mystics of Islām*. London: Luzac & Co., 1950.

Other Works

Carl W. Ernst, *The Shambhala Guide to Sufism*. Boston: Shambhala, 1997.

Bruce B. Lawrence, *Notes from a Distant Flute: The Extant Literature of Pre-Mughal Indian Sufism*. Tehran: Imperial Iranian Academy of Philosophy, 1978.

Saiyid Athar Abbas Rizvi, *A History of Sufism in India*. Two volumes. Delhi: Munshiram Manoharlal, 1997.

R. C. Zaehner, *Hindu and Muslim Mysticism*. Reprint edition. Delhi: Research Press, 1999.

Sources of Texts and Translations

90	*Kashf al-Mahjub*, ch. 14, 19, 15, 25	Nicholson 186–88, 307–08, 270–71, 415–16
91	*Fawā'id al-Fu'ād* 4.28, 2.9, 4.8, 1.14	Lawrence 258, 142–43, 225, 95
92	*Maktūbāt-i ṣadī*, letters 1, 15	Jackson 12–15, 64–67
93	*Risala-i muraqaba*	Ernst 55–58
94	Quatrains 10, 26, 34; *Ghazal*	Hasrat 148, 153, 156, 144
95	*Risālat al-Ṣāḥibiyya*	Smith 131–32
96	*Al-Tafhīmāt al-ilāhiyya*	Hermansen 338–40

Part Four

Reformulations

12

உடம்பினை முன்னம் இழுக்கென் றிருந்தேன்
உடம்பினுக் குள்ளே யுறுபொருள் கண்டேன்.

Mistakenly I believed the body to be imperfect,
But within it I realized the Ultimate Reality.

Tirumular, *Tirumantiram* 725

Siddhas, Yogis and Others

PSYCHO-PHYSICAL practices aiming at establishing a link between the human individual and a higher presence or power had been current in India for centuries before Patanjali systematised them in the *Yoga Sūtra*. Most early practices of which we have record involved ascetic discipline and the renunciation of the life of the world. The rise of Tantrism towards the middle of the first millennium brought in more positive attitudes. The body was viewed not as an encumbrance but as a means of perfection, while the world was viewed as a real manifestation of the power of the divine principle.

The philosophy and practices of Buddhist and Hindu Tantrism were set forth in Sanskrit texts that were accessible only to a few; but the tantric dispensation was spread also by means of poetry and songs in the regional languages. In this section are gathered together works from four traditions of popular tantric mysticism as well as one individual mystic. Though only indirectly related, they may be viewed as varied expressions of a single development. That this movement was pan-Indian is shown by the fact that the texts featured come from all four corners of the country: Tamil Nadu, Maharashtra, Kashmir and Bengal. Though they are often hard to date, it is fairly certain that most of them were composed between the tenth and seventeenth centuries.

The traditions selected are those of the Tamil *siddhas*, the *nāth yogīs*, the *vaiṣṇava sahajiyās*, and the *bāuls*. The teachings of Lalla have much in common with these traditions, but much that is unique to her. Indeed, the teachings of these mystics are so distinctive that their grouping together might be questioned. But along with their differences they have a number of striking similarities. First, all of them were unorthodox and opposed to mechanical devotion and ritualism. Though associated with the shaiva or vaishnava traditions, they did not view the Supreme as an object of worship but as a living presence within. Instead of scriptures, they relied on human gurus or the inner guide; instead of ritual or worship, they emphasised practices that opened the way to mystical experience. Since they viewed the Godhead as a principle within them, they gave a good deal of importance to the body, which they regarded both as a vessel of divinity and a means for its attainment. The practices they promoted included *prāṇāyāma*, and (in some cases) esoteric sexuality. To all of them, the body was an instrument of progress, and its perfection was part of the goal. Many of them considered salvation not as freedom after death or while living in a body doomed to die, but perfection in an immortal body. This lead many to experiment with alchemy and to seek extraordinary powers or *siddhi*s.

After leaving the rounds of conventional life, most of these mystics spent their time wandering from place to place, transmitting their teachings in gnomic verses or songs. These are among the earliest surviving examples of four of the country's regional languages: Tamil, Marathi, Kashmiri and Bengali. The texts use images drawn from daily life, which have special meanings to initiates. Something of their beauty, and a hint of their mystical sense, comes through even in English translation.

TIRUMULAR AND THE TAMIL SIDDHAS

Like many of the other mystics studied in this section, Tirumular is claimed by several different traditions. To orthodox followers of Tamil Shaiva Siddhanta, he is a semi-divine founder-figure, and also is revered as one of the sixty-three *nāyaṉār*s or Tamil shaiva saints. In addition, he is an authority on tantric theory and practice, giving a more detailed exposition of the "eight-limbed" yoga than Patanjali. Finally, he is regarded as the first of the Tamil *siddha*s, most of whom were active several centuries after his death. It is as a *siddha* that he is discussed below.

A *siddha* (Tamil: *cittar*) is one who has attained perfection or *siddhi* by means of yogic practice. The term is applied to members of several different traditions: the eighty-four *mahāsiddha*s of Vajrayana Buddhism (see section 7), the north Indian nath yogis or siddhas (see below), the Indian alchemists or *rasasiddha*s, and the eighteen siddhas of South India. The number eighteen, like the number eighty-four, is doubtless conventional. The membership of both groups varies from list to list; but just as Gorakhnath is rarely absent from catalogues of the eighty-four northern siddhas, Tirumular is rarely omitted from the southern eighteen.

Among the other siddhas found on the southern list are the authors of a body of popular literature that is best characterised in negative terms: anti-establishment, anti-ritual, anti-caste, anti-brahmin, non-devotional, relativistic and pessimistic. The best known of these siddhas are Sivavakkiyar, Pattinattar and Pampattic-cittar. They and the other Tamil siddhas were wandering tantric adepts who sang in rough popular idiom about the abuses of society, the glory of God, and the need to seek freedom and immortality by means of yogic practices.

[97]

Tirumular

Of the historical Tirumular, virtually nothing is known. Most scholars place him in the sixth or seventh century and take seriously the legend that has him leaving Mount Kailas, that is, the far North, and settling in the South. The book ascribed to him, the *Tirumantiram*, is a vast compendium of philosophy, morality, yoga, tantrism, siddha doctrines, and more. The title means "Sacred Utterance", from *tiru*, an honorific, and *mantiram*, the Tamil for *mantra*. It consists of more than 3000 quatrains arranged in nine *tantra*s or books. The selections below are from three different *tantra*s. The first explains salvation in terms of the Shaiva Siddhanta trinity of *pati* (Lord Shiva), *pāśa* (bondage), and *paśu* (the bound individual). The second and third give expression to the experiential side of siddha-yoga practice. Translated from the Tamil by B. Natarajan.

They speak of the Three — Pati, Pasu and Pasa;
Beginningless as Pati, Pasu and Pasa are:
But the Pasu – Pasa nears not the Pati supreme:
Let but Pati touch! the Pasu – Pasa is as nought. . . .

Our intelligence entangled in the senses
Finds itself in very deep waters,
But inside our consciousness is a deeper Consciousness,
Which the supreme Grace stimulates. . . .

Space intermingling with space,
Nectar drowning in nectar,
Light dissolving in light:

The elect are they, the Siva-Siddhas,
Who attain this glorious state.

*

The Mighty Lord, the Great Nandi,
Granted me His Feet of indescribable bliss;
And in Ocean of Grace immersed me;
Freeing me from all illusions,
And secretly guarding me in safety,
He bore me to the holy banks of Silence
That indeed was an Experiment Divine. . . .

Into the Goal beyond goals,
Into the Assembly where none assemble,
Into the Knowledge beyond knowledge,
I loosened myself,
In single-minded thought;
I merged in Holy Nandi's Grace,
There in Pervasiveness beyond pervasiveness
Was Siva.

*

Ended the birth; sundered the bonds;
God and I became one;
No more for me the way of rebirth;
I have met Siva the Auspicious. . . .

None can intimidate me hereafter,
The Lord came and entered my thoughts,
There will I sport and wander in joy;
No more will I be with anyone else.

I freed myself of fetters
The Creator bound me with,
I learned the way of reaching Siva;
I smote Karmas with the sharp sword of mind,
I stood ego-lost;
And now I hasten towards the City of God.

[98]

Sivavakkiyar

Nothing reliable is known about the life of Sivavakkiyar or indeed any of the Tamil siddhas. The oldest of the group after Tirumular, he may have lived as early as the ninth or tenth century. His *Pāṭal* or "Song" consists of 527 stanzas written in a rough, sometimes crude idiom. Disdainful of the vedic as well as the orthodox shaiva religion, he sings powerfully of the need to seek God within and not by means of outward ceremonies and observances. Translated from the Tamil by Kamil V. Zvelebil.

In the Four Eternal Vedas,
In the study and reading of scripts,
In sacred ashes and in Holy Writs
And muttering of prayers
You will not find the Lord!
Melt with the Heart Inside
and proclaim the Truth.
Then you will join the Light—
Life without servitude.

*

He is not Hari, He is not the Lord Śiva.
He is the Ultimate Cause,
In the Beyond of Beyond,
Transcending Blackness, Redness, and Whiteness.
Immovable.
Try to understand:
He is not big, He is not small.
He is Infinite Distance,
Immovable,
Transcending even
Supreme Quiescence.

*

The slothful
    sluggards
    say: He is far, far, far
    away!
But the Supreme It

is spread everywhere
on Earth and in Heavens.
O you poor dumb ones,
running
stunned and suffering
through towns and fields and forests
in Search!
He is right there
within you!
Stand still
and feel Him,
feel!

[99]

Pattinattar

The name Pattinattar seems to have been borne by two different poets. One, who lived around the tenth century, is venerated by orthodox shaiva siddhantins. The other, apparently four centuries younger, was an opponent of orthodoxy in all its forms. Several translations from the works of this second Pattinattar are reproduced here. Filled with world-disgust and pessimism, Pattinattar's verses sometimes hint at the peace and bliss of inner spiritual fulfilment. Translated by Kamil V. Zvelebil.

O Lord of Madurai! O Lord of Madurai!

I do not know the origin,
I do not know the end,
I only know, o Lord,
That there's much suffering in the world.

The filth of ignorance, o Lord,
Has all the powers of my wit destroyed,
Through the results of sticking deeds
A deranged madman I became, o Lord!

By body and its actions was I stupefied,
Caught in the nets of secret rules I lied.

I roam about in jungles — Great Illusions,
sick in this world created by Confusion.

I can't forget my children and my relatives,
Attachment to the land and king does never cease.

The wish to master science does not halt,
I wish to possess Powers undissolved.

O Lord of Madurai,
O Lord!

*

I left the world.
I do not wish the two-fold deeds.
I do not mix with idle, useless men.
I do not listen to their speech.

I touched the state
when only Truth
remains.
I swept away
pleasures and pains.
The Highest
which is beyond the reach
of the four ancient Vedas
came
    here
        to me!

*

The eightfold Yoga
the six regions of the body
the five states
they have all left and gone
totally erased
and in the open
Void
I am left
amazed.

There is but a red rounded Moon
A fountain of white milk
for delight
The unobtainable Bliss
has engulfed me
A precipice
of light.

[100]

Akkapey-cittar

Some of the Tamil siddhas are known by the tag-lines found in their songs. The siddha known as Aggapey-cittar addressed his songs to the "demon of the soul". His nihilistic view of world and salvation is in some ways reminiscent of the more polished thought of that earlier south Indian mystic, Nagarjuna. Translated by Kamil V. Zvelebil.

I do not exist
The Lord does not exist
The Self does not exist
The Teacher does not exist

Mantras do not exist
Experience does not exist
Tantras do not exist
Doctrines have been destroyed

Rites are just devil's play
Knowledge — a hollow stable
The Lord is but an illusion
Everything is like that

Why and whatfor to study?
Why and whatfor to act?
All set rules and all forms
have been burnt and annulled

All manifested actions
you see are only Void
Those which in fact do not appear
will appear in Pure Nothingness

[101]

Pampattic-cittar

The word *pāmpāṭṭi* means "the one who makes snakes dance" or, simply, snake-charmer. The poet of the "song of the snake-charmer" was a siddha who lived between the fifteenth and eighteenth centuries. Each of the 129 stanzas of his still-popular song ends with the refrain "Dance, snake, dance!" These words, which a snake-charmer might use to control his cobra, hint at the siddha's effort to control his wandering mind, and evoke also the Kundalini Shakti of Tantrism and the creative – destructive Dance of Shiva. Translated by David C. Buck.

make the horse
called mind
a mount,

insert the bit
called intellect
in its mouth,

mount gracefully
into the saddle
called anger,

ride to the
Clear Place,
and
dance,
snake!
dance!

*

we placed our feet
on the sandals of desire,

and stamped to ruins
the thorny forest of vanity;

we kindled a fire
in the grass of evil traits,

and transcended
time,
so
dance,
snake!
dance!

*

in the mountain
called eternity
we stood fast;

we accomplished
whatever we thought;
we were
purified;

truthfully,
our body
won't be
destroyed;

we'll even live
forever,
so
dance,
snake!
dance!

THE NATH YOGIS

Claiming descent from the sage Gorakhnath, who, among other things, is credited with the discovery of *haṭhayoga* (see Chapter 8), the *nāth yogī*s or *nāth siddha*s have practised an eclectic blend of physical and mental disciplines since the eleventh or twelfth century. Those initiated into the sect add the suffix "nath" to their names and wear rings in their pierced ears.

Hence they are popularly known as *nāth* or *kānphaṭa* ("split ear") *yogīs*. Their beliefs and practices seem to come, on the one hand, from Vajrayana Buddhism, and, on the other, from shaiva cults like the *pāśupatas*. The *nāth yogīs* are known to have been active across north India from Bengal to Punjab, as well as in Maharashtra. They are still active today, though it is difficult to say how much the contemporary cult preserves the earlier doctrines and practices. Although technically shaivite, the *nāths* do not worship Shiva or any other divinity, since they believe that human beings are potentially gods in their own bodies. This conviction, which they share with the Tamil siddhas, determines both their practices and their goal. By means of *prāṇāyāma* and other hathayogic techniques they hope to arrive at mastery of the five or ten subtle "breaths" and other components of an intricate inner physiology. This will lead them to freedom from physical limitations, the development of the eight extraordinary powers or *siddhis*, the ecstasy of *samādhi*, and finally physical immortality.

[102]

Songs of "Jnandev"

Legend links Jnandev, the Maharashtrian philosopher and mystical poet (see Chapter 13), with the *nāth yogīs*. The historical Jnandev certainly knew about the sect and about the practices of tantric yoga. His masterwork, the *Jñāneśvarī*, contains a description of the ascent of the *kuṇḍalinī* and a passing mention of "the secrets of the convention of the *nāths*". Jnandev is also said to be the author of a series of songs that are informed with secret nath teachings. There is reason to doubt whether the man who wrote the *Jñāneśvarī* was also the author of the songs, but they remain interesting examples of popular nath teachings. The following selections are from a collection called the *Lākhoṭā* or "Sealed Letter", which may date from as early as the thirteenth century. The songs are filled with esoteric imagery, which would require the instruction of a nath guru to be fully understood. Translated from the Marathi by Catharina Kiehnle.

See the eye in the eye, the end of the voids, the blue dot, clear and sparkling.
Consciousness reached there to take rest. Know [that] positively with experience!
Ādināth showed [the sign] for the sake of Pārvatī. [It] accrued to Jñāndev by Nivṛtti's compassion.

*

The one whose nature is the Self flooded the river of the sky. The
seer drowned the moment he saw.
While [he] sees the waves of consciousness [they] suddenly
[become] like the water of the deluge,
or [like] pearls, scattered in the sky. [They] are visible but do not
come to [one's] hands.
One should get to know and take up the sign through the mouth
of the *guru*, and see the state of the liberated in this very body.
Jñāndev says, the generous Nivṛtti made me understand my very
essence.

*

Neither colour nor manifestation, immeasurable, of innate lustre:
this is the secret of the *santa*s, consisting in the Self.
The ocean of the pearl / an ocean of pearls filled into the ten
directions: as soon as [one] sees [it] the condition of the soul
drowns.
My [own] eyes showed that sign [to me], a mine of jewels of
consciousness opened up.
Jñāndev attained the grace of Nivṛtti, he became happy by that joy.

*

[When] I saw [the highest reality] in the courtyard of the eye,
[then,] know, the ten directions brightened.
All is cast as large as the universe—mind and intellect do not
embrace [it].
Jñāndev attained that knowledge through his [own] eyeball(s).
Nivṛtti gave it, holding [him] by [his] hand.

LALLA

Little is known of the life of the woman whom Kashmiri Hindus call Lalleswari, Kashmiri Muslims Lalla Arifa, and both Lal Ded ("Granny Lal") or simply Lalla. She was born near Srinagar in the fourteenth century, apparently in a brahmin family. Married off while still young, she proved an intractable daughter-in-law, and after a few years of domestic life, she renounced the world and became a wandering ascetic. On the basis of a single line in one of her *vākh*s or sayings, she is supposed to have danced or wandered about in the nude; but the line in question perhaps means simply that she disrobed herself of all worldly attachments. Lalla undoubtedly knew something of the teachings of Kashmir Shaivism, though not through Sanskrit texts, and she also may have had some knowledge of Sufism; but it is clear from her sayings that she was not the follower of any single tradition. The guru she sometimes mentions may have been a human teacher, but it seems likely that most of her knowledge came from inner practice and experience. Like the *siddha*s of Tamil Nadu and the North she mentions breath-control and other tantric practices, which suggests a pan-Indian movement of popular tantrism, of which she was a part.

[103]

Lalla's *Vakh*s

The sayings of Lalla (*Lallā Vākh* or, in Sanskrit, *Lallā-vākyāni*), is a collection of some hundred-fifty verses that were transmitted orally for four hundred years before being written down early in the twentieth century. Composed in old Kashmiri, they were modernised by successive singers, with the result that, barring a word here and there, they can be understood by any modern Kashmiri. And no modern Kashmiri is unaware of Lalla's *vākh*s, many of which have become proverbial sayings. Using ordinary language and everyday images, she gives expression to her own spiritual strivings, and to the insights she arrived at through tantric practice and spontaneous inner illumination. Translated by Jaishree Kak Odin.

I pull the boat with untwisted yarn
Will God hear and help me across
Water leaks from unbaked clay saucers
My heart desires to go home

*

I, Lalla, set out in the hope of blooming like a cotton flower
Ginner and carder gave me hard blows
The female spinner spun me into fine yarn
In the weaver's shop I was stretched on the loom

*

The washerman then dashed me on a slab of stone
Rubbing me with much soap and washing soda
Then the tailor cut me into bits with scissors
And only then I, Lalla, attained supreme bliss

*

Awakening in the early dawn
I summoned the restless mind
Enduring the pain I devoted myself to God
By saying "I am Lalla, I am Lalla," I awakened my darling
By becoming one with Him, I purified my mind and body

*

I took the reins of the mind-horse
Through practice, I learned breath control
Then only the orb of moon melted and flowed down into my body
Nothingness merged with nothingness

*

Cold changes water into ice or snow
Discernment shows the three states though different are not really different
When the sun of consciousness shines,
The plurality is dissolved into oneness
Then the universe appears throughout permeated with Shiva

*

When teachings disappear, the mantra remains
When the mantra disappears, consciousness remains
When consciousness disappears, nothing remains
Nothingness merges with nothingness

*

Easy to read but difficult to follow
Attaining self-knowledge is subtle and difficult
Absorbed in practice, I forgot the scriptures
Consciousness-bliss I realized

*

I, Lalla, entered the door to the garden of my mind
I saw Shiva and Shakti in communion
I became immersed in the nectar of bliss
I died while still alive
Nothing worries me

*

You are the sky and you are the earth
You are the day, the night and the wind
You are the grain, sandalwood, flowers, and water
You are everything, then what should I offer to you

*

Slowly through the practice of breath control
The lamp shone and I saw my true nature
Inner light I realized
Caught it in the darkness and seized it

*

Why are you groping like the blind
If you are wise, you will turn your attention within
Shiva is there, you need not go anywhere else
Believe my simple words

THE VAISHNAVA SAHAJIYAS

Popular Tantrism took different forms in combination with different traditions. Emerging from the matrix of southern Shaiva Siddhanta, it expressed itself in the songs of the Tamil *siddha*s. Developing under the influence of Gorakhnath and the Buddhist *mahāsiddha*s, it developed into the cult of the *nāth yogī*s. In Bengal, where the teachings of shakta tantrics competed with those of Krishna-devotees, it took the form of the *vaiṣṇava sahajiyā* cult. The original sahajiyas were vajrayana Buddhists who believed that the innate or spontaneous nature of existence was perfect Bliss. The doctrines of the Buddhist sahajiyas left their trace in eastern India in the teachings of the nath yogis and other yogic cults after Buddhism had become little more than a memory. Vaishnavism, the worship of Vishnu, particularly in his form of Krishna, became the leading form of Hinduism in the region. Poets of Bengal, Bihar, and Assam celebrated the mystic love of Krishna and Radha, and their songs were taken up by the mystic Chaitanya, whose cult of Krishna-devotion spread throughout eastern India (see Chapter 13). In the fifteenth or sixteenth century, a hybrid tradition took form which interpreted the love of Radha and Krishna in a radically tantric way. Radha was the human *rūpa* or form; Krishna the true form (*svarūpa*) — not so much a god as a pure cosmic principle. The goal of existence was to find *svarūpa* in the *rūpa*, and since each woman was Radha and each man Krishna, this could be done by means of ritual coitus. Sahajiya *sādhana*, abhorred by the orthodox, was practiced in strict secrecy, and its doctrines were transmitted in treatises and songs that made use of a code that only initiates could understand.

[104]

Songs of "Chandidas"

The sahajiyas read the songs of the vaishnava *bhakta*s in their own tantric light, and also composed new lyrics in the name of those older poets. Chandidas (see selection 130) has ascribed to him a number of sahajiya songs, most of which apparently were written a century or two after his death. In them the "humanistic" doctrines of the cult come to the fore: "Man" is the highest thing there is, because he can, in a finite body, realise or become the Infinite. Radha, the archetypal Woman, is the means by which this supreme goal can be reached. These three songs, attributed to Chandidas, but probably by a sixteenth- or seventeenth-century mystic, were translated from the Bengali by Deben Bhattacharya.

All go chattering
Man, man, man,
The word
That hides the deepest of thoughts.
Man is a resident
Of the greatest height,
Above and beyond
Everything else.
If you should know
Who is housed
In the depth
Of the deep, deep sea of love,
The nature of man
Might reveal itself.
The laws of the Vedas
And the wisdom of Vishnu
Throw no light
On the substance called man.
Man is unique
And a joy to the universe.

*

Who can know
The creation — woman?
Even the god
Who brought her into being
Has no clue at all.
Poison and nectar
Were blended into one.

The lamp that throws light,
Holds a flame in her heart
And the loving moth
Wanders to his fiery death.
A man can march
To his funeral, in lust.
But a lover drinks the nectar
Sieving poison out. . . .

*

The essence of beauty
springs
from the eternal play
of man as Krishna
and woman as Rādhā.
Devoted lovers
in the act of loving,
seek to reach
the goal.
Who is devoted
To whom and how
Is of no interest.
Dedicate your soul
to the service of loving.
Love was born to Rādhā
as one by one,
her eight friends helped.
If your senses
and the mind
can grasp the essence
Krishna is reached.

Says Chandidās:
Listen, O, brother man,
Man is the greatest Truth
Of all, nothing beyond.

THE BAULS

Of all the traditions brought together in this section, none resist classification more than the *bāuls*. Wandering musicians and mystics of rural Bengal, they are regarded by some as vaishnava devotees, by others as sahajiyas. Some scholar underline their kinship with the *nāth yoga* tradition, others stress their sufi characteristics. It may be said that the bauls have absorbed something from all these traditions, but that they remain irreducibly bauls. The word *bāul* means "mad", and doubtless was applied to them because of their unconventional language and behaviour. The figure of the "crazy-wise" mystic is an established one in India and Tibet. The bauls exemplify it not only in their wild ways and "upside-down" speech, but in the mystical method of their madness. For their doctrines are not incoherent. Like other tantrics, they view the body as a microcosm of the universe. Within it resides the Divine, called by them the "Man of the Heart". This is the object of their adoration and also the goal of their *sādhana*, which includes the practice of *prāṇāyāma* as well as ritual sex. The bauls do not hope for freedom after death, but long instead for the state of *jiyānta morā* — "being dead while yet alive".

[105]

Songs of the Bauls

The songs of the bauls were not written down until the end of the nineteenth century, when they were "discovered", and romanticised, by scholars like Kshitimohan Sen and poets like Rabindranath Tagore. It is impossible to determine how long the bauls have existed as such. There is evidence of them from as early as the fifteenth century, but the first well-attested baul, Lalan Shah, died in 1890. Many baul songs carry the signature line of the composer, and these at least sometimes are of known historical individuals. But many of the songs cannot be dated: they may be as much as three hundred or as little as thirty years old. Asked by Kshitimohan Sen why they did not keep better records, a baul singer replied "We follow the *sahaj* (simple) way and so leave no trace behind us. . . . Do the boats that sail over flooded river leave any mark? . . . All the streams that flow into the Ganges become the Ganges. So must we lose ourselves in the common stream, else it will cease to be living" (Sen 1931: 213–14). These songs by known and unknown bauls were translated from the Bengali by Deben Bhattacharya.

Scanning the cosmos
you waste your hours:
he is present
in this little vessel.

He does not dwell
in the complex of stars
nor in limitless space;
he is not found
in the ethical scriptures
nor in the text of the *Vedas*.
He lives beyond the existence
of all.

He is here
in his form without form
to adorn the hamlet of limbs,
and the sky above
is the globe of his feelings
the platform of spontaneous matter.

*

Those who are dead
and yet fully alive
and know the flavors of feelings
in loving,
they will cross the river.
Gazing at the stream of life
and death,
they seek integrity.
They have no wish
for happiness,
walking against the wind.

They kill lust
with lust,

and enter the city of love
unattached.

*

My soul cries out,
snared by the beauty
of the formless one.
As I cry by myself,
night and day,
beauty amassed before my eyes
surpasses numberless moons and suns.
If I look at the clouds in the sky,
I see his beauty afloat;
and I see him walk on the stars
blazing my heart.

*

The nectar of the moon
and the honey in the lotus,
how do they meet —
the moon from the sky
and the lotus from the lake?

*

Build a bridge
over the river
of life and death
to reach beyond.

FURTHER READING

Source Materials

Deben Bhattacharya, trans., *Love Songs of Chandidās: The Rebel Poet-Priest of Bengal*. New York: Grove Press, 1970.

Deben Bhattacharya, trans., *The Mirror of the Sky: Songs of the Bāuls of Bengal*. Prescott, AZ: Hohm Press, 1999.

David C. Buck, *dance, snake! dance!: A Translation with Comments of the Song of Pāmpāṭṭi-Cittar*. Calcutta: Writers Workshop, 1976.

Catharina Kiehnle, ed. and trans., *Songs on Yoga: Texts and Teachings of the Mahārāṣṭrian Nāths*. Stuttgart: Franz Steiner Verlag, 1997.
B. Natarajan, trans., *Tirumantiram: A Tamil Scriptural Classic*. Madras: Sri Ramakrishna Math, 1991.
Jaishree Kak Odin, *To the Other Shore: Lalla's Life and Poetry*. New Delhi: Vitastā, 1999.
Kamil V. Zvelebil, *The Poets of the Powers*. London: Rider and Co., 1973.

Other Works

George Weston Briggs, *Gorakhnāth and the Kānphaṭa Yogīs*. Reprint edition. Delhi: Motilal Banarsidass, 1998.
Sasibhusan Dasgupta, *Obscure Religious Cults*. Reprint edition. Calcutta: Firma K. L. Mukhopadhyay, n.d.
Edward C. Dimock, Jr., *The Place of the Hidden Moon: Erotic Mysticism in the Vaiṣṇava-Sahajiyā Cult of Bengal*. Reprint edition. Delhi: Motilal Banarsidass, 1991.
T. N. Ganapathy, *The Philosophy of the Tamil Siddhas*. New Delhi: Indian Council of Philosophical Research, 1993.
Jayalal Kaul, *Lal Ded*. New Delhi: Sahitya Akademi, 1973.
Kshiti Mohan Sen, "The Baül Singers of Bengal". In Rabindranath Tagore, *The Religion of Man*. London: George Allen & Unwin, 1931.

Sources of Texts and Translations

97	*Tirumantiram* 115, 119, 124; 2635, 2638; 2958, 2960–61	Natarajan 18–20, 408, 454
98	*Pāṭal* 30, 9, 27	Zvelebil 84, 83, 82
99	*Aruḷ pulampal*; *Potu* 24–25	Zvelebil 93–94, 101–02
100	*Akapēycittar* 70–72, 77, 88	Zvelebil 110
101	Song of *Pāmpāṭṭiccittar* 78, 79, 77	Buck 94–96
102	*Lākhoṭā* 2, 4–6	Kiehnle 204–05
103	*Lallā Vākh* (ed. Odin) 2, 13, 14, 30, 34, 39, 41, 52, 58, 59, 65, 97	Odin 103, 109, 117, 119, 122, 123, 128, 131, 132, 135, 151
104		Bhattacharya (1967) 164, 165, 167
105	Anon., Haridās, Fikirchānd, Ramanadās, Rāmalāl	Bhattacharya (1999) 43, 102, 85, 201

13

सगुन ध्यान रुचि सरस नहिं निर्गुन मन ते दूरि।
तुलसी सुमिरहु राम को नाम सजीवन मूरि॥

When contemplation of the Personal brings no joy, and the Impersonal remains out of reach, Tulsi says, remember Ram — his name is the medicine that gives life.

Tulsidas, *Dohāvalī* 8

The Bhakti Movement

THE ATTEMPT to approach the Divine by establishing a personal relationship with a particular form of the godhead has been part of Indian religion since the time of the *Ṛg Veda*. In most vedic hymns, the gods are looked upon as powerful beings that must be propitiated by sacrifice; but sometimes they are addressed as "friends". In some of the later *upaniṣad*s the word *bhakti* is used to designate the love that a human worshipper can feel for a higher or divine being. *Bhakti* usually is translated as "devotion", but the root-sense is "participation" in the godhead through intense attachment and love. *Bhakti* was a major component of the bhagavata and shaiva cults that arose in the last centuries before the Common Era. The *Bhagavad Gītā* combines bhagavata devotionalism, samkhya philosophy and yoga techniques; in a number of verses, it puts forward *bhakti* to Krishna as the supreme way for humans to approach the divine. The *Lotus Sutra* and other Mahayana texts recommend and exemplify a similar devotion to the Bodhisattvas and Celestial Buddhas.

In the post-classical period, devotional religion was given new forms in different sorts of Sanskrit texts: the narratives of the *purāṇa*s, the esoterism of the *tantra*s, the *stotra*s of Hindus, Buddhists and Jainas. But the principal developments in the religions of *bhakti* were recorded in poems, songs and sayings in the emerging regional languages. In a famous puranic passage it is stated that Bhakti was "born in the Tamil country and attained maturity in Karnataka". Afterwards, she gained some respect in Maharashtra and reached old age in Gujarat, before being born again in Vrindavan, the village in the North where Krishna passed his youth (*Bhāgavata-Māhātmya 43–50; cf. Padma Purāṇa 6.189–90*). These legendary wanderings of a personified Bhakti correspond roughly to the historical spread of *bhakti* from Tamil Nadu to the Deccan and thence to the North and East.

In this chapter, works by most of the more important *bhakta*s of the various regions and traditions are reproduced. These saints (as they often are called in English) have enough in common for the phrase "bhakti movement" to be meaningful; but it should not be imagined that it was the undifferentiated spread of a single mode of worship. Wherever bhakti arose, it found expression in accordance with the period, place, and personality of worshipper and worshipped. Some *bhakta*s adored God in a particular form; others gave their devotion to the Formless. Some formal worshippers preferred Vishnu or his incarnations, others Shiva, and still others the Mother Goddess. Some pursued a path of quiet inwardness, others the demonstrative expression of intense emotion. Despite these and other differences, the various bhakti traditions had a number of things in common. Most gave considerable importance to the Name of the Divine, which was considered not a label but a living portion of the godhead. Chanting the Name and singing songs about the beauty and majesty of the chosen deity (*iṣṭadevatā*) were frequent forms of worship. Temple ritual, though often given a place, was regarded as inferior to direct communion with the *iṣṭa devatā*. Accordingly, the offices of the priest were considered less important than the initiation and guidance of a *guru*. Most bhakti traditions were open to men and women of all castes; a number of influential bhaktas were women or outcastes. On account of this comparative freedom from the strictures of the Hindu social system and from temple organisation and Sanskrit learning, the bhakti movement was implicitly revolutionary and in some cases actively anti-establishment.

The notes that follow contain biographical information about all the bhaktas included, along with remarks about their background and works. For most of these saints, the chief biographical sources are hagiographies written long after their deaths. These works generally contain more legend than verifiable fact. While I avoid making statements that are historically unsound, I occasionally cite exemplary stories that may be assumed to have some basis in fact.

THE SOUTH

The earliest surviving bhakti songs are those of the shaiva and vaishnava devotional traditions of Tamil Nadu. Both took lasting form in the sixth century CE, though there are evidences that they go back a few centuries earlier. This was the age of the Pallava Dynasty, famous for the architecture and sculpture of its artisans as well as the poetry and sanctity of its saints. A new movement of shaiva devotion began in Karnataka four centuries later, followed by an outburst of vaishnava bhakti poetry in the Kannada and Telugu languages, which lasted almost until the modern period.

THE NAYANARS

The Tamil word *nāyaṉār*, meaning "leader" or "master", is applied to sixty-three shaiva saints, the most celebrated of whom are Appar, Sambandar and Sundarar. These three, whose hymns make up the *Tēvāram*, the main scripture of Tamil Shaivism, were born in the seventh and eighth centuries in central and northern Tamil Nadu. They are often grouped together with Manikkavachakar, a later saint who is revered almost as much as they. The principal characteristic of all four saints is their intense, overwhelming love for Shiva. There was nothing abstract in this devotion. They wandered from temple to temple throughout the Tamil country, singing the praises of the form of Shiva therein enshrined, whom they looked on as a parent or master or friend. The intimacy of this relationship between the human person and a divine personality was something novel in Indian religion, and it remained part of the bhakti movement wherever it spread. The songs of the nayanars and of Manikkavachakar began to be sung in temples not long after their composition, and are still sung, and broadcast in amplified form, during Tamil religious festivals. The same songs, as interpreted by Tamil theologians, are treated as fundamental texts of the Shaiva Siddhanta school of philosophy.

[106]

Appar

At the beginning of the seventh century, when Marunikkiyar was born, Jainism and Buddhism were powerful religions in the Tamil country. Marunikkiyar became a Digambara monk and rose to be head of a monastery. Then, while suffering from seemingly incurable colitis, he entered a Shiva temple and burst into song. Cured of his disease by Shiva, he became an opponent of Jainism under the name of Tirunavukkaracar ("Lord of Speech"). More familiarly, he is known as Appar ("Father"). According to legend, Appar converted the Pallava king to Shaivism after undergoing various forms of torture and emerging unscathed. Whatever the truth of this story, it is a fact that, owing to the appeal of the religions of bhakti, Jainism and Buddhism were soon extinct in Tamil Nadu. The following extracts from Appar's songs were translated from the Tamil by Indira Viswanathan Peterson.

O devotees who pass your time
in useless talk of worldly things
and in the care of this despicable frame,
in multiplying your karma,
in fattening the belly,
in getting entangled in family affairs!
Be saved! Smear the sacred ash
on yourselves,
become faithful devotees at the shade
of the feet of the Lord who dwells
in Ārūr of lotus ponds!

*

When I think of the skullbearer
who wears a wreath of flowers in his hair,
the Lord with the white moon who likes to live
in Veṇṇi's ancient city,
a flood of ambrosia
wells up in my tongue.

*

I hold none dearer to me
than myself; yet within my self
there is one dear to me —
Iṉṉampar's Lord
who is the breath of life,
which enters and leaves me,
and abides within.

[107]
Sambandar

The legends of Sambandar reveal little of his historical circumstances, except that he was born in a brahmin family in Sirkazi, south of

Chidambaram. While still a child, he adopted Shiva and Parvati as his parents, lauding them in his sometimes sensuous songs. It was he who gave the name of Appar to his elder contemporary. Like Appar, he often railed against the Jainas, as the second of these extracts shows. Translated by Indira Viswanathan Peterson.

He wears a woman's earring on one ear;
riding on his bull,
crowned with the pure white crescent moon,
his body smeared with ash from the burning-ground,
he is the thief who stole my heart.
He is the Lord who lives in fine Piramapuram,
where he once blessed with his grace
Brahmā of the lotus seat
who worshipped him.

*

Lord who holds the fawn and the axe,
Primal Being who dwells in southern Ālavāy!
May your glory reign supreme in the world!
Is it your gracious will,
that I should annihilate in debate
those great sinners
who neglect the Vedic rite and wear mats as robes,
the base men who pluck the hair from their heads?

*

Cast into the bright flames
the holy name of Naḷḷāṟu's Lord
whose body is cool and gleaming
from embracing the beautiful, cool, lustrous breasts
of the mountain's daughter,
woman who glows with the loveliness
of a young sprout!
It will emerge unharmed —
This is the truth!

[108]

Sundarar

Nambi Arurar, later known as Sundarar or Sundaramurti, was born around the beginning of the eighth century. The story of his life forms the most colourful chapter of the *Periya Purāṇam*, the canonical hagiography of the Tamil shaiva saints. This legendary account emphasises his familiarity with Shiva, whom he addressed as "friend" and even went so far as to use him as a go-between in his amours. In this extract, translated from the Tamil by Vidya Dehejia, Sundarar sings of his first blissful surrender to Shiva.

O madman
on whose locks
rests the crescent moon
Sovereign Lord
of grace abounding
Never more
will I forget you
You are enshrined
in my heart and
in my mind.
In the holy temple of Arul Turai
in the heart of Vennai Nallur
on the south banks of the Pennar
you do abide.
Father
no more can I deny you
To you I have
surrendered.

Through many arid days
I wandered
restless as a ghost
groped in vain
aimlessly
with little thought of you
Such grace as none may hope to win
I won from you.

In the holy temple of Arul Turai
in the heart of Vennai Nallur
where bamboos fringe the flowing Pennar
do you abide.
Father
no more can I deny you
To you I have
surrendered.

[109]

Manikkavachakar

Born near Madurai about a century after Sundarar, and so not included in Sundarar's authoritative list of nayanars, Manikkavachakar ("he whose words are rubies") was minister to one of the Pandya kings. Seduced by Shiva in the form of a guru, he abandoned his duties, was thrown into prison, but eventually was released and allowed to become a wandering singer and saint. These extracts from his principal work, the *Tiruvācakam*, were translated from the Tamil by Vidya Dehejia, Glenn E. Yocum and M. Dhavamony.

Like oil
consumed by flames
I was scorched
by the fire
of women's eyes
now you have forsaken me
O Lord of lotus feet
your grace
made me one with the saints
who worship
your fragrant feet
O Lord, my Master
full of faults
though I be
forsake me not
your praises
ever will I sing.

*

Like a fly
caught in honeyed jack-fruit
I succumbed
to fawn-eyed maidens
with budding breasts
so you have forsaken me—
but if you go away
I'll revile you
Black-throated One
who drank
The poison of the seas
One without character
Mere mortal
Wearer of the crescent moon
Great One
gone astray
With these names
shall I reproach you.

*

While unperishing love melted my bones,
    I cried
I shouted again and again,
    louder than the waves of the billowing sea,
I became confused,
    I fell,
    I rolled,
    I wailed,
Bewildered like a madman,
Intoxicated like a crazy drunk,
    so that people were puzzled
    and those who heard wondered.
Wild as a rutting elephant which cannot be mounted,
    I could not contain myself.

*

You made me yours
thrilling my frame through every pore
You are my Lord
who melting my bones
entered my Self
as a shrine.

THE ALVARS

Around the time that the nayanars began singing the glories of Shiva, a group of vaishnava devotees were doing the same for their own chosen deity. Called *āḻvārs* ("those who are immersed or drowned in devotion"), these saints released a current of devotion that would influence the author of the *Bhāgavata Purāṇa* and the philosopher Ramanuja and, through them, much of the rest of India. Like the nayanars, the alvars exemplified an emotional form of bhakti that expressed itself in songs chronicling the pain of separation and the joy of union. There were in all twelve alvars. The first three, called Poikai, Bhutam and Pey, lived probably in the seventh century. The dates and sequence of the others is disputed; they stretch, roughly, from the eighth to the tenth centuries. To pious southern vaishnavas, the alvars are regarded as partial incarnations of Vishnu's attributes and companions. Their works are collected in the *Divya Prabandham* or "Divine Treatise".

[110]

Andal

Daughter or foster daughter of Periyalvar, the "Great Alvar", Andal was born in Srivilliputtur in the south of Tamil Nadu in the eighth or ninth century. According to legend, while still a child she decided she would marry no one but Vishnu. Her poetry is filled with sensuous bridal imagery showing that, in terms of inner experience, she was indeed the Lord's beloved. The most famous of her works is the *Tiruppāvai*, a song still sung during the Marlaki festival by girls hoping for a happy marriage. Andal's other work is a series of hymns called the *Nācciyār Tirumoḻi* or "Sacred Song of the Lady". This passage from one of the *Tirumoḻi* hymns makes use of a familiar device of Sanskrit love poetry: an isolated lover sending a messenger to the beloved one. Translated by Vidya Dehejia.

Pining for
Mādhava of eternal fame

dark as the blue sapphire,
crowned with a cluster of gems,
is it right
that the conch shell bangles
should slip off my wrists?
Koelbird who lives in flowery groves
of laurel, pear, wild poppy and *ñāḻal*,
fly to my lord of the coral lips
stay with him,
call his names repeatedly,
ask him
to hasten to my side. . . .

My bones melt,
my beautiful lance-like eyes
have known no sleep
for many nights.
Sunk in the sea of sorrow,
I whirl round and round —
I do not see
the boat named Vaikuṇṭa.
O koel, you know well
the pangs of parting
from the beloved.
Go to the lord whose emblem
is golden-hued Garuḍa,
ask that holy one
to come to me. . . .

So great is my desire
to unite with the lord
who rests upon the milky ocean
that emotion chokes my breath,
my breasts rise and fall
and quiver in joy.
O dainty koel,
what do you gain
by hiding from me?
If you will go
to him who holds

conch, discus and mace,
ask him to come to me,
great indeed will be your merit. . . .

I yearn for him
who once measured the worlds.
He has me in his thrall,
I cannot resist his power.
I know not how
the moon and the southern breeze
add to my heartache.
O koel,
do not linger in this grove
and add to my anguish,
go bring Nārāyaṇa to me
else I shall drive you away.

[111]

Tirumangai

Little is known about Tirumangai Alvar, who is supposed to have lived during the eighth century. In the hagiographies, he is said to have been a local ruler who turned to robbery to feed the devotees of Vishnu. More than a thousand of his stanzas are included in the *Divya Prabandham*. These extracts were translated by Vidya Dehejia.

Weary was I
sad, weary and worn
sunk in deep sorrow
I sought the company of young women
thinking only of
the pleasures they bring —
I wanted to escape
I ran and ran
I discovered the knowledge,
the greatest of all,
I searched and searched —
I realized
the sacred name of Narayana.

I became a thief
deceitful, dishonest
I wandered hither and thither
yet light dawned upon me —
I reached your feet
and instantly your grace fell upon me
with melting heart and choked voice
your praises I sing
body bathed in streaming tears
I repeat day and night
the sacred name of Narayana.

*

What need of penance harsh
flesh wasting, senses impaired
weakened with fasting
barely alive?
If you but reach Chitrakutam
king of the *devas* you can be —
that sacred town
whose mansions' banners fly
where in green flooded fields
kayal fish leap and play
where bees hum
peacocks dance in the woods —
go to that Tillai Chitrakutam.

What need of such penance
feeding for many a year
on fruit and berries
braving the sharp gusting winds?
standing before the five fires?
Retain in your mind
the sacred form of the Lord
Go to Tillai
where brahmins of hoary fame
chant all day the Vedas
and guard the holy fires —
As grows the fire, so grows the fame
of Tillai Citrakutam.

[112]

Nammalwar

Greatest of the alvars both in output and reputation, Nammalvar ("our alvar") was born in the southern part of Tamil Nadu, apparently towards the end of the ninth century. The speaker in many of his songs is a lovesick girl who condemns the tricks, and laments the absence, of her beloved. These delicate works are much revered by southern vaishnavas, whose theologians have built round them a dense mass of interpretation. The most important of Nammalvar's works, the *Tiruvāymoḻi*, comprises more than a quarter of the *Divya Prabandham*. These extracts were translated from the Tamil by A. K. Ramanujan.

Don't tell us those lies,

heaven and earth
  know your tricks.

Just one thing,
my lord of the ancient wheel
  that turns at your slightest wish:

while all those girls
—their words pure honey—
stand there
wilting for love of you,

don't playact here and sweet-talk
  our lisping mynahs,
  our chattering parrots!

*

Look here:

  being naughty,
    grabbing our dolls
      and doing wild things

  won't get you anywhere;

we know you
   from old times,
how can we stand your pranks,
   your airs?

There are any number
   of lovely women,
      queens of the three worlds;

so don't torment
   this plain crowd.
Such stuff is childish,
   even for you.

*

Pure one,
   you devoured once
      the sea-surrounded world.

Great one,
   it isn't right to grab
      our dolls and toys.

What's wrong is wrong
      even for you.

You tease us with sweet talk:
if my brothers hear of it,

they won't wait to see
   right and wrong,
they'll just bring out
      their sticks

and beat you up.

*

While I was waiting eagerly for him
   saying to myself,

"If I see you anywhere
I'll gather you
and eat you up,"

he beat me to it
and devoured me entire,

my lord dark as raincloud,
my lord self-seeking and unfair.

*

I don't understand why,

while all the worlds
live within him

and he lives within them
by birthright,

our lord of Kāṭkarai,
of gardens blowing with fragrance,

should assault
and devour this poor little
soul of mine
with his grace.

THE VIRASHAIVA TRADITION

The virashaiva or lingayat faith is a form of Shaivism prevalent in Karnataka, which was founded in the twelfth century by Basavanna and others. Initiated members of the virashaiva community wear a small *liṅga* or symbol of Shiva around their necks at all times. As a result they are known popularly as lingayats or "*liṅga*-wearers". Like other forms of Shaivism, such as Tamil Shaiva Siddhanta and Kashmir Shaivism, Virashaivism is based on the tradition of the shaiva *āgama*s, and it accepts many doctrines common to the other shaiva schools, such as the thirty-six *tattva*s and the supremacy of Shiva. But the real source-texts of Virashaivism are the Kannada *vacana*s or "sayings" that were composed by its founding teachers. The doctrines and practices of Virashaivism differ in a number of respects from those of other forms of Shaivism. Most noteworthy among these distinctive characteristics are its uncompromising rejection of image-worship and of the authority of the Vedas, and its non-acceptance (at least in its original formulation) of caste distinctions. Bhakti for Shiva has always had a central place in virashaiva practice, and the *vacana*s in which the virashaiva saints gave expression to their devotion are among the greatest accomplishments of Kannada literature.

[113]

Devara Dasimayya

Born a century or more before Basavanna, Devara Dasimayya ("God's Dasimayya") is regarded as a precursor of the twelfth century *vacanakāra*s. His sayings, filled with psychological insight, are addressed to Ramanatha or Shiva as the lord and advisor of Rama. Translated from the Kannada by A. K. Ramanujan.

I'm the one who has the body,
you're the one who holds the breath.

You know the secret of my body,
I know the secret of your breath.

That's why your body
is in mine.

You know
and I know, Rāmanātha,

the miracle

of your breath
in my body.

*

In the mother's womb
the child does not know
his mother's face

nor can *she* ever know
his face.

The man in the world's illusion
does not know the Lord

nor the Lord him,

Rāmanātha.

[114]

Basavanna

Greatest among the founder-figures of Virashaivism, Basava (called familiarly Basavanna or respectfully Basaveshvara) was born in the beginning of the twelfth century in northern Karnataka. At the age of sixteen, he removed his brahminical thread and went to Kudalasangama, at the confluence of three rivers, where he studied under a guru for several years. Having realised that Shiva was the only God and the *liṅga* his only symbol, Basava went to Kalyan, where his uncle was serving as the king's minister. Eventually succeeding him to the ministership, Basava established an Anubhava Mantapa or Hall of Spiritual Experience, which became the centre of the virashaiva faith. Arousing the ire of brahminical orthodoxy by his opposition to the caste system, he was obliged to flee from Kalyan to Kudalasangama, where he died around 1167. All his *vacana*s are addressed to Kudalasangama Deva, Shiva as the Lord of the Meeting Rivers. Translated by A. K. Ramanujan.

Don't you take on
this thing called bhakti:

like a saw
it cuts when it goes

and it cuts again
when it comes.

If you risk your hand
with a cobra in a pitcher
will it let you
pass?

*

The rich
will make temples for Śiva.
What shall I,
a poor man,
do?

My legs are pillars,
the body the shrine,
the head a cupola
of gold.

Listen, O lord of the meeting rivers,
things standing shall fall,
but the moving ever shall stay.

*

When
like a hailstone crystal
like a waxwork image
the flesh melts in pleasure
how can I tell you?

The waters of joy
broke the banks
and ran out of my eyes.

I touched and joined
my lord of the meeting rivers.
How can I talk to anyone
of that?

[115]

Mahadeviyakka

Virashaivism, unlike many other Hindu sects, admits women as full members of the religious community. There are a number of women among the *vacanakāras* or makers of the virashaiva *vacanas*. The greatest of them was Mahadeviyakka, who was a younger contemporary of Basava. Though she had betrothed herself to Shiva Mallikarjuna, she was pursued by human suitors. Rejecting a society that allowed women only the role of wife and mother, she went to Kalyan where she was accepted by Allama Prabhu as a member of the virashaiva faith. Her *vacanas*, considered by some to be the most poetic in the virashaiva corpus, are addressed to Shiva Mallikarjuna (rendered by the translator, A. K. Ramanujan, as "The Lord White as Jasmine").

O twittering birds,
don't you know? don't you know?

O swans on the lakeshore,
don't you know? don't you know?

O high-singing koils,
don't you know? don't you know?

O circling swooping bees,
don't you know? don't you know?

O peacocks in the caverns,
don't you know?
don't you know?

Tell me if you know:
where is He,
my lord
white as jasmine?

*

He bartered my heart,
looted my flesh,
claimed as tribute

my pleasure,
took over
all of me.

I'm the woman of love
for my lord, white as jasmine.

*

Like
treasure hidden in the ground
taste in the fruit
gold in the rock
oil in the seed

the Absolute hidden away
in the heart

no one can know
the ways of our lord

white as jasmine.

[116]

Allama Prabhu

The *vacana*s of Allama contain no biographical references. The deficiency has been made up by a host of legends, all of which portray him as a master (*prabhu*) of yogic concentration and power. After receiving initiation from his guru, he wandered as a shaiva ascetic until he reached Kalyan, where he became the head of the Anubhava Mantapa. His *vacana*s, notable for their accomplished mysticism, are addressed to Guhesvara, Shiva as Lord of the Cave. Translated by A. K. Ramanujan.

Looking for your light,
I went out:

it was like the sudden dawn
of a million million suns,

a ganglion of lightnings
for my wonder.

O Lord of Caves,
if you are light,
there can be no metaphor.

VAISHNAVA BHAKTI IN ANDHRA AND KARNATAKA

By the fifteenth century, the bhakti movement had exponents in every region of India and in every sect of Hinduism. In Andhra and Karnataka, the main mediaeval Vishnu-bhaktas were Annamacharya of Tirupati, and the Kannada-speaking saints of the Haridasa sect, in particular Purandaradasa and Kanakadasa. These bhaktas lived during the flowering of the Vijayanagara empire, which dominated peninsular India between 1336 and 1565. During this period, while most of the North was controlled by Muslim rulers, Hindu religion, literature, art and music flourished in Vijayanagara. Annamacharya and Purandaradasa contributed greatly to the development of Carnatic music, as did the composer and Ram-bhakta Tyagaraja, who was born in the eighteenth century.

[117]

Annamacharya

Born in what is now the Cuddapah district of Andhra Pradesh, Annamacharya (1408–1503) became devoted while still a child to Lord Venkateshvara, Vishnu as the Lord of the Tirumala Hills. As a youth Annamacharya went to Tirumala's Tirupati temple, where he met his guru and was initiated into the Srivaishnava sect of Ramanuja. Forced by his family to marry, he remained at Tirumala, composing thousands of songs in which he expressed the many moods of his love for Lord Venkateshvara. Translated from the Telugu by William J. Jackson.

Doubt has vanished, now I feel satisfaction
Now I've attained holy bliss — *brahmānanda*

Since you've put the words of sweet songs in my mouth
I believe that you really will protect me
Because you accepted me in my youth
I am convinced you will save me, surely

Doubt has vanished, now I feel satisfaction
Now I've attained holy bliss — brahmananda

Ever since your form, O consort of Lakshmi
Came into my mind I am certain you are mine
I am known as your servant, near you in this world
I know you'll protect me without being asked twice

Doubt has vanished, now I feel satisfaction
Now I've attained holy bliss — brahmananda

You became accessible, gave me orders in a dream,
Lord Venkatesha, now I believe you're with me always
Now I always am before you, and that is the way
I've become purified and how I attained fame

Doubt has vanished, now I feel satisfaction
Now I've attained holy bliss — brahmananda

[118]

Purandaradasa

Purandaradasa (1485–1565) lived in the heart of the Vijayanagara empire during its sixteenth-century heyday. According to tradition he was a tight-fisted merchant who, in unusual circumstances, became a devotee of Vitthala, a form of Vishnu. Renouncing his riches, he joined the Haridasas or Servants of Hari (Vishnu), a devotional sect based on the teachings of the thirteenth-century philosopher Madhva, who stressed the eternal difference between the human soul and the Divine. Regarded by many as the founder of the Carnatic school of music, Purandaradasa composed hundreds of songs in praise of Vishnu. Translated from the Kannada by William J. Jackson.

What's the use of chanting a mantra
if one has no purity of mind
What's the use of sipping holy tirtha water
if one has no cleanliness of body
What's the use of excessive bathing
in the water like a big or little fish
What's the use of standing still as a crow

in Shrisaila keeping your eye alert for food
outside you take a holy bath
inside you're not clean
Purandara Vithala saw phonies like these
and they made him start to laugh

*

I feasted my eyes upon Lord Venkateshvara
until my mind was fully satisfied

I saw the pure one with his hair tuft in a knot
I feasted my eyes . . .

I saw the one who enjoys boiled rice
and who uses
wealth without giving up even a penny
the one who causes folks to sell rice and *dosas*
the one who dances joyfully in the company
of dasas — I feasted my eyes . . .

I saw the one who wears an upper cloth with knots
of pure gold
the one who goes hunting, and enjoys
the sound of bells, the one who declares
with his right hand that this place is really
heaven on earthly land — I feasted my eyes . . .

I saw the one who lives in the hills
who is favourable to his devotees, the one who
keeps his promises, the Lord of the universe,
Purandara Vithala, I feasted my eyes
upon Lord Venkateshvara
until my mind was fully satisfied

[119]

Kanakadasa

Unlike Annamacharya and Purandaradasa, both of whom were brahmins, Kanakadasa (sixteenth century) lived outside the pale of Hindu society. Born a member of the Koruba clan of herdsmen and hunters, he became a revenue official and soldier. Wounded in battle, he was given up for dead, but heard the voice of Vishnu asking him to become his servant. Kanakadasa agreed, regained his health and (after suffering the scorn of high-caste worshippers) was initiated as a Haridasa. His bhakti was so great that (according to a famous legend) Krishna turned around to look at him when Kanakadasa, the Koruba, had *darśan* through a chink in the back wall of the temple. Translated from the Kannada by William J. Jackson.

Are you inside illusion or is illusion inside you?

Are you inside the body or is the body inside you?

Is the open space in the house, or
is the house in the open space, or
are both in the eyes beholding them?
Is the eye inside the buddhi, or
is the buddhi inside the eye, or
are both inside you Lord Hari

Is the sweetness in the sugar, or
is the sugar in the sweetness, or
are both on the tasting tongue?
Is the tongue inside the mind, or
the mind inside the tongue, or
are both inside you Lord Hari?

Is the fragrance in the flower, or
is the flower in the fragrance, or
are both inside the sense of smell?
Unique Lord Keshava of Kaginele,
life-breath is not just deep within me
it is deep within you too.

*

I am saved now I am saved
my worldly existence is finished

I received the grace
of Lord Padmanabha's feet

I received the prasad offering and the
tirtha water — my tongue tasted them
My ears received the nectar of Hari nama
Haridasas have become my kith and kin
The Vaishnava emblem branded in my skin
during initiation — that's my ornament
I am saved . . .

One hundred and one generations of
my ancestors have won liberation, and I
have become fit for *muktimārga*. My mind
has become finely tuned in devotion
to Shri Hari; Rukmini's Lord, Krishna has
become accessible, possession of him
is in my palm — I am saved . . .

Today my life, my very soul, is blessed
with all fulfilments and prosperity, today
my future life has become fruitful
My father, Lord Adikeshava, today has been
installed in the shrine of my heart
This is the day all has come to fruition

I am saved now I am saved
my worldly existence is finished.

[120]

Tyagaraja

After the fall of the Vijayanagara Empire, Hindu culture was kept alive in the South by the Nayak and Maratha kings of Thanjavur. Born in Tiruvarur, a town not far from Thanjavur, Tyagaraja (1767–1847) absorbed everything there was to learn about Carnatic music, Sanskrit and Telugu literature, and devotion to Ram. His songs are regarded as the supreme accomplishments of Carnatic composition and also as expressions of musical mysticism, in which the vibrations of euphonious sound are regarded as a subtle form of the Divine. Translated from the Telugu by William J. Jackson.

The wisdom of music's art and science
is the bestower of the ecstasy
of sharing in the beloved's divinity
O mind

That music, soaked in the ocean of *ānanda*
which is the story of Rāma
full of the love pangs of separation
and the other emotions
has a wisdom which is
the bestower of the ecstasy
of sharing in the beloved's divinity
O mind

It gives *prema* and *bhakti*,
affection to the virtuous,
it brings the grace of Lakṣmī's consort
It gives self-control, peace of mind,
and the wealth which is fame —
That wisdom, learned by the knowing Tyāgarāja
and drenched in the Rāma-story sea,
is the bestower of the ecstasy
of coming face to face with divinity

THE WEST

A number of devotional schools arose in western India between the thirteenth and seventeenth centuries. The most important were associated with the worship of Vishnu and gave utterance to an extensive literature in Marathi. Around the middle of the same period, some individual bhaktas sang of their love of Krishna in mediaeval Gujarati.

THE VARKARI TRADITION

The shrine of Vitthala or Vitthoba in Pandharpur (southern Maharashtra) has been a centre of devotion for Marathi- and Kannada-speaking bhaktas since at least the thirteenth century. Originally a local deity, Vitthoba is now looked on as a form of Krishna. Each year, Vitthoba's worshippers flock to Pandharpur to worship him, singing the songs of the *vārkarī* ("pilgrim") bhaktas, most of which were composed by between the fourteenth and seventeenth centuries. The earlier mystic philosopher and poet Jnandev is regarded as the founder of the *vārkarī* school, though his major, unquestioned, works are not songs.

[121]

Jnandev

Jnandev or Jnaneshwar was born and died in Alandi, Maharashtra, towards the end of the thirteenth century. His commentary on the *Bhagavad Gītā*, the *Jñāneśvarī* (completed in 1290), was the first important work of Marathi literature. Jnandev also was the author of a mystical poem, the *Anubhavāmṛt*, and a shorter poem called the *Cāngdevpāsaṣṭi*. To him also are attributed a number of songs in the *vārkarī* style, and others giving expression to the doctrines of the *nāth yogīs*. It is a matter of scholarly debate whether the author of the *Jñāneśvarī*, who is said to have died at the age of twenty-one, was actually the creator of all these works. Some *nāth* songs attributed to Jnandev are reproduced in Chapter 12; the work of the historical Jnandev is represented here by extracts from the *Anubhavāmṛt*. This work, commonly but incorrectly called the *Amṛtānubhav*, is composed of eight hundred stanzas that set forth a non-dual shaivite philosophy. The title means "Immortal Experience" or "The Nectar of Experience", and the poem clearly is infused with Jnandev's own experiential insights. Translated from the Marathi by Dilip Chitre.

She is her lover's body:
Her lover is the grace of her being:
They feast on each other
Blended together:

As wind is always with its motion,
As gold is always with its glow,
So are Shiva and Shakti
A totality:

*

Touch to the hand:
Image to the eye:
Sweetness to the tongue:
Is that One: . . .

But the instant the senses
Connect with their object,
Their contact becomes
Their being one: . . .

Here motive ceases:
Yet one does not turn away:
Everything is turned
Into Self-experience:
Unity becomes
A playground of duality:
The more the differentiation
The greater the fusion!

The Self's savouring of the senses
Surpasses Absolute Bliss:
God and devotee blend
In that home of Bhakti: . . .

If he desires to create
A faithful devotee to serve Him:
God alone has to become
That devotee:

To recite his own names:
To meditate upon Himself:
To have unflinching faith:
There is God alone: . . .

Wherever one goes
It is Shiva's pilgrimage:
And going to Shiva is
Not going anywhere:

Walking and sitting
Both become one:
In this place
Wonder does not cease:

Whatever one sees
And whatever its form:
One celebrates
Seeing Shiva: . . .

O Shiva my Lord! O Almighty one!
You have made one the sole ruler
Of this realm
Of absolute bliss!

You have electrified awareness:
You have put the unconscious to sleep:
One has oneself become
Your miracle:

[122]

Namdev

The first important bhakta of the *vārkarī* school was Namdev, who is said by some to have been born in 1270, by others a century or more later. According to tradition, he was a tailor who joined a gang of thieves before turning to a life of devotion. His *abhaṅg*s or Marathi devotional hymns express his devotion to Vitthala and other forms of Vishnu. Also attributed to Namdev are a number of Hindi songs in the style of the *nirguṇ* tradition of bhakti (see Chapter 14). The *abhaṅg*s reproduced below were translated by Justin E. Abbot.

"My heart is attached to sensual things.
It will not give itself to contemplate Thee, O Lord of Paṇḍharī.

I have many kinds of evil thoughts,
That cause me great sorrow.

O God, what a sinner and evil doer I am!
How can I expect Thee, O God [to meet me].

Life is slipping away, but not my evil thoughts.
And I am suffering many forms of anguish.

As I experience birth, death, and hardships in my distresses,
My rebirths become a succession of sufferings.

My heart wanders and takes pleasure in illusory seductions.
I have missed what was for my good, O God.

Thou art the advocate of the helpless, therefore, run to my help,
Deliver me, O God," says Nāmā.

*

The mother bird goes early in the morning for food.
The chicks, hungry, wait for her coming.

Just so my heart longs for Thee.
Day and night I think of Thy feet.

The infant calf is tied at home, O God!
In its heart it is calling to its mother.

Says Nāmā, "Thou art my close friend, O Keshava,
Do not turn me away, O Protector-of-the-helpless."

[123]

Chokhamela

Namdev, like many of the bhakta-saints, belonged to an inferior caste. His contemporary Chokhamela came from a still more despised community: he was a member of the "untouchable" *mahār* class, whose traditional work is removing dead bodies and tanning leather. Chokhamela lived in the holy city of Pandharpur, and was filled with devotion for Vitthoba. Despite the disadvantages of his status, he was able to achieve a level of spirituality that in the end even brahmins had to acknowledge. These Marathi *abhaṅg*s by Chokhamela were translated by Charlotte Vaudeville.

We know neither science nor Purāṇas,
About the words of the Veda, we know nothing—
The intricacies of the Āgamas and the secrets of the Nigamas
And all the truths contained in the Śāstras, we do not know!
Of Yoga and of sacrifices, of the eight spiritual paths,

Of alms, of vows and austerities, we know nothing!
Says Cokhā, O God, in my candid devotion,
I'll simply sing Your Name, O Keśava!

*

Look at the wonder, look at the wonder!
He who had gone to see sees nothing!
In the Invisible, the Visible is found, in the Visible the Invisible,
For the essence of both is just the same.
Says Cokhā, while seeing, one ceases to see—
As the soul reflects the Soul.

*

In my own body I have found Him, that Lord of Paṇḍharī,
The Self, the Eternal, He is standing on the brick!
Know that He, Pāṇḍurang, is the supreme Soul
And his wife Rukmiṇī is the Peace of my heart!
What had taken a visible Form has now vanished,
Now I contemplate Viṭṭhala as the eternal Soul:
In such guise did Viṭṭhala take hold of my heart and mind—
And Cokhāmeḷā clasps His feet!

[124]

Eknath

During Jnandev's lifetime, the Yadava dynasty held sway over central Maharashtra. The fall of the Yadavas, followed by the collapse of Vijayanagara, meant that the entire Deccan was under Muslim rule. For a time the *vārkarī* tradition suffered an eclipse, but it reemerged towards the end of the sixteenth century. The main figure in this renaissance was Eknath, who was born in Paithan, central Maharashtra, around 1548. A Sanskrit scholar as well as a devotee of Vishnu, Eknath translated the eleventh book of the *Bhāgavata Purāṇa* into Marathi, and composed several philosophical works. Also attributed to him are a number of devotional *abhaṅg*s, of which these two, translated by Justin E. Abbot, are examples.

O Merciful One, Purifier-of-the-Sinner,
Give attention to my words.

I am lowly, poor, the lowest of the low.
Therefore, it is that I have come to Thee.

Freeing me from my distresses, O God,
Make me to serve Thee with all my heart.

This is my, Ekā Janārdan's, fixed thought,
And I have no secret to keep from Thee.

*

Thy fame is in the Three worlds,
That Thou hast saved innumerable sinners.

It is because my heart has already believed
That I cling tightly to Thy feet.

I, Ekā Janārdan, am Thy darling child,
So now take care of me.

[125]
Tukaram

The most beloved of the *vārkarī* bhaktas, Tukaram (1608–1649) was born in Dehu, a village near Pune. Following in his father's footsteps, he became a petty merchant and prospered briefly before being crushed by misfortune: the death of his parents, the failure of his business, the loss his wife during a famine. In the midst of this crisis, he turned to Vitthoba and soon became his fervent worshipper. Tukaram's *abhaṅgs*, of which there are more than a thousand, range in tone from the didactic to the devotional. More than the other *vārkarī* singers, he referred frequently to his own spiritual experiences. Translated by J. Nelson Fraser and K. B. Marathe.

I was born in a Sūdra family, thus was set free from all pride.
Now it is thou who art my father and mother, O Lord of Paṇḍharī!
I have no authority to study the Vedas; I am helpless in every way,
humble in caste, says Tukā.

*

I obey your injunctions, nevertheless I am greatly afraid of you.
So I make your feet my familiar friends; I do not ask to sit beside you.
With folded hands, I stand waiting before you.
Tukā says, O ye saints, I am a sinful man.

*

This was the original step that averted my pangs; I presented my body at your feet; I was set free from toil and redeemed.
Now I shall not suffer my own authority to guide me.
Tukā stands apart from the world, far from all its worries.

*

I have found a sea of love, an inexhaustible flood; I have opened a treasure of spiritual knowledge which diffuses the lustre of a million suns, arisen in thy worshippers' souls.
Unexpectedly and without an effort, I have heard the eternal secret and have learned to know God.
The seed of the sublime reunion has been enfolded in my own destiny.
I have now beheld him in whose sight is all goodness, a sea of happy augury, the supreme power of mystic words.
I have attained him whose name is nectar, whose nature is pure, who is intellect free from passion.
The very joy of peace and compassion is found in this joy of being and knowing God; this Puṇḍalik declares.
Lo! Paṇḍharī has unfolded the delight of infinite bliss!
I myself do not know the stage beyond desire that is needed by the faithful; I do not know the universal brotherhood of living things.
Tukā says, O Lord of Paṇḍharī, let me now dwell with the saints!

*

Every action should be offered to God; this is the only worship that reaches him.
Every action is perfected by this rule of conduct, that the worshippers have union with God.
This is the one secret; this is the message of religion.
Tukā says, It is true; it is true; three times I say it is true.

*

This is our delight, to show the world what is right, to make those ashamed who have strayed from the path.
How can a man be injured by delivering his message? What harm can the anger of the world do me?
What can the exertions of ignorance attain, so sharp are the arrows of Krishna's name?
Tukā says, This is a shop where genuine goods are sold; no false wares will be accepted here.

[126]

Bahina Bai

The comparative rarity of works by woman saints in India is due largely to the fact that their biographies and texts were not preserved as well as those of their male compeers. Bahina Bai (1628–1700) left behind not only a collection of devotional *abhaṅgs* but also an autobiography. From this we learn that, while a young wife in Kolhapur, she became fascinated by the *abhaṅgs* of Tukaram. Her wish to go to Dehu to meet him was rejected by her husband, as they were brahmins and Tukaram was a shudra. A short while later, Tukaram appeared to her in a dream, and gave her a mantra of initiation (see the first extract below). Bahina Bai's devotional *abhaṅgs*, of which the second extract is an example, show her unwavering dedication to Vishnu in various forms. Translated by Justin E. Abbot.

I began to experience great sorrow in my heart. Why, O Viṭṭhal, have you forsaken me.
I am all in a heat from the three fevers of life. What matters it, let me die!
But just then on the seventh day, repeating aloud the names and praises of God, Tukārām appeared in a vision before my eyes, and said: "Remember the first lines [of the calf's *śloka*].
Do not be troubled, I am beside you. Take from my hand this nectar.
When a calf puts its mouth to the cow, a stream of milk flows. This is excellent nectar, drink it."
With this he placed his hand upon my head and whispered a *mantra* in my ear.
I then placed my head on his feet. He gave me a book called the Mantra *Gītā*.
This vision in a dream occurred through the *guru's* favour on a Sunday, on the fifth day of the dark half of the moon in the month of Kārtika.

My heart rejoiced. It fixed itself on Brahma, Pure Intelligence. I sat up astonished.
I recollected the *mantra*. Tukobā, in the form of a vision, had manifested to me his abundant mercy in this dream.
He had fed me with nectar, which to the taste was unlike anything else. He only can appreciate this who experiences it.
Says Bahiṇī, "Such was the mercy of the *sadguru*. Tukārām had truly shown it abundantly."

*

I have turned my eyes to the meditation of God (Keshava) and my ears to listening to the praises of God (Hari).
Right-thinking has shown my organs of sense and action the way of happiness, and having connected them [with that happiness] they think of nothing else.
It has turned my power of speech into praising God's name, and the service of God (Keshava) with free hands.
It has turned my feet to visit sacred bathing places and places of pilgrimage, there to see God. My organs of action are to be judged by these uses.
Right-thinking has turned to use all my ten organs of sense and action. So, Oh *manā*, because of this, you have lost your power.
Says Bahiṇī, "The senses which have been appointed by me to do the bidding of *viveka* will not now come back to serve sensual desires."

KRISHNA-BHAKTI IN GUJARAT

The bhakti impulse reached Gujarat in the fifteenth century, mainly in the form of ecstatic devotion to Krishna. The chief bhaktas who sang in Old Gujarati or Old Western Rajasthani (the precursor of the modern language) were Narsi Mehta and Mira Bai. The language of Mira's songs is now generally considered to be a dialect of western Hindi, so her life and works are discussed below in the section devoted to the North. The pre-modern movement of Krishna-bhakti in Gujarat lasted until the early nineteenth century. Its last great proponent, Dayaram, died just four years before the formal establishment of the British Indian Empire.

[127]

Narsi Mehta

Born near Junagadh to an orthodox family of Nagar Brahmins, Narasimha Mehata or Narsi Mehta (1414–1480) spent much of his youth in the company of *sādhus*. Originally a Shiva worshipper, he became a devotee of Krishna after Shiva granted him a vision of Krishna's *rāsa-līlā*. Afterwards, he used to dress up as a *gopī* and dance while chanting Krishna's name. Like most other bhaktas, he was indifferent to caste-restrictions and was excommunicated by his family when he entered the house of an untouchable. Many of his songs are based on the tenth book of the *Bhāgavata Purāṇa*, others on the *Gīta-govinda* of Jayadeva. Almost all express an intense emotional attachment to Krishna. Translated by K. M. Munshi.

Look at the sky, see Who pervades it,
    uttering the words: "I am He", "I am He".
At the feet of the Dark One, would I die;
    for there is none here who can compare with Krishna.
My mind, lost in one endless festive mood,
    cannot fathom the great, dark splendour.
Know the animate and the inanimate as one;
    lovingly hold fast to the life eternal.
Look there—where the flaming light shines out of a million rising suns;
    where the heavens are ablaze with a golden mantle;
There, the Supreme sports in joy,
    swinging in a golden cradle.
There, without wick or oil or thread, burns bright
    the fiery lamp, unwavering and everlasting.
Let us see, but not with eyes, Him who is Formless.
    Let us drink in the delicious joy of this vision, but not with tongues.
He is the Unknowable, the Deathless
    swinging high and low.
The Lord of Narsaiyā is omnipresent. The saints alone
    can catch Him in the web of their love.

[128]

Dayaram

The last of the great bhakti-poets of Gujarat, Dayaram or Kavi Dayarambhai (1777-1852), was, unlike his predecessors Narsi Mehta and Mira Bai, closely connected with a Hindu sectarian group. During the sixteenth century, the Pushtimarga or "way of well-being" — a sect based on the teachings of the southern Vedantin Vallabhacharya — began to spread throughout Gujarat. Followers of the Pushtimarga seek Krishna by means of intense and sometimes sensuous love and devotion. Since the world is a gift from Krishna, worldly life should be enjoyed to its full. This unascetic path was well suited to Dayaram, who was a connoisseur of fine clothes and beautiful women. But the ultimate object of his love was Krishna, the Lord of Delight. These two songs by Dayaram were translated by Rachael Dwyer.

O Rājeśvara, you look beautiful, coming to my house.
Refrain

Dressed in a beautiful gold-embroidered tunic,
With a golden turban tied on your head,
Wearing a beautiful scarf, you tempt my mind.

The garland of roses on your breast gives off perfume,
The thief detains my mind,
Flower-ornaments on both your hands delight my mind.

Holding a beautiful gold stick,
You move swaying with an elephant's gait,
Singing softly, you have stolen my mind.

Nātha, Dayā's Beloved, I am devoted to your lotus face,
Which surpasses all others,
You invited me with love, soothing my affliction.

*

What does the pandit know? What does the pandit know about anything?
A jar filled with ghee cannot taste it.
Refrain

The cooking pot can't eat beautifully spiced vegetables,
The kindling stick does not enjoy the fire that lives inside it.

The deer does not delight in the musk of its own navel,
Dayo says, the rich man who buries great wealth is called
poor.

THE EAST

The most popular deities of eastern India are Krishna (or other forms of Vishnu) and Kali (or other forms of the Mother Goddess). To people from outside the region, the combination might seem strange. Krishna is an embodiment of all that is beautiful, sweet and delightful, Kali an incarnation of the forces of destruction and death. Yet in Bengal, Assam and Orissa, the cults of Krishna and Kali not only flourish side by side but are often embraced by the same worshippers. Starting in the late twelfth century, Krishna-bhakti found expression in works written in Sanskrit, Maithili, Bengali and other languages. Kali-bhakti had to wait until the eighteenth century before it was given accomplished literary expression by the Bengali bhakta Ramprasad.

KRISHNA-BHAKTI IN BENGAL

After the founding of the Sena dynasty in the mid eleventh century, Vaishnavism replaced Buddhism as the main recipient of state patronage in Bengal. One beneficiary of Sena largesse was the poet Jayadeva, who towards the end of the twelfth century wrote the *Gīta-govinda*, a Sanskrit poem that had an enormous influence on the development of Krishna-bhakti throughout India. It was in Jayadeva's poem that Radha, the beloved of Krishna, first made her appearance in courtly literature. Two centuries later, after Bengal had come under Muslim rule, songs of popular bhakti were composed in Maithili, a language of eastern Bihar, as well as in Bengali. The central theme of these works is Radha's pain of separation and her bliss of reunion with Krishna. Most of them are characterised by sensuous imagery and highly emotional expression.

[129]

Vidyapati

Born in the Mithila or Tirhut region of Bihar, apparently in the middle of the fourteenth century, Vidyapati became a court poet and scholar under the Hindu overlord of the region. Turning from the Sanskrit of the court to the language of the people, he composed hundreds of songs that chronicle the love of Radha and Krishna, from the first childish stirrings in her heart to their final ecstatic union. Some doubt whether Vidyapati should be regarded as a mystic, or whether the erotic poetry he pioneered ought to be considered an expression of bhakti. Too little is known about the man to decide the first point, but there is no doubt that his songs were an inspiration to many mystics, most notably Chaitanya. These selections were translated from the Maithili by Deben Bhattacharya.

Nocturnal spirits are abroad.
Fierce snakes
Wander in darkness
And only lightning
Lifts the gloom.
Through the thick night
You bravely go.
O friend,
Who is that treasure among men
Who stole your heart,
To whom you hurry
Eager to be loved?
Before you flows the Jamnā
Fraught with perils
And you must cross its dreaded stream
To offer him your joys.
Beside you goes the guardian god
Armed with flower-arrows.
Have no fear and yet
I tremble for you.

*

As I near the bed,
He smiles and gazes.
Flower-arrows fill the world.
The sport of love,
Its glow and luxuries
Are indescribable, O friend,
And when I yield myself,
His joy is endless.

Freeing my skirt,
He snatches at my garland.
My downcast mind
Is freed of frontiers,
Though my life is held
In the net of his love.
He drinks my lips.
With heart so thrilled,
He takes my clothes away.
I lose my body
At his touch
And long to check
But grant his love.

Says Vidyāpati:
Sweet as honey
Is the talk of a girl in love.

[130]

Chandidas

Apparently a younger contemporary of Vidyapati, Chandidas was born in western Bengal towards the end of the fourteenth century. He was, according to tradition, a priest in a village temple who fell in love with the washerwoman Rami, conceiving of their relationship as a human counterpart of the love of Krishna and Radha. Needless to say, his clansmen were scandalised by the liaison; but Chandidas persisted, abandoning neither his priestly duties nor his beloved. There is a large body of songs containing his signature-line, in which the author sings of his love for Rami and of Radha's love for Krishna. Many of these are certainly the work of later poets, some of whom were connected with the vaishnava sahajiya sect. Some sahajiya songs attributed to Chandidas are given in Chapter 12; here, songs expressing the more conventional but still intense emotions of vaishnava bhakti are reproduced. Translated from the Bengali by Deben Bhattacharya.

One day
Walking with my sister-in-law,
I thought of beloved Shyām.
Emotions filled my heart

And I stood still.
My body went beyond control
Trembling, trembling.

*

Never have I seen such love,
Nor heard.
Even a blink's delay contains eternity.
Clasped to my breasts you are far from me.
Stay as my veil close to my face,
How I fear when you turn your eyes away!
We spend the night: one body,
Sinking in the fathomless ocean of joy.
As the dawn comes our anxious hearts watch
Life deserting us.

*

The morning crows and the *kokila* cried
The end of the night.
My lover was up and hastily left
Fixing his dishevelled hair.
I cannot describe my suffering, O friend!
My dark lover left me saying not a word,
My heart was aching.
Resting in lassitude
My eyes were heavy,
As I discovered his clothes on me.

My people at home are eager to blame,
What can I do with his dress on me?

Chandidās says with a joyful heart,
Suffering leads to the treasures of love.

[131]

Chaitanya

From the early sixteenth century, a great wave of vaishnava bhakti spread throughout eastern India and into other regions. The protagonist of this movement was the Bengali mystic Sri Krishna Chaitanya

(1486–1533). Born Vishvambara Mishra in Navadvip, Bengal, a centre of Sanskrit learning, he became a master of the New Logic school of philosophy, and a famous and arrogant teacher. When he was twenty-two, he went to Gaya to perform his father's death-anniversary rites. While there he had an overwhelming spiritual experience, after which he asked to be initiated into Krishna worship. For the rest of his life he was a God-intoxicated man, living out the separations and unions exemplified by Radha's love for Krishna. He and his followers practised a form of worship called *saṁkīrtana*, which involves the communal singing of songs or chanting of mantras, often while dancing. Chaitanya wrote almost nothing, transmitting his teachings by means of sermons and the example of his highly emotional devotion. (His followers later developed his thought into a full-fledged philosophy and a complex cartography of devotional states.) The most important of his hagiographies, the *Caitanya-Caritāmṛta* of Krishna Das Kaviraj (1517–1582), contains many of his discourses and a number of scenes in which the intensity of his bhakti is apparent. This example was translated from the Bengali by Jadunath Sarkar.

The Master told his disciples of the sweet life of Madhav Puri. . . .

So saying the Master recited a stanza of the Puri's composition, which has lighted the world like the moon. Discourse on the stanza only revealed its full beauty, just as the odour of the sandal spreads with rubbing. I deem this stanza the rarest gem in poetry. Radha speaks it through the mouth of Madhavendra. How did Chaitanya relish it! None besides these three can know its full flavour. He finally attained to the supreme knowledge by reciting this stanza:

> O Lord! Gracious to the lowly! thou art now in Mathura.
> When wilt thou come to me?
> Darling mine! my heart runs about in pain of longing to see thee.
> What shall I do?

On reciting the stanza the Master fell down on the ground in a trance, senseless with the intensity of love. Nityananda hurriedly took Him up in his arms. Chaitanya rose weeping, and ran hither and thither in a transport of devotion, shouting, laughing, dancing, and singing. Oft did He repeat the first word of the stanza, His voice choked with emotion and tears running down His cheeks. He trembled, perspired, wept with joy, stood still, changed colour, —now showing remorse, now grief, now stupor, now pride or meekness. The stanza opened the gate of His love. The servitors of Gopinath gazed on the Master's outpouring of love. But He came back to Himself on seeing a crowd gathering. The *bhog* was performed, then the *ārati*. The priest laid the god to rest, came out of the shrine and laid the twelve pots of kshir before the Master, who joyfully took five pots for Himself and His disciples and returned the other seven to the priest. True, the sight of Gopinath had been food enough for Him; but He now drank the kshir as a mark of reverence. The night was passed in singing the Name. In the morning He attended the *maṅgal ārati* and then departed.

[132]

Govindadas

Little is known about Govindadas (1537–1612), a Bengali exponent of vaishnava bhakti from the generation after the death of Chaitanya. His songs follow the conventions established by Vidyapati and Chandidas, but do so with great perfection and charm. Translated by Edward C. Dimock, Jr., and Denise Levertov.

When they had made love
she lay in his arms in the *kuñja* grove.
Suddenly she called his name
and wept — as if she burned in the fire of separation.
The gold was in her anchal
but she looked afar for it!
— Where has he gone? Where has my love gone?
O why has he left me alone?
And she writhed on the ground in despair,
only her pain kept her from fainting.
Krishna was astonished
and could not speak.

Taking her beloved friend by the hand,
Govinda-dāsa led her softly away.

*

Let the earth of my body be mixed with the earth
my beloved walks on.
Let the fire of my body be the brightness
in the mirror that reflects his face.

Let the water of my body join the waters
of the lotus pool he bathes in.
Let the breath of my body be air
lapping his tired limbs.
Let me be sky, and moving through me
that cloud-dark Shyāma, my beloved.

Govinda-dāsa says, O golden one,
Could he of the emerald body let you go?

DEVI-BHAKTI IN BENGAL

Goddess-worship has been prevalent in Bengal since the sixth or seventh century, finding expression in the songs of the Buddhist *mahāsiddhas* and the manuals and *stotras* of Hindu tantrics. The goddess Kali was popular, especially in the villages, but her terrible aspect made it difficult for her worshippers to approach her on the intimate level required for emotional bhakti. Ramprasad Sen was the first to sing of her as a tender loving mother or even as a little girl. After him, a school of shakta poets continued the Kali-bhakti tradition.

[133]

Ramprasad

Ramprasad Sen (1718?–1775) lived in a tumultuous era, during which the indigenous Muslim rulers of Bengal were replaced by the British East India Company. Through the changes of those years he remained so absorbed in his devotion that he seems to have taken little notice. Born to a family of tantric worshippers in a town thirty miles north of Kolkata, he studied Sanskrit, Bengali, Hindustani and Persian as a child. Obtaining a position as a clerk, he proved ill-suited to the job. According to a famous story, he filled the margins of his account book with poems in praise of Kali. Moved by his devotion, his employer discharged him with a pension. This allowed him to practice his *sādhana* and to compose the songs that helped to transform the Kali of popular worship from a terrible distant goddess to a fierce but approachable mother. Translated from the Bengali by Swami Budhananda.

O mind, you do not know how to farm!
Fallow lies the field of your life.
If you had only worked it well,

How rich a harvest you might reap!
Hedge it about with Kali's name
If you would keep your harvest safe;
This is the stoutest hedge of all,
For Death himself cannot come near it.

Sooner or later will dawn the day
When you must forfeit your precious field;
Gather, O mind, what fruit you may,
Sow for your seed the holy Name
Of God that your Guru has given to you,
Faithfully watering it with love;
And if you should find the task too hard
Call upon Ramprasad for help.

*

Once for all, this time, I have thoroughly understood:
From one who knows it well, I have learnt the secret of bhava.
A man has come to me from a country where there is no night,
And now I cannot distinguish day from night any longer;
Rituals and devotions have all grown profitless for me.

My sleep is broken: how can I sleep any more?
For now I am wide awake in the sleeplessness of yoga.
O Divine Mother, made one with Thee in yoga-sleep at last,
My slumber I have lulled asleep for evermore.

I bow my head, says Prasad, before desire and liberation;
Knowing the secret that Kali is one with the highest Brahman,
I have discarded, once for all both righteousness and sin.

THE NORTH

The bhakti impulse penetrated the Hindi-speaking North in the fifteenth century. By that time, the region had been under Muslim rule for two hundred years. The governing élite patronised Islamic artists, writers and teachers, and for the most part simply ignored what they called "Hindu" (indigenous Indian) religion and culture. Hindu culture still flourished in the South and, to a lesser extent, the West and East, but was by and large moribund in the North. The first stirrings of new spiritual vigour came in the decades after 1450 and are attributed to a monk named Ramanand, who is supposed to have initiated many of the principal figures of the fifteenth-century north Indian bhakti movement. Most important among these were Raidas and Kabir, who, as bhaktas of the *nirguṇ* or "formless" tradition, are dealt with in the next chapter. In the present chapter, three important Hindi-speaking bhaktas of the *saguṇ* tradition, who worshipped God in different forms, are considered. These three, Surdas, Mira Bai and Tulsidas, did their work during the sixteenth and early seventeenth centuries.

[134]

Surdas

With Surdas, as with most of the bhakti singers, the dearth of biographical data is more than made up for by an abundance of legend. He is said to have been born in 1483 in a town near Delhi. Scholars agree that he died in 1563. All accounts of his life say that he was blind, probably from birth. His songs, written in the Braj dialect of Hindi, give expression to his profound love for Krishna. The most famous of them feature the child whose pranks are recounted in the *Bhāgavata Purāṇa*, but others are about the love of the grown-up Krishna and Radha. His works are collected in the *Sur-sāgar* or "Ocean of Sur". These selections were translated from the Hindi by J. S. Hawley and Mark Juergensmeyer.

Gopal has slipped in and stolen my heart, friend.
He stole through my eyes and invaded my breast
    simply by looking — who knows how he did it? —
Even though parents and husband and all
    crowded the courtyard and filled my world.
The door was protected by all that was proper;
    not a corner, nothing, was left without a guard.
Decency, prudence, respect for the family —
    these three were locks and I hid the keys.
The sturdiest doors were my eyelid gates —
    to enter through them was a passage impossible —
And secure in my heart, a mountainous treasure:
    insight, intelligence, fortitude, wit.

And then, says Sur, he'd stolen it —
  with a thought and a laugh and a look —
    and my body was scorched with remorse.

*

She's found him, she has, but Radha disbelieves
That it's true, what she sees when her eyes behold
  her master's moonlike face.
Her gaze is fixed, but her mind is glazed;
  her eyes refuse to close;
And her intellect wages a raging debate:
  Is it a dream? Or is this her true Lord?
Her eyes fill and fill with beauty's high pleasure,
  then hide it away in her breast:
Like bees driven wild by any distance from honey
  they dart back and forth from the hoard to the source.
Sometimes she musters her thoughts; she wonders:
  "Who does he love? Who can this Hari be?"
For love, says Sur, is an awkward thing.
  It ripples the mind with waves.

*

Until you wake up to what you really are
You'll be like the man who searches the whole jungle
  for a jewel that hangs at his throat.
Oil, wick, and fire: until they mingle in a cruse
  they scarcely produce any light,
So how can you expect to dissipate the darkness
  simply by talking about lamps?
You're the sort of fool who sees your face
  in a mirror, befouled by inky filth,
And proceeds to try to erase the blackness
  by cleaning the reflection to a shine.
Surdas says, it's only now the mind can see —
  now that so countless many days are lost and gone —
For who has ever recognized the brilliance of the sun
  but by seeing it through eyes gone blind?

[135]

Mira Bai

The basic outline of Mira Bai's life is well known, even if few hard facts about her have survived. She was born in a town in Rajasthan around 1498, the daughter of a Rajput chief. Given in marriage to the son of the Rana or ruler of Mewar, she was widowed before becoming a mother. Unwilling to accept the circumscribed life of a high-caste Hindu widow, she left her apartments, sought out the company of holy-men, and danced before the image of Krishna. Even when persecuted by her husband's family, she persisted in her "shameful" ways. Eventually (it is said) she became a wandering ascetic and went to Brindavan and other places where Krishna had passed his life on earth. Most of her songs are addressed to Giridhara Gopal, "He who held up the mountain", and express the many moods of her love and longing for union with Krishna. Translated by A. J. Alston.

O my companion,
Strange is the behaviour of my eyes.
That sweet form has entered my mind
And pierced its way into my heart.
How long have I been standing in my house
Gazing down the road?
My very existence depends on Shyām, the Beloved.
He is the herb that grants me life.
Mīrā has become the personal property of Giridhara:
The people say she is mad.

*

O my companion, all I can see is Shyām,
All I can think of is Shyām.
Wherever my feet tread the earth
I am dancing in his honour.
Mīrā's Lord is the courtly Giridhara:
In His company
She is walking the woods and lanes.

*

Come to my house, O Krishna,
Thy coming will bring peace.
Great will be my joy if I meet Thee,

And all my desires will be fulfilled.
Thou and I are one,
Like the sun and its heat.
Mīrā's heart cares for nothing else,
It only wants the beautiful Shyām.

*

That dark Dweller in Braj
Is my only refuge.
O my companion,
Worldly comfort is an illusion,
As soon you get it, it goes.
I have chosen the Indestructible for my refuge,
Him whom the snake of death
Will not devour.
My Beloved dwells in my heart,
I have actually seen that Abode of Joy.
Mīrā's Lord is Hari, the Indestructible.
My Lord, I have taken refuge with Thee,
Thy slave.

[136]

Tulsidas

More orthodox in belief and observance than most other bhaktas, Tulsidas (1532–1625) passed most of his life in Benares. His poetry, written in Avadhi, an eastern dialect of Hindi, is regarded as the greatest achievement of mediaeval Hindi literature. He is remembered chiefly for his translation or adaptation of the Ramayana, the *Rāmcaritmānas*; but he also composed a number of songs giving more direct and personal expression to his devotion to Ram. These selections were translated by J. S. Hawley and Mark Juergensmeyer.

You are the pitying, I the pitiful one,
    you the beneficent, I the one who begs;
I am notoriously fallen,
    and you dash away mountains of sin.
You are the father of those without fathers,
    and who could be more orphaned than I?

No one is so downtrodden — none more than I —
    and you are the one who lifts the heavy weight.
You are all life, I am one life;
    you are the master and I the servant;
You are mother and father, teacher and friend:
    in every connection my lot is relieved.
We are bound by numerous ties, you and I,
    so choose whichever you please.
Somehow, says Tulsi, oh you who send mercy,
    let me find at your feet a refuge of peace.

*

The flame offered to Ram
    extinguishes the flame of pain;
It burns up sin and sorrow,
    burns down to the root of lust.
In a lovely mist of incense,
    in a row of splendid lamps
Its ritual rhythm — the hand-claps —
    scares the bird of sin away.
It dissipates the darkness, the dumbness,
    from the house, the heart, of devotees;
    it casts wide the net of purest truth.
It is the frosty night that chills
    the lotuses of this dark age:
    the lurching, the drunkenness, the rage.
It is the messenger girl of liberation
    embodied in a flash of lightning,
The fingers of the moon spread out to catch
    and lift the lotuses of the night —
    the forest of those who flee for refuge.
It is the force of a multitude of Kalis
    pitted against the buffalo of Tulsi's pride.

FURTHER READING

Source Materials

Justin E. Abbot, *Stotramālā: A Garland of Hindu Prayers*. Poona: Scottish Mission Industries, 1929.

Justin E. Abbot, *Bahiṇā Bāī: A Translation of her Autobiography and Verses*. Reprint edition. Delhi: Motilal Banarsidass, 1985.

A. J. Alston, trans., *The Devotional Songs of Mīrābāī*. Delhi: Motilal Banarsidass, 1980.

Deben Bhattacharya, trans., *Love Songs of Chantidās: The Rebel Poet-Priest of Bengal*. New York: Grove Press, 1970.

Deben Bhattacharya, trans., *Love Songs of Vidyāpati*. London: George Allen and Unwin, 1963.

Swami Budhananda, *Ramprasad: The Melodious Mystic*. New Delhi: Ramakrishna Mission, 1982.

Dilip Chitre, ed. and trans., *Sri Jnandev's Anubhavamrut*. New Delhi: Sahitya Akademi, 1996.

Vidya Dehejia, *Slaves of the Lord: The Path of the Tamil Saints*. Delhi: Munsihram Manoharlal, 1988.

Vidya Dehejia, *Āṇṭāḷ and Her Path of Love*. Albany, NY: State University of New York Press, 1990.

Wilbur Stone Deming, ed., *Selections from Tukārām* [translations by J. Nelson Fraser and K. B. Marathe]. Madras: Christian Literature Society for India, 1932.

Edward C. Dimock, Jr., and Denise Levertov, trans., *In Praise of Krishna: Songs from the Bengali*. Chicago: University of Chicago Press, 1967.

Rachael Dwyer, *The Poetics of Devotion: The Gujarati Lyrics of Dayaram*. London: Curzon, 2001.

William J. Jackson, *Tyāgarāja: Life and Lyrics*. Delhi: Oxford University Press, 1991.

William J. Jackson, *Songs of Three Great South Indian Saints*. Delhi: Oxford University Press, 1998.

J. S. Hawley and Mark Juergensmeyer, trans., *Songs of the Saints of India*. New York: Oxford University Press, 1988.

Kanaiyalal M. Munshi, *Gujarāt and its Literature*. Bombay: Bharatiya Vidya Bhavan, 1954.

Indira Viswanathan Peterson, *Poems to Śiva: The Hymns of the Tamil Saints*. Princeton: Princeton University Press, 1989.

A. K. Ramanujan, trans., *Hymns for the Drowning: Poems for Viṣṇu by Nammalvar*. Princeton: Princeton University Press, 1981.

A. K. Ramanujan, trans., *Speaking of Śiva*. Harmondsworth, England: Penguin, 1973.

Jadunath Sarkar, *Chaitanya's Pilgrimages and Teachings: From his Contemporary Biography the Chaitanya-charit-amrita: Madhya-lila*. Calcutta: M. C. Sarkar, 1913.

Charlotte Vaudeville, *Myths, Saints and Legends in Medieval India*. Delhi: Oxford University Press, 1999.

Other Works

Kshitimohan Sen, *Mediaeval Mysticism of India*. New Delhi: Oriental Books Reprint Corporation, 1974.

M. Sivaramkrishna and Sumita Roy, eds., *Poet Saints of India*. New Delhi: Sterling Publishers, 1996.

H. Thipperudra Swamy, *The Vīraśaiva Saints: A Study*, translated by S. M. Angadi. Mysore: Rao and Raghavan, 1968.

Sources of Texts and Translations

106	*Tēvāram*, Appar 4.103.1, 5.131.2, 5.135.1	Peterson 254, 210, 209
107	*Tēvāram*, Campantar 1.1.1, 3.266.3, 3.345.1	Peterson 270–71, 280
108	*Tirumuṟai* VII, hymn 36	Dehejia (1988) 53
109	*Tiruvācakam* 6.44, 46; 3.150–56; 37.10	Dehejia (1988) 62–63, 65, 66
110	*Nācciyār Tirumoḻi* 5.1, 4, 7, 10	Dehejia (1990) 91–94
111	*Periya Tirumoḻi* 1.1.1, 5; 3.2.1, 2	Dehejia (1988) 102–04
112	*Tiruvāymoḻi* 6.2.5–7, 9.6.10, 4	Ramanujan (1981) 22–24, 69, 6
113	Haḷakoṭṭi 120, 23	Ramanujan (1973) 106, 97
114	Basavanāḷ 212, 820, 847	Ramanujan (1973) 79, 88, 89
115	Basavarāju 73, 88, 2	Ramanujan (1973) 115, 121, 12
116	Basavarāju 972	Ramanujan (1973) 148
117	*Sandehamu*	Jackson (1998) 63
118	*Upabhoga* 10, *Dhaniye*	Jackson (1998) 153, 89
119	*Ni vayiyilaga*; *Badukidenu*	Jackson (1998) 201, 175–6
120	*Saṅgīta śastrajñanamu*	Jackson (1991) 315

121	*Amṛtānubhav* 40–41; 714, 717, 728–30, 739–40, 752–54, 764–65	Chitre 30–31, 199–200, 202–03, 205, 208–09, 211–212
122	Avate 1416, 1575	Abbot (1929) 13, 15
123	*Sakalasanta gāthā* 1, Cokhāmeḷā 47, 70, 76	Vaudeville 233–35
124	*Eknāthāche Abhaṅg* (ed. Avate) 1915–16	Abbot (1929) 28
125	Indu Prakash edn. 2765, 3543, 88, 672, 280, 834	Deming 39–40, 56, 38, 114, 69, 41
126	*Ātmanivedan* 25; *Manaḥpar abhaṅgs* 136	Abbot (1985) 19–20, 79
127	*nirkhane gaganamāṁ koṇ ghumī rahyo*	Munshi 198
128	*rūḍā dīso cho rājeśvara; vediyo vaiyākaraṇīya*	Dwyer 256–57, 356–57
129		Bhattacharya (1963) 103, 107
130		Bhattacharya (1967) 63, 61, 112
131	*Caitanya-caritāmṛta, Madhya-līlā* 2	Sarkar 19–21
132		Dimock and Levertov 23, 58
133	*man re kṛṣi kāj jān nā*	Budhananda 53, 68
134	NPS 2490, 2741, 368	Hawley and Juergensmeyer 109, 107, 115
135	*ālī rī mhāre ṇeṇāṃ, sakhi mhāṃro sāmariyā ṇai, mhāra ājyo jī rāmāṃ, mhāro sāṃvaro braja-vāsī*	Alston 38, 41, 80, 116
136	*Vinaya Patrikā* 79, 48	Hawley and Juergensmeyer 168–69

14

दह दिसि रांम रह्यौ भरपूरि। संतनि नेरै साकत दूरि॥

Ram pervades the entire universe, but he is close to the *sants* and far from the wicked.

Namdev, *Hindī Padāvalī*

The Sants

ALL THE BHAKTAS discussed in the previous chapter worshipped God in a particular form: as Shiva or Vishnu or one of Vishnu's incarnations or the Mother Goddess. An important group of bhaktas, who flourished especially in the Hindi-speaking North between the fourteenth and eighteenth centuries, gave their devotion instead to a God without form, the *nirguṇ* (attributeless) divinity. The bhaktas of this movement often called themselves, and were called by others, *sants*, a word that means a good or wise or holy person, and is often translated by "saint". Four notable Hindi-speaking sants — Kabir, Raidas, Dadu and Paltu Sahib — are dealt with the present chapter. Guru Nanak, a sant who founded a tradition that became a separate religion, is considered in Chapter 15.

The distinction between the *nirguṇ* and the *saguṇ* (personal) trends of bhakti is by no means absolute. Kabir often sounds very much like a vaishnava devotee; Appar, Tukaram and Surdas, famous for celebrating particular forms of the godhead, sometimes uttered sant-like expressions. Devotees of both the "schools" (a term used for want of a better) preferred songs in living languages over Sanskrit scriptures, and placed their hopes for salvation in the grace of God rather than the intercession of priests. Still, there is an evident difference between the tone of an Andal or Manikkavachakar and that of a Kabir or Nanak. The heart of the *saguṇ* school is attachment to a name and form of the Divine, often of a particular avatar. Its bhaktas gave expression to the moods and emotions of specific human relationships: pupil and teacher, child and mother, lover and beloved. In contrast to this, the bhaktas of the *nirguṇ* school turned away from God as Form, giving their attention to God as Name. The Divine of their conception was impersonal and featureless, yet somehow still interested in them and their trials, and willing to come to their aid. There is, to be sure, something paradoxical about the idea of establishing a personal relationship with the Impersonal, and some critics have doubted whether such a thing could really exist. The only answer to this objection is that for several hundred years there have been devotees of the Divine Name who had no interest in the Divine Form, and the literature they produced shows that they knew what they were talking about.

The bhaktas of the *saguṇ* school have for the most part been assimilated into mainstream Hinduism. Indeed, one could say that the devotionalism of the bhakti movement, increasingly mediated by priests and organisations, is the principal component of contemporary Hinduism. The sant tradition, on the other hand, has remained outside the mainstream. The more important sants stand at the head of their own *panth*s or paths, which reject the primary determinant of membership in Hinduism: acceptance of the authority of the Veda. More than most other bhaktas, the sants were open to influences from marginal Hindu and even non-Hindu sources, for instance the *nāth yogī*s and the sufis. At the same time, they served as a conduit of Hindu ideas to those beyond the pale of organised Hinduism. Practically all the sants were from "inferior" social situations. Some, like Raidas, came from the very bottom of the Hindu social order; others, like Kabir and Dadu, were artisans and probably of Muslim birth. Yet these unorthodox figures are now regarded by many Hindus as equal in sanctity to anyone in the higher castes—and are sometimes given a brahminical pedigree to justify this.

The songs of the sants are composed in rough, energetic Hindi, and were often transmitted orally for centuries before finally being written down. The themes of these songs are so diverse that it is impossible to speak of a single path of the sants, but most sants would agree that God is without form, gender or attributes; God does not reside in images and does not take birth as an avatar; God is to be found not in outward practices but within oneself, in the *sadguru* or true guru, and in the Name.

The first generation of north Indian sants, which included Kabir and Raidas, appeared in the region of Benares towards the middle of the fifteenth century. They were preceded by two thirteenth- or fourteenth-century figures: Namdev and Ramanand. Namdev is known chiefly as one of the *vārkarī* bhaktas (see Chapter 13), to whom the name "sant" is often applied. These Maharashtrian sants were for the most part of *saguṇ* tendency. Namdev was the exception; he wrote, along with his Marathi *abhang*s, a number of *nirguṇ* songs in Hindi. He is said to have spent some time in the North, thus forming a bridge between the western and northern groups of sants. But the figure generally placed at the head of the sant tradition is not Namdev but Ramanand, a vaishnava ascetic who, according to tradition, initiated Raidas, Kabir and several other sants. Though certainly historical, Ramanand is a somewhat shadowy figure, whose life-story is told in different ways by his line of "Ramanandi" monks, and by the sants and Sikhs, who regard him as a forerunner. He is believed by most to have been a vaishnava brahmin, fifth in preceptorial descent from the philosopher Ramanuja (see Chapter 10). He thus is regarded as a link between the bhakti of the South and the Gangetic region. Settling in Benares to study and to teach, Ramanand accepted students of all castes, a fact that did little to endear him to the orthodox. Those said to be his disciples include the Jat farmer Dhana, the outcaste cobbler Raidas, the Muslim weaver Kabir, and Padmavati, a woman.

These traditional disciples of Ramanand (whether or not they actually were initiated by him) formed the first generation of sants, who may be placed in the late fifteenth century. The dominant figure of the next generation was Guru Nanak (1469–1539). Over the next three centuries, the sant tradition was kept alive by a number of individual singers, as well as by the *panth*s that formalised the teachings of Kabir, Dadu and others.

Kabir

Kabir is sometimes considered an "apostle of Hindu–Muslim unity", but he in fact was opposed to orthodoxy in all its forms, whether found in mosque, temple or elsewhere. Born in Benares, probably towards the middle of the fifteenth century, he was brought up as a *julahā* or weaver. It is all but certain that his family was Muslim, though his knowledge of the religion of Muhammad was superficial and his familiarity with vaishnava Hinduism and the doctrines of the nath yogis fairly extensive. The path of the sants has been called a synthesis of vaishnava bhakti, the teaching of the naths, and popular sufism. In Kabir these three elements first appear together; he may thus be called the creator of the sant synthesis.

In Kabir the vaishnava influence is most evident in songs in which he addresses Ram or Hari, though to him these are the names not of avatars of Vishnu but of the formless Absolute. His love and longing for the divine Beloved is sometimes expressed in terms that recall those of sufi poets (as in the first two *dohā*s below); but the primary element in the make-up of his thought and practice was the popular Tantrism of the nath yogis. This comes out particularly in songs employing the vocabulary of the naths, such as the second to last *pad* below. But Nathism underlies Kabir's whole path, which he calls, using an important tantric term, the path of *sahaj*.

Kabir's diction is rough, sometimes even crude, but always infused with a frankness and vitality that, to many modern ears, is startlingly contemporary. Generally straightforward, Kabir sometimes uses the cryptic "upside-down" language found also in other popular tantric texts (see for example the second *pad* below). On account of his influence and popularity, many later singers added his signature-line to their poems, with the result that many well-known "songs of Kabir" (including most of those translated by Tagore in a popular collection) are probably not by Kabir. His genuine works, written in a mixed old Hindi dialect, are found in three collections: the *Ādi Granth* or sacred book of the Sikhs; the *Pañc-vāṇī* or book of the Dadu panth of Rajasthan, which provides the text of the standard *Kabīr-granthāvalī*; and the *Bījak* or special scripture of the Kabir panth. In each of these collections, the compositions are arranged by type of composition: *dohā*s or couplets and *pad*s or songs. The same convention is followed here.

[137]

*Dohā*s of Kabir

*Dohā*s are couplets: in the original Hindi they occupy two lines. *Dohā*s are given different names in different collections. In the *Ādi Granth*, they are called *ślok*s and in the *Bījak* and *Pañc-vāṇī*, *sākhī*s. Kabir's *dohā*s are often aphoristic, with an ironical turn at the end. Of the twelve reproduced here, the first group, from the *Ādi Granth*, was translated by Nirmal Dass, the second group, from the *Bījak*, by Linda Hess and Shukdev Singh, and the third, from the *Kabīr-granthāvalī*, by Charlotte Vaudeville.

Kabir,
separation from the Beloved
coils around my heart
like a snake.
No mantras work.
I cannot live without Ram.
If I go on living,
I'll go mad.

*

I lower
my eyes in shyness —
my Beloved is in my body.
I enjoy all pleasures
with my Beloved —
I tell no one.

*

Kabir,
the physician died,
the patient died,
the whole wide world died.
Only Kabir did not die,
for whom
there were no mourners.

*

Kabir says,
"By saying, 'You, You,'
I have become You.
'I am' is in me no longer.
When the difference
between us was erased,
I saw You everywhere."

* * *

Use the strength of your own arm,
stop putting hope in others.
When the river flows through your own yard,
how can you die of thirst?

*

Human birth is hard to attain,
you don't get a second chance.
Once a ripe fruit falls,
it won't jump back to the branch.

*

They searched and searched, searched some more —
it just kept disappearing.
After all that search, when they couldn't find it,
they gave up and said, "Beyond."

*

Sun sinks, day fades,
dusk has fallen.
From screwing too many lovers,
the whore is barren.

* * *

Kabīr's house is on the top,
    where the path is slippery:
An ant cannot hold its footing
    and they go with loaded bullocks!

*

In myself, there is nothing of mine,
    all there is is Thine:
Whatever I offer Thee is Thine already,
    how can the gift be mine?

*

When I was, Hari was not,
    now Hari is and I am no more:
All darkness vanishes
    when I found the Lamp within my heart.

*

Him whom I went out to seek,
    I found just where I was:
He now has become myself
    whom before I called "Another"!

[138]

*Pad*s of Kabir

*Pad*s (poems, songs or hymns) are compositions in varying forms and lengths, which often are set to music. Most of them contain a refrain, sometimes indicated by "Rest". The *pad*s below are from all three of the main collections of Kabir's works. The first group, from the *Ādi Granth*, was translated by Nirmal Dass, the second group, from the *Bījak* (where *pad*s are known as *śabda*s or *ramainī*s), was translated by Linda Hess and Shukdev Singh, and the last group, from the *Kabīr-granthāvalī*, was translated by Charlotte Vaudeville.

Make your heart Mecca
and your body the Ka'aba.
Make consciousness
its primal guru.

Hey, mullah, give the call for prayers:
One mosque, ten doors. (Rest)

Do away with sacrifice,
doubt and inner filth.
Make patience
your five daily prayers.

The Master of Hindus and Turks
is one and the same.
What use is being
a mullah or sheikh?

Kabir, say,
"I have become insane.
Slowly, slowly my heart
has blended with the Infinite."

*

The wife gives birth to her husband;
the child bounces
his father on his knee.
The breastless woman gives suck.

O people, behold the ways of the present Age:
The son marries his own mother. (Rest)

The man with no feet jumps;
the mouthless man howls with laughter.
A man slumbers without sleeping;
milk is churned without a churn.

The udderless cow gives milk;
the long journey is taken without a road.
The way can't be found without the True Guru—
Kabir speaks so that you may understand.

*

Over there,
there is no rain, ocean, sunshine, or shade.

Over there,
there is no creation or destruction,
neither living nor dying,
neither the touch of sorrow or joy.
Over there,
there is neither solitude nor meditation.

Hard to describe that eternal peace:
Over there,
nothing is measured, nothing depleted,
nothing is light, nothing heavy. (Rest)

Over there,
none is high or low.
Over there,
there is neither night nor day.
Over there,
there is neither water, air, nor fire.
Over there,
only the True Guru permeates all.

Unaccessible, beyond thought
is the Eternal One;
He can be found
by the guru's grace.
Kabir, say,
"I sacrifice myself
for my Guru—
may I blend with His true being."

* * *

Pandit, do some research
and let me know
how to destroy transiency.
Money, religion, pleasure, salvation—
which way do they stay, brother?
North, South, East or West?
In heaven or the underworld?
If Gopal is everywhere, where is hell?

Heaven and hell are for the ignorant,
not for those who know Hari.
The fearful thing that everyone fears,
I don't fear.
I'm not confused about sin and purity,
heaven and hell.
Kabir says, seekers, listen:
Wherever you are
is the entry point.

*

Pandit, you've got it wrong.
There's no creator or creation there,
no gross or fine, no wind or fire,
no sun, moon, earth or water,
no radiant form, no time there,
no word, no flesh, no faith,
no cause and effect, nor any thought
of the Veda. No Hari or Brahma,
no Shiva or Shakti, no pilgrimage
and no rituals. No mother, father
or guru there. Is it two or one?
Kabir says, if you understand now,
you're guru, I'm disciple.

*

Saints, if I speak
who will believe it?
If I lie
it passes for truth.
I glimpsed a jewel,
unpierced and priceless,
without buyer or seller.
Glittering, gleaming, it flashed
in my eyes, and filled
the ten directions.
A touch of grace
from the guru:
the invisible, markless
appeared.

Simple meditation,
absolute stillness
awakened. Simply
I met Ram.
Wherever I look,
only this, only this.
The diamond pierced
my ruby heart.
Through the guru
comes the supreme.
Thus teaches Kabir.

* * *

Hari, the Thug,
  has tricked the whole world—
Yet, away from Him, I cannot live,
  O my Friend! *refrain*

Who has a husband?
  who has a wife?
Think well about it
  and search your own soul.

Who has a son?
  who has a father?
Who is it who suffers,
  who is it who dies?

Says Kabīr, with that Thug,
  my heart is well pleased—
And the thuggery was over
  when I recognized the Thug.

*

If there be a saint in whose heart the bliss of Sahaj is born,
  I'll give Him all litanies and penance as brokerage:
Let He but give me a single drop of Rām's Liquor
  as the Liquor-girl pours out a drink!

For the sake of money, that Liquor-girl of the body
 had taken the Guru's Word as sugar:
Greed, lust, anger, envy and pride, she's ground them fine
 and used them as toning up.

From the fourteen worlds, she made her still
 and she lit the Fire of Brahman:
In the vat sealed with *mudrā*, the sound of the Sahaj rose up,
 Sushumnā itself was the worm.

The spring flowed, ambrosia oozed out,
 on such a drink, the Prince got drunk —
Says Kabīr, such a flavour is hard to find:
 the all-knowing Guru alone masters the art!

*

I am in all, all are in me,
I am in each and every one — Ho!
Let one call me "Kabīr",
let another call me "Rām-Rāī" — Ho!

Neither a child nor an old man am I,
 nor a father of young children — Ho! —
Sent away, I don't go, sent for, I don't come:
 easily, I remain in the whole world — Ho!

All I wear is a loin-cloth
 and people say it's whole — Ho!
Yet the Weaver couldn't weave it whole:
 So he tore it in ten places — Ho!

Since I merged into that Fruit which is Quality-less,
 my Name is "Rām-Rāī" — Ho!
I see the world, the world does not see me:
 that little bit Kabīr has secured — Ho!

[139]

Raidas

References to Kabir in Raidas's songs make it apparent that he was Kabir's younger contemporary. Raidas also lived in Benares, but there is no historical evidence that the two ever met. Legend connects Raidas not only with Kabir but with Ramanand (who is supposed to have been his guru) and with Mira Bai (who is supposed to have been his disciple). Those who accept both of these stories are obliged to give Raidas a life span of a hundred-twenty years or more. Hagiography aside, the only source of information on Raidas's life are his songs and those of later sants. All agree that he was a *camār* or leather-worker and cobbler and thus (because of his contact with animal carcasses) an untouchable. The other thing that emerges clearly from Raidas's songs is his acquaintance with the *nirguṇ* and *saguṇ* devotional traditions, and the practices and experiences of nath yoga. Few give better accounts of the experience of mystical union, which he frequently refers to as *sahaj*—the state in which the truths of the many and the One spontaneously blend. About a hundred of Raidas's songs have been preserved in the *Pañc-vāṇī* of the Dadu panth and the *Ādi Granth* of the Sikhs. (In the *Ādi Granth*, and in other sources, Raidas is called Ravidas.) These selections from the *Pañc-vāṇī* were translated from the Hindi by Winand M. Callewaert and Peter G. Friedlander.

Creator, I am Your wretched servant!
Grant Your vision to this hopeful one.
My soul is restless for Your vision. *refrain*

You are first and last, God and man,
You manifest as angel and man.
You are the refuge sought by Pīrs and prophets,
What have I, poor and dirty, to fear?
You are the manifest Lord, the One Yogi,
there is no other like You.
For him whose love has no effect,
what is prayer and worship?
Till now I was an unhonoured shoemaker,
a wretched servant of yours.
I can get no answer at Your door,
Raidās says, I am wretched.

*

God, if I did not sin, Infinite One,
how could Your Name be "Uplifter of the fallen"? *refrain*

How can there be a difference
between "You" and "I", "I" and "You",
Gold and bracelet, water and wave?
In You there are several men, Indweller —
Through the master the servant is known,
through the servant the master.
You are in everything and everything is in You,
your servant Raidās says in confusion:
where are You?

*

How can I offer worship to Rām?
I cannot find perfect fruits or flowers. *refrain*

Milk is defiled by the calf at the udder,
flowers are polluted by the bee,
water by the fish.
The serpent has coiled around the sandal-wood,
poison and nectar are mixed together.
Through the mind alone there is worship,
through the mind alone incense is offered.
Through the mind alone
I serve the essence of *sahaj*.
I do not know how to adore or worship you, Rām.
Raidās says, what is to be my fate?

*

Mādhav! What can be said? This delusion is such
that whatever I say You are, You are not! *refrain*

A king slept comfortably on his bed
and dreamt he was a beggar.
He still had a kingdom but was very distressed —
my condition has become like that.
When I exist You do not,
only You exist and I do not.
A river flows into the waves of the ocean,

only water in water.
Like rope and snake by night or light,
some of the mystery is now made known to me.
I understood gold and ornaments,
I no longer say what I once said.
There is One Creator, brother, who experiences the world,
He is the only one in every body, in every way.
Raidās says, devotion is all that has arisen,
whatever is exists through *sahaj*.

*

What shall I sing? There is nothing I can sing—
I sing of the beauty of *sahaj*. *refrain*

There is no heaven, no mountain, no earth,
no body filled with breath, no moon,
no Rām, no Krishna, no *guṇs*, brother,
when spontaneity speaks.
There are no Vedas, no scriptures, no Koran,
within the *sahaj śūnya*, brother.
There is no "I" or "You", no "You" or "I",
whom can I tell this to?
Raidās says, what shall I sing?
Singing, singing I am defeated.
How long shall I consider and proclaim:
absorb the self into the Self?

*

This experience is such,
that it defies all description.
I have met the Lord,
Who can cause me harm? *refrain*

Hari in everything, everything in Hari—
For him who knows Hari and the sense of self,
no other testimony is needed:
the knower is absorbed.
I shall live along with the magician,
I have understood the secret of the show.
Though the magic is false, the magician is real,

I know the state and my mind believes.
When the mind is stilled why do you not realise:
the knower knows?
Raidās says, in the bliss of pure discernment,
I contemplate the essence of *sahaj*.

[140]

Dadu

Born in Ahmedabad a century after Kabir, Dadu (1544 – 1603) was by profession a cotton carder. Although apparently of Muslim birth, he is given brahmin parentage and a miraculous origin by the members of his panth. Dadu's Hindi hagiographies continue in the same strain, making it difficult to arrive at a clear picture of his life. It seems certain that at a relatively early age, he became a wandering mendicant, eventually settling in Rajasthan. There he became known as Dadu Dayal, or Dadu the compassionate. Clearly influenced by Kabir, Dadu sang in the sant mode, stressing that God is to be found not through rituals or scriptures but rather by inner experience. These selections from his *Vāṇī* or "Utterances" were translated from the Hindi by Ahmad Shah and E. W. Ormerod.

All sing praises with their body, but with soul scarce one sings the praise.
To keep before the soul the One Essence, this, O Dadu, is hard.
Dadu, all know how to praise the dwelling of the earthly.
But one can sing the place of soul-God, alone, unique.
While, Dadu, the material body persists, then all things are apparent.
Before the spiritual body fearless, alone His Essence *is*.
For him who knows no more his existence, the world is done away.
Whom one knows himself as spirit, alone the formless *is*.
In the body sing the praises, while the body is in health.
When praises spring up within the soul, then all else is tasteless.

*

Then was I one with Him, O brother: I met my love and found true knowledge.
By the touch of the magic stone I was the giver of bliss: then the folly of distinction was cast away.

In Malayagiri I found the secret: then delusions of race, and caste and family were done away.
The water, brought near to the ocean of Hari, to the uttermost drop was absorbed therein.
Vanished the secrets of all varied illusions: then in the one colour Dadu was dyed.

*

Caught in the wave of love and borne into the lover's presence,
My soul, as a maiden, with her lover finds joy, O Dadu Das.
Maiden and Lover are made one: for her the bridal bed is spread.
With her lover she tastes the sweets of love: Dadu how blest her lot.
O Dadu, the maiden with her body should render service to her Lord.
Inebriate with her lover's love, drinking deep of love's nectar.
O Dadu, the maid is perfect, perfect too the spouse.
From the union of perfections a perfect love flows forth.
The maid of surpassing brightness — surpassing bright her Lord.
Upon a bed of brightness, the festival they kept.
Lover and maid united know but one state of bliss.
Ever in her lover's arms, no one is so blest as she.

[141]

Paltu Sahib

As with most of the sants, little is known about Paltu Sahib beyond what can be gleaned from his songs. A shopkeeper by trade, he lived in Ayodhya during the eighteenth century. It is said that the priests of that famous pilgrimage centre were so offended by his unorthodox teachings that they brought about his death. His songs, noted for their literary craftsmanship, stress the importance of the *śabd* or Word, the *sadguru* or true teacher, and the need of yogic self-discipline. These selections were translated from the Hindi by Issac A. Ezekiel.

At times Saints face starvation; at times they roll in wealth.
At times they roll in wealth, but neither joy nor sorrow affects them.
Empty or full, they ever possess the treasure of contentment.

Sometimes their couch is bedecked with flowers, and they ride caparisoned elephants.
Sometimes they sleep on raw ground and they walk with bare feet.
At times they wear gold-embroidered garments,
At times, all but naked, they warm themselves before fire.
O Paltu, both the states are alike to them; they blame not their destiny.
At times saints face starvation; at times they roll in wealth.

*

The Melody of the Word pierced him like an arrow and Paltu died that very moment.
Paltu died the very moment he set his foot on the battlefield.
His head was the first to go and then he fought with his trunk.
Wounded in every pore of the body, his entrails came out and trailed along the field.
The beholders, stricken with awe, wondered at the fierce battle Paltu fought.
It was, indeed, the Master who shot him right in the heart with an arrow.
The arrow went whizzing like a whirlwind and piercing his heart went deep within.
Words are easy as the wind, the number of those who merely preach is legion.
But Paltu gave away his life the moment the Melody of the Word pierced him like an arrow.

FURTHER READING

Source Materials

Winand M. Callewaert and Peter G. Friedlander, *The Life and Work of Raidās*. Delhi: Manohar Book Publications, 1992.

Nirmal Dass, *Songs of Kabir from the Adi Granth*. Reprint edition. Delhi: Sri Satguru Publications, 1992.

Isaac A. Ezekiel, *Saint Paltu: His Life and Teachings*. Dera Baba Jaimal Singh, Punjab: Radha Soami Satsang Beas, 1979.

Linda Hess and Shukdev Singh, *The Bījak of Kabir*. Reprint edition. Delhi: Motilal Banarsidass, 1986.

Ahmad Shah and E. W. Ormerod, *Hindi Religious Poetry*. Cawnpore [Kanpur]: n.p., 1925.

Charlotte Vaudeville, *A Weaver Named Kabir*. Delhi: Oxford University Press, 1997.

Other Works

David N. Lorenzen, *Praises to a Formless God: Nirguṇī Texts from North India*. Reprint edition. Delhi: Sri Satguru Publications, 1997.

Karine Schomer and W. H. McLeod, eds., *The Sants: Studies in a Devotional Tradition of India*. Reprint edition. Delhi: Motilal Banarsidass, 1987.

Charlotte Vaudeville, *Kabir*. Oxford: Clarendon Press, 1974.

Sources of Texts and Translations

137	*Ādi-granth*, *Śloks* of Kabir, 76, 234, 69, 204; *Bījak*, *Śākhīs* 277, 115, 343, 51; *Kabīr Granthāvalī*, *Śākhīs*	Dass 274, 310, 272, 303; Hess and Singh 122, 102, 130, 94; Vaudeville 179, 176, 178, 179
138	*Ādi-granth*, Rag Bhairo 4, Rag Basant 3, Rag Gauri 48; *Bījak*, *Śabdas* 42, 43, 7; *Kabīr Granthāvalī* (2) 49, 51, 53	Dass 229, 242, 77; Hess and Singh 55–56, 44; Vaudeville 245–46, 262–63, 294–95
139	*Vāṇī* 65, 34, 39, 57, 26, 10	Callewaert and Friedlander 143, 125–28, 139, 118–119, 110–111
140	*tan soṁ sumiraṇ sab karen, tab hum ek bhaye re bhāī, prem lahari gahi le gaī*	Shah and Ormerod 92, 98, 94
141	*Palṭū Sāhib ki Bānī*, Pt. I, *kuṇḍli* 30; Pt. I, *kuṇḍli* 105	Ezekiel 199–200, 120–21

15

ਭੈ ਨਾਸਨ ਦੁਰਮਤਿ ਹਰਨ ਕਲਿ ਮੈ ਹਰਿ ਕੋ ਨਾਮੁ ॥
ਨਿਸਿ ਦਿਨੁ ਜੋ ਨਾਨਕ ਭਜੈ ਸਫਲ ਹੋਹਿ ਤਿਹ ਕਾਮ ॥

The divine Name in this dark age
dispels fear and ignorance.
Says Nanak, they who recite It night and day,
triumph in every action.

Guru Tegh Bahadur, shalok 20

The Sikh Gurus

OF THE VARIOUS *panth*s or paths based on the teachings of *sant*s who adored the Formless God and the Name, the only one that has established itself as a thriving separate religion is the *panth* of Guru Nanak (1469–1539). The followers of Nanak and his nine successor Gurus are called *sikh*s or "disciples"; the system of belief and practice based on the teachings of the Sikh Gurus is known in English as Sikhism.

The Sikh religion took form during the sixteenth and seventeenth centuries—a tumultuous period that witnessed the fall of the Delhi Sultanate and the rise of the Mughal dynasty. During most of its early life, the new *panth* had to fight for its existence, with the result that the gentle and tolerant teachings of Nanak became imbued with a martial spirit. This remains a key element in the ethos of the contemporary Sikh community.

One may distinguish four stages in the early history of the Sikhs. First came the mysticism and ministry of Guru Nanak. After his death in 1539, the new faith was consolidated under Angad, Amar Das and Ram Das, the second, third and fourth Gurus (1539–1581). During these years, a number of important institutions were established, such as the *Guru kā laṅgar* or casteless dining room, while the town that would become the Sikh capital, Amritsar, was founded. Consolidation continued under Arjan, the fifth Guru (1581–1606), whose greatest achievement was the compilation of the *Ādi Granth*, the Sikhs' scripture. From 1605 began a period of persecution, during which Angad and the ninth Guru, Tegh Bahadur, became martyrs to the faith. Moulded into a cohesive community by the tenth Guru, Gobind Singh, the Sikhs survived to become the major power in the region during the early nineteenth century.

Despite its combative history, Sikhism began as a devotional and contemplative path. This orientation is apparent in the hymns of Guru Nanak and his successors, which make up the bulk of the *Ādi Granth* or "Primordial Book" of the Sikhs. Since the death of the last personal Guru in 1708, the *Ādi Granth* has been regarded as the Guru of the Sikhs, and as such is known as the *Gurū Granth Sāhib*. Along with the hymns of Nanak and four of his successors, the *Ādi Granth* contains three hundred hymns by Namdev, Kabir, Ravidas/Raidas and other sants, as well as works by the sufis Sheikh Farid and Sheikh Bhikan. This inclusion of texts by members of different traditions shows the tolerance and inclusiveness of Sikhism, and also indicates the sources that were available to Guru Nanak as he gave shape to his own *panth*. Chief among these were the bhakti movement, in particular the *nirguṇ* tradition of Kabir and Ravidas, who were alive when Nanak was born. The second was the contemplative practices of the *nāth yogī*s, which Nanak seems to have been drawn to at an early stage of his development. Finally there was Islam, which at the time of his birth was the religion of the northern Indian élite, and also (in the form of popular sufism) an important element in the life of village and town.

What Guru Nanak gave his followers was a path of salvation by means of meditation on the Name. The unique Godhead is revealed in this divine self-expression and also in the promptings of the inner *sadguru*. By repetition of the Name, which is nothing less than the self-expression of the nature and being of God, one can achieve the experience of God's existence and freedom from the cycles of rebirth. The Name may be repeated inwardly or audibly, alone or in congregation. This is the sole and sufficient means of liberation. Image-worship, rituals and ascetic practices are useless. In principle, all Sikhs have an equal chance at salvation, since all are equal before Guru and God. There is thus no room in Sikhism for the caste-system or for the systematic subordination of women.

[142]

Guru Nanak

Born in 1469 in a village near Lahore, Nanak was the son of a village official who worked as a revenue collector. According to the Sikh hagiographic tradition, preserved in the *janam sākhī*s or "birth testimonies", Nanak was of a contemplative cast of mind from childhood. Finding him unsuited to accountancy, his father gave him the work of grazing cattle. One day, while bathing in a river, Nanak had the experience of the Presence of God, and received the gift of the Name. When he came back to his normal consciousness, the first words that he uttered were "There is no Hindu, there is no Muslim". Afterwards, in the immemorial tradition of India, he became a wandering mystic. Accompanied by his minstrel, he moved from place to place, singing hymns in praise of the Formless God, the Name, and the inner Guru. Many tales are told of his travels throughout India and as far west as Baghdad and Mecca. During these journeys he attracted the first of his disciples or *sikhs*. Eventually he returned to the Punjab and settled in Kartarpur on the banks of the Ravi. Here he began to systematise the beliefs and practices that became the basis of the Sikh religion. Before his death in 1539, he named one of his disciples, Angad, to be his successor.

Guru Nanak is the author of 974 hymns of the *Ādi Granth*, including the first hymn, called *Jap* or, respectfully, *Japjī*. At the head of this is placed the *mūl mantra* or "fundamental creed" of Sikhism, which begins *ek oṅkar*, "There is One Being". This statement of the indescribable nature of God is followed by the beautiful and evocative stanzas of the *Japjī*, which sketch, with a profusion of poetic images, the outlines of That which is beyond human conception. Nanak's other *pads* or hymns, of which two are given after the extracts from the *Japjī*, make use of metaphors drawn from the common pool of poetic figures that by the sixteenth century was shared by bhaktas, sufis and sants. The language used by Guru Nanak is an early form of Punjabi closely related to old Hindi. Translated by Nikky-Guninder Kaur Singh.

There is One Being
Truth by Name
Primal Creator
Without fear
Without enmity
Timeless in form
Unborn
Self-existent
The grace of the Guru.

MEDITATE
Truth before time
Truth throughout time
Truth here and now
Says Nanak, Truth is evermore.

Thought cannot think,
    nor can a million thoughts.
Silence cannot silence,
    nor can seamless contemplation.
Greed is not made greedless,
    not by the wealth of all the world.
Though a thousand mental feats become a million,
    not one can go with us.
How then to be true?
    How then to break the wall of lies?
By following the Will.
    Says Nanak, this is written for us.

By the divine Will, all forms were created;
    what that Will is, no one can say.
By that Will, all life is formed
    and, by that Will, all are exalted.
The Will determines what is high and what is low;
    the Will grants all joy and suffering.
Some are blessed by the Will,
    others migrate from birth to birth.
All are within the Will, none stands apart.
Says Nanak, by recognizing the Will,
    we silence our ego. . . .

Filled with might, they sing praise of the Might,
Seeing the signs, they sing praise of the Bounty,
Perceiving the virtues, they sing praise of the Glory.
Some sing praise through high philosophy,
Some sing praise of the power that creates and destroys,
Some sing in awe of the giving and taking of life.
Some sing of the thereness, the utter transcendence,
Some sing of the hereness, the close watch over all.
Stories and stories add one to another,
Preaching and preaching lead nowhere.
The Giver gives, the receivers tire of receiving;
Age upon age they eat and eat the gifts.
All are directed by that Will;
Says Nanak, the Carefree is ever in bliss.

The True Sovereign, Truth by Name,
    infinite love the language.
Seekers forever seek gifts
    and the Giver gives more and more.
What can we offer for a glimpse of the Court?
What can we say to win divine love?
In the ambrosial hour, exalt and reflect upon the True Name.
Through actions each is dressed in a body,
    but liberation comes only from the Gaze of grace.
Says Nanak, know the Absolute thus.

That One cannot be moulded or made,
Alone immaculate and self-existent.
Those who serve receive honours.
Nanak says, sing of the Treasure of virtues,
Sing, listen, and hold love in the heart
So sorrow is banished, joy ushered in.
Through the Guru comes the sacred Word,
    through the Guru comes the scripture,
    through the Guru, That One is experienced in all.
The Guru is Shiva, the Guru is Vishnu, the Guru is Brahma,
    the Guru is Parvati, Laxmi and Sarasvati.
Were I to comprehend, I'd still fail to explain,
    for That One is beyond all telling.
Guru, let me grasp this one thing:
All creatures have one Provider,
    may I not forget this. . . .

Countless are the ways of meditation,
    and countless the avenues of love,
Countless the ways of worship,
    and countless the paths of austerity and sacrifice.
Countless the texts, and countless the Vedic reciters,
Countless the yogis turning away from the world,
Countless the devout reflecting on virtue and knowledge,
Countless the pious, and countless the patrons,
Countless the warriors, faces scarred by iron
Countless the sages sunk in silent trance.
How can I express the Primal Power?
I cannot offer myself to you even once.

Only that which pleases You is good.
You are for ever constant, Formless One. . . .

Infinite is Your glory, and infinite the ways to sing
Your praise,
Infinite are the deeds, and infinite the gifts,
Infinite is the seeing, and infinite the hearing,
And infinite are the workings of That Mind.
Infinite is the variety of forms,
Infinite are the edges of the universe.
And how many yearn to comprehend the limits?
Even their end is not to be found.
The end eludes all,
The more it is expressed, the farther it extends.
The Sovereign is great and high in station,
Yet higher still is the Name.
If we could ever reach that height,
Then only would we know the Highest of the high.
Expansive as It is, That One alone can know Itself.
Nanak says, we are graced with the gift of the Gaze. . . .

Priceless are the virtues, priceless their trade,
Priceless are the dealers, priceless the treasures in store,
Priceless are they who come for this trade,
priceless what they take away,
Priceless is love, priceless those immersed in it,
Priceless is the law, and priceless the court,
Priceless are the scales, priceless the weights,
Priceless is the bounty, priceless the seal,
Priceless is the favour, priceless the command,
How priceless the Priceless One is, no one can say,
Those who try are lost in silence.
Vedas and Puranas have also sought to say,
Scholars say in their texts and discourses,
Brahmas say, Indras say,
Gopis and Krishnas say,
Shivas say, Siddhas say,
Innumerable Buddhas say,
The demons say, the gods say,
The virtuous, wise and devout say.

How many speak and begin to speak,
Many have spoken and gone,
And if their numbers were doubled again,
Still no one could say.
That One is as great as It chooses to be,
Nanak says, only the True One knows Itself.
That babbler who presumes to say
Is marked as the fool of fools. . . .

Wear contentment as your yogi earrings,
    let honest actions be your pouch and begging bowl,
    make inner contemplation your penitential ashes.
Death shall be the cloak you wear,
    pure living your yogic discipline,
    and faith the staff you lean upon.
Accept all humans as your equals,
    and let them be your only sect.
    Conquering ourselves, we conquer the world.
Salutations!
Salutations to That One who is primal, immaculate,
    immortal, immutable, constant throughout the ages. . . .

In the Realm of Knowledge, knowledge blazes forth,
Here reign mystic melodies and myriad sports and joys.
Now the Realm of Beauty is beauty itself,
Here the faculties are honed in unmatched splendour.
Words fail to describe,
They who try lament their lack.
Here consciousness, wisdom, mind and discernment are honed,
Awareness sharpened like that of the gods and mystics.

The Realm of Grace is full of force,
Here is the One with no other.
Here heroes and mighty warriors dwell,
Inspired by Rama.
Here are Sita and women of her fame and virtue,
Their beauty beyond words.
They do not die, they are not beguiled,
For Rama is in their hearts.

Saints from many worlds live in this Realm of Grace.
They know bliss, for the True One
    is imprinted on their minds.
In the Realm of Truth, the Formless One is at home,
Gazing upon Its creation.
Here are continents, constellations, and universes
Whose limits cannot be told.
Here are creatures of various forms,
All acting according to the Will.
That One watches, rejoices
    and contemplates Its own creation.
Nanak says, to describe this is as hard as iron.

Let continence be your smithy, and patience your goldsmith.
Let wisdom be your anvil, and knowledge your hammer.
Let awe be the bellows, and inner control the blazing fire.
In the crucible of love, let the ambrosia flow,
In this true mint, forge the Word,
Such fulfilment comes to those blessed with the Gaze.
Says Nanak, happy are they who are gazed upon.

EPILOGUE

Air is our Guru, water our father,
and the great earth our mother.
Day and night are the female and male nurses
in whose laps the whole universe plays.
Good and bad deeds are all disclosed
in the presence of Righteousness.
Our actions take us near or far.
Those who remember the Name earn true success.
Nanak says their faces shine,
and they take many with them to liberation.

*

This body of mine is steeped in illusion,
    the clothes I wear are dyed with greed.
My Beloved does not like my dress,
    how then can this bride enter the nuptial bed?

I offer myself to You, Compassionate One,
I offer myself to You.
I offer myself even to those who remember Your Name.
To those who remember Your Name,
I offer myself a hundred times.

If my body were a vat, and the crimson of the Name
were poured into it,
And if the dyer were my Sovereign,
such a brilliant colour would never have been seen.

Those who wear clothes so dyed,
have the Beloved ever close to them.
This is Nanak's plea,
may I receive the dust of their feet.

That One creates, That One colours,
That One bestows the loving Gaze.
Nanak says, if a woman pleases the Husband
then the Beloved makes love to her.

*

If I make of my mind a temple,
and of my body a hermit's robe,
if I bathe in the fount of myself,
If the One Word dwells in my breath,
I will not return to the circle of life.

Mother, my mind is pierced
with love for the Compassionate One.
But who can know another's pain?
The Divine is my only concern.

You who are unfathomable, unknowable, ineffable, infinite,
do watch over us.
You pervade the waters and the lands and the air above,
Your Light shines in each and every heart.

All teaching, all wisdom, all enlightenment is Yours,
all temples and shelters are Yours.

My Sovereign, I know no one else but You,
and I sing your glory forever.

All creatures seek refuge in Your lap,
responsibility for all rests with You.
Whatever pleases You is good,
This is all Nanak has to say.

[143]
Guru Ram Das

All the hymns of the Sikh Gurus carry the signature-line of Nanak regardless of the actual author. This is a sign that the successor Gurus are in a sense the same Guru in different bodies. The fourth "Nanak" was Ram Das, who lived from 1534 to 1581 and was Guru from 1574 until his death. He is remembered for excavating the holy tank around which grew the city of Amritsar ("Ambrosial or Immortal Lake"). Guru Ramdas was the author of 697 hymns of the *Ādi Granth*, of which this paean to the Name is an example. Translated from the Punjabi by Nikky-Guninder Kaur Singh.

Devotees, True Guru, True Creator, I beseech You,
Like worms we seek shelter in the True Guru,
Have compassion, and grant us the radiance of the Name.

My Enlightening Friend, grant me the radiance
of the divine Name.
The Name taught by the Guru is the breath of my life,
To praise the One is my daily custom.

Fortunate are the devotees, wrapped in faith, thirsty
for the Divine.
Hearing the Name, their thirst is quenched,
Meeting with the faithful, their virtues sparkle.

They who do not taste the elixir of the Name
Are unfortunate, they are with the god of death.
They who do not seek the lap of the True Guru,
nor the company of the pious, are accursed in this life,
accursed in their life to come.

The foreheads of the devotees who seek the Truth Guru
glow with fortune written from the dawn of time.
Blessed, blessed is the true company
in which the elixir is tasted.
Nanak says, in such company, the Name is revealed.

[144]

Guru Arjan

Youngest son of Guru Ram Das, Arjan (1563–1606) was appointed by his father to be his successor in 1581. One of the most energetic Gurus, he built the Harimandir or Golden Temple and compiled the *Ādi Granth*, thus providing the Sikhs with their principal holy place and their holy book. As Guru during the reign of the broad-minded emperor Akbar, he promoted the new religion and played an active role in the community's secular affairs. After the ascension of Jehangir in 1605, Arjan came into conflict with the Mughal administration. Refusing to compromise, he was tortured to death. Arjan was the author of 2218 hymns of the *Ādi Granth*, of which the following selections are examples. The second item comprises the last of the twenty-four sections of an extended composition called *Sukhmaṇi* or "Pearl of Peace", which celebrates the divine Name. Translated by Nikky-Guninder Kaur Singh.

My mind pines for a vision of the Guru,
It wails like the chatrik bird.
My thirst is unquenched, and I find no peace
without sight of the beloved saint.

May I offer myself again and again
for a vision of the beloved and holy Guru.

Your face is beautiful, and the music of Your sweet Word
brings peace within.
It has been so long since I caught a glimpse of You,
I yearn for You as a soaring bird for water.
Blessed is the land where You dwell,
my good and beloved Friend.

May I offer myself again and again,
my Guru, my good and beloved Friend.

A moment without sight of You passes painfully
as a long dark age.
When shall I see you now, my blessed Beloved?
My nights are a torment, I cannot sleep a wink
without a glimpse of the Court.

May I offer myself again and again
to the True One's Court.

By good fortune I have met the holy Guru,
And I have found the Immortal in my own house.
May I always serve You,
never parting for a minute
or moment, Nanak is Your humble slave.

May I offer myself again and again,
Nanak is Your humble slave.

*

We revere the Absolute, whose Name is absolute too. Says Nanak, we win the Absolute, if we sing the praise of that Absolute.

Listen to the teaching of the Absolute Guru,
Let us see the Transcendent intimately within us.
Let us remember the Protector with every breath,
So shall our worries depart.
Let us discard our desires rolling like waves,
Let us yearn for the company of the faithful.
Abandoning our ego, let us pray
That we swim across the ocean of fiery waves.
Let us fill our treasury with the Name,
Says Nanak, my homage to the Absolute Guru.

As we remember the Transcendent with the faithful,
Comfort, peace and eternal bliss are ours,
Hell is evaded, life redeemed,
We sing divine praise, and we drink the ambrosial nectar.

Our mind contemplates the Supreme One,
The Formless One of so many different colours.
Preserver of all, compassionate of the lowly,
You annul our suffering, our absolute and beneficent One.
Let us remember Your Name again and again,
Says Nanak, for this is our only support.

The words of the faithful are glorious,
They are jewels most precious.
Listening to them and abiding by them,
We liberate ourselves and we liberate others.
They whose minds are suffused with radiance,
Are triumphant, triumphant are their friends.
They who resonate with the unstruck melody,
Hear the One, they enjoy supreme bliss,
Their foreheads shine with revelation,
Says Nanak, we too are liberated by their presence.

Hearing of You as our Refuge, we have come to You,
Have compassion on us, that we may unite with You.
We have expelled hate, we welcome humility,
In the company of the faithful,
    we sing Your ambrosial Name.
By pleasing You, our supreme Guru,
The devotion of Your devotees is fully fulfilled.
We are freed from all entanglements and vice
As we hear Your Name and recite Your praise.
Through compassion, You bestow Your grace,
Says Nanak, so we profit in our trade.

My good friends, let us sing divine praise,
With single mind, ever alert.
The pearls of peace shine on the thread of the Name,
Those who wear them are treasuries of wealth,
All their desires are fulfilled,
They are exalted and celebrated through all the worlds,
They win the highest station,
Are subject to birth and death no more.
Only they who receive your gifts,
Says Nanak, walk away with the sacred wealth.

Comfort, peace, riches, the nine treasures,
Intelligence, wisdom, the various miraculous powers,
The merit of knowledge, austerity, penance and contemplation,
Of supreme discernment, and most sacred ablution,
Life with its four goals, the self ever blossoming like a lotus,
Living in the midst of all yet free from all constraints,
Beauty, cleverness, insight into the essence,
An equal regard for everyone —
All these fruits are garnered by those,
Says Nanak, who recite and hear the Name.

Few recite this precious treasure within,
They live freely in all ages,
Their speech resounds with the praise of the Name,
As Smritis, Shastras and Vedas have declared.
The Name is the omega of all faiths,
Dwelling in the mind of the faithful.
The company of the faithful dispels countless faults,
Their grace saves us from the snare of death.
Those whose foreheads shine with the divine gift,
Says Nanak, they alone seek the company of the faithful.

They who cherish this treasure within, who hear it lovingly,
They remember the Divine constantly.
Freed from the suffering of life and death,
Their precious body is instantly liberated.
Their fame is unblemished, their words ambrosial,
For the One Name pervades them.
Suffering, sickness, fear and duality depart,
They are known as the faithful, all their actions are good.
They receive the highest glory.
No wonder, says Nanak,
the Name is the pearl of peace — *sukhmaṇi*.

[145]

Guru Tegh Bahadur

After the martyrdom of Guru Arjan, the Sikhs were obliged to develop the martial virtues for which they became famous. Guru Arjan's successor Guru Hargobind (1595–1664) shifted the throne of the

Gurus to the Shivalik Hills, where it remained for more than fifty years. The ninth Guru, Tegh Bahadur (1621–75), returned to the plains after he became Guru in 1664. This led to increased conflict with the Mughal authorities and Tegh Bahadur's eventual martyrdom. Fifty-nine hymns and fifty-six couplets by Guru Tegh Bahadur were included by his son Guru Gobind Singh in the final edition of the *Ādi Granth*. These couplets, composed not long before his execution, were translated by Nikky-Guninder Kaur Singh.

Unless we sing divine praise
our life passes in vain;
Says Nanak, love the Divine, my mind,
as a fish loves water.

Why are we caught in worldly delights?
Why can't we be free for a moment?
Says Nanak, love the Divine, my mind;
be saved from the snare of death. . . .

This body in which we take such pride,
vanishes in an instant, my friend.
Says Nanak, they who exalt the Divine,
they conquer the world.

They who enshrine the Divine in their self,
know them as liberated.
Says Nanak, know this for sure,
between the Divine and them, no difference lies. . . .

Friends and relatives desert,
none is our ally for ever.
Says Nanak, in times of distress
You are our only shelter.

The Name is eternal, the faithful are eternal,
eternal is the sustaining Guru.
Says Nanak, there are few in this world
who remember the Guru's Word.

Let us enshrine the Name in our hearts,
    for none is its equal.
The Name dispels our suffering;
    the Name brings us the sight of You.

[146]

Guru Gobind Singh

Born in Patna while his father, Guru Tegh Bahadur, was visiting eastern India, Gobind Rai, later known as Guru Gobind Singh (1666–1708) was not yet nine when his father was executed. Installed as Guru in March 1676, he spent his youth preparing himself for a life of spiritual and military leadership. He is remembered chiefly as the creator of the military brotherhood known as the Khalsa ("the Pure"), which remains the principal order of the Sikh religion and a focus of Sikh identity. Boys initiated into the Khalsa agree never to cut their hair or beards, and to wear four insignia that mark them out as committed Sikhs. All of them take the surname Singh, after the order's founder. (Woman initiates take the surname Kaur.) Guru Gobind Singh is the author of the *Dasam Granth* or "Tenth Book" of the Sikhs. The two excerpts from the *Dasam Granth* are from the *Savayye* or Quatrains, which form part of the Sikhs' morning prayers, and from the *Jāp*, a poetic catalogue of the attributes of God. Translated by Nikky-Guninder Kaur Singh.

There is One Being. Victory to the wonderful Guru.
The composition of the Tenth Guru.
My wonderful Guru, I recite the Savayye by Your grace.

I have seen hosts of purists and ascetics,
    I have visited the homes of yogis and celibates.
Heroes and demons, practitioners of purity
    and drinkers of ambrosia, hosts of saints
    from countless religions, I have seen them all.
I have seen religions from all countries,
    but I have yet to see followers of the Creator.
Without love for the Almighty,
    without grace from the Almighty,
    all practices are without a grain of worth.

Drunken elephants draped in gold,
 first among giants in blazing colours,
Herds of horses, sprinting like gazelles,
 swifter than the wind,
The people bow their heads to strong-armed rulers,
But what if they be such mighty owners;
 at the last, they depart barefoot from the world.

Conquerors of the world march triumphant
 to the beat of kettle-drums.
Their herds of handsome elephants trumpet,
 their royal steeds lustily neigh.
These rulers of past, future and present
 can never be counted.
Without worshipping the supreme Sovereign,
 all end in the house of death. . . .

How futile to sit in contemplation,
 like a stork with both eyes closed.
While trying to bathe in the seven seas,
 we lose this world and the next.
How futile to sink in misdeeds,
 we only waste away our life.
I tell the truth, do listen to me,
 they alone who love, find the Beloved.

Some worship stones, some bear them on their heads;
 some wear phalluses around their necks.
Some claim to see the One in the south;
 some bow their heads to the west.
Some worship idols, some images of animals;
 some run to worship the dead and their graves.
The entire world is lost in false ritual;
 none knows the mystery of the Almighty One.

*

You have no trait, no trace whatsoever,
 no colour, caste or family.
How to describe Your features or complexion,
 the lines on Your palms or Your garb?

You are called eternal, self-illumined, of infinite power,
Supreme among countless deities, Ruler among rulers,
Guardian of the three worlds—gods, humans and
    demons, tiny blades of grass and towering forests
    all proclaim Your infinity.
Who can recount all Your names?
The wise name You from Your actions.

Salutations to You, the Timeless
Salutations to You, the Merciful
Salutations to You, the Formless
Salutations to You, the Incomparable . . .

Formless
Incomparable
Immovable
Transcendent

Without description
Without attire
Without name
Without desire

Inconceivable
Mysterious
Unassailable
Fearless

You are exalted in all three worlds
You are the precious Treasure
You encompass all three goals of life
You were never born . . .

Primal Form, timeless Profile, unborn, infinite Being,
Divinity of the three worlds, extolled by all,
    unknown, primal, bountiful,
Nourisher of all, Vanquisher of all, Destroyer of all,
Omnipresent, most fervent Ascetic, most ardent Reveller.

Nameless, placeless, casteless,

without form, colour or contour,
Expansive timeless Being,
unborn, primal, and absolute,
Confined to no country or garb,
to no form, shape or attachment,
The Embodiment of Love
extends to all lands, to every nook and cranny. . . .

Primal Being
Whose origin cannot be told
You shatter evil in an instant
Mighty and timeless are You

Your glory resounds in every home
Your Name beats in every heart
Ageless Body
You are utterly independent . . .

Salutations to the Revered One
who destroys us all,
Salutations to the invincible Nameless One
who exists everywhere,
Salutations to the desireless Treasure
who is manifest everywhere,
Salutations to the Destroyer of evil
who fosters goodness.

Forever truth, consciousness and bliss,
vanquishing enemies,
Abounding in gifts, You create us all,
You dwell in us all,
Of wondrous glory, furious against tyrants,
Our Destroyer, our Creator, full of benevolence,
full of compassion.

Present in all four directions, rejoicing in all four directions,
Self-illumined, most beautiful, forever tied to each of us,
Freeing us from the pain of birth and death,
Compassion itself,
For ever by our side, Radiance eternal.

FURTHER READING

Source Materials

Nikky-Guninder Kaur Singh, *The Name of My Beloved: Verses of the Sikh Gurus*. San Francisco: HarperSanFrancisco, 1995.

Other Work

W. H. McLeod, *Gurū Nanak and the Sikh Religion*. Reprinted, with three other works, in *Sikhs and Sikhism*. Delhi: Oxford University Press, 1999.

Sources of Texts and Translations

142	*Ādi Granth*, *Jap* 1–5, 17, 24, 26, 28, 36; Rag Tilang, Mahalla 1; Rag Bilaval, Mahalla 1	Singh 47–49, 52–53, 55–62, 69, 72–73
143	*Ādi Granth*, Rag Gujri, Mahalla 4	Singh 118
144	*Ādi Granth*, Rag Majh, Mahalla 5; *Sukhmaṇi* 24	Singh 67–68, 237–40
145	*Ādi Granth*, shaloks 1–2, 42–43, 55–57	Singh 163, 168, 170
146	*Dasam Granth*, *Savayye* 1–3, 9–10; *Jāp* 1, 29–32, 79–80, 167–68, 197–99	Singh 109, 110; 77, 81, 87–88, 100, 104–05

16

باجھوں مرشد کجھ ناں حاصل توڑے راتیں جاگ پڑھیوے ہو
مریئے مرن تھیں اگے باہو تاں رب حاصل تھیوے ہو

Nothing is gained without a guide, even if one stays up nights
in study.
Let us die before dying, Bahu, only then is the Lord attained.

Sultan Bahu

Popular Sufism

DURING the first five hundred years of its development, South Asian sufism was (culturally speaking) part of the flowering of the Islamic mystical tradition of Persia and Central Asia. Indian sufis were children of the land of their birth, but their religious orientation was towards Mecca and Medina, and their philosophical vocabulary was drawn from thinkers of the vast Islamic world: from the Iberian Ibn al-Arabi and the Iraqi al-Junayd to the Afghan-born, Lahore-domiciled al-Hujwiri. When sufis of Bihar or the Deccan wrote accounts of their experiences or gave advice to their disciples, they did so in Persian, the language of Iranian mystics as well as of officials in Delhi. They had little interest in other religious traditions. If they felt any influence from Hinduism, Buddhism and Jainism, it was indirect and relatively minor.

This situation changed during the Mughal dynasty. From the mid sixteenth century there were extensive and often respectful contacts between Hindus and Muslims at every level of society. In constructing his Divine Faith or *Dīn-i Ilāhī*, Akbar was influenced by Hindus, Jainas and Parsis. His great-grandson Dara Shikuh was both a Qadiri initiate and a translator of the *upaniṣad*s and *Bhagavad Gītā*. Away from the urban centres, interaction between Muslim and Hindu mystics was even more widespread. Sufis and yogis exchanged notes on meditation-methods and the uses of the divine Name. Bhaktas influenced, and were influenced by, the devotional poetry and practices of the sufis. In this atmosphere, it was natural that syncretic cults should arise. Kabir and Guru Nanak arrived at a middle ground between the Hindu and Muslim traditions, rejecting the rituals but accepting the inner truths of both.

From around the fifteenth century, sufis in the villages of Punjab, Sind and Bengal began to express themselves in the emerging languages of those regions. The result was a popular literature that articulated their experiences and insights in a way that the common people, Hindu and Muslim alike, could appreciate. The Indo-Persian strand of sufism continued till the end of the Mughal period, especially in the cities; but the concurrent popular sufism of village and town proved more vigorous and, in the long run, more influential. In this chapter, several songs composed by Punjabi and Sindhi sufis are followed by works in Urdu by two sufis from the Delhi region.

Popular sufism took different forms wherever it arose; indeed, its genius was to give expression to the beliefs and practices of a certain sufi order in a given cultural environment. In India, the orders included the Chishtiyah, the Qadiriyah and the Shattariyah; the environment was a land in which the population was largely Hindu but the ruling class predominantly Muslim. The beliefs and practices of the religion from the West were communicated to the common people through the teachings of the sufis. Many of them were villagers themselves, and they used the idiom and folklore of rural life to express themselves to their neighbours. This meant drawing from Hindu as well as Muslim sources, as is demonstrated by this passage from the Sindhi mystic Sachal Sarmast (Schimmel 1975: 394):

> He is Abū Ḥamīfa and He is Hanuman,
> He is the Koran and He is the Vedas,
> He is this and He is that,
> He is Moses and He is Pharaoh.

To the Muslims of cities, many of whom were under the sway of the neo-orthodoxy of Ahmad Sirhindi, such lines would have been simple blasphemy. Writing as he did in a remote village in the "rustic" Sindhi language, Sachal managed to escape condemnation. So also, in the Punjab, Bulleh Shah could sing of the sound of Krishna's flute as naturally as Mira Bai or Narsi Mehta. Closer to Delhi, Ghauth Ali Shah was as familiar with Vedantic as with Islamic forms of meditation. Despite this syncretism, however, Indian sufis remained Muslims. If they were critical of hidebound orthodoxy, they venerated the Prophet and studied the *Qur'ān*. Yet the basis of their practice was not uninformed belief, but personal conviction and experience.

POPULAR SUFISM IN PUNJAB

The land of the five rivers was under continuous Muslim rule from the founding of the Delhi Sultanate till the rise of the Sikh state five hundred years later. Much of the population converted to Islam, particularly in the western districts. Largely rural and agricultural, Punjab had its own distinctive culture but was slow to develop its own language. One of the first to use a dialect similar to modern Punjabi was the sufi Shaikh Farid, some of whose works are preserved in the *Ādi Granth*. The Sikh Gurus added their own Punjabi songs during the sixteenth century. Somewhat later, sufis like Sultan Bahu and Bulleh Shah gave expression to their devotional moods and inner experiences in songs that still are sung by peasants as well as professional *qawāl*s.

[147]

Sultan Bahu

Born near Jhang (now in Pakistan) in the beginning of the seventeenth century, Bahu came under the influence of a sufi teacher while still a young man. Aware of his student's unusual capacity, the teacher sent him to Delhi to study under a Qadiri *murshid*. Returning to the Punjab after completing his studies, Bahu wrote dozens of works in Persian; but he is remembered today primarily for his Punjabi *abyāt* or stanzas, in which he gave expression to his mystical longings and experiences. He said more than once that to learn *alif*, the first letter of the Arabic alphabet and the first letter of the word *Allah*, was worth more than mastering whole libraries. Most of his lines end with "*bāhū*", which is at once the name his mother gave him, the Persian phrase "with Him", and (in Arabic) the prayer-formula "O He!". The themes of his poems are disillusionment with formal religion, reverence for the human master, and longing for union with the Divine. Somewhat conventional and didactic, they are remarkable for using images that could be understood by any peasant. In some, Bahu speaks with the voice of a lovelorn woman. This device, common in the songs of vaishnava bhakti, was new in sufi poetry, and later was developed in openly Krishnaite ways by Bulleh Shah. Sultan Bahu died in 1691. These selections from his *Abyāt* were translated from the Punjabi by Jamal J. Elias.

The heart is a register of unity, so study it always.
Your entire life was spent in study, passed in ignorance.
Keep only the name "Allah" as your one lesson to contemplate.

Both worlds are slaves of those, Bahu, who guard Allah in their hearts.

*

Having learned wisdom from a thousand books, they become great scholars.
They cannot learn one letter of love — the wretches wander in ignorance.
If a lover glances just once, he can swim a hundred million rivers.
If the scholar looks a hundred million times, he cannot reach the other bank.
Between learning and love is an arduous journey, with many miles of distance.
Whoever does not gain love, Bahu, is a loser in both worlds.

*

Lovers are never free from the mysteries of the Beloved.
Sleep is forbidden to those who obtain the name of the Essence.
They do not rest for a single instant, wandering in lamentation day and night.
What good fortune is theirs, Bahu, who have learned the *alif* correctly!

*

I knew God well when love flashed before me.
It gives me strength by night and day, and shows what lies ahead.
In me are flames, in me is fuel, in me is smoke.
I only found my Beloved, Bahu, when love made me aware.

*

There is no room for rationality where there is the glorious mystery of divine unity.
Here there are neither mullahs, pandits, and astrologers, nor the outward meaning of the Qur'an.
When Ahmad appears as the One, all else is destroyed.
Perfect knowledge is obtained, Bahu, by those who close the revealed scriptures.

*

When You made a show of unity, I was lost to myself.
Neither intimacy nor union, stage nor goal, body nor soul remain.
Nor is there love of any kind, nor place, nor being.
In that instant, Bahu, I was faced with the secret of divine unity.

[148]

Bulleh Shah

Like Sultan Bahu, Bulleh Shah (1680–1758) was initiated into the mysteries of sufism by a Qadiri master. This man, Inayat Shah, was a grocer, and Bulleh Shah, as a *sayyid* or descendent of the Prophet, had to endure much humiliation for surrendering to him. Many of his songs express the various moods of his love for his master. As in the songs of the sants and Sikh Gurus, the love of a human teacher becomes an analogue for the love of God. In contrast to this, *mullah*s (Qur'anic experts) and *qāzi*s (legal scholars) were to him "thugs" who robbed him of his spiritual treasures. Bulleh Shah drew many of his images from the Punjab countryside, alluding often to popular folklore, like the story of the lovers Hir and Ranjha, and borrowing images and ideas from his Hindu neighbours. There is a strong monistic current in his songs that may reflect an indirect influence from Vedanta; but when he spoke of loss of "I-ness", he based himself not on Muslim or Hindu scriptures but his own understanding and feelings. These songs were translated from the Punjabi by J. R. Puri and T. R. Shangari.

Come, Friend, I crave Your help,
My life is wrapped in troubles!

In sleep, I got separated from You,
Waking, I have lost trace of You.
Isolated, I have been robbed, my Lord!
Thieves and dacoits have encircled me.

Mullahs and *qazis* mislead me
To the labyrinth of religious rituals.
They are thugs, they are the hunters of sparrows;
They cast their nets on all the sides.
They teach me the so-called ways of piety,
Which serve as fetters around my feet.

Love does not care for caste or creed;
Love is the foe of orthodox canon.
The land of the Beloved is across the river;
And the waves of avarice have engulfed me.
The Master is holding the boat; why do you tarry?
Why do you tarry, why this delay?

O Bullah, you will realize the Lord, for sure;
Boldly announce this to your heart.
The Beloved is right within you!
Whom do you search from outside?
Why get deluded in broad daylight?

Come, Friend, I crave Your help,
My life is wrapped in troubles.

*

O friends, I am lost to myself;
Lifting my veil I dance in the open.

Wherever I look, Him alone I see;
By Him I swear, none else exists.
"He is with you" went round the world,
When the Master read from the scroll.
O friends, I am lost to myself;
Lifting my veil I dance in the open.

O friends, no trace of I-ness is left!
The secret I tell you, do not disclose.
Give not a hint of it to anyone,
That Bullah has well realized the Truth.

O friends, I am lost to myself;
Lifting my veil I dance in the open.

*

Repeating the name of the Beloved,
I have become the Beloved myself;
Whom shall I call the Beloved now?

Separation and union — I give up both,
Whom should I belong to now?
Like Majnun, the mad one in love,
Become Laila yourself.

O Bullah, the Beloved has come to my house,
Why should I now suffer the taunts of others?

Repeating the name of the Beloved,
I have become the Beloved myself;
Whom shall I call the Beloved now?

POPULAR SUFISM IN SIND

The first region of South Asia to come under Muslim rule, Sind has been a centre for the practice of sufism for more than a millennium. An unusual composite culture developed in this desert land, in which sufis learned from yogis, and Hindus took sufi masters. This cultural blending is symbolised by the Sindhi language itself. Though written in a modified Arabic script, it has a more Sanskritic vocabulary than most north Indian languages. Two sufi saints were among the founders of Sindhi literature: Shah Abdul Latif of Bhit and Sachal Sarmast.

[149]

Shah Abdul Latif

Born in a family of sufis near Hyderabad (Sind), Shah Abdul Latif (1689–1752) learned Arabic and Persian as a youth, but abandoned this conventional education for the life of a wandering holy man. Travelling in the company of yogis (of whom he spoke with great respect), he visited Muslim and Hindu shrines in Sind, Baluchistan, Gujarat and other places. Everywhere he sought the One Beloved. Settling down near his birthplace in the village of Bhit, he passed his life in prayer and meditation. Around him gathered a circle of disciples, attracted more by his personal sanctity than by his status as a *sayyid* and son of a sufi. His songs, which are considered the crown of Sindhi literature, tell the struggles and joys of the God-seeker and God-lover in terms familiar to the peasants of his homeland. These extracts were translated from the Sindhi by Annemarie Schimmel.

The knees of the Sanyasis are Mount Sinais,
In prostration they put on blisters.
"And it was two bows' length or less" [Qur'ān 53: 9], thus the naked bow down,
"Whatever is on it, is vanishing" [Qur'ān 55: 26] — there remains none.
"God is the friend of those who believe and leads them from the darkness to the light" [Qur'ān 2: 258] — they walk in this style.
"Moses fell down swooning" [Qur'ān 7: 139] — the groups of Yogis burn.
"The eye did not rove nor did it turn away" [Qur'ān 53: 17] — such walking they go.
Without regarding, without hearing, without meeting they sit,
Without going, without talking do they go thus —
Sayyid says: How can you get information about them?

*

From unity came multiplicity, multiplicity is all union;
Reality is one: do not be mistaken!

He is "Mighty is His Greatness" (*jalāl*), He is all Beauty (*jamāl*),
He is the image of the beloved, He is perfection of loveliness (*kamāl*)

He Himself becomes master and disciple, He is all imagination,
And through Him the state of all things becomes known.

He is this, and He is that, He is God, and He is death,
He the Beloved, He the breath, He the enemy, and He the helper.

*

God, as Thy name is, so I have great hope.
Creator, there is no limit nor end to Thy patience,
Thy name, o Lord — I have put it into the soul.

Great is Thy strength, with graces art Thou filled,
Do not lift Thy kindness from me — I am Thine.

As sweet as Thy name, as great is my hope,
No door is like to Thee, I have seen many other doors

Do not make loose, o Lover, the relation with this poor one;
The miserable one has no salvation but Thee.
Only Thy name, I grasp it constantly

Cover, o Coverer! I am naked!
Cover, o Coverer! Give me the hem of Thy protection!

*

My Prince will give me protection,
therefore my trust is in God.
The beloved will prostrate, will lament and cry,
therefore my trust is in God.
Muhammad, the pure and innocent, will intercede there for his people,
therefore my trust is in God.
When the trumpet sounds, the eyes all will be opened —
therefore my trust is in God,
The pious will gather, and Muhammad, full of glory —
therefore my trust is in God,
Will proceed for every soul to the door of the Benefactor —
therefore my trust is in God,
And the Lord will honor him and forgive us all our sins —
therefore my trust is in God.

[150]

Sachal Sarmast

There is a story that in his old age Shah Abdul Latif met a youth named Abdul Wahab, whom he prophesised would complete his mission. The story was probably invented to explain the event; for Abdul Wahab, later known as Sachal Sarmast, did become Latif's spiritual and poetic successor. Born in a village in upper Sind, Sachal (1739 – 1826) never left the region. Learned in Persian and Arabic, he wrote poetry in those languages as well as five regional tongues and dialects. Of all this poetical output, it is mainly his mystical songs in Sindhi that are remembered. They are signed Sachal or Sachu, "man of truth" — possibly an allusion to Mansur al-Hallaj, the Iranian sufi who was executed for declaring "I am the Creative Truth". Trained in Islamic theology, Sachal became aggressively anti-clerical, but he managed to avoid Hallaj's fate. His songs are filled with mystical ecstasy, from which comes his second epithet: Sarmast, "the intoxicated one".

These three extracts were translated by Annemarie Schimmel, N. B. Butani and Kalyan B. Advani.

I do not know, o sisters, what I really am.
Perhaps I am a puppet, perhaps the thread on which it hangs,
perhaps a ball in the hand of the Beloved,
perhaps a yoke with heavy burden,
perhaps the castle where the king sits and thinks and talks about many things to get new information.
Perhaps I am a horse which some rider guides,
perhaps a wave of the ocean which drowns the outward being,
perhaps a henna-flower with red coloring,
perhaps a rose, the head full of scent.
Perhaps I am a fountain, filled by a cloud, in which the sun is reflected and the moon as well.
Perhaps I am the mirror of God since pre-eternity which is beyond all words—
perhaps I am not at all!

*

Open your eyes; behold the show; all is a picture of the Lord.
Here, there, and everywhere, is that Heart-ravisher, all around.
In some places He is a nightingale; in some, a flower; in some, a garden and springtime verdure. . . .
In some, He wears the coarse cloth of a dervish; in some He wears silk.
In some, He speaks all tongues; in some, He is dumb.
In some, He is a Sunni; in some, a Shia; in some, He has the true insight.
In some, He is a lover; in some, a beloved; in some, He is all blandishments and coquetry.
In some, He shows Himself in one way; in others, in some other; my beloved is a great deceiver.
He is like cloth of one name, with innumerable patterns on it.

*

In that state, there is neither affliction nor comfort;
Neither this nor that, neither attributes nor arts;
Neither prayer nor devotion, neither revelations nor miracles;
Neither pain nor feeling, neither sorrow nor joy;

Neither vision nor view, neither pleasure nor enjoyment;
Neither body nor soul, neither life nor languor;
Neither happiness nor misery, neither feeling nor agony;
Neither mystery nor modesty, all is wonderment:
Sachu! It is pure Truth, it is all Tranquillity.

MYSTICAL EXPRESSION IN URDU

Though Urdu originally took form as a military lingua franca, by the end of the sixteenth century it was being employed for serious poetry. During the late Mughal period, mystics like Shah Wali Allah (see Chapter 11) began writing some of their works in this hybrid tongue. Wali Allah's younger contemporary Khwaja Mir Dard was the first to use Urdu for mystical poetry. A mystical strand also is found in the work of the greatest Urdu poet, Mirza Ghalib (1797–1869). Sufis of the post-Mughal period, such as Ghauth Ali Shah, used popular Urdu for everyday speech as well as for their spiritual teachings.

[151]

Khwaja Mir Dard

Like his contemporary Shah Wali Allah (see Chapter 11), Khwaja Mir Dard (1721–1785) attempted to bridge the gulf between Ibn al-Arabi's "unity of being" and the more orthodox notion of subjective "unity of experience". Dard himself went through a period of mystical "intoxication", but he spoke of this later as a childlike phase that had to be passed through before one reached the calm of sobriety. His *murshid* was his father, a military officer who retired to devote himself to poetry and contemplation. Under his tutelage, Dard became a master of Arabic and Persian: in the first he wrote his spiritual autobiography, in the second, numerous works of poetry and prose; but he is remembered today chiefly for his Urdu *Dīvān*, which contains his gem-like couplets and *ghazal*s. Many of these have a mystical flavour. Though he lived through frequent pillages of Delhi and saw the dismemberment of the Mughal Empire, he rarely mentioned these events in his poetry. Instead he took the classic images of Arabic and Persian verse — "nightingale" for soul, "rose" for the beauty of God — and made them speak of his own joys and pains. "Pain" is, in fact, the meaning of his literary epithet, "Dard". These couplets from his Urdu *Dīvān* were translated by Annemarie Schimmel.

Whether madrasa or monastery, whether Ka'ba or idol-temple:
They were all guest-houses, but you are the owner of the house.

*

My turpitude is the place of manifestation for the lights of purity;
As much as I am iron, I can become a mirror.

*

We have no desire to be angels and reach heaven —
This is the heart's wish: to reach Thy feet!

*

If we not see Thee in Thy manifestation,
It is alike whether we see the world or not.

*

In the garden of the World we are rose, and we are thorn,
Where there is a friend, it's us, where a rival: it is us.

*

We ourselves were the veil before our friend's face —
We opened our eyes, and no veil was left.

*

In the state of collectedness the single beings of the world are one:
All the-petals of the rose together are one.

[152]

Ghauth Ali Shah

In sufi parlance, a *qalandar* is a homeless wandering sage; used as a title, the term designates a high-ranking spiritual master. Ghauth Ali Shah Qalandar (1804–1880) lived during a period of general decline in Indian life, during which the country became an impoverished British possession. He was initiated into several sufi orders and learned from Hindu philosophers and yogis; but he kept himself free from all forms of organised religion. Settling down in Panipet, near Delhi, he gave his teachings to a circle of students who gathered round him. Some of his discourses and parables were recorded by one of them, Gul Hasan, in a book called the *Tadhkira Ghauthya* or Tree of

Gnosis. This recalls, in its immediacy, such Indo-Persian *malfuzāt* as the *Fawā'id al-Fu'ād* (see Chapter 11). Long forgotten, the *Tadhkira Ghautya* was recently translated from the Urdu by Hasan Askari, from whose rendering these selections are drawn.

Once Ghauth Ali Shah was asked about unveiling. Thereupon he said that unveiling is of two kinds—one of the cosmos and another of the self. In the first unveiling the cosmos reveals its secrets gradually in accord with the seeker's levels of development. The unveiling of the self is in reality a reference to the Divine Essence. As soon as one concentrates on the Divine Essence, there is a flood of lights and darknesses. This is the realm of attributes. The traveller should move ahead and concentrate on pure simplicity, on oneness without any attribution. One now goes through emptiness and fullness of being. A state of bewilderment descends. Only a few stand firm and reach their ultimate goal. Others, those who are sincere, remain perpetually restless as they are unable to rise above their sense of wonder. Let one who aspires to such heights seek a person of God and surrender to his guidance and gnosis so that one day the image is absorbed in the original. If one stays in the certitude of knowledge, one is far away from one's goal. If one goes to the certitude of vision, then one is near. But the one who reaches the certitude of essence has already arrived. . . .

When someone raised the question of the variety of paths and techniques linked with several doctrines, Ghauth Ali Shah set them all aside by a gesture of his hand. Of course, he said, there are some who believe that God alone is all-powerful and humanity has no free will. Some say that both God and humanity have free will but humanity is subservient to God. There are those who regard goodness as originating from God whereas they attribute evil, if any, to themselves. Likewise regarding attainment, they have various doctrines.

On the subject of Divine Unity, some discourse about the unity of All-Being; others aspire to its vision; some strive for union; and there are those who are incarnationists. Some are satisfied with the image of unity in their souls, and others go for Essence. Some say, "That is" and do not say more. "All is from that" or "All is that"; such is the variety of insights.

So let them all strive, he said, in their own ways towards that mystery—the traditionalists with their obedience to the law and ritual, and mystics with their meditations and aspirations, and the madmen with their eyes filled with wonder. *We are of God, and unto God we all return* [*Qur'ān* 2.156].

When asked about those who are on the right path and those who go astray, he cited the Qur'anic utterance that all things that move are held by God and God is on the straight path [*Qur'ān* 11.56]. Asked about how the truth of the Divine Reality is manifested in creation, he cited Junaid when he said, "Look around! It is the truth."

Once Ghauth Ali Shah said that there are two kinds of people who practise poverty: those who strive, and those who are resigned to the divine decree. Then he smiled and said that even those who make an effort are pulled by divine attraction. However, he added, both of them should know that they already possess within themselves what they strive for, or rest upon. When asked how far the perfect ones go, he replied that they all go up to the divine threshold, the stage of the ultimate attainment of their selfhood, and beyond that nobody knows.

FURTHER READING

Source Materials

Kalyan B. Advani, *Sachal Sarmast*. New Delhi: Sahitya Akademi, 1997.

Hasan Askari, ed. and trans., *Solomon's Ring: The Life and Teachings of a Sufi Master*. Walnut Creek, CA: AltaMira Press, 1998.

N. B. Butani, "Sufism–II". In *The Cultural Heritage of India*, volume IV. Calcutta: The Ramakrishna Mission Institute of Culture, 1993, pp. 597–610.

Jamal J. Elias, ed. and trans., *Death before Dying: The Sufi Poems of Sultan Bahu*. Berkeley: University of California Press, 1998.

J. R. Puri and T. R. Shangari, *Bulleh Shah: The Love Intoxicated Iconoclast*. Dera Baba Jaimal Singh, Punjab: Radha Soami Satsang Beas, 1995.

Annemarie Schimmel, *Sindhi Literature*. Wiesbaden: Otto Harrassowitz, 1974.

Annemarie Schimmel, *Mystical Dimensions of Islam*. Chapel Hill: University of North Carolina Press, 1975.

Annemarie Schimmel, *Pain and Grace: A Study of Two Mystical Writers of Eighteenth-Century Muslim India*. Leiden: E. J. Brill, 1976.

Other Works

Mustansir Mir, "Teachings of Two Punjabi Sufi Saints". In Donald S. Lopez, Jr., ed., *Religions of India in Practice*. Princeton, NJ: Princeton University Press, 1995.

Annemarie Schimmel, "Khwaja Mir Dard: Poet and Mystic". In *German Scholars on India*, vol. 1. Varanasi: The Chowkhamba Sanskrit Series Office, 1973, pp. 279–93.

H. T. Sorley, *Shāh Abdul Latīf of Bhit*. Reprint edition. New Delhi: Ashish Publishing House, 1984.

Sources of Texts and Translations

147	*Abyāt-i Bāhū*	Elias 121, 48, 87, 32, 85, 36
148	*Kalam-i-Bulleh Shah*, p. 15; *Qanum-i-Ishq*, p. 348; *Faqir Mohd. Kulliyat*, p. 66	Puri and Shangari 187–88, 245, 274
149	*Risalo*	Schimmel (1976) 224, 193, 240, 258
150	*Risalo*	Schimmel (1974) 22; Butani 598; Advani 19
151	*Urdu Dīvān*	Schimmel (1976) 139; Schimmel (1975) 382; Schimmel (1976) 145, 77, 143; Schimmel (1975) 382
152	*Tadhkira Ghauthya*, chapter 6 (selections)	Askari 169–72 passim

Part Five

Continuity and Innovation

17

All reality, all experience must indeed, to be held as true, be capable of verification by a same or similar experience; so, in fact, all men can have a spiritual experience and can follow it out and verify it in themselves, but only when they have acquired the capacity or can follow the inner methods by which that experience and verification are made possible.

Sri Aurobindo, *The Life Divine*

Twelve Mystics of Modern India

MODERNITY in India is generally supposed to have begun with the arrival of European traders in the seventeenth century. This privileging of European "advancement" and "enlightenment" ignores the fact that the Mughal Empire in its prime was in many ways more advanced than Europe, and that the Portuguese Inquisition and English Civil War can hardly be held up as models of enlightenment. It is true, however, that the introduction of European ideas, generally in the wake of European conquests, marked an era in the intellectual and even the spiritual history of India.

During the seventeenth and eighteenth centuries, there was comparatively little contact between the thoughts and beliefs of the intruders from the West and those of the people whom they met. Islam was familiar to them already through a millennium of conflict and competition; Buddhism, so far as it survived in the subcontinent, appeared to be in a state of terminal decline. Hinduism was vigorous but at the same time incomprehensible; Europeans looked on this religion (for they viewed it as a single monolithic whole) with a mixture of outrage and wonder. Against these Eastern traditions, the traders and soldiers from Portugal, England and France opposed their twin orthodoxies — Christianity and Enlightenment rationality. Both of these became powerful influences in India in the eighteenth century. Somewhat ironically, in the field of spirituality it was

European secular thought rather then European religion that left the more lasting mark.

The story of the discovery of Oriental languages and literatures by European scholars has been told many times and need not be repeated here. The realisation that Sanskrit was a sister-language of Greek and Latin gave special interest to their study of ancient Indian literature. For many years most texts read and translated by European Orientalists were religious classics such as the *Ṛg Veda*, the *upaniṣad*s, and the *Bhagavad Gītā*, along with the occasional legal text, such as the *Mānavadharmaśāstra*, or literary work, such as Kalidasa's *Śakuntalā*. The preponderance of texts that were wholly or partly religious helped create the stereotypes of "spiritual India" and "the mystic East" that have coloured European thinking ever since. These same texts, some of which had long ceased to be widely studied, provided educated Indians with a glorious past about which they could be proud even as their country fell under foreign sway. The Europeans might be supreme in the outward sphere of trade and politics, but in the inward sphere of experience, thought and devotion, traditional India remained unconquered. Had not Schopenhauer and Deussen declared their indebtedness to the *upaniṣad*s? Was not "*Ex Oriente Lux*" the slogan of the hour?

The European infatuation with the Wisdom of the East was short-lived and was counterbalanced, even while current, by an attack against almost every aspect of Indian life by colonial administrators and missionaries. As interest in Indian spirituality waned in Europe, it was taken up with vigour and sometimes with brilliance by India's new English-educated élite. Ram Mohan Roy (1777–1833) translated several *upaniṣad*s into Bengali and English and declared that they were the basis of a universal religion, of which popular Hinduism was a corruption. Other members of the Bengal Renaissance, such as Devendranath Tagore and Keshab Chandra Sen, along with scholars in Maharashtra, Tamil Nadu and other regions, identified spirituality as the primary component of Indian "traditional" culture, and promoted it in various ways. At the same time, members of the urban élite turned their back on traditional customs that they had learned (under the influence of Enlightenment philosophy) to regard as a blot on India's name. This was the start of the nineteenth-century movement of social reform, which helped bring about the abolition of the rite of *sati*, the raising of the legal age of marriage, the promotion of widow remarriage, etc.

By the middle of the nineteenth century these trends had affected most members of the English-educated élite. Some of them promoted European values as the key to the transformation of an inequitable and impoverished society. Others declared that Hindu religion, as presented in Sanskrit texts, was the eternal and unchanging law, *sanātana dharma*, which alone of the religious and social systems of the world could be considered true. Most thinkers avoided these two extremes, working out an amalgam of Enlightenment values and traditional beliefs that suited their temperaments. Virtually all Indian religious and social institutions were affected to some extent by the opposing pressures of these two trends.

Indian mystics who emerged during the nineteenth and twentieth centuries were not insulated from the characteristics of their age. If in their personal experience they were alone with the Divine, they were obliged, when they attempted to explain their insights to others, to make use of the modern idiom. Many went beyond this passive or involuntary modernity by trying actively to relate their inner experiences to the changing world around them.

The present chapter consists of works of twelve mystics of nineteenth- and twentieth-century India, who display a variety of responses to the challenges of modernity. Four of them — Sai Baba of Shirdi, Ramana Maharshi, Anandamayi Ma and Nisargadatta Maharaj — appear to have differed very little from such pre-modern predecessors as Gautama Buddha, Mahadeviyakka and Kabir. On second look, however, it becomes clear that Mahadeviyakka would not have had the freedom to travel around the country in a bullock-cart, much less an automobile, while Ramana Maharshi is unlikely to have given his message to tens of thousands if he had not been "discovered" by Indian and foreign admirers, who wrote volumes about his silence. Three other mystics — Sri Ramakrishna, Swami Ramdas and Swami Yogananda — followed traditional yogic paths but chose as their primary audience the non-traditional élite. The remaining five — Ramalinga Swami, Sri Aurobindo, Inayat Khan, Krishnamurti and Gopi Krishna — began their practice along traditional lines, but broke free from these moorings in their individual *sādhana* and in the communities or organisations that they founded or were founded around them. One sign of their freedom from tradition is linguistic. Four of the last group, along with two from the second group, used English as their primary language of instruction.

The twelve mystics chosen for inclusion drew their inspiration from a number of sources and engaged in a variety of spiritual practices. Several were representatives of the traditions of Hindu *bhakti*, cultivating intense personal relations with a form of Vishnu or Shiva; others became absorbed in the experience of the formless *brahman*; yet others practised tantric or *siddha* techniques. A few claimed the freedom of the wandering ascetic; others followed the instructions of a *guru* or *murshid*; still others rejected all religious formalism. Most of these mystics in fact drew from more than one source and practised an eclectic blend of techniques. The boundaries between spiritual traditions have become blurred during the modern period. This has led some mystics to speak of a "universal religion", at the base of which are subjective spiritual experiences, which, in principle, are available to all humans.

RAMALINGA SWAMI

One of the most striking features of modern religious movements is the way they situate themselves in a line going back untold ages, yet give themselves the freedom to depart from tradition when modern circumstances require it. The most revolutionary departures are justified by appeal to ancient scriptures. Mystics who start movements often claim this sort of continuity with the past and do not hesitate to quote from scripture to justify their innovations; but they also claim another source of authority. Their own inner experience gives them the freedom to innovate.

Ramalinga Swami began his career as a traditional shaivite bhakta with leanings towards the Tamil siddha tradition; he ended it as a revolutionary reformer, reviled by the orthodox who considered themselves the custodians of the tradition he was rooted in. Born in a village near Chidambaram, Tamil Nadu, in 1823, he was deeply influenced by the *bhaktas* of that region, such as Sambandar and Manikkavachakar (see Chapter 13), and also by Tirumular and the other Tamil siddhas (see Chapter 12). His father, Ramayya Pillai, died shortly after his birth, and the family went to live near Chennai. Ramalinga showed little interest in his studies, but still managed to become a master of Tamil literature. His early poetry reveals a highly sensitive soul, repelled by the coarseness of the ordinary life and filled with an overwhelming love for Shiva. The young man passed much of his time worshipping at a nearby temple and studying the *Tēvāram*, *Periya Purāṇam* and other shaiva classics. His family arranged for him to be married, but (according to a famous story) he spent his wedding-night reading the *Tiruvācakam* to his bride, who soon disappeared from his life.

When he was around thirty-five, Ramalinga Swami (as he was now called) left the increasingly urbanised suburbs of Chennai, and settled in Karunkuzhi, a village near his birthplace. Here he lived a simple life, wearing a plain white *lungi* and body-cloth, and eating almost nothing. By now he had attracted a number of disciples, to whom he taught a plain creed of devotion, moral living and compassion for all living creatures. In 1865 he established the Samarasa Sanmarga Satya Sangam or Society for Truth and Righteous Living, which was open to members of all religions. Its credo proclaims that there is only one God, who should be worshipped as Light by means of love. Living creatures should not be offered as sacrifices to the gods, nor should their flesh be eaten. The dead should not be cremated but buried. Differences of creed, sect and caste should be ignored; all humans should be treated alike in a spirit of universal brotherhood.

According to Ramalinga Swami, the key to righteous living is compassion, and an essential mark of compassion is feeding the hungry. Two years after the foundation of the Sangam, he established a Satya Dharma Salai or House of Charity. Here the poor of the area were (and are) given free meals. Around 1870, the Swami withdrew from Karunkuzhi to the hamlet of Mettukkupam, near Vadalur. Here, in 1872, he founded the last and most remarkable of his institutions: the Satya Gnana Sabhai. This "Shrine of Divine Knowledge" consists of a hall of meditation, at the centre of which is a simple oil lantern which stands for God as Light. In front of the lantern are seven curtains, which represent the veils of illusion that have to be pierced before the seeker can perceive the divine light. Every year, at a special ceremony, the veils are removed to permit devotees to have *darśan* of the Lord as Light.

In his early poetry, Ramalinga approached God in the manner of a traditional shaivite bhakta. He gave special attention to Shiva as Lord of Dance (*naṭarāja*), the form in which he is worshipped at Chidambaram. His songs of this period are very much in the style of the *nayaṉār*s and Manikkavachakar. But later he came to feel that Shaivism, like other forms of religion, was an obstacle rather than helper on the way. "You know what faith I once had in the Shaiva religion," he told his followers. "See how that faith is completely gone now." He asked them not to rely on books, "which are intent upon hiding the truth", and to avoid seeking *siddhi*s or miraculous powers, which were a distraction on the road to God. They should avoid all creeds, because "through them you will never experience the Living Truth or Nature of Reality". He himself was a witness to this Truth, because God in his Grace had given him the experience of the divine nature (Thangappa 1990: 17–18).

Such teachings brought Ramalinga into conflict with the priestly establishment. His enemies circulated pamphlets against him and even took him to court on a trumped-up charge. His disciples began to make extravagant claims about his powers and, against his wishes, to worship him as a deity. Eventually he closed the Gnana Sabhai and devoted himself exclusively to his own *sādhana*. In his last sermon, delivered in January 1894, he said: "Friends, I opened a shop but there was none to purchase; so I have closed it. I will not be visible to your eyes for a certain period, although I will be universally present in the world. . . . Worship God in the form of light and attain salvation" (Francis 1990: 17). He then entered his room and told his disciples to lock the door from outside. When the door was opened a few days later, it was found that his body had disappeared. His disciples believed that he had performed the *siddhi* of dematerialisation.

Ramalinga Swami's principal work is *Tiruvarutpa* or "Songs of Grace", a collection of nearly 7000 poems written in clear and mellifluous Tamil. The text is divided into six books, only five of which were published during his lifetime. The early poems are confessional and devotional; the later ones deeply mystical. A number give accounts of his personal practice and experiences; others tell of his hopes for the Universal True Path of Gnosis. These extracts were translated from the Tamil by G. Vanmikanathan.

[153]

The Awakening

In these extracts from different books of the *Tiruvarutpa*, Ramalinga Swami writes about his early life, his first turning to the path, and his developing love for Shiva (Tamil: Civa).

Fearing that if I looked on
the extrovert life of this world
my mind would be disturbed,
I spent every day, all the day-light hours,
seeking [solitude in] the gardens
on the outskirts of the city
and wandering in other places.
Not only in the daytime but at night as well
I wandered in many many places.
What need for this slave to say all this?
This is nothing but what is known to You.

*

Oh mind of mine!
What profit did you find
in getting infatuated by the eyes
of women with brows shaped like bent bows,
and suffering at the hands
of those perfidious ones
and yet daily yearning for them?
Go with me to beauteous Otriyoor
and meditate chanting
"Om Civa Shanmuka Civa Om, Om Ci-vaa-ya,
Who are sweeter than honey-filled sugar-cane
and Who, saturating the minds of your devotees,
are arisen thereon."

*

Oh Sky which pours ever-increasing great [flood of] grace!
Oh Gnosis which occurs
in the state of union with You!
Oh Civan risen in the middle of my heart
with Your hundred-petalled twin feet

well established in my hundred-petalled heart!
Oh Spouse Who enslaved me
at a tender age of ignorance,
bestowing on me a special privilege!
Oh transcendent Being
capable of raising to the status of gods
those devotees
who do not tread the path of attachments!
Oh Joy rare to be gained by those
who argue saying: "this boon can be gained there,
nay, this boon can be gained here"!
Oh Fullness Who fills everywhere
as embodiment of bliss,
and as ether transcending even that!
Oh Succourer Who held in Your arms
this youngster who was asleep,
and, bidding me wake up,
got rid of my sleep!
Oh great Being established
in the ethereal turiya space,
Oh Guru Who is Nataraja
of effulgent grace!

*

Ha! this is a marvel! this is a marvel!
What shall I say about it!
You made me rejoice,
making this mean fellow
ignorant of gnosis, learn gnosis
        by showing me,
          Oh Gem with the matted locks
          on which the moon shines,
          Your feet and crown as well,
        showing me this
          and showing me that,
        revealing to me my state as well,
        showing me the special guile
          of the self-complacent miracle-mongers,
        showing me the state of deathlessness,
        showing me Your natural state,

and the place where the mind,
which resembles the rushing wind,
melts away.
Who has got the magnanimity of Your grace!

[154]

Ascension

In the sixth book of the *Thiruvarutpa*, Ramalinga Swami recounts his experiences of mystical union with Shiva. In this passage he addresses Shiva both as Father and as Lover, speaking in the voice of a young girl who is amazed and overjoyed by the "affinity" that has developed between her and her Lord.

There was a high pillar
with no peer to it here on earth.
As I shinned up and up the pillar,
it tapered to the size of a thread.
When I faltered to go further up,
and was perturbed and grieved,
ridding me of my perturbation,
You lifted me up and placed me on high,
that I may be well established [atop that pillar]!
What kind of an affinity is this affinity
between You and me?
Is this affinity an affinity
which others in the world can gain? . . .

Oh King! Desire wells up in me to embrace You.
On account of the certainty that I will embrace You,
my life lingers on.
My hand stretches forward in a hurry
to take hold of the fragrant feet.
Whenever my hand reaches it and grasps them,
joy reigns in my mind!
What kind of an affinity . . .

If I forget You, Oh my Father,
will my soul dwell in the body?
Will my mind ever think about anyone but You?

With what idea did You accept me
when I offered myself to You?
Oh my Father, will You come today
to give Yourself to me?
        What kind of an affinity . . .

Tightly have I taken hold of Your feet,
would I ever let them go any more?
Would I ever touch anything else
with the hand which has grasped those feet?
Death, afraid to approach me,
has run away in consternation!
Oh King, Your gracious effulgence of gnosis
has become mine!
        What kind of an affinity . . .

Oh just Effulgence Who forcibly enslaved me!
Oh immaculate Effulgence Who brings me up
      to sing to You!
Oh righteous Effulgence Who came and protected me
      like a very mother!
Oh Effulgence Who bestowed on me
      omnipotent mystic powers!
        What kind of an affinity . . .

Oh Effulgence Who taught me the art of not dying!
Oh Effulgence Who placed on my head
      a crown just like the crown of Yours!
Oh Effulgence Who raised me to the golden seat
      of one-pointed contemplation!
Oh Effulgence Who bestowed on me
      rule over mystic powers!
        What kind of an affinity . . .

Obeisance to You, the Just Effulgence
      of the Pure Blissful True Creed!
Obeisance to the Effulgence in the Hall of Gnosis
      Who bestowed on me a life of joy!
Obeisance to the Effulgence
      Who dances in the Golden Hall scintillating with purity!

Obeisance to the Effulgence
    Who shines that all other effulgences may shine!
        What kind of an affinity . . .

[155]

From "The Garland of Experience"

These stanzas are from a section of the sixth book of the *Thiruvarutpa* known as the *Anubhava Mālai* or Garland of Experience. It contains one of Ramalinga's most powerful accounts of his love-relation with Shiva.

I have returned after beholding
the colour of the sacred body of my Spouse
Who performs an illuminating dance [of gnosis]
in the middle of the eternal sacred assembly [of devotees]!
Oh my dear, what can I say,
Oh my companion,
about the nature of the colour
of that holy body!
Shall I say
that it is the colour which will shine
if countless crores of moons,
suns, fires, lightning
were to join together?
Even if I say so, it will not be adequate!
That colour, even the Upanishads cannot describe!
Who else, indeed, can describe the colour
of that Great Effulgence of Grace? . . .

*

After reaching my house,
when He embraced me on the flower-strewn bed,
I never consciously felt separate
and thought of that as my Spouse's body
and of this as my body!
If I was not conscious of myself even the least,
how was I going to be conscious of other things?
Not even a whit of differentiated feeling is in me;
how am I, therefore, going to tell you

how the Lord of mukti united with me!
If He embraces you,
I will ask you a similar question;
then your knowledge and my knowledge
will be the same knowledge! . . .

*

You ask:
"Oh damsel with a waist like an hour-glass,
tell me, what is the reason
for this pride that has come over you!"
Vishnu, Brahma, the heavenly ones, sages and others,
having gained the privilege
of standing at the foot of the golden steps
leading to the Presence of my Husband
with sacred-ash-dust-laden form,
are filled with pride like the king of lightning.
I [on the other hand], to the amazement of all,
have ascended the steps to His Presence
and am drinking the ambrosia
seeping from the holy feet of the Chief!
What is the need to say the reason for my pride? . . .

*

When I went in,
while all those who had clung to falsehood
were staying outside,
and, witnessing the dance on the Hall,
was rejoicing in my mind,
my Bridegroom said:
"Oh you who have apprehended Reality,
blessed be you!
Do shine in the world
that the Universal True Creed may shine therein",
and took hold of my hand;
and I, in turn, took hold of His feet!
Saying: "Rejoice,
We will nevermore desert you,
We are garlanding you [in token of marriage]
with all the men of darkness-filled eyes

of all the world as witness",
He garlanded me!

While all the unfit people were standing outside,
but I went in and was standing there
watching with rejoicing the dance in the Hall,
the unique Chief came deliberately near me
and took hold of my hand,
and I, in turn, took hold of His blossomy feet,
Saying: "Do not grieve,
do not get confused any more,
look, undying life has come to you alone;
with all the world respecting you,
live long with your ideas blossoming",
He gave me a ring,
and clasped a golden bangle also on my wrist;
look at it, Oh my companion! . . .

*

Oh Lord, today, with You instructing me, out of love,
the true state,
I learnt exactly what You, dwelling in my mind,
had instructed me in the very beginning,
that all the theological rubbish
which has marked out many streets in castes and creeds
is worthless,
and I arrived at the Universal Pure Creed
which those who have realised it by study praise!
I got the opportunity to behold the Assembly of Gnosis,
and I received within me
the King of the dance of effulgence
Who is the Reality,
my Spouse, the Life of my life,
the Fullness of true bliss,
and I rejoice thereat! . . .

*

I have experienced the state of transcendental wakefulness
which is still a subject of research to others,
I have experienced the state of transcendental dreaming,

I have experienced the state
of transcendental deep sleep,
I am experiencing the great Fourth state,
I have joined the Universal True Path,
and, gaining the embrace of my Husband
Who is dancing the dance of grace on the Hall,
I have become His form;
I live, delighting in it,
a life that has no match to it,
Oh my companion!

In a unique pure wakeful state of bliss
I remained alone,
I attained the pure dream state of bliss,
I delighted in the state of bliss
of the fruitful true pure state of deep sleep,
I blended with the pure Fourth state of bliss,
and in the pure blissful state
transcending the Fourth state of bliss,
I became IT,
I became the birthless ONE,
I became everything and nothing,
and gained FRUITION
as the very embodiment of Civam.
As a result of gaining
the sweet-tasting Lord of the Hall of Gnosis,
I gained all these
and am with you here,
Oh my companion!

At the moment
when I stood embracing the golden body
of the Chief of the Effulgence of Grace,
the Husband full of love to me,
gone were all tattvas of the breed of dark ignorance!
everywhere, everything was transformed
into a great light.
There, at the moment when He,
ridding me of the taint of delusion,
had union with me,

I gained FRUITION,
becoming transformed into the form
of eternal bliss that is CIVAM.
I entered along with my Husband
the sacred Assembly of Universal True Creed
which flourishes on the strength of gnosis.

That moment when my Husband
had external union with me
is the moment when I partook of the fresh ambrosia
and exulted.
About the joy of the moment
when, transforming me into remarkable EXPERIENCE,
He had internal union with me,
how can I relate it?
This is not a matter like other unions.
[A flood of] great enjoyment, great bliss
swelled up and filled everywhere.
It is the state where,
without any feeling of obstruction,
I become IT,
IT becomes me,
We became embodiment of gnosis,
and IT BECAME IT!

[156]

The Universal True Creed

In these stanzas from the sixth book of the *Tiruvarutpa*, Ramalinga sang of his Universal True Creed which he hoped would replace "superstitious" forms of worship.

I am telling you what I have experienced
out of a sense of oneness with you;
I am a kinsmen to you indeed,
do not take me for an enemy.
Oh men of the world!
You see the learned and the unlearned perish!
Is death,
which comes confusing all your faculties of understanding,

acceptable to you?
My mind will not agree to this even the least;
I do not know whether your mind
is a stony mind or a callous mind.
Today this can be thwarted;
come and join me;
my Creed is the death-dispelling True Creed indeed! . . .

*

It is my desire, Oh my Father
to have union with You
in this world rife with living creatures,
to remain inseparably united with You
through aeons and aeons,
to sing about You only and dance and dance about
on this vast earth and rejoice very much,
to eradicate the troubles
when others are beset by them,
and to make them possessed of love
for Your sacred Hall of Gems!

It is my desire, Oh my Father,
to consider the lives
of all the throng of creatures
as my very own life
and to bring joy to them,
to eradicate the troubles
which beset those creatures
and to dispel their fears,
and, becoming immaculate in heart,
to sing of Your sacred feet,
to dance chanting "Civa-Civa",
and, with surging joy,
to remain imperishably eminent
here on earth.

It is my desire, Oh my Father, that all
who had intimately associated with me,
beginning from the time I gained adolescence
and ending with the day

I gained gnosis of You,
who had thoughts for me only,
and who had sought my company only
but have later parted from me,
should now gather here sincerely
and live paying obeisance to You
with boundless great love!

It is my desire, Oh my Father
to renovate, according to the rules laid down
in the vast Vedas and the Agamas
the great temple called Chitambaram where shines
the divinity-invested sacred Hall of Gnosis
and to make it shine brighter
than a fragrant flower,
to behold the hue of Your body
and delight therein,
and to witness the spectacle of the festivals
in this world teeming with life!

It is my desire, Oh my Father,
that I should found the society
of Universal Pure True Path of Gnosis
consisting of men who are verily like gold,
and rejoice thereat,
that I should raise a sacred temple
pertaining to that society
that the purity-invested society
should flourish eternally,
and that this slave of yours,
should sing about you and dance
in that society to the delight of my limbs.

FURTHER READING

Source Materials

G. Vanmikanathan, *Pathway to God Trod by Raamalinga Swaamikal.* Bombay: Bharatiya Vidya Bhavan, 1976.

Other Sources

T. Dayanandan Francis, *The Mission and Message of Ramalinga Swamy*. Delhi: Motilal Banarsidass, 1990.

M. L. Thangappa, *Songs of Grace*. Pondicherry: All India Books, 1985.

Vallalar's Home Page <http://www.vallalar.org>

Sources of Texts and Translations

153	*Tiruvarutpa* 3457; 794; 3684; 3038	Vanmikanathan 34, 61, 492, 359
154	*Tiruvarutpa* 4964, 4970, 4975, 5020, 5060–61, 5063	Vanmikanathan 651–54
155	*Tiruvarutpa, Anubhava Mālai* 11, 16, 53, 56–57; 92, 95–98	Vanmikanathan 692–733 passim
156	*Tiruvarutpa* 5601, 3402–06	Vanmikanathan 678, 406–08

RAMAKRISHNA PARAMAHANSA

The middle of the nineteenth century is remembered as a time of revolutionary change in Bengal, during which that province opened up to new ideas from the West and rediscovered (with Western help) its own past. Ramakrishna Paramahansa was virtually untouched by these changes. His spiritual roots were in the shakta and vaishnava traditions of Bengal, and he had little knowledge of the social, economic and intellectual forces that were transforming Bengal and India. His spiritual teachings, based largely on his own knowledge and experience, might well have been addressed to the contemporaries of Ramprasad Sen (whose songs he loved); but they were heard by a generation that had been educated in Kolkata colleges, to whom his voice became the call of resurgent India. He is sometimes acclaimed as the originator of the nineteenth-century "Hindu revival", but it would be better to regard him as one who saw all religions as possible means of enlightenment. His great maxim was *jato mat tato path*: each way of thinking has its own means of realisation.

Ramakrishna was born in 1836 in a village in the Hooghly district, about a hundred kilometres north of Kolkata. His father, Khudiram Chatterjee, was a poor but pious brahmin, who died when Ramakrishna, then known as Gadadhar, was only seven. In order to provide for the family, Gadadhar's eldest brother Ramkumar went to Kolkata, where he opened a school. Later he became the priest at a temple complex in Dakshineshwar, a little north of Kolkata. When Ramkumar died in 1856, Ramakrishna succeeded him as priest of Dakshineshwar's Kali temple.

Ramakrishna made an unusual priest. He knew no Sanskrit; indeed, he could not read Bengali. But he had an extraordinary ability to channel his emotional energy in the service of his *sādhana* or spiritual practice. At Dakshineshwar he performed the temple rituals with utmost sincerity, not as obligatory observances but as means of achieving union with the Divine. One day, brought to the point of suicide by his longing, he had the experience of Kali as the universal Mother. For weeks he remained in a God-intoxicated state, which made it impossible for him to lead a normal life. At the suggestion of those around him, he underwent treatment by a local doctor, and later went to his village for a year and a half. At this time he was married to a young girl, who remained with her family. Returning to Dakshineshwar, Ramakrishna resumed his *sādhana*. Over the next five years he practised Tantrism under a female adept, experienced the *bhāva*s of vaishnava bhakti with a wandering *sādhu*, and achieved union with Brahman under the direction of a *jñāna-yogī*. He even briefly practiced Islam and Christianity as he conceived them. Asked why one who had achieved union with Kali had to follow other paths, he replied: "Although I had realised Her and felt Her presence always by my side, a strong desire arose in me to experience Her, who is of multifarious forms and relations, in as many of such forms and relations as She would be pleased to reveal to me" (Saradananda 1978: 280).

Around 1875 Ramakrishna began to visit Kolkata, where he met the intellectual and cultural élite of Bengal. Keshab Chandra Sen, head of the Brahmo Samaj of India, became his admirer and helped introduce him to a wider audience. Within a few years a circle of young disciples gathered round him. Among them was Narendranath Dutt, a bright student who approached the things of the spirit with a questioning mind. "Have you seen God?" he asked Ramakrishna, point-blank, at one of their meetings. "Yes, I have seen God," Ramakrishna answered. "In fact I see him more clearly than I see you. And if you so wish, I can show him to you also"(Lokeswarananda 1997: 38). Narendranath soon became Ramakrishna's leading disciple. As Swami Vivekananda, he helped spread his master's teachings to all parts of India and to America and Europe.

While at Dakshineshwar Ramakrishna was looked after by one of the temple trustees, then by his nephew, and finally by his wife and disciples. Developing cancer of the throat in 1885, he was removed to Kolkata, where he received medical treatment. This did not arrest the progress of the disease, and he died, surrounded by his disciples, the next year.

Ramakrishna wrote nothing. His teachings consist of parables, advice and recollections given orally to those who came to see him. During the last four years of his life, many of his conversations were noted down by Mahendranath Gupta, an English-educated disciple who was head of an educational institution. After Ramakrishna's death, Mahendranath, or "M", as he signed himself, worked up these notes into a book he called *Śrī Śrī Rāmakṛṣṇa Kathāmṛta*, which was first published in 1897. In 1944 an English translation was published under the title *The Gospel of Sri Ramakrishna*. The first full-scale Bengali biography of Ramakrishna was Swami Saradananda's *Śrī Śrī Rāmakṛṣṇa Līlāprasaṅga*, which was translated into English as *Sri Ramakrishna: The Great Master*. Both books include accounts by Ramakrishna himself of his experiences. Critics have claimed that these two books do not reveal all that Ramakrishna said, veiling in particular the tantric foundations of his *sādhana*. Others have noted that the translations turn his vigorous and occasionally coarse Bengali into English of near-Victorian propriety. To be sure, the existing texts do not give all that Ramakrishna said, and the renderings into English do not convey as much as the Bengali originals. Nevertheless, the accounts of M and Saradananda remain documents of considerable value, which have allowed Ramakrishna to speak to a worldwide audience in the twentieth and twenty-first centuries with something of the immediacy with which he spoke to his disciples at the end of the nineteenth.

[157]

From *Sri Ramakrishna: The Great Master*

Swami Saradananda, who wrote the principal biography of Sri Ramakrishna, the *Śrī Śrī Rāmakṛṣṇa Līlāprasaṅga*, became his disciple while he was still in his teens. He began working on the book more than twenty years after Sri Ramakrishna's death, using material that he and his brother disciples had heard and gathered. In it he reproduced, within quotation marks, a number of passages in which Ramakrishna spoke about himself. These passages include accounts of Ramakrishna's early, spontaneous spiritual experiences, as well as some he had while doing *sādhana* on his own or under the yogin Tota Puri. Six such passages are reproduced here. Translated from the Bengali by Swami Jagadananda.

"In that part of the country [Kamarpukur] children are given parched rice to eat, in small baskets. Those who have no such baskets in their houses eat it from the folds of their cloth. While loitering about in the fields, some boys eat it from the baskets and others from the folds of their cloth. I was then six or seven years old. One morning I took the parched rice in a small basket and was eating it while walking on the narrow balks in the corn fields. It was the month of Jyaishtha or Ashadh. In one part of the sky there appeared a beautiful black rain cloud. I was looking at it while eating the rice. Very soon the cloud covered almost the whole sky, when a flock of milk-white cranes flew against the background of that black cloud. It looked so beautiful that I became very soon absorbed in an extraordinary mood. Such a state came on me that my external consciousness was lost. I fell down and the rice got scattered near the balk. People saw this and carried me home. This was the first time that I lost external consciousness in ecstasy."

*

He used to say, "There was then an intolerable anguish in my heart because I could not have Her vision. Just as a man wrings a towel forcibly to squeeze out all the water from it, I felt as if somebody caught hold of my heart and mind and was wringing them likewise. Greatly afflicted with the thought that I might never have Mother's vision, I was in great agony. I thought that there was no use in living such a life. My eyes suddenly fell upon the sword that was there in the Mother's temple. I made up my mind to put an end to my life with it that very moment. Like one mad, I ran and caught hold of it, when suddenly I had the wonderful vision of the Mother, and fell down unconscious. I did not know what happened then in the external world — how that day and the next slipped away. But, in my heart of hearts, there was flowing a current of intense bliss, never experienced before, and I had the immediate knowledge of the Light that is Mother."

On another occasion the Master described to us in detail his wonderful vision mentioned above. He said, "It was as if the houses, doors, temples and all other things vanished altogether; as if there was nothing anywhere! And what I saw was a boundless infinite Conscious Sea of Light! However far and in whatever direction I looked, I found a continuous succession of Effulgent Waves coming forward, raging and storming from all sides with great speed. Very soon they fell on me and made me sink to the Abysmal Depths of Infinity. I panted and struggled, as it were, and lost all sense of external consciousness." The Master told us that at that time he saw a luminous sea of Consciousness. But what about the Divine Mother's form consisting of pure Consciousness only — the form of Hers with hands that give boons and freedom from fear? Did the Master then have the vision of that form also in that sea of Light? It appears that he had; for as soon as he had the slightest consciousness at the time of his first vision, he, we are told, uttered repeatedly the word "Mother" in a voice choked by emotion.

*

He said, "I used to show to my mind the image of the Bhairava in meditation pose on the parapet of the roof of the music hall and say to it, 'You must be firm and motionless like that and meditate on Mother's Lotus Feet.' No sooner had I sat down for meditation than I heard clattering sounds produced in the joints of my body and limbs from the direction of the legs upwards; and they got locked one after another as if some one from within turned the keys. As long as I meditated, I had no power to move my body and change my posture even slightly or give up meditation and go elsewhere or do anything else at will. I was, as it were, forcibly made to sit in the same posture, as long as the joints did not make clattering sounds as before and were unlocked, this time from the direction of the head to the legs. When I sat and meditated, I had, in the beginning, the vision of particles of light like groups of fire-flies; I saw sometimes all quarters covered with masses of mist-like light; and at other times I perceived that all things were pervaded by bright waves of light like molten silver. I saw these things sometimes with my eyes shut and sometimes with my eyes open. I did not understand what I saw nor did I know whether it was good or bad to have such visions. I therefore prayed to Mother with a troubled heart, 'I don't understand, Mother, what is happening to me; I don't know Mantras etc., by which to call Thee; please teach me personally what may enable me to realize Thee. Mother! if Thou dost not teach me, who else will? For, there is no refuge for me except Thee.' I used to pray thus with a concentrated mind and weep piteously on account of the eagerness of my heart."

*

"At the time of performing Sandhya and worship," said the Master, "I used to think, according to scriptural prescription, that the Papa-purusha within had been burnt up. Who knew then that there was actually a Papa-purusha within the body and that it could be actually burnt and destroyed? A burning sensation came on the body from the beginning of the Sadhana. I thought, 'What is this disease?' It increased by degrees and became unbearable. Various kinds of oils prescribed by physicians were used; but it could by no means be alleviated. One day, while I was sitting under the Panchavati, I saw that a jet-black person with red eyes and a hideous appearance came reeling, as if drunk, out of this [showing his own body] and walked before me. I saw again another person of placid mien in ochre-coloured dress, with a trident in his hand similarly coming out of my body. He vehemently attacked the other and killed him. The burning sensation in the body decreased for a short time after I had that vision. I suffered from that burning sensation continually for six months before the Papa-purusha was burnt up."

*

We have said before that during the first four years of his Sadhana the Master depended for God-realization mainly on his intense eagerness. No one came to him at that time to help him in his spiritual progress by guiding him along the path prescribed by the scriptures. Therefore, the only means he had recourse to was the intense longing, which is the common requisite of all Sadhanas. As the Master had the vision of the Divine Mother with the help of this longing only, it is also proved that an aspirant may have God-vision similarly, even without any external aid. But we forget very often to reflect how great must be the degree of intensity of this eagerness in order that one may reach one's end that way. This becomes clear to us if we study the Master's life at this time. We have seen how under the intensity of this longing, firmly established habits of life and modes of thought, together with the mental impressions at their back, disappeared from him altogether. He paid no attention even to the preservation of his life, let alone physical health. The Master said, "As no attention was bestowed on the cleaning of the body, the hairs on the head became long and got matted owing to dirt and dust adhering to them. At the time of meditation the body used to become motionless like the trunk of a tree. Thinking it to be an inert thing, birds came and remained sitting on the head without any hesitation and stirred up the dust in the hair in search of particles of rice! Again, impatient on account of the separation from the divine Lord, I rubbed my face against the ground so vehemently that it got cut and bruised and bled in many places. I had no consciousness of how the whole day slipped away in prayer, meditation, devotional exercises, offering of the self, and so on. When afterwards at the approach of the evening, conch-shells were blown and bells rung, I remembered that the day was at an end. Another day passed in vain; and I had not yet seen the Mother. Intense sorrow seized me and made the heart so restless that I could no longer remain calm. I threw myself violently on the ground, saying, 'Mother, Thou hast not shown Thyself to me even yet!' I filled the quarters with wailing and struggled on account of pain. People said, 'He has got colic pain and that is why he is crying so much'."

*

Tota tried to make the Master attain Samadhi on that day with the help of various arguments and conclusive quotations from the scriptures. We were informed by the Master that Tota strove his best on that occasion to put him immediately into the state of non-dual consciousness to which he himself had attained through lifelong Sadhana. "After initiating me," said the Master, "the naked one taught me many dicta conveying the conclusions of the Vedanta, and asked me to make my mind free of function in all respects and merge it in the meditation of the Self. But, it so happened that when

I sat for meditation, I could by no means make my mind go beyond the bounds of name and form and cease functioning. The mind withdrew itself easily from all other things, but, as soon as it did so, the intimately familiar form of the universal Mother consisting of the effulgence of pure consciousness, appeared before it as a living presence and made me quite oblivious of the renunciation of names and forms of all description. When I listened to the conclusive dicta and sat for meditation, this happened over and over again. Almost despairing of the attainment of the Nirvikalpa Samadhi, I then opened my eyes and said to the naked one, 'No, it cannot be done; I cannot make the mind free from functioning, and force it to dive into the Self.' Scolding me severely, the naked one said very excitedly, 'What! It can't be done! What nonsense!' He then looked about in the hut, and finding a broken piece of glass, took it in his hand and forcibly pierced my forehead with its needle-like pointed end between the eye-brows and said, 'Collect the mind here at this point.' With a firm determination I sat for meditation again, and as soon as the holy form of the Divine Mother appeared now before the mind as previously, I looked upon knowledge as a sword and cut the form mentally in two with that sword of knowledge. There remained then no function in the mind, which transcended quickly the realm of names and forms, making me merge in Samadhi."

[158]

From *The Gospel of Sri Ramakrishna*

Mahendranath Gupta first met Sri Ramakrishna in 1882, after Ramakrishna had become fairly well known among the Kolkata middle class. Mahendranath (or "M") soon became a frequent visitor at Ramakrishna's room in Dakshineshwar, and he noted down the master's remarks in a personal shorthand. Afterwards he expanded these notes into the *Śrī Śrī Rāmakṛṣṇa Kathāmṛta*, five editions of which appeared between 1897 and 1932. In each edition, the reports were published not chronologically but in an order decided on by M. In the English edition, the reports were rearranged in chronological order, in the form of a diary or memoir. Each of the extracts reproduced below comprises or includes a quotation from a talk by Sri Ramakrishna, in which he refers to past or present experiences. Translated by Swami Nikhilananada.

"Rādhā was mad with prema, ecstatic love of God. But there is also the madness of bhakti. Hanumān's was such. When he saw

Sītā entering the fire he was going to kill Rāma. Then, too, there is the madness of Knowledge. I once saw a jñāni behaving like a madman. He came here very soon after the temple garden was dedicated. People said he belonged to the Brāhmo Sabhā of Rammohan Roy. He had a torn shoe on one foot, a stick in one hand, and a potted mango-plant in the other. After a dip in the Ganges he went to the Kālī temple where Haladhari was seated. With great fervour he began to chant a hymn to the Divine Mother. Then he went up to a dog, held it by the ear, and ate some of its food. The dog didn't mind. Just at that time I too was about to experience the state of divine madness. I threw my arm around Hriday's neck and said, 'Oh, Hridē! Shall I too fall into that plight?'

"I became mad. Narayan Shastri came here and saw me roaming about with a bamboo pole on my shoulder. He said to the people, 'Ah, he is mad!' In that state I could not observe any caste restrictions. The wife of a low-caste man used to send me cooked greens, and I ate them.

"I touched my head and lips with the leaf-plates from which the beggars ate their food in the guest-house of the Kālī temple. Thereupon Haladhari said to me: 'What have you done? You have taken the food left by beggars. How will you marry off your children?' These words aroused my anger. Haladhari was my cousin, older than myself. But could that restrain me? I said to him: 'You wretch! Isn't it you who take pride in the study of the *Gītā* and the Vedānta? Isn't it you who teach people that Brahman alone is real and the world illusory? And yet you imagine that I shall beget children! May your mouth that recites from the *Gītā* be blighted!"

*

"The Divine Mother revealed to me in the Kālī temple that it was She who had become everything. She showed me that everything was full of Consciousness. The Image was Consciousness, the altar was Consciousness, the water-vessels were Consciousness, the door-sill was Consciousness, the marble floor was Consciousness — all was Consciousness.

"I found everything inside the room soaked, as it were, in Bliss — the Bliss of Satchidānanda. I saw a wicked man in front of the Kālī temple; but in him also I saw the Power of the Divine Mother vibrating.

"That was why I fed a cat with the food that was to be offered to the Divine Mother. I clearly perceived that the Divine Mother Herself had become everything — even the cat. The manager of the temple garden wrote to Mathur Babu saying that I was feeding the cat with the offering intended for the Divine Mother. But Mathur Babu had insight into the state of my mind. He wrote back to the manager: 'Let him do whatever he likes. You must not say anything to him.'

"After realizing God, one sees all this aright — that it is He who has become the universe, living beings, and the twenty-four cosmic principles. But what remains when God completely effaces the ego cannot be described in words. As Rāmprasād said in one of his songs, 'Then alone will you know whether you are good or I am good!' I get into even that state now and then.

"A man sees a thing in one way through reasoning and in an altogether different way when God Himself shows it to him."

*

"God made me pass through the disciplines of various paths. First according to the Purāna, then according to the Tantra. I also followed the disciplines of the Vedas. At first I practised sādhanā in the Panchavati. I made a grove of tulsi-plants and used to sit inside it and meditate. Sometimes I cried with a longing heart, 'Mother! Mother!' Or again, 'Rāma! Rāma!'

"While repeating the name of Rāma, I sometimes assumed the attitude of Hanumān and fixed a tail to the lower end of my backbone. I was in a God-intoxicated state. At that time I used to put on a silk robe and worship the Deity. What joy I experienced in that worship!

"I practised the discipline of the Tantra under the bel-tree. At that time I could see no distinction between the sacred tulsi and any other plant. In that state I sometimes ate the leavings from a jackal's meal, food that had been exposed the whole night, part of which might have been eaten by snakes or other creatures. Yes, I ate that stuff.

"Sometimes I rode on a dog and fed him with luchi, also eating part of the bread myself. I realized that the whole world was filled with God alone. One cannot have spiritual realization without destroying ignorance; so I would assume the attitude of a tiger and devour ignorance.

"While practising the disciplines of the Vedas, I became a

sannyāsī. I used to lie down in the chandni and say to Hriday: 'I am a sannyāsī. I shall take my meals here.'

"I vowed to the Divine Mother that I would kill myself if I did not see God. I said to Her: 'O Mother, I am a fool. Please teach me what is contained in the Vedas, the Purānas, the Tantras, and the other scriptures.' The Mother said to me, 'The essence of the Vedānta is that Brahman alone is real and the world illusory.' The Satchidānanda Brahman described in the Vedas is the Satchidānanda Śiva of the Tantra and the Satchidānanda Krishna of the Purāna. The essence of the *Gītā* is what you get by repeating the word ten times. It is reversed into 'tāgi', which indicates renunciation.

"After the realization of God, how far below lie the Vedas, the Vedānta, the Purāna, the Tantra! [*To Hazra*] I cannot utter the word 'Om' in samādhi. Why is that? I cannot say 'Om' unless I come down very far from the state of samādhi.

"I had all the experiences that one should have, according to the scriptures, after one's direct perception of God. I behaved like a child, like a madman, like a ghoul, and like an inert thing.

"I saw the visions described in the scriptures. Sometimes I saw the universe filled with sparks of fire. Sometimes I saw all the quarters glittering with light, as if the world were a lake of mercury. Sometimes I saw the world as if made of liquid silver. Sometimes, again, I saw all the quarters illumined as if with the light of Roman candles. So you see my experiences tally with those described in the scriptures.

"It was revealed to me further that God Himself has become the universe and all its living beings and the twenty-four cosmic principles. It is like the process of evolution and involution.

"Oh, what a state God kept me in at that time! One experience would hardly be over before another overcame me. It was like the movement of the husking-machine: no sooner is one end down than the other goes up.

"I would see God in meditation, in the state of samādhi, and I would see the same God when my mind came back to the outer world. When looking at this side of the mirror I would see Him alone, and when looking on the reverse side I saw the same God."

*

"Formal worship drops away after the vision of God. It was thus that my worship in the temple came to an end. I used to worship the Deity in the Kālī temple. It was suddenly revealed to me that everything is Pure Spirit. The utensils of worship, the altar, the door-frame — all Pure Spirit. Men, animals, and other living beings — all Pure Spirit. Then like a madman I began to shower flowers in all directions. Whatever I saw I worshipped.

"One day, while worshipping Śiva, I was about to offer a bel-leaf on the head of the image, when it was revealed to me that this Virāt, this Universe, itself is Śiva. After that my worship of Śiva through the image came to an end. Another day I had been plucking flowers, when it was revealed to me that the flowering plants were so many bouquets."

*

"Oh, what a state I passed through! I passed some days absorbed in Śiva and Durgā, some days absorbed in Rādhā and Krishna, and some days absorbed in Sītā and Rāma. Assuming Rādhā's attitude, I would cry for Krishna, and assuming Sītā's attitude, I would cry for Rāma.

"But līlā is by no means the last word. Passing through all these states, I said to the Divine Mother: 'Mother, in these states there is separation. Give me a state where there is no separation.' Then I remained for some time absorbed in the Indivisible Satchidānanda. I removed the pictures of the gods and goddesses from my room. I began to perceive God in all beings. Formal worship dropped away. You see that bel-tree. I used to go there to pluck its leaves. One day, as I plucked a leaf, a bit of the bark came off. I found the tree full of Consciousness. I felt grieved because I had hurt the tree. One day I tried to pluck some durvā grass, but I found I couldn't do it very well. Then I forced myself to pluck it."

*

Sri Ramakrishna then described to Girish, M., and the other devotees his own experience of mahābhāva.

MASTER [*to the devotees*]: "My joy after that experience was equal to the pain I suffered before it. Mahābhāva is a divine ecstasy; it shakes the body and mind to their very foundation. It is like a huge elephant entering a small hut. The house shakes to its foundation. Perhaps it falls to pieces.

"The burning pain that one feels when one is separated from God is not an ordinary feeling. It is said that the fire of this anguish in Rupa and Sanātana scorched the leaves of the tree under which they sat. I was unconscious three days in that state. I couldn't move. I lay in one place. When I regained consciousness, the Brāhmani took me out for a bath. But my skin couldn't bear the touch of her hand; so my body had to be covered with a heavy sheet. Only then could she hold me with her hand and lead me to the bathing-place. The earth that had stuck to my body while I was lying on the ground had become baked.

"In that state I felt as if a ploughshare were passing through my backbone. I cried out: 'Oh, I am dying! I am dying!' But afterwards I was filled with great joy."

*

"Once a sādhu of Hrishikesh came here. He said to me: 'There are five kinds of samādhi. I find you have experienced them all. In these samādhis one feels the sensation of the Spiritual Current to be like the movement of an ant, a fish, a monkey, a bird, or a serpent.'

"Sometimes the Spiritual Current rises through the spine, crawling like an ant.

"Sometimes, in samādhi, the soul swims joyfully in the ocean of divine ecstasy, like a fish.

"Sometimes, when I lie down on my side, I feel the Spiritual Current pushing me like a monkey and playing with me joyfully. I remain still. That Current, like a monkey, suddenly with one jump reaches the Sahasrāra. That is why you see me jump up with a start.

"Sometimes, again, the Spiritual Current rises like a bird hopping from one branch to another. The place where it rests feels like fire. It may hop from Mulādhāra to Svādhisthāna, from Svādhisthāna to the heart, and thus gradually to the head.

"Sometimes the Spiritual Current moves up like a snake. Going in a zigzag way, at last it reaches the head and I go into samādhi.

"A man's spiritual consciousness is not awakened unless his Kundalini is aroused.

"The Kundalini dwells in the Mulādhāra. When it is aroused, it passes along the Sushumnā nerve, goes through the centres of Svādhisthāna, Manipura, and so on, and at last reaches the head. This is called the movement of the Mahāvāyu, the Spiritual Current. It culminates in samādhi.

"One's spiritual consciousness is not awakened by the mere reading of books. One should also pray to God. The Kundalini is aroused if the aspirant feels restless for God. To talk of Knowledge from mere study and hearsay! What will that accomplish?

"Just before my attaining this state of mind, it had been revealed to me how the Kundalini is aroused, how the lotuses of the different centres blossom forth, and how all this culminates in samādhi. This is a very secret experience. I saw a boy twenty-two or twenty-three years old, exactly resembling me, enter the Sushumnā nerve and commune with the lotuses, touching them with his tongue. He began with the centre at the anus and passed through the centres at the sexual organ, navel, and so on. The different lotuses of those centres — four-petalled, six-petalled, ten-petalled, and so forth — had been drooping. At his touch they stood erect.

"When he reached the heart — I distinctly remember it — and communed with the lotus there, touching it with his tongue, the twelve-petalled lotus, which was hanging head down, stood erect and opened its petals. Then he came to the sixteen-petalled lotus in the throat and the two-petalled lotus in the forehead. And last of all, the thousand-petalled lotus in the head blossomed. Since then I have been in this state."

*

Question: Sir, how do you feel in samādhi?

"You may have heard that the cockroach, by intently meditating on the bhramara, is transformed into a bhramara. Do you know how I feel then? I feel like a fish released from a pot into the water of the Ganges."

Q: Don't you feel at that time even a trace of ego?

"Yes, generally a little of it remains. However hard you may rub a grain of gold against a grindstone, still a bit of it always remains. Or again, take the case of a big fire; the ego is like one of its sparks. In samādhi I lose outer consciousness completely; but God generally keeps a little trace of ego in me for the enjoyment of divine communion. Enjoyment is possible only when 'I' and 'you' remain.

"Again, sometimes God effaces even that trace of 'I'. Then one experiences jaḍa samādhi or nirvikalpa samādhi. That experience cannot be described. A salt doll went to measure the depth of the ocean, but before it had gone far into the water it melted away. It became entirely one with the water of the ocean. Then who was to come back and tell the ocean's depth?"

*

"God has covered all with His māyā. He doesn't let us know anything. Māyā is 'woman and gold'. He who puts māyā aside to see God, can see Him. Once, when I was explaining God's actions to someone, God suddenly showed me the lake at Kāmārpukur. I saw a man removing the green scum and drinking the water. The water was clear as crystal. God revealed to me that Satchidānanda is covered by the scum of māyā. He who puts the green scum aside can drink the water.

"Let me tell you a very secret experience. Once I had entered the wood near the pine-grove, and was sitting there, when I had a vision of something like the hidden door of a chamber. I couldn't see the inside of the chamber. I tried to bore a hole in the door with a nail-knife, but did not succeed. As I bored, the earth fell back into the hole and filled it. Then suddenly I made a very big opening."

Uttering these words, the Master remained silent. After a time he said: "These are very profound words. I feel as if someone were pressing my mouth. . . . I have seen with my own eyes that God dwells even in the sexual organ. I saw Him once in the sexual intercourse of a dog and a bitch.

"The universe is conscious on account of the Consciousness of God. Sometimes I find that this Consciousness wriggles about, as it were, even in small fish."

The carriage came to the crossing at Shovābāzār in Calcutta. The Master continued, saying, "Sometimes I find that the universe is saturated with the Consciousness of God, as the earth is soaked with water in the rainy season."

*

"I experienced one of my first ecstasies when I was ten or eleven years old, as I was going through a meadow to the shrine of Viśālākshi. What a vision! I became completely unconscious of the outer world.

"I was twenty-two or twenty-three when the Divine Mother one day asked me in the Kālī temple, 'Do you want to be *akṣara*?' I didn't know what the word meant. I asked Haladhari about it. He said, '*kṣara* means jīva, living being; *akṣara* means *Paramātman*, the Supreme Soul.'

"At the hour of the evening worship in the Kālī temple I would climb to the roof of the kuthi and cry out: 'O devotees, where are you all? Come to me soon! I shall die of the company of worldly people!' I told all this to the 'Englishmen'. They said it was all an illusion of my mind. 'Perhaps it is', I said to myself, and became calm. But now it is all coming true; the devotees are coming.

"The Divine Mother also showed me in a vision the five suppliers of my needs; first, Mathur Babu, and second, Sambhu Mallick, whom I had not then met. I had a vision of a fair-skinned man with a cap on his head. Many days later, when I first met Sambhu, I recalled that vision; I realized that it was he whom I had seen in that ecstatic state. I haven't yet found out the three other suppliers of my wants. But they were all of a fair complexion. Surendra looks like one of them.

"When I attained this state of God-Consciousness, a person exactly resembling myself thoroughly shook my Iḍā, Piṅgalā, and Sushumnā nerves. He licked with his tongue each of the lotuses of the six centres, and those drooping lotuses at once turned their faces upward. And at last the Sahasrāra lotus became full-blown.

"The Divine Mother used to reveal to me the nature of the devotees before their coming. I saw with these two eyes — not in a trance — the kirtan party of Chaitanya going from the banyan-tree to the bakul-tree in the Panchavati. I saw Balaram in the procession and also, I think, yourself [meaning M.]. Chuni's spiritual consciousness and yours, too, have been awakened by frequent visits to me. In a vision I saw that Sashi and Sarat had been among the followers of Christ."

*

"I went to Vrindāvan with Mathur Babu. The moment I came to the Dhruva Ghāt at Mathurā, in a flash I saw Vasudeva crossing the Jamunā with Krishna in his arms.

"One evening I was taking a stroll on the beach of the river. There were small thatched huts on the beach and big plum-trees. It was the 'cow-dust' hour. The cows were returning from the pasture, raising dust with their hoofs. I saw them fording the river. Then came some cowherd boys crossing the river with their cows. No sooner did I behold this scene than I cried out, 'O Krishna, where are You?' and became unconscious.

"I wanted to visit Śyāmakunda and Rādhākunda; so Mathur Babu sent me there in a palanquin. We had a long way to go. Food was put in the palanquin. While going over the meadow I was overpowered with emotion and wept: 'O Krishna, I find everything the same; only You are not here. This is the very meadow where You tended the cows.' Hriday followed me on foot. I was bathed in tears. I couldn't ask the bearers to stop the palanquin.

"At Śyāmakunda and Rādhākunda I saw the holy men living in small mud huts. Facing away from the road lest their eyes should fall on men, they were engaged in spiritual discipline. One should visit the 'Twelve Grove'.

"I went into samādhi at the sight of the image of Baṅkuvihāri. In that state I wanted to touch it. I did not want to visit Govindaji twice. At Mathurā I dreamt of Krishna as the cowherd boy. Hriday and Mathur Babu had the same dream."

*

MASTER: "Well, Keshab, say something! They are eager to hear your words."

KESHAB [*humbly, with a smile*]: "To open my lips here would be like trying to 'sell needles to a blacksmith'."

MASTER [*smiling*]: "But don't you know that the nature of devotees is like that of hemp-smokers? One hemp-smoker says to another, 'Please take a puff for yourself and give me one.' " [*All laugh.*]

It was about four o'clock in the afternoon. They heard the music from the nahabat in the temple garden.

MASTER [*to Keshab and the others*]: "Do you hear how melodious that music is? One player is producing only a monotone on his flute, while another is creating waves of melodies in different rāgas and rāginis. That is my attitude. Why should I produce only a monotone when I have an instrument with seven holes? Why should I say nothing but, 'I am He, I am He'? I want to play various melodies on my instrument with seven holes. Why should I say only, 'Brahma! Brahma!'? I want to call on God through all the moods—through śānta, dāsya, sakhya, vātsalya, and madhur. I want to make merry with God. I want to sport with God."

Keshab listened to these words with wonder in his eyes and

said to the Brāhmo devotees, "I have never before heard such a wonderful and beautiful interpretation of jñāna and bhakti."

KESHAB [*to the Master*]: "How long will you hide yourself in this way? I dare say people will be thronging here by and by in great crowds."

MASTER: "What are you talking of? I only eat and drink and sing God's name. I know nothing about gathering crowds. Hanumān once declared: 'I know nothing about the day of the week or the position of the moon and stars in the sky. I simply meditate on Rāma.'"

KESHAB: "All right, sir, I shall gather the crowd. But they all must come to your place."

MASTER: "I am the dust of the dust of everybody's feet. If anyone is gracious enough to come here, he is welcome."

KESHAB: "Whatever you may say, sir, your advent cannot be in vain."

In the mean time the devotees had arranged a kirtan. Many of them had joined it. The party started at the Panchavati and moved toward the Master's room. Hriday blew the horn, Gopidas played the drum, and two devotees played the cymbals.

Sri Ramakrishna sang:

O man, if you would live in bliss, repeat Lord Hari's name;
Then you will lead a life of joy and go to paradise,
And feed upon the fruit of moksha evermore:
Such is the glory of His name!
I give you the name of Hari, which Śiva, God of Gods,
Repeats aloud with His five mouths.

The Master danced with the strength of a lion and went into samādhi. Regaining consciousness of the outer world, he sat down in his room and began to talk with Keshab and the other devotees.

MASTER: "God can be realized through all paths. It is like your coming to Dakshineswar by carriage, by boat, by steamer, or on foot. You have chosen the way according to your convenience and taste; but the destination is the same. Some of you have arrived earlier than others; but all have arrived."

*

About seven o'clock in the morning Sri Ramakrishna felt a little better. He talked to the devotees, sometimes in a whisper, sometimes by signs. Narendra, Rakhal, Latu, M., Gopal of Sinthi, and others were in the room. They sat speechless and looked grave, thinking of the Master's suffering of the previous night.

MASTER [*to the devotees*]: "Do you know what I see right now? I see that it is God Himself who has become all this. It seems to me that men and other living beings are made of leather, and that it is God Himself who, dwelling inside these leather cases, moves the hands, the feet, the heads. I had a similar vision once before, when I saw houses, gardens, roads, men, cattle—all made of One Substance; it was as if they were all made of wax.

"I see that it is God Himself who has become the block, the executioner, and the victim for the sacrifice."

As he describes this staggering experience, in which he realizes in full the identity of all within the One Being, he is overwhelmed with emotion and exclaims, "Ah! What a vision!"

Immediately Sri Ramakrishna goes into samādhi. He completely forgets his body and the outer world. The devotees are bewildered. Not knowing what to do, they sit still.

Presently the Master regains partial consciousness of the world and says: "Now I have no pain at all. I am my old self again."

FURTHER READING

Source Materials

Mahendranath Gupta [M], *The Gospel of Sri Ramakrishna*, tr. Swami Nikhilananda. Two volumes. Madras: Sri Ramakrishna Math, n.d.

Swami Saradananda, *Sri Ramakrishna: The Great Master*, tr. Swami Jagadananda. Two volumes. Madras: Sri Ramakrishna Math, [1978].

Other Sources

Christopher Isherwood, *Ramakrishna and his Disciples*. Calcutta: Advaita Ashrama, 1974.

Sudhir Kakar, *The Analyst and the Mystic: Psychoanalytic Reflections on Religion and Mysticism*. New Delhi: Viking, 1991.

Swami Lokeswarananda, *Ramakrishna Paramahansa*. New Delhi: Sahitya Akademi, 1997.

Sri Ramakrishna Math <www.sriramakrishnamath.org>

Ramakrishna-Vivekananda Center of New York <www.ramakrishna.org>

Sources of Texts and Translations

157 Saradananda 115, 162–63, 164–65, 171–72, 181–82, 290
158 M. Gupta 548, 345–46, 543–45, 396, 687, 747, 829–30, 196–97, 260, 933–34, 361–62, 1009–10, 941–42

SAI BABA OF SHIRDI

One day, probably in 1854, residents of Shirdi, Maharashtra, noticed a young *faqīr* sitting under a tree outside the village. There was nothing remarkable in this; *sādhu*s, *sannyāsī*s and *faqīr*s are familiar figures in the Indian landscape, and this one, like others before him, soon moved on. Four years later, however, he came back to Shirdi, and this time he followed a marriage procession into the village. A man who had seen him earlier greeted him with a cordial "*Ya Sāi*", Sāi being a term of address for Muslim holy men. The appellation stuck, and soon everyone was calling him Sai Baba. (*Bābā* or father is a term of respect.) He spent the rest of his life in Shirdi, dying there in 1918.

Nothing is known for sure about Sai Baba's antecedents. He must have been born around 1838, apparently in what is now eastern Maharashtra. He spoke of being raised by an (apparently Muslim) *faqīr*, and many of his habits point to Muslim spiritual training: he dressed like a sufi, said prayers in Persian and Arabic, and generally addressed God as Allah. On the other hand he had an (apparently Hindu) guru, from whom he learned the way of devotion. In Shirdi he loved to sing and dance to the songs of Kabir, and once spoke of himself as following the Kabir "religion"; but like Kabir himself, he was given a brahmin parentage by the Hindus who made up most of his following. He did occasionally speak of himself as a brahmin, but he seems to have used the term in its original sense: a man of developed spiritual knowledge.

For a few years after his arrival in Shirdi, Baba spent his time wandering in the forest or sitting in contemplation. At one point, he decided to stay in a local temple; but his way was barred by the priest, who considered him a Muslim. Unconcerned, Baba moved into a dilapidated mosque, which became his permanent home. His simple life, great powers of intuition, and ability to achieve results that others found miraculous, caused people to regard him as a wise and powerful holy man. As his reputation grew, men and women from other parts of the country began coming to Shirdi to see him. Most arrived in search of cures for themselves or their loved ones, or in hopes of success in their careers. Baba seems to have regretted this, but he met his devotees on their own terms, and many of them went away satisfied.

A few devotees came to Baba with spiritual yearnings. Sometimes he answered their questions about philosophical and religious topics. These replies show his acquaintance with the *advaita* and *bhakti* traditions. More usually, however, he gave his teachings in the form of riddles or parables or symbolic acts. Once, for instance, an unbeliever came to see what the celebrated *faqīr* was like. He found Baba washing pots and placing them upside down. "What is all this?" asked the visitor. "Every pot coming to me comes with mouth downwards", Baba replied, with obvious reference to the visitor's lack of receptivity (Narasimhaswami 1944: 37).

No matter how celebrated Sai Baba became, he never changed his lifestyle: begging for his food, which he always shared with others; walking in a garden that he cultivated himself; performing secret rites that only he understood; and giving advice and blessings to those who came to see him. Many have noted that being in Baba's presence was enough to give them contentment.

The chief sources for Sai Baba's life and teachings are the *Shri Sai Satcarita*, a hagiography in Marathi verse, and *Sri Sai Baba's Charters and Sayings*, a collection of anecdotes and aphorisms in English translation. The incidents and teachings found in these books are reproduced in countless pamphlets and tracts, which present Sai Baba as a modern wonder-worker, who performed, and still performs, innumerable miracles for those who have faith in him. Such publications tend to obscure the simple sanctity and unostentatious benevolence of the *faqīr* who settled down in Shirdi.

[159]

From *Sri Sai Baba's Charters and Sayings*

The following extracts from Narasimhaswami's *Charters and Sayings* give some idea of Sai Baba's relationship with his guru, his spiritual status, and his methods of teaching.

For 12 years I waited on my Guru who is peerless and loving. How can I describe his love to Me? When he was *dhyānastha* [*i.e.*, in love-trance], I sat and gazed at him. We were both filled with Bliss. I cared not to turn my eye upon anything else. Night and day I pored upon his face with an ardour of love that banished hunger and thirst. The Guru's absence, even for a second made me restless. I meditated on nothing but the Guru, and had no goal, or object, other than the Guru. Unceasingly fixed upon him was my mind. Wonderful indeed, the art of my Guru! I wanted nothing but the Guru and he wanted nothing but this intense love from me. Apparently inactive, he never neglected me, but always protected me by his glance. That Guru never blew any mantra into my ear. By his grace, I attained to my present state. Making the Guru the sole object of one's thoughts and aims one attains Paramartha, the Supreme Goal. This is the only truth the Guru taught me. The four sadhanas and six sastras are not necessary. *Trusting in the Guru fully is enough.*

*

My master told me to give bounteously to all that ask. No one listens to me or wisdom. My treasury is open. None brings carts to take from it. I say dig; none will take any pains. I said dig out the treasure and cart it away. Be the real and true sons of the mother and fully stock your magazine. What is to become of us, *i.e.*, this bodily life? Earth will return to the earth; and the air [breath] will return to the air. This opportunity will not return.

*

A devotee objected to people going to Baba for temporal benefit, e.g., *employment, money, children, cure of disease.*

Do not do that. My men first come to me on account of that only. They get their heart's desires fulfilled; and comfortably placed in life, they then follow me and progress further. I bring my men to me from long distances under many pleas. I seek them and bring them to me. They do not come [of their own accord]. I bring them to me.

However distant — even thousands of miles away — my people might be, I draw them to myself, just as we pull birds to us with a string tied to their foot.

*

Question: Baba, who are you? Whence?

[*In the mood of the Absolute*] I have no residence. I am the attributeless Absolute — Nirguna. [*Again, in the mood of Duality*] By the action of Karma I got embroiled and came to a body. My name is "The embodied" (dehī). The world is my abode. Brahman is my father, and Maya my mother. By their interlocking I got this body. The world is mutable, evanescent.

[*To a devotee*] Allah or the Nirguna [Parabrahma] became saguna Parabrahma [known as] Mohiniraja at Nivas. Go and bow before him. God manifests all his powers for the benefit of his devotees.

*

I am the Progenitor of God. Meditate on me as pure Ananda Nirakara: but if you cannot do so, meditate on this Sai body exactly as it is.

*

You have been with me eighteen years. Does "Sai" mean to you only this 3½ cubits height of body?

I am in the ant and fly.

Whenever you see this sign, remember that I am there and that I can eat food through ants, flies etc.

*

To know me, constantly think "Who am I?" by Sravana and Manana.

Who are we? What are we? Where am I? Where are you? Where is all the world?

Think, think on all your husband said [*viz., that, in reality, you are not different from God*].

*

Q: What am I?

I am you, You are I. There is no difference between you and me. That which constitutes me constitutes you.

*

Q: Baba, what is God like?

[*Not addressing the visitor but addressing a certain devotee*] Go to Bagchand Marwadi and tell him Baba wants Rs. 100/–and bring the money.

Devotee [returning in a minute]: The Marwadi says he has no money and sends his namaskars.

Go to the next money lender and ask him for a loan of Rs. 100/– for me.

Devotee [returning in a minute]: He says he has not got the money.

Fetch Nana Saheb Chandorkar. [*When Nana came*] Nana, I want Rs. 100/–.

Nana wrote a chit to Bagchand Marwadi for a loan of Rs. 100. The money was at once sent by the Marwadi.

All is like this in the world.

*

Two Parables

I once changed the lower part of my body for that of a parrot, and after a year's experience, I discovered that it was a serious loss. I lost a lakh of rupees.

A person rode on a camel. It passed excreta. I gathered all the excreta and ate them up. My belly was puffed up — swollen. I felt listless. Then the rider took pity upon me. He gave me four grains of Bengal gram and I ate them and drank water. Thus my vehement turbulence ceased. My swollen belly subsided. Now hereafter it will be cured.

*

> *Q: Enough of this Samsara for me. As the Sastras describe it,* saṁsāra *is really* nissāra *[i.e., worthless]. Break its fetters off from me, Baba. What first seems to be joy here is seen to be but sorrow at the end. Fate leads us a nice dance here and there. I cannot discover even a bit of happiness in this Samsara. I am quite disgusted, I do not wish to touch it, Baba, any further.*

What crazy and delusive talk is yours! There is some truth in it — mixed up with error. As long as the body remains, samsara remains. None escapes it. How can you? Even I am caught up in it. Samsara is of various sorts. It is like the surface of the body. Kama (desire) krodha (anger) etc., and any mixture of these is samsara. All mental and bodily processes are samsara. The contact of any two things is samsara. By going away to a forest you cannot escape samsara. Your present condition has been brought about by yourself. What is the use of irritation at it? This *deha prārabdha* is the result of the karma done by you in former births. This body was, therefore, born. The Jiva takes birth in body to work out former Karma. Without suffering the results of Prarabdha Karma, you cannot get rid of it. All persons, all creatures differ in form etc. Why? Because of previous Karma of each. Differences between species, like differences between individuals are due to the same cause. See the difference between the rich man's dog lolling on sofa and the poor man's running about in search of crumbs. That is due to *deha prārabdha*.

*

Q: Pray, tell us about Suddha Chaitanya, *what it is.*

That is the origin, the essence, the foundation and the permeator of the entire universe, sentient and insentient, as also the end of it. The source is Suddha Chaitanya. You cannot exactly describe "Chaitanya", but every moment it exists in your existence. There is no place without it but it has no form or name. In that it resembles air, which has no colour or form to be seen, and whose existence however is unquestionable. Suddha Chaitanya is called Brahman. The wise do upasana of it under the name Brahman and then, are called Brahmavit. Vegetable, animal, human and all other lives are contained within it. It is the original cause of all appearances, perceptions and knowledge. It is the one root of the many. It pervades everything. It may be characterised as Sat (reality), Chit (consciousness), Ananda (bliss) and Ekatva (unity). All of us are that. We are not distinct from it.

FURTHER READING

Source Materials

B. V. Narasimhaswami, *Sri Sai Baba's Charters and Sayings*. Fifth edition. Madras: All India Sai Samaj, 1944.

Other Sources

Govind R. Dabholkar [Hemad Pant], *Shri Sai Satcharita: The Life and Teachings of Shirdi Sai Baba*, translated by Indira Kher. New Delhi: Sterling Publishers Private, Ltd., 1999.

Antonio Rigopoulos, *The Life and Teachings of Sai Baba of Shirdi*. Albany: State University of New York Press, 1994.

Shirdi Sai Baba Homepage <http://www.shirdibaba.org>

Shirdi Sai Baba <http://www.saibaba.org>

Sources of Texts

159 Narasimhaswami, pp. 59–60, 7, 8, 23–24, 17, 12, 18, 19, 38, 270, 271, 19–20, 31

SRI AUROBINDO

In 1872, when Aurobindo Ghose was born in Kolkata, Bengal had been under British rule for more than a century. His father was one of the first Indians to go to Britain for higher education. When he returned to Bengal, he was so enamoured of British ways that he forbade his sons from speaking Bengali at home. Hoping that one of them would enter the élite Indian Civil Service, he took them to England in 1879 and left them in the care of a Manchester clergyman. Aurobindo excelled as a scholar at St. Paul's School, London, and King's College, Cambridge, mastering Latin, Greek and French along with English; but he knew almost nothing about the languages, culture and people of India. Nevertheless he nourished patriotic feelings, and dreamed of bringing about a revolution in his homeland in the manner of a Mazzini or Joan of Arc. Selected for the Indian Civil Service in 1890, he completed the course but neglected to take the riding examination and was rejected. Finding employment in the service of the Maharaja of Baroda, he returned to India in 1893.

Aurobindo remained in Baroda for thirteen years, working in various government departments and teaching at the local college. He also read deeply in English, Sanskrit and Bengali literature, and wrote poetry, essays and translations. From around 1902 he began to organise a secret society that, in the wake of the government's partition of Bengal, took part in some small revolutionary acts (all of them failures). At this time Aurobindo left his job in Baroda, went to Kolkata and became one of the most outspoken publicists of the Extremist wing of the Indian National Congress. His plans for turning the Congress into a dynamic organisation dedicated to the attainment of complete independence were derailed when an attempt at political assassination led to his arrest and imprisonment.

Three years before his arrest, Aurobindo had begun the practice of yoga with the idea of getting power to help him in his work. After a few years of solitary *sādhana* he met a Maharashtrian yogin named V. B. Lele, who showed him how to silence his mind. This led to the experience of the "passive Brahman", in which the Divine alone is seen as true, while the universe appears to be unreal. A few months later, while in jail awaiting trial for conspiracy, Aurobindo had the wider experience of the Divine as simultaneously transcendent of and immanent in the universe. This came to him as a vision of Krishna in all things and beings. Further realisations followed, which revealed to him the higher levels of consciousness that link the manifested world to the unmanifest Divine. One of these, the supermind, became the key to his future *sādhana* and the central term of his philosophy. Supermind, "the truth of that which we call God", is "the intermediary power between that self-possession of the One and this flux of the Many" (*Life Divine* 132, 122). Aurobindo believed that this power could transform human life into a divine existence. The goal of spiritual discipline was not an escape from the rounds of *saṁsāra* but a state of individual and collective perfection in the body and on earth.

By the time he was released from jail in 1909, Aurobindo's outlook on life and the world had radically changed. He now saw his work as a form of *karmayoga* or action in obedience to the divine will. For a year he felt impelled to continue his nationalist work, then, following what he termed an *ādeśa* or inner command, he left Kolkata and settled in Pondicherry, a French enclave in south India. Here he passed the remainder of his life, absorbed in his personal *sādhana*, which was also, he said, a "*sādhana* for the earth-consciousness" (*On Himself* 144). At the same time he wrote and published numerous works of philosophy, scriptural exegesis, political science, literary and cultural criticism and poetry.

In 1914 Aurobindo met a Frenchwoman named Mirra Alfassa, who had studied occultism in Algeria with a Kabbalistic master, and had contact with teachers like the sufi Hazrat Inayat Khan and Abdul Baha, the leader of the Bahais. In 1920 Mirra settled in Pondicherry, where she became the centre of the spiritual community that was forming around Aurobindo. In 1926 he handed over the charge of this ashram to Mirra, now called the Mother, and retired from public view. For the next twenty-four years, he remained in an apartment in his house, practising yoga, writing poetry, and answering questions posed by disciples. A selection of his letters, ranging in subject from metaphysics to the minutiae of daily life, were later published in five large volumes. Sri Aurobindo (as he was called after 1926) spent the last years of his life working on a symbolic epic poem, *Savitri*. He died of kidney failure in 1950.

The writings of Sri Aurobindo are extensive and diverse. His *Life Divine* presents a spiritual metaphysics, founded on the insights of the *upaniṣads* but affirming, against Shankara's *advaita*, the reality and value of the world. *The Synthesis of Yoga* considers the four main paths of yoga: the way of works (as taught by the *Bhagavad Gītā*), the way of knowledge (as put forward by the *upaniṣads* and similar texts), the path of love (as formulated by Bengal Vaishnavism and other schools of *bhakti-yoga*), and the path of self-perfection (such as was practised by tantric yogis and siddhas). Showing that each of these paths can lead to the Divine, he proposed a synthetic yoga in which every power of human consciousness is put to spiritual use. He also noted the progress of his own *sādhana* in a spiritual diary, published posthumously as *Record of Yoga*. This document chronicles the ups and downs of his own daily practice, providing an unprecedented glimpse into the inner life of an advanced practitioner. Some of his poems likewise are autobiographical records of his spiritual experiences. More explicitly than many other spiritual teachers, Sri Aurobindo affirmed that such experiences were the basis of his philosophy and yoga.

[160]

From *Uttarpara Speech*

Shortly after his release from jail in 1909, Aurobindo was invited to give a speech in Uttarpara, a suburb of Kolkata. Here he spoke of his experience of the cosmic consciousness during his imprisonment. This was the first time he had spoken in public of his spiritual experiences.

When I was arrested and hurried to the Lal Bazar hajat, I was shaken in faith for a while, for I could not look into the heart of His intention. Therefore I faltered for a moment and cried out in my heart to Him, "What is this that has happened to me? I believed that I had a mission to work for the people of my country and until that work was done, I should have Thy protection. Why then am I here and on such a charge?" A day passed and a second day and a third, when a voice came to me from within, "Wait and see." Then I grew calm and waited. I was taken from Lal Bazar to Alipore and was placed for one month in a solitary cell apart from men. There I waited day and night for the voice of God within me, to know what He had to say to me, to learn what I had to do. . . . Then He placed the Gita in my hands. His strength entered into me and I was able to do the *sādhana* of the Gita. I was not only to understand intellectually but to realise what Srikrishna demanded of Arjuna and what He demands of those who aspire to do His work, to be free from repulsion and desire, to do work for Him without the demand for fruit, to renounce self-will and become a passive and faithful instrument in His hands, to have an equal heart for high and low, friend and opponent, success and failure, yet not to do His work negligently. . . .

Therefore this was the next thing He pointed out to me, — He made me realise the central truth of the Hindu religion. He turned the hearts of my jailers to me and they spoke to the Englishman in charge of the jail, "He is suffering in his confinement; let him at least walk outside his cell for half an hour in the morning and in the evening." So it was arranged, and it was while I was walking that His strength again entered into me. I looked at the jail that secluded me from men and it was no longer by its high walls that I was imprisoned; no, it was Vasudeva who surrounded me. I walked under the branches of the tree in front of my cell, but it was not the tree, I knew it was Vasudeva, it was Srikrishna whom I saw standing there and holding over me His shade. I looked at the bars of my cell, the very grating that did duty for a door and again I saw Vasudeva. It was Narayana who was guarding and standing sentry over me. Or I lay on the coarse blankets that were given me for a couch and felt the arms of Srikrishna around me, the arms of my Friend and Lover. This was the first use of the deeper vision He gave me. I looked at the prisoners in the jail, the thieves, the murderers, the swindlers, and as I looked at them I saw Vasudeva, it was Narayana whom I found in these darkened souls and misused bodies. Amongst these thieves and dacoits there were many who put me to shame by their sympathy, their kindness, the humanity triumphant over such adverse circumstances. One I saw among them especially who seemed to me a saint, a peasant of my nation who did not know how to read and write, an alleged dacoit sentenced to ten years' rigorous imprisonment, one of those whom we look down upon in our Pharisaical pride of class as *chhotalok*. Once more He spoke to me and said, "Behold the people among whom I have sent you to do a little of my work. This is the nature of the nation I am raising up and the reason why I raise them."

When the case opened in the lower court and we were brought before the Magistrate I was followed by the same insight. He said to me, "When you were cast into jail, did not your heart fail and did you not cry out to me, where is Thy protection? Look now at the Magistrate, look now at the Prosecuting Counsel." I looked and it was not the Magistrate whom I saw, it was Vasudeva, it was Narayana who was sitting there on the bench. I looked at the Prosecuting Counsel and it was not the Counsel for the prosecution that I saw; it was Srikrishna who sat there, it was my Lover and Friend who sat there and smiled. "Now do you fear?" He said, "I am in all men and I overrule their actions and their words. My protection is still with you and you shall not fear. This case which is brought against you, leave it in my hands. It is not for you. It was not for the trial that I brought you here but for something else. The case itself is only a means for my work and nothing more."

[161]

Extracts from Letters to Disciples

Between 1926 and 1950, Sri Aurobindo never left his three-room apartment, seeing and speaking to no one but the Mother and a few personal attendants. During these years, he stayed in contact with the members of his ashram by means of correspondence. Most of his replies to their questions and comments are brief, but he also wrote longer letters in which he explained the fundamentals of his yoga. In these he occasionally referred to his own spiritual experiences, which, as he explained in the first of these extracts, were the basis of his yoga and teaching.

I began my Yoga in 1904 without a Guru; in 1908 I received important help from a Mahratta Yogi and discovered the foundations of my Sadhana; but from that time till the Mother came to India I received no spiritual help from anyone else. My Sadhana before and afterwards was not founded upon books but upon personal experiences that crowded on me from within. But in the jail I had the Gita and the Upanishads with me, practised the Yoga of the Gita and meditated with the help of the Upanishads; these were the only books from which I found guidance; the Veda which I first began to read long afterwards in Pondicherry rather confirmed what experiences I already had than was any guide to my Sadhana.

*

I am glad you are getting converted to silence, and even Nirvana is not without its uses — in my case it was the first positive spiritual experience and it made possible all the rest of the Sadhana; but as to the positive way to get these things, I don't know if your mind is quite ready to proceed with it. There are in fact several ways. My own way was by rejection of thought. "Sit down," I was told, "look and you will see that your thoughts come into you from outside. Before they enter, fling them back." I sat down and looked and saw to my astonishment that it was so; I saw and felt concretely the thought approaching as if to enter through or above the head and was able to push it back concretely before it came inside.

In three days — really in one — my mind became full of an eternal silence — it is still there. . . .

*

Now to reach Nirvana was the first radical result of my own Yoga. It threw me suddenly into a condition above and without thought, unstained by any mental or vital movement; there was no ego, no real world — only when one looked through the immobile senses, something perceived or bore upon its sheer silence a world of empty forms, materialised shadows without true substance. There was no

One or many even, only just absolutely That, featureless, relationless, sheer, indescribable, unthinkable, absolute, yet supremely real and solely real. This was no mental realisation nor something glimpsed somewhere above, — no abstraction, — it was positive, the only positive reality, — although not a spatial physical world, pervading, occupying or rather flooding and drowning this semblance of a physical world, leaving no room or space for any reality but itself, allowing nothing else to seem at all actual, positive or substantial. I cannot say there was anything exhilarating or rapturous in the experience, as it then came to me, — (the ineffable Ananda I had years afterwards), — but what it brought was an inexpressible Peace, a stupendous silence, an infinity of release and freedom. I lived in that Nirvana day and night before it began to admit other things into itself or modify itself at all, and the inner heart of experience, a constant memory of it and its power to return remained until in the end it began to disappear into a greater Superconsciousness from above. But meanwhile realisation added itself to realisation and fused itself with this original experience. At an early stage the aspect of an illusionary world gave place to one in which illusion[1] is only a small surface phenomenon with an immense Divine Reality behind it and a supreme Divine Reality above it and an intense Divine Reality in the heart of everything that had seemed at first only a cinematic shape or shadow. And this was no reimprisonment in the senses, no diminution or fall from supreme experience, it came rather as a constant heightening and widening of the Truth; it was the spirit that saw objects, not the senses, and the Peace, the Silence, the freedom in Infinity remained always with the world or all worlds only as a continuous incident in the timeless eternity of the Divine.

Now, that is the whole trouble in my approach to Mayavada. Nirvana in my liberated consciousness turned out to be the beginning of my realisation, a first step towards the complete thing, not the sole true attainment possible or even a culminating finale. It came unasked, unsought for, though quite welcome. I had no least idea about it before, no aspiration towards it, in fact my aspiration was towards just the opposite, spiritual power to help the world

[1] In fact it is not an illusion in the sense of an imposition of something baseless and unreal on the consciousness, but a misinterpretation by the conscious mind and sense and a falsifying misuse of manifested existence. [*Sri Aurobindo's note*]

and to do my work in it, yet it came — without even a "May I come in" or a "By your leave". It just happened and settled in as if for all eternity or as if it had been really there always. And then it slowly grew into something not less but greater than its first self. How then could I accept Mayavada or persuade myself to pit against the Truth imposed on me from above the logic of Shankara?

*

To return to the supramental: the supramental is simply the direct self-existent Truth-Consciousness and the direct self-effective Truth-Power. There can therefore be no question of jugglery about it. What is not true is not supramental. As for calm and silence, there is no need of the supramental to get that. One can get it even on the level of Higher Mind which is the next above the human intelligence. I got these things in 1908, 27 years ago, and I can assure you they were solid enough and marvellous enough in all conscience without any need of supramentality to make it more so. Again, "a calm that looks like action and motion" is a phenomenon of which I know nothing. A calm or silence that is what I have had — the proof is that out of an absolute silence of the mind I edited the *Bande Mataram* for 4 months and wrote 6 volumes of the *Arya*, not to speak of all the letters and messages etc. I have written since. If you say that writing is not an action or motion but only something that seems like it, a jugglery of the consciousness, — well, still out of that calm and silence I conducted a pretty strenuous political activity and have also taken my share in keeping up an Ashram which has at least an appearance to the physical senses of being solid and material! If you deny that these things are material or solid (which, of course, metaphysically you can), then you land yourself plump into Shankara's Illusionism, and there I will leave you.

You will say, however, that this is not the supramental but at most the Overmind that helped me to these non-nebulous motions and action. But the Supermind is by definition a greater dynamic activity than mind or Overmind. I have said that what is not true is not supramental; I will add that what is ineffective is not supramental. And, finally, I conclude by saying that I have not told X that I have taken complete possession of the supramental — I only admit to be very near to it. But "very near" is — well, after all — a relative phrase like all human phrases.

*

I have no intention of achieving the Supermind for myself only — I am not doing anything for myself, as I have no personal need of anything, neither of salvation (Moksha) nor supramentalisation. If I am seeking after supramentalisation, it is because it is a thing that has to be done for the earth-consciousness and if it is not done in myself, it cannot be done in others. My supramentalisation is only a key for opening the gates of the supramental to the earth-consciousness; done for its own sake, it would be perfectly futile. But it does not follow either that if or when I become supramental, everybody will become supramental. Others can so become who are ready for it, when they are ready for it — though, of course, the achievement in myself will be to them a great help towards it. It is therefore quite legitimate to have the aspiration for it — provided:

1. One does not make a too personal or egoistic affair of it turning it into a Nietzschean or other ambition to be a superman.
2. One is ready to undergo the conditions and stages needed for the achievement.
3. One is sincere and regards it as part of the seeking of the Divine and consequent culmination of the Divine Will in one and insists on no more than the fulfilment of that will whatever it may be, psychicisation, spiritualisation or supramentalisation. It should be regarded as the fulfilment of God's working in the world, not as a personal chance or achievement.

*

It is not for personal greatness that I am seeking to bring down the Supermind. I care nothing for greatness or littleness in the human sense. I am seeking to bring some principle of inner Truth, Light, Harmony, Peace into the earth-consciousness; I see it above and know what it is — I feel it ever gleaming down on my consciousness from above and I am seeking to make it possible for it to take up the whole being into its own native power, instead of the nature of man continuing to remain in half-light, half-darkness. I believe the descent of this Truth opening the way to a development of divine consciousness here to be the final sense of the earth evolution. If greater men than myself have not had this vision and this ideal before them, that is no reason why I should not follow my Truth-sense and Truth-vision. If human reason regards me as a fool for trying to do what Krishna did not try, I do not in the least care. There is no question of X or Y or anybody else in that. It is a question between the Divine and myself — whether it is the Divine Will or not, whether I am sent to bring that down or open the way for its descent or at least make it more possible or not. Let all men jeer at me if they will or all Hell fall upon me if it will for my presumption, — I go on till I conquer or perish. This is the spirit in which I seek the Supermind, no hunting for greatness for myself or others.

*

I have never said that my Yoga was something brand new in all its elements. I have called it the integral Yoga and that means that it takes up the essence and many processes of the old Yogas — its newness is in its aim, standpoint and the totality of its method. In the earlier stages which is all I deal with in books like the "Riddle" or the "Lights" or in the new book to be published there is nothing in it that distinguishes it from the old Yogas except the aim underlying its comprehensiveness, the spirit in its movements and the ultimate significance it keeps before it — also the scheme of its psychology and its working: but as that was not and could not be developed systematically or schematically in these letters, it has not been grasped by those who are not already acquainted with it by mental familiarity or some amount of practice. The detail or method of the later stages of the Yoga which go into little known or untrodden regions, I have not made public and I do not at present intend to do so.

I know very well also that there have been seemingly allied ideals and anticipations — the perfectibility of the race, certain Tantric Sadhanas, the effort after a complete physical Siddhi by certain schools of Yoga, etc., etc. I have alluded to these things myself and have put forth the view that the spiritual past of the race has been a preparation of Nature not merely for attaining the Divine beyond the world, but also for this very step forward which the evolution of the earth-consciousness has still to make. I do not therefore care in the least, — even though these ideals were, up to some extent parallel, yet not identical with mine, — whether this Yoga and its aim and method are accepted as new or not, that is in itself a trifling matter. That it should be recognised as true in itself by those who can accept or practise it and should make itself true by achievement is the one thing important; it does not matter if it is called new or a repetition or revival of the old which was forgotten. I laid emphasis on it as new in a letter to certain Sadhaks so as to explain to them that a repetition of the aim and idea of the old Yogas was not enough in my eyes, that I was putting forward a thing to be achieved that has not yet been achieved, not yet clearly visualised, even though it is the natural but still secret outcome of all the past spiritual endeavour.

It is new as compared with the old Yogas:

1. Because it aims not at a departure out of world and life into Heaven or Nirvana, but at a change of life and existence, not as something subordinate or incidental, but as a distinct and central object. If there is a descent in other Yogas, yet it is only an incident on the way or resulting from the ascent—the ascent is the real thing. Here the ascent is the first step, but it is a means for the descent. It is the descent of the new consciousness attained by the ascent that is the stamp and seal of the Sadhana. Even the Tantra and Vaishnavism end in the release from life; here the object is the divine fulfilment of life.
2. Because the object sought after is not an individual achievement of divine realisation for the sake of the individual, but something to be gained for the earth-consciousness here, a cosmic, not solely a supra-cosmic achievement. The thing to be gained also is the bringing in of a Power of Consciousness (the Supramental) not yet organised or active directly in earth-nature, even in the spiritual life, but yet to be organised and made directly active.
3. Because a method has been preconized for achieving this purpose which is as total and integral as the aim set before it, viz., the total and integral change of the consciousness and nature, taking up old methods but only as a part action and present aid to others that are distinctive. I have not found this method (as a whole) or anything like it professed or realised in the old Yogas. If I had, I should not have wasted my time in hewing out a road and in thirty years of search and inner creation when I could have hastened home safely to my goal in an easy canter over paths already blazed out, laid down, perfectly mapped, macadamised, made secure and public. Our Yoga is not a retreading of old walks, but a spiritual adventure.

[162]

Sri Aurobindo's Teaching and Method of Sadhana

Sri Aurobindo wrote this essay in August 1934 to explain his philosophy and yoga to the general public. First published anonymously in a daily newspaper (hence his use of the third person), it was later included among his collected works.

The teaching of Sri Aurobindo starts from that of the ancient sages of India that behind the appearances of the universe there is the Reality of a Being and Consciousness, a Self of all things, one and eternal. All beings are united in that One Self and Spirit but divided by a certain separativity of consciousness, an ignorance of their true Self and Reality in the mind, life and body. It is possible by a certain psychological discipline to remove this veil of separative consciousness and become aware of the true Self, the Divinity within us and all.

Sri Aurobindo's teaching states that this One Being and Consciousness is involved here in Matter. Evolution is the method by which it liberates itself; consciousness appears in what seems to be inconscient, and once having appeared is self-impelled to grow higher and higher and at the same time to enlarge and develop towards a greater and greater perfection. Life is the first step of this release of consciousness; mind is the second; but the evolution does not finish with mind, it awaits a release into something greater, a consciousness which is spiritual and supramental. The next step of the evolution must be towards the development of Supermind and Spirit as the dominant power in the conscious being. For only then will the involved Divinity in things release itself entirely and it become possible for life to manifest perfection.

But while the former steps in evolution were taken by Nature without a conscious will in the plant and animal life, in man Nature becomes able to evolve by a conscious will in the instrument. It is not, however, by the mental will in man that this can be wholly done, for the mind goes only to a certain point and after that can only move in a circle. A conversion has to be made, a turning of the consciousness by which mind has to change into the higher principle. This method is to be found through the ancient psychological discipline and practice of Yoga. In the past, it has been attempted by a drawing away from the world and a disappearance into the height of the Self or Spirit. Sri Aurobindo teaches that a descent of the higher principle is possible which will not merely release the spiritual Self out of the world, but release it in the world, replace the mind's ignorance or its very limited knowledge by a supramental Truth-Consciousness which will be a sufficient instrument of the inner Self and make it possible for the human being to find himself dynamically as well as inwardly and grow out of his still animal humanity into a diviner race. The psychological discipline of Yoga can be used to that end by opening all the parts of the being to a conversion or transformation through the descent and working of the higher still concealed supramental principle.

This, however, cannot be done at once or in a short time or by any rapid or miraculous transformation. Many steps have to be taken by the seeker before the supramental descent is possible. Man lives mostly in his surface mind, life and body, but there is an inner being within him with greater possibilities to which he has to awake — for it is only a very restricted influence from it that he receives now and that pushes him to a constant pursuit of a greater beauty, harmony, power and knowledge. The first process of Yoga is therefore to open the ranges of this inner being and to live from there outward, governing his outward life by an inner light and force. In doing so he discovers in himself his true soul which is not this outer mixture of mental, vital and physical elements but something of the Reality behind them, a spark from the one Divine Fire. He has to learn to live in his soul and purify and orientate by its drive towards the Truth the rest of the nature. There can follow afterwards an opening upward and descent of a higher principle of the Being. But even then it is not at once the full supramental Light and Force. For there are several ranges of consciousness between the ordinary human mind and the supramental Truth-Consciousness. These intervening ranges have to be opened up and their power brought down into the mind, life and body. Only afterwards can the full power of the Truth-Consciousness work in the nature. The process of this self-discipline or Sadhana is therefore long and difficult, but even a little of it is so much gained because it makes the ultimate release and perfection more possible.

There are many things belonging to older systems that are necessary on the way — an opening of the mind to a greater wideness and to the sense of the Self and the Infinite, an emergence into what has been called the cosmic consciousness, mastery over the desires and passions; an outward asceticism is not essential, but the conquest of desire and attachment and a control over the body and its needs, greeds and instincts are indispensable. There is a combination of the principles of the old systems, the way of knowledge through the mind's discernment between Reality and the appearance, the heart's way of devotion, love and surrender and the way of works turning the will away from motives of self-interest to the Truth and the service of a greater Reality than the ego. For the whole being has to be trained so that it can respond and be transformed when it is possible for that greater Light and Force to work in the nature.

In this discipline, the inspiration of the Master, and in the difficult stages his control and his presence are indispensable — for it would be impossible otherwise to go through it without much stumbling and error which would prevent all chance of success. The Master is one who has risen to a higher consciousness and being and he is often regarded as its manifestation or representative. He not only helps by his teaching and still more by his influence and example but by a power to communicate his own experience to others.

This is Sri Aurobindo's teaching and method of practice. It is not his object to develop any one religion or to amalgamate the older religions or to found any new religion — for any of these things would lead away from his central purpose. The one aim of his Yoga is an inner self-development by which each one who follows it can in time discover the One Self in all and evolve a higher consciousness than the mental, a spiritual and supramental consciousness which will transform and divinise human nature.

[163]

From *The Life Divine*

Sri Aurobindo's most important prose writing is *The Life Divine*, a thousand-page work of spiritual philosophy, whose principal purpose is to explain the relationship between the Absolute Brahman and the manifested universe. In contrast to the illusionistic *advaita* of Shankara, Aurobindo's "realistic *advaita*" accepts the existence and value of the world. First published chapter-by-chapter in a monthly journal between 1914 and 1920, *The Life Divine* was revised and enlarged before being published as a book in 1939–40.

The possibility of a cosmic consciousness in humanity is coming slowly to be admitted in modern Psychology, like the possibility of more elastic instruments of knowledge, although still classified, even when its value and power are admitted, as a hallucination. In the psychology of the East it has always been recognised as a reality and the aim of our subjective progress. The essence of the passage over to this goal is the exceeding of the limits imposed on us by the ego-sense and at least a partaking, at most an identification with the self-knowledge which broods secret in all life and in all that seems to us inanimate. Entering into that Consciousness, we may continue to dwell, like It, upon universal existence. Then we become aware — for all our terms of consciousness and even our sensational experience begin to change, — of Matter as one existence and of bodies as its formations in which the one existence separates itself physically in the single body from itself in all others and again by physical means establishes communication between these multitudinous points of its being. Mind we experience similarly, and Life also, as the same existence one in its multiplicity, separating and reuniting itself in each domain by means appropriate to that movement. And, if we choose, we can proceed farther and, after passing through many linking stages, become aware of a supermind whose universal operation is the key to all lesser activities. Nor do we become merely conscious of this cosmic existence, but likewise conscious in it, receiving it in sensation, but also entering into it in awareness. In it we live as we lived before in the ego-sense, active, more and more in contact, even unified more and more with other minds, other lives, other bodies than the organism we call ourselves, producing effects not only on our own moral and mental being and on the subjective being of others, but even on the physical world and its events by means nearer to the divine than those possible to our egoistic capacity.

Real then to the man who has had contact with it or lives in it, is this cosmic consciousness, with a greater than the physical reality; real in itself, real in its effects and works. And as it is thus real to the world which is its own total expression, so is the world real to it; but not as an independent existence. For in that higher and less hampered experience we perceive that consciousness and being are not different from each other, but all being is a supreme consciousness, all consciousness is self-existence, eternal in itself, real in its works and neither a dream nor an evolution. The world is real precisely because it exists only in consciousness; for it is a Conscious Energy one with Being that creates it. It is the existence of material form in its own right apart from the self-illumined energy which assumes the form, that would be a contradiction of the truth of things, a phantasmagoria, a nightmare, an impossible falsehood.

But this conscious Being which is the truth of the infinite supermind, is more than the universe and lives independently in Its own inexpressible infinity as well as in the cosmic harmonies. World lives by That; That does not live by the world. And as we can enter into the cosmic consciousness and be one with all cosmic existence, so we can enter into the world-transcending consciousness and become superior to all cosmic existence. And then arises the question which first occurred to us, whether this transcendence is necessarily also a rejection. What relation has this universe to the Beyond? . . .

*

It has been held that ecstasy is a lower and transient passage, the peace of the Supreme is the supreme realisation, the consummate abiding experience. This may be true on the spiritual-mind plane: there the first ecstasy felt is indeed a spiritual rapture, but it can be and is very usually mingled with a supreme happiness of the vital parts taken up by the Spirit; there is an exaltation, exultation, excitement, a highest intensity of the joy of the heart and the pure inner soul-sensation that can be a splendid passage or an uplifting force but is not the ultimate permanent foundation. But in the highest ascents of the spiritual bliss there is not this vehement exaltation and excitement; there is instead an illimitable intensity of participation in an eternal ecstasy which is founded on the eternal Existence and therefore on a beatific tranquillity of eternal peace. Peace and ecstasy cease to be different and become one. The Supermind, reconciling and fusing all differences as well as all contradictions, brings out this unity; a wide calm and a deep delight of all-existence are among its first steps of self-realisation, but this calm and this delight rise together, as one state, into an increasing intensity and culminate in the eternal ecstasy, the bliss that is the Infinite. In the gnostic consciousness at any stage there would be always in some degree this fundamental and spiritual conscious delight of existence in the whole depth of the being; but also all the movements of Nature would be pervaded by it, and all the actions and reactions of the life and the body: none could escape the law of the Ananda. Even before the gnostic change there can be a beginning of this fundamental ecstasy of being translated into a manifold beauty and delight. In the mind, it translates into a calm of intense delight of spiritual perception and vision and knowledge, in the heart into a wide or deep or passionate delight of universal union and love and sympathy and the joy of beings and the joy of things. In the will and vital parts it is felt as the energy of delight of a divine life-power in action or a beatitude of the senses perceiving and meeting the One everywhere, perceiving as their normal aesthesis of things a universal beauty and a secret harmony of creation of which our mind can catch only imperfect glimpses or a rare supernormal sense. In the body it reveals itself as an ecstasy pouring into it from the heights of the Spirit and the peace and bliss of a pure and spiritualised physical existence. A universal beauty and glory of being begins to manifest; all objects reveal hidden lines, vibrations, powers, harmonic significances concealed from the normal mind and the physical sense. In the universal phenomenon is revealed the eternal Ananda.

*

The hard logical and intellectual notion of truth as a single idea which all must accept, one idea or system of ideas defeating all other ideas or systems, or a single limited fact or single formula of facts which all must recognise, is an illegitimate transference from the limited truth of the physical field to the much more complex and plastic field of life and mind and spirit.

This transference has been responsible for much harm; it brings into thought narrowness, limitation, an intolerance of the necessary variation and multiplicity of viewpoints without which there can be no totality of truth-finding, and by the narrowness and limitation much obstinacy in error. It reduces philosophy to an endless maze of sterile disputes; religion has been invaded by this misprision and infected with credal dogmatism, bigotry and intolerance. The truth of the spirit is a truth of being and consciousness and not a truth of thought: mental ideas can only represent or formulate some facet, some mind-translated principle or power of it or enumerate its aspects, but to know it one has to grow into it and be it; without that growing and being there can be no true spiritual knowledge. The fundamental truth of spiritual experience is one, its consciousness is one, everywhere it follows the same general lines and tendencies of awakening and growth into spiritual being; for these are the imperatives of the spiritual consciousness. But also there are, based on those imperatives, numberless possibilities of variation of experience and expression: the centralisation and harmonisation of these possibles, but also the intensive sole following out of any line of experience are both of them necessary movements of the emerging spiritual Conscious-Force within us. Moreover, the accommodation of mind and life to the spiritual truth, its expression in them, must vary with the mentality of the seeker so long as he has not risen above all need of such accommodation or such limiting expression. It is this mental and vital element which has created the oppositions that still divide spiritual seekers or enter into their differing affirmations of the truth that they experience. This difference and variation is needed for the freedom of spiritual search and spiritual growth: to overpass differences is quite possible, but that is most easily done in pure experience; in mental formulation the difference must remain until one can exceed mind altogether and in a highest consciousness integralise, unify and harmonise the many-sided truth of the Spirit.

[164]

From *Talks with Sri Aurobindo*

After an accident in 1938, Sri Aurobindo permitted a few of his disciples to attend on him during his convalescence. With them he had wide-ranging conversations, mostly about what was going on in the world, but sometimes also about his inner experiences.

Question: What happens when the human consciousness is replaced by the divine consciousness?

One feels a perpetual calm, perpetual strength, one is aware of infinity and lives not only in infinity but also in eternity. One feels immortality and does not care about the death of the body. And then one has the consciousness of the One in all. Everything becomes the manifestation of the Brahman. For instance, as I look round this room, I see everything as the Brahman. No, it is not mere thinking, it is a concrete experience. Even the wall, the books are the Brahman. I see you no more as Dr. Manilal but as the Divine living in the Divine. It is a wonderful experience.

[165]

Four Sonnets

Sri Aurobindo began to write poetry as a schoolboy in England, and continued for the rest of his life. During the 1930s he wrote a series of sonnets in which he explored spiritual themes, often with reference to his own experience.

Nirvana

All is abolished but the mute Alone.
The mind from thought released, the heart from grief
Grow inexistent now beyond belief;
There is no I, no Nature, known-unknown.
The city, a shadow picture without tone,
Floats, quivers unreal; forms without relief
Flow, a cinema's vacant shapes; like a reef
Foundering in shoreless gulfs the world is done.

Only the illimitable Permanent
Is here. A Peace stupendous, featureless, still,
Replaces all, — what once was I, in It
A silent unnamed emptiness content
Either to fade in the Unknowable
Or thrill with the luminous seas of the Infinite.

Transformation

My breath runs in a subtle rhythmic stream;
It fills my members with a might divine:
I have drunk the Infinite like a giant's wine.
Time is my drama or my pageant dream.
Now are my illumined cells joy's flaming scheme
And changed my thrilled and branching nerves to fine
Channels of rapture opal and hyaline
For the influx of the Unknown and the Supreme.

I am no more a vassal of the flesh,
A slave to Nature and her leaden rule;

I am caught no more in the senses' narrow mesh.
My soul unhorizoned widens to measureless sight,
My body is God's happy living tool,
My spirit a vast sun of deathless light.

The Indwelling Universal

I contain the wide world in my soul's embrace:
In me Arcturus and Belphegor burn.
To whatsoever living form I turn
I see my own body with another face.

All eyes that look on me are my sole eyes;
The one heart that beats within all breasts is mine.
The world's happiness flows through me like wine,
Its million sorrows are my agonies.

Yet all its acts are only waves that pass
Upon my surface; inly for ever still,
Unborn I sit, timeless, intangible;
All things are shadows in my tranquil glass.

My vast transcendence holds the cosmic whirl;
I am hid in it as in the sea a pearl.

Bliss of Identity

All Nature is taught in radiant ways to move,
All beings are in myself embraced.
O fiery boundless Heart of joy and love,
How art thou beating in a mortal's breast!

It is Thy rapture flaming through my nerves
And all my cells and atoms thrill with Thee;
My body Thy vessel is and only serves
As a living wine-cup of Thy ecstasy.

I am a centre of Thy golden light
And I its vast and vague circumference;
Thou art my soul great, luminous and white
And Thine my mind and will and glowing sense.

Thy spirit's infinite breath I feel in me;
My life is a throb of Thy eternity.

FURTHER READING

Source Materials

Sri Aurobindo, *Karmayogin: Political Writings and Speeches 1909–1910*. Pondicherry: Sri Aurobindo Ashram, 1997.

Sri Aurobindo, *The Life Divine*. Pondicherry: Sri Aurobindo Ashram, 1972.

Sri Aurobindo, *On Himself*. Pondicherry: Sri Aurobindo Ashram, 1972.

Sri Aurobindo, *Sonnets*. Pondicherry, India: Sri Aurobindo Ashram, 1980.

Nirodbaran, *Talks with Sri Aurobindo*. Two volumes. Pondicherry: Sri Aurobindo Ashram, 2001.

Other Sources

Peter Heehs, *The Essential Writings of Sri Aurobindo*. Delhi: Oxford University Press, 1997.

Stephen H. Phillips, *Aurobindo's Philosophy of Brahman*. Leiden: E. J. Brill, 1986.

Website of Sri Aurobindo Ashram <www.sriaurobindoashram.org>

The Integral Yoga of Sri Aurobindo and the Mother <www.miraura.org>

Sources of Texts and Translations

160 *Karmayogin* 5–7

161 *On Himself* 68, 82–83, 101–02, 162–63, 144–45, 143–44, 107–09

162 *On Himself* 95–97

163 *Life Divine* 21–22, 990–91, 887–88

164 *Talks* 19

165 *Sonnets* 3, 1, 19, 20

RAMANA MAHARSHI

Many spiritual teachers of nineteenth- and twentieth-century India expressed themselves in ways that declare their modernity. Others seem to belong to no particular era. When one reads the talks of Ramana Maharshi, one can easily forget that they were spoken by a particular individual: a man born in southern Tamil Nadu in a family of shaiva brahmins at the end of the nineteenth century. They seem rather to come from a timeless spiritual consciousness, which expresses itself here in the Sanskrit of the *upaniṣad*s and there in contemporary Tamil or Telugu.

Ramana Maharshi, or Venkataraman Ayyar as he originally was known, was born in 1879. His father died when he was twelve, and he and his family went to Madurai, where he continued his education. Ventakaraman found school-work uninteresting, but he did enjoy reading the hagiography that tells the stories of Appar, Sundarar and other shaiva saints. He also read the Bible (he was attending an American mission school) and bits of the siddha-inspired poetry of Tayumanava, as well as the *Tēvāram*; nevertheless he showed no interest in or special aptitude for the spiritual life. Then, when he was sixteen, he had an unexpected experience. One day, for no particular reason, he became convinced he was going to die. Instead of abandoning himself to his fear, he lay down and considered the fact of death. That which died, he realised, was the body, but the body was not the "I". Continuing his self-inquiry, he saw that the "I", which did not die, was the one transcendent Spirit. This self-realisation, which came to him as a direct intuitive perception and not as the result of logical analysis, never left him for the rest of his life.

After his experience, Venkataraman's interest in school and family life lapsed, and he spent most of his time in solitary contemplation. Finally he resolved to leave his home and go to Arunachala, a sacred hill in the northern part of Tamil Nadu. Slipping out one afternoon, he travelled by train and by foot to Tiruvannamalai, the town that lies in the shadow of Arunachala. Taking up residence in the ancient Shiva temple of Tiruvannamalai, he became absorbed in contemplation of the deathless Spirit which he was. He took no interest in his body, which soon was covered with insect-bites. He ate only a part of the food that people brought for him to eat, and, being disinclined to speak, said nothing.

Venkataraman, soon shortened to Ramana, spent next fifty-four years living on or near Arunachala, which he regarded as a manifestation of Shiva. Soon he attracted the attention of curiosity-seekers as well as a few serious devotees. One of them declared that Ramana was a *mahārṣi* or "great sage", who, unhelped, had realised the truths of Vedanta. Ramana Maharshi had in fact no knowledge of Vedanta or any other system. He later said he was lucky that he never made a study of philosophy. If he had done so, he "would probably be nowhere". Instead his inherent tendencies caused him "directly to enquire 'Who am I?' ", and by that means he attained self-realisation (*Talks* 377).

After living for many years in shrines or in caves, the Maharshi settled at a place at the foot of Arunachala where his mother, who had joined him, had been buried. An ashram gradually developed here and, as he became well known in India and abroad, hundreds of aspirants came to see him. He always remained accessible for part of the day to his disciples as well as visitors. Though he denied he was anyone's *guru*, he took seriously the spiritual and even the material welfare of those who came to him.

In 1949, the Maharshi developed a tumour on his arm. After permitting an unsuccessful operation, he told those concerned about his health: "There is no cause for alarm. The body itself is a disease. Let it have its natural end" (Osborne 1970: 180). He died peacefully in April 1950.

Ramana Maharshi taught mainly by silence. People would come to him with questions in their heads or anguish in their hearts. After sitting before him, they would feel their questions vanish and their anguish disappear. When he did reply, his method was not to give a "satisfactory" answer but to undermine the question, forcing his visitors to ask the only one that mattered: "Who am I?" During his later years, his talks became more extensive, and some were noted down by disciples and published. These talks form the bulk of his teachings. He also wrote a few short works in Tamil prose and poetry, along with the occasional poem in Telugu or Malayalam. Despite his lack of interest in philosophy and scripture, he sometimes went through books that others brought him, acquiring in this way a good knowledge of Indian spiritual literature. Prompted by disciples, he made a number of translations of Sanskrit texts into Tamil or, more rarely, Telugu and Malayalam. His *Complete Works*, which is composed of these writings and translations, comprises only some three hundred pages.

[166]

The Awakening

This is the Maharshi's own account of his first awakening at the age of sixteen. Translated from the Tamil.

It was about six weeks before I left Madura for good that the great change in my life took place. It was quite sudden. I was sitting alone in a room on the first floor of my uncle's house. I seldom had any sickness, and on that day there was nothing wrong with my health, but a sudden violent fear of death overtook me. There was nothing in my state of health to account for it, and I did not try to account for it or to find out whether there was any reason for the fear. I just felt "I am going to die" and began thinking what to do about it. It did not occur to me to consult a doctor, or my elders or friends; I felt that I had to solve the problem myself, there and then.

The shock of the fear of death drove my mind inwards and I said to myself mentally, without actually framing the words: "Now death has come; what does it mean, What is it that is dying? The body dies." And I at once dramatized the occurrence of death. I lay with my limbs stretched out stiff as though *rigor mortis* had set in and imitated a corpse so as to give greater reality to the enquiry. I held my breath and kept my lips tightly closed so that no sound could escape, so that neither the word "I" nor any other word could be uttered. "Well then", I said to myself, "this body is dead. It will be carried stiff to the burning ground and there burnt and reduced to ashes. But with the death of this body am I dead? Is the body I? It is silent and inert but I feel the full force of my personality and even the voice of the "I" within me, apart from it. So I am Spirit transcending the body. The body dies but the Spirit that transcends it cannot be touched by death. That means I am the deathless Spirit." All this was not dull thought; it flashed through me vividly as living truth which I perceived directly, almost without thought-process. "I" was something very real, the only real thing about my present state, and all the conscious activity connected with my body was centered on that "I". From that moment onwards the "I" or Self focussed attention on itself by a powerful fascination. Fear of death had vanished once and for all. Absorption in the Self continued unbroken from that time on.

[167]

Who Am I?

The Maharshi's first works are transcripts of verbal exchanges he had with people who came to him during his early years in Tiruvannamalai. *Nān Yār?* ("Who Am I"), a series of twenty-eight questions and answers, dates from the period around 1902, and remains one of his best-known works. In his replies, he presented the method of self-enquiry, which is the basis of his spiritual teaching. Here seven of the twenty-eight exchanges are reproduced. Translated from the Tamil.

Question: Who am I?

The gross body which is composed of the seven humours (*dhātus*),

I am not; the five cognitive sense-organs, viz. the senses of hearing, touch, sight, taste, and smell, which apprehend their respective objects, i.e. sound, touch, colour, taste, and odour, I am not; the five conative sense-organs, viz. the organs of speech, locomotion, grasping, excretion, and procreation, which have as their respective functions speaking, moving, grasping, excreting and enjoying, I am not; the five vital airs, *prāṇa*, etc., which perform respectively the five functions of in-breathing, etc., I am not; even the mind which thinks, I am not; the nescience too, which is endowed only with the residual impressions of objects, and in which there are no objects and no functionings, I am not.

Q: If I am none of these, then who am I?

After negating all of the above-mentioned as "not this", (*neti-neti*), that Awareness which alone remains—that I am. . . .

Q: What is the nature of the mind?

What is called "mind" is a wondrous power residing in the Self. It causes all thoughts to arise. Apart from thoughts, there is no such thing as mind. Therefore, thought is the nature of mind. Apart from thoughts, there is no independent entity called the world. In deep sleep there are no thoughts, and there is no world. In the states of waking and dream, there are thoughts, and there is a world also. Just as the spider emits the thread [of the web] out of itself and again withdraws it into itself, likewise the mind projects the world out of itself and again resolves it into itself. When the mind comes out of the Self, the world appears. Therefore, when the world appears [to be real], the Self does not appear; and when the Self appears [shines] the world does not appear. When one persistently inquires into the nature of the mind, the mind will end leaving the Self [as the residue]. What is referred to as the Self is the *Atman.* The mind always exists only in dependence on something gross; it cannot stay alone. It is the mind that is called the subtle body or the soul (*Jīva*).

Q: What is the path of inquiry for understanding the nature of the mind?

That which rises as "I" in this body is the mind. If one inquires as to where in the body the thought "I" rises first, one would discover that it rises in the heart. That is the place of the mind's origin. Even if one thinks constantly "I" "I", one will be led to the place. Of all the thoughts that arise in the mind, the "I"-thought is the first. It is only after the rise of this that the other thoughts arise. It is after the appearance of the first personal pronoun that the second and third personal pronouns appear; without the first personal pronoun there will not be the second and third.

Q: How will the mind become quiescent?

By the inquiry "Who am I?". The thought "Who am I?" will destroy all other thoughts, and, like the stick used for stirring the burning pyre, it will itself in the end get destroyed. Then, there will arise Self-realization. . . .

Q: What is the nature of the Self?

What exists in truth is the Self alone. The world, the individual soul, and God are appearances in it, like silver in mother-of-pearl; these three appear at the same time, and disappear at the same time.

The Self is that where there is absolutely no "I"-thought. That is called "Silence". The Self itself is the world; the Self itself is "I"; the Self itself is God; all is Siva, the Self. . . .

Q: What is happiness?

Happiness is the very nature of Self; happiness and the Self are not different. There is no happiness in any object of the world. We imagine through our ignorance that we derive happiness from objects. When the mind goes out, it experiences misery. In truth, when its desires are fulfilled, it returns to its own place and enjoys the happiness that is the Self. Similarly, in the states of sleep, *samādhi* and fainting, and when the object desired is obtained or the object disliked is removed, the mind becomes inward-turned and enjoys pure Self-Happiness. Thus the mind moves without rest, alternately going out of the Self and returning to it. Under the tree the shade is pleasant; out in the open the heat is scorching. A person who has been going about in the sun feels cool when he reaches the shade. Someone who keeps on going from the shade into the sun and then back into the shade is a fool. A wise man stays permanently in the shade. Similarly, the mind of the one who knows the truth does not leave *Brahman*. The mind of the ignorant, on the contrary, revolves in the world, feeling miserable, and for a little time returns to *Brahman* to experience happiness. In fact, what is called the world is only thought. When the world disappears, i.e. when there is no thought, the mind experiences happiness; and when the world appears, it goes through misery.

[168]

From *Spiritual Instruction*

Upadeśa Mañjari or "Spiritual Instruction" consists of answers by the Maharshi to questions posed by various devotees. They were noted down by a disciple, who later expanded them and arranged them in four sections. The work was published in 1934 after it had been seen and approved of by the Maharshi. The following extracts are from the end of the first and the beginning of the second sections. Translated from the Tamil.

Q: What is the mark of the ego?

The individual soul of the form of "I" is the ego. The Self which is of the nature of intelligence (*cit*) has no sense of "I". Nor does the insentient body possess a sense of "I". The mysterious appearance of a delusive ego between the intelligent and the insentient being the root cause of all these troubles, upon its destruction by whatever means, that which really exists will be seen as it is. This is called liberation (*mokṣa*).

Q: What is the method of practice?

As the Self of a person who tries to attain Self-realization is not different from him and as there is nothing other than or superior to him to be attained by him, Self-realization being only the realization of one's own nature, the seeker of liberation realizes, without doubts or misconceptions, his real nature by distinguishing the eternal from the transient, and never swerves from his natural state. This is known as the practice of knowledge. This is the enquiry leading to Self-realization.

[169]

From *Maharshi's Gospel*

These extracts are from a group of translated questions and answers, which were published under the editorial title *Maharshi's Gospel* in 1939.

Q: How can I attain Self-realization?

Realization is nothing to be gained afresh, it is already there. All that is necessary is to get rid of the thought "I have not realized".

Stillness or Peace is Realization. There is no moment when the Self is not. So long as there is doubt or the feeling of non-Realization, the attempt should be made to rid oneself of these thoughts. They are due to the identification of the Self with the not-Self. When the not-Self disappears, the Self alone remains. To make room, it is enough that the cramping be removed; room is not brought in from elsewhere.

Q: Since Realization is not possible without vāsanā-kṣaya, *how am I to realize that state in which the* vāsanās *are effectively destroyed?*

You are in that state now!

Q: Does it mean that by holding on to the Self, the vāsanās *should be destroyed as and when they emerge?*

They will themselves be destroyed if you remain as you are.

Q: How shall I reach the Self?

There is no reaching the Self. If the Self were to be reached, it would mean that the Self is not here and now but that it is yet to be obtained. What is got afresh will also be lost. So it will be impermanent. What is not permanent is not worth striving for. So I say the Self is not reached. You *are* the Self; you are already That.

The fact is, you are ignorant of your blissful state. Ignorance supervenes and draws a veil over the pure Self which is Bliss. Attempts are directed only to remove this veil of ignorance which is merely wrong knowledge. The wrong knowledge is the false identification of the Self with the body, mind etc. This false identification must go, and then the Self alone remains.

Therefore Realization is for everyone; Realization makes no difference between the aspirants. This very doubt, whether you can realize, and the notion "I-have-not-realized" are themselves the obstacles. Be free from these obstacles also.

Q: What is the use of samādhi *and does thought subsist then?*

Samādhi alone can reveal the Truth. Thoughts cast a veil over Reality, and so It is not realized as such in states other than *samādhi.*

In *samādhi* there is only the feeling "I AM" and no thoughts. The experience "I AM" is being still.

> *Q: How can I repeat the experience of* samādhi *or the stillness that I obtain here?*

Your present experience is due to the influence of the atmosphere in which you find yourself. Can you have it outside this atmosphere? The experience is spasmodic. Until it becomes permanent, practice is necessary.

> *Q: One has at times vivid flashes of a consciousness whose centre is* outside *the* normal self, *and which seems to be all-inclusive. Without concerning ourselves with philosophical concepts, how would Bhagavan advise me to work towards* getting, retaining *and* extending *those rare flashes? Does* abhyāsa *in such experience involve* retirement?

Outside! For whom is the inside or outside? These can exist only so long as there are the subject and object. For whom are these two again? On investigation you will find that they resolve into the subject only. See who is the subject; and this inquiry leads you to pure Consciousness beyond the subject.

The *normal self* is the mind. This mind is with limitations. But pure Consciousness is beyond limitations, and is reached by investigation as above outlined.

Getting: The Self is always there. You have only to remove the veil obstructing the revelation of the Self.

Retaining: Once you realize the Self, it becomes your direct and immediate experience. It is never lost.

Extending: There is no extending of the Self, for it is as ever, without contraction or expansion.

Retirement: Abiding in the Self is solitude. Because there is nothing alien to the Self. Retirement must be from some one place or state to another. There is neither the one nor the other apart from the Self. *All* being the Self, retirement is impossible and inconceivable.

Abhyāsa is only the prevention of disturbance to the inherent peace. You are always in your natural State whether you do *abhyāsa* or not.... To remain as you are, without question or doubt, is your natural State.

> *Q: On realizing* samādhi, *does not one obtain* siddhis *also?*

In order to display *siddhis*, there must be others to recognize them. That means, there is no *jñāna* in the one who displays them. Therefore, *siddhis* are not worth a thought; *jñāna* alone is to be aimed at and gained.

Q: Does my Realization help others?

Yes, and it is the best help that you can possibly render to others. Those who have discovered great truths have done so in the still depths of the Self. But really there are no "others" to be helped. For the Realized Being sees only the Self, just as the goldsmith sees only the gold while valuing it in various jewels made of gold. When you identify yourself with the body, name and form are there. But when you transcend the body-consciousness, the "others" also disappear. The Realized One does not see the world as different from himself.

Q: Would it not be better if the saints mix with others?

There are no "others" to mix with. The Self is the only Reality.

Q: Should I not try to help the suffering world?

The Power that created you has created the world as well. If it can take care of you, it can similarly take care of the world also. . . . If God has created the world, it is His business to look after it, not yours.

Q: Is it not our duty to be patriots?

Your duty is *to be*, and not to be this or that. "I AM THAT I AM" sums up the whole truth: the method is summarized in "*be still.*"

And what does Stillness mean? It means "Destroy yourself"; because, every name and form is the cause of trouble. "I-I" is the Self. "I am this" is the ego. When the "I" is kept up as the "I" only, it is the Self. When it flies off at a tangent and says "I am this or that, I am such and such", it is the ego.

Q: Who then is God?

The Self is God. "I AM" is God. If God be apart from the Self, He must be a Selfless God, which is absurd. All that is required to realize the Self is to *be still*. What can be easier than that? Hence *ātma-vidyā* is the easiest to attain.

*

Q: How can I get peace? I do not seem to obtain it through vicāra.

Peace is your natural state. It is the mind that obstructs the natural state. Your *vicāra* has been made only in the mind. Investigate what the mind is, and it will disappear. There is no such thing as mind apart from thought. Nevertheless, because of the emergence of thought, you surmise something from which it starts and term that the mind. When you probe to see what it is, you find there is really no such thing as mind. When the mind has thus vanished, you realize eternal Peace.

Q: Through poetry, music, japa, bhajana, *the sight of beautiful landscapes, reading the lines of spiritual verses, etc., one experiences sometimes a true sense of all-unity. Is that feeling of deep blissful quiet (wherein the personal self has no place) the same as the entering into the Heart of which Bhagavan speaks? Will practice thereof lead to a deeper* samādhi *and so ultimately to a full vision of the Real?*

There is happiness when agreeable things are presented to the mind. It is the happiness inherent to the Self, and there is no other happiness. And it is not alien and afar. You are diving into the Self on those occasions which you consider pleasurable; that diving results in self-existent bliss. But the association of ideas is responsible for foisting that bliss on other things or occurrences while, in fact, that bliss is within you. On these occasions you are plunging into the Self, though unconsciously. If you do so consciously, with the conviction that comes of the experience that you are identical with the happiness which is verily the Self, the one Reality, you call it Realization. I want you to dive consciously into the Self, i.e., into the Heart.

*

Q: To me sleep is a mere blankness.

That is so, because your waking state is a mere effervescence of the restless mind.

Q: What I mean by blankness is that I am hardly aware of anything in my sleep; it is for me the same as nonexistence.

But you did exist during sleep.

Q: If I did, I was not aware of it.

You do not mean to say in all seriousness you ceased to exist during your sleep! [*Laughing*] If you went to sleep as Mr. X, did you get up from it as Mr. Y?

Q: I know my identity, perhaps, by an act of memory.

Granting that, how is it possible unless there is a continuity of awareness?

Q: But I was unaware of that awareness.

No. Who says you are unaware in sleep? It is your mind. But there was no mind in your sleep? Of what value is the testimony of the mind about your existence or experience during sleep? Seeking the testimony of the mind to disprove your existence or awareness during sleep is just like calling your son's evidence to disprove your birth!

Do you remember, I told you once previously that existence and awareness are not two different things but one and the same? Well, if for any reason you feel constrained to admit the fact that you existed in sleep be sure you were also aware of that existence.

What you were really unaware of in sleep is your bodily existence. You are confounding this bodily awareness with the true Awareness of the Self which is eternal. *Prajñāna*, which is the source of "I-am"-ness, ever subsists unaffected by the three transitory states of the mind, thus enabling you to retain your identity unimpaired.

Prajñāna is also beyond the three states, because it can subsist without them and in spite of them.

It is that Reality that you should seek during your so-called waking state by tracing the *aham-vṛtti* to its source. Intense practice in this inquiry will reveal that the mind and its three states are unreal and that you are the eternal, infinite consciousness of Pure Being, the Self or the Heart.

[170]

From *Talks with Sri Ramana Maharshi*

During his later years in Tiruvannamalai, the Maharshi settled down at the foot of Arunachala, where an ashram gradually grew around him. People from all over India and around the world came to see him. At certain times during the day, he received ashram-members and visitors in a large hall. As always, silence and not speech was his preferred means of communication, but he did answer all sorts of questions that people put to him. Between 1935 and 1939, Munagala S. Venkataramiah noted down more than six hundred of the Maharshi's talks, often directly in English translation. These were published in English in 1955 as *Talks with Sri Ramana Maharshi*, a book that remains perhaps the best introduction to his teaching.

> *Q: I once before told Sri Bhagavan how I had a vision of Siva about the time of my conversion to Hinduism. A similar experience recurred to me at Courtallam. These visions are momentary. But they are blissful. I want to know how they might be made permanent and continuous. Without Siva there is no life in what I see around me. I am so happy to think of him. Please tell me how his vision may be everlasting to me.*

You speak of a vision of Siva. Vision is always of an object. That implies the existence of a subject. The value of the vision is the same as that of the seer. (That is to say, the nature of the vision is on the same plane as that of the seer.) Appearance implies disappearance also. Whatever appears must also disappear. A vision can never be eternal. But Siva is eternal. . . .

The vision implies the seer. The seer cannot deny the existence of the Self. There is no moment when the Self as Consciousness does not exist; nor can the seer remain apart from Consciousness. This Consciousness is the eternal Being and the only Being. The seer cannot see himself. Does he deny his existence because he cannot see himself with the eyes as *pratyakṣa* [in vision]? No! So, *pratyakṣa* does not mean seeing, but BE-ing.

"TO BE" is to realise. Hence I AM THAT I AM. I AM is Siva. Nothing else can be without Him. Everything has its being in Siva and because of Siva.

Therefore enquire "Who am I?". Sink deep within and abide as the Self. That is Siva as BE-ing. Do not expect to have visions of Him repeated. What is the difference between the objects you see and Siva? He is both the subject and the object. You cannot be without Siva. Siva is always realised here and now. If you think you have not realised Him it is wrong. This is the obstacle for realising Siva. Give up that thought also and realisation is there.

Q: Yes. But how shall I effect it as quickly as possible?

This is the obstacle for realisation. Can there be the individual without Siva? Even now He is you. There is no question of time. If there be a moment of non-realisation, the question of realisation can arise. But as it is you cannot be without Him. He is already realised, ever realised and never non-realised.

Surrender to Him and abide by His will whether he appears or vanishes; await His pleasure. If you ask Him to do as you please, it is not surrender but command to Him. You cannot have Him obey you and yet think that you have surrendered. He knows what is best and when and how to do it. Leave everything entirely to Him. His is the burden: you have no longer any cares. All your cares are His. Such is surrender. This is *bhakti*.

Or, enquire to whom these questions arise. Dive deep in the Heart and remain as the Self. One of these two ways is open to the aspirant.

[*Sri Bhagavan also added*:] There is no being who is not conscious and therefore who is not Siva. Not only is he Siva but also all else of which he is aware or not aware. Yet he thinks in sheer ignorance that he sees the universe in diverse forms. But if he sees his Self he is not aware of his separateness from the universe; in fact his individuality and the other entities vanish although they persist in all their forms. Siva is seen as the universe. But the seer does not see the background itself. Think of the man who sees only the cloth and not the cotton of which it is made; or the man who sees the pictures moving on the screen in a cinema show and not the screen itself as the background; or again the man who sees the letters which he reads but not the paper on which they are written. The objects are thus Consciousness and forms. But the ordinary person sees the objects in the universe but not Siva in these forms. Siva is the Being assuming these forms and the Consciousness seeing them. That is to say, Siva is the background underlying both the subject and the object, and again Siva in Repose and Siva in Action, or Siva and Sakti, or the Lord and the Universe. Whatever it is said to be, it is only Consciousness whether in repose or in action. Who is there that is not conscious? So, who is not realised? How then can questions arise doubting realisation or desiring it? If "I" am not *pratyakṣa* to me, I can then say that Siva is not *pratyakṣa*.

These questions arise because you have limited the Self to the body, only then the ideas of within and without, of the subject and the object, arise. The objective visions have no intrinsic value. Even if they are everlasting they cannot satisfy the person. . . .

*

Q: Can I engage in spiritual practice even remaining in saṁsāra*?*

Yes, certainly. One ought to do so.

Q: Is not saṁsāra *a hindrance? Do not all the holy books advocate renunciation?*

Saṁsāra is only in your mind. The world does not speak out, saying: "I am the world". Otherwise, it must be ever there — not excluding your sleep. Since it is not in sleep it is impermanent. Being impermanent it has no stamina. Having no stamina it is easily subdued by the Self. The Self alone is permanent. Renunciation is non-identification of the Self with the non-self. On the disappearance of ignorance the non-self ceases to exist. That is true renunciation.

Q: Why did you then leave your home in your youth?

That is my *prārabdha* [fate]. One's course of conduct in this life is determined by one's *prārabdha*. My *prārabdha* is this way. Your *prārabdha* is that way.

Q: Should I not also renounce?

If that had been your *prārabdha*, the question would not have arisen.

Q: I should therefore remain in the world and engage in spiritual practice. Well, can I get realisation in this life?

This has been already answered. You are always the Self. Earnest efforts never fail. Success is bound to result. . . .

[171]

Five Stanzas on the One Self

The Maharshi wrote these verses in Telugu at the request of a devotee, and later translated them into Tamil. His last poetic composition, they contain the same teachings as those he gave his earliest disciples. Translated by K. Swaminathan.

When, forgetting the Self, one thinks
That the body is oneself and goes
Through innumerable births
And in the end remembers and becomes
The Self, know this is only like
Awaking from a dream wherein
One has wandered over all the world.

One ever is the Self. To ask oneself
"Who and whereabouts am I?"
Is like the drunken man's enquiring
"Who am I?" and "Where am I?"

The body is within the Self. And yet
One thinks one is inside the inert body,
Like some spectator who supposes
That the screen on which the film is thrown
Is within the picture.

Does an ornament of gold exist
Apart from the gold? Can the body exist
Apart from the Self?
The ignorant one thinks "I am the body";
The enlightened knows "I am the Self".

The Self alone, the Sole Reality,
Exists for ever.
If of yore the First of Teachers
Revealed it through unbroken silence
Say who can reveal it in spoken words?

FURTHER READING

Source Materials

Ramana Maharshi, *Collected Works of Ramana Maharshi*. Tiruvannamalai: Sri Ramanasramam, 1996.
Ramana Maharshi, *Maharshi's Gospel*. Tiruvannamalai: Sri Ramanasramam, 2000.

Ramana Maharshi, *Talks with Sri Ramana Maharshi.* Tiruvannamalai: Sri Ramanasramam, 2000.

Ramana Maharshi, *The Teachings of Bhagavan Ramana Maharshi in His Own Words*, ed. Arthur Osborne. Tiruvannamalai: Sri Ramanasramam, 1971.

Other Sources

Arthur Osborne, *Ramana Maharshi and the Path of Self-Knowledge.* New Delhi: B. I. Publications, 1994.

T. M. P. Mahadevan, *Bhagavan Ramana.* Tiruvannamalai: Sri Ramanasramam, 1989.

Sri Ramanasramam <http://www.ramana-maharshi.org>

Sources of Texts and Translations

166 *Teachings* 2–3
167 *Collected Works* 39–48 passim
168 *Collected Works* 56–57
169 *Maharshi's Gospel* 22–25, 31, 67–68
170 *Talks* 440–43, 218–19
171 *Collected Works* 137–38

HAZRAT INAYAT KHAN

Listening to music (*samā'*) has long been a part of sufi practice. Although frowned on by some of the orders, like the Naqshbandhiya and Qadiriyah, the audition of sacred poetry set to music is regarded by many as a powerful means for approaching the Beloved. For the sufi it is the *samā'* or "listening" that is important, but the music also must be properly performed. For this reason many musicians have been sufis, and some sufis have presented their teachings in the form of music.

The most prominent sufi-musician of the early twentieth century was Hazrat Inayat Khan. Born in Baroda in 1882, Inayat was the grandson of Maula Bakhsh, still remembered as one of the greatest musicians of the period as well as an accomplished sufi. Trained in Hindustani music by his grandfather, father and uncle, Inayat was exposed in his youth to an eclectic blend of cultures: the Islam of his forefathers, the Hinduism of his neighbours, and the Western affectations of nineteenth-century urban India. Around the turn of the century, he became a professor of music in an academy founded by his grandfather. Though absorbed in his profession, he had a mystical opening which showed itself in visions and voices. Driven to seek a *murshid*, he eventually found one in the Chishti sufi Abu Hashim Madani, with whom he studied for four years. Before his death, Abu Hashim told Inayat: "You are gifted in music, you are gifted in philosophy; combine these two, go abroad and bring better understanding between East and West" (Keesing 1981: 42).

For the next few years, Inayat wandered through India, meeting with sufis, visiting holy places, and occasionally giving recitals, which were always highly regarded. In 1910 he and some other musicians went to America, where they performed before uncomprehending audiences. His main interest, however, was to introduce sufi thought and practice to the West. He was, he later said, "at this time a mystic in the guise of a musician" (Keesing 1981: 69). A year after his arrival in America he began to accept Western students of Sufism.

In 1912, Inayat Khan went to Europe, where he became something of a celebrity as a musician and as a mystical teacher. In 1915 he founded the Sufi Society, reorganised in 1917 as the Sufi Order. The membership of this group was made up almost entirely of middle- and upper-class urban Europeans and Americans. To them he presented a simplified form of sufism, divested of most of its Islamic character; for his idea at the time was "to simplify mysticism through a logical and scientific training" (Keesing 1981: 103). He continued to work in the West until 1926, when he came back to India. Falling ill not long after his return, he died in Delhi in 1927.

[172]

From *The Sufi Message of Hazrat Inayat Khan*

Books in English by Inayat Khan began to appear from 1914. Most of the early ones were co-authored by his English or American disciples. Later, as his English improved, he dispensed with such help. Almost all of his works are based on his lectures, which were delivered in English. They present the great themes of Sufism in universal garb, seeking always to break down the barriers between different cultures, religions and ways of life.

The whole idea of the Sufi is to cover his imperfect self even from his own eyes by the thought of God; and that moment when God and not his own self is before him, is the moment of perfect bliss. My murshid, Abu Hashim Madani, once said that there is only one virtue and one sin for a soul on this path: virtue when he is conscious of God and sin when he is not. No explanation can describe the truth of this except the experience of the contemplative, to whom, when he is conscious of God, it is as if a window is open which is facing heaven, and when he is conscious of the self the experience is the opposite. For all the tragedy of life is caused by the consciousness of the self. All pain and depression are caused by this, and anything that can take away the thought of self helps to a certain extent to relieve man from pain; but God-consciousness gives perfect relief.

*

I first believed without any hesitation in the existence of the soul, and then I wondered about the secret of its nature. I persevered and strove in search of the soul, and found at last that I myself was the cover over my soul. I realized that that in me which believed and that in me which wondered, that which persevered in me, and that which found, and that which was found at last, was no other than my soul. I thanked the darkness that brought me to the light, and I valued the veil which prepared for me the vision in which I saw myself reflected, the vision produced in the mirror of my soul. Since then I have seen all souls as my soul, and realized my soul as the soul of all; and what bewilderment it was when I realized that I alone was, if there were anyone; that I am whatever and whoever exists; and that I shall be whoever there will be in the future. And there was no end to my happiness and joy.

Verily, I am the seed and I am the root and I am the fruit of this tree of life.

*

To attain spirituality is to realize that the whole universe is one symphony in which every individual is one note. His happiness lies in becoming perfectly harmonious with the symphony of the universe. It is not following a certain religion that makes one spiritual, or having a certain belief, or being a fanatic in regard to one idea, or by becoming too good to live in this world. Many good people there are, who do not even understand what spirituality means. They are very good, but they do not yet know what ultimate good is. Ultimate good is harmony itself. For instance, all the different principles and beliefs of the religions of this world, taught and proclaimed by priests and teachers — but which men are not always able to follow and express — come naturally from the heart of a man who attunes himself to the rhythm of the universe. His every action, every word he speaks, every feeling he has, every sentiment he expresses, is all harmonious; it is all virtue, it is all religion. It is not following a religion, it is living a religion, making one's life a religion, which is necessary.

Music is the miniature of the whole harmony of the universe, for the harmony of the universe is music itself; and man, being the miniature of the universe, must show the same harmony. In his pulsation, in the beat of his heart, and in his vibration he shows rhythm and tone, harmonious or inharmonious chords. His health or illness, his joy or discomfort — all show the music or lack of music in his life.

What does music teach us? Music helps us to train ourselves in some way or other in harmony, and it is this which is magic, or the secret behind music. When you hear music that you enjoy, it tunes you and puts you in harmony with life. Therefore man needs music; he longs for music. Many say that they do not care for music, but these have not heard music! If they really hear music, it will touch their souls, and then certainly they cannot help loving it. If not, it only means that they have not heard music sufficiently and have not made their heart calm and quiet in order to listen to it, to enjoy and appreciate it. Besides, music develops that faculty by which one learns to appreciate all that is good and beautiful. In the form of art and science, in the form of music and poetry, in every aspect of beauty one can then appreciate it. What deprives man of all the beauty around him is his heaviness of body, or heaviness of heart. He is pulled down to earth, and by that everything becomes limited. When he shakes off that heaviness and feels joyous, he feels light. All good tendencies, such as gentleness and tolerance, forgiveness, love, and appreciation — all these beautiful qualities — come by being light, light in mind, soul, and body.

Where does music come from? Where does the dance come from? It all comes from the natural spiritual life which is within. When that spiritual life springs forth, it lightens all the burdens that man has. It makes his life smooth, floating on the ocean of life. The faculty of appreciation makes one light. Life is just like the ocean. When there is no appreciation, no receptivity, man sinks like a piece of iron to the bottom of the sea. He cannot float like the boat which is hollow, which is receptive.

The difficulty in the spiritual path is always what comes from ourselves. Man does not like to be a pupil; he likes to be a teacher. If man only knew that the greatness and perfection of the great ones, who have come from time to time to this world, was in their pupilship, and not in teaching! The greater the teacher, the better the pupil he was. He learned from everyone, the great and the lowly, the wise and the foolish, the old and the young. He learned from their lives and studied human nature in all its aspects.

The one who learns to tread the spiritual path must become as an empty cup in order that the wine of music and harmony may be poured down into his heart. You may ask: "How can one become an empty cup?" I shall tell you how cups show themselves filled, instead of being empty. Often a person comes to me and says: "Here I am. Can you help me spiritually?" And I answer: "Yes." But then he says: "I want to know first of all what you think about life and death, or about the beginning and the end." And then I wonder what his attitude will be if his previously conceived opinion does not agree with mine. He wants to learn, yet he does not want to be empty. That means, going to the stream of water with one's cup covered up: wanting the water, and yet the cup is closed, filled with preconceived ideas. Where have the preconceived ideas come from? No idea can be called one's own! All ideas have been learned from one source or another, but in time one comes to think that they are one's own. For these ideas one will argue and dispute, although they do not satisfy fully. At the same time, they are one's battleground, and all the time they will keep the cup covered up.

Mystics therefore have adopted a different way. They have learned a different course, and that course is self-effacement, or, in other words, unlearning what one has learned. They say in the East that the first thing that is learned is to understand how to become a pupil. They do not first learn what God is, or what life is. The first thing to learn is how to become a pupil. One may think that in this way one loses one's individuality. But what is individuality? Is it not that which is collected? What are one's ideas and opinions? They are just collected knowledge. This should be unlearned.

How can one unlearn? You would say that the character of the mind is such that what one learns is engraved upon it, and how then can one unlearn it? Unlearning is completing knowledge. To see a person and say: "That person is wicked" — that is learning. To see further, and recognize something good in that person — that is unlearning. When you see the goodness in someone whom you have called wicked, you have unlearned. You have unraveled that knot. You have once said: "I hate that person" — that is learning. And then you say: "Oh no, I can like him, or I can pity him." When you say that, you have seen with two eyes. First you learn by seeing with one eye; then you learn to see with two eyes. That makes sight complete.

All that we have learned in this world is partial knowledge, and when this is uprooted by another point of view, then we have knowledge in its completed form. That is called mysticism. Why is it called mysticism? Because it cannot be put into words. Words will show us one side of it, but the other side is beyond words.

The whole manifestation is duality, the duality which makes us intelligent, and behind the duality is unity. If we do not rise beyond duality and go towards unity, we do not attain the perfection which is called spirituality.

This does not mean that our learning is of no use. It is of great use. It gives us the power of discrimination and of discerning differences. This makes the intelligence sharp and the sight keen, so that we understand the value of things and their use. It is all part of human evolution, and all useful. So we must learn first, and unlearn afterwards. You do not look first at the sky when you are standing on the earth. First look at the earth, and see what it offers you to learn and to observe, but at the same time do not think that your life's purpose is fulfilled by looking only at the earth. The fulfillment of life's purpose is in looking at the sky.

What is wonderful about music is that it helps man to concentrate or meditate independently of thought. Therefore music seems to be the bridge over the gulf between the form and the formless. If there is anything intelligent, effective, and at the same time formless, it is music. Poetry suggests form, line and color suggest form, but music suggests no form.

Music also produces that resonance which vibrates through the whole being. It lifts the thought above the denseness of matter; it almost turns matter into spirit, into its original condition, through the harmony of vibrations touching every atom of one's whole being.

Beauty of line and color can go so far and no further. The joy of fragrance can go a little further. Music touches our innermost being, and in that way produces new life, a life that gives exaltation to the whole being, raising it to that perfection in which lies the fulfillment of human life.

FURTHER READING

Source Materials

Elisabeth Keesing, *A Sufi Master Answers: On the Sufi Message of Hazrat Inayat Khan*. Delhi: Motilal Banarsidass, 1997.

Hazrat Inayat Khan, *The Heart of Sufism: Essential Writings of Hazrat Inayat Khan*. Boston: Shambhala, 1999.

Other Sources

Elisabeth Keesing, *Hazrat Inayat Khan: A Biography*. Delhi: Munshiram Manoharlal, 1981.

Sufi Order International <http://www.sufiorder.org>

Sources of Texts

172 *Sufi Message* IX: 115; VIII, 231 (*Sufi Master Answers* 213); *Sufi Message* V: 137, *Sufi Message* II (rev. edition): 109–14 (*Heart of Sufism* 225–26, 269–73)

SWAMI RAMDAS

The Hindu *dharma-śāstra*s or books of traditional law lay down innumerable rules governing the conduct of life from birth to cremation. The duties of the student, the householder and the retired person are defined with such precision that there would seem to be little room for freedom of choice. But there is a saving clause. Those who feel an inner impulsion to pursue the spiritual life are allowed to become renunciates (*sannyāsin*s), abandoning their family duties and devoting themselves exclusively to the pursuit of the Divine. Hindu society as a whole approves of and honours the *sannyāsin*, though the families of those who decide to renounce generally oppose the decision of the renouncer. Still, hundreds of people enter the path of *sannyāsa* every year. Many of them are goaded by disappointment or bereavement or by a simple inability to cope; but some are impelled by an imperative inner aspiration for deeper things. Whatever may have been the original impulsion, a few succeed in channelling their energies to the divine pursuit, in the end attaining union with the object of their search.

A remarkable renunciate of the early twentieth century was Swami Ramdas, born P. Vittal Rao in Kanhangad, Kasaragod, north Kerala, in 1884. Vittal Rao was sent to a local school, where he was an indifferent scholar, though his love of reading gave him a good command of English. After failing his matriculation examination, he entered a technical college, where he obtained a diploma in textile manufacture. Over the next ten years he worked in a number of mills, got married and had a daughter. Though often out of work, he was noted for his sense of humour. A talented raconteur, he would keep his friends in stitches with his stories.

In 1917 Vittal Rao went to Mangalore to join his father-in-law's business. Failing in this he went into business on his own, and failed in that as well. By this time his domestic life had begun to fall apart. More and more, he was filled with dissatisfaction about the life he led. The only times he felt release were when he was singing devotional songs and chanting the name of Ram, whom he conceived of as "the only Truth — the only Reality" (*In Quest of God* 3). Around this time, his father gave him this *mantra* "*Śrī Rām jaya Rām jaya jaya Rām*". He took this as an initiation, and became absorbed in the recitation of the *mantra*.

Sometime in 1921, Vittal Rao abruptly left his life in Mangalore. Boarding a train, he set off with no clear idea of where he would go. Arriving in the temple-city of Srirangam, he donned the orange robe of a *sannyāsin* and took the name Ramdas, "Servant of Ram". For the next year, following the guidance of Ram, whom he saw in every form and every action, he wandered around India, meeting holy men and reprobates, and finding the face of Ram everywhere. This pilgrimage is the subject of *In Quest of God*, from which most of the selections below are drawn.

Ramdas returned to Mangalore in 1922. Instead of rejoining his family, he retired to a cave outside the town, where he passed some months in the performance of difficult austerities. Then he was off again, visiting pilgrimage places throughout the country, with an occasional stop back in north Kerala. Whenever he settled down for a while, he was surrounded by aspirants who wished to serve and learn from him. The most prominent of these disciples was Krishna Bai (1903–1989), with whom he founded in 1931 the Anandashram in Kanhangad. This period of his life is the subject of *In the Vision of God.*

For the remainder of his life, Ramdas spent most of his time at the ashram, guiding those who came to him for spiritual uplift and direction. He also made a number of tours, one of which took him around the world. His talks with his followers have been published in several volumes, among them *God-Experience*. Swami Ramdas died in 1963.

[173]

From *In Quest of God*

Swami Ramdas wrote *In Quest of God* in English in 1922 and 1923, after returning from the pilgrimage around the country that is the subject-matter of most of its chapters. In this as in his other books he referred to himself as "Ramdas". Those he met along the way were also seen and sometimes addressed as forms of Ram, for example the "Sadhuram" (Ram in the form of a *sādhu*) who is mentioned in the third passage below.

It was about two years ago that Ram first kindled in the heart of His humble slave, Ramdas, a keen desire to realise His Infinite Love. To strive to approach and understand Ram is to recede from the world of vanishing forms, because Ram is the only Truth — the only Reality. Ram is a subtle and mysterious power that pervades and sustains the whole universe. . . .

*

For nearly a year, Ramdas struggled on in a world full of cares, anxieties and pains. It was a period of terrible stress and restlessness — all of his own making. In this utterly helpless condition, full of misery, "Where is relief? Where is rest?" was the heart's cry of Ramdas. The cry was heard, and from the Great Void came the voice "Despair not! Trust Me and thou shalt be free!" — and this was the voice of Ram. These encouraging words of Ram proved like a plank thrown towards a man struggling for very life in the stormy waves of a raging sea. The great assurance soothed the aching heart of helpless Ramdas, like gentle rain on thirsting earth. Thenceforward, a part of the time that was formerly totally devoted to worldly affairs was taken up for the meditation of Ram who, for that period, gave him real peace and relief. Gradually love for Ram — the Giver of peace — increased. The more Ramdas meditated on and uttered His name, the greater the relief and joy he felt. Nights, which are free from worldly duties were, in course of time, utilised for Rambhajan with scarcely one or two hours' rest. His devotion for Ram progressed by leaps and bounds.

During the day, when cares and anxieties were besetting him due to monetary and other troubles, Ram was coming to his aid in unexpected ways. So, whenever free from worldly duties — be the period ever so small — he would meditate on Ram and utter His name. Walking in the streets he would be uttering, "Ram, Ram". Ramdas was now losing attraction for the objects of the world. Sleep, except for one or two hours in the night, was given up for the sake of Ram. Fineries in clothes and dress were replaced by coarse khaddar. Bed was substituted by a bare mat. Food, first, two meals were reduced to one meal a day and after sometime this too was given up for plantains and boiled potatoes — chillies and salt were totally eschewed. No taste but for Ram; meditation of Ram continued apace. It encroached upon the hours of the day and the so-called worldly duties.

At this stage one day, Ramdas' father came to him, sent by Ram, and calling him aside, gave him the *upadeś* of Ram Mantram — "Sri Ram, Jai Ram, Jai Jai Ram!" assuring him that if he repeated this Mantram at all times, Ram would give him eternal happiness. This initiation from the father — who has thereafter been looked upon by Ramdas as Gurudev — hastened on the aspirant in his spiritual progress. Off and on he was prompted by Ram to read the teachings of Sri Krishna — "The Bhagavad Gita," Buddha — "Light of Asia," Jesus Christ — "New Testament", Mahatma Gandhi — "Young India" and "Ethical Religion." The young plant of *bhakti* in Ram was thus nurtured in the electric atmosphere created by the influence of these great men on the mind of humble Ramdas. It was at this time that it slowly dawned upon his mind that Ram was the only Reality and all else was false. Whilst desires for the enjoyment of worldly things were fast falling off, the consideration of me and mine was also wearing out. The sense of possession and relationship was vanishing. All thought, all mind, all heart, all soul was concentrated on Ram, Ram covering up and absorbing everything.

*

Ramdas made up his mind to give up for the sake of Ram, all that he till then hugged to his bosom as his own, and leave the samsaric world. During this period, he was very simple in his dress which consisted of a piece of cloth covering the upper part of the body and another wound round the lower part. Next day, he got two clothes of this kind dyed in gerrua or red ochre, and the same night wrote two letters—one to his wife whom Ram had made him look upon for sometime past as his sister—and another to a kind friend whom Ram had brought in touch with Ramdas for his deliverance from debts. The resolution was made. At five o'clock in the morning he bade farewell to a world for which he had lost all attraction and in which he could find nothing to call his own. The body, the mind, the soul—all were laid at the feet of Ram—that Eternal Being, full of love and full of mercy.

*

The morning train carried Ramdas away from Mangalore and dropped him in the evening at Erode—a railway junction. He had taken with him a sum of Rs. 25 and a few books including the Gita and the New Testament. At Erode he found himself strangely helpless without any plans or thought for the future. He did not know where he was being led by Ram. He wandered about for sometime and when darkness fell, he approached a small, low hut on the road-side and finding at its entrance a middle-aged mother, requested her to give him some food. The kind mother at once welcomed him into her hut and served him with some rice and curds. The mother was very kind. With great difficulty could she be induced to accept some money for the food supplied by her.

On leaving the hut, he proceeded to the Railway station. He laid himself down in a corner in the station and took rest for sometime. He did not know what to do or where to go. At midnight, a bell rang to announce the arrival of a train. He got up and found near him a Tamilian who inquired of him regarding his movements. Ramdas was unable to say anything in reply. Ram alone could determine his future. Here this friend promised Ramdas to take him with him as far as Trichinopoly for which place he was bound. Money was given him for the purchase of a ticket for Ramdas, and both boarded the train. It was evening when the train reached Trichinopoly station. Alighting from the train, he proceeded to the city. All the time, all the way from Mangalore, the divine mantram of Sri Ram was on his lips. He could never forget it. The utterance of Ram's name alone sustained and cheered him. Taking rest for the night on the verandah of a house by the road-side, next morning he started on foot to Srirangam about 7 miles from Trichy. He reached the place at about 8 o'clock.

Here Ramdas was first let into the secret of Ram's purpose in drawing him out from the sphere of his former life and surroundings, and that purpose was to take him on a pilgrimage to sacred shrines and holy rivers. At Srirangam the beautiful river Kaveri was flowing in all her purity and majesty. Going up to the river, he bathed in its clear waters. Here on the banks of the Kaveri he assumed, by Ram's command, the robe of a *sannyāsin*. It was a momentous step by taking which Ram gave him an entirely new birth. The white clothes previously worn by him were offered up to the Kaveri — who carried them away in her rushing waters. The gerrua or orange-coloured clothes were put on and the following prayer went up to the feet of Almighty Ram:

O Ram! O Love Infinite — Protector of all the worlds! it is by Thy wish alone that Thy humble slave has been induced to adopt *sannyās*. In Thy name alone, O Ram, he has given up *saṁsāra*, and cut asunder all bonds, all ties.

*

The thrills of a new birth, a new life, with the sweet love of Ram was felt. A peace came upon Ramdas' struggling soul. The turmoil ceased. Ram's own hands seemed to have touched the head of his slave — Ram blessed. O tears, flow on, for the mere joy of a deliverance! Sorrow, pain, anxiety and care — all vanished, never to return. All glory to Thee, Ram. The great blessing came from Ram: "I take thee under my guidance and protection — remain ever my devotee — thy name shall be Ramdas."

Yes, Ramdas, what a grand privilege it is to become the *dās* of Ram who is all love — kindness — all mercy — all forgiveness!

*

One day, the kind Sadhuram took him for the *darśan* of a famous Saint of the place, named Sri Ramana Maharshi. His ashram was at the foot of the Tiruvannamalai mountains. It was a thatched shed. Both the visitors entered the ashram, and meeting the Saint, fell prostrate at his holy feet. It was really a blessed place where that great man lived. He was young but there was on his face a calmness, and in his large eyes a passionless look of tenderness, which cast a spell of peace and joy on all those who came to him. Ramdas was informed that the Saint knew English. So he addressed him thus:

"Maharaj, here stands before thee a humble slave. Have pity on him. His only prayer to thee is to give him thy blessing".

The Maharshi, turning his beautiful eyes towards Ramdas, and looking intently for a few minutes into his eyes as though he was pouring into Ramdas his blessing through those orbs, shook his head to say that he had blessed. A thrill of inexpressible joy coursed through the frame of Ramdas, his whole body quivering like a leaf in the breeze. O Ram, what a love is Thine! Bidding farewell to the *mahātmā*, the Sadhuram and he returned to the goldsmith's residence. . . .

*

Now, at the prompting of Ram, Ramdas desiring to remain in solitude for some time, placed the matter before the Sadhuram. The Sadhuram was ever ready to fulfil his wishes. Losing no time, he took Ramdas up the mountain behind the great temple. Climbing high up, he showed him many caves. Of these, one small cave was selected for Ramdas which he occupied the next day. In this cave he lived for nearly a month in deep meditation of Ram. This was the first time he was taken by Ram into solitude for His *bhajan*. Now, he felt most blissful sensations since he could here hold undisturbed communion with Ram. He was actually rolling in a sea of indescribable happiness. To fix the mind on that fountain of bliss — Ram, means to experience pure joy!

Once, during the day, when he was lost in the madness of Ram's meditation, he came out of the cave and found a man standing a little away from the mouth of the cave. Unconsciously, he ran up to him and locked him up in a fast embrace. This action on the part of Ramdas thoroughly frightened the friend who thought that it was a mad man who was behaving in this manner and so was afraid of harm from him. It was true, he was mad — yes, he was mad of

Ram, but it was a harmless madness which fact the visitor realised later. The irresistible attraction felt by him towards this friend was due to the perception of Ram in him. "O Ram, Thou art come, Thou art come!" with this thought Ramdas had run up to him. At times, he would feel driven to clasp in his arms the very trees and plants growing in the vicinity of the cave. Ram was attracting him from all directions. Oh, the mad and loving attraction of Ram! O Ram, Thou art Love, Light and Bliss. Thus passed his days in that cave.

*

Now the train carried Ramdas to the Junagadh station. It was midday. He was without a guide. At the city gate he inquired of a policeman if there was a *Rām-mandir* in that place. He replied that there was a *Rām-mandir* about two miles from the gate and he pointed out the way leading to it. Ramdas walked on, making frequent inquiries on the way. At last, he reached the high gateway of the *Rām-mandir*. Entering, he was welcomed by the *mahant* of the ashram, with whom he remained for about a week. Here he had the benefit of the society of six other Sadhus who were also there as the guests of the kind-hearted *mahant*. All of them were very kind to Ramdas.

Ram here performed two wonderful miracles — one of these Sadhus had an attack of fever from a fortnight and in spite of various kinds of treatment he was as bad as ever. He was bedridden, emaciated and pale. Besides, he was disheartened and was fretting over his illness. Seeing his condition Ramdas could not resist going to his bed, and, sitting near him and offering himself for his service, began pressing his legs lightly. Coming to know of this the ailing Sadhu sat up and remonstrated, saying that he was quite unworthy to receive such attention from him. He only asked for a blessing from Ramdas that he should be all right by the following day. Ramdas said that he was only a humble slave of Ram and had no right to bless anybody.

"Do bless in the name of Ram," he appealed.

"Well, brother," said Ramdas, "may Sri Ram, the Protector of all, bless you with health by tomorrow morning"

That night Ram was perhaps busy setting the Sadhu right, for next morning he was entirely free from fever and was moving about in good cheer and health. This marvellous cure by Ram, for working which he had made humble Ramdas his tool, made quite a sensation in the ashram. So he became the object of considerable attention and love from all in the ashram. About three or four days later, another Sadhu fell ill. He too asked Ramdas to bless him in the same way as he had done the other one. Ramdas prayed again to Ram as requested. O Ram, what a powerful being Thou art! The second Sadhu also recovered by the following morning. All glory to Thee, Ram!

*

Now, news reached Mangalore that Ramdas was staying at the Mutt at Hubli. His former wife, but present mother (as all women are mothers to Ramdas) and his child came there to fetch him. Sri Siddharudha Swami was appealed to by them in the matter and the kind-hearted Saint advised him to go with them to Mangalore. Ramdas submitted to the order, feeling that it came from Ram Himself. Ram always means well and He does everything for the best. The mother [i.e., Ramdas' former wife] proposed to him to return to *saṁsāra*, to which he replied:

"O mother, it is all the work of Ram. Ram alone has freed humble Ramdas from the bonds of samsaric life, and he resides now at Ram's holy feet. He is now the slave of Ram and prays to Him always to keep him as such. To trust and acknowledge His supreme powers of protection over all, and believe that He alone is the doer of all actions and possessor of all things is the only way to be rid of the miseries of life. Therefore, O mother, throw off your burden of cares and anxieties and approaching the divine feet of Ram, live there always in peace and happiness. This is all poor Ramdas can ask you to do."

Now, under the kind care and escort of the mother, he started by train and reaching Mormugoa embarked upon a steamboat which took them in due course to Mangalore. As the party came up to the *bundar*, Ramdas, as bid by Ram, walking in advance, directed his steps straight to the Kadri hills, where he remained for the night. Next day, by Ram's will, he visited the house of brother Sitaram Rao — a brother by the old relation and a great *bhakta* of Ram. A few days later, he had the happiness of the *darśan* of his Gurudev (father by old relationship) who had given him the *upadeś* of the divine Rammantram. Now, Ramdas stays by Ram's command in a cave called "Panch Pandav Cave" on the Kadri hill, and lives there a serene life, devoting his whole time in talking about, writing of and meditating on that all-loving and glorious Ram.

[174]

From *In the Vision of God*

In the Vision of God, subtitled "Experiences in continuation of 'In Quest of God'", deals with Swami Ramdas's life from 1923 until the early 1930s. During this period he visited a number of holy places but always returned to Kasaragod, where in 1931 he founded an ashram. The two passages reproduced below deal with his austerities in the Panch Pandav Cave and the nature of the *samadarśan* or "true vision" that became established in him at that time.

Ramdas . . . would rise at about three o'clock early morning and run down directly to the water tanks for bath. Though the path to the tanks was rough and risky, he would not forego his morning dip even in the darkest night. After bath he would sit in asan for meditation till day-break. For some days his meditation consisted of only the mental repetition of Ram-mantram. Then the mantram having stopped automatically, he beheld a small circular light before his mental vision. This yielded him thrills of delight. This experience having continued for some days, he felt a dazzling light like lightning, flashing before his eyes, which ultimately permeated and absorbed him. Now an inexpressible transport of bliss filled every pore of his physical frame. When this state was coming on, he would at the outset become oblivious of his hands and feet and then gradually his entire body. Lost in this trance-state he would sit for two to three hours. Still a subtle awareness of external objects was maintained in this state.

Some friends would pay him visits early in the morning when he was absorbed in the trance, and he had at the time a hazy recognition of their presence. He could hear sounds of talk, if any, mere sounds without sense or meaning for him. Whenever he fell into the trance he would feel its grip so firmly that he could not easily shake it off. At the longest it would not last more than three hours. After returning to body-consciousness he would be engaged in singing to himself some hymns glorifying God, and also in the loud recitation of the mantram. In fact, except when conversing, reading or writing, he used to utter the mantram ceaselessly throughout the day.

The trance experience brought about another change, viz.,

sleep thereafter became a state of half-wakefulness or awareness during which he was filled with pure ecstasy. Sometimes, at dead of night, a friend would pay him a surprise visit. Although Ramdas was in the trance-state, he could know the friend's approach even when he was yet a furlong from the cave. . . .

*

For two years from the time of the significant change which had come over him, Ramdas had been prepared to enter into the very depths of his being for the realization of the immutable, calm and eternal sprit of God. Here he had to transcend name, form, thought and will — every feeling of the heart and faculty of the mind. The world had then appeared to him as a dim shadow — a dreamy nothing. The vision then was mainly internal. It was only for the glory of the Atman in His pristine purity, peace and joy as an all-pervading, immanent, static, immortal and glowing spirit.

In the earlier stages this vision was occasionally lost, pulling him down to the old life of diversity with its turmoil of like and dislike, joy and grief. But he would be drawn in again into the silence and calmness of the spirit. A stage was soon reached when this dwelling in the spirit became a permanent and unvarying experience with no more falling off from it, and then a still exalted state came on; his hitherto inner vision projected outwards. First a glimpse of this new vision dazzled him off and on. This was the working of divine love. He would feel as though his very soul had expanded like the blossoming of a flower and, by a flash as it were, enveloped the whole universe embracing all in a subtle halo of love and light. This experience granted him a bliss infinitely greater than he had in the previous state. Now it was that Ramdas began to cry out "Ram is all, it is He as everybody and everything." This condition was for some months coming on and vanishing. When it wore away, he would instinctively run to solitude. When it was present, he freely mixed in the world preaching the glory of divine love and bliss. With this externalised vision started Ramdas' mission. Its fullness and magnificence was revealed to him during his stay in the Kadri cave, and here the experience became more sustained and continuous. The vision of God shone in his eyes and he would see none but Him in all objects. Now wave after wave of joy rose in him. He realized that he had attained to a consciousness, full of splendour, power and bliss.

Ramdas gave up the cave and set forth once again on a wandering life. He gave a touch of the inexpressible bliss he was enjoying to all who came in contact with him. Vast crowds thronged around him wherever he went. Divine love thrilled his entire being at the sight of big multitudes. In a state of perfect ecstasy he delivered himself out in accents of love and joy.

[175]

From *God-Experience*

After 1931 Ramdas spent most of his time in his ashram in north Kerala. Here he held *satsaṅg* (meetings with chanting and discussion of spiritual topics) with people attracted by his frankness, benevolence and devotion. Transcripts of these informal talks were later published in books like *God-Experience*, the first volume of which contains talks of 1961. The following extracts are from that book.

Question: What is God-consciousness?

You should know you are not the body, but the divine reality, pure wisdom, all-pervading light, infinite love, everlasting joy, all put together. *That* you are. Ordinarily man thinks he is a body subject to birth, growth, decay, disease and death. But he is truly the changeless, birthless, deathless Atman, whose nature is bliss and peace. To realize this is to attain God-consciousness. Man, in his state of ignorance, dwells in body-consciousness. When he rises to God-consciousness, he knows he is God. How very different one is from the other! When Ramdas visited the house of a devotee in Seattle in America, the person who introduced Ramdas to a group of spiritual aspirants told them, "I have brought God to show you." She was a lady and the leader of that group. Ramdas said, "God has come to see God."

*

In taking Ram Nam you think you are taking the name of the deity living in some far-off heaven. But you are really repeating the name of your own immortal Self, that is, Atma Ram. You do not know that you are Ram. So, you must ceaselessly remember Him until you are awakened to the consciousness that you are Ram yourself. How can you remove forgetfulness? By continuous remembrance of the Atman until you know that you are the Atman. Suppose there is a purse containing money in your pocket and you have forgotten about it. When you recollect it, you put your hand in the pocket and it is there. So remembrance gives you awareness. It is already there. You were ignorant of it; you had forgotten about it. Forgetfulness can be removed by remembrance; ignorance by awareness or knowledge.

So you are repeating the name of your own immortal, infinite, eternal Self. Do not take the Name thinking that the Name is of one who is far away from you, of one who is other than you. Know that you are taking your own name. Ram is a synonym for Self or Atman. You are already the Self. You can be conscious of your Self by constantly remembering the Self. Gradually the body-consciousness leaves you and you attain Jnana, which means knowledge of the Self. You cannot realize the all-comprehensive being of God unless you attain Jnana. That is the basis for knowing God, as both Purusha and Prakriti. This grants you the vision of the world-lila in the state of Para-Bhakti. Bhakti is the root; Vairagya is the trunk; Jnana is the flower and Para-Bhakti is the fruit. In Para-Bhakti, Purusha and Prakriti are realized as one. Here, Prakriti is not Mithya. God not only pervades the universe but transcends it to infinity. Being all the worlds, He is still beyond all limitations or boundaries — limitless expanse of divine existence. . . .

*

One who has realized the Truth cannot express what it is. Therefore Buddha has said, "Do not dip the string of thought into the unfathomable. He who questions errs, he who answers errs." No question is to be put and no answer is to be given. Buddha did not believe in a personal God. He attained the impersonal Reality. That state, he called Nirvana. He said this is liberation gained by the annihilation of desire. He never tried to define what Nirvana is. All-pervading, formless, still, calm — these are mere words. They convey nothing to you. If you want to know what it is, you must experience it. Hence if you are asked to describe what is Moksha or Jnana, you keep quiet. If you say anything about it, it is not that, because it is beyond thought and expression. Mouna is Brahman. If one simply quotes Slokas from books, it shows one is still in the intellectual plane. Those who have gone beyond it will merely keep silent, if asked what Brahman is.

FURTHER READING

Source Materials

Swami Ramdas, *In Quest of God*. Kanhangad, Kasaragod, Kerala: Anandashram, 1998.
Swami Ramdas, *In the Vision of God*. Kanhangad, Kasaragod, Kerala: Anandashram, 1998.
Swami Ramdas, *God-Experience*, vol. 1. Kanhangad, Kerala: Anandashram, 1998.

Others Sources

Swami Ramdas, *Swami Ramdas on Himself*. Kanhangad, Kasaragod, Kerala: Anandashram, 1996.
Anandashram <http://www.anandashram.org>

Sources of Texts and Translations

173 *Quest* 1, 3–5, 8–12 passim, 31–34, 125–26, 163–65
174 *Vision* 7–8, 13–14
175 *God-Experience* 64, 126–27, 256

PARAMAHANSA YOGANANDA

From at least the time of the *upaniṣads*, the preferred method of transmission of spiritual teachings in India has been verbal instruction from teacher to pupil. Whether referred to as *ācārya*, *guru*, *murshid* or by some other title, the teacher is believed to be one who has experienced the inner truths of the doctrines after being initiated by a perfected master. The fit pupil — *śisya*, *sādhaka*, *murīd* — is one who has passed through some preliminary training and been found suitable, morally and otherwise, to receive the secret teachings. Important in Vedanta, Buddhism and Jainism, the master became indispensable in Tantrism, with its highly technical *kriyā*s or practices. In later cults the *guru* was elevated to almost divine status. To the *sant*s, the Sikhs and numerous Hindu sects, the *sadguru* is not just a channel but an embodiment of the Presence and Power. More recently, Indian *guru*s have been successfully marketed by public-relations teams; despite this triumph of Western commercialism, the traditional *guru-śisya* relationship is still alive. A modern example of this ancient institution is provided by the lives of Paramahansa Yogananda and his teacher Swami Sri Yukteswar Giri.

Yogananda was born Mukunda Lal Ghosh in Gorakhpur (Uttar Pradesh) in 1893. The son of pious middle-class Bengalis, he was attracted to spiritual life while still a child. His parents were lay disciples of Shyama Charan Lahiri (generally known as Lahiri Mahashay, 1828–1895), a Bengali yogin of Benares who taught a form of practice called *kriyā yoga*, literally "the attainment of union by means of a certain technique". According to Yogananda, this particular *kriyā yoga* is "a simple psychophysical method by which human blood is decarbonized and recharged with oxygen" (*Autobiography* 235). Based evidently on the principles of *prāṇāyāma* as codified by Patanjali, Gorakshanatha and others, this method was taught by Lahiri Mahashay to laypersons like Yogananda's parents as well as to advanced disciples like Sri Yukteswar (original name Priya Nath Karar, 1855–1936).

Yogananda met Yukteswar in 1910 after several years of seeking for a master. Their relationship, true to the pattern found in the songs of Jnandev, Bulleh Shah and others, was characterised by intense love on the one hand and no-nonsense discipline on the other. Yukteswar initiated Yogananda into the Swami order of monks, giving him the name by which he is known. He also insisted that his disciple, a mediocre student, take the degree-course at Calcutta University. Diploma in hand, Yogananda set up an experimental school in Ranchi (Jharkhand). Two years later he was invited to Boston as a delegate to an international conference of religions. After the conference he stayed on to spread Kriya Yoga in the West, as Yukteswar had said he was destined to do. With the exception of eighteen months during which he toured Europe and India, he remained in the

Unites States for the rest of his life.

In 1920 Yogananda founded the Self-Realization Fellowship, and four years later established its international headquarters in Los Angeles. This became the base of his activities over the next twenty-six years. During the thirties he drew back from his hectic round of lectures and classes in order to devote more time to contemplation and writing. The most important of the books written at this time is *Autobiography of a Yogi*, first published in 1946 and never out of print since. Written in fluent, sometimes humorous English, the *Autobiography* recounts Yogananda's youth and early seeking, his meeting and life with Sri Yukteswar, and his subsequent mission abroad. In 1952 Yogananda died suddenly and peacefully in Los Angeles.

[176]

From *Autobiography of a Yogi*

This extract from a chapter of the *Autobiography* entitled "An Experience in Cosmic Consciousness" describes an occasion when Sri Yukteswar transmitted a certain spiritual experience to Yogananda. The ability of *guru*s to transmit psychological states, curative forces, etc. by means of instruction, touch or mental power is often alluded to in yogic literature.

"I am here, Guruji." My shamefacedness spoke more eloquently for me.

"Let us go to the kitchen and find something to eat." Sri Yukteswar's manner was as casual as though hours and not days had separated us.

"Master, I must have disappointed you by my abrupt departure from my duties here; I thought you might be angry with me."

"No, of course not! Wrath springs only from thwarted desires. I do not expect anything from others, so their actions cannot be in opposition to wishes of mine. I would not use you for my own ends; I am happy only in your own true happiness."

"Sir, one hears of divine love in a vague way, but today I am indeed having a concrete example of it from your angelic self! In the world, even a father does not easily forgive his son if he leaves his parent's business without warning. But you show not the slightest vexation, though you must have been put to great inconvenience by the many unfinished tasks I left behind."

We looked into each other's eyes, where tears were shining. A blissful wave engulfed me; I was conscious that the Lord, in the form of my guru, was expanding the small ardours of my heart to the vast reaches of cosmic love.

A few mornings later I made my way to Master's empty sitting room. I planned to meditate, but my laudable purpose was unshared by disobedient thoughts. They scattered like birds before the hunter.

"Mukunda!" Sri Yukteswar's voice sounded from a distant balcony.

I felt as rebellious as my thoughts. "Master always urges me to meditate," I muttered to myself. "He should not disturb me when he knows why I came to his room."

He summoned me again; I remained obstinately silent. The third time his tone held rebuke.

"Sir, I am meditating," I shouted protestingly.

"I know how you are meditating," my guru called out, "with your mind distributed like leaves in a storm! Come here to me."

Thwarted and exposed, I made my way sadly to his side.

"Poor boy, mountains could not give you what you want." Master spoke caressingly, comfortingly. His calm gaze was unfathomable. "Your heart's desire shall be fulfilled."

Sri Yukteswar seldom indulged in riddles; I was bewildered. He struck gently on my chest above the heart.

My body became immovably rooted; breath was drawn out of my lungs as if by some huge magnet. Soul and mind instantly lost their physical bondage and streamed out like a fluid piercing light from my every pore. The flesh was as though dead, yet in my intense awareness I knew that never before had I been fully alive. My sense of identity was no longer narrowly confined to a body but embraced the circumambient atoms. People on distant streets seemed to be moving gently over my own remote periphery. The roots of plants and trees appeared through a dim transparency of the soil; I discerned the inward flow of their sap.

The whole vicinity lay bare before me. My ordinary frontal vision was now changed to a vast spherical sight, simultaneously all-perceptive. Through the back of my head I saw men strolling far down Rai Ghat Lane, and noticed also a white cow that was leisurely approaching. When she reached the open ashram gate, I observed her as though with my two physical eyes. After she had passed behind the brick wall of the courtyard, I saw her clearly still.

All objects within my panoramic gaze trembled and vibrated like quick motion pictures. My body, Master's, the pillared courtyard, the furniture and floor, the trees and sunshine, occasionally became violently agitated, until all melted into a luminescent sea; even as sugar crystals, thrown into a glass of water, dissolve after being shaken. The unifying light alternated with materializations of form, the metamorphoses revealing the law of cause and effect in creation.

An oceanic joy broke upon calm endless shores of my soul. The Spirit of God, I realized, is exhaustless Bliss; His body is countless tissues of light. A swelling glory within me began to envelop towns, continents, the earth, solar and stellar systems, tenuous nebulae, and floating universes. The entire cosmos, gently luminous, like a city seen afar at night, glimmered within the infinitude of my being. The dazzling light beyond the sharply etched global outlines faded slightly at the farthest edges; there I saw a mellow radiance, ever undiminished. It was indescribably subtle; the planetary pictures were formed of a grosser light.

The divine dispersion of rays poured from an Eternal Source, blazing into galaxies, transfigured with ineffable auras. Again and again I saw the creative beams condense into constellations, then resolve into sheets of transparent flame. By rhythmic reversion, sextillion worlds passed into diaphanous lustre, then fire became firmament.

I cognized the centre of the empyrean as a point of intuitive perception in my heart. Irradiating splendour issued from my nucleus to every part of the universal structure. Blissful *amṛta*, nectar of immortality, pulsated through me with a quicksilverlike fluidity. The creative voice of God I heard resounding as *Aum*, the vibration of the Cosmic Motor.

Suddenly the breath returned to my lungs. With a disappointment almost unbearable, I realised that my infinite immensity was lost. Once more I was limited to the humiliating cage of a body, not easily accommodative to the Spirit. Like a prodigal child, I had run away from my macrocosmic home and had imprisoned myself in a narrow microcosm.

My guru was standing motionless before me; I started to prostrate myself at his holy feet in gratitude for his having bestowed on me the experience in cosmic consciousness that I had long passionately sought. He held me upright and said quietly:

"You must not get overdrunk with ecstasy. Much work yet remains for you in the world. Come, let us sweep the balcony floor; then we shall walk by the Ganges."

I fetched a broom; Master, I knew, was teaching me the secret of balanced living. The soul must stretch over the cosmogonic abysses, while the body performs its daily duties.

When Sri Yukteswar and I set out later for a stroll, I was still entranced in unspeakable rapture. I saw our bodies as two astral pictures, moving over a road by the river whose essence was sheer light.

"It is the Spirit of God that actively sustains every form and force in the universe; yet He is transcendental and aloof in the blissful uncreated void beyond the worlds of vibratory phenomena," Master explained. "Those who attain Self-realization on earth live a similar twofold existence. Conscientiously performing their work in the world, they are yet immersed in an inward beatitude.

"The Lord has created all men from the illimitable joy of His being. Though they are painfully cramped by the body, God nevertheless expects that men made in His image shall ultimately rise above all sense identifications and reunite with Him."

The cosmic vision left many permanent lessons. By daily stilling my thoughts, I could win release from the delusive conviction that my body was a mass of flesh and bones, traversing the hard soil of matter. The breath and the restless mind, I saw, are like storms that lash the ocean of light into waves of material forms—earth, sky, human beings, animals, birds, trees. No perception of the Infinite as One Light can be had except by calming those storms.

As often as I quieted the two natural tumults, I beheld the multitudinous waves of creation melt into one lucent sea; even as the waves of the ocean, when a tempest subsides, serenely dissolve into unity.

A master bestows the divine experience of cosmic consciousness when his disciple, by meditation, has strengthened his mind to a degree where the vast vistas would not overwhelm him. Mere intellectual willingness or open-mindedness is not enough. Only adequate enlargement of consciousness by yoga practice and devotional *bhakti* can prepare one to absorb the liberating shock of omnipresence.

The divine experience comes with a natural inevitability to the sincere devotee. His intense craving begins to pull at God with an irresistible force. The Lord as the Cosmic Vision is drawn by that magnetic ardour into the seeker's range of consciousness. . . .

Sri Yukteswar taught me how to summon the blessed experience at will, and also how to transmit it to others when their intuitive channels are suitably developed.

For months, after the first time, I entered the state of ecstatic union, comprehending daily why the *Upanishads* say that God is *rasa*, "the most relishable". One morning however, I took a problem to Master.

"I want to know, sir — when shall I find God?"

"You have found Him."

"O no, sir, I don't think so!"

My guru was smiling. "I am sure you aren't expecting a venerable Personage, adorning a throne in some antiseptic corner of the cosmos! I see, however, that you are imagining that possession of miraculous powers is proof that one has found God. No. One might gain the power to control the whole universe — yet find the Lord elusive still. Spiritual advancement is not to be measured by one's displays of outward powers, but solely by the depth of his bliss in meditation.

FURTHER READING

Source Material

Paramahansa Yogananda, *Autobiography of a Yogi*. Mumbai: Jaico Publishing House, 1997.

Other Sources

Sananda Lal Ghose, *"Mejda": Sri Sri Paramahansa Yogananda: His Family and Early Life*. Mumbai: Jaico Publishing House, 2001.

Self-Realization Fellowship <http://www.yogananda-srf.org>

Source of Text

176 *Autobiography* 140–144, 147

J. KRISHNAMURTI

The relationship between spiritual teacher and seeker of enlightenment can take many forms. In the tantric, *bhakti*, *sant* and Sikh traditions, the *guru* is regarded as the equivalent of the Divine, by whose grace alone the aspirant can receive power or knowledge or peace. This divinisation of the human *guru* has led to exaggerated claims on the part of some masters, and exaggerated expectations on the part of many disciples. Reliance on the *guru* leads often to a state of helpless dependence, in which the disciple feels no need to do anything at all. But the aspirant's personal effort is always necessary; without it, the greatest guru can do nothing.

In his youth, J. Krishnamurti was proclaimed a "world teacher", one who would lead humanity, in particular the members of an organisation of which he was the head, to enlightenment and transformation. As a man of thirty-five he dissolved this group and told his followers that they could not approach Truth "by any path whatsoever, by any religion, by any sect" (selection 177). He urged them to strive after Truth on their own, free from organisations, dogmas, beliefs and sure-fire techniques. This approach was not altogether novel. Other Indian teachers, from the Buddha to Ramana Maharshi, have insisted on the primary importance of self-enquiry, and showed by their own *sādhana* that the instructions of a *guru* were not indispensable. Krishnamurti's originality was to frame this message without reference to any past tradition, using a language that was meaningful to thousands of present-day men and women.

Jiddu Krishnamurti was born in 1895 in the town of Madanapalle in the hill-country of southern Andhra Pradesh. His father, a struggling clerk, was a member of the Theosophical Society. After his retirement, he took Krishna and three of his other children to the society's head-quarters in Chennai, where he had found employment. Soon after their arrival, C. W. Leadbeater, a prominent Theosophist, became convinced that Krishna was meant to be the vehicle of the World Teacher that he and his colleagues were awaiting. Soon Krishna had been adopted by Annie Besant, the President of the Theosophical Society, who became his legal guardian. In 1911 an organisation called the Order of the Star in the East was founded with Krishna at its head. The same year he was taken to England, where he lived for the next ten years. Tutored by members of the Society, he grew up in an atmosphere surcharged with occult mysteries. He also received a conventional education, but repeatedly failed his examinations.

In 1922, while staying in California, Krishnamurti had a three-day-long spiritual experience that utterly transformed him. He wrote of this later: "The fountain of Truth has been revealed to me and the darkness has been dispersed. . . . I have drunk at the fountain of Joy and eternal Beauty. I am God-intoxicated" (Lutyens 1983: 7). He now accepted that he was indeed a world-teacher, though perhaps not in the way that had been expected of him.

For several years Krishnamurti spoke at meetings and conventions of the Order of the Star in the East, but he became increasingly disenchanted with the Order, the Theosophical Society, and its hierarchy. Finally, in 1929, he dissolved the Order, returned the properties and funds he had been given, and began to teach to the general public on his own. Over the next fifty-five years he addressed many hundreds of meetings and spoke with thousands of individuals in North America, Europe and India. To all he gave the same fundamental message: an individual in search of truth must not depend on outward authority, whether religious, political, moral, intellectual or other. To find what is not known there must be freedom from the known, from the past, from the web of time. To become aware of *what is*, one must put an end to the known by means of "meditation", which is not a state brought on by concentration or any form of practice, but a natural, effortless "emptying of the content of consciousness — which means the fears, the anxieties, the conflicts in relationship — the ending of sorrow and, therefore, compassion. The ending of the content of consciousness is complete silence" (*Total Freedom* 320). In this silence one can find the immensity or benediction of that which *is*.

Krishnamurti had virtually no knowledge of spiritual traditions, Indian or other. He deliberately avoided reading scriptural texts, which he saw as so many cages for the imprisonment of consciousness. He was scathing in his dismissal of ritualistic religion. To an audience in Mumbai he said in 1957: "Any intelligent man can see that going to temples, doing *pūjā*, and all the other nonsense that goes on in the name of religion is not religion at all; it is merely a social convenience" (*Total Freedom* 192). Yet he did not condemn "religion" itself, for "if there is no religion then the culture dies, civilisation goes to pieces" (*Total Freedom* 315). True religion, that indispensible thing, was "the search for God, or truth, or whatever one might like to name it — and not the mere acceptance of belief and dogma" (*Total Freedom* 99).

Krishnamurti continued to give talks until the last year of his life. He died in California in 1986.

Krishnamurti's teachings consist mostly of transcripts of his talks and dialogues. Available now in the form of CD-ROMs, they are said to comprise the equivalent of 200 volumes. Krishnamurti also wrote a number of books as well as three journals (one of which was dictated and not written by hand). Characterised by frugality and incisiveness, his prose demonstrates his keen powers of observation of the natural and psychological worlds. All but one of the selections below are taken from Krishnamurti's journals and other writings. Although perhaps not typical of his work as a whole, they provide a first-person perspective on his teachings, sometimes revealing the mystical sources from which they are drawn.

[177]

Truth is a Pathless Land

The opening of a talk delivered on 2 August 1929, when Krishnamurti dissolved the Order of the Star in the East.

We are going to discuss this morning the dissolution of the Order of the Star. Many people will be delighted, and others will be rather sad. It is a question neither for rejoicing nor for sadness, because it is inevitable, as I am going to explain.

You may remember the story of how the devil and a friend of his were walking down the street when they saw ahead of them a man stoop down and pick up something from the ground, look at it, and put it away in his pocket. The friend said to the devil, "What did that man pick up?" "He picked up a piece of Truth," said the devil. "That is a very bad business for you, then," said his friend. "Oh, not at all," the devil replied, "I am going to let him organize it."

I maintain that Truth is a pathless land, and you cannot approach it by any path whatsoever, by any religion, by any sect. That is my point of view, and I adhere to that absolutely and unconditionally. Truth, being limitless, unconditioned, unapproachable by any path whatsoever, cannot be organized; nor should any organization be formed to lead or to coerce people along any particular path. If you first understand that, then you will see how impossible it is to organize a belief. A belief is purely an individual matter, and you cannot and must not organize it. If you do, it becomes dead, crystalized; it becomes a creed, a sect, a religion, to be imposed on others. This is what everyone throughout the world is attempting to do. Truth is narrowed down and made a plaything for those who are weak, for those who are only momentarily discontented. Truth cannot be brought down; rather, the individual must make the effort to ascend to it. You cannot bring the mountaintop to the valley. If you would attain to the mountaintop you must pass through the valley, climb the steeps, unafraid of the dangerous precipices. You must climb toward the Truth, it cannot be "stepped down" or organized for you. Interest in ideas is mainly sustained by organizations, but organizations only awaken interest from without. Interest, which is not born out of love of Truth for its own sake, but aroused by an organization, is of no value. The organization becomes a framework into which its members can conveniently fit. They no longer strive after Truth or the mountaintop, but rather carve for themselves a convenient niche in which they put themselves, or let the organization place them, and consider that the organization will thereby lead them to Truth.

[178]

The Awareness of *What Is*

From the introduction to *The First and Last Freedom*, a book first published in 1954.

To communicate with one another, even if we know each other very well, is extremely difficult. I may use words that may have to you a significance different from mine. Understanding comes when we, you and I, meet on the same level at the same time. That happens only when there is real affection between people, between husband and wife, between intimate friends. That is real communion. Instantaneous understanding comes when we meet on the same level at the same time.

It is very difficult to commune with one another easily, effectively, and with definitive action. I am using words which are simple, which are not technical, because I do not think that any technical type of expression is going to help us solve our difficult problems; so I am not going to use any technical terms, either of psychology or of science. I have not read any books on psychology or any religious books, fortunately. I would like to convey, by the very simple words which we use in our daily life, a deeper significance; but that is very difficult if you do not know how to listen.

There is an art of listening. To be able really to listen, one should abandon or put aside all prejudices, preformulations, and daily activities. When you are in a receptive state of mind, things can be easily understood; you are listening when your real attention is given to something. But unfortunately most of us listen through a screen of resistance. We are screened with prejudices, whether religious or spiritual, psychological, or scientific; or with our daily worries, desires, and fears. And with these for a screen, we listen. Therefore, we listen really to our own noise, to our own sound, not to what is being said. It is extremely difficult to put aside our training, our prejudices, our inclination, our resistance, and, reaching beyond the verbal expression, to listen so that we understand instantaneously. That is going to be one of our difficulties.

If, during this discourse, anything is said which is opposed to your way of thinking and belief, just listen; do not resist. You may be right and I may be wrong; but by listening and considering together we are going to find out what is the truth. Truth cannot be given to you by somebody. You have to discover it; and to discover, there must be a state of mind in which there is direct perception. There is no direct perception when there is a resistance, a safeguard, a protection. Understanding comes through being aware of *what is*. To know exactly *what is*, the real, the actual, without interpreting it, without condemning or justifying it, is, surely, the beginning of wisdom. It is only when we begin to interpret, to translate according to our conditioning, according to our prejudice, that we miss the truth. After all, it is like research. To know what something is, what it is exactly, requires research—you cannot translate it according to your moods. Similarly, if we can look, observe, listen, be aware of, *what is*, exactly, then the problem is solved. And that is what we are going to do in all these discourses. I am going to point out to you *what is*, and not translate it according to my fancy; nor should you translate it or interpret it according to your background or training.

Is it not possible, then, to be aware of everything as it is? Starting from there, surely, there can be an understanding. To acknowledge, to be aware of, to get at that which is, puts an end to struggle. If I know that I am a liar, and it is a fact which I recognize, then the struggle is over. To acknowledge, to be aware of what one is, is already the beginning of wisdom, the beginning of understanding, which releases you from time. To bring in the quality of time—time, not in the chronological sense, but as the medium, as the psychological process, the process of the mind—is destructive, and creates confusion.

So, we can have understanding of *what is* when we recognize it without condemnation, without justification, without identification. To know that one is in a certain condition, in a certain state, is already a process of liberation; but a man who is not aware of his condition, of his struggle, tries to be something other than he is, which brings about habit. So, then, let us keep in mind that we want to examine *what is*, to observe and be aware of exactly what is the actual, without giving it any slant, without giving it an interpretation. It takes an extraordinarily astute mind, an extraordinarily pliable heart, to be aware of and to follow *what is;* because *what is* is constantly moving, constantly undergoing a transformation, and if the mind is tethered to belief, to knowledge, it ceases to pursue, it ceases to follow the swift movement of *what is*. *What is* is not static, surely it is constantly moving, as you will see if you observe it very closely. To follow it, you need a very swift mind and a pliable heart — which are denied when the mind is static, fixed in a belief, in a prejudice, in an identification; and a mind and heart that are dry cannot follow easily, swiftly, that which is.

[179]

From *Krishnamurti's Notebook*

Between June 1961 and January 1962, Krishnamurti kept a written journal, in which he noted his mental and physical states and recorded his reflections on his surroundings and events. During this period, the "process", a mysterious physical pain to which he had been subject since his transformative experience of 1922, resumed with some intensity.

16th

The whole process went on most of the night; it was rather intense. How much can the body stand! The whole body was quivering and, this morning, woke up with the head shaking.

There was, this morning that peculiar sacredness, filling the room. It had great penetrating power, entering into every corner of one's being, filling, cleansing, making everything of itself. The other felt it too. It's the thing that every human being craves for and because they crave for it, it eludes them. The monk, the priest, the sanyasi torture their bodies and their character in their longing for this but it evades them. For it cannot be bought; neither sacrifice, virtue nor prayer can bring this love. This life, this love cannot be if death is the means. All seeking, all asking must wholly cease.

Truth cannot be exact. What can be measured is not truth. That which is not living can be measured and its height be found.

17th

We were going up the path of a steep wooded side of a mountain and presently sat on a bench. Suddenly, most unexpectedly that sacred benediction came upon us, the other felt it too, without our saying anything. As it several times filled a room, this time it seemed to cover the mountainside across the wide, extending valley and beyond the mountains. It was everywhere. All space seemed to disappear; what was far, the wide gap, the distant snow-covered peaks and the person sitting on the bench faded away. There was not one or two or many but only this immensity. The brain had lost all its responses; it was only an instrument of observation, it was seeing, not as the brain belonging to a particular person, but as a brain which is not conditioned by time-space, as the essence of all brains.

It was a quiet night and the whole process was not so intense. On waking this morning, there was an experiencing whose duration was perhaps a minute, an hour or timeless. An experiencing that is informed with time ceases to be experiencing; what has continuity ceases to be the experiencing. On waking there was in the very depths, in the measureless depth of the total mind, an intense flame alive and burning furiously, of attention, of awareness, of creation. The word is not the thing; the symbol is not the real. The fires that burn on the surface of life pass, die away, leaving sorrow and ashes and remembrance. These fires are called life but it's not life. It's decay. The fire of creation that is destruction is life. In it there is no beginning, no ending, neither tomorrow or yesterday. It's there and no surface activity will ever uncover it. The brain must die for this life to be.

[180]

From *Krishnamurti's Journal*

For several weeks in 1973 and 1975, Krishnamurti again kept a diary. Many of the entries of these years take their start from natural scenery, which inspired him to write some of his most beautiful and most revealing prose. Here, as elsewhere, he often referred to himself as "he".

September 17, 1973

That evening, walking through the wood there was a feeling of menace. The sun was just setting and the palm trees were solitary against the golden western sky. The monkeys were in the banyan tree, getting ready for the night. Hardly anyone used that path and rarely you met another human being. There were many deer, shy and disappearing into the thick growth. Yet the menace was there, heavy and pervading: it was all around you, you looked over your shoulder. There were no dangerous animals; they had moved away from there; it was too close to the spreading town. One was glad to leave and walk back through the lighted streets. But the next evening the monkeys were still there and so were the deer and the sun was just behind the tallest trees; the menace was gone. On the contrary, the trees, the bushes and the small plants welcomed you. You were among your friends, you felt completely safe and most welcome. The woods accepted you and every evening it was a pleasure to walk there.

Forests are different. There's physical danger there, not only from snakes but from tigers that were known to be there. As one walked there one afternoon there was suddenly an abnormal silence; the birds stopped chattering, the monkeys were absolutely still and everything seemed to be holding its breath. One stood still. And as suddenly, everything came to life; the monkeys were playing and teasing each other, birds began their evening chatter and one was aware the danger had passed.

In the woods and groves where man kills rabbits, pheasants, squirrels, there's quite a different atmosphere. You are entering into a world where man has been, with his gun and peculiar violence. Then the woods lose their tenderness, their welcome, and here some beauty has been lost and that happy whisper has gone.

You have only one head and look after it for it's a marvellous thing. No machinery, no electronic computers can compare with it. It's so vast, so complex, so utterly capable, subtle and productive. It's the storehouse of experience, knowledge, memory. All thought springs from it. What it has put together is quite incredible: the mischief, the confusion, the sorrows, the wars, the corruptions, the illusions, the ideals, the pain and misery, the great cathedrals, the lovely mosques and the sacred temples. It is fantastic what it has done and what it can do. But one thing it apparently cannot do: change completely its behaviour in its relationship to another head, to another man. Neither punishment nor reward seem to change its behaviour; knowledge doesn't seem to transform its conduct. The me and the you remain. It never realises that the me is the you, that the observer is the observed. Its love is its degeneration; its pleasure is its agony; the gods of its ideals are its destroyers. Its freedom is its own prison; it is educated to live in this prison, only making it more comfortable, more pleasurable. You have only one head, care for it, don't destroy it. It's so easy to poison it.

He always had this strange lack of distance between himself

and the trees, rivers and mountains. It wasn't cultivated: you can't cultivate a thing like that. There was never a wall between him and another. What they did to him, what they said to him never seemed to wound him, nor flattery to touch him. Somehow he was altogether untouched. He was not withdrawn, aloof, but like the waters of a river. He had so few thoughts; no thoughts at all when he was alone. His brain was active when talking or writing but otherwise it was quiet and active without movement. Movement is time and activity is not.

This strange activity, without direction, seems to go on, sleeping or waking. He wakes up often with that activity of meditation; something of this nature is going on most of the time. He never rejected it or invited it. The other night he woke up, wide awake. He was aware that something like a ball of fire, light, was being put into his head, into the very centre of it. He watched it objectively for a considerable time, as though it were happening to someone else. It was not an illusion, something conjured up by the mind. Dawn was coming and through the opening of the curtains he could see the trees.

*

October 2, 1973

Consciousness is its content; the content is consciousness. All action is fragmentary when the content of consciousness is broken up. This activity breeds conflict, misery and confusion; then sorrow is inevitable.

From the air at that height you could see the green fields, each separate from the other in shape, size and colour. A stream came down to meet the sea; far beyond it were the mountains, heavy with snow. All over the earth there were large, spreading towns, villages; on the hills there were castles, churches and houses, and beyond them were the vast deserts, brown, golden and white. Then there was the blue sea again and more land with thick forests. The whole earth was rich and beautiful.

He walked there, hoping to meet a tiger, and he did. The villagers had come to tell his host that a tiger had killed a young cow the previous night and would come back that night to the kill. Would they like to see it? A platform on a tree would be built and from there one could see the big killer and also they would tie a goat to the tree to make sure that the tiger would come. He said he wouldn't like to see a goat killed for his pleasure. So the matter was dropped. But late that afternoon, as the sun was behind a rolling hill, his host wished to go for a drive, hoping that they might by chance see the tiger that had killed the cow. They drove for some miles into the forest; it became quite dark and with the headlights on they turned back. They had given up every hope of seeing the tiger as they drove back. But just as they turned a corner, there it was, sitting on its haunches in the middle of the road, huge, striped, its eyes bright with the headlamps. The car stopped and it came towards them growling and the growls shook the car; it was surprisingly large and its long tail with its black tip was moving slowly from side to side. It was annoyed. The window was open and as it passed growling, he put out his hand to stroke this great energy of the forest, but his host hurriedly snatched his arm back, explaining later that it would have torn his arm away. It was a magnificent animal, full of majesty and power.

Down there on that earth, there were tyrants denying freedom to man, ideologists shaping the mind of man, priests with their centuries of tradition and belief enslaving man; the politicians with their endless promises were bringing corruption and division. Down there man is caught in endless conflict and sorrow and in the bright lights of pleasure. It is all so utterly meaningless — the pain, the labour and the words of philosophers. Death and unhappiness and toil, man against man.

This complex variety, modified changes in the pattern of pleasure and pain, are the content of man's consciousness, shaped and conditioned by the culture in which it has been nurtured, with its religious and economic pressures. Freedom is not within the boundaries of such a consciousness; what is accepted as freedom is in reality a prison made somewhat livable in through the growth of technology. In this prison there are wars, made more destructive by science and profit. Freedom doesn't lie in the change of prisons, nor in any change of gurus, with their absurd authority. Authority does not bring the sanity of order. On the contrary it breeds disorder and out of this soil grows authority. Freedom is not in fragments. A non-fragmented mind, a mind that is whole is in freedom. It does not know it is free; what is known is within the area of time, the past through the present to the future. All movement is time and time is not a factor of freedom. Freedom of choice denies freedom; choice exists only where there is confusion. Clarity of perception, insight, is the freedom from the pain of choice. Total order is the light of freedom. This order is not the child of thought for all activity of thought is to cultivate fragmentation. Love is not a fragment of thought, of pleasure. The perception of this is intelligence. Love and intelligence are inseparable and from this flows action which does not breed pain. Order is its ground.

*

April 10, 1975

In the silence of deep night and in the quiet still morning when the sun is touching the hills, there is a great mystery. It is there in all living things. If you sit quietly under a tree, you would feel the ancient earth with its incomprehensible mystery. On a still night when the stars are clear and close, you would be aware of expanding space and the mysterious order of all things, of the immeasurable and of nothing, of the movement of the dark hills and the hoot of an owl. In that utter silence of the mind this mystery expands without time and space. There's mystery in those ancient temples built with infinite care, with attention which is love. The slender mosques and the great cathedrals lose this shadowy mystery for there is bigotry, dogma and military pomp. The myth that is concealed in the deep layers of the mind is not mysterious, it is romantic, traditional and conditioned. In the secret recesses of the mind, truth has been pushed aside by symbols, words, images; in them there is no mystery, they are the churnings of thought. In knowledge and its action there is wonder, appreciation and delight. But mystery is quite another thing. It is not an experience, to be recognised, stored up and remembered. Experience is the death of that incommunicable mystery; to communicate you need a word, a gesture, a look, but to be in communion with *that*, the mind, the whole of you, must be at the same level, at the same time, with the same intensity as that which is called mysterious. This is love. With this the whole mystery of the universe is open.

This morning there wasn't a cloud in the sky, the sun was in the valley and all things were rejoicing, except man. He looked at this wondrous earth and went on with his labour, his sorrow and passing pleasures. He had no time to see; he was too occupied with his problems, with his agonies, with his violence. He doesn't see the tree and so he cannot see his own travail. When he's forced to look, he tears to pieces what he sees, which he calls analysis, runs away from it or doesn't want to see. In the art of seeing lies the miracle of transformation, the transformation of "what is". The "what should be" never is. There's vast mystery in the act of seeing. This needs care, attention, which is love.

[181]

From *Krishnamurti to Himself*

In 1983, Krishnamurti was given a tape-recorder so that he could continue his journal without having to write. The entries of this period often begin with accounts of remembered landscapes, and then became more reflective.

Wednesday, April 20, 1983

At the end of every leaf, the large leaves and the tiny leaves, there was a drop of water sparkling in the sun like an extraordinary jewel. And there was a slight breeze but that breeze didn't in any way disturb or destroy that drop on those leaves that were washed clean by the late rain. It was a very quiet morning, full of delight, peaceful, and with a sense of benediction in the air. And as we watched the sparkling light on every clean leaf, the earth became extraordinarily beautiful, in spite of all the telegraph wires and their ugly posts. In spite of all the noise of the world, the earth was rich, abiding, enduring. And though there were earthquakes here and there, most destructive, the earth was still beautiful. One never appreciates the earth unless one really lives with it, works with it, puts one's hands in the dust, lifting big rocks and stones — one never knows the extraordinary sense of being with the earth, the flowers, the gigantic trees and the strong grass and the hedges along the road.

Everything was alive that morning. As we watched, there was a sense of great joy and the heavens were blue, the sun was slowly coming out of the hills and there was light. As we watched the mockingbird on the wire, it was doing its antics, jumping high, doing a somersault, then coming down on the same spot on the wire. As we watched the bird enjoying itself, jumping in the air and then coming down circling, with its shrill cries, its enjoyment of life, only that bird existed, the watcher didn't exist. The watcher was no longer there, only the bird, grey and white, with a longish tail. That watching was without any movement of thought, watching the flurry of the bird that was enjoying itself.

We never watch for long. When we watch with great patience, watch without any sense of the watcher, watch those birds, those droplets on the quivering leaves, the bees and the flowers and the long trail of ants, then time ceases, time has a stop. One doesn't take time to watch or have the patience to watch. One learns a great deal through watching — watching people, the way they walk, their talk, their gestures. You can see through their vanity or their negligence of their own bodies. They are indifferent, they are callous.

There was an eagle flying high in the air, circling without the beat of the wings, carried away by the air current beyond the hills and was lost. Watching, learning: learning is time but watching has no time. Or when you listen, listen without any interpretation, without any reaction, listen without any bias. Listen to that thunder in the skies, the thunder rolling among the hills. One never listens completely, there is always interruption. Watching and listening are a great art — watching and listening without any reaction, without any sense of the listener or the see-er. By watching and listening we learn infinitely more than from any book. Books are necessary, but watching and listening sharpen your senses. For, after all, the brain is the centre of all the reactions, thoughts and remembrances. But if your senses are not highly awakened you cannot really watch and listen and learn, not only how to act but about learning, which is the very soil in which the seed of goodness can grow.

When there is this simple, clear watching and listening, then there is an awareness — awareness of the colour of those flowers, red, yellow, white, of the spring leaves, the stems, so tender, so delicate, awareness of the heavens, the earth and those people who are passing by. They have been chattering along that long road, never looking at the trees, at the flowers, at the skies and the marvellous hills. They are not even aware of what is going on around them. They talk a great deal about the environment, how we must protect nature and so on, but it seems they are not aware of the beauty and the silence of the hills and the dignity of a marvellous old tree. They are not even aware of their own thoughts, their own reactions, nor are they aware of the way they walk, of their clothes. It does not mean that they are to be self-centered in their watching, in their awareness, but just be aware.

When you are aware there is a choice of what to do, what not to do, like and dislike, your biases, your fears, your anxieties, the joys which you have remembered, the pleasures that you have pursued; in all this there is choice, and we think that choice gives us freedom. We like that freedom to choose; we think freedom is necessary to choose — or, rather, that choice gives us a sense of freedom — but there is no choice when you see things very, very clearly.

And that leads us to an awareness without choice — to be aware without any like or dislike. When there is this really simple, honest, choiceless awareness it leads to another factor, which is attention. The word itself means to stretch out, to grasp, to hold on, but that is still the activity of the brain, it is in the brain. Watching, awareness, attention, are within the area of the brain, and the brain is limited — conditioned by all the ways of past generations, the impressions, the traditions and all the folly and the goodness of man. So all action from this attention is still limited, and that which is limited must inevitably bring disorder. When one is thinking about oneself from morning until night — one's own worries, one's own desires, demands and fulfilments — this self-centredness, being very, very limited, must cause friction in its relationship with another, who is also limited; there must be friction, there must be strain and disturbances of many kinds, the perpetual violence of human beings.

When one is attentive to all this, choicelessly aware, then out of that comes insight. Insight is not an act of remembrance, the continuation of memory. Insight is like a flash of light. You see with absolute clarity, all the complications, the consequences, the intricacies. Then this very insight is action, complete. In that there are no regrets, no looking back, no sense of being weighed down, no discrimination. This is pure, clear insight — perception without any shadow of doubt.

Most of us begin with certainty and as we grow older that certainty changes to uncertainty and we die with uncertainty. But if one begins with uncertainty, doubting, questioning, asking, demanding, with real doubt about man's behaviour, about all the religious rituals and their images and their symbols, then out of that doubt comes the clarity of certainty. When there is clear insight into violence, for instance, that very insight banishes all violence. That insight is outside the brain, if one can so put it. It is not of time. It is not of remembrance or of knowledge, and so that insight and its action changes the very brain cells. That insight is complete and from that completeness there can be logical, sane, rational, action.

This whole movement from watching, listening, to the thunder of insight, is one movement; it is not coming to it step by step. It is like a swift arrow. And that insight alone can uncondition the brain, not the effort of thought, which is determination, seeing the necessity for something; none of that will bring about total freedom from conditioning. All this is time and the ending of time. Man is time-bound and that bondage to time is the movement of thought. So where there is an ending to thought and to time there is total insight. Only then can there be the flowering of the brain. Only then can you have a complete relationship with the mind.

[182]

The Core of Krishnamurti's Teaching

Krishnamurti wrote this short summary of his teachings in London in 1980. He began by correcting a draft written by his biographer Mary Lutyens, but ended up producing his own concise summary of his teachings.

The core of Krishnamurti's teaching is contained in the statement he made in 1929 when he said "Truth is a pathless land." Man cannot come to it through any organization, through any creed, through any dogma, priest, or ritual, nor through any philosophical knowledge or psychological technique. He has to find it through the mirror of relationship, through the understanding of the contents of his own mind, through observation, and not through intellectual analysis or introspective dissection. Man has built in himself images as a sense of security — religious, political, personal. These manifest as symbols, ideas, beliefs. The burden of these dominates man's thinking, relationships, and daily life. These are the causes of our problems, for they divide man from man in every relationship. His perception of life is shaped by the concepts already established in his mind. The content of his consciousness *is* this consciousness. This content is common to all humanity. The individuality is the name, the form, and superficial culture he acquires from his environment. The uniqueness of the individual does not lie in the superficial but in the total freedom from the content of consciousness.

Freedom is not a reaction; freedom is not choice. It is man's pretense that because he has choice he is free. Freedom is pure observation without motive; freedom is not at the end of the evolution of man, but lies in the first step of his existence. In observation one begins to discover the lack of freedom. Freedom is found in the choiceless awareness of our daily existence.

Thought is time. Thought is born of experience, of knowledge, which are inseparable from time. Time is the psychological enemy of man. Our action is based on knowledge and, therefore, time, so man is always a slave to the past.

When man becomes aware of the movement of his own consciousness he will see the division between the thinker and the thought, the observer and the observed, the experiencer and the experience. He will discover that this division is an illusion. Then only is there pure observation, which is insight without any shadow of the past. This timeless insight brings about a deep radical change in the mind.

Total negation is the essence of the positive. When there is negation of all those things which are not love — desire, pleasure — then love is, with its compassion and intelligence.

FURTHER READING

Source Materials

J. Krishnamurti, *Krishnamurti's Notebook*. Madras: Krishnamurti Foundation India, 1982.

J. Krishnamurti, *Krishnamurti's Journal*. Madras: Krishnamurti Foundation India, 1982.

J. Krishnamurti, *Krishnamurti to Himself: His Last Journal*. New York: HarperSanFrancisco, 1993.

J. Krishnamurti, *Total Freedom: The Essential Krishnamurti*. New York: HarperSanFrancisco, 1996.

Other Sources

Mary Lutyens, *Krishnamurti: The Years of Awakening*. New York: Avon Books, 1976.

Mary Lutyens, *Krishnamurti: The Years of Fulfilment*. New York: Avon Books, 1983.

Krishnamurti Foundation Trust <http://www.kfoundation.org>

Krishnamurti Foundation of America <http://www.kfa.org>

Sources of Texts and Translations

177 *Total Freedom* 1–2
178 *Total Freedom* 60–61
179 *Krishnamurti's Notebook* 24–25
180 *Krishnamurti's Journal* 14–15, 40–41, 91–92
181 *Krishnamurti to Himself* 71–74
182 *Total Freedom* 257–58

ANANDAMAYI MA

Some form of *sādhana* — inner effort or practice — seems to be required to free the human being from the limitations of the "ordinary" mind, life and body. If, however, as many mystics have claimed, the (liberated) human being is not different from the Divine, who is it that makes the effort or engages in spiritual practice? One possible solution to this problem is that it is the Divine itself that does *sādhana* in the apparent individual. In a few rare cases, there is more — what seems to be a spontaneous self-emergence of the Divine in a human being. In Hinduism, such divine manifestations are known as *avatār*s — a term originally reserved for incarnations of Vishnu, but increasingly used of human beings who are proclaimed by their followers to be the Divine in human form. Chaitanya (see selection 131) was one of the first well-known individuals about whom such a claim was made. In the nineteenth and twentieth centuries, assertions of avatarhood have been made on behalf of Sri Ramakrishna, Sai Baba of Shirdi, Sri Aurobindo, Ramana Maharshi and many others. In each of these instances, the guru (if there was a guru at all) played a relatively minor role; there was instead a sudden self-emergence of the spiritual personality, which soon overshadowed the ordinary humanity of the seeker.

A striking example of such spontaneous self-emergence is found in the life of the Bengali woman who became known as Anandamayi Ma. Born in 1896 in a remote village in East Bengal (now Bangladesh), Nirmala Sundari was the daughter of a devout orthodox vaishnava brahmin named Bipin Bihari Bhattacharya. As a girl, Nirmala was considered remarkable, if at all, mostly for her sunny disposition. She was, as was the custom, given little education, and married off to an older man when she was not yet thirteen. She remained in her father's house for several years, and then went to live with her sister-in-law, whose duty it was to turn her into a proper Hindu wife. Finally, in 1914, Nirmala went to live with her husband. By this time she had shown herself to be an unusual young woman, given to visions and trances. Recognising her spiritual qualities, her husband kept his distance, and it is assumed that the marriage was never consummated.

From around 1918, Nirmala's "play of sadhana" began in earnest. As she later explained: "One day at Bajitpur . . . the *kheyāla* suddenly came to me, 'How would it be to play the role of a *sādhikā* [a woman who practises *sādhana*]?' And so the *līlā* began" (Lipski 1977: 10). *Kheyāla*, a term used frequently by Anandamayi Ma and her followers, means normally a sudden desire. In her case it referred to a spontaneous manifestation of the will of the Divine, which she invariably obeyed.

Over the next few years, in obedience to her *kheyāla*, Nirmala performed various forms of *sādhana*, often without knowing exactly what she was doing. Those around her sometimes worried that she was losing her balance; but when spiritual experts were consulted, they declared that she not only was sane but in fact was an unusually advanced soul. During this period, she became spontaneously aware of mantras that had to be repeated and rituals that had to be performed. Finally, in 1922, she became her own *guru* by initiating herself. There followed a stage in which she was moved to traverse "the paths of all religions and faiths apart from the varieties of all forms of Hinduism. She had the *kheyāla* to experience, as it were, the trials, hardships, and despairs of the pilgrim in search of God and also his state of blissful excitement" (B. Mukherji, quoted in Hallstrom 40). During this period she manifested a therapeutic power that benefited many people. Soon her spiritual accomplishments were on everyone's lips, but she remained withdrawn from the public.

In 1924 her husband found work in Dhaka and she followed him there. Her *līlā* or "play" continued in Dhaka for another year; but then her realisation became stable and the unusual occurrences that had accompanied her *sādhana* ceased. By this time she was famous in Dhaka, and there was an unending flow of people who wanted to have her *darśan*, that is, to have a sanctifying glimpse of her. In 1926, following her *kheyāla*, she began to go out on tour, visiting pilgrim centres in Bengal, Bihar and Uttar Pradesh. Wherever she went, hundreds of people thronged to meet her, drawn by her reputation and charisma. During these travels, her devotees began to refer to her as *Mā* or Mother. To this the epithet *Ānandamayī*—"permeated with bliss"—was soon added.

For some time, Anandamayi Ma returned periodically to Dhaka, but from 1932 till her death in 1982 she was always on the move, never remaining in one place for more than two weeks. Accompanied by a band of disciples, who looked after and shielded her, she met with those who approached her, the famous as well as the obscure. Her teachings were given mostly in the form of answers to their questions. At first she spoke only in Bengali; later she mastered Hindi as well. Many collections of her "words" have appeared in these languages and in translations into other Indian languages as well as English and other European tongues. The extracts below are from such collections of sayings as well as from biographies and reminiscences. All have been translated into English from the original Bengali or Hindi. In many of the passages, Anandamayi Ma refers to herself as "this body".

[183]

Talks on Sadhana

These four passages are each from a different source. In the first three, Anandamayi Ma refers to a stage of her *sādhana* or period of spiritual striving. In the last she describes the state when one has gone beyond *sādhana* altogether.

Question: Kusum Brahmachari says your sādhana *was no real* sādhana *because all the obstacles and difficulties that arise from within us when we set out to practise* sādhana *were non-existent in your case.*

Why should this be so? When the play of *sādhana* commenced within this body, did it not live with a good number of people? This body resided in the midst of Bholānath's large family. Every type of work was performed by this body. But when this body played the role of a *sādhaka*, it assumed every detail necessary for each particular *sādhana*. For instance, marks on the forehead like *tilak, svarūpa, tripuṇḍra*, all appeared one by one. . . . About the *āsanas* (yogic postures) that formed spontaneously I have already told you previously. Some people spend a lifetime in acquiring the art to perform one such *āsana* to perfection. But when this body became a *sādhaka*, it was seen that one *āsana* after another was executed and each of them to perfection. All your questions have now been replied to.

*

All these *āsanas* and so forth were not done of my own volition. Indeed, I was unable to do anything with my own hands. I saw that this body was bending and performing various *āsanas*. Every day a variety of *āsanas* was performed. One day, a particular *āsana* occurred, but another time when the same *āsana* began again, I thought I would watch what happened. I supplied extra support with my hand and readjusted slightly. This caused a severe pull to my leg and I was hurt. Even now it feels sensitive at that spot. At that time I didn't know what *āsanas* were, but various kinds formed of themselves. Till then I had not been informed externally as to how many kinds of *āsana* existed nor what their names were. After that I began to hear and understand clearly from within what was going on. The body was being twisted and turned to perform *āsanas* in such a way that it was entirely boneless and only thus was it possible for it to contort in that way. It was turned topsy-turvy in all kinds of positions. The head would bend backwards and remain touching the middle of the back. The hands were bent so sharply that it was stunning to watch.

This body has not followed one particular line of *sādhana* only, but has covered all known lines. It passed through all the different varieties of practice referred to by the sages of ancient times. This body successfully went through *nāma sādhana, haṭha yoga* with its numerous *āsanas* and through the diversity of yogas, one after another. In order to attain to a particular stage along only one of those lines an ordinary individual may have to be born again and again, but in this body it was a matter of seconds. Moreover, the different forms of *sādhana* that this body has been seen to practise were not meant for this body; they were meant for you all.

This body has no desire, no intention or set purpose—everything occurs spontaneously.

Whether this body talks to you or laughs or lies down to sleep, or whether it sinks to the ground and rolls about, as sometimes happened during *kīrtan*, no matter how many different states and conditions this body may appear to be in, it nevertheless remains always in the one state. Indeed everything arises out of one Being.

*

When *pūjā* and similar rites were spontaneously performed by this body then the particular characteristics of the deity worshipped, the *āsanas* and *mudrās*, the display of power and so on, specific to that deity, everything manifested through this body in exactly the prescribed manner. But all this, far from being the product of imagination, was as real as you are here right now before me. Every detail necessary for the ceremony not only appeared of itself, in fact it issued from this body. Even the forms (*mūrti*) of gods and goddesses were taken out of this body and made to sit down and then were worshipped. Again, when the *pūjā* had been completed they merged into this body exactly from where and in the same way in which they had emerged. It has to be borne in mind that everything is possible.

*

At the stage of the *sādhaka* there is progression towards a goal. But here, one cannot speak either of a stage or stagelessness, neither of a goal nor aimlessness. Just as when lighting a lamp every object in a dark room can be clearly seen one by one, it is exactly like this. But while still treading the path of the aspirant, it is not possible to perceive all details. Many kinds of obstacles have to be overcome while advancing. There is an outer current and there is another one that leads within. But here, there is no question of this either.

Here, the veins are myself, the nerves are myself, the movement is myself, and the witness of it all is also myself. Of course, the word, "myself", is used only because some language has to be employed.

[184]

Paramahansa Yogananda meets Anandamayi Ma

Paramahansa Yogananda (see selection 176) met Anandamayi Ma in Kolkata in December 1935. Afterwards she visited his school in Ranchi. A decade or more later, Yogananda described these meetings in two passages of his *Autobiography of a Yogi.*

Ananda Moyi Ma was standing in an open-topped automobile, blessing a throng of about one hundred disciples. She was evidently on the point of departure. Mr. Wright parked the Ford some distance away, and accompanied me on foot, toward the quiet assemblage. The woman saint glanced in our direction; she alighted from her car and walked toward us.

"Father, you have come!" With these fervent words (in Bengali) she put her arm around my neck and her head on my shoulder. Mr. Wright, to whom I had just remarked that I did not know the saint, was hugely enjoying this extraordinary demonstration of welcome. The eyes of the hundred chelas were also fixed with some surprise on the affectionate tableau.

I had instantly seen that the saint was in a high state of *samādhi.* Oblivious to her outward garb as a woman, she knew herself as the changeless soul; from that plane she was joyously greeting another devotee of God. She led me by the hand into her automobile.

"Ananda Moyi Ma, I am delaying your journey!" I protested.

"Father, I am meeting you for the first time in this life, after ages!" she said. "Please do not leave yet."

We sat together in the rear seats of the car. The Blissful Mother soon entered the immobile ecstatic state. Her beautiful eyes glanced heavenward and, half-opened, became stilled, gazing into the near-far inner Elysium. The disciples chanted gently: "Victory to Mother Divine!"

I had found many men of God-realization in India, but never before had I met such an exalted woman saint. Her gentle face was burnished with the ineffable joy that had given her the name of Blissful Mother. Long black tresses lay loosely behind her unveiled head. A red dot of sandalwood paste on her forehead symbolized the spiritual eye, ever open within her. Tiny face, tiny hands, tiny feet — a contrast to her spiritual magnitude!

I put some questions to a nearby woman chela while Ananda Moyi Ma remained entranced.

"The Blissful Mother travels widely in India; in many parts she has hundreds of disciples," the chela told me. "Her courageous efforts have brought about many desirable social reforms. Although a Brahmin, the saint recognizes no caste distinctions. A group of us always travel with her, looking after her comforts. We have to mother her; she takes no notice of her body. If no one gave her food, she would not eat, or make any inquiries. Even when meals are placed before her, she does not touch them. To prevent her disappearance from this world, we disciples feed her with our own hands. For days together she often stays in the divine trance, scarcely breathing, her eyes unwinking. One of her chief disciples is her husband. Many years ago, soon after their marriage, he took the vow of silence." . . .

*

"It is beautiful here," Ananda Moyi Ma said graciously, as I led her into the main building. She seated herself with a childlike smile by my side. The closest of dear friends, she made one feel, yet an aura of remoteness was ever around her — the paradoxical isolation of Omnipresence.

"Please tell me something of your life."

"Father knows all about it; why repeat it?" She evidently felt that the factual history of one short incarnation was beneath notice.

I laughed, gently repeating my request.

"Father, there is little to tell." She spread her graceful hands in a deprecatory gesture. "My consciousness has never associated itself with this temporary body. Before I came on this earth, Father, 'I was the same'. As a little girl, 'I was the same'. I grew into womanhood, but still 'I was the same'. When the family in which I had been born made arrangements to have this body married, 'I was the same'.

"And, Father, in front of you now, 'I am the same'. Ever afterward, though the dance of creation change around me in the hall of eternity, 'I shall be the same'."

Ananda Moyi Ma sank into a deep meditative state. Her form was statue-still; she had fled to her ever-calling kingdom. The dark pools of her eyes appeared lifeless and glassy. This expression is often present when saints remove their consciousness from the physical body, which is then hardly more than a piece of soulless clay. We sat together for an hour in the ecstatic trance.

[185]

Replies to Questions

These exchanges are taken from two English books comprising Anandamayi Ma's answers to questions put to her by devotees and visitors. Translated anonymously from the Hindi or Bengali.

Q: At the time of parting, when with a broken heart I did praṇāma *to you, I knew that I had found something, but I also felt as if I were losing something. In this mood I went my way.*

Where nothing is, there is everything. All efforts are for the sake of this realization only. To do *pranāma* means to pour oneself out at His feet, to become closely bound to them and thereby united to Him, to become His, who alone IS. When doing *pranāma* in a temple or anywhere else, you should not hold back anything, but give yourself without reserve.

Q: To know you are always near, although physically you may be far away, this experience can only come by your Grace. It seems impossible for me to attain it through my own efforts.

You must know Him in such a way that no place remains where He is not. According to Vaishnavite terminology there is *viraha* and *milana* [separation and union]. But this *viraha rasa*, this experience of profound yearning for God after having known union, is not like the worldly sense of separateness, which means not knowing the other, being unfulfilled.

Everything comes by His Grace alone — this of course is a fact. You experience as your own the power He has vested in you. Apply it in His service to the utmost of your capability, whatever be the nature of your approach, whatever your line.

Q: While I was near you, I forgot all about my home. I did not give a single thought to my family affairs and cares.

But the nearer the train carries me to my home, the more my domestic hopes and worries crowd into my mind.

Just as thoughts about your home crowd into your mind as you draw nearer to your dwelling-place, so also the closer you get to God, the greater grows the joy derived from the ever-increasing variety of experiences of the Divine. Indeed as you advance toward your real home, you realize more and more of this Joy. You are on the way to finding yourself, be it as the servant of the Lord, or as a part of Him, or as the ONE SELF. You must seek what will take you to *eka rasa*, the state of undifferentiated Being, of Oneness, where nothing remains to be known, to be attained.

Q: Grant me the strength, the power to become firmly established in pure devotion, in truthfulness and sincerity. I desire no other wealth except the abandonment of myself at the Feet of the Lord.

All desire must be for God only. Whatever you do whether with your hands or with your brain, do it as His service. Whatever you accept, physically or mentally, accept it as God coming to you in this shape. If anything is to be given, it is a surrender of yourself at His feet.

*

Q: How can we get Self-realization?

Not by anything. "Something" means a little. By doing something, you will get something which is not worth anything. God is Wholeness, Totality. When the clouds fade away He stands revealed. In very truth there is One Self, duality has no real existence. *Durbuddhi*, evil-mindedness and stupidity, arise from the conception of duality — mine and thine. As a result there is *durgati*, hardship and misery, and *durbodha*, difficulty in understanding. The two, the pairs of opposites (*dvandva*) are nothing but blindness (*andha*).

*

Q: "What does Mataji consider to be the most essential thing in life?"

To try to find out "who I am"! To endeavour to know that which has brought into existence the body that I know: The Search after

God. But first of all one must conceive the desire to know oneself. When one finds one's Self, one has found God; and finding God one has found one's Self, the one Ātmā.

Q: Are there many people who succeed in this?

Quite a few attain to some perfection (*siddhi*) or liberation (*mukti*). But complete Realization is very, very rare indeed—one in ten millions.

Q: Does Mataji think that she herself has attained to that complete perfection?

[*Laughs.*] Whatever you believe me to be, that I am.

*Q: [*to the translator*]: It means that she does think so, otherwise she would have said "No!"*
*[*To Mataji*]: From what moment did you have that Realization?*

When was I not?

*

Q: Surely, one who has become established in the Self will naturally forget the world?

In the kingdom of forgetting one forgets. So long as you are identified with the body (*deho*), it is your very nature to call out, "give, give!" (*"deo, deo"*!). You say, "give!" because you are in want. Where want exists, there must needs be error and ignorance; and where error and ignorance abide, there will most certainly be forgetting. When in the midst of all this you practise *sādhana* in order to realize your Self, or rather, when by God's Grace *sādhana* comes about,—for to be able to engage in *sādhana* is itself the Grace of God—then, after having worked through layers and layers of ignorance, you discover: "I am in fact the whole". I am: this is why there are trees and plants and everything that exists, however manifold. Every single form is in fact I.

Where I am conscious of separateness, my natural expression is to want. Even in this condition I am infinite. In the very form of the human body lie moods of endless variety and numberless modes of expression. Indeed, all existing forms are infinite, and I am likewise infinite. All forms and distinctive marks I see to be myself:

eternally, therefore, I exist. So then I have discovered this, and that I am of many forms — infinite forms indeed, with infinite modes of appearance. They exist within me in ways of infinite diversity, and yet I myself am all of these. Within me exist the separate modes of display — in endless variation none are excluded. When the like is directly perceived and all manifold aspects are recognized as a whole, then the One will certainly be revealed. How can the One be distinct from the infinite multiplicity? The many exist in the One and the One in the many.

This is why, when you can visualize five hundred of your former births, you are still limited by number; for there is so very much more than this! When you have discovered yourself in all the untold forms, you realize that the Lord is present in every one of them. When the essential nature of infinity and finiteness becomes fully revealed, you see that there is finiteness in infinity and infinity in the finite. Now you are in a position to resolve the polarity of *Sākāra* (God-with-form), and *Nirākāra* (God-without-form).

Look, if there were no veil of ignorance for the individual, how could God's *Līlā* be carried on? When acting a part one must forget oneself; the *Līlā* could not proceed without the covering veil of ignorance. Consequently it is but natural that the veil should be there. So, the world is the perception by the senses of what is projected (*sṛṣṭi-dṛṣṭi*). To be a separate individual means to be bound, and that which binds is the veil of ignorance: Here is the clue to the forgetting about which you asked.

*

> *Q: I have read in books that some say they have to descend in order to act in the world. This seems to imply that although they are established in Pure Being, they have to take the help of the mind when doing work. Just as a king, when acting the role of a sweeper, has for the time being to imagine he is a sweeper.*

In assuming a part, surely, there is no question of ascending or descending. Abiding in His own Essential Being (*Svarūpa*), He Himself plays various parts. But when you speak of ascending and descending, where is the state of Pure Being? Can there be duality in that state? Brahman is One without a second. Though from your angle of vision, I grant, it does appear as you put it.

Q: You have explained this from the level of ajñāna. *Now be pleased to speak from the level of the Enlightened* (Jñānī)*!*

[*Laughing*]: What you say now, I also accept. Here [*pointing to Herself*] nothing is rejected. Whether it is the state of Enlightenment or of ignorance, everything is all right. The fact is that you are in doubt. But here there is no question of doubt. Whatever you may say — and from whatever level — is THAT, THAT and only THAT.

Q: If this is so, is it of any use to ask you further questions?

What is, Is. That doubts should arise is natural. But the wonder is, where THAT is, there is not even room for different stands to be taken. Problems are discussed, surely, for the purpose of dissolving doubts. Therefore it is useful to discuss. Who can tell when the veil will be lifted from your eyes? The purpose of discussion is to remove this ordinary sight. This vision is no vision at all, for it is only temporary. Real vision is that vision where there is no such thing as the seer and the seen. It is eyeless — not to be beheld with these ordinary eyes, but with the eyes of wisdom. In that vision without eyes there is no room for "di-vision".

Here [*pointing to Herself*] there is no question of giving and taking, neither of serving. On your level they exist; from there these topics arise.

*

Pitājī, when you asked: "Tell me your experience," it would imply that the experiencer has still remained. This cannot be so here; furthermore, the question of transmission of power by the Guru to the disciple is equally non-existent. If there is no body, this question cannot be there either. There is no question of a physical or any other body. What is beyond even that cannot be put into words of any language. Whatever can be expressed in words or speech is a creation of the mind. *Pitājī*, as to the saying, "There is only one Brahman without a second", in the Self there is no possibility at all of a "second". The notion of the "two" has come about through the operating of reason. Just as you say: "Without feet He walks and without eyes He sees".

This body maintains that whatever anyone may say from the plane of reason — with the idea that the body exists, from the standpoint of the disciple — can be supported on the level of reasoning. For one's vision is conditioned by the spectacles one uses. This body declares that, whatever theory anyone may hold is based on reasoning, which presupposes the existence of a residue of the mind and of *prārabdha*. But where THAT stands revealed, it is quite otherwise. There, to discriminate or speculate is impossible. Beyond reason, beyond points of view, there is a state where none of these can be. *Pitājī*, in very truth, in THAT there is no room for words, language, or discrimination of any kind. Whether one says "there is not" or "there is" — these are also merely words, words floating on the surface. Therefore it is said that here, words, language, utterances of any type have no place. This is the truth, *Pitājī*, do you understand?

*

Q: Am I right to believe that you are God?

There is nothing save Him alone, everyone and everything are but forms of God. In your person also He has come here now to give darshan.

Q: Then why are you in this world?

In this world? I am not anywhere. I am myself reposing within myself.

Q: What is your work?

I have no work. For whom can I work since there is only ONE?

Q: Why am I in the world?

He plays in infinite ways. It is His pleasure to play as He does.

Q: But I, why am I in the world?

That is what I have been telling you. All is He, He plays in countless forms and ways. However, in order to find out for yourself why you are in the world, to find out who you are in reality, there are the various *sādhanas*. You study and you pass your exams, you earn money and enjoy the use of it. But all this is within the realm of death in which you continue life after life, repeating the same kind of thing again and again. Then there is another path as well, the path of Immortality, which leads to the knowledge of what you really are.

Q: Can anyone help me in this or must each one find out for himself?

The professor can teach you only if you have the capacity to learn. Of course, he can give you help but you must be able to respond, you must have it in you to grasp what he teaches.

Q: Which is the best path to Self-knowledge?

All paths are good. It depends on a man's *saṁskāras*, his conditioning, the tendencies he has brought over from previous births. Just as one can travel to the same place by plane, railway, car or cycle, so also different lines of approach suit different types of people. But the best path is the one which the Guru points out.

Q: When there is only ONE, *why are there so many different religions in the world?*

Because He is infinite, there is an infinite variety of conceptions of Him and an endless variety of paths to Him. He is everything, every kind of belief, and also the disbelief of the atheist. Your belief in non-belief is also a belief. When you speak of disbelief it implies that you admit belief. He is in all forms and yet He is formless.

Q: From what you said I gather that you consider the formless nearer to Truth than God with form?

Is ice anything but water? Form is just as much He as the Formless. To say that there is only One Self (*Ātmā*) and all forms are illusion would imply that the formless was nearer to Truth than God-with-form. But this body declares: every form and the formless are He and He alone.

Q: What have you to say about those who insist that only one religion is the right one?

All religions are paths to Him.

Q: I am a Christian . . .

So am I; a Christian, a Muslim, anything you like.

Q: Would it be right for me to become a Hindu or is my approach by the Christian way?

If you are fated to become a Hindu it will happen in any case. Just as you cannot ask: "What will happen in case of a car accident?" When the accident occurs, you will see.

Q: If I feel the urge to become a Hindu, should I give way to it or is it right to suppress it, since it is said that everyone has been born where it is best for him?

If you really felt the urge to become a Hindu, you would not ask this question but would just go ahead with it.

Yet there is also another side to this problem. It is true that you are a Christian, but something of a Hindu is in you as well, otherwise you could not even know anything about Hinduism. Everything is contained in everything. Just as a tree yields seed and from a single seed hundreds of trees may develop, so the seed is contained in the tree and the whole of the tree potentially in the tiny seed.

Q: How can I find happiness?

First tell me whether you are willing to do as this body bids you to do?

Q: Yes, I am.

Are you really? Very well. Now suppose I ask you to remain here, will you be able to do it?

*Q: No, I will not [*laughter*].*

You see, happiness that depends on anything outside of you, be it your wife, children, money, fame, friends, or anything else, cannot last. But to find happiness in Him who is everywhere, who is all pervading—your own Self, this is real happiness.

Q: So you say happiness lies in finding my Self?

Yes. Finding your Self, discovering who you really are, means to find God, for there is nothing outside of Him.

Q: You say all are God! But are not some people more God than others?

For him who asks such a question, this is so. But in actual fact God is fully and equally present everywhere.

Q: Is there no substance to me as an individual? Is there nothing in me that is not God?

No. Even in "not being God" there is only God alone. Everything is He.

Q: Is there no justification at all for professional or any other mundane work?

Occupation with worldly things acts like slow poison. Gradually, without one's noticing it, it leads to death. Should I advise my friends and my fathers and mothers to take this road? I cannot do so. What this body says is: Choose the path to Immortality, take any path that according to your temperament, will lead you to the Realization of your Self.

Nevertheless, even while working in the world, you can do one thing. Whatever you do throughout the day, endeavour to do it in a spirit of service. Serve God in everyone, regarding everyone and everything as manifestations of Him and serve Him by whatever work you undertake. If you live with this attitude of mind, the path to Reality will open out before you.

FURTHER READING

Source Materials

Anandamayi Ma, *Words of Sri Anandamayi Ma*, translated and compiled by Atmananda. Calcutta: Shree Shree Anandamayee Charitable Society, 1982.

Anandamayi Ma, *Matri Vani*, vol. II: Calcutta: Shree Shree Anandamayee Charitable Society, 1993.

Anandamayi Ma, *As the Flower Sheds its Fragrance* (*Diary Leaves of a Devotee*). Calcutta: Shree Shree Anandamayee Charitable Society, 1994.

Paramahansa Yogananda, *Autobiography of a Yogi*. Mumbai: Jaico Publishing House, 1997.

Other Sources

Alexander Lipski, *Life and Teaching of Śrī Ānandamayī Mā*. Delhi: Motilal Banarsidass, 1977.

Lisa Lassell Hallstrom, *Mother of Bliss: Ānandamayī Mā (1896–1982)*. Delhi: Oxford University Press, 1999.

Richard Lannoy, *Anandamayi: Her Life and Wisdom*. Shaftsbury, Dorset: Element, 1996.

Sri Sri Anandamayi Ma's Darshan <http://www.anandamayi.org>

Sources of Texts and Translations

183 A. K. Das Gupta, quoted in Hallstrom 182; text quoted in Lannoy 3–4; *Matri Vani*, vol. II: 278–80, 284

184 Yogananda 447–49, 450

185 *As the Flower* 31–32, 78, 181; *Words* 153–54, 45–46, 60–61; *As the Flower* 127–30

SRI NISARGADATTA MAHARAJ

Popular conceptions of how a holy man or woman ought to look and act are often coloured by romantic stereotypes picked up from books and films. But, as the author of the *Bhagavad Gītā* points out, those who are "firmly fixed in wisdom" are to be recognised not by outward appearances but by their psychological and spiritual condition. The "sage of stable intelligence", is one who is "satisfied in the self by the self" (*Gītā* 2.54–55). This phrase may be used to describe the inner state of Nisargadatta Maharaj, a *jñānī* or man of yogic knowledge who, at least at first sight, was the antithesis of the stereotypical yogin. Nisargadatta lived most of his life in a run-down neighbourhood of Mumbai, where he made his living selling *bidi*s or country cigarettes. He looked "no different from the crowds of the lower middle class people who live in the lanes and by-lanes of his locality" (S. S. Dikshit in *Presentation Volume*: 2), yet he spoke on spiritual things with the authority that comes from personal experience of the Self.

Born in Mumbai in 1897, Nisargadatta — or Maruti, as he was then known — was the son of Shivarampant, a peasant from rural Maharashtra, who had come to the city to work as a domestic servant. Later Shivarampant took the family back to the village, where he eked out a living as a farmer. When he was old enough, Maruti used to help around the farm. He received virtually no education, but always listened with interest when a friend of the family spoke about spiritual subjects.

Shivarampant died when Maruti was eighteen, and the young man was obliged to go to Mumbai to find work. After a short stint in an office, he opened a shop where he sold clothing, tobacco and *bidi*s. This provided him with sufficient money to support a wife and four children. His life went on in the usual grooves, until one day a friend introduced him to Siddharameshwar Maharaj, a *nāth yogī* belonging to the Inchgeri lineage of the Navnath order. Siddharameshwar initiated Maruti, giving him a mantra to repeat, and instructing him to attend carefully to the sense of self. This Maruti did with great tenacity, with the result that within three years he was liberated from his ego-personality and united with the *ātman* or Self.

For a while, Nisargadatta continued to ply his trade; but after the death of his guru in 1936, he became a wandering mendicant. He resolved to pass the remainder of his life as a renunciate in the Himalayas, but was convinced by a brother-disciple that renunciation in the midst of worldly activities was a greater, if more difficult, path. Returning to Mumbai, he reopened his shop, earning enough to provide for his family and for himself. Whenever he was not busy, he retired to a tiny loft he had built above his room, where he performed daily worship and meditated on the Self. Occasionally he spoke to customers and others about spiritual things.

As more and more people began coming to see him, these impromptu teaching-sessions were moved to his loft. By the end of the 1950s, he had gained some reputation as an unorthodox holy man; but he never changed his mode of life, dressing simply and eating very little. He continued to sell, and to smoke, country cigarettes, and gave spiritual initiation while reading the newspaper. Every day he worshipped the photograph of his guru and sang devotional songs; but, paradoxically, he told others that such practices had nothing to do with the attainment of self-realisation. Although labelled a vedantin he had little knowledge of Vedanta and never quoted from Sanskrit scriptures. His basic teaching never varied over the years: "All I can truly say is 'I am', all else is inference. But the inference has become a habit. Destroy all habits of thinking and seeing. The sense of 'I am' is a manifestation of a deeper cause which you may call self, God, Reality, or by any other name" (*Frydman and Dikshit* 1997: 199).

In 1973, a series of talks by Nisargadatta, translated from the Marathi into English, were published as *I Am That*. This attracted devotees and admirers from different parts of India as well as other countries. His way of instruction was not so much to answer the questions he was posed as to show how the questions, whether intellectual, moral or other, were simply ways of avoiding the only question that mattered: Who or what am "I"? In the early 1980s, Nisargadatta was diagnosed with cancer, but he continued to speak to those who came to sit in his loft in Mumbai. His last recorded talks, given shortly before his death in 1983, are as clear and insightful as his first.

[186]
From *I Am That*

These extracts are translations of conversations between Sri Nisargadatta Maharaj, who spoke only in Marathi, and visitors to his tenement-loft, some of whom spoke in English or other languages. When necessary, questions or answers or both were interpreted by people who were present. The talks were held during the late sixties and early seventies. The English edition, based on tape-recordings of the original conversations, was translated by Maurice Frydman, and revised and edited by Sudhakar S. Dikshit.

Question: Are we permitted to request you to tell us the manner of your realization?

Somehow it was very simple and easy in my case. My Guru, before he died, told me: Believe me, you are the Supreme Reality. Don't doubt my words, don't disbelieve me. I am telling you the truth—

act on it. I could not forget his words and by not forgetting—I have realized.

Q: But what were you actually doing?

Nothing special. I lived my life, plied my trade, looked after my family, and every free moment I would spend just remembering my Guru and his words. He died soon after and I had only the memory to fall back on. It was enough.

Q: It must have been the grace and power of your Guru.

His words were true and so they came true. True words always come true. My Guru did nothing; his words acted because they were true. Whatever I did, came from within, unasked and unexpected.

Q: The Guru started a process without taking any part in it?

Put it as you like. Things happen as they happen — who can tell why and how? I did nothing deliberately. All came by itself — the desire to let go, to be alone, to go within.

Q: You made no efforts whatsoever?

None. Believe it or not, I was not even anxious to realize. He only told me that I am the Supreme and then died. I just could not disbelieve him. The rest happened by itself. I found myself changing — that is all. As a matter of fact, I was astonished. But a desire arose in me to verify his words. I was so sure that he could not possibly have told a lie, that I felt I shall either realize the full meaning of his words or die. I was feeling quite determined, but did not know what to do. I would spend hours thinking of him and his assurance, not arguing, but just remembering what he told me.

Q: What happened to you then? How did you know that you are the Supreme?

Nobody came to tell me. Nor was I told so inwardly. In fact, it was only in the beginning when I was making efforts, that I was passing through some strange experiences; seeing lights, hearing voices, meeting gods and goddesses and conversing with them. Once the Guru told me: "You are the Supreme Reality", I ceased having visions and trances and became very quiet and simple. I found myself desiring and knowing less and less, until I could say in utter astonishment: "I know nothing, I want nothing."

*

Q: How does one come to know the knower?

I can only tell you what I know from my own experience. When I met my Guru, he told me: "You are not what you take yourself to be. Find out what you are. Watch the sense 'I am', find your real self". I obeyed him, because I trusted him. I did as he told me. All my spare time I would spend looking at myself in silence. And what a difference it made, and how soon! It took me only three years to realize my true nature. My Guru died soon after I met him, but it made no difference. I remembered what he told me and persevered. The fruit of it is here, with me.

Q: What is it?

I know myself as I am in reality. I am neither the body, nor the mind, nor the mental faculties. I am beyond all these.

Q: Are you just nothing?

Come on, be reasonable. Of course I am, most tangibly. Only I am not what you may think me to be. This tells you all.

*

Until I met my Guru I knew so many things. Now I know nothing, for all knowledge is in dream only and not valid. I know myself and I find no life nor death in me, only pure being — not being this or that, but just *being*. But the moment the mind, drawing on its stock of memories, begins to imagine, it fills the space with objects and time with events. As I do not know even this birth, how can I know past births? It is the mind that, itself in movement, sees everything moving, and having created time, worries about the past and future. All the universe is cradled in consciousness (*mahā-tattva*), which arises where there is perfect order and harmony (*mahā-sattva*). As all waves are in the ocean, so are all things physical and mental in awareness. Hence awareness itself is all important, not the content of it. Deepen and broaden your awareness of yourself and all the blessings will flow. You need not seek anything, all will come to you most naturally and effortlessly. The five senses and the four functions of the mind — memory, thought, understanding and selfhood;

the five elements — earth, water, fire, air and ether; the two aspects of creation — matter and spirit, all are contained in awareness.

Q: Yet, you must believe in having lived before.

The scriptures say so, but I know nothing about it. I know myself as I am; as I appeared or will appear is not within my experience. It is not that I do not remember. In fact there is nothing to remember. Reincarnation implies a reincarnating self. There is no such thing. The bundle of memories and hopes, called the "I", imagines itself existing everlastingly and creates time to accommodate its false eternity. To *be*, I need no past or future. All experience is born of imagination; I do not imagine, so no birth or death happens to me. Only those who think themselves born can think themselves re-born. You are accusing me of having been born — I plead not guilty!

*

Q: I find it hard to grasp what exactly do you mean by saying that you are neither the object nor the subject. At this very moment, as we talk, am I not the object of your experience, and you the subject?

Look, my thumb touches my forefinger. Both touch and are touched. When my attention is on the thumb, the thumb is the feeler and the forefinger — the self. Shift the focus of attention and the relationship is reversed. I find that somehow, by shifting the focus of attention, I become the very thing I look at and experience the kind of consciousness it has; I become the inner witness of the thing. I call this capacity of entering other focal points of consciousness — love; you may give it any name you like. Love says: "I am everything". Wisdom says: "I am nothing". Between the two my life flows. Since at any point of time and space I can be both the subject and the object of experience, I express it by saying that I am both, and neither, and beyond both.

Q: You make all these extraordinary statements about yourself. What makes you say those things? What do you mean by saying that you are beyond space and time?

You ask and the answer comes. I watch myself — I watch the answer and see no contradiction. It is clear to me that I am telling you the truth. It is all very simple. Only you must trust me that I mean what I say, that I am quite serious. As I told you already, my Guru showed me my true nature—and the true nature of the world. Having realized that I am one with, and yet beyond the world, I became free from all desire and fear. I did not reason out that I should be free—I found myself free—unexpectedly, without the least effort. This freedom from desire and fear remained with me since then. Another thing I noticed was that I do not need to make an effort; the deed follows the thought, without delay and friction. I have also found that thoughts become self-fulfilling; things would fall in place smoothly and rightly. The main change was in the mind; it became motionless and silent, responding quickly, but not perpetuating the response. Spontaneity became a way of life, the real became natural and the natural became real. And above all, infinite affection, love, dark and quiet, radiating in all directions, embracing all, making all interesting and beautiful, significant and auspicious.

*

I am now 74 years old. And yet I feel that I am an infant. I feel clearly that in spite of all the changes I am a child. My Guru told me: that child, which is you even now, is your real self (*svarūpa*). Go back to that state of pure being, where the "I am" is still in its purity before it got contaminated with "this I am" or "that I am". Your burden is of false self-identifications—abandon them all. My Guru told me—"Trust me. I tell you; you are divine. Take it as the absolute truth. Your joy is divine, your suffering is divine too. All comes from God. Remember it always. You are God, your will alone is done." I did believe him and soon realized how wonderfully true and accurate were his words. I did not condition my mind by thinking: "I am God, I am wonderful, I am beyond". I simply followed his instruction which was to focus the mind on pure being "I am", and stay in it. I used to sit for hours together with nothing but the "I am" in my mind and soon peace and joy and a deep all-embracing love became my normal state. In it all disappeared—myself, my Guru, the life I lived, the world around me. Only peace remained and unfathomable silence.

Q: It all looks very simple and easy, but it is just not so. Sometimes the wonderful state of joyful peace dawns on

> *me and I look and wonder: how easily it comes and how intimate it seems, how totally my own. . . . Yet how soon it all dissolves. . . . Maybe some unique experience is needed to fix me for good in the new state. . . .*

Your expectation of something unique and dramatic, of some wonderful explosion, is merely hindering and delaying your self-realization. You are not to expect an explosion, for the explosion has already happened — at the moment when you were born, when you realized yourself as being-knowing-feeling. There is only one mistake you are making: you take the inner for the outer and the outer for the inner. What is in you, you take to be outside you and what is outside, you take to be in you. The mind and feelings are external, but you take them to be intimate. You believe the world to be objective, while it is entirely a projection of your psyche. That is the basic confusion and no new explosion will set it right. You have to think yourself out of it. There is no other way.

*

Q: Is the search for it worth the trouble?

Without it all is trouble. If you want to live sanely, creatively and happily and have infinite riches to share, search for what you are.

While the mind is centred in the body and consciousness is centred in the mind, awareness is free. The body has its urges and mind its pains and pleasures. Awareness is unattached and unshaken. It is lucid, silent, peaceful, alert and unafraid, without desire and fear. Meditate on it as your true being and try to be it in your daily life, and you shall realize it in its fullness.

Mind is interested in what happens, while awareness is interested in the mind itself. The child is after the toy, but the mother watches the child, not the toy.

By looking tirelessly, I became quite empty and with that emptiness all came back to me except the mind. I find I have lost the mind irretrievably.

Q: As you talk to us just now, are you unconscious?

I am neither conscious nor unconscious, I am beyond the mind and its various states and conditions. Distinctions are created by the mind and apply to the mind only. I am pure Consciousness itself, unbroken awareness of all that is. I am in a more real state than yours. I am undistracted by the distinctions and separations which constitute a person. As long as the body lasts, it has its needs like any other, but my mental process has come to an end.

Q: You behave like a person who thinks.

Why not? But my thinking, like my digestion, is unconscious and purposeful.

Q: If your thinking is unconscious, how do you know that it is right?

There is no desire, nor fear to thwart it. What can make it wrong? Once I know myself and what I stand for, I do not need to check on myself all the time. When you know that your watch shows correct time, you do not hesitate each time you consult it.

Q: At this very moment who talks, if not the mind?

That which hears the question, answers it.

Q: But who is it?

Not who, but what. I am not a person in your sense of the word, though I may appear a person to you. I am that infinite ocean of consciousness in which all happens. I am also beyond all existence and cognition, pure bliss of being. There is nothing I feel separate from, hence I am all. No thing is me, so I am nothing.

The same power that makes the fire burn and the water flow, the seeds sprout and the trees grow, makes me answer your questions. There is nothing personal about me, though the language and the style may appear personal. A person is a set pattern of desires and thoughts and resulting actions; there is no such pattern in my case. There is nothing I desire or fear — how can there be a pattern?

Q: Surely, you will die.

Life will escape, the body will die, but it will not affect me in the least. Beyond space and time I am, uncaused, uncausing, yet the very matrix of existence.

Q: May I be permitted to ask how did you arrive at your present condition?

My teacher told me to hold on to the sense "I am" tenaciously and not to swerve from it even for a moment. I did my best to follow his advice and in a comparatively short time I realized within myself the truth of his teaching. All I did was to remember his teaching, his face, his words constantly. This brought an end to the mind; in the stillness of the mind I saw myself as I am — unbound.

Q: Was your realization sudden or gradual.

Neither. One is what one is timelessly. It is the mind that realizes as and when it gets cleared of desires and fears.

*

Q: Admitted that the world in which I live is subjective and partial, what about you? In what kind of world do you *live?*

My world is just like yours. I see, I hear, I feel, I think, I speak and act in a world I perceive, just like you. But with you it is all, with me it is almost nothing. Knowing the world to be a part of myself, I pay it no more attention than you pay to the food you have eaten. While being prepared and eaten, the food is separate from you and your mind is on it; once swallowed, you become totally unconscious of it. I have eaten up the world and I need not think of it any more.

Q: Don't you become completely irresponsible?

How could I? How can I hurt something which is one with me. On the contrary, without thinking of the world, whatever I do will be of benefit to it. Just as the body sets itself right unconsciously, so am I ceaselessly active in setting the world right.

Q: Nevertheless, you are aware of the immense suffering of the world?

Of course I am, much more than you are.

Q: Then what do you do?

I look at it through the eyes of God and find that all is well.

Q: How can you say that all is well? Look at the wars, the exploitation, the cruel strife between the citizen and the state.

All these sufferings are man-made and it is within man's power to put an end to them. God helps by facing man with the results of his actions and demanding that the balance should be restored. *Karma* is the law that works for righteousness; it is the healing hand of God.

*

Q: Your words are wise, your behaviour noble, your grace all-powerful.

I know nothing about it all and see no difference between you and me. My life is a succession of events, just like yours. Only I am detached and see the passing show as a passing show, while you stick to things and move along with them.

Q: What made you so dispassionate?

Nothing in particular. It so happened that I trusted my Guru. He told me I am nothing but my self and I believed him. Trusting him, I behaved accordingly and ceased caring for what was not me, nor mine.

Q: Why were you lucky to trust your teacher fully, while our trust is nominal and verbal?

Who can say? It happened so. Things happen without cause and reason and, after all, what does it matter, who is who? Your high opinion of me is your opinion only. Any moment you may change it. Why attach importance to opinions, even your own?

Q: Still, you are different. Your mind seems to be always quiet and happy. And miracles happen round you.

I know nothing about miracles, and I wonder whether nature admits exceptions to her laws, unless we agree that everything is a miracle. As to my mind, there is no such thing. There is consciousness in which everything happens. It is quite obvious and within the experience of everybody. You just do not look carefully enough. Look well, and see what I see.

Q: What do you see?

I see what you too could see, here and now, but for the wrong focus of your attention. You give no attention to your self. Your mind is all with things, people and ideas, never with your self. Bring your self into focus, become aware of your own existence. See how you function, watch the motives and the results of your actions. Study the prison you have built around yourself, by inadvertence. By knowing what you are not, you come to know your self. The way back to your self is through refusal and rejection. One thing is certain: the real is not imaginary, it is not a product of the mind. Even the sense "I am" is not continuous, though it is a useful pointer; it shows where to seek, but not what to seek. Just have a good look at it. Once you are convinced that you cannot say truthfully about your self anything except "I am", and that nothing that can be pointed at, can be your self, the need for the "I am" is over — you are no longer intent on verbalizing what you are. All you need is to get rid of the tendency to define your self. All definitions apply to your body only and to its expressions. Once this obsession with the body goes, you will revert to your natural state, spontaneously and effortlessly. The only difference between us is that I am aware of my natural state, while you are bemused. Just like gold made into ornaments has no advantage over gold dust, except when the mind makes it so, so are we one in being — we differ only in appearance. We discover it by being earnest, by searching, enquiring, questioning daily and hourly, by giving one's life to this discovery.

*

Q: Are you not afraid of death?

I am dead already.

Q: In what sense?

I am double dead. Not only am I dead to my body, but to my mind too.

Q: Well, you do not look dead at all!

That's what you say! You seem to know my state better than I do!

Q: Sorry. But I just do not understand. You say you are bodiless and mindless, while I see you very much alive and articulate.

A tremendously complex work is going on all the time in your brain and body, are you conscious of it? Not at all. Yet for an outsider all seems to be going on intelligently and purposefully. Why not admit that one's entire personal life may sink largely below the threshold of consciousness and yet proceed sanely and smoothly?

Q: Is it normal?

What is normal? Is your life—obsessed by desires and fears, full of strife and struggle, meaningless and joyless—normal? To be acutely conscious of your body is it normal? To be torn by feelings, tortured by thoughts: is it normal? A healthy body, a healthy mind live largely unperceived by their owner; only occasionally, through pain or suffering they call for attention and insight. Why not extend the same to the entire personal life? One can function rightly, responding well and fully to whatever happens, without having to bring it into the focus of awareness. When self-control becomes second nature, awareness shifts its focus to deeper levels of existence and action.

Q: Don't you become a robot?

What harm is there in making automatic, what is habitual and repetitive? It is automatic anyhow. But when it is also chaotic, it causes pain and suffering and calls for attention. The entire purpose of a clean and well-ordered life is to liberate man from the thraldom of chaos and the burden of sorrow.

Q: You seem to be in favour of a computerized life.

What is wrong with a life which is free from problems? Personality is merely a reflection of the real. Why should not the reflection be true to the original as a matter of course, automatically? Need the person have any designs of its own? The life of which it is an expression will guide it. Once you realize that the person is merely a shadow of the reality, but not reality itself, you cease to fret and worry. You agree to be guided from within and life becomes a journey into the unknown.

[187]

From *Consciousness and the Absolute*

The conversations below were held in May and November 1980. Nisargadatta Maharaj spoke in Marathi. The English edition was prepared by Jean Dunn using tape-recordings of the talks, which were interpreted at the time or translated later.

Q: How does a jñānī see the world?

A jñānī is aware of the origin and the value of consciousness, this beingness, which has spontaneously dawned on him. This same consciousness plays a multitude of roles, some happy, some unhappy; but whatever the roles, the jñānī is merely the seer of them. The roles have no effect on the jñānī.

All your problems are body-mind problems. Even so, you cling to that body. Since you identify with the body-mind, you follow certain polite modes of expression when you talk. I do not. I might embarrass you; you may not be able to take what I say. I have no sense of propriety.

You are bound by your own concepts and notions. Actually, you love only this sense of "I"; you do everything because of this. You are not working for anybody, nor for the nation, but only for this sense of "I" which you love so much.

Q: But I like to act; I like to work.

All these activities go on, but they are only entertainment. The waking and deep sleep states come and go spontaneously. Through the sense of "I", you spontaneously feel like working. But find out if this sense of "I" is real or unreal, permanent or impermanent.

The "I" which appears is unreal. How unreal it is I have proven. The moment the "I" is proven unreal, who is it who knows that the "I" is unreal? This knowledge within you that knows the "I" is unreal, that knowledge which knows change, must itself be changeless, permanent.

You are an illusion, *māyā*, an imagination. It is only because I know that I'm unreal that I know you also are unreal. It is not like this: Because I am real, you are unreal. It is like this: Because I am unreal, everything is unreal.

Consciousness depends on the body; the body depends on the essence of food. It is the Consciousness which is speaking now. If the food-essence is not present, the body cannot exist. Without the body, would I be able to talk?

Can you do anything to retain this sense of "I"? As it came spontaneously, so will it go. It will not forewarn you by announcing, "I am going tomorrow."

A doubt has arisen and you are trying to find the solution, but who is it who has this doubt? Find out for yourself.

*

My present outlook is without limitation, total freedom.

Ultimately one must go beyond knowledge, but the knowledge must come, and knowledge can come by constant meditation. By meditating, the knowledge "I Am" gradually settles down and merges with universal knowledge, and thereby becomes totally free, like the sky, or space.

Those who come here with the idea of getting knowledge, even spiritual knowledge, come here as individuals aspiring to get something; that is the real difficulty. The seeker must disappear.

When you know your real nature the knowledge "I Am" remains, but that knowledge is unlimited. It is not possible for you to acquire knowledge, you *are* knowledge. You are what you are seeking.

*

Whatever I had thought earlier has now changed. What is happening now is that even the slightest touch of individuality has completely disappeared, and it is consciousness as such which is spontaneously experiencing. The result is total freedom. All the time there was complete conviction that it was consciousness which was experiencing; but that "I" which the consciousness was experiencing was there. Now that has totally disappeared; therefore, whatever happens in the field of consciousness, I, who am there before consciousness, am not concerned in any way. The experience is of consciousness experiencing itself.

Nevertheless, understand what consciousness is, even if consciousness is not an individual. The basis and source of consciousness is in the material. What I say is still in the conceptual world, and you need not accept it as truth. Nothing in the conceptual world is true.

Once the disease was diagnosed, the very name of the disease started various thoughts and concepts. Watching those thoughts and concepts I came to the conclusion that whatever is happening is in the consciousness. I told the consciousness, "It is you who are suffering, not I." If consciousness wants to continue to suffer, let it remain in the body. If it wants to leave the body, let it. Either way, I am not concerned.

FURTHER READING

Source Materials

Jean Dunn, ed., *Consciousness and the Absolute: The Final Talks of Sri Nisargadatta Maharaj*. Bombay: Chetana, 1994.

Maurice Frydman and Sudhakar S. Dikshit, eds. and trans., *I Am That: Talks with Sri Nisargadatta Maharaj*. Bombay: Chetana, 1997.

Other Sources

Sri Nisargadatta Maharaj Presentation Volume: 1980. Bombay: Sri Nisargadatta Adyatma Kendra, 1980.

Sri Nisargadatta Maharaj <http://www.realization.org/page/topics/nisargadatta.htm>

Sources of Texts and Translations

186 *I Am That* 390–91, 301–02, 261–62, 268–69, 239–40, 221–23, 24, 4–5, 32–33

187 *Consciousness and the Absolute* 1–2, 13–14, 16

PANDIT GOPI KRISHNA

The practices and doctrines that are taught by mystics and prophets, or that develop around their teachings, are intended to help aspirants come in touch with the Divine and to remain in touch once the initial contact has been made. Unfortunately, these practices and ideas tend to become stagnant or to dry up altogether, leaving only dead formulas or rituals. When these remnants of spiritual teachings are systematised and defended by scriptures, priesthoods, and organisations, they become religions.

Religions often retain enough of their original inspiration to serve as guide-posts to people who are drawn to the spiritual life; but just as often they hinder rather than help. Many men and women with a natural spiritual bent are never drawn to traditional religion or deliberately reject the religions they were born to. A striking feature of nineteenth- and twentieth-century spirituality has been the appearance of mystics who disclaim any connection with traditional religion. This rejection of revealed certainties does not eliminate the need of a foundation on which the mystic can base his or her teachings. In non-religious mysticism, this foundation is often found in the verifiable certainties of science. To "scientific" mystics, the statements of older mystics are not falsehoods but pre-rational expressions of scientific facts.

One twentieth-century mystic who reformulated a traditional teaching in scientific terms was Pandit Gopi Krishna. Born in a brahmin family in Srinagar in 1903, he passed his first eleven years in the Kashmir valley. In 1914, his family moved to Lahore, where he attended school and college. During his childhood he had accepted the popular Hinduism of his mother, but when he began to read his college textbooks, his critical mind awoke, and he ended up considering himself an agnostic, albeit one who "thirsted for rationality in religion" (Gopi Krishna 1970: 35). Failure in his examinations drove him to take stock of his life. He resolved to live simply and austerely. Meditation became part of his daily routine; but he saw it not as a religious practice but a means of mental self-discipline. Returning to Srinagar, he found employment in the public works department of the Maharaja's government. A number of relatively uneventful years passed. He married and raised a family.

In 1937, during his regular morning meditation, Gopi Krishna experienced the first opening of a powerful force within him, which he recognised as the *kuṇḍalinī śakti* that is spoken of in tantric texts. What happened subsequently is the subject of his autobiography *Kundalini: The Evolutionary Energy of Man*, from which most of the passages below have been taken. There is no need to comment on the author's vivid descriptions of the physical and mental states that accompanied the manifestation of this power. It is interesting however to note that he had no special knowledge of tantric teachings when his *kuṇḍalinī śakti* awoke. He later commented that the information in tantric texts about the shapes, colours and mantras of the *cakra*s or energy-centres did not correspond to his own experience. On the other hand he affirmed that the *kuṇḍalinī śakti* itself, along with the *cakra*s and *nāḍī*s or energy-channels were facts of the (subtle) human organism, as real on their own plane as the brain and nervous system are in the physical body.

It took Gopi Krishna almost a decade to assimilate the workings of the *kuṇḍalinī śakti*. He continued to work in his government office and in 1946 founded an organisation that sought to bring about reforms in the social life of Kashmir, opposing the dowry system and promoting widow remarriage. A few years later he took early retirement to devote himself entirely to this work. Around the same time, he made his first attempts to express his inner experiences in English prose and poetry. Later, encouraged by friends and admirers, he undertook the writing of his autobiography, which was published in India in 1967. Foreign editions followed, and before long Gopi Krishna was delivering his message to appreciative audiences in the West.

During the last decade of his life, Gopi Krishna travelled frequently, and wrote more than a dozen books. Most of these were concerned with the evolutionary importance of Kundalini, which he viewed as the source of individual genius, and also as the key to a radical solution of the political and social problems of the world. Neither science nor religion alone could solve of the world's ills, he asserted. What was needed was a scientific study of that which was at the root of the religious impulse in man, namely the *kuṇḍalinī śakti*, a biological phenomenon that was the "guardian of human existence and evolution". By harnessing its power, humankind could get beyond "the conflicting ideologies and divergent systems of government" whose conflict endangered life on earth, and "the revolt against the major religions, and their proliferation into innumerable creeds and cults", which has left society without a stable ethical foundation (Gopi Krishna in Kieffer, ed., 1996: 25–49). Gopi Krishna continued to preach this message till the last year of his life. He died in Srinagar of a lung infection in 1984.

[188]

From *Kundalini: The Evolutionary Energy in Man*

These passages are from Gopi Krishna's autobiography, which was published in 1967, thirty years after his first experience of the *kuṇḍalinī śakti*. The book is in the form of a chronological narrative, with occasional passages of critical reflection.

One morning during the Christmas of 1937 I sat cross-legged in a small room in a little house on the outskirts of the town of Jammu, the winter capital of the Jammu and Kashmir State in northern India. I was meditating with my face towards the window on the east through which the first grey streaks of the slowly brightening dawn fell into the room. Long practice had accustomed me to sit in the same posture for hours at a time without the least discomfort, and I sat breathing slowly and rhythmically, my attention drawn towards the crown of my head, contemplating an imaginary lotus in full bloom, radiating light.

I sat steadily, unmoving and erect, my thoughts uninterruptedly centered on the shining lotus, intent on keeping my attention from wandering and bringing it back again and again whenever it moved in any other direction. The intensity of concentration interrupted my breathing; gradually it slowed down to such an extent that at times it was barely perceptible. My whole being was so engrossed in the contemplation of the lotus that for several minutes at a time I lost touch with my body and surroundings. During such intervals I used to feel as if I were poised in mid-air, without any feeling of a body around me. The only object of which I was aware was a lotus of brilliant colour, emitting rays of light. This experience has happened to many people who practise meditation in any form regularly for a sufficient length of time, but what followed on that fateful morning in my case, changing the whole course of my life and outlook, has happened to few.

During one such spell of intense concentration I suddenly felt a strange sensation below the base of the spine, at the place touching the seat, while I sat cross-legged on a folded blanket spread on the floor. The sensation was so extraordinary and so pleasing that my attention was forcibly drawn towards it. The moment my attention was thus unexpectedly withdrawn from the point on which it was focused, the sensation ceased. Thinking it to be a trick played by my imagination to relax the tension, I dismissed the matter from my mind and brought my attention back to the point from which it had wandered. Again I fixed it on the lotus, and as the image grew clear and distinct at the top of my head, again the sensation occurred. This time I tried to maintain the fixity of my attention and succeeded for a few seconds, but the sensation extending upwards grew so intense and was so extraordinary, as compared to anything I had experienced before, that in spite of myself my mind went towards it, and at that very moment it again disappeared. I was now convinced that something unusual had happened for which my daily practice of concentration was probably responsible.

I had read glowing accounts, written by learned men, of great benefits resulting from concentration, and of the miraculous powers acquired by yogis through such exercises. My heart began to beat wildly, and I found it difficult to bring my attention to the required degree of fixity. After a while I grew composed and was soon as deep in meditation as before. When completely immersed I again experienced the sensation, but this time, instead of allowing my mind to leave the point where I had fixed it, I maintained a rigidity of attention throughout. The sensation again extended upwards, growing in intensity, and I felt myself wavering; but with a great effort I kept my attention centered round the lotus. Suddenly, with a roar like that of a waterfall, I felt a stream of liquid light entering my brain through the spinal cord.

Entirely unprepared for such a development, I was completely taken by surprise; but regaining self-control instantaneously, I remained sitting in the same posture, keeping my mind on the point of concentration. The illumination grew brighter and brighter, the roaring louder, I experienced a rocking sensation and then felt myself slipping out of my body, entirely enveloped in a halo of light. It is impossible to describe the experience accurately. I felt the point of consciousness that was myself growing wider, surrounded by waves of light. It grew wider and wider, spreading outward while the body, normally the immediate object of its perception, appeared to have receded into the distance until I became entirely unconscious of it. I was now all consciousness, without any outline, without any idea of a corporeal appendage, without any feeling or sensation coming from the senses, immersed in a sea of light simultaneously conscious and aware of every point, spread out, as it were, in all directions without any barrier or material obstruction. I was no longer myself, or to be more accurate, no longer as I knew myself to be, a small point of awareness confined in a body, but instead was a vast circle of consciousness in which the body was but a point, bathed in light and in a state of exaltation and happiness impossible to describe.

After some time, the duration of which I could not judge, the circle began to narrow down; I felt myself contracting, becoming smaller and smaller, until I again became dimly conscious of the outline of my body, then more clearly; and as I slipped back to my old condition, I became suddenly aware of the noises in the street, felt again my arms and legs and head, and once more became my narrow self in touch with body and surroundings. When I opened my eyes and looked about, I felt a little dazed and bewildered, as if coming back from a strange land completely foreign to me. The sun had risen and was shining full on my face, warm and soothing. I tried to lift my hands, which always rested in my lap, one upon the other, during meditation. My arms felt limp and lifeless. With an effort I raised them up and stretched them to enable the blood to flow freely. Then I tried to free my legs from the posture in which I was sitting and to place them in a more comfortable position but could not. They were heavy and stiff. With the help of my hands I freed them and stretched them out, then put my back against the wall, reclining in a position of ease and comfort. . . .

*

Whenever my mind turned upon itself I always found myself staring with growing panic into the unearthly radiance that filled my head, swirling and eddying like a fearsome whirlpool; even found its reflection in the pitch darkness of my room during the slowly dragging hours of the night. Not infrequently it assumed horrible shapes and postures, as if satanic faces were grinning and inhuman forms gesticulating at me in the blackness. This happened night after night for months, weakening my will and sapping my resistance until I felt unable to endure the fearful ordeal any longer, certain that at any moment I might succumb to the relentlessly pursuing horror and, bidding farewell to my life and sanity, rush out of the room a raving maniac. But I persisted, determined to hold on as long as I had a vestige of will power, resolved at the first sign of breaking to surrender my life rather than lose myself in the ghastly wilderness of insanity.

When it was day I longed for the night and during the night I fervently prayed for the day. As the time wore on, my hope dwindled and desperation seized me. There was no relaxation in the tension or any abatement in the ceaselessly haunting fear or any relief from the fiery stream that darted through my nerves and poured into my agonized brain. On the other hand, as my vitality ebbed as a result of fasts, and my resistance weakened, the malady was aggravated to such a pitch that every moment I expected the end. . . .

Pulling the cover over my face, I stretched myself to my full length on the bed, burning in every fibre, lashed as it were by a fiery rain of red-hot needles piercing my skin. At this moment a fearful idea struck me. Could it be that I had aroused Kundalini through *piṅgalā* or the solar nerve which regulates the flow of heat in the body and is located on the right side of *suṣumnā*? If so, I was doomed, I thought desperately and as if by divine dispensation the idea flashed across my brain to make a last-minute attempt to rouse *iḍā*, or the lunar nerve on the left side, to activity, thus neutralizing the dreadful burning effect of the devouring fire within. With my mind reeling and senses deadened with pain, but with all the will-power left at my command, I brought my attention to bear on the left side of the seat of Kundalini, and tried to force an imaginary cold current upward through the middle of the spinal cord. In that extraordinarily extended, agonized, and exhausted state of consciousness, I distinctly felt the location of the nerve and strained hard mentally to divert its flow into the central channel. Then, as if waiting for the destined moment, a miracle happened.

There was a sound like a nerve thread snapping and instantaneously a silvery streak passed zigzag through the spinal cord, exactly like the sinuous movement of a white serpent in rapid flight, pouring an effulgent, cascading shower of brilliant vital energy into my brain, filling my head with a blissful lustre in place of the flame that had been tormenting me for the last three hours. Completely taken by surprise at this sudden transformation of the fiery current, darting across the entire network of my nerves only a moment before, and overjoyed at the cessation of pain, I remained absolutely quiet and motionless for some time, tasting the bliss of relief with a mind flooded with emotion, unable to believe I was really free of the horror. Tortured and exhausted almost to the point of collapse by the agony I had suffered during the terrible interval, I immediately fell asleep, bathed in light and for the first time after weeks of anguish felt the sweet embrace of restful sleep. . . .

*

Days and weeks passed, adding to my strength and to the assurance that I was in no imminent mental or physical danger. But my condition was abnormal, and the more I studied it with growing clarity of mind, the more I wondered and the more uncertain I became about the outcome. I was in an extraordinary state: a lustrous medium intensely alive and acutely sentient, shining day and night, permeated my whole system, racing through every part of my body, perfectly at home and absolutely sure of its path. I often watched the marvellous play of this radiant force in utter bewilderment. I had no doubt that Kundalini was now fully awake in me, but there was absolutely no sign of miraculous psychic and mental powers associated with it by the ancients. I could not detect any change in me for the better; on the contrary, my physical condition had considerably deteriorated and my head was yet far from steady. I could not read attentively or devote myself with undivided mind to any task. Any sustained effort at concentration invariably resulted in an intensification of the abnormal condition. The halo in my head increased enormously in size after every spell of prolonged attention, creating a further heightening of my consciousness with a corresponding increase in the sense of fear now present only occasionally, and that, too, in a very mild form. . . .

At last mustering my courage, I wrote to one of the best-known modern saints of India, the author of many widely read books in English on Yoga, giving him full details of my extraordinary state and sought for guidance. I waited for his reply in trepidation, and when it failed to come for some days, I sent a telegram also. I was passing a very anxious time when the answer came. It said that there was no doubt that I had aroused Kundalini in the Tantric manner and that the only way for me to seek guidance was to find a Yogi who had himself conducted the Shakti successfully to the Seventh Centre in the head. I was thankful for the reply which fully confirmed my own opinion, thereby raising my hopes and self-confidence. It was obvious that the symptoms mentioned by me had been recognized as those characterizing the awakening, thereby giving to my weird experience a certain appearance of normality. If I were passing through an abnormal condition, it was not an isolated instance nor was the abnormality peculiar to me alone, but must be a necessary corollary to the awakening of Kundalini, and with modifications suited to different temperaments must have occurred in almost all those in whom awakening had taken place. But where was I to find a Yogi who had raised the Shakti to the Seventh Centre? . . .

*

The magnitude of the risk that one has to run in the event of a powerful awakening all of a sudden, can be gauged from the fact that simultaneously with the release of the new energy, profound functional and structural changes begin to occur in the delicate fabric of the nervous system with such rapidity and violence as to be sufficient to cause unhinging of the brain instantaneously if the organism as a whole does not possess enough power of adjustment to bear the tremendous strain, as actually happens in a large percentage of cases. Among the inmates of mental hospitals there are often some who owe their malady to a prematurely active or morbidly functioning Kundalini.

With the restoration of my faculties and the growing clarity of mind I began to speculate about my condition. I read all that came my way pertaining to Kundalini and Yoga, but did not come across any account of a similar phenomenon. The darting warm and cold currents, the effulgence in the head, the unearthly sounds in the ears, and the gripping fear were all mentioned, but there was no sign in me of clairvoyance or of ecstasy or of communication with disembodied spirits or of any other extraordinary psychic gift, all considered to be the distinctive characteristics of an awakened Kundalini from the earliest times.

*

As I still failed to notice the development of any extraordinary talent or supernormal faculty, I continued to be tormented by serious doubts about the actual nature of the abnormality of which I was the victim. The ever-present radiation, bathing my head with lustre and glowing along the path of countless nerves in the body, streaming here and there in a most wonderful and sometimes awe-inspiring manner, had little in common with the effulgent visions described by yogis and mystics. Beyond the spectacle of a luminous circle around the head, which was now constant in me, and an extended consciousness, I felt and saw nothing extraordinary in the least approaching the supernatural, but for all practical purposes was the same man that I had always been. The only difference was that I now saw the world reflected in a larger mental mirror. It is extremely difficult for me to express adequately this change in my cognitive apparatus. The best I can do is to say that it appeared as if an enlarged picture of the world was now being formed in the mind, not enlarged in the sense of magnification by a microscope, but as if the world image was now presented by a wider conscious surface than before. In other words, the knowing self appeared to have acquired distinctly extended proportions. . . .

As the alteration in the state of my consciousness is the most important feature of my experience to which I wish to draw attention, having far-reaching results, it is necessary to say more about this extraordinary development, which for a long time I considered to be an abnormality or delusion. The state of exalted and extended consciousness, permeated with an inexpressible, supermundane happiness which I experienced on the first appearance of the serpent fire in me, was an internal phenomenon, subjective in nature, indicating an expansion of the field of awareness, or the cognitive self, formless, invisible, and infinitely subtle, the observer in the body, always beyond scrutiny, impossible to delineate or depict. From a unit of consciousness, dominated by the ego, to which I was habituated from childhood, I expanded all at once into a glowing conscious circle, growing larger and larger, until a maximum was reached, the "I" remaining as it was, but instead of a confining unit, now itself encompassed by a shining conscious globe of vast dimensions. For want of a better simile, I should say that from a tiny glow the awareness in me became a large radiating pool of light, the "I" immersed in it yet fully cognizant of the radiantly blissful volume of consciousness all around, both near and far. Speaking more precisely, there was ego consciousness as well as a vastly extended field of awareness, existing side by side, both distinct yet one. . . .

In this manner a prey to doubts and uneasiness I continued to pass my time until one sunny day, when on my way to the office, I happened to look at the front block of the Rajgarh Palace, in which the Government offices were located, taking in my glance the sky as well as the roof and the upper part of the building. I looked casually at first, then struck by something strange in their appearance, more attentively, unable to withdraw my gaze, and finally rooted to the spot I stared in amazement at the spectacle, unable to believe the testimony of my eyes. I was looking at a scene familiar to me in one way before the experience and in another during the last few months, but what I now saw was so extraordinary as to render me motionless with surprise. I was looking at a scene belonging not to the earth but to some fairyland, for the ancient, weather-stained front of the building, unadorned and commonplace, and the arch of sky above it, bathed in the clear light of the sun, were both lit with a brilliant silvery lustre that lent a beauty and a glory to both and created a marvellous light and shade effect impossible to describe.

Wonderstruck, I turned my eyes in other directions, fascinated by the silvery shine which glorified everything. Clearly I was witnessing a new phase in my development; the lustre which I perceived on every side and in all objects did not emanate from them but was undoubtedly a projection of my own internal radiance.

*

In November 1949 I again went to Jammu with the office. My wife chose to stay at Srinagar to look after the house and children. She had grown confident of my health and ability to look after myself in view of the endurance displayed by me during the past two years. . . .

Profiting by the awful experience I had undergone previously, I made absolutely no attempt to meditate as before. What I did now was quite different. Without any effort and sometimes even without my knowing it, I sank deeper and deeper within myself, engulfed more and more by the lustrous conscious waves, which appeared to grow in size and extent the more I allowed myself to sink without resistance into the sea of consciousness in which I often found myself immersed. After about twelve years a curious transformation had occurred in the glowing circle of awareness around my head which made me constantly conscious of a subtle world of life stretching on all sides in which I breathed, walked, and acted without either in any way affecting its all-pervasive homogenous character or being affected by it in my day-to-day transactions in the world. Speaking more clearly, it seemed as if I were breathing, moving, and acting surrounded by an extremely subtle, viewless, conscious void, as we are surrounded by radio waves, with the difference that I do not perceive or feel the existence of the waves and am compelled to acknowledge their presence by the logic of certain facts; in this case I was made aware of the invisible medium by internal conditions, as if my own confined consciousness, transcending its limitations, were now in direct touch with its own substance on all sides, like a sentient dewdrop floating intact in an ocean of pure being without mingling with the surrounding mass of water.

*

. . . In the middle of the meal, while still in the same condition of semientrancement, I stopped abruptly, contemplating with awe and amazement, which made the hair on my skin stand on end, a marvellous phenomenon in progress in the depths of my being. Without any effort on my part and while seated comfortably on a chair, I had gradually passed off, without becoming aware of it, into a condition of exaltation and self-expansion similar to that which I had experienced on the very first occasion, in December 1937, with the modification that in place of a roaring noise in my ears there was now a cadence like the humming of a swarm of bees, enchanting and melodious, and the encircling glow was replaced by a penetrating silvery radiance, already a feature of my being within and without.

The marvellous aspect of the condition, lay in the sudden realization that although linked to the body and surroundings I had expanded in an indescribable manner into a titanic personality, conscious from within of an immediate and direct contact with an intensely conscious universe, a wonderful inexpressible immanence all around me. My body, the chair I was sitting on, the table in front of me, the room enclosed by walls, the lawn outside and the space beyond including the earth and sky appeared to be most amazingly mere phantoms in this real, interpenetrating and all-pervasive ocean of existence which, to explain the most incredible part of it as best I can, seemed to be simultaneously unbounded, stretching out immeasurably in all directions, and yet no bigger than an infinitely small point. From this marvellous point the entire existence, of which my body and its surroundings were a part, poured out like radiation, as if a reflection as vast as my conception of the cosmos were thrown out upon infinity by a projector no bigger than a pinpoint, the entire intensely active and gigantic world picture dependent on the beams issuing from it. The shoreless ocean of consciousness in which I was now immersed appeared infinitely large and infinitely small at the same time, large when considered in relation to the world picture floating in it and small when considered in itself, measureless, without form or size, nothing and yet everything.

*

In the course of time I came more and more towards the normal, while retaining the heightened state of consciousness inviolate, and descending mentally from a state of intoxication to one of sobriety. I became more keenly conscious of the fact that though my psychophysiological equipment had now attained a condition that made it possible for me on occasions to transcend the boundary rigidly confining the mental activity of my fellow beings, I was essentially in no way different from or superior to them. . . .

Warned by the ill effects that followed my excessive absorption in the superconscious at Jammu, I tried and gradually succeeded in exercising restraint and moderation on the supersensory activity of my mind by keeping myself engaged in healthy temporal pursuits and the work of the organization. The exhausting mental effort needed for the reception of compositions in languages other than those known to me was too high a price to be paid for a performance which at the most had only a sensational or surprise value for others. I found in the course of time that only a slight knowledge of a language was sufficient to enable me to receive passages in verse without straining the memory or causing a harmful fatigue of the sensitive brain. Perhaps because of the possibility of injury, due to the strenuous mental exertion required in the reception of unknown languages, this phase of the newly developed psychic activity ceased after a while. Passages in the known languages continued to come off and on, especially during the three months of winter, when probably owing to a greater adaptability to cold than to heat my system can sustain the higher moods more easily than in summer. But whether summer or winter, it is essential for the supersensual play of my mind that the body be in normal health, entirely free of sickness and infection.

The luminous glow in the head and cadence in the ears continue undiminished. There is a slight variation in the lustre as well as in the quality of the sounds during bodily or mental disturbance, which clearly indicates at least as close a relationship between the now highly extended consciousness and organism as existed between the two before the awakening. My reaction to infection and disease is slightly different; first, an utter absence of or only a slight rise in temperature during illness, with an abnormal rapidity of pulse, secondly, my inability to undergo a fast with safety. It appears that the drain on the vital fuel in my system to feed the ever-burning flame across the forehead is too excessive and the reserve of energy too small to allow it to carry on the highly increased vital activity for lengthy periods without replenishment. This susceptibility of the organism might be because of the tremendous strain borne or even slight damage sustained by my nervous system on more than one occasion, owing to my unconscious violation of the conditions governing my new existence, or to the inherent weakness of some vital organ, or to both. For this reason in any disorder of the system I have to be extremely careful about diet and regularity. . . .

The one really remarkable change I perceive in myself is that, not by my own effort but by what at present I can only call grace, as the result of a day-to-day observable but still incomprehensible activity of a radiant kind of vital energy, present in a dormant form in the human organism, there has developed in me a new channel of communication, a higher sense. Through this extraordinary and extremely sensitive channel an intelligence, higher than that which I possess, expresses itself at times in a manner as surprising to me as it might be to others, and through which again I am able on occasions to have a fleeting glimpse of the mighty, indescribable world to which I really belong, as a slender beam of light slanting into a dark room through a tiny hole does not belong to the room which it illuminates, but to the effulgent sun millions and millions of miles away. I am as firmly convinced of the existence of this supersense as I am of the other five already present in every one of us. In fact on every occasion when I make use of it, I perceive a reality before which all that I treat as real appears unsubstantial and shadowy, a reality more solid than the material world reflected by the other senses, more solid than myself, surrounded by the mind and ego, more solid than all I can conceive of including solidity itself. Apart from this extraordinary feature, I am but an ordinary human being with a body perhaps more susceptible to heat and cold and to the influence of disharmonious factors, mental and physical, than the normal one.

[189]

From Later Writings

During the last decade of his life, Gopi Krishna was called upon to address audiences of many different types, from academic gatherings to government organisations, and to write essays for different publications. The first passage below is from an incomplete essay written in 1983, the last year of his life, at the invitation of *Impact*, a UNESCO journal. In it Gopi Krishna speaks of his inner condition after the awakening of Kundalini had become stable. The second passage is from notes for a proposed further volume of his autobiography, which was discovered among his papers after his death.

In my autobiography, I have described my fluctuating mental condition in the beginning. This fluctuation was due to alterations occurring in my pranic spectrum. It was this slow transformation of the element constituting my personality that ultimately resulted in the state of radiancy in my interior that I never possessed before.

After my first experience, however, I oscillated between life and death, sanity and insanity, for nearly twelve years and experienced the indescribable ecstasies of the mystics on the one hand and the agonies of the mentally afflicted on the other. For part of this period my mental state became so acute that, when retiring to bed at night, I was never sure whether I would rise alive or sane in the morning. But almost by a miracle my reason and judgment remained unimpaired, which allowed me always to evaluate my mental condition day and night. I clearly saw my own organism battling with a new situation in my interior, as if a new and powerful psychic energy were operating in my brain and nerves in place of the former, much weaker current, whose passage I could not feel at all.

But the powerful energy now circulating in my system filled my head with a silvery luster and darted through my nerves and organs in flashes of light. At the same time, I started to hear an inner cadence, varying in tone and pitch, from time to time, which has lasted to this day. This play of sound is known as unstruck melody in all the books on Kundalini, and it is an unmistakable sign of the awakening of this power.

Inner light is an invariable feature of mystical experience. In the mystical trance, the subject finds his visionary experiences bathed in a heavenly luster and sometimes hears voices or sounds coming out of empty space around. After nearly twelve years of uncertainty and suspense, I found myself well established in a new state of perception resulting from a continued biological transformation that had occurred during this long period and of which, in my ignorance, I could not make head or tail, as the whole province of this extraordinary potential in the human body is still shrouded in mystery.

I now came to realize that every panorama of nature had a beauty for me that I had never noticed before. Every landscape or scene I observed, and every object I saw was bathed in a milky luster that enchanted me, and I could hardly take my eyes from it, so fascinating was the spectacle at times. My ears were always listening to an enrapturing melody, except at times when I had some health problem. Then the sounds became somewhat discordant and harsh, as if to warn me that something was amiss in my interior. This helped me times out of number to assess the condition of my health and to take precautions in time.

At last I arrived at a fairly stable mental condition, but the process of expansion still continued, almost imperceptibly, without causing any disturbance or anguish, except during rare periods of ill health. Finally a stage came in the evolution of my mind where, whether sitting in my room or in movement outside, whenever I turned my attention upon myself, I experienced the same oceanic expansion, the same thrill, the same wonder, and the same radiance as I did on the day when Kundalini irradiated my brain and wafted me to lustrous planes of eternal being for the first time.

It is only now that I am able to assign a reason for this unbalanced state of mind that defied all my efforts to understand at that time. The awakening of Kundalini does not only mean the activation of a dormant force in the body, but also an altered activity of the entire nervous system and the opening of a normally silent center in the brain. The repeated allusion in the Yoga texts to the central conduit, designated as Sushumna, and the outer channels, Ida and Pingala, to chakras or nerve plexuses, controlling the vital organs—lungs, heart, liver, kidney, digestive tract, etc.—and to particular areas in the brain, like the Brahmarandhra, provides clear corroboration for what I say.

What I would wish now, with all my heart, is that this transformation be recognized and accepted as a possibility for every individual. I believe it is often to this transformation that the books on alchemy and occultism refer in the West and those on Yoga and the tantras in the East. My conclusion is that the brain has a potential unknown to science that can radically change the personality of a human being.

*

The main purpose of my writings is to bring this exceptional condition of my consciousness to the notice of the learned. It definitely is not an abnormality, since in all other respects my mind and my body function in a strictly normal way. The change did not occur all at once. For years after the awakening, I could only observe a chalky whiteness on every object at which I looked. It seemed as if my vision had become affected in some way. I always felt my head filled with luster, and my thought images stood against a luminous background. But there was no brightness of the external objects and no alluring veneer of light, which now holds me spellbound when I look at a grand spectacle of nature on a clear day.

Even the sky overcast with clouds, with the flashes of lightning and the roar of clouds assumes an aspect of such sublimity and grandeur that my mind almost reels at the impact. I feel as if the darkened sky, the flashing lightning, and the roaring thunder are not external or away from me but that all the awe-inspiring events are taking place in my own soul.

It is a transformation so extraordinary that I feel at a loss to make it intelligible to my fellow human beings. When I say that "My inner self is now wrapped in a sheath of light," I wonder if it would be possible for others to grasp what I mean. What I came to realize afterward is that from the very day of the awakening, my consciousness started to expand. My trials and suffering stem from the fact that I had no awareness of what had happened, what forces were now active in my body, and what the target of this activity was. . . .

The paramount importance of a scientific investigation into the phenomenon of Kundalini will become obvious as soon as it is proved that there does exist an evolutionary tendency in the human brain. This will have the effect of an electric shock in all religions also. There is hardly any sphere of human thought that has been exploited by unscrupulous, clever individuals as that of religion. Deep religious feeling and the desire for spiritual experience have provided tempting baits from immemorial times for false prophets, pseudosaints, tricksters, and impostors to prey upon the gullibility of the searching crowds.

If religion were really the crop of a holy impulse, installed by heaven in the human mind as a means to achieve the union of the human soul with its Maker, that is the Lord of Creation, then there would occur no deviations from the straight path connecting the two. The priesthood in every religion that is supposed to be conversant with ecclesiastic canons and the ways of God has seldom if ever shown a greater penetration into the mystery of creation than normal human beings. . . .

The human brain is molding itself imperceptibly in the direction of a superior type of consciousness able to apprehend the subtler levels of creation. Compelled by the limited range of our senses to perceive only a fraction of the universe, we are duped into the belief that what we experience throughout our lives is the whole of creation and there is nothing beyond it, hidden from us due to our inability to apprehend beyond the circumscribed periphery. The present-day trends in science to confine itself only to what is perceptible to our senses has been a grave error, of which the vicious harvest is before our eyes in the explosive condition of the world. . . .

This is the province of science as well as of religion. Why science should ignore some of the most important issues of human existence no one has dared to answer. And why religion should be satisfied with explanations for these riddles, offered thousands of years ago, when space was flat, atoms were solid, and earth was the center of the universe, is equally unintelligible. . . .

FURTHER READING

Source Materials

Gopi Krishna, *Kundalini: The Evolutionary Energy in Man*. Boston: Shambhala, 1997.

Gene Kieffer, ed., *Kundalini: Empowering Human Evolution: Selected Writings of Gopi Krishna*. St. Paul, MN: Paragon House, 1996.

Other Sources

Gopi Krishna, *The Secret of Yoga*. London: Turnstone Books, 1972.

The Kundalini Research Foundation, Ltd. <http://www.renature.com/krf/Welcome.html>

Sources of Texts and Translations

188 Gopi Krishna 11–13; 62–66; 84–93 passim; 117; 137–42 passim; 198–99; 206–07; 227–33 passim

189 Kieffer, ed. 178–180; 209–213 passim

18

মন দিয়ে যার নাগাল নাহি পাই,
গান দিয়ে সেই চরণ ছুঁয়ে যাই,
সুরের ঘোরে আপনাকে যাই ভুলে,
বন্ধু ব'লে ডাকি মোর প্রভুকে॥

I touch by the edge of the far spreading wing of my song thy feet which I could never aspire to reach.

Drunk with the joy of singing I forget myself and call thee friend who art my lord.

Rabindranath Tagore, *Gītāñjalī*

Four Mystic Poets

MOST of the men and women whose works are included in this anthology transmitted their teachings by means of poetry. Indeed, the use of prose for the expression of mystical thought and emotion was relatively unusual before the nineteenth century. There are a number of reasons for this. Classical texts were transmitted orally for centuries, sometimes millennia, before being written down. Metrical language is easier to memorise and recite accurately than prose. Moreover, rhythmical language seems particularly appropriate for the subject-matter of religious and spiritual texts, as anyone who has listened to the recitation of vedic hymns or Mahayana *sūtra*s can affirm. The ancients explained the appropriateness of rhythmic language not in aesthetic but in mystical terms. The verses or *mantra*s of the vedic hymns, as well as their rhythms or *chanda*s, were believed to issue from the spiritual depths of being. The very word *brahman*, the vedantic term for the Absolute, meant in the Vedas "sacred word" or "prayer". The prestige of poetic language and the belief in the efficacy of the *mantra* prompted the authors of the *purāṇa*s and *tantra*s to compose their works in metrical form. Philosophers, as a rule, preferred to systematise by means of prose commentaries, but mystical philosophers like Nagarjuna and

Utpaladeva wrote their most remarkable works in verse. When mystics began to express themselves in vernacular languages towards the end of the first millennium, they invariably chose to express themselves in metrical couplets and songs. The rhythms of the Apabhramsa *dohās* of Saraha and the other Buddhist *siddhas* are echoed eight hundred years later in the Hindi *dohās* of Tulsidas.

The mystics of South Asia who used poetry as a means of expression did not think of themselves as "poets" in the modern sense of the term. The notion of the autonomous artist in solitary communion with his (not usually her) Muse is a nineteenth-century European concept. "Mystic poetry" is an even more modern idea. This is not, of course, to say that there were no poets before the Romantic movement, or that "mystic poetry" was not written before the critical category had been created. But it is still somewhat anachronistic to speak of Pattinatar or Purandaradasa or Dadu or Sachal as "mystic poets" instead of mystics who expressed themselves in verse.

The same problem does not arise when dealing with the poetry of mysticism of the nineteenth and twentieth centuries. Along with mystics who wrote in poetry, such as Ramalinga Swami and Sri Aurobindo, there were a number of important poets who wrote works of mystic inspiration. The four writers chosen for inclusion in this chapter were all poets of the first rank, each being credited with the creation or transformation of the modern poetic literature of his language. While none of them may be considered mystics in the usual sense of the term, they each had moments of mystical insight, to which they gave utterance in memorable verse.

The poets chosen are from three different corners of the subcontinent—Rabindranath Tagore from the East, Subramania Bharati from the South, and Muhammad Iqbal and Bhai Vir Singh from the North-West. Each revolutionised the literature of his language—Bengali, Tamil, Urdu, Punjabi—but each also was fluent in the language of the colonial rulers. English became their gateway to European science and philosophy, and also to European journalism and politics. All four of them were involved in the Indian freedom movement, and used journalistic prose as well as patriotic poetry to move the hearts of their compatriots. Like the mystics in the previous chapter, they were children of modernity, but at the same time representatives and champions of a traditional culture.

The selection with which the chapter begins helps to clarify the distinction between mystics who wrote poetry and poets who wrote in a mystic strain. Rabindranath Tagore was the most important Bengali writer of the nineteenth and twentieth centuries, arguably the most important Indian writer of that period. Religious sentiment and mystical insight infuse much of his greatest work, but only his most ardent admirers would claim he was a mystic in the same way that, say, Kabir (some of whose songs he translated) was a mystic. In the extract reproduced here from *The Religion of Man*, Tagore provides a beautiful description of an experience he had in his youth, as well as two similar epiphanies before and after. There is little in his biography to suggest that he penetrated further than this into the realms of spiritual experience; but he did give expression to mystical themes in a number of his poems and songs. Finally, however, it makes little difference whether one calls Tagore or Singh or Iqbal or Bharati "mystic poets" or mystics who wrote in poetry. What matters is the beauty and significance of their works, and these are accessible to all who read them.

RABINDRANATH TAGORE

Born in Kolkata in 1864, Rabindranath Tagore was the son of a leader of the Brahmo Samaj, a Hindu reform group that played an important role in the so-called Bengal Renaissance. Exposed to the best of Bengali culture in his youth, he began to publish books of poetry during his twenties. By 1890 he had taken his place as the leading poet of his generation. During the last decade of the century he lived mostly in his family's country estates. Contact with the landscape and people of rural Bengal brought new breadth and colour to his writing. In 1901 he founded an experimental school, "Santiniketan", which thereafter became his base. Always a supporter of cultural and political nationalism, he was active for a while in the agitation against the Partition of Bengal (1905), but drew back when he saw that the movement was becoming dominated by race-hatred and violence.

Tagore's lifetime literary output is astounding: a thousand poems, two thousand songs (for which he wrote both words and music), two dozen plays, eight novels, as many collections of short stories, and numerous essays and other works. In each of these genres he made notable contributions, but it was as a poet that he won his most lasting fame. In 1913 he was awarded the Nobel prize for literature, primarily for *Gitanjali*, his own translations into English of some of his more mystical poems. Though not the only or even the dominant strand of his genius, Tagore's mysticism was deeply rooted and genuine. It may be said to have had three sources: his personal disposition, his Brahmo environment, and his reading of mystical literature. The most important of these literary influences were the songs of the *bāul*s and of the vaishnava bhaktas of Bengal; but this cosmopolitan poet also absorbed mystical elements from the literatures of other cultures of East and West.

The selection below is from a lecture delivered in 1930, in which Tagore explained to an English audience the genesis of his personal religion. It contains his own translation of one of his early mystical poems.

[190]

A Poet's Religion

It is evident that my religion is a poet's religion, and neither that of an orthodox man of piety nor that of a theologian. Its touch comes to me through the same unseen and trackless channel as does the inspiration of my songs. My religious life has followed the same mysterious line of growth as has my poetical life. Somehow they are wedded to each other and, though their betrothal had a long period of ceremony, it was kept secret to me.

When I was eighteen, a sudden spring breeze of religious experience for the first time came to my life and passed away leaving in my memory a direct message of spiritual reality. One day while I stood watching at early dawn the sun sending out its rays from behind the trees, I suddenly felt as if some ancient mist had in a moment lifted from my sight, and the morning light on the face of the world revealed an inner radiance of joy. The invisible screen of the commonplace was removed from all things and all men, and their ultimate significance was intensified in my mind; and this is the definition of beauty. That which was memorable in this experience was its human message, the sudden expansion of my consciousness in the super-personal world of man. The poem I wrote on the first day of my surprise was named "The Awakening of the Waterfall". The waterfall, whose spirit lay dormant in its ice-bound isolation, was touched by the sun and, bursting in a cataract of freedom, it found its finality in an unending sacrifice, in a continual union with the sea. After four days the vision passed away, and the lid hung down upon my inner sight. In the dark, the world once again put on its disguise of the obscurity of an ordinary fact.

When I grew older and was employed in a responsible work in some villages I took my place in a neighbourhood where the current of time ran slow and joys and sorrows had their simple and elemental shades and lights. The day which had its special significance for me came with all its drifting trivialities of the commonplace life. The ordinary work of my morning had come to its close, and before going to take my bath I stood for a moment at my window, overlooking a marketplace on the bank of a dry river bed, welcoming the first flood of rain along its channel. Suddenly I became conscious of a stirring of soul within me. My world of experience in a moment seemed to become lighted, and facts that were detached and dim found a great unity of meaning. The feeling which I had was like that which a man, groping through a fog without knowing his destination, might feel when he suddenly discovers that he stands before his own house.

I still remember the day in my childhood when I was made to struggle across my lessons in a first primer, strewn with isolated words smothered under the burden of spelling. The morning hour appeared to me like a once-illumined page, grown dusty and faded, discoloured into irrelevant marks, smudges and gaps, wearisome in its moth-eaten meaninglessness. Suddenly I came to a rhymed sentence of combined words, which may be translated thus — "It rains, the leaves tremble". At once I came to a world wherein I recovered my full meaning. My mind touched the creative realm of expression, and at that moment I was no longer a mere student with his mind muffled by spelling lessons, enclosed by classroom. The rhythmic picture of the tremulous leaves beaten by the rain opened before my mind the world which does not merely carry information, but a harmony with my being. The unmeaning fragments lost their individual isolation and my mind revelled in the unity of a vision. In a similar manner, on that morning in the village the facts of my life suddenly appeared to me in a luminous unity of truth. All things that had seemed like vagrant waves were revealed to my mind in relation to a boundless sea. I felt sure that some Being who comprehended me and my world was seeking his best expression in all my experiences, uniting them into an ever-widening individuality which is a spiritual work of art.

To this Being I was responsible; for the creation in me is his as well as mine. It may be that it was the same creative Mind that is shaping the universe to its eternal idea; but in me as a person it had one of its special centres of a personal relationship growing into a deepening consciousness. I had my sorrows that left their memory in a long burning track across my days, but I felt at that moment that in them I lent myself to a travail of creation that ever exceeded my own personal bounds like stars which in their individual fire-bursts are lighting the history of the universe. It gave me a great joy to feel in my life detachment at the idea of a mystery of a meeting of the two in a creative comradeship. I felt that I had found my religion at last, the religion of Man, in which the infinite became defined in humanity and came close to me so as to need my love and co-operation.

This idea of mine found at a later date its expression in some of my poems addressed to what I called *Jīvan devatā*, the Lord of my life. Fully aware of my awkwardness in dealing with a foreign language, with some hesitation I give a translation, being sure that any evidence revealed through the self-recording instrument of poetry is more authentic than answers extorted through conscious questionings

Thou who art the innermost Spirit of my being,
art thou pleased,
        Lord of my Life?
For I gave to thee my cup
filled with all the pain and delight
that the crushed grapes of my heart had surrendered,
I wove with the rhythm of colours and songs the cover for thy bed,
and with the molten gold of my desires
I fashioned playthings for thy passing hours.

I know not why thou chosest me for thy partner,
        Lord of my life!
Didst thou store my days and nights,
my deeds and dreams for the alchemy of thy art,
and string in the chain of thy music my songs of autumn and spring,
and gather the flowers from my mature moments for thy crown?

I see thine eyes gazing at the dark of my heart,
        Lord of my Life,
I wonder if my failures and wrongs are forgiven.
For many were my days without service
and nights of forgetfulness;
futile were the flowers that faded in the shade not offered to thee.
Often the tired strings of my lute
slackened at the strain of thy tunes.
And often at the ruin of wasted hours
my desolate evenings were filled with tears.

But have my days come to their end at last,
        Lord of my life,
while my arms round thee grow limp,

my kisses losing their truth?
Then break up the meeting of this languid day.
Renew the old in me in fresh forms of delight;
and let the wedding come once again
in a new ceremony of life.

You will understand from this how unconsciously I had been travelling toward the realization which I stumbled upon in an idle moment on a day in July, when morning clouds thickened on the eastern horizon and a caressing shadow lay on the tremulous bamboo branches, while an excited group of village boys was noisily dragging from the bank an old fishing-boat; and I cannot tell how at that moment an unexpected train of thoughts ran across my mind like a strange caravan carrying the wealth of an unknown kingdom.

BHAI VIR SINGH

Standing at the head of modern Punjabi literature, Bhai Vir Singh occupies a position in his home state similar to that of Tagore in Bengal. Although comparatively little known outside Punjab, he is regarded by many of his co-religionists as the most influential Sikh of the twentieth century. By means of articles, tracts, biographies and critical studies, he initiated a fruitful confrontation between traditional Sikh thought and modernity. In his novels, his plays and above all his poetry, he drew on the core of Sikh belief as preserved in the *Ādi Granth* and renewed it in his own vision and experience.

Vir Singh was born in 1872, twenty-three years after the British annexation of Punjab. At this time many Sikhs had begun to question the value of their religion, which was under attack by British and Hindu critics. On completion of his studies, he decided not to apply for a comfortable government job. Instead he started his own printing press, which in 1892 began issuing a series of religious tracts, most of them written by him. A few years later he launched a newspaper, the *Khālsā Samācār*, which became the voice of Sikh renewal, and also helped in the development of modern Punjabi prose. His contributions to literature went far beyond journalism, however. His *Sundarī* was the first novel in Punjabi, his *Rana Surat Singh* its first epic, and his shorter poems the first attempts to adopt stanzas like the Persian *rubai* into Punjabi verse. In these lyrics, particularly those in his last collection *Mere Saian Jio* ("O My Beloved"), he "interprets sacred themes from the Guru Granth, in a modern, secular and poetic voice" (Kaur Singh 1999: 143). The Infinite is seized in the things of the world by means of the poet's heightened powers of vision. Bhai Vir Singh died, old and honoured, in 1957. These four selections from his poetry were translated by Gurbachan Singh Talib and Harbans Singh.

[191]

Four Poems

The Momentary Flash

As your manifestation flashed on my eyes
The sliver fell from my hand,
The hum of the spinning-wheel ceased;
My eyes fell into a daze as they saw you descend on earth;
My vision trembled as my being melted into yours.
Drowned in a flood of ecstasy,
Lost, absorbed!
Though you became one with me
The vision blinds me yet,
Stunning the senses.

Broodings

Your memory is always with me,
Felt in my innermost being.
To what shall I compare these reveries?
To the sinuous movement of a symphony's music,
Lifting the soul to sight of the Divine;
To a goblet of heady wine;
To the vibration of a vina's strings?
A sweet, struggling pain,
Yet blissful ecstasy!

Invisible Bliss

A touch like a scarcely perceptible breeze
Fell on my half-opened lips
And brushed them with unutterable joy,
Stirring vibrations as on a vina's strings.
A storm set every hair erect,
A sweet and tremulous ecstasy.
Joy transformed this frame in every limb;
Bliss upon bliss inspired self-adoration:
Waves of nectar,
Joy sweeping all before it in spate.
He is invisible, inscrutable, the One
From whom this bliss poured down in showers;
He baffles thought, imagination, sense.

Ecstasy

The Master raised the chalice to my lips,
Full of the holy drug of drunkenness.
It took me riding through the celestial realms on the swing of ecstasy.
Master, give me more of this gift,
A few sips, a draught —
Keep me for ever on these dizzy heights
So may I never touch the earth again.

MUHAMMAD IQBAL

Only a stone avoids contradictions, Muhammad Iqbal once observed, and he did not hesitate to take contradictory positions during his active, productive life. An early admirer of Persian sufi poetry, he later condemned it as emasculating. A vigorous proponent of a pan-Islamism that would transcend national boundaries, he later called for the establishment of a state where the Muslims of north-west India could live their separate lives. Iqbal was born in Sialkot, Punjab (now in Pakistan) in 1877. Educated in Lahore, Cambridge and Munich, he began his career as a teacher in Lahore, but later shifted to the legal profession. Soon he became known as the leading poet of his generation in Persian as well as in Urdu. His early poetry laments the degenerate state of contemporary Islam, and calls for a renewal by means of personal and social-political striving. Eventually his stress on the necessity of a developed selfhood (*khudi*), and the activism it makes possible, caused him to condemn the apparently pantheistic mysticism of such sufis as Hafiz. In his philosophical poem *Asrar-i Khudi* ("Secrets of the Self"), which brought him international fame after its publication in Persian in 1915 and in English five years later, he developed this idea of Ego or Self, which in the human being is "partly free and partly determined, and reaches fuller freedom by approaching the Individual who is most free—God" (Iqbal 1985: xx–xxi). In a later poem he tempered this extreme individualism with the idea of Selflessness (*bikhudi*), arguing that the highest ideals of Islam were self-surrender and brotherhood. His conviction that Islam needed to reassert itself drove him to enunciate the ideal of pan-Islamism, but also to propose, in 1930, that the Muslim-majority areas of north-west India should form a separate state. Iqbal's support of the Pakistan movement gave it a respectability it had hitherto lacked, and helped make the new state a reality in 1947. Iqbal died in Lahore in 1938. His early Urdu poetry, much of it influenced by sufism and Romanticism, was published in *Bang-i Dara* ("Caravan Bells") in 1924. During the years of his maturity he preferred Persian for poetic expression, but towards the end of his life returned to Urdu in *Bal-i Jibril* ("Gabriel's Wing"). The five poems reproduced here are from these two Urdu collections. Translated by Mustansir Mir.

[192]

Five Poems

Reason and Heart

One day reason said to the heart:
"I am a guide for those who are lost.
I live on earth, but I roam the skies—
Just see the vastness of my reach.
My task in the world is to guide and lead,
I am like Khizr of blessed steps.
I interpret the book of life,
And through me Divine Glory shines forth.
You are no more than a drop of blood,
While I am the envy of the priceless pearl!"

The heart listened, and then said:
"This is all true,
But now look at me,
And see what I am.
You penetrate the secret of existence,
But I see it with my eyes.
You deal with the outward aspect of things,
I know what lies within.
Knowledge comes from you, gnosis from me;
You seek God, I reveal Him.
Attaining the ultimate in knowledge only makes one restless —
I am the cure for that malady.
You are the candle of the Assembly of Truth;
I am the lamp of the Assembly of Beauty.
You are hobbled by space and time,
While I am the bird in the Lotus Tree.
My status is so high —
I am the throne of the God of Majesty!"

Man

Nature has played a strange and wanton joke —
Making man a seeker of secrets,
But hiding the secrets from his view!
The urge for knowledge gives him no rest,
But the secret of life remains undiscovered.
Wonder is at the beginning and the end —
What else is there in this house of mirrors?
The wave of the river glides along,
The river follows its course to the ocean,
The wind sweeps the clouds along,
Bearing them on its shoulders,
The stars are drunk with the wine of fate,
And lie chained in the sky's prison;
The sun, a worshipper who gets up at dawn,
And calls out the message "Arise!",
Is hiding in the western hills,
Drinking a cup of reddish wine.
All things delight in their very existence,

They are drunk with the wine of being.
But there is no one to drive away his sorrow —
How bitter are the days of man!

Listen to Me!

Whether or not it moves you,
At least listen to my complaint —
It is not redress this free spirit seeks.
This handful of dust,
This fiercely blowing wind,
And these vast, limitless heavens —
Is the delight You take in creation
A blessing or some wanton joke?
The tent of the rose could not withstand
The wind blowing through the garden:
Is this the spring season,
And this the auspicious wind?

I am at fault, and in a foreign land,
But the angels never could make habitable
That wasteland of yours.
That stark wilderness,
That insubstantial world of Yours
Gratefully remembers my love of hardship.
An adventurous spirit is ill at ease
In a garden where no hunter lies in ambush.
The station of love is beyond the reach of Your angels,
Only those of dauntless courage are up to it.

The Dervish *of the Kingdom of Birds*

I have turned away from that place on earth
Where sustenance takes the form of grain and water.
The solitude of the wilderness pleases me —
By nature I was always a hermit —
No spring breeze, no one plucking roses, no nightingale,
And no sickness of the songs of love!

One must shun the garden-dwellers —
They have such seductive charms!
The wind of the desert is what gives
The stroke of the brave youth fighting in battle its effect.
I am not hungry for pigeon or dove —
For renunciation is the mark of an eagle's life.
To swoop, withdraw and swoop again
Is only a pretext to keep up the heat of the blood.
East and West — these belong to the world of the pheasant,
The blue sky — vast, boundless — is mine!
I am the *dervish* of the kingdom of birds —
The eagle does not make nests.

Beyond the Stars

Other worlds exist beyond the stars —
More tests of love are still to come.
This vast space does not lack life —
Hundreds of other caravans are here.
Do not be content with the world of colour and smell,
Other gardens there are, other nests, too.
What is the worry if one nest is lost?
There are other places to sigh and cry for!
You are an eagle, flight is your vocation:
You have other skies stretching out before you.
Do not let mere day and night ensnare you,
Other times and places belong to you.
Gone are the days when I was alone in company —
Many here are my confidants now.

SUBRAMANIA BHARATI

During his brief life span, Subramania Bharati transformed the Tamil language, long hobbled by academic conventionalism, into a powerful means of popular expression, which he used to give voice to his patriotic, social, literary and mystical interests. Born in southern Tamil Nadu in 1882, Bharati did poorly at school but won early fame as a literary prodigy. Settling in Chennai in 1904, he found work as a translator and journalist. At that time south India was comparatively untouched by the breath of cultural and political nationalism that was blowing through Bengal and Maharashtra. Bharati and his associates got in touch with the leaders of the Nationalist Party and promoted their views in Tamil newspapers. The patriotic poems that Bharati published at this time were soon on the tongue of every Tamilian. Forced to flee to French Pondicherry in 1910, he came in touch with Sri Aurobindo, who nurtured his interest in the Vedas and other Sanskrit scriptures. But Bharati's primary literary influences remained the Tamil classics and, even more, the poetry of the Tamil siddhas. "Not only the form and language of some of [Bharati's] songs, but to a great extent the imagery and the content is derived directly from Siddha poetry" (Zvelebil 1973: 121). Bharati liked to speak of himself as a siddha and in the first poem reproduced below paid tribute to his seventeenth-century predecessor Tayumanava, whose poems are coloured by the style and ideas of the siddhas. Bharati also loved the poems of the alvars and seems to have drawn upon them while writing his own songs of Krishna-bhakti. Perhaps the most remarkable of his mystical works are a series of prose poems that give expression to his feelings of intuitive insight into the beauty and goodness of Nature. Bharati returned to British India from Pondicherry in 1919. Two years later he was killed in Chennai by a temple elephant. These three selections from Bharati's poetry were translated by Prema Nandakumar.

[193]

Three Poems

Tayumanava

You willed to live for ever,
    A symbol of sweet Tamil.
You are young even today,
    deathless like Tamil.
You knew that the One is That,
    and That is utter Bliss.
Part of the undying heavens,
    abide with our transience too!

Krishna the Omnipresent

I see your complexion, Krishna,
In the crow's dark feathers.

I see the divine green, O Krishna,
In the leaves of all the trees.

'Tis thy music, Krishna, that I hear
In all the sounds of the world.

And I thrill with your touch, Krishna,
When my finger feels the flame.

Joy

The world is charged with sweetness.
The sky is sweetly fashioned.
The air is sweet.
Fire, water, earth,
All is sweet.
The sun is beneficent, the moon is beneficent.
The stars in the sky are wondrous beautiful.
Sweet is rain, lightning, thunder.
Sweet is ocean, mountain, forest.
Rivers are joy-giving.
Ore, tree, plant, creeper,
Flower, fruit,
All give joy.
Bird, insect, animal,
All, all good creatures are.
Fishes and the denizens of the deep are good.
Men are very good too.
Male and female are alike good.
Childhood is blessed.
Sweet is youth, and age is sweet.
Welcome life, and welcome, death!

FURTHER READING

Source Materials

Mustansir Mir, *Tulip in the Desert: A Selection of the Poetry of Muhammad Iqbal*. London: Hurst & Company, 2000.

Prema Nandakumar, *Poems of Subramania Bharati*. New Delhi: Sahitya Akademi, 1977.

Gurbachan Singh Talib and Harbans Singh, *Bhai Vir Singh: Poet of the Sikhs*. Delhi: Motilal Banarsidass, 1976.

Rabindranath Tagore, *The Religion of Man*. London: George Allen and Unwin, 1931.

Other Works

Muhammad Iqbal, *The Secrets of the Self*, translated from the Persian by R. Nicholson. Lahore, Sh. Muhammad Ashraf, 1985.

Iqbal Singh, *The Ardent Pilgrim: An Introduction to the Life and Work of Mohammed Iqbal*. Delhi: Oxford University Press, 1997.

Nikky-Guninder Kaur Singh, "Poetry Urges Poetry: From the Guru Granth to Bhai Vir Singh". In Kerry Brown, ed., *Sikh Art and Literature*. London: Routledge, 1999.

Kamil V. Zvelebil, *The Poets of the Powers*. London: Rider and Company, 1973.

Sources of Texts and Translations

190	Tagore 93–98	
191	*Achancheti jhalka*, *Yād*, *Andittha Ras-dātā*, *Be-khudi*	Singh Talib and Singh 2, 15, 60, 62
192	*Bang-i Dara* 72–73, 152–53; *Bal-i Jibril* 348, 495, 389–90	Mir 59, 47, 18, 94, 96
193		Nandakumar 129, 93, 90

INDEX OF PROPER NAMES

Names of persons, places, texts and major religions. Texts by known authors are listed under the author. Religious sects and schools are listed under the religion.

INDEX AND GLOSSARY OF TERMS

Terms occurring once or twice that are adequately defined in the text are not included. Definitions cover significances encountered in this book only. Non-English terms (Sanskrit unless otherwise indicated) are spelled using the appropriate formal transliteration system. Informal spellings are given only when they differ markedly from the formal one.

guru: spiritual teacher, 194, 304, 450, 510, 516, 550, 551, 552, 554, 558

ḥadīth qudsī (Arabic): "hallowed *ḥadīth*": an extra-Qur'anic saying of the Prophet in which he reports the words of Allah, 276
hājat (Hindi): police lock-up, 457
Hari: a name of *Kṛṣṇa* or *Viṣṇu*, 158, 285, 324, 326, 327, 337, 349, 351, 359, 362, 446; to the *sants* and Sikhs, a name of the formless God, 365, 366, 370, 372
Haridāsa: "servant of *Hari*", a member of a south Indian *vaiṣṇava* sect, 324, 326
haṭhayoga: a system of *yoga* that relies especially on physical and psycho-physical practices such as *āsana* and *prāṇāyāma*, 10, 52, 137, 204–06, 290
Hīnayāna: "the lesser vehicle", the Mahayana name for Theravada Buddhism, 168
homa: sacrifice by offering oblations into the fire, 201, 203

iḍā: in Tantrism, the *nāḍī* or subtle nerve-channel on the left side of the body, 444, 569, 578; the left nostril, 206
Indra: god of rain and storm, often depicted as lord of the gods, 41, 42, 46, 47–49, 70, 210
īśvara (Ishwara): the Lord; God, 132, 137, 163

japa: repetition of a *mantra*, 200, 203, 484
jhāna (Pali = Sanskrit *dhyāna*): meditation; (level of) meditative absorption, 115, 116, 123, 124
Jina: "victorious one", in Jainism, a title given to Mahavira and other *Tīrthaṅkaras*, 90, 92, 94, 98, 230, 232, 233; in Buddhism, a title of the Buddha, 179
jīva: living being: in Jainism, soul, sentient being, 30, 99, 230; in Hinduism, the individual soul, 163, 199, 243, 244, 245, 444
jñāna: (spiritual) knowledge, 155, 483, 508
jñānayoga: the *yoga* of knowledge, 148
jñānī: one who possesses spiritual knowledge, in particular, the knowledge of the Self, 543, 549, 561

kaivalya: aloneness, isolation, freedom, 9, 10, 30, 31, 85, 132, 133, 136, 137, 141
Kālī: "the black one", a name given to the terrible form of the Goddess, 340, 346, 347, 430, 437, 440, 443, 444
kāma: (the satisfaction of) desire, one of the four ends of human existence, 202
kamma (Pali = Sanskrit *karma*): action, 105, 111
karman (nominative case, *karma*): action, the residual effects of action that bind one to the cycle of birth-and-death, 59, 60, 80, 105, 111, 112, 113, 189, 196, 201, 212, 241, 284, 306, 451, 453, 558; in Jainism, *karma* is conceived of as a fine form of matter that adheres to the *jīva*, causing bondage, 60, 97, 99, 101, 230, 231
kaula: a school of Tantrism that emphasises esoteric rites, 198, 199, 201, 203, 204, 247
kaulika: of the *kaula* school of Tantrism, 203

Keśava (Keshava): "long haired", a name of *Viṣṇu* or *Kṛṣṇa*, 326, 332, 337
kevala: aloneness, isolation; in Jainism, the state of omniscience achieved when one is isolated from karmic impurity (in full, *kevala-jñāna*), 7, 10, 30, 90, 91, 97, 98, 132, 136; in Shaivism, a similar state of perfect consciousness, 197
kevala-jñāna: in Jainism, omniscience, 91
kevalin: one who has achieved *kevala*, 98
kheyāla (Bengali): whim; sudden impulsion to action, 533, 534
Khizr (Persian): name given to a person mentioned in the *Qur'ān* who is appointed by God to initiate Moses; he is the guide and rescuer of those who have lost their way, 590
kīrtan(a): singing of devotional songs, 444, 446, 530, 536
Kṛṣṇa (Krishna): a popular Hindu god, who takes many forms and is prominent in many different legends; he is regarded as an incarnation of *Viṣṇu*, 147, 213, 295, 337, 340, 342, 341, 344, 455, 348; to the *vaiṣṇava sahajiyās*, the masculine divine principle 292, 297
kṣara (Kshara): the mutable soul in nature, 444
kṣatriya: a member of the second order of society, a warrior, 57, 89, 148
ksīr (kshir) (Bengali): thickened milk, 345
kulācāra: the practice of *kaula* Tantrism, 204
kuṇḍalinī: a power visualised as a snake coiled up in the lowest *cakra* that brings extraordinary knowledge and power when it rises (in full, *kuṇḍalinī śakti*), 291, 441, 442
kuṇḍalinī śakti: the power of *kuṇḍalinī*, 199, 289, 564, 565
kuṭir (kuthi) (Bengali): hut, cottage, 444

Lakṣmī (Lakshmi): a name of the Goddess as consort of *Viṣṇu*, 217, 324
līlā: play; the action of the divine on earth, 440, 533
līlā-vibhūti: the playful efflorescence of the Divine's powers, 242
liṅga: mark, symbol; the penis (the mark of manhood); a symbol of *Śiva* in the form of a phallus, 210–213, 317, 319

Mādhav(a): "descendent of Madhu", a name of *Kṛṣṇa*, 369
madhur(a): the "sweet" sentiment or attitude, one of the *bhāva*s or attitudes of devotion, that of the lover for the beloved, 445
Mādhyamika: the "middle" school of Buddhism, formalised by Nagarjuna and sometimes known as *śūnyavāda*, 169, 172, 222, 223, 224, 233
madrasa (Arabic): a Muslim college, 406
mahābhāva: intense ecstatic love for God, 440
mahāsiddha: a great adept, who has attained perfection (*siddhi*), 189, 282, 295
mahāsukha: "great bliss", the goal of some forms of Tantrism, 189, 190
mahāvāyu: in Tantrism, the spiritual current, 441